For a
Friendship
Remembrance –

Donald
+
Francis

Sarasota,
November 21, 2000.

Concert Life in Puerto Rico
1957-1992

Views and Reviews

·

DONALD THOMPSON

·

FRANCIS SCHWARTZ

EDITORIAL DE LA UNIVERSIDAD
DE PUERTO RICO

First Edition, 1998
©1998, University of Puerto Rico

Library of Congress Cataloging-in Publication Data

Thompson, Donald, 1928-
    Concert Life in Puerto Rico, 1957-1992 : views and reviews / by Donald Thompson and Francis Schwartz. — 1st ed.
        p.   cm.
    Includes bibliographical references (p.   ) and index.
    ISBN 0-8477-0320-7 (pbk. : alk. paper)
    1. Music—Puerto Rico—20th century—History and criticism. 2. Concerts—Puerto Rico—Reviews.   I. Schwartz, Francis. II. Title
ML207.P8T56   1998
780'.97295'09045—dc21   97-45086
                                         CIP
                                         MN

Tipography and design: Héctor R. Pérez

Printed in the United States of America

The University of Puerto Rico Press acknowledges the generosity of *The San Juan Star* for the use of photographic material.

UNIVERSITY OF PUERTO RICO PRESS
PO Box 23322
San Juan, Puerto Rico 00931-3322

Administration: Tel. (787) 250-0550 Fax (787) 753-9116
Sales Dept.: Tel. (787) 758-8345 Fax (787) 751-8785

To the countless colleagues
–instrumentalists, singers,
composers, conductors, scholars,
critics and administrators–whose
work during the centuries has
enriched Puerto Rico's musical
cosmos.

Contents

Praeludium xv

VIEWS AND REVIEWS

Puerto Rico Toasts Casals 3
Laud Ode by Campos-Parsi 8
Memorable Piano Recital 10
Clarinet Recital Pleases 11
Strings Plucked Skillfully 12
Horszowski and Casals Excel 15
The Maestro Plays 17
Superb Segovia 19
Figueroas Gratify 21
String Congress is Unique School 23
Casals, Brahms and Mozart 27
Festival Finale: The Bach Passion 30
High Spirited Climax for Concert Season 33
Electronic Music Comes to Town 35
Chávez Concerto at UPR 37
Don Pablo Evokes Great Emotion 39
Ormandy Conducts—and Conquers 41
How Long Can Puerto Rico Ignore Twentieth-Century Music? 43
The Plight of a Young Composer 47
Carnival Accompanies Concert 50

Chamber Orchestra at UPR	52
Final Chamber Festival Concert	54
Modern Music Concert	56
War Gloom Hits Festival	59
Musicians Explore Vast Horizons	61
Orford Quartet	63
The Festival Begins	65
UPR Amphitheater: Odnoposoff, Sanromá	68
Chamber Music at the Tapia	69
Figueroas and the Rain	71
Frederick King and the New Sound of Percussion	73
Handel and Davidovsky at the Institute	76
Casals Festival: Whatever Happened to the Twentieth Century?	78
Chamber Orchestra in Concert	81
Institute Concert Reveals Progress	83
The Next Decade: An Exciting Era Shaping Up	85
UPR Hears Madrigalists	89
Díaz May Become One of the Great Bassos	91
Music of Our Century: The Third Concert	93
Elvira in Recital	96
Opera 68: *I Pagliacci*	98
Mandolinist and Pianist Give Imaginative Recital	100
A Mediocre Performance	102
Symphony Season Closes With Thud	104
Important Musical Era Ends	106
Casals Festival: Where Have The People Gone?	108
Casa Blanca: Music for a Sunday Afternoon	110
Romantic Music Series Lacks Sense of Purpose	112
Locally Styled *Viet-Rock* is Scathing Attack on Military	114
Chamber Orchestra at Casa Blanca	116
The Casals Festival	119
Ferré: La Fortaleza's Best Musician	122
Concert Honors Massacred Pilgrims	125
Exhilarating Verdi at Festival	127
Casals Festival Applauded for New Works	129

Festival Fizzles	131
Setting the Facts Straight	133
The Future of the Casals Festival	135
Tosca: Alive and Well in San Juan	138
Eaton Displays Art of Electronic Music	140
Five Figueroas and a Varied Program	143
The "Popularization" of WIPR	145
Cathedral Acoustics Mar Concert	147
The Terrible Trauma That Trapped Tristan Trimble	148
World Harmony Defeated	151
New World Work Marks Casals Festival First	153
Festival Program Evokes Yawns	155
When is a Festival Not a Festival?	157
For the Birds	162
What Does a Tricycle Have to Do With Music?	163
Maestro's Favorites are Played in Homage	166
Butterfly Feebly Flutters	168
Symphony Concert Hits Sour Note	170
Meeting of Musical Minds	172
Fine Performance, Poor Attendance	174
Casals Festival: Empty Seats and Nothing Memorable	176
A TV-Eye View of the Casals Festival	178
Dull Performance Concludes Festival	180
A Proposal to Save the Casals Festival	182
A Praiseworthy *Figaro*	188
Casals Festival: The View From the Courtyard	190
Perlman Shines at Festival	192
Casals Festival Questions	194
Martínez Zarate Quartet: Four Guitars	198
The Vienna Choirboys	200
Politics and Music: The Proposed Casals Foundation	202
Variety of Singers Adds Spice to Met Auditions	206
Otello Takes Much Moor Than Local Casting Gives	209
Odón Alonso Conducts PRSO	211
Double Bass Recital a Rare Event	213

Glosses, Muddles, Spirited Youth at Festival 215
Children's Choir, Rampal at Festival 217
Rostropovich: Knockout Performance 219
Betty Allen 221
New Horizons For Casals Festival? 225
Casals Festival: A Political Picnic With Incidental Music 231
Opera de Cámara: A New Force 235
Serrano and the PRSO 237
Pabón Lends Fresh Style 239
Soprano Evangelina Colón: Warmth and Clarity 241
Cellist Norma Erickson: First Rate Recital 243
Contemporary Chamber Music 245
Margarita Castro Offers Varied Program at UPR 248
Experimental Music 250
Musical Archaeology, Fine Talent Bring *Macías* To Life 252
A Musical Conversation Among Equals 255
Opera Stars Spellbind Audience 257
A Fitting Finale for Island's First Music Biennial 259
Audacious, Unprecedented, Innovative and Successful 261
Sarmientos and the PRSO 265
Caballé: High Point of the Season 268
The Collapse of a Festival 270
   I. The Background 270
   II. The Puerto Rico Symphony Orchestra And How it
        Got That Way 273
   III. And Now What? 277
Opera de San Juan: *Don Pasquale* 281
Niculescu and Elvira for Pro Arte 283
An Amateur Endeavor 286
The Culture Bills 288
   I. Measure for Measure, for Better or Worse 288
   II. A Long Look at the Institute of Puerto Rican Culture 292
Bravos to Alonso and Orchestra 296
Second Biennial at Midpoint 298
Patio Theater Concerts Regain Dignity 301

Marina	303
The Indestructible *Danza*	305
A Plenitude of Pluckers	307
Pabón Conducts Self, Orchestra Well	309
Mezzo Isales, One of the Island's Finest Talents	311
Pedro Navaja: Musical Satire Sets High Note	312
Gary Karr, Double Bass Virtuoso	315
Encore: New Music	317
Quintón	319
Of the Arts, Politics and Elitism	322
Arts Center Opening	325
Two Island Tenors: Vázquez and Soto	328
Festival Opens on Discordant Note	332
Kudos to Two Performers	335
Lack of Professional Input in Festival Planning	338
A Concert of Great Contrasts	342
Fleischer and the PRSO	344
A Bartók Commemoration	347
Schwartz at the Institute	349
Forrester and the PRSO	352
Accomplished Soprano: Susan Pabón	354
PRSO: A Nicely Balanced Concert	356
Gym Audience Sweaty but Smiling	358
On the Road with the San Juan Children's Choir	360
John Cage Week	364
Yvonne Figueroa and the PRSO	367
Casals Opener Signals Shift in Artistic Direction	370
Impressions Following the Casals Festival	372
Operatic *Déjà Vu*	378
Out of Season Offering	381
A Week of Twentieth Century Chamber Music	384
Ohlsson and the Bösendorfer; A Week With the PRSO	387
Viva Sanromá!	390
The Biennial: A Month of Unusual Concerts	392
Inaccurate View of Campos-Parsi	396

Third Music Biennial	399
Daughter of the Regiment: A Fresh Offering	403
Zabaleta, A Most Welcome Visitor	406
Pro Arte: A Pillar of Culture	408
A New *Schwartzwerk* and a *Bassmeister*	410
Ho Hum	414
Evita Enters the Electronic Age	419
Die Fledermaus: A Grand Homecoming For Island Singers	423
Mignon Dunn Illuminates the Best *Aida* Yet	426
Out of Limbo But Not Out of the Woods	430
Pro Arte's Fiftieth Anniversary	434
Kronos; Tevah and the PRSO	438
José Enrique Pedreira	440
Memorable Concert Best Forgotten	443
A Musical Homecoming	446
The Verdi Requiem	448
A Winning Team	451
Grimaces	454
Camerata Caribe	460
This is a Festival?	462
Electronic Shlockburger	464
Turandot: An Exotic Fantasy	466
Homage to Ginastera	469
Sanromá	472
Antidogma	474
Bravo *Figaro*	476
Iannelli and Martínez, Two Welcome Soloists	478
A Privileged Voice	480
Doña Francisquita: Still a Winner	482
A Fitting Performance	485
Festival Long Ago Ceased to Serve Its Purpose	488
Rosado With Style and Zeal	491
What **IS** a Puerto Rican Work?	493
Foundation Keeps the Flame Burning	495
Present Evokes Past	497

Quintet of the Americas	499
Latin Pops	501
Ringing Out the Old: 1985 in Music	504
Tocata	510
Poles: A Unified Ensemble	512
Homage to Pepito	514
Continuum: In Honor of Berg	516
Bravos for APOS	518
The Organ at UPR	521
Baritone and Pianist in Song Cycle	523
Play it Again, Mónica!	525
The Fauré Requiem	527
A Memorable Guitar Recital	529
The Good, the Bad and the Thoughtful	532
Three Premieres	535
A New Ensemble Emerges	538
More Surprises in Music Biennial	540
First of the Super-Pops	542
Canadians Bring a Mixed Bag of Music	544
Tocata: A Sunday Treat	547
Otello is Best on Stage	549
David Krakauer, Clarinetist	553
PRSO Pension Gala Raises Retirement Funds	555
Beaux Arts Trio	558
Melody Reigns Supreme	560
UPR Chorus Celebrates First Fifty Years	563
Special	565
Friend of Music	567
Lucia: Italian Opera at Its Sweetest	569
Raunchy Zarzuela	571
Alonso Overcomes	573
Monteverdi Vespers	576
Island Composers Featured	579
Caballé: Memorable Recital	582
A Nineteenth-Century Ponce Home Musicale	584

Old Vivaldi Was Right	587
An Ivesian Cheer for Harold Lewin and the LAFCM	589
Symphony Orchestra Launches UPR Concerts	592
Piano and Violin	595
Forum Draws Caribbean Composers	597
Elvira Exhibits Craft in PRSO Appearance	600
Los Gavilanes Offers a Good Idea of the Zarzuela	602
Casals Festival Off to Splendid Start	604
Stykhira—From Russia With Love	607
The Three C's at the Casals Festival	609
Casals Festival: Lightweight Programming	611
Stormy PRSO Opening	613
Into the Realm of Bel Canto Opera	617
A Festival?	620
Spanish Guitarist's Gifts Have Deepened	623
It's Refreshing to See a Maverick Thrive	625
Tribute to Vázquez	629
P.D.Q. Bach: A Rich World of Musical Parody	631
Schwartz's Long History of New Ideas	634
Soprano Colón Superb in *Luisa Fernanda*	639
Freni in Top Form	641
Symphony Orchestra Sounds Final Notes of UPR Series	643
A World Far From Tense Concert Atmosphere	646
Márquez Performance a Reunion	648
TV's Drawbacks	650
Gabrieli Does Its Namesake Proud	652
A Stirring Rendition of Prokofiev Cantata	654
Starker's Unforgettable Subtlety	656
Pre-National Universality	658
Morton Gould at UPR	660
Talented Cast Makes *Merry Widow* a Success	663
Puerto Rico to be Included in Spanish Music Encyclopedia	666
PRSO Presents Lyrical Spanish Music	668
PRSO: Retirees and a Rite of Passage	671
Casals Festival Opening Night: A Revelation	674

Gabrieli Significance	677
Bach Provides Splendid Festival Fare	679
Restored Tapes of an Amazing Time	681
Tchaikovsky Loud and Disorderly	683
Pro Arte Lírico and *Rosa la China*	685
Castro's Music Shines With the PRSO	688
Forum's Final Concerts	691
Composers Forum: More Than Music	693
Camerata Caribe Honors Memory of Sanromá	696
A Revelation in Castanets	698
Chamber Music at the Casa del Libro	701
Mezzo Bartoli at the Tapia	704
Soloists Save the Day	706
Sala Casals	708
Guitar Trio Delivers	710
Schola Antiqua Digs Deep For Repertory	712
The 1991 Casals Festival	714
San Juan Pops	718
Ana María Martínez	721
Principal Singers Come Through in *Tosca*	723
Brain Drain Affecting the PRSO?	725
A Curious Concert	728
Children's Choir: Artistic Excellence	731
Concerto Fills Musical Niche	733
A Refreshing Sample of Modern Music	736
A Schwartz Cantata and the Puerto Rico Youth Choir	740
Opera Concert Soars With Valente and Golden	743
Alonso Enriched PRSO and Its Audience As Well	745
Donald Thompson, Man of Notes	749
Index	755

Praeludium

The period covered by this selection of reviews and articles witnessed a great intensification and diversification of concert life on the Caribbean island of Puerto Rico.

Mainly for economic reasons, musical performance during the immediately preceding decades had become rather sharply limited to activities at the University of Puerto Rico, concerts sponsored by the Pro Arte Musical Society, the presentations of resident and visiting lyric theater companies at the San Juan Municipal Theater and occasional musical events in other island centers.

Pro Arte, as the San Juan concert society is familiarly known, had been organized in 1932, a few years after the University of Puerto Rico's cultural activities series, and the two concert cycles nicely complemented each other for many years in the presentation of resident and touring instrumental soloists, singers, dancers, chamber ensembles and an occasional orchestra. Pro Arte itself sponsored the formation of a concert orchestra in the late 1930s, but this promising initiative soon succumbed to difficulties created by World War II. Pro Arte societies also existed in the island cities of Ponce and Mayagüez, and often joined the San Juan organization in engaging the same soloists for performances in the three centers. The Ateneo Puertorriqueño, active as a vital San Juan cultural and intellectual center since 1875, was the site of occasional musical performances as well, as were other scattered island venues.

During most of the period covered by the present selection, the principal settings for San Juan's concert and theatrical activity were the venerable San Juan Municipal Theater at Plaza Colón in Old San Juan, in existence since 1832 and seating some 800 patrons, and the University of Puerto Rico Theater in Río Piedras, a product of federal U.S. relief and reconstruction work in Puerto Rico in the 1930s. The Institute of Puerto Rican Culture, established in 1955, gradually developed an interest in concert life, providing performance opportunities for island singers and instrumentalists at its Patio Theater in San Juan and in affiliated cultural centers throughout Puerto Rico. These three centers (the Patio Theater, the small Municipal Theater and the spacious University of Puerto Rico Theater) have brought their great usefulness into the present, to be joined in 1987 by the three new theaters of the Performing Arts Center (Centro de Bellas Artes) in Santurce, constructed and operated by the insular government.

In the 1950s, when the present accounts begin, Puerto Rico was experiencing the euphoria of great economic activity resulting from a rapidly developing governmental industrialization program and from a rapidly increasing transfer of funds provided by a wide array of U.S. federal agencies. The island had entered a new era of relative prosperity marked by new levels of social and economic mobility, by a great investment of energy in planning and development and by the rapid expansion of educational and cultural initiatives. This period extended through three decades, slowing only during the political apprehensions and economic uncertainties of the present and the recent past. The effects on the arts of the innovations of the 1950s were soon felt, with results which are explored in the present accounts.

The writers whose observations are reprinted in the present collection were not only observers but also participants—and sometimes, prime movers—in Puerto Rico's increasingly vigorous musical life during this vital period. Donald Thompson, an instrumentalist with a background in historical musicology, joined the University of Puerto Rico faculty in 1954 and was a pioneer force in the creation of the music department of that institution. From 1980 until his retirement in 1985 he served as department chairman. He was named Professor Emeritus of the University of Puerto Rico in 1995. Throughout the entire period and in addition to his university commitments, he has been active as an instrumentalist, conductor, organizer, researcher, editor and critic.

Francis Schwartz, pianist and composer, joined the University of Puerto Rico music faculty in 1966, serving as its chairman from 1971 to 1980. He then became Director of the university's Cultural Activities program. In 1995 he was named to the post of Dean of the Faculty of

Humanities of the same institution. Both within the university and in Puerto Rico's broader musical circles, Schwartz has been a major figure in the advancement and encouragement of contemporary music, while his own works have enjoyed worldwide circulation and performance, often with himself as pianist or conductor.

Our writers are close colleagues, then, whose tenure as music critics for the daily *The San Juan Star*, the main source of the present writings, tended to alternate as determined by the commencement of their respective academic leaves as periodically granted by the University of Puerto Rico. In addition, occasional substitutions occurred when the critic of record was not available to cover one or another specific event. And finally, both Thompson and Schwartz occasionally opined on musical subjects of the moment in the pages of *The San Juan Star* and other island newspapers when not serving in the critical capacity.

Colleagues, yes, but colleagues with widely differing points of view and sometimes wildly differing opinions. Their judgments as musicians tended to coincide in the generally favorable evaluation of the work of professional artists who performed in Puerto Rico. However, in at least one case the reviewer was merciless when an amateur performer who needed neither the work nor the exposure was somehow engaged for a concert series designed for young professionals. On the other hand, the reviewers' premises, and therefore their conclusions, differed widely when taking the long view of certain institutionalized island musical initiatives. For example, they came to view the function of the annual Puerto Rico Casals Festival in very different terms, and their writings on this subject reflect this basic difference. Schwartz saw this brief annual observance, mounted annually at government expense in honor of the great Catalan cellist Pablo Casals (1876-1973), as a general music festival which should treat all eras and all types of concert music equally, including the avant-garde. Thompson, on the other hand, believed that the festival should emphasize music which could logically be associated with the tastes and the teachings of Casals himself: chamber music, orchestral music and choral music of the late baroque, classical and very early romantic periods in European concert music. Thompson, with his own agenda (now it can be told), began very early to urge instead that the Puerto Rico Symphony Orchestra, originally a subsidiary of the Casals Festival Corporation itself, be properly subsidized and properly developed by the insular government for the presentation of a comprehensive musical repertory, with broad educational functions and during a long season. The brief Puerto Rico Casals Festival, then, could perhaps be maintained as an appropriately conservative monument both to Casals' memory and to his own conservative musical tastes. The perceptive reader will encounter other examples of differences of opinion between our reviewers, differences which can usually be traced to differences between the premises upon which the opinions themselves are based.

Did our reviewers' solemn pronouncements and gratuitous recommendations, extending over a period of three decades, have any effect at all on the course of governmental involvement in Puerto Rico's concert life? This is impossible to determine with any degree of certainty, partly due to the chronic inertia of policy change in government branches. Thompson began urging in the early 1960s that the post of orchestra manager be created for the Puerto Rico Symphony Orchestra, but the most minute details of the orchestra's life continued to be determined in New York City until 1975, when such a post, based in San Juan, was finally created. Was this a case of slow reaction, or rather of a sudden and independent bureaucratic inspiration? Beginning with his first reviews in the mid-1960s Schwartz insisted that the annual Casals Festival expand its programmatic horizons to include music characteristic of the twentieth century, but he had to wait until 1972 to see his vision realized. Was this managerial innovation due to Schwartz' insistence, or was it completely irrelevant to it? A query directed to the festival management on this point would probably have evoked the same response as is often uttered by performers: "So who reads reviews?" (always excepting the favorable ones, naturally).

According to the folklore of concert life in Puerto Rico, at least one high governmental arts functionary indeed read reviews. It is said that on being told "Schwartz is leaving *The San Juan Star*," the functionary exclaimed "That's wonderful!" "But Thompson's returning." "That's terrible!"

Thompson and Schwartz were occasionally called upon to review each other's work, and a number of those reviews can be seen in the present selection. In addition they periodically interviewed each other, and some of these friendly exchanges can also be found herein as well as some frankly autobiographical exercises. The present selection represents approximately half of the writers' work in newspaper and magazine writing during the period, and has been made mainly for the purpose of historical documentation. Reviews, interviews and newspaper feature articles represent the warm and living "today" of current events in the world of music as seen by articulate and informed commentators; if this "today" is not preserved in some such way as the present volume it soon fades into the cold realm of forgotten history. The recent history of music in Puerto Rico deserves better.

Some editing has taken place for the present collection, mainly in correcting typographical errors and in abbreviating a number of painfully long or painfully repetitive articles. However, editorial autoretrocorrection of early misjudgments now recognized in the light of subsequent developments has not been permitted; opinions rendered in the full and splendorous dignity of youthful confidence have been retained as a confirmation of the fallibility of human judgment and possibly as a lesson for young and confident critics themselves.

On the other hand, the titles of newspaper reviews have been freely modified for the present selection. These titles were not the authors' work originally; now free of the constraint of column widths, it has been possible in many cases to provide titles which better reflect the salient points of the reviews themselves.

Our reviewers' work frequently evoked reactions from readers, both *pro* and *contra* and occasionally followed by rebuttals by the reviewers themselves or by comments by other readers. These exchanges have been reluctantly excluded from the present compilation, but might be seen along with some 300 reviews and articles not included herein, in preserved numbers of *The San Juan Star*.

The vast preponderance of the present writings first appeared in the pages of the daily *The San Juan Star*, which has been a pillar of English-language journalism in Puerto Rico since its appearance in 1959. Except where so indicated, the writings first appeared in that publication. The authors are grateful to Andrew Viglucci, editor of the newspaper, for permission to reprint this material.[1]

---

1. A critic's view of the period 1946-1959, slightly overlapping the present selection, may be seen in Alfredo Matilla Jimeno, *De Música*, ed. Alfredo Matilla Rivas (Río Piedras: University of Puerto Rico Press, 1992), reprinting a selection of his reviews in the daily *El Mundo* (San Juan). An index to critical writing and other newspaper references to musical activity in nineteenth-century Puerto Rico is

Annie F. Thompson, *Puerto Rican Newspapers and Journals of the Spanish Colonial Period as Source Materials for Musicological Research: An Analysis of Their Musical Content* (Ph.D. dissertation, The Florida State University, 1980). The remaining newspaper gap, covering almost five decades (1898-1946), as well as coverage since 1992, will eventually be filled by new research and new compilations. A key to non-newspaper sources of information is Donald Thompson and Annie F. Thompson, *Music and Dance in Puerto Rico From the Age of Columbus to Modern Times: An Annotated Bibliography* (Metuchen and London: The Scarecrow Press, 1991).

Views and Reviews

Puerto Rico Toasts Casals

Latin American Report (New Orleans)
June, 1957   By Donald Thompson

    SAN JUAN, PUERTO RICO. As the lights dimmed and the packed auditorium hushed, the concertmaster looked around at his colleagues, gazed one last time at the bare podium and gave the signal to play. With rare artistry the 47-member festival orchestra then brought to life J.S. Bach's Suite No. 1 in C Major, thus fixing the standard for the next eleven concerts of the Puerto Rico Casals Festival. Their inspiration was Pablo Casals, a man whose musical standards are superlative. The festival's opening work was to have been a solo presentation by the maestro himself, regarded by colleagues, critics and audiences the world over as the greatest living cellist. Instead, the eighty year old virtuoso lay under an oxygen tent at his suburban San Juan home, recovering from a coronary thrombosis. The attack struck down the famed musician during the orchestra's first rehearsal, a week before the festival's opening date. As he was borne from the auditorium the maestro rolled his head and sighed "What a pity . . . what a pity . . . such a marvelous orchestra. . . ."

    When it became evident that Casals would not be able to perform or conduct, modifications were reluctantly made by the festival committee. Works which required the cellist's performance were deleted from the program "in homage to the maestro." In further tribute to Casals, the podium remained unoccupied. The orchestra took its cues from Alexander Schneider, occupying his chair as concertmaster. Schneider, the close friend of Casals who had persuaded the cellist to hold the renowned festivals in Prades, France, had also had a leading role in organizing the Puerto Rico festival.

    To ensure the festival's success and compensate in some measure for the maestro's absence, the soloists and orchestra members—recruited mainly in the United States—vowed to redouble their efforts. Pianist Rudolf Serkin summed up the musicians' feelings when he said "We will play twice as well as we have ever done."

The idea of a music festival in tropical Puerto Rico occurred to Casals during a visit to the island last winter. The visit brought the fulfillment of a long standing Casals dream: to pay homage to his mother's birthplace and meet his Puerto Rican cousins. His mother, Pilar Defilló, was born in Mayagüez, Puerto Rico's third largest city, but left as a young girl for the Catalonia of her parents, never to return. The house of her Mayagüez childhood still stands, however; to its memories new echoes sound, for Casals was so deeply moved on his first visit that he gave an impromptu concert there. Greatly attracted by the island's mild climate, its people's ways and the proximity of music lovers the length of the Western Hemisphere, the cellist felt that this would be a good place to establish his winter home and launch a series of festivals, a Caribbean counterpart of those which he had directed in Prades annually since 1950.

That year was a joyous one for music lovers around the globe. After eleven years of self-imposed seclusion, the great cellist consented to perform in public again.

In 1939, when the Spanish Civil War ended in victory for the forces of General Francisco Franco, Casals abandoned his career in mute protest against the dictator's action and went into voluntary exile in Prades, across the French border from his native Catalonia. He devoted himself and his substantial savings to the aid of other Spanish exiles. Except for a few concerts in London and Paris after World War II and the intimate Prades festivals, he had steadfastly resisted the pleas of impresarios for performances, particularly in countries which have recognized the Franco regime in Spain. Nonetheless, Casals has periodically renewed his Spanish passport at the Spanish consulate in Perpignan. Asked why he did not relinquish it, Casals replied: "It is my country. Let Franco give up *his* passport!"

No politician but a moralist of strong convictions, Casals sees his action as the only way in which he can protest against political oppression in his native country. For this reason he has refused to return to Spain; for this reason he cut short extensive plans for launching a new career in England after an auspicious beginning in 1945; and for this reason he has stoutly and repeatedly refused to appear in the continental

United States.

"I have great affection for the United States," Casals said in an interview on his eightieth birthday last December. "But as a refugee from Franco Spain I cannot condone the United States' support of a dictator who sided with that country's enemies, Hitler and Mussolini. Franco's power would surely collapse today without American aid."

However, since Casals' comments have been disseminated through the press during the past months, a body of comment has arisen. It has been pointed out that France, Casals' residence since 1939, was much more instrumental than the United States in aiding the Franco regime to establish itself, failing in many instances to support anti-Franco forces when opportunities arose. Moreover, Puerto Rico and the United States share the same foreign policies, for the Commonwealth conducts no foreign relations apart from those enunciated in Washington. Despite these arguments, Casals maintains his personal boycott of the United States while admiring this nation's democratic principles from his home in its tiny Caribbean island partner. He describes the Puerto Rican people as "walking with dignity . . . with the great help of the United States," and adds "One cannot witness the degree of autonomy and self-government which little Puerto Rico has without recognizing that here we have a relationship between a great power and a small state that is an example for the whole world."

Skeptics suggest that even if Casals were to lift his ban of U.S. concert halls his appearances would be few. After all, at 80 he could hardly be expected to tour as indefatigably as he did at the height of his virtuoso career in the 1920s. Those who have made the pilgrimage to Prades, however, claim that the many years Casals has spent in low-pressure music making have added depth to his musical conception while detracting not one whit from the dazzling technical perfection which he developed in his youth.

Whether as cellist or as conductor, Casals' musical efforts have been directed toward one end: to extract from the written page the essence of the music which it represents, without undue flourish, extraneous contortion or externally imposed personality. This fundamental honesty, coupled with the distrust of any traditional interpretation until it proves its worth, results in the constant reexamination of works in hopes of discovering a different nuance which might shed new light on a passage. This can result in long and grueling orchestra rehearsals, for during these tense sessions hardened players have verged on tears of frustration from trying to achieve the maestro's exacting requirements. As a result, however, performances under Casals' baton are marked by freshness, sincerity and the absence of cliché.

News of Casals' illness shocked the world, and particularly the island which has taken the cellist to its heart. Notes from well-wishers have poured in by the hundreds. Several of his students spent the first nights following the attack at their master's bedside. The island legislature stood in silent prayer for the recovery of the renowned cellist. Governor and Mrs. Muñoz Marín, close friends of Casals, have been frequent visitors at the beachfront cottage where Casals is convalescing. And along the sandy beaches and shaded streets in his neighborhood, where the bald little man with the black umbrella had become a familiar figure, his everyday neighbors miss him.

Physicians attending Casals have issued a guarded answer to the universal question regarding his state of health. Dr. Paul Dudley White, the Boston specialist who had attended President Eisenhower, was brought in by the insular government to examine the eminent musician. Dr. White opined that following a long convalescence, Pablo Casals might be able to resume his work on a limited scale. This, the specialist added, was "provided that there were no complications and that the heart is not appreciably enlarged."

In another sense, there are thousands who hold the conviction that the Casals heart could be no bigger. Luis Quintanilla, the Spanish painter who had finished a portrait of the maestro shortly before his illness, described the cellist as "one of these exceptional men who radiate affection. His voice, his manner, his facial expressions and his laughter are affectionate. When you have been in his company for a few minutes you really love him." For admirers the world over of Casals the virtuoso, of Casals the uncompromising and of Casals the gentle, the vigil will be a devoted one.

Catalan cellist **Pablo Casals** and his wife **Marta Montañez Casals**.

Laud Ode by Campos-Parsi

The San Juan Star
December 21, 1959 By Donald Thompson

Saturday night the Puerto Rico Symphony Orchestra, two thirds of the way through its two-week season and in the second of three programs in the University of Puerto Rico Theater, racked up another first performance of a Puerto Rican work in what we hope will be a perennial policy of Puerto Rican premieres.

Last year the new work was Héctor Campos-Parsi's charming *Divertimento del Sur*; on Saturday the same composer's new *Ode to Cabo Rojo* was given a rousing send-off by this orchestra. The one movement work for full orchestra consists of a number of alternating martial and lyric sections, and makes references in rhythms and melodies to the folk music of southwestern Puerto Rico. Far from being simply a potpourri of folksy tunes in mildly dissonant contemporary harmonic dress, however, this *Ode* attains a truly noble stature at times, and in its best moments sings in broad cantilena recalling the lyric flow of last year's *Divertimento*.

In Saturday's premiere the piece's carpentry, the joints between sections, showed through in mildly disconcerting fashion. This was perhaps due to last-minute changes in the order of sections, a not uncommon occurrence in the preparation of premiere performances, and will no doubt be ironed out before the *Ode to Cabo Rojo* receives the future performances which it deserves.

Noteworthy to chroniclers of Puerto Rico's cultural history is the emergence in recent years of island-born, continent-trained violinist Henry Hutchinson from an overshadowed position here to one of firm leadership in musical affairs. Historically, Puerto Rico has not been one of the world's great musical marketplaces to put it mildly, and opportunities for solo performance and artistic growth have been few, far between, and the objects of strenuous if subtle competition.

Through it all, Mr. Hutchinson has been quietly building a reputation as a skilled, artistic and reliable performer, one not given to flashy display for its own sake nor to the use of his fiddle to wring tears of soggy sentiment from audiences. His sterling performance Saturday night of the warhorse G Minor Concerto of Max Bruch was, I hope, as satisfying to Mr. Hutchinson as it was to his audience and to this reviewer.

This work, a product of the moistly sentimental or "pocket-handkerchief" school of late nineteenth-century German composition, has long been a favorite vehicle for technical display, serving the same function for violinists that the Liszt E Flat Concerto, the waggishly-dubbed "Concerto for Triangle" has for pianists. It was inevitable, I suppose, that it turn up here sooner or later on its rounds.

Saturday's audience was fortunate that the difficult virtuoso solo part was in the capable hands of Mr. Hutchinson, whose clean technique and overall artistic sense, abetted by the able work of conductor Alexander Schneider and the excellent orchestra, balanced a great deal of the schmaltz inherent in the piece and made of it an exciting, first rate performance.

Opening the concert was Mendelssohn's sunny Symphony No. 4, which forms an excellent opener for any concert and which is apparently on its way to becoming a standard item in the Puerto Rican repertory, having appeared here last year during the Puerto Rico Casals Festival. If we must have a standard repertory of repeated works, let it include such lovely music as this.

And providing a fiery finale to the concert was Rimsky-Korsakov's peppery fantasy in the "Spanish" style, *Capriccio Espagnol*. This piece, which provided audiences of seventy years ago with headaches and three generations of composers with orchestration lessons, was given a rousing good reading by Mr. Schneider and the orchestra.

Solo passages featured the excellent playing of virtually all of the orchestra's first desk players and by courageous young Mike Tschudin of this city, who performed the tricky and exposed drum solos.

♪

Memorable Piano Recital

The San Juan Star
April 25, 1960 By Donald Thompson

A memorable recital was offered yesterday afternoon to a full house at the Institute of Puerto Rican Culture by distinguished pianist Jesús María Sanromá.

Beginning with a majestic and old fashioned prelude by Pablo Casals (which if unidentified would be taken for Rachmaninoff) and ending with two beautifully played Debussy encores, the program probed many corners of the soloist's immense repertory and exhibited his admirable skill and great sensitivity. From the polyphonic roulades of Bach to the rumbling rhetoric of Villa-Lobos, Sanromá's musicianship and authority were evident in virtually every passage.

For the second half of the concert Sanromá removed his coat (audiences but not performers are cooled by a breeze in the Institute hall) and demonstrated his familiarity and ease with the music of more recent times.

The witty Shostakovich preludes (the first of which sounds like the Stravinsky Circus Polka might if played upside down) sparkled with piquant but harmless dissonances, while the *Danza* of Villa-Lobos grumbled along in percussive and jazzy thumps and crashes.

An unexpected dividend of pleasure was the level of dignity and calm attained by the simple absence of photographic expeditions down the aisle during the course of the concert. The necessities of the publicity office were presumably discharged before or after the event, and much better so. Sanromá's views on this matter are known, and it is probably to him that thanks are due. May other performers take a similar position with regard to this undeniably necessary adjunct to the music business.

Clarinet Recital Pleases

The San Juan Star
May 11, 1960   By Donald Thompson

It is not often that one hears a recital of clarinet music tossed off as well and with as little apparent effort as the one presented yesterday by UPR teacher Roger Martínez in the hall of the Institute of Puerto Rican Culture.

For my taste, a program of clarinet music could not have been better chosen. The gallant sonata of Johann Wanhall (1739-1813) contains all of the polite turns and trills associated with the Austro-Bohemian school of eighteenth-century composers, and sounds like something Haydn himself might have written on a busy Tuesday morning. The wistful second movement is pure Italian opera, while the bouncy rondo finale appropriately alternates a rollicking street song with mock solemnities in minor mode. The whole sonata is a jewel.

Only in the incredibly long phrases of the Brahms sonata could the shadow of misstep be detected: the soloist's tendency to stray from his normally faultless intonation by forcing the volume of clarinet tone beyond its normal limit. This sort of variation, however, might even be considered a virtue, by someone more susceptible than I to devices of romantic expression.

In the *Duo Concertante* of C.M. von Weber the hard work is more equally distributed between clarinet and piano, and pianist Irma Isern held up her end with the skill for which she has become rightly noted.

Strings Plucked Skillfully

The San Juan Star
May 16, 1960   By Donald Thompson

Well, sir, I have often heard Beethoven scraped, Brahms scratched and Bach violated, but never before Sunday's Institute of Puerto Rican Culture concert had I ever had the pleasure of hearing Vivaldi plucked.

The occasion was a fine performance by a group with a wide following hereabouts: Maestro Jorge Rubiano's Rondalla Puerto Rico.

Consisting of fifteen fresh faced and well trained players, the Rondalla contains many different varieties of plucked string instruments played in as many different fashions, and is as much fun to see as to hear.

Due to the steadily rising prestige of the bowed strings (principally the violin) and to the development of grandiose forms of concert music during the past several centuries, one tends to forget that the guitars and mandolins, sounded directly by the fingers or by a plectrum, have led long and honorable lives on the concert stage. Well into the violin era, such composers as Handel, Vivaldi, Mozart and Beethoven wrote music especially for the pearshaped mandolin, while Boccherini, Paganini and a score of others down to our own time have persistently regarded the guitar as a worthy companion to the violin in chamber music.

Yesterday the Puerto Rican *danzas* of Morel Campos, Tavárez and Maestro Rubiano sounded especially well in the Rondalla's warm arrangements. But the ensemble sonority of plucked strings makes Rubiano's fantasy on Schubert melodies sound like music from outer space: the effect of hearing that noble cello theme of the Unfinished Symphony come rippling out of the mandolins can only be described as unearthly.

The real prize of the concert was the Vivaldi concerto. Originally composed for two solo mandolins with standard string orchestra accompaniment, the work was presented on this occasion with the orchestral parts skillfully rewritten for supporting guitars, *cuatros*, and a *laúd*.

Gustavo Batista and Jaime Camuñas played their solo parts with skill and elegance and were well supported by the ensemble's rhythmic strumming and melodic inner counterpoint, which sounded as if Vivaldi himself might have written it that way.

Puerto Rico's first opera star at New York's Metropolitan Opera: Graciela Rivera.

Horszowski and Casals Excel

The San Juan Star
June 13, 1960   By Donald Thompson

Saturday's Casals Festival concert began with the orchestra's marvelous horn quartet chiming forth the misty fanfares of Weber's Der Freischütz Overture, beautifully supported later in the piece by soaring strings and the three noble trombones. Juan José Castro conducted, as did he Mozart's Piano Concerto in G Major (K 453) with Mieczyslaw Horszowski as soloist.

Horszowski played like the complete master that he is: the concerto's introspective slow movement sobbed in profound recitative, and the finale, a stunning set of variations which includes everything from the deceptively folksy to the mock martial, was put forth in all its contrast and clarity.

Beethoven's explosive and tender Seventh Symphony closed the concert and marked the festival's halfway point. Castro conducted vividly, with a barely perceptible drop of the wrist here, there perhaps a violent leap into the air or a "Statue of Liberty" baton thrust. The results were remarkable, and the ripping scherzo demonstrated some of the finest orchestral rapport and ensemble playing yet heard in these concerts.

Friday night's near capacity audience appeared only mildly disappointed when pianist Claudio Arrau was unable to appear for his opening concert because of illness. Festival old-timer Horszowski was called on to substitute. He collaborated masterfully with cellist Pablo Casals, violinist Alexander Schneider and violist Walter Trampler in an appropriately moody performance of Brahms' foreboding Quartet in G Minor.

Soprano Graciela Rivera, making her first appearance on the island in several years, appeared a bit nervous as she negotiated the soulful phrases of Handel's "Care Selve" and the runs and trills of a pair of

Mozart arias with but minor slips in the latter's most treacherous passages.

Opening Friday's concert was Corelli's warm hearted Concerto Grosso Op. 6 No. 1, with occasional solos for Alexander Schneider, Sidney Harth and cellist Victor Gottlieb emerging from the finely spun body of string orchestra sound.

The Maestro Plays

The San Juan Star
June 16, 1960 By Donald Thompson

On Tuesday evening, the beloved Pablo Casals walked serenely onto the University Theater stage for his only appearance this season as soloist with the festival orchestra—and into a standing ovation by orchestra and public. The work was the Cello Concerto of Antonin Dvořák, the orchestra was conducted by Alexander Schneider, and the audience fell into an immediate and expectant hush as the introduction began; but these are only the dry facts, the empty statistics.

The occasion was nothing so simple as a performance of a difficult work by a celebrated virtuoso, but represented to Tuesday's audience the noble and stirring song of a man whose long and productive life has been tenaciously focused on one point: music. What came across the stage during the work's finest moments was not simply the sound of a violoncello accompanied by an orchestra, but a concentrate of all the wisdom, the human experience and the joy of a musician whose lifetime, beginning when *Aida* was but five years old and Brahms still had three symphonies to compose, spans what would normally be two or three full and rich careers. Who is to say that the performance was technically flawless? Tuesday's audience could not have cared less about such petty matters; it wanted Casals, it got Casals, and it loved Casals.

The "Great" C Major Symphony of Schubert, so designated to distinguish it from another Schubert symphony of the same key but of more modest dimensions, formed the entire first half of the concert. This is a difficult work to conduct and a demanding one to play, but for all the wrong reasons, as it were.

True, it requires skill and concentration (as what great musical work doesn't?), but certainly not to a degree beyond that which is second nature to this fine orchestra. The difficulty lies, I believe, in its very magnitude, coupled with certain aspects of its structure.

This symphony is a grand outpouring of Schubertian song; a prodigy combining only the most chaste of melodies and the sweetest of harmonies with the simplest of rhythms, the whole cast in an immense frame requiring (or generously offering, depending on the point of view) seemingly endless recapitulation. Herein lies the problem: that of keeping the orchestra afloat and moving forward through such a delicious and unruffled sea of pure song. To this listener, at least, the earnest efforts of conductor Schneider and the great accumulation of skill represented by this orchestra were not enough to make the work move on Tuesday.

Superb Segovia

The San Juan Star
June 20, 1960   By Donald Thompson

Friday's Casals Festival concert opened with a moving performance of the rarely heard Adagio and Fugue of Mozart by the orchestral strings, conducted by Alexander Schneider. This marvelous work presents a dark side of Mozart which is seldom revealed, although a few chamber music movements and the G Minor Symphony certainly hint at its existence.

There is little joy in this music; instead, it approaches grinding despair and bleak resignation by routes not fully explored by composers until nearly a century after Mozart's death. The performance was perfection itself: powerful, poignant and intense.

Andrés Segovia, looking scholarly and lonely on the wide stage of the University Theater, occupied the central portion of the program with a group of his own subtle transcriptions for guitar of music borrowed from other branches, mainly the keyboard. Regardless of the original nature of these pieces, Segovia has the extraordinary ability of making everything he plays sound as if it had been written especially for the guitar—and for him.

Segovia's playing can only be described as hauntingly beautiful, while his technical mastery calls into play all of the varied effects possible on the guitar: from hard and brittle sounds to soft and sweet; from muffled and distant to clear and bell-like, with an occasional thrummed accent or a touch of warm vibrato.

Happily, Segovia never exploits these devices as ends in themselves, but introduces them modestly and for sound musical reasons. Beautifully adapted, and beautifully played on Friday, were an Air and Variations by seventeenth-century organist-composer Girolamo Frescobaldi and two lovely sonatas by Domenico Scarlatti.

Pablo Casals conducted the full festival orchestra in the concert's closing work, the broadly expansive Symphony No. 5 ("From the New World") of Antonin Dvořák. Despite all conscious efforts to suppress extramusical identifications and to listen to the music for its own sake, this work persists in bringing to mind Conestoga wagons, the broad Mississippi, waving prairies and crafty redskins. Such is the subtle and enduring power of western movies and of the elementary school "music appreciation" of some years back. The performance of this warhorse on Friday night was superb, and Leonard Arner beautifully played the second movement's luscious English horn solo.

Figueroas Gratify

The San Juan Star
July 12, 1960   By Donald Thompson

Sunday's concert at the Institute of Puerto Rican Culture consisted of a well played program by one of the island's hardest working ensembles, the Figueroa Quartet.

A performance by this group, composed entirely of brothers, invariably brings to mind the gentle pastimes of a bygone day, when whole families would tune their instruments after dinner and address themselves to the music of Haydn and Mozart, or Schultz and Schmidt. Today, we prefer to sink passively into the furniture and attain a Nirvana of sorts at the modest cost in energy and concentration of turning a knob to revive the TV from its diurnal sleep. Alas, the family musicale (private *or* public) has become pretty much a thing of the past. And anyway, how many of today's certified individualists could even stand the thought of a two-hour rehearsal with their own brothers and sisters?

The Figueroas, including three pianists in addition to the present string quartet, are a remarkable family, and for several decades they have been among the mainstays of Puerto Rico's musical microcosm. It is good to see them on the Institute's series of intimate Sunday matinees.

Sunday's program began with Mozart's Quartet in B Flat Major (K 458), great stretches of which consist of solo violin supported in delicate accompaniment by the other three instruments. José Figueroa, as first violin, played these charming passages with singing tone and true elegance. At times, however, he seemed in danger of being swamped by his husky brothers.

It is never an easy task for three supporting players to maintain an unrelieved oom-pah-pah for many measures, with expression always at the pianissimo. Sheer rhythmic repetition seems to physically demand—and seemed on Sunday to get—an automatic increase of volume, which can mar an otherwise fine performance. The Mozart quartet's breakneck finale redeemed all; its stunning syncopations came popping out of a truly unified ensemble, with pairs of instruments emerging, then falling back in splendid interplay.

The rest of the program consisted of two broadly romantic and mellifluous works, the tunefully fusty "American" Quartet of Antonin Dvořák and a sweetly nostalgic quartet by late Puerto Rican composer José Quintón. The latter is an especially well knit piece of nineteenth-century music written many years too late; its date of composition is given as 1913 (the fateful year of Stravinsky's Rite of Spring!), but its vocabulary, without a hint of harmonic spice, is that of Mendelssohn.

Both quartets were well played on Sunday. The Figueroas are at their best in this expansively romantic idiom, and they made of these warm and flowing works their best performance within recent memory.

String Congress is Unique School

The San Juan Star
July 26, 1960   By Donald Thompson

For anyone wishing to observe one of the most impressive concentrations of youthful musical talent ever assembled in one place, the trip over the mountains to San Germán is strongly urged. It is there, you see, that the International String Congress is in full session under the direction of distinguished U.S. composer Roy Harris.

The String Congress constitutes a unique summer school of orchestral technique, drawing its student body of 102 violinists, cellists, violists and bass players from all parts of the United States, from Canada, Puerto Rico, and one each from Italy and Chile.

These are no run of the mill music students. Chosen on the basis of indicated talent and proven ability, they represent the cream of orchestral material between the ages 15 and 21 years. Furthermore, they are all here on full scholarships, covering travel from their homes and back again, maintenance while in San Germán and tutoring by a splendid faculty of instrumental artists.

Why on full scholarships? According to the sponsors (the American Federation of Musicians, Inter American University and the Commonwealth of Puerto Rico), the aim is to locate trained and talented youngsters, get them together for eight weeks of intensive and spirited music making in pleasant and thought provoking surroundings, and interest them in considering orchestral playing as a career. The aim is noteworthy, for the need is great; although many thousands of young people are studying orchestral instruments, an almost incredible increase in the number of functioning symphony orchestras over the past decade has produced a critical shortage of able and willing personnel, notably in the strings.

Being chosen to attend is high recognition in itself, while the eight week session certainly provides a concentrated dose of fine music and fine playing. And the results? A number of students accepted orchestra positions after last year's course (the first, at Greenleaf Lake, Oklahoma), while this year, inquiries from orchestra managements are already coming in at mid-session.

On the Inter American University campus, students' time is absorbed in a rigorous round of musical activities relieved by an organized social program and by the excursions to mountains and beach long beloved by islanders. With weekday mornings devoted to orchestra rehearsals, afternoons to private lessons, individual practice or excursions and evenings to concerts, recording sessions or faculty programs, students virtually breathe music.

One result has been a series of concerts and recordings notable for their marvelous precision and youthful vigor. Concerts are given both on the Inter American campus (before audiences of a thousand or more, drawn from the university's regular summer school, from San Germán and from the rest of the island) and at other points in Puerto Rico. Recordings, made in a unique studio whose essential characteristics were conceived by Harris himself, are destined for broadcast on Monitor (NBC), in nationwide educational broadcasts, and by the U.S. State Department abroad.

By the end of the congress, a total of eighteen concerts will have been presented in Puerto Rico, six by the orchestras and twelve, consisting largely of contemporary music, by faculty ensembles.

The String Congress teaching faculty is remarkable, and their names constitute a roster of section heads of leading U.S. orchestras. In addition, pianists Johana Harris and Jesús María Sanromá participate actively in chamber music coaching, in faculty programs and in orchestra concerts. The collaboration of members of the IAU music faculty, of soprano María Esther Robles and of Ponce flutist Miguel Besosa has assured students and public a tremendous variety of skilled soloists and chamber music players.

Composer Harris, who intends to make his home in San Germán as soon as he can slow down enough to get moved in, directs the String Congress with the vigor and forthright enthusiasm which have long marked his music. A recent two day period, typical of the way in which he strides along, saw Harris conducting a three-hour rehearsal after dinner Thursday and a public concert by the two orchestras on Friday morning. Friday afternoon was spent in consultation with faculty members and administrative aides in settling details of projected island concerts, and that evening he conducted a recording session devoted to Héctor Campos-Parsi's *Divertimento del Sur*.

Everyone connected with the String Congress, from students and faculty to sponsors and public, seems overjoyed by the prospect of its becoming a fixture in the musical life of Puerto Rico. And a fixture it is apparently destined to become, for it has been announced that this is to be the first of ten on the IAU campus.

Pianist **Jesús María Sanromá**, **Pablo Casals** and soprano **María Esther Robles** discuss performance details in a 1961 rehearsal.

Casals, Brahms and Mozart

The San Juan Star
June 3, 1963   By Donald Thompson

The seventh annual Puerto Rico Casals Festival is in session at the University Theater with a program of seven musical events designed to reflect the high and conservative taste of the festival's central figure and guiding force, the famed Catalan cellist-conductor, Pablo Casals.

A glance at this season's program book reveals many parallels to festivals of recent years. Concerts will consist of large and middle-sized orchestral favorites from the core of the standard concert repertory interspersed with Baroque miniatures; some pleasant surprises are in store here. A handful of virtually unknown works of high merit, peripheral to the standard repertory and in the present context somewhat daring, will make their appearance in the middle reaches of the short series and an extended finale of three evenings devoted to monumental works with chorus, orchestra and soloists will round off the festival in spectacular fashion.

Sadly missing from this festival are the glorious evenings of chamber music which were for several years and for many listeners the high points of the series. The Budapest Quartet, Andrés Segovia, Maria Stader, Mieczyslaw Horszowski, Casals himself and many others are remembered here for their excellence in this intimate art, whose unexplained passing from the Casals Festival is deeply mourned by many.

Still and all, Casals Festival remains a musical force to be reckoned with. The festival orchestra, now more than ever before the center of the whole thing, is a marvel. This orchestra is composed of masters: of seasoned artists in their own right who together create an ensemble whose precision, flexibility and purity of tone are beyond description.

Such was the orchestra which under Casals' direction closed the first concert of the present festival. One would think that such an old favorite as the First Symphony of Brahms could hold few surprises. Under Casals' direction, however, new and brilliant facets of the symphony were revealed: the total impression was one of irrepressible youthfulness and vigor. It's remarkable that while the rest of us pile up the years as we stagger forward, Pablo Casals at 87 seems to be shucking them off. Especially notable on Friday was the grand swing and flow of the symphony's final movement—an irresistible and exultant stream which even had some of the audience unconsciously tapping their feet and singing along with the familiar theme.

The rest of the opening pair of concerts was dominated by the pianists Serkin: father Rudolf and son Peter. Friday's concert opened with Rudolf Serkin, a perennial fixture of these festivals, and the festival orchestra conducted by Alexander Schneider, in the First Piano Concerto of Brahms. Then on Saturday father and son, singly and together, filled the solo positions in the evening's three Mozart concertos.

A bit of a gamble, this: scheduling an eveningful of works in the same form by the same composer and with the same soloists. The Serkins carried it off successfully, together with the festival orchestra, now reduced to Mozartean proportions and again conducted by Schneider.

Young Peter Serkin led off, with the brisk and cheerful Concerto in D Major (K 451) by Mozart, a work more characteristic of Haydn than of most of Mozart's music in its use of solo winds in incidental passages, its third movement's almost crudely folksy rhythm, and its splendidly unabashed swagger throughout. Serkin the younger played crisply and ably, with an enthusiasm nicely suited to the piece and with all the technical equipment necessary for its realization.

And then, the father came on. The elder Serkin's offering was the Concerto in A Major (K 414), a more "Mozartean" Mozart with its many rhythmic and harmonic subtleties and its caressing melodic flow. Serkin played as his son might someday when he has more years and more experience on him: that is to say, with great subtlety, faultless instinct and complete authority.

Saturday's concert closed with the elegant and spirited Concerto for Two Pianos and Orchestra (K 365), in a performance of which half the fun was precisely this contrast between the generations: the younger Serkin thrusting onward with the impetuous and sometimes brittle enthusiasm of youth; the elder, when his turn came, balancing it off with the mellow wisdom of maturity. A gratifying contrast; the work, after all, was written for two human pianists, not for a twenty-fingered Martian. At the end, soloists, conductor and orchestra shared repeated calls from the captivated audience.

Festival Finale: The Bach Passion

The San Juan Star
June 17, 1963   By Donald Thompson

    Whatever else might be said of them, eighteenth-century Lutherans possessed two sterling virtues: a deep love of music and great physical stamina. The two final evenings of this year's Casals Festival were devoted to the presentation of a masterpiece which in its original context—and with a sermon into the bargain—occupied a single sitting: the Good Friday *Passion According to Saint Matthew* by Johann Sebastian Bach. The work recounts the betrayal, trial, crucifixion and burial of Christ.
    On Thursday and Friday the mighty work, dramatic in concept and operatic in design, was conducted by Pablo Casals, and involved almost the entire Casals Festival Orchestra (divided according to the demands of the score into two smaller units), the miraculous Cleveland Orchestra Chorus of Robert Shaw (also divided into two groups), and six solo voices.
    Among the soloists, the warm, limpid and secure soprano of Olga Iglesias and the rich bass of William Warfield will long be remembered; notable also was the success with which Maureen Forrester's fine contralto has accomplished the adjustment from the deep heroic (last week's Wagner songs) to the lighter style of Bach. Ara Berberian's bass appeared at a disadvantage due to a treacherous cold; even so, it came into its own in Friday's "Come Blessed Cross." Mr. Berberian's lighter voice has an appeal of its own as has that of Raymond Murcell, bass, who also had a supporting role in last year's performance of Casals' *El Pessebre*. It would be a pleasure to hear more of Mr. Murcell, whose appearances here have given little more than a sample of his abilities.
    The narrative of the Passion is carried forward by the recitatives of the Evangelist, here tenor Ernst Haeflinger, whose ringing voice, tending

toward the grandly heroic style, was also heard in a number of arias throughout the work.

But the spiritual and musical foundation of the Saint Matthew Passion is to be found in the work's many chorales, sung by the entire chorus and supported by the massed double orchestra. Of four-square construction, straightforward harmony and stately motion, the chorales symbolize the participation of the church congregation in the unfolding of the Good Friday ritual. Robert Shaw's Cleveland Orchestra Chorus sounds like no conceivable earthly congregation of worthy burghers, but is instead as close to the celestial choir as most of us will ever come to hearing. In other sections of the oratorio, one or the other half of the chorus is entrusted with the dramatic utterances of witnesses and participants in the trial and crucifixion: "the people," priests, elders and bystanders; the Cleveland singers' thundering polyphony and stark interjections dramatically punctuated the expressive flow of solo voice throughout the two evenings.

Still, despite the length of the Saint Matthew Passion and the grand total of forces used in its presentation here, its general conception was that of something approaching chamber music. Each of the two orchestras was of "chamber orchestra" size and their union but seldom required, while each of the two choruses was of a size with which clear counterpoint can still be obtained. Too, the largest ensemble of solo voices in the composition is a moving duet of soprano and contralto, while most of the oratorio is borne forward on light instrumental accompaniment. Admirable throughout the two Bach evenings was the really solid and subtle union of cellist Frank Miller, harpsichord Robert Conant and organist Paul Wolfe, who together provided the nucleus around which the entire performance was built.

Within seconds after Bach's final phrase had melted away in sweet resolution, the entire capacity of the University Theater was on its feet in mutual respect and honor: orchestra, soloists, Robert Shaw's marvelous chorus, Mr. Shaw himself and Saturday's large audience; with final and highest honors for the diminutive giant who had brought them all together: Pablo Casals.

Thus ended the Saint Matthew Passion of Bach, and with it the seventh annual Puerto Rico Casals Festival. In looking back over this seventh season, certain elements stand out. Certainly, this year's festival cannot expect to be remembered for having introduced a new roster of soloists to its local public; the annual appearance of several of the festival regulars is, in fact, a contributing factor to the festival's having taken such firm root in Puerto Rican soil. Regular attendance at the concerts has come to mean participation in an annual conclave of old and beloved friends; at the very least it increases concertgoers' familiarity with cornerstones of the musical art in performances which can be considered definitive, a blessing not to be taken lightly.

Nor can it be said that this year's Festival Orchestra has improved over last year's or the one before that. Perfection is not a matter of degree, and a festival orchestra which is a marvel by the very nature of its components, is not going to vary in overall effect from one year to the next. Conceived in greatness, this orchestra remained great in its seventh season, and that's about all that can be said of it in retrospect.

Still, some specific performances of this season persist in the memory. Pablo Casals' youthful direction of Brahms' First Symphony was a revelation to this listener as was his intimate conception of the Saint Matthew Passion: intimate conception and intimate knowledge, in both cases the result of Casals' long and loving familiarity with the music.

Alexander Schneider, assistant musical director and a central force in guiding the destinies of the Casals Festival, served this year both as conductor (most effectively in the works of Mozart, Bach, Vivaldi, and Handel which occupied the middle of the series) and as soloist, collaborating gloriously with Isaac Stern and Sidney Harth in a program of Vivaldi miniatures.

Rudolf Serkin, that genial figure who places the firm stamp of absolute mastery on everything he touches, made a celebrated contribution in an evening of Mozart concertos; the genius of Mozart (itself reason enough for a hundred festivals) was also tellingly represented by the "Prague" Symphony directed by Juan José Castro, who in addition introduced an oddment by Monteverdi: the *Sonata sopra Sancta Maria* for women's voices, strings, and the festival orchestra's superb brass section.

High Spirited Climax for Concert Season

The San Juan Star
March 23, 1966   By Francis Schwartz

The Tapia Theater, filled to capacity Monday night, hosted the final concert in the regular season of the Puerto Rico Symphony Orchestra. The orchestra, under the baton of Victor Tevah, and the audience were in high spirits, and it was a fitting climax to a rewarding two months of listening during the present brief orchestral season.

Schubert's Symphony No. 4, the "Tragic," began the evening. The conception was lean, correct, and based more on strict metrical adherence than relaxed lyricism, in the spirit of Teutonic athleticism rather than Viennese *Gemütlichkeit*.

Following on the program was Rimsky-Korsakov's *Capriccio Espagnol*, an old warhorse of the orchestral repertoire. The *Capriccio* never loses its charm in spite of countless hearings because the rhythms are alive and the flamboyant orchestration absolutely batters the audience into submission.

The orchestra played beautifully. Not content with emphasizing the musical robustness, the woodwind section delivered first-class solo work in the sensuous melodic sections. And two French horn phrases in the second section were downright delicious. Rather a sweet and pungent Rimsky-Korsakov.

The power and drive of the finale brought tingles to many a spine and one can only say it was wonderful to hear this inspired playing.

After intermission, the Third Piano Concerto of Serge Prokofiev was brought into the spotlight. The soloist for the evening was Irma Vallecillo, a twenty year old pianist currently studying at the Juilliard School of Music in New York City. To use the word "student" is very misleading, for she is just a step away from full membership in the professional ranks. Miss Vallecillo has very good technical equipment and sufficient power to do justice to Prokofiev's musical brawn.

The concerto is a curious combination of neo-classicism structurally, modernism harmonically, and romanticism in melody and atmosphere. The biting percussiveness constantly gives way to dreamy tonal explorations moving the music nervously from high point to low. Rhythmically the electric motor pulsations act as a directional propellant.

Fortunately, the soloist understands the tensile strength of the music. She selected her fortes with good taste and never allowed the music to degenerate into an orgy of banging.

The first movement was excellent. It had the necessary ingredients of accuracy, imagination and flair. The second had a weak spot or two but on the whole was good. For some reason the third variation moved sluggishly and was underplayed in tone and rhythm. The fourth scintillated with delicate sounds flexibly embroidering the theme. The final movement closed with energy and rhythmic punch.

It was a very fine evening for piano playing, and in this reviewer's opinion, Irma Vallecillo has a very promising musical future.

Electronic Music Comes to Town

The San Juan Star
March 28, 1966 By Francis Schwartz

Electronic music? The coming of a new era? Well, we had better see about that. Saturday evening, four musicians entered the Puerto Rico Conservatory of Music (one had to be carried in) for the first performance of an all electronic music concert in Puerto Rico. The non-mobile member was a tape recorder, lovingly cared for by Messrs. Milton Babbitt, Vladimir Ussachevsky and Mario Davidovsky, composers represented on the program.

Electronic music is produced by the alteration of sound waves by complex electronic means. The raw sonic material may be taken from a bell, a voice, a sneeze (musique concrète) and is then altered by the composer; or it may be taken from the pure oscillations of sound which pass through the entrails of an electronic music synthesizer.

Bulent Arel's Electronic Music No. 1 opened this historic, never to be forgotten program. Imagine 400 innocent, well-meaning concertgoers facing a stage devoid of life except for two electronic speakers. Then conjure up the quaint combination of a hoarse vacuum cleaner, a rhinoceros with a bad cold, the hysterical shriek of a woman being strangled, the scrape of a fingernail against a blackboard; all this accompanied by a chorus of 200 voices gargling in unison: and you have a vivid image of Saturday night's performance.

Oh brave new world! If this is the future of music we may end up tone-deaf!

Realistically, electronic music is a new musical pathway which after rejection and modification, will inevitably be accepted. This listener feels that the future of this musical genre lies in integration with conventional instruments. The most enjoyable and possibly the most important compositions were Davidovsky's *Sincronismos 1 & 3*, ably performed by flutist Felix Skowronek and cellist Adolfo Odnoposoff; and Babbitt's *Vision and Prayer*, with soprano Ethel Casey doing beautiful work in the difficult vocal part.

When mirrored against the human performer, electronic music creates an eerie, fantastic atmosphere. The pointillistic effects bring out a clarity and one perceives a cohesive quality; a quality sadly lacking in the other, purely electronic, works.

As for the composers, one must salute their valor and energy in the pursuit of this experiment. The electronic medium has a future, but it must become more personalized, more recognizably expressive, and ultimately, more useful. The tape recorder can be an effective instrument in the orchestra; Respighi realized the value of recorded sound early in the century. But to exclude the entire realm of instruments relegating the musical past to a dusty library vault is sheer folly.

This reviewer thought to himself, as he watched the tape recorder smugly blipping and waffling its way through the concert (at the risk of incurring the wrath of Federal security agencies), . . . just one small, strategically-placed power failure in Hato Rey. . . .

Controversial ideas of the present are the conservative ideas of the future. We need more exposition to these new musical explorations and hope that Puerto Rico will stay in the musical mainstream by continuing this imaginative program of contemporary music.

Chávez Concerto at UPR

The San Juan Star
April 2, 1966   By Francis Schwartz

The University of Puerto Rico Theater, filled with illustrious figures of the music world on Thursday night, was the scene of the Hispanoamerican premiere of Carlos Chávez's Violin Concerto, performed by the Puerto Rico Symphony Orchestra under the direction of Victor Tevah, with Georges Tessier as soloist.

To open the program was Antonio Tauriello's Symphonic Overture, whose most commendable quality was its brevity.

Flashy orchestration is no substitute for musical substance and this listener was waiting for twenty thousand gladiators to come streaming out of the wings with a movie director in hot pursuit.

The Chávez concerto came as a surprise. One associates Chávez with raw, granitic rhythms; orchestration teeming with percussive devices; and a musical brightness which is blinding to the ear (if one can use such a phrase). But this work is permeated with a lush romantic quality and filled with violinistic delicacies. This is the music of the early twentieth century, music which usually finds its spiritual home in the nationalistic schools.

The form of the work, which in reality is a huge one movement design, is clearly outlined by the use of the theme and variations technique. Unfortunately, many of the rapid variations use the same violinistic vocabulary and tend to sound repetitive. Rhythmically the composition is exciting. Chávez may try to be more melodiously mellow but he cannot suppress those wonderful driving rhythms which give life to his compositions.

As for Georges Tessier, the violin soloist, one can sum up his performance in one word: brilliant. He is a masterful technician with a sweet sound. He has a nervous vibrato which borders on St. Vitus dance, at times disturbing the tranquility of a slow melody. Tessier's intonation was excellent, amazingly so because of the music's countless leaps and running note passages. It was an advantage to have such a convincing artist perform the concerto and no doubt Maestro Chávez, sitting in the audience, was satisfied.

Juan Orrego Salas's Piano Concerto was given a fine performance by Elías López Sobá. The work is gay, unpretentious, and evoked a Poulencian atmosphere. Perhaps "Concertino" would be a more accurate title for the work than "Concerto."

Concluding the program with a huge work is a fine idea, but Roque Cordero's Second Symphony proved too much for this reviewer. It is certainly filled with imagination, clever technical tricks and interesting orchestration. But how many times can one repeat a musical idea without running it into the ground? Bach had the good sense not to overdo his ground basses. Cordero chose to push it beyond the three mile limit. The fault lies in the handling of the musical architecture, not in lack of inventiveness, and certainly not a lack of personality. In this festival, this composer has demonstrated one of the most forceful musical personalities; one would like to hear his work in the shorter forms.

Don Pablo Evokes Great Emotion

The San Juan Star
June 10, 1966   By Francis Schwartz

There was a moment of great emotion when ailing don Pablo Casals walked onto the stage Wednesday night at the University Theater. Recovering from his recent illness, the intrepid maestro made his first festival appearance conducting Beethoven's Fifth Symphony. It could not have been more appropriate: a heroic symphony by a heroic composer conducted by a heroic human being. Everyone's heart was up on the podium and players were on the edges of their chairs.

The Beethoven was powerful, hypnotizing. What dynamism Casals projected and how the orchestra played for him! Every note was played to the utmost and the expressivity was breathtaking. No longer in the realm of performance, the musical experience was more like a communion of souls, a merging of personalities in order to achieve something beautiful. And it was achieved.

The ovation for the Maestro was explosive. People were yelling, stomping, beating their hands purple, and some, crying. A moving experience.

Casals' presence inspired everyone. Alexander Schneider conducted a scintillating Marriage of Figaro Overture. The tempo was not hasty and one heard everything, in a performance marked by charm, grace and elegance. Excellent Mozart.

Next came the Mozart D Major Flute Concerto with John Wummer as soloist. This man is one of the world's great flutists. He played with joy and enthusiasm. The tone and the rhythmic lilt which came from that flute, paired with imaginative orchestral work, made for a splendid performance. The cadenzas sparkled and the bouncing joviality of the final allegro was humorous Mozart playing at its best.

Apparently the magical effect extended to young Soviet artist Igor Oistrakh, who, in contrast to his previous performance, really opened up musically in the Brahms Violin Concerto. He was daring, full of excitement, and showed no timidity concerning slides or vibrato. It was a big, assured Brahms which he conveyed and his reception was indeed merited. Especially fine playing was done by the horn section and the oboist, Harry Shulman.

This was the Casals Festival. This was the kind of playing that sends the audience out of the hall afire with the beauties of music. Assembled here are some of the world's finest, and one demands the very finest from them. Wednesday night they fulfilled every hope. Of this they can be proud for it was the highest tribute they could pay to the man whom they so deeply revere.

Ormandy Conducts—and Conquers

The San Juan Star
June 18, 1966   By Francis Schwartz

It was a night of reformation, transformation and definitely, elevation. Maestro Eugene Ormandy, who on Thursday evening conducted the Puerto Rico Casals Festival Orchestra, thrilled a teeming University Theater audience with his interpretive mastery and personal magnetism.

The program began with the overture to Weber's opera *Der Freischütz*. Filled with the macabre and rooted in an incipient nationalism, this work was the turning point for romantic German opera. Its influence on the more hysterical side of German romanticism (including Austro-Hungarians), is obvious with its use of magic heroism and the importance of the horn. Wagner was ecstatic about the work and even the counter-school of Schumann-Brahms was somewhat molded by the legacy of Weber.

Ormandy's interpretation was nothing less than brilliant. Contrasting the bright, optimistic sections with the more mysterious, the conductor wove a spell that was not short-lived. The orchestra was a great instrument tuned to perfection, working with clock-like precision. The horn section solo at the beginning of the overture was exquisite, and you will not hear finer horn playing anywhere in the world. The violins had a rich, full sound splendidly executing their theme of hope and courage. Perhaps the greatest moment of all occurred when nobody played. Yes! The poignant silences before the finale robbed one's breath in anxious anticipation of the climax. Truly a beautifully conceived performance.

Following the overture was the "Reformation" Symphony, No. 5, of Felix Mendelssohn. This large composition is based on Lutheran church music and may have been a commemorative work of the Augsburg Reforms.

Ormandy brought out the towering spirituality of the symphony. After the quasi-invocation style of the first *andante*, the orchestra pounced insistently onto the forceful *allegro*. The second movement had bucolic charm; played not too fast, as it often is, and allowing the music to breathe. There was breadth in the finale with exciting brass work heightening the tension and forging a resounding ring of finality.

Using the intermission to recover from the much-welcomed musical onslaught, the audience returned to hear the Seventh Symphony of Beethoven. It was the highest type of musicianship that one heard, for every orchestral line stood out with the greatest clarity. The violas bolted from the orchestral fabric to emphasize their phrase-closing importance, which is often neglected. Nothing marred the transition from the sustained opening to the bouncing, dotted-rhythm *vivace*.

Ormandy drew huge crescendos which seemed to emanate from beneath the stage, so great was their range. The precision which accompanied the difficult dotted-rythm entrances awed this listener. Ormandy gets exactly what he wants from an orchestra with apparent ease, and his knowledge of what to conduct and what not to conduct when dealing with a fine orchestra exemplifies his professional expertise.

Beethoven's *allegretto* marking of the second movement has caused many a heated word in the world of music. Some conductors feel that it is misplaced and play the movement very slowly. Others take the indication as license to fly through at a hectic pace. Ormandy chose a happy medium, pushing the music ahead by allowing enough time for all of the instrumental interplay to be heard. It was nice to hear the triplets at the bottom of the string section for a change. The musicians played with great enthusiasm; such was the enthusiasm, in fact, that a couple of violinists gave us a bonus of an additional counterpoint at the close of the movement.

The final two movements were majestic, representing the best in Beethoven playing. A salute to Ormandy and to the orchestra. They were, without reservation, superb.

How Long Can Puerto Rico Ignore Twentieth-Century Music?

The San Juan Star
August 7, 1966   By Francis Schwartz

At a recent concert a prominent local composer who had just returned from the Caracas Music Festival exclaimed with mixed feelings of hope and anguish, "We are still in the nineteenth century. We don't even know what is going on in the world."

As an observation this is quite accurate; as a situation it is entirely unnecessary. Puerto Rico is living in a musical world which ended before the invention of the airplane. The public remains unaware of the new and not-so-new developments in the Orphean art, and there is not much concern regarding this antiquated position. If the same condition existed in industrial techniques or clothing styles, expenditures of funds and energy would seek ways of modernization.

What has happened in the world outside? Twentieth-century composers have created many styles: atonality, polytonality, chance music, electronic music. A host of experiments have taken place, have been modified and have absorbed and given birth to new experiments in turn.

The composer of this century has had to find a way to express the phenomena of two world wars, the age of flight, universal political upheavals, racial strife, the atomic age, automation, population explosion, the exploration of space. Quite obviously he could no longer work with nineteenth-century forms without alienating himself from the flow of historical events and the dynamic novelty of his environment. Thus he broke with the immediate past.

Many trends formed. The composer's desire to jettison all Romantic trappings led him to primitivism, the use of savage rhythms and acerbic dissonances. This was the primeval home from which music sprang and Bartók, Stravinsky and Prokofiev employed this style in an attempt to purge the past.

The Austro-Germanic atonalists turned music upside down by wiping out 500 years of tonal striving only to impose a strict theoretical code. Arnold Schoenberg, with his pupils Berg and Webern, initiated this important temporary force.

The movement of the "Neo," Neo-Classicism, Neo-Gothic, Neo-Baroque, found expression in the works of Stravinsky, Hindemith, Bloch and Prokofiev. A search was on for the incorporation of new, freely conceived techniques within the architectonic concepts of past eras.

The nationalism of the twentieth century was accompanied by a resurgence of nationalistic music. Prokofiev, Bartók, Copland, Chávez and Vaughan-Williams delved into the richness of folklore and folk music to establish a native means of expression, a musical confirmation of national pride.

Edgard Varèse concatenated sounds, whether from musical instruments, sirens, tire screeches or coughs, brilliantly opening another path in the already vital modernism.

The composer of our century feels free to experiment in all realms, and we encounter specific composers cataloged among several modern trends because they have tried the many ways available to them.

Since the end of World War II new composers with exciting new ideas have come upon the scene. Karlheinz Stockhausen, Milton Babbitt, Christoph Caskel, Mario Davidovsky and Otto Luening have ventured into the world of electronic music, artificially creating sounds with enormously complex machines. Perhaps this was a logical development in an age which has come to rely upon the machine for practically all tasks.

Others who choose to stay closer to the human element are Gunther Schuller, Luigi Nono, Hans Werner Henze, Ben Weber, Pierre Boulez, Witold Lutoslawski and John Cage. These men, well schooled in the techniques of the past, are experimenting with new forms, new instruments, new combinations of elements. They seek a solution to the problem of expressing this fantastic world which dramatically changes before our very eyes. They are achieving their goal, and their work will in turn foster new modes of musical creation. It is the pattern of music's history.

For Puerto Rico, with two thirds of the century already recorded, these men and their music do not exist. An average concert program here consists of one part classical music, one part romantic and just a pinch of the Baroque (if that pinch happens to be Bach or Handel).

The situation is seriously debilitating, for it leaves the public ignorant of cultural forces which have proven themselves internationally over the past 66 years. It creates an intolerable atmosphere for the local composer who either has no contact with vital developments in his art or is intimidated into composing old, "likable" music that everyone will accept.

This is the crisis here and now. New works are primarily *danzas* or *plenas* dressed up in slightly more modern costume, expressions of nineteenth-century musical ideas with compositional techniques of the 1920s. With the vast change in living patterns on the island, the growth of industrialization, the shattering of insularity by modern travel facilities, it is simply not enough to orchestrate something that reminds one of "No Me Toques," toss in a few dissonances for contemporary "authenticity" and hold the work up as a composer's reflection of this environment.

The community of composers has been loath to try anything new; consequently their output is small with little variety. Recently there have been some stirrings which bode well for the future, if continued. Héctor Campos-Parsi, in his recent trio, *Petroglifos*, took a long step toward the present and indications are that he may continue his new line of endeavor. My own chamber work *Antigone* will be introduced this winter, representing a new form of modern expression used only in Europe at present. Perhaps other composers will become curious and delve into this vast sea of modernity, bringing vitality to the local musical life.

The situation must be changed. It can be changed without a great deal of difficulty, needing only intelligent planning and an adventurous spirit. The following steps are recommended.

1. Modern works should be included with frequency in the programs of the better known musical organizations, such as the Puerto Rico Symphony Orchestra, the Puerto Rico Casals Festival and the University of Puerto Rico concert series. This would gradually expose the public and musicians to the new art and awaken their interest.

2. Concerts for school children should include contemporary works. Youth apparently readily comprehends modern music, while their elders are often hampered by prejudice.

3. Internationally active composers should be invited here to lecture, premiere new works and discuss their techniques with local composers and performers.

4. Commissions for new works should be more numerous. Considering the soaring wealth of Puerto Rico, patronage of new compositions is disappointingly small.

5. A competition should be established inviting participants from all over the world. It would give the local composer an opportunity to compete on the highest levels. Nothing could be healthier for his development.

6. Individual performers and soloists, out of duty to the perpetuation of their art, should endeavor to present twentieth-century works. One may not prefer the modern school but one should not be fossilized mentally and should be aware of all art.

Many organizations can begin programs fostering development of contemporary music: universities, government, conservatories, private enterprise and cultural societies.

Puerto Rico must be brought into the twentieth century and cease being a musical anachronism. The talent of the present and the future depends upon the island's ability to face the realities of a new world, a world whose complexities and marvels will fire the imagination of composers, stimulating new creations and shaping historical landmarks of man's nobler ways.

The Plight of a Young Composer

The San Juan Star
September 24, 1966   By Francis Schwartz

    Musical composition in Puerto Rico is dying. For a serious composer, the conservatism which characterizes our musical institutions presents an almost insurmountable barrier. To the creator who moves with the innovations of the world, our current tastes are a Dantean torture. To the composer who seeks professional debate, technical interchange, contributions by fellow composers against which to measure one's own work, Puerto Rico is a desert.

    What happens to an art when it depends exclusively upon public approval for its stylistic base? What happens to creativity when the self takes refuge in a romantic past? The result is a meaningless output of mediocre quality; a futile exercise in nostalgia which leads nowhere. And that is the situation of our community of composers.

    What is truly astonishing is that the composer, who presumably is propelled by an adventuresome spirit, has become so domesticated. He writes (when he writes) harmless salon pieces more appropriate to Madame du Pompadour's gatherings than the dynamic world of the twentieth century. Controversy is to be avoided at all costs. No radical techniques, no unpopular literary overtones, no political references outside of the acceptable. The lion has turned vegetarian.

    To understand the seriousness of the situation one has only to analyze some of the opinions presented by composers regarding contemporary techniques. In regard to serialism and twelve-tone writing, which has had international acceptance for more than a quarter century this writer was privileged to hear, "I wrote a piece during my conservatory years using this technique. It just doesn't fit my personality." A student exploration of the revolutionary musical system led to instant rejection. As if such a monumental procedure could be absorbed and comprehended with a few work hours. Can one imagine Monteverdi saying, "I tried out the major-minor system a couple of times but you know, it just isn't me." Or perhaps Richard Wagner commenting, "this chromaticism is all very stimulating intellectually, but I'll take the classics, thank you."

Ridiculous? Of course. To create, the composer must be open to all new ideas; to experiment, reject, modify, worry, struggle; until he emerges with some inkling of the music's validity. Then, and only then, is he prepared to utilize those elements compatible with his own artistic beliefs and responsibly reject the rest.

Another attitude detrimental to progress is the prejudice toward new instruments and electronic sounds. "It's noise, anti-art. A joke." "I dabbled a bit but returned to the beauty of melody."

New instrumental sounds have been accompanied through the ages by jeers and scoffing. The saxophone, invented in 1842, had to bear the brunt of this narrow-mindedness. And at the moment electronic sounds, whether the amplification of standard instruments by electronic means or the use of electrical synthesizers which work with pure electronically made sounds, are firing the imaginations of composers the world over. Here it is foolishly ridiculed.

Do the traditionalists think that their "valid" instruments sprang from the forehead of Zeus? Don't they realize that instruments have undergone periodic changes; that what was considered acceptable by one generation was insufficient for the next? In a world filled with electronically produced sounds from TV, radio, phonographs, one cannot ignore their importance to daily life and must consider their possibilities as musical elements.

As for "dabbling a bit" that is like being a "little bit dead." When you experiment you plunge into a new idea as if it were Truth made music, simultaneously trying to verify and destroy its elements. In art there is no room for dabbling.

Another serious obstacle to creativity is the "political hangup." I have spent countless hours hearing composers rant about the intolerable political situation in Puerto Rico. Feelings are intense on the subject and politics is of importance in the composer's life. What is terribly disappointing about the parlor revolutionaries is that their fervent political feelings remain neatly tucked away while they continue to produce timid works. Political viewpoints are not important. What is vital is that the artists utilize their conflicts with the world; not to hide in the comfort of blandness but to speak out according to conscience. To do less is to betray their belief.

It is impossible to separate the works of Beethoven, Wagner, Verdi from the socio-political ferment of their times. There is no need to sloganize in music for it to be politically motivated. If the artist feels the violence and injustice of his surroundings, he must sacrifice in order to voice his ideas. If the composer seeks comfort instead of truth he ceases to be an artist.

What will the future hold for Puerto Rico's composers? The picture is gloomy. At present Rafael Aponte-Ledée is working with serialism and the electronic medium; the writer of this article is composing with the fusion of electronic sounds and conventional instruments. Two men under the age of thirty, but only two.

The older generation has frozen. Veray, Campos-Parsi, Délano, Ramírez, give us the same tired formulas year after year. They have ceased to contribute anything new in the artistic sense. It is doubtful whether the bulk of their music will be anything more than historical references in the next century.

Until the public, composers and organizational potentates wake up to the fact that art cannot be outmoded; if convenience rules instead of artistic conscientiousness, then the reign of mediocrity will continue undisturbed.

In the words of Debussy's Monsieur Croche, "Discipline must be sought in freedom, and not within the formulas of an outworn philosophy only fit for the feebleminded. Give ear to no man's counsel; but listen to the wind which tells in passing the history of the world."

Carnival Accompanies Concert

The San Juan Star
February 5, 1967 By Francis Schwartz

In the annals of music history there abound performance stories with riots, stage mishaps, backstage romances and so on. Certainly, the Friday night concert at the Tapia Theater will take its place among the most entertaining of these tales.

The Claremont Quartet, playing splendidly in the Ravel String Quartet, found themselves suddenly accompanied by a choir of motorcycles, skybombs and marching bands. Contributing to the general harmony were the periodic cheers which hailed the passing carnival queen. Ravel would have been fascinated by the coloristic effects; the police whistles would probably have suggested an orchestral version of the quartet.

After the last hurrah, the Claremont returned to complete the program. The Ravel was beautifully played. The shadings were subtle and quite audible. The musicians maintained a fine balance of sound and conceptually held the large form tightly (but no stiffly) in place. In the last movement, the biting rhythm blended exquisitely into the lyrical section, and then out again into an exciting undulating pattern. Fine control.

Bartók's Third String Quartet (1927) closed the program. Without any doubt this work is one of the best string quartets written in the twentieth century. Bartók is without peer in the quartet form; to find a comparable master of chamber strings one must look back to Brahms and Beethoven. The Hungarian composer's immense conception of string possibilities has enriched the musical vocabulary of modern composers and his mastery of the form is awesome, for the music appears in fractured, spasmodic sections: yet the quartet is completely unified.

The performance was brilliant. Combining excellent ensemble with emotional sweep, the Claremont rendered outstanding service to Bartók and to the audience.

Laila Storch joined three members of the string group for a performance of Mozart's Quartet for Oboe and Strings (K 370). Unfortunately this listener was unable to reach the theater for the Mozart, due to a traffic jam of Wagnerian magnitude.

The selection of another concert site would have been more logical on such a night as the Carnival Queen Coronation, but at least music history was made. Assuredly both audience and artists will not forget Friday the Third: the night Ravel caused dancing in the streets of San Juan.

Chamber Orchestra at UPR

The San Juan Star
February 15, 1967   By Francis Schwartz

    The largest audience seen during the present San Juan Chamber Music Festival flocked to the University of Puerto Rico theater for the Monday night concert of the Paris Chamber Orchestra. The orchestra, a relatively young group of musicians under the baton of Paul Kuentz, presented a tasteful, varied program with works ranging from Torelli to Bartók.
    The overall impression which the Paris orchestra gives is that of control, for Kuentz terraces his dynamics carefully within narrow limits. What he achieves in subtle contrasts is admirable, considering his self-imposed bounds. Rhythmically, the group is quite deliberate, emphasizing pulse in a heavy manner. For the Baroque period this is fine though in the classicism of Mozart it becomes ponderous. The ensemble produces a nice smooth sound with no ragged edges.
    The evening began with a solid performance of Rameau's Concerto No. 6, "La Poule." The tempi were well chosen and never hurried, thus allowing the charm of the music to come through.
    In the Torelli Trumpet Concerto, trumpeter Adolf Scherbaum proved himself an exciting soloist. His tone is large but not harsh; excellent breath control allows him to shade and contrast phrases, while his musical delivery is with the utmost of clarity. Kuentz coordinated the counterparts skillfully.
    Bach's Violin Concerto in D, with Monique Frasca-Colombier as soloist, began at a slow, almost too slow, pace. One wondered if the interpretation could hold up under such metrical stress. Fortunately the beat was relentless and the first movement concluded well. It is a tribute to the fine musicianship of these artists that they are able to create a

feeling of long line at such a tempo. Playing fast makes it much easier. Miss Frasca-Colombier's playing is again exemplary of the tight control which reigns throughout the orchestra. Every phrase was well thought out, each nuance correctly placed, and her tone appropriately blended into the orchestral sound. What was lacking in spontaneity was present in solid, intellectual musicianship.

After intermission, Scherbaum performed the Trumpet Concerto of Telemann. And again, he did wonderful things with the work. It was in the Mozart Serenade (K 239), where one felt the musical control a bit overbearing. Even the planned *ritard* at each entrance of the first rondo theme became matter-of-fact, because after several repetitions it lost its piquant flavor, its coquettishness. In general the Mozart needed more life, more gaiety *a la italiana*.

The final work, Bartók's Rumanian Dances, represents the composer's own orchestral transcription of a work originally conceived for piano. Using folk material collected on his many musicological surveys, Bartók created six dances of exotic melodiousness and rhythmic power. The Paris Chamber Orchestra felt at home with this music, interpreting it with spirit and emotion. One could take issue with Mr. Kuentz's ideas on the second dance, "Braul." Usually one expects a pause after each phrase which is intimately tied up with its dance qualities. The conductor chose to maintain a steady beat, which would be a dancer's nightmare.

For those who attended, the concert was a treat; we hope that the Paris Chamber Orchestra will visit us again.

Final Chamber Festival Concert

The San Juan Star
February 21, 1967 By Francis Schwartz

Sunday afternoon's concert at the Puerto Rico Conservatory of Music brought to a close the First San Juan Chamber Music Festival. Under the directorship of Kachiro Figueroa, the Institute of Puerto Rican Culture Chamber Orchestra presented three compositions from the Italian Baroque and one early romantic surprise, Bellini's *Concerto for Oboe and Strings*.

Alessandro Scarlatti's Concerto Grosso in F opened the program. The performance was adequate though not imaginatively conceived; there were few dynamic subtleties and the most that can be said is that the playing was accurate and had steady rhythm.

The Concerto for Oboe and Strings of Benedetto Marcello, with Laila Storch as soloist, did not fare well. The Baroque concerto concept is to pit the orchestral mass against the soloist or soloists. There is an emphasis on contrast, on musical competition. Mr. Figueroa took this duel quite seriously, almost annihilating the soloist. Every diminuendo, every phrase ending in the oboe part was swallowed up by the thick string sound. And the beat was so inflexible. It is bad enough for a violinist to hurriedly search for new positions because of rhythmic rigidity, but in the case of a wind instrument it is worse. Breath is involved; breath which influences tone and line. This situation hampered Miss Storch considerably. Her musicianship came warmly through in the *adagio*, for it was there, and only there, that she had enough freedom to sing.

Bellini's Concerto for Oboe and Strings is an operatic work; so operatic is it that we expected the Druids (from Bellini's opera *Norma*) to form a circle after the opening *larghetto*. There is great lyricism in the work and the closing *allegro* has its charm. Here the soloist played with verve and articulated with skill. Again the accompaniment was heavy handed.

José Figueroa, Henry Hutchinson and Guillermo Figueroa joined the orchestra for the Vivaldi Concerto for Three Violins in F. The performance lacked clarity and suffered from bad intonation. It was impossible to make any sense out of the music.

Thus closes the San Juan Chamber Music Festival. We have complained considerably during the last year of the dearth of chamber music in our musical life and the dull programming. The Festival has offered many types of chamber ensembles, music from several eras, and has proved beyond doubt that the public will support this intimate art. Perhaps this mass support might even encourage the Casals Festival to again undertake the presentation of chamber music.

A word of thanks to the University of Puerto Rico, the Puerto Rico Conservatory of Music and the Institute of Puerto Rican Culture for their excellent efforts in the service of art and the community.

Modern Music Concert

The San Juan Star
May 17, 1967 By Francis Schwartz

The Institute of Puerto Rican Culture was the scene Sunday afternoon of a contemporary music concert performed by the newly-formed Trío de Puerto Rico. The trio, composed of violinist José Figueroa, cellist Adolfo Odnoposoff and pianist Elías López Sobá, forged their way through three trios which they had recently played in a music festival in Venezuela.

Musically, the program went from better to worse. The concert began with Campos-Parsi's *Petroglifos*, which is a moderately experimental work using new techniques such as emulation of electronic sound waves; fists, forearms, and fingernails as pianistic armament; and the older Bartókian concept of enmeshed harmonic and slide playing. Divided into five brief movements, the music is fragmented, bursting into sudden rages only to subside into a dry musical abruptness. The instruments are balanced in importance and worked together nicely due both to the writing and to the ensemble work of the Trío de Puerto Rico.

The composer's decision to be terse enabled him to capture his audience's attention. Brevity is one of the most controversial subjects of contemporary music. Historically, the Greeks would listen to their quasi-religious dramatic and musical celebrations for days on end. In the eighteenth and nineteenth centuries, musical programs would last four or five hours without any discomfort to the public. But the twentieth century has created the one and-a-half hour concert, and with its new mode of musical expression, even this duration taxes the listener.

Since the destruction of recognizable melodic ideas and its ever present companion, musical repetition, the listener has been left in a state of suspended animation. He no longer knows what to listen for, and unless he is one of the initiates who can sit down with the score to follow the technical marvels in detail, he may feel in the midst of musical bedlam. On the conscious level the mind can absorb new material only to a limited extent, and brevity becomes a musical necessity if there is to be a true communication between the modern experimental composer and his public.

And this brings us to the other works. Sergio Cervetti's Cinco Episodios was an abstract, spatial work which this listener will not presume to judge until another hearing. From the point of view of effects, it is very interesting. But effects alone do not a piece of music make.

The Trio, Op. 58 of Juan Orrego Salas was disappointing. Like his piano concerto, this work is a potpourri of musical styles. The musical hodge-podge consisted of Bartókian melody (it sure sounded like the Concerto for Orchestra), a Golliwog Cakewalk rhythm (credit to Mr. Debussy), and a hybrid harmonic palette of Schoenberg and Poulenc. Professor Orrego is a well schooled musician and an admirable teacher. What can possibly induce him to produce this kind of music?

It is heartening to see the formation of the Trío de Puerto Rico. They, of course, are fine professional players and one looks forward to many future concerts of modern music as well as the other musical epochs.

Two Casals Festival favorites, **Isaac Stern** and **Yehudi Menuhim** in conversation.

War Gloom Hits Festival

The San Juan Star
June 8, 1967 By Francis Schwartz

A cloud of gloom descended upon the fourth Casals Festival concert, Tuesday night. Many musicians were actively concerned about the outbreak of war in the Middle East and in order to express their desire for peace, the orchestra changed the program to one of a more solemn nature.

Alexander Schneider led the opening work, Beethoven's Egmont Overture. It was a somber performance without the vitality one expects from the music. Even the ensemble work was on the light side. Obviously everyone worked, but the result was not happy.

Isaac Stern, noted violinist, strode onto the stage and performed the D Minor Chaconne from Bach's Second Violin Partita. His technical expertise coupled with an imaginative understanding of the musical form gave birth to a highly sensitive, moving Bach. The shadings and phrasings were ingeniously applied, as were the occasional pullings at the rhythmical fabric, stretching a cadence for a more decisive effect. It was beautifully done: introspective and deeply felt.

In order to participate in this placation of the god Mars, Maestro Casals made an unscheduled appearance, conducting the "Air" from the Third Orchestral Suite of Bach. The interpretation was lush and romantic, the type of Bach which Casals has repeatedly advocated. No one has been able to dissuade the maestro from his interpretative ideas, so let it suffice to say that there are other valid ways to play the music of Bach.

Stern returned to deliver a lovely reading of Dvořák's Romanze for Violin and Orchestra. The composition is certainly worthy and its neglect can only be a loss for the music world. Stern and Schneider worked together successfully, the violin carefully terraced above the orchestral mass but never so forcefully as to interrupt the Elysian mood.

The evening closed with Stern as soloist in the first movement of Beethoven's Violin Concerto.

At this point one must speak out. That the players wished to make an offering for peace bespeaks their nobility. Artists must participate in society and fulfill their tasks as citizens. If they feel they must emphasize their beliefs by an artistic gesture, fine, as long as the art does not base itself constantly on a political premise. The evening's program was completely altered in order to better emulate the seriousness of the moment. Again fine. But why chop up musical works? What greater expression of humanity than the entire Beethoven concerto? That it ends with a joyful movement in no way conflicts with the search for peace. On the contrary, it is an expression of hope, of optimism in the ability of man to live in brotherhood. And why not the entire Bach orchestral suite? After all he was a fairly competent composer. There was no need to dissect the composition.

This writer is in complete sympathy with the expression extolling the virtues of peace, but not the vehicle used. And rehearsal problems do not justify a fragmented program. Both Stern and the orchestra have played the Beethoven many times, and given their high professional quality, could have played a gratifying performance. Nobody would be nit-picking on such an occasion.

Which brings us to the final point. We had the unpleasant experience of sitting in the midst of a new breed of concert-goer: the young dilettante. The Young D, as we shall refer to said organism in the future, is a person who has read several record jackets, a virtuoso of hi-fi button manipulation, a master of the studied smirk, and whose profound musical opinions are based on opinions heard five minutes before. Arrogant Young D thinks it chic not to applaud the great artists who appear in concert, or to do so with a careful nonchalance so that everyone will take notice of his or her discernment in cultural matters.

These people might take a course in good manners. You may violently disagree with an interpretation or dislike a performance, but when an artist walks onto the stage you owe him the courtesy of a welcome. And one might add, the honesty of your feelings.

Musicians Explore Vast Horizons

The San Juan Star
September 21, 1967 By Francis Schwartz

Sunday afternoon at the Institute of Puerto Rican Culture, a dynamic young group of performers called The Composers Group for International Performance presented one of the year's most important concerts.

The music, representing composers born in the 1930s, centered around the latest experiments involving use of traditional instruments, the combination of electronic sounds with instruments, new performing functions for the instrumentalists, and visual additions to the customary aural indications of the composer.

One element stands out in the evaluation of this music. It is the use of electronic sounds combined with voice or instruments, which opens a new world of possibilities. The employment of this medium is as revolutionary, as potentially rewarding as was the first combination of voice with a primitive instrument or the first use of scenery with music.

When Mario Davidovsky and Milton Babbitt brought their electronic-live performer music to San Juan less than two years ago, their ideas seemed powerful, though exotic. Today, with the performance of Jacob Druckman's (U.S.A.) *Animus* for trombone and electronic sounds; and Rafael Aponte-Ledée's (Puerto Rico) *Presagio de Pájaros Muertos* for speaking voice and electronic sounds the ideas seem so valid that one wonders how the original doubt could have arisen.

Both Druckman and Aponte-Ledée use the taped sound in contrapuntal fashion. There is an interplay of instrument and tape; an interplay which demands incredibly accurate ensemble work. Perhaps nobody in the audience would be able to detect a missed entrance upon one or two hearings, but after knowing the piece one expects the same accuracy as in a Mozart quartet. The Aponte and Druckman pieces have a tendency to be lengthy and perhaps this is the one negative quality.

There seems to be a proportional relationship between brevity and accessibility in the new medium. And in spite of the fascinating sounds produced, the listener tends to lose the thread upon overexposure. Or perhaps because of the variety of sounds, the listener cannot easily assimilate and mentally catalog them. There is a time barrier.

In the Druckman work the trombonist, Per Brevig, left the stage during the solo electronic section. The impact was immense. There were no visual distractions, a stage devoid of life; only the multi-ranged sounds coming from the amplifiers. It was an imaginative device of the composer and highly successful.

The Composers Group is an important organization. All of the members are performing musicians and most are composers. They are all trained in the traditional repertoire and can play a Beethoven quintet as easily as a Davidovsky piece.

Thus there exists no charlatanism. These serious musicians are moving with the times, exploring vast horizons, and educating audiences and musicians throughout the hemisphere.

The members are Alcides Lanza (Argentina), director; Per Brevig (Norway), trombone; Efraín Guiguí (Argentina), clarinet; David Gilbert (U.S.A.), flute; Carla Hubner (Chile), piano; Rogelio Terán (Panama), percussion.

Bravo and please come back.

Orford Quartet

The San Juan Star
February 10, 1968   By Francis Schwartz

    The Faithful Hundred, those hardy souls who brave foul weather and foul traffic to attend all concerts on the San Juan music scene, were treated to a chamber concert of great merit at the Conservatory of Music on Wednesday evening. The occasion marked the Puerto Rico debut of the Orford String Quartet, a group of young Canadian musicians who are participating in an interchange between the University of Toronto and the Institute of Puerto Rican Culture.
    The quartet (Andrew Dawes, first violin; Kenneth Perkins, second violin; Terence Helmer, viola; Marcel St. Cyr, cello) is undoubtedly one of the most promising young groups this listener has heard in some time. Their playing throbs with vitality, they are not afraid to take chances, and they are able to keep the music under rein. Their musicianship belies their age (they must be all in their twenties).
    One knew from the outset of Haydn's Quartet Op. 54, No. 1 that this was no ordinary group. Their sense of pace, of musical logic, lent plasticity to the performance, which sparkled as a result. It was witty, puckish, carefree playing, perfectly adapted to a clever score. Haydn's fourth to tritone tease, a bit of clever Haydnesque deviltry, was seized upon with relish by the quartet. The *presto* finale flew past at breakneck speed but always under control. Highly effective playing.
    Bartók's string quartets have a special place in the heart of any twentieth-century music enthusiast. The work's monumental technical accomplishments stagger the imagination, whereas its powerful expressive qualities underline the presence of authentic genius. The Second Quartet, completed in 1917, is as fascinating today as ever. Bartók's uncanny ear for sonorities, coupled with his rhythmic concepts of

steamroller force and complex permutations, provides chamber music vitality at a level equaled by few other composers. The members of the Orford quartet played with drive and were amazingly faithful to the composer's wishes. Their accuracy in the second movement, where a miscue can bring everything to a standstill, was praiseworthy.

The final work, Mendelssohn's lovely A Minor Quartet, Op. 13, received a passionate reading. No victims of the "anti-romantic syndrome" which plagues many young artists today, the Orford quartet played with sweep and lyricism (non-syrup variety).

This quartet will certainly develop a more homogeneous sound in the future. There are moments when the playing is on the gritty side, a bit forced in quality. But time and growth will take care of that. This listener would say that we are hearing a great string quartet of the future; let those who missed the concert gnash their teeth in remorse.

The Festival Begins

The San Juan Star
May 26, 1968   By Francis Schwartz

Speculative thinking about the role of the Puerto Rico Casals Festival in our society is in order as the twelfth festival season begins.

The Casals Festival enjoys more prestige and receives more publicity (not to speak of money) than any other cultural organization functioning in Puerto Rico. The participating artists are of international renown, automatically creating a special atmosphere, and the government, committed to a successful musical program, has taken the festival under Fomento's wing.

This mixture of governmental cooperation, outstanding performers and a public which has shown its willingness by ever-growing attendance, should yield splendid results.

But something has gone wrong.

Instead of the expected enthusiasm among festival devotees, we find discontent. People are complaining, rightfully so, that the programs have become increasingly unimaginative.

The main problem is: Where can our public hear orchestral concerts of excellence except in this festival? The Puerto Rico Symphony Orchestra, with its miniature season, gives no more than five yearly concerts in any one of the metropolitan areas, and less than five in most locations. And this orchestra, in its early growing stage, cannot tackle much of the symphonic repertoire with the same facility as the festival orchestra.

If the festival orchestra does not include all major and important minor composers from the romantic, impressionistic, and modern periods, then, where are we going to hear them? It is too great a luxury to maintain such a specialized repertoire in an area where the public has no access to these masterworks. Thus, the Casals Festival does not fulfill its role as an educational force by presenting a partial view of music.

This limited musical scope affects more than the listening public. Its influence extends to the student class, the future professionals who should be vitally involved in music past and present. But the apathy one encounters among these future performers and teachers regarding innovations in their chosen profession is astonishing.

Were these students exposed to twentieth-century ideas in the festival, they would take greater interest in keeping abreast of their field. They should know that Serkin is as masterly in the Bartók concertos as in Brahms; that Stern is unrivaled in his interpretation of the Berg violin concerto. They should have the opportunity to hear these performances and see rehearsals in which prestigious artists commit themselves to new ideas. It is the unreal atmosphere that the Casals Festival creates by its restricted programming, which distorts the public's view of its musical heritage.

Examining this year's program we find certain positive elements. A night of chamber music will be offered which is most welcome. Too, Sibelius and Mahler make their debuts (on the same evening) forming the most attractive concert in the series. Even Tchaikovsky found a place on the program. At least some new (new!!) composers are being considered.

On the negative side, the inclusion of the Brahms First Symphony for the fourth time is beyond belief. While it is an exquisite work, there exist many other compositions which we could have enjoyed, for the first time. This is simply irresponsible programming, which ignores the needs of our concert life. Several other works will also be repeated for the second or third time. The inclusion of Beethoven's Choral Fantasy seems like such a misuse of energy and time. So obviously below Beethoven's Olympian par, this work was merely a warm-up for the Ninth Symphony. Musically, it has little to recommend itself.

What then is to be done?

If the Casals Festival is to survive in a future era, it will need all the public support available. Ignoring the public need is the surest way to alienate the base support which the festival must have.

How can the Casals Festival answer these needs?

1. Include symphonic works from all eras, excluding no particular school. This would offer a varied repertoire to an audience eager for it.

2. The revival of once popular works, now forgotten. Let us hear

some works of Joachim, Stradella, Stamitz, Reger, Raff. Butler University has enjoyed great success in unearthing unusual works. This festival can do the same.

3. Commission a work by an internationally prominent composer annually. Bring new ideas into our musical life and assist in the patronage of new compositions.

4. The inclusion of an operatic production, either fully staged or in concert version. Opera is dead in Puerto Rico and shamefully so, since the island has enjoyed a rich operatic tradition. Surely private industry, in cooperation with the festival, would sponsor such a project. Choruses can be prepared here, as in the past, and soloists are available both here and abroad.

If some imaginative step is not taken to rejuvenate the Casals Festival, the time will come when everybody will be sitting around in silence wondering what happened. This would be tragic and every person who cherishes the festival would be wise to consider the problem and try to find a solution.

UPR Amphitheater: Odnoposoff, Sanromá

The San Juan Star
October 11, 1968   By Francis Schwartz

The UPR Amphitheater hosted one of the finest recitals of the present season with the presentation of cellist Adolfo Odnoposoff. Odnoposoff, assisted at the piano by Jesús María Sanromá, performed sonatas by Brahms, Shostakovich and Rachmaninoff.

Intelligence and refinement are the trademarks of Odnoposoff's playing. He produces a warm, rich sound, and though the volume is never great, within the defined limits the cellist creates variety and subtle shadings. The Brahms *Sonata* proved an appropriate vehicle for such playing. The interpretation had drive, held together as a formal unit, and captured that ineffable quality and mystique that imbues music of the Romantic Era.

Shostakovich's Cello Sonata is a fine example of outstanding craftsmanship. The musical material is not particularly noteworthy, and some themes are downright trite. But what the composer is able to do with them is truly fascinating. The work seems fun to perform: a cellistic "Much Ado About Nothing." Again Odnoposoff controlled his execution masterfully and performed with the flexibility necessary to breathe life into the score.

Closing the evening was Rachmaninoff's Sonata, Op. 19. This was the least satisfactory work of the evening. If one is going to play such a heart-on-the-sleeve composition, then one should surrender to Dionysus and let the music run its inevitable course. But to play with too much control, too much taste, robs the expression of its irrational element: its passion. Rather like eating fried chicken with a knife and fork: you never get into it in order to completely enjoy it.

Sanromá sensitively collaborated at the keyboard.

Chamber Music at the Tapia

The San Juan Star
November 23, 1968   By Francis Schwartz

The third Festival of Puerto Rican Music opened at the Tapia Theater Tuesday night with a chamber music concert of serious music. We use the word "serious" to differentiate between so-called art music and the popular styles. Not that popular music cannot be frivolous; it just makes for a handy label.

For example, we had the performance of Lito Peña's Suite Antillana, which was often accoutered in popular style. There exists a curious relationship between Peña's vocabulary and the Gershwin Preludes for Piano. In both works we encounter the popular music element woven into a "serious" pianistic context.

However, the melodic factor in the Suite Antillana does not sustain interest while the harmony is not sufficiently dominant to make the piece a success. Hopefully, the composer will continue his serious excursions for he obviously has a talent to develop.

Amaury Veray's Allegro, for cello and piano, was an incredible example of time hopping. The work sounds like fair-to-middling Mendelssohn with a dash of Von Weber. One marvels at Veray's contemporaneity with these nineteenth century composers and wonders how is it possible. Though the Allegro may be a work of youth, the composer necessarily would have to be one hundred and sixty years old to coordinate his earlier years with historical reality. In an age of transplants, the Allegro belongs to the chronological genre.

The premiere of Luis Antonio Ramírez' Sonata Elegíaca for cello and piano signaled once again that the composer is working and progressing. It is his best work to date. There are still several weaknesses, such as the inability to develop musical material and the occasional use of stereotyped harmonies. Perhaps the greatest problem is that of thematic evolution. The composer applies the academic rules to his ideas: some sequence, diminution, a bit of juxtaposition, etc. But the result is forced, artificial. One does not feel that the composition has organically grown. The cello was well used in a tradition fashion and the piano writing adequate.

Also programmed were works of Aponte-Ledée, Campos-Parsi and Cordero.

Figueroas and the Rain

The San Juan Star
January 30, 1969   By Francis Schwartz

The Figueroa Quintet, back from a tour of Central America, encountered inclement weather in their Sunday afternoon Conservatory of Music concert, which reduced the size of the audience (still respectable in number). A fitting program would have been Handel's Water Music, or even more appropriate, Stravinsky's The Flood.

The quintet is composed of brothers José and Kachiro, violins; Guillermo, viola; Rafael, cello; and Narciso, piano.

Opening with Shostakovich's Quintet Op. 57, the players showed that their enthusiasm had been dampened, for the performance was lackluster, without drive, and deficient in coloration. The *scherzo* is a clever piece of writing and should be played wittily, but there was little appreciation of the humor. As for the structure, the Figueroa quintet ably blocked out formal units and in the Intermezzo created a directional force. Yet the concluding movement returned again to the controlled, rather bland approach which slakes no musical thirst.

José Quintón's String Quartet (1913) is one of the most important works in the Puerto Rican repertory. As we have mentioned on previous occasions, the composition is well made, shows melodic flair, and an understanding of the string idiom. It is painful to ponder the situation of such a composer, for he had no opportunity to travel abroad and study in such great centers of music as Berlin, Leipzig, Paris. Had Quintón been privileged to undertake this training, the results would have been amazing.

In their performance of this piece, the string players performed carefully and correctly. The second movement sang expressively and achieved a good balance. The other movements lacked clarity of texture and crystalline execution which is implicit in the score.

Frederick King and the New Sound of Percussion

The San Juan Star
March 2, 1969   By Francis Schwartz

"You are a percussionist? Oh, you play drums!" A look of anguish spreads across the face of Frederick L. King, the new percussion professor at the Puerto Rico Conservatory of Music. King, who has winced at this concept of his professional duties thousands of times, is a man with a mission. He is determined to set the record straight on the role of the percussionist and to define with exactitude the instruments which are his professional tools, his musical implements.

King, who arrived in Puerto Rico last August to assume his current teaching post, has an impressive academic and performance background. After receiving bachelor's and master's degrees in percussion and orchestral conducting from the University of Iowa, the percussionist continued his postgraduate studies at the prestigious Juilliard School of Music under the tutelage of New York Philharmonic timpanist Saul Goodman. Interest in the newly expanding field of ethnomusicology led King to Columbia University where he is presently a doctoral candidate.

His work with the New York Pro Musica, specialists in Medieval and Renaissance music, was particularly rewarding. "What an experience to work under [conductor] Noah Greenberg. He was a strong personality but always allowed his musicians freedom. He respected the integrity of each artist; consequently we gave him everything we had."

King has performed under the batons of such distinguished musicians as Dmitri Mitropolous and Edgard Varèse in the serious orchestral field; and also has wide experience in jazz. This flexibility is a main premise in King's philosophy of education.

"Only one percent of trained percussionists find employment in symphony orchestras," he says, "The rest must be adequately prepared to deal with popular, jazz, and Afro-Indo repertoire. We must instill in students the desire to achieve the highest standards no matter what their job may be."

One of the reigning myths which piques the percussion professor is the equation of percussion with drums. Truly, the drum family makes up an important part of the percussion section but there are also the mallet-struck instruments such as xylophone, vibraphone, marimba and chimes. Gongs, castanets, metal triangles and wood blocks also are the percussionist's responsibility. In the Afro-Indo-New World category we find bongos, maracas, steel drums, güiros and tablas. The percussion section is undoubtedly the most varied of the orchestral body. And since a composer may call for any or all these instruments in a score, the professional must be able to effectively discharge his duties.

Percussion pedagogy is relatively new. The last fifteen years have witnessed the spread of teachers throughout university music faculties and a growing importance in conservatory curricula. Not only are serious contemporary composers experimenting more with percussion than before; the TV and radio industries are using a great deal of percussion as background music. This has created a demand for competent, versatile players.

"Conservatories are generally conservative in their musical outlook. Often, the timpani professor had symphonic experience limited to the classical repertoire," says King. "While often outstanding in his field, he could not really prepare the students for, let's say, the jazz world or the popular music world. Even many new percussion ideas were outside the realm of the classical percussionist because he had a fixed idea what technique should be. Often composers would go to percussionists outside of the symphony orchestras in order to find flexibility. I must say that the administration here, at the Conservatory of Music, has been most cooperative. Dean José Gueits has extended every courtesy and has given me freedom in my teaching methods. I am quite pleased."

King is forming a percussion ensemble with his advanced students and plans to give a concert at the earliest opportunity.

"I have some very talented people in my class. If we work hard, we can do some exciting things."

There are many works by Varèse, Chávez, Ginastera, Wuorinen,

Harrison and others which could be performed by such a group. Also, the existence of a percussion ensemble would provide an excellent vehicle for the composers of Puerto Rico. King already has begun a campaign to stimulate the composition of new works, offering his cooperation in technical matters and putting into composers' hands new material in the field.

What difference is there between the "old" and "new" styles of percussion? The percussionist of the standard repertoire was restricted to a few basic movements. He perhaps would worry about stick coordination while playing tympani. And this would be limited to a basic rhythmic pattern. The "new" percussionist often has to carry several rhythms simultaneously.

His foot may be performing rhythm "A" on the bass drum pedal, his right hand playing "B" on the wood block, while a third rhythm is executed by the left hand on the bells. This is multiple percussion and the strain it places on the performer is obvious. Thus the classical, European-based rhythms which have served as the basis for standard performance practices are no longer adequate in preparing the percussionist for the new professional demands. Coupled with the standard training must be jazz, improvisation, and the study of African and Indian music with their subtle, complex rhythms.

"The world is growing smaller. We are becoming aware that a wonderful body of music exists outside the Western European culture, and we are beginning to perform it," says King, "It's a universal approach. And that is what I want to give my students."

Handel and Davidovsky at the Institute

The San Juan Star
April 5, 1969   By Francis Schwartz

Two off-the-beaten-path treats were offered at an Institute of Puerto Rican Culture concert Sunday afternoon. Handel's *No Se Emendará Jamás* and Mario Davidovsky's *Sincronismo Núm. 2* were the piquant additives to the imaginative musical fare.

Handel, that eighteenth-century internationalist, never felt bound by the narrow strictures of nationalism. He was German-born, Italian-trained, and opted for British nationality. As if this were not enough, he continued to demolish the barriers of nationality and language further by composing a cantata for guitar, soprano, and continuo, with a Spanish text. We hear Handel in English, Italian, and German; indeed, why not Spanish?

Camelia Ortiz del Rivero, soprano, rendered an intelligent, carefully measured reading of the work, though a bit more dramatic projection would have been in order. Guitarist Federico Cordero and cellist Rafael Figueroa effectively collaborated and the three musicians achieved good musical rapport. Their interpretation shunned any demonstrative posture, dwelling on the intimacy of the music.

Mario Davidovsky's *Sincronismo Núm 2*, for clarinet, flute, violin, cello, and electronic sounds, received excellent treatment in the hands of conductor Efraín Guiguí, whose musical intelligence was matched by his solid baton technique. It is no mean feat to hold the complex score together and Guiguí rose admirably to the task.

The music is beautifully conceived, making sporadic use of electronic sounds, which creates a fascinating counterpoint between the timbral qualities of the traditional instruments and the resonant sounds produced by an electronic musical synthesizer.

In my opinion this amalgamative approach is much more successful than electronic music alone, for the electronic sounds are much more accessible when fused with those of traditional instruments. It gives the listener a frame of reference whereas in a completely electronic score one can wander aimlessly upon a sea of unfamiliar sonoral patterns.

Also, from the audience's point of view, the participation of human beings in the musical activity permits identification with the performers. This would be impossible in the case of a stage populated exclusively by loudspeakers. Hopefully, we have not reached that state of automation as thinking creatures.

Respighi's *Il Tramonte*, as performed by soprano Luisita Rodríguez and the Figueroa string quartet, was adequate. The soprano sang with warmth and sureness of pitch, but the string players' intonation could have been more exact.

Closing the program was Brahms' Quintet for Piano and Strings, Op. 34, which this listener was unable to hear.

Casals Festival:
Whatever Happened to the Twentieth Century?

The San Juan Star
May 25, 1969   By Francis Schwartz

We are rapidly approaching the May 29 opening of the thirteenth Puerto Rico Casals Festival. Festival followers will undoubtedly be pleased with the appearance of some new composers in the programs. Too, there are such notable artists as Yehudi Menuhin, Alexander Schneider, Sir John Barbirolli, William Steinberg, María Esther Robles, Victor Tevah and Daniel Barenboim to give life to the printed musical page. No doubt most of maestro Casals' orchestral family will be returning for their yearly participation in Puerto Rico's most prestigious musical event.

On examining the program, we find a slight variation in the repertory with the inclusion of works by Elgar, Schoenberg, Sibelius and Vaughan-Williams. Variation seems more appropriate than change because, instead of a much needed musical face-lifting, the festival has merely used new makeup. The flirtation with composers who have lived in the present century but whose works reflect nineteenth-century philosophies, is not the answer to the festival's fossilized musical ideas. What twentieth-century reality does the Sibelius Symphony No. 5 reflect? Does the Elgar concerto illustrate the magnificent revolution that has taken place in our six decades? Does the post-romantic chromaticism of Schoenberg's *Transfigured Night* fall into the category of this master's innovative works? One must realize that these so-called modern works have precious little to say regarding the changes of our century.

What has happened to the Casals Festival? The answer is simple and disagreeable. Maestro Casals, whose hostility to the repertory of the twentieth century is well known, has fomented a policy of conservatism. He has refused to comprehend the great developments of our time and has publicly declared that no great composer has appeared on the scene in the twentieth century. This pronouncement includes such "non-greats" as Stravinsky, Bartók, Schoenberg, Debussy, Ravel and Webern. His complete control of the festival programming has resulted in an imposed artistic policy, because practically all of the participating musicians have performed music of our time in concert.

Is this a healthy situation? Should the public be spoon-fed a decidedly limited diet of pre-twentieth-century pabulum? Should one man impose his ideas on a public which has little opportunity to hear concerts of festival caliber during the rest of the year? I emphatically answer in the negative. The essence of cultural progress lies in the open presentation of a multiplicity of ideas, the weighing of these ideas, and their eventual acceptance or rejection. If freedom does not reign in the world of art the result is stagnation, and stagnation is what we are experiencing in the festival at this time.

Of course much of the blame must fall upon the concert-going public who have docilely accepted the criteria of the festival. There is much criticism in private, but few people are willing to state their dissatisfaction in public. No manifestation of dissent has emerged from the cocoon of apathy. Public debate, so necessary to betterment of policy, is shunned. No doubt it is considered unwise to voice opposition to Maestro Casals' ideas as he enjoys an international reputation. However, music is greater than any one of its stellar figures, and the future of the art demands the interchange of opinions, of dissent. If it is in bad taste to criticize Casals, then it is equally wrong for the maestro to relegate the music of many great men to a position of unimportance.

Why does the programming reflect exclusively European creations? Ironically, our festival takes place in the heart of the Americas. Why, then, are the works of Chávez, Ginastera, Copland, Villa-Lobos not presented? It is unrealistic to deny the cultural contribution of the hemisphere in which we live. If we are privileged to hear Vaughan-Williams then any one of the aforementioned composers of the Americas could also be enjoyed.

As for the music of our time, it is most important that Penderecki, Xenakis, Foss, Berio, Davidovsky and other composers of this caliber be represented in the festival concerts. Do not Tanglewood and Salzburg include contemporary works without suffering a loss of purity? The Festival Casals must not be a museum piece. It must have vitality and must answer the needs of our public.

Immediate steps should be taken to redesign the Festival Casals. Maestro Casals should understand that freedom in the concert hall is as important as freedom in society. Every listener, every contributor, has the right to pass individual judgment on all music, from all epochs. Nobody should decide for the public.

In 1970, the festival will be devoted to the works of Beethoven, in celebration of the 200th anniversary of his birth. Splendid. But no stone should be left unturned in an attempt to present a new and more realistic series of festival concerts in 1971. The time to work is now. The house of music has many mansions. Let us not practice segregation here.

Chamber Orchestra in Concert

The San Juan Star
July 29, 1969 By Francis Schwartz

It has been over a year since we last heard the Chamber Orchestra of the Institute of Puerto Rican Culture, and the first time under the direction of its new musical director, Augusto Rodríguez. Sunday afternoon's concert at the Institute revealed that many problems which have beset this group in the past years are still present in epidemic proportions.

The program was selected in imaginative fashion, fielding music of the Baroque and the twentieth century including the magnificent concerto for keyboard instrument and string orchestra of J.S. Bach, with Jesús María Sanromá at the piano. Perhaps this performance exemplified the great weaknesses which exist at this time in the orchestra and which point the way to future betterment. Mr. Sanromá played very well: shading, forging contrasts, driving forward in dynamic fashion. However, his efforts were often thwarted by the orchestra's thick, unyielding blanket of sound. There was no dialogue between soloist and the instrumental mass and the orchestra was unresponsive to the conductor's signals.

Obviously the musicians must watch the conductor if any solid ensemble is to be achieved. And more rehearsal time must be allotted for the interpretations to jell into performable entities. The intonation (often in quarter tones reminiscent of Hindu music) must improve. The violas and several violins were especially guilty of these aural assaults. To build this orchestra into a first rate chamber group is a herculean task, but it can be done. With work and discipline much will be gained. Hopefully, Maestro Rodríguez will achieve what has eluded others in the past.

Hindemith's Five Pieces for String Orchestra were far from ideal, but the final section began to take shape and one could concentrate on interpretation rather than technical execution. Without technical solidity all the musicality a musician may possess will fail to impress itself on the listener, and it is the same with an orchestra. No matter how much the players feel the music, there is no substitute for correct execution. From this base grow imaginative interpretations.

If the Institute wants an orchestra of which it can be proud and which can render service to the community, then it must demand more from these musicians. They are capable of playing at a much higher level.

Also programmed were works by Scarlatti, Cowell, Ramírez and Benjamin.

Institute Concert Reveals Progress

The San Juan Star
October 17, 1969 By Francis Schwartz

We didn't think it could happen in such a short time. Whether Maestro Augusto Rodríguez resorted to witchcraft, brute force or prayers is as yet unknown. What can be asserted publicly and should be proclaimed from San Juan rooftops is that the Chamber Orchestra of the Institute of Puerto Rican Culture finally sounds like a professional group!

A recent Sunday afternoon concert at the Institute of Puerto Rican Culture revealed the progress made during the past two months. This writer strongly criticized the orchestra in their August concert and it is with great pleasure that we can report that a transformation has occurred. A great deal of the out of tune playing has been corrected. Entrances are more exactly coordinated, though still lacking sufficient precision. The sound produced is more homogeneous than before.

The program featured music of the Americas plus a curtsy to Spain. The *Obertura Española* (1772) of Ventura Galván sounded spirited, clearly blocked and rather clean in execution. The music demands the clarity and balance typical of the classical epoch; both conductor and orchestra achieved this.

Guillermo Figueroa's arrangement for string orchestra of Jose Quintón's *Puerto Rico Quartet* proved pleasing and intelligently scored. Maestro Rodríguez could have been more pliant in his approach to the long lined melody, for one sought more breath, more ease in the unfolded line. Often clipped phrase endings marred the pacific nature of the movement. The American Suite by Charles Wakefield Cadman harkened back to the American past, with music of U.S. Indians, Negroes and the country fiddler. Admittedly, this music is not profound, and from the 1969 vantage point, is a bit ludicrous. The Indian dance sounded like background music from "Son of Geronimo"; and the fiddler, like "Grand Ole Opry." The players responded enthusiastically.

The Next Decade: An Exciting Era Shaping Up

The San Juan Star
November 2, 1969 By Francis Schwartz

Music in Puerto Rico is deeply integrated into the fabric of the island's culture and intimately identified with its people. The importance of music in any society depends on many factors: class structure, the economic condition, technological advancement, national historic experience. The absorption of outside influences is a salient feature of all musical development and Puerto Rico has been caught in the crosscurrents of many trends.

Undeniably a great debt is owed to Spain. Through four centuries of imperial presence, Iberian taste and Iberian art reigned as the dominant cultural force. Too, visiting opera companies and performing soloists came to these Caribbean shores, especially in the late nineteenth century, bringing other European styles. For the past 71 years, the U.S. presence has created an influx of new ideas which have permeated all areas of the musical arts: classical, popular, even folk songs. Most Puerto Rican performers and composers have at one time studied and worked in the continental U.S. and have been influenced by teachers and colleagues. Popular music is largely influenced by the Angloamerican modes of expression, themselves closely related to the Anglo-American dominance in the field of recording companies, distributors and concert managements.

The various waves of influence which have swept the island are not new in the world of music. Every major country experienced the same phenomenon, and was able to express its individuality by adapting ideas of foreign origin to existing needs.

In the sixties, an era of industrial expansion in which wealth was more widely distributed than ever before, music in Puerto Rico began to prosper. While concert series had been sponsored in earlier decades, at times under heroic conditions, never had so much Orphean activity taken place. The Puerto Rico Conservatory of Music began to function as an educational institution (1959), and the University of Puerto Rico Music Department received formal baptism in 1965 (though it had existed for many years under the Fine Arts wing). The Puerto Rico Symphony Orchestra (1958) expanded both its season and its repertoire, the Casals Festival played to ever-growing audiences, the UPR Chorus sang scores of concerts winning laurels here and abroad, the Institute of Puerto Rican Culture developed a music series (1966), the UPR Cultural Activities program invited great artists throughout the world for its concerts, the Madrigalists and Grupo Fluxus were born (1968) and the Free Schools of Music were developing a more intensive program for public school students who desired to pursue careers in music. There was even an Inter American Festival held in San Juan in 1966, which attracted many renowned composers and performers. Clearly these endeavors have been of great value in developing musical life here and one can consider the Sixties as a testing ground for the institutions which were destined to drastically alter cultural life in the next decade.

Predictions as to what might come to pass within the confines of a ten-year period are always dangerous. Musical oracles have often had to consume rather large portions of newsprint sandwiches after making rash statements. However, there are several unmistakable tendencies which, barring unexpected reversals, will forge the type of musical life we will enjoy until 1980. The following comments are this writer's humble predictions of what we might expect during the next decade.

The most powerful institution in Puerto Rico's music field is Casals Festival Inc., which comprises the two week summer festival itself, the Puerto Rico Conservatory of Music and the Puerto Rico Symphony Orchestra. The umbrella institution will attempt to continue its conservative policies, but both public and governmental pressure will cause reforms. The great weakness to date has been the Casals Festival, Inc.'s pedagogical flabbiness. While the summer festival has been considered mainly a tourist attraction, the other two appendages, i.e., the orchestra and the conservatory, have suffered from insufficient attention. While Puerto Rico can take pride in hosting an international festival, the benefit derived year round from this agency is minimal. Obviously, in terms of Puerto Rico and its needs, both the educational institution and the orchestral performing body are infinitely more important than a two week showcase, as enjoyable as it may be in itself. Any music educator will confirm this. Not that a festival is undesirable, but there is a question of priorities. Any region which does not enjoy a full orchestral season and which spends more from its public funds in two summer weeks than it does for the entire orchestral year, must reexamine the purpose of its commitment. Is Casals Festival, Inc. to exist for publicity purposes or should it be so structured as to render maximum benefit to its host area? It is only when Casals Festival, Inc. becomes more responsive to local needs that it will merit the praise too charitably heaped upon it in the past.

In this decade, the Puerto Rico Symphony Orchestra will achieve a 36 to 44 week season and may even free itself from the control of Casals Festival, Inc. This would sow the seeds of excellence for the ninth decade.

Music teaching in the seventies will find both the UPR Music Department and the Conservatory offering masters degrees, with applied music coming into the university. The public schools are in desperate need of music teachers. In this age of violence, educators are realizing the importance of Aristotle's maxim about music's function in the formation of the student's character; we shall find greater disbursement of funds for art programs. New programs utilizing the latest audiovisual methods coupled to better prepared classroom personnel will introduce music to countless young people. The humanistic side of study will become more important, attaining a balance in the educational system. Nobody wishes to produce automatons. If a student is unable to appreciate the beauty of art and has no one to guide him, he may become a rather heartless drone in an already gigantic beehive.

As for concert life aside from the Symphony Orchestra, the UPR cultural activities office will continue to serve the community with high quality concerts; the Institute of Puerto Rican Culture will promote its sometimes interesting series (though recent budget slashes do not augur well for the future), and more small groups will launch themselves on the perilous path of artistic and economic success. The big question mark at present is whether an opera group can be established on a permanent basis, performing regularly. All the elements for success are here: singers, conductors, orchestra players, designers, etc. However, financial sponsorship is lacking and it seems tragic that Puerto Rico with a rich operatic tradition should not be able to sustain one small opera company. A few groups will try for success but will encounter innumerable hardships.

Puerto Rico lacks a tradition of private patronage of the musical arts. Wealthy families here have been paragons of stinginess where adequate artistic sponsorship is concerned. Now artistic patronage may become a status symbol and it would not be surprising to find industrial tycoons competing among themselves in the backing of this music group or that sculptor, as they now do with yachts, homes and automobiles. When the economic elite enters the horse race of art, then exciting things will happen which are not currently possible, due to artists' financial limitations or to restrictions imposed by governmental sponsorship.

This decade will see the emergence of exciting new stars in the musical firmament and many of Puerto Rico's best known musicians, now in their late sixties, will begin to curtail their activities, leaving room for the younger generation to try their wings in the limelight. Puerto Rico will not lack musical controversies, so vital to artistic growth. There will be schools of composition clearly defined, and the battle for esthetic dominance will continue.

Summing up, we are at the beginning of an exciting era, an era which promises the birth of new careers, new institutions; a musical flood covering the island; of new competitions born on this soil. Puerto Rico, in the eighth decade of the twentieth century, will bathe in the delights of music as never before in her history.

UPR Hears Madrigalists

The San Juan Star
November 30, 1969   By Francis Schwartz

A heady and provocative mixture of music filled the University of Puerto Rico Theater when the Madrigalists of Puerto Rico, under the direction of Sergije Rainis, made their university debut. This recently born group (May 1969) enjoys the participation of such excellent professional singers as María Esther Robles, Flavia Acosta, Camelia Ortiz del Rivero, Luisita Rodríguez, Raquel Gandía, to mention but a few; plus the collaboration of an able and enthusiastic group of amateurs.

Henry Purcell's operatic gem, *Dido and Aeneas* (1689) opened the program. This work, written for a girls' school performance, contains some of the English master's finest phrases, and it seems a pity that Purcell chose Nahum Tate's pedestrian libretto for a literary base. The dramatic interest never flags and the expressive vocal writing ideally moves the listener in the best Baroque tradition.

The performance was enjoyable. The singing was at times dynamic, at times delicate. Rainis molded his chorus well and achieved proper balance.

Miss Rodríguez, as Dido, sang freely and accurately with an occasional overindulgence in slides. Alex Vázquez proved to be an able Aeneas. Adolfo Odnoposoff, cello, and Cecilia Talavera, harpsichord, were the instrumental soloists.

Vivaldi's *Gloria in D* filled the rest of the program. While singing ably, the group failed to capture the enthusiasm of the score. A more vigorous approach was needed.

Justino Díaz at the Metropolitan Opera House in New York City.

Díaz May Become One of the Great Bassos

The San Juan Star
February 10, 1970   By Francis Schwartz

Hundreds of friends and concertgoers turned out Friday night to hear bass Justino Díaz' recital at the University of Puerto Rico Theater. It was an event of considerable importance since the singer is one of Puerto Rico's most famous personages the world over. Díaz was up to the occasion.

Handel's cantata *Dalla Guerra Amorosa* began the program. The singer showed good breath control, a flexible technique and intelligence in his phrasing. Díaz never fought the music, which is an accomplishment, considering some of the rapid passage work which appeared so early in the evening. The voice resounded and always possessed an evenly rounded quality.

Four Brahms lieder demonstrated the bass' skill with the German language. The diction was faultless, the appreciation of the dramatic content sensitive. "O Liebliche Wangen" had drive and breadth.

Díaz is an actor with a beautiful voice. Naturally this makes him at home in the operatic form. It was precisely when he could put his histrionic talents to use that he achieved that special excitement which brought the audience to fever pitch. His performances of arias from *Simon Boccanegra* (Verdi), *La Sonnambula* (Bellini) and *Faust* (Gounod) showed the singer's dramatic flair: his obvious relish of bringing a stage character to life. Díaz possesses the power of effective gesture and can appear nonchalant as he leans against the piano, or devilishly aggressive as he jabs the air to drive home his point. Combined with a splendid voice, these qualities are unbeatable.

Mention must be made of the three Monsalvatge songs based on Antillean poetry. Díaz showed wisdom in this selection, for he tossed them off as child's play to the delight of all. Again he gestured, contorted, lifted eyebrows, clapped: all geared effectively to the style at hand.

Accompanying at the piano was the very sensitive Donald Nold, a first-class musician. Also programmed were four songs of Fauré.

Justino Díaz at the age of thirty has the world at his feet. He has grown musically in the past five years. His interpretations show more thought, more exploration of the musical content of his repertoire. However, he has not fallen into the trap of pedantry and evokes a youthful, buoyant spirit. This listener feels that Díaz has the possibility to become one of the great basses of opera. And one does not refer to fame, which is fleeting and can be generated by a flood of publicity. One thinks of the high standard which the artist sets for himself and with which only he can come to terms. Fame should not deter this young artist and if he continues to battle with the elements of his art he will achieve that honored place in the pantheon of great singers.

Music of Our Century: The Third Concert

The San Juan Star
February 23, 1970   By Francis Schwartz

Is simplicity the essence of greatness? Does the artist seek out cumbersome complexities merely to disguise a thin idea? These questions came to mind at Thursday evening's University of Puerto Rico Theater concert, the third in the Music of Our Century series.

Pianist Héctor Tosar performed two works of Arnold Schoenberg: the six Op. 19 pieces, and the Five Pieces, Op. 23. The former work is concise in expression, atonal; saying with a few notes and piquant silences everything that Romantic bombast had said, but in a more economical fashion. In short, it is the antithesis of Wagnerian grandiloquence, though there are elements of the former style embedded in certain melodic fragments and expressive devices.

Twelve years later, Schoenberg put into practice his famous "twelve-tone system," a compositional method which overturned four centuries of tonal thinking. In the Op. 23 we find a thicker, more intricate arrangement of sounds; one feels that while the system may be unfolding according to plan, the result is musically unsatisfactory. The system becomes a procrustean bed which adapts communicative ideas to the method.

Many twelve-toners will scream at this comment, but the method, if not flexibly used, ends in a musical cul-de-sac. Fortunately, Schoenberg and his gifted disciples, Berg and Webern, overcame these limitations on countless occasions.

Tosar's playing was sensitive and his tempi always on the slow side, especially in the Op. 19. He lavished care on each melodic fragment, and experimented with coloration. The Op. 23 went well, although it is not as interesting as the former work.

Música Nocturna, by the contemporary Argentine composer Gerardo Gandini, was conducted by Efraín Guiguí. The work, scored for flute, violin, piano, cello and viola, uses the highly coloristic vocabulary of the sixties' instrumental writing. The audience received the fine rendition enthusiastically and the communication between players and public was genuine. It only proves that contemporary expression finds acceptance when adequately presented. It is the same in all the arts.

Also programmed were works by Gregory Tucker, Paul Hindemith and Alban Berg. Guillermo Figueroa Jr. merits praise for his performance of the Hindemith Violin Sonata, Op. 31, No. 1. Though the piece is the epitome of tedium, the young player effectively put his talents to use. He bears watching.

Opera star **Pablo Elvira**.

Elvira in Recital

The San Juan Star
April 4, 1970 By Francis Schwartz

"A touch of the poet" could well summarize the singing style of Pablo Elvira, Puerto Rican baritone, whose Tuesday night University of Puerto Rico recital revealed a voice of quality and an uncommon musical intelligence.

Elvira selected Brahms' *Zigeunerlieder* (Gypsy Songs) for his opening number. These songs, completed during the composer's final decade of life, are inspired by Hungarian lyrics and attempt to capture the essence of Gypsy music without merely imitating its salient features. *Zigeunerlieder* contains the ideal balance between the academic solidity of the art song and the expressive force of a folk-based idiom. The performance was impassioned, well paced and interestingly shaded. The baritone never allowed the dramatic tension to wane.

Elvira's voice projected well, had a warm quality and exhibited great flexibility. There were times when he would reach for a soft high note and the resultant sound came out thin and "whitish." However, he immediately corrected the fault and achieved a full tone. It happened on several occasions during the night and one wonders if Elvira prefers this approach. He has the technical equipment to avoid it.

The four songs of Richard Strauss which followed were exquisitely sung, especially "Befreit," which showed the singer at his best. He was deeply involved with the text and the music sailed forth with all the tenderness and feeling one could wish for. It was really a beautiful performance.

In the two arias from Mozart's *The Marriage of Figaro*, the singer's acting ability often overshadowed the singing. Personally this listener found the arias a bit on the thin side, lacking resonance at times, with some unprepared notes interspersed along the way.

Elvira has a fine future. He is proof again that Puerto Rico has the highest per capita production of fine singers of any spot on this weary planet.

Opera 68: *I Pagliacci*

The San Juan Star
April 9, 1970   By Francis Schwartz

While the clown (pagliaccio) cries on the Tapia Theater stage, all of Puerto Rico can smile, for we have in our midst an operatic hit. The Thursday night performance of Leoncavallo's most famous opera, *I Pagliacci*, by the Opera 68 company, proved to be an experience of considerable pleasure.

Featured in the leading roles were Robert Kelly (Canio), Camelia Ortiz del Rivero (Nedda), Abraham Lind Oquendo (Tonio), Alex Vázquez (Silvio) and Johnny Soto (Beppo).

The opera belongs to the Italian "Verismo" genre which occurred at the end of the 19th century. A slice of actual life, a dramatic look at raw human passion, shocking revelations, are the ingredients of this opera which deals with the murder of a faithless wife and her lover by the outraged husband. Leoncavallo based his libretto on a case which appeared in the judicial district of his father, who was a judge.

The drama is simple in content, no Freudian subtleties à la Richard Strauss' *Salomé* or *Electra*; rather, an open and shut case of jealousy and violence.

The portrayal of the malicious Tonio by Abraham Lind was excellent. He sang well, with a full booming voice, acting the role to villainous perfection. Some of his gestures were a bit obvious such as the statement to the audience "Actors are of flesh and blood," while dangling his hand for all to ogle. But the characterization had impact.

Miss Ortiz del Rivero sang with surety and a cool, refined tone. One wishes that her histrionic efforts were more spontaneous. There is too obvious an awareness of stage positions, of the conductor, of stances. Musically, she rendered meritorious service.

Mr. Kelly has a light tenor voice and was not sufficiently forceful in his role. His diction often lacked clarity. Dramatically, Kelly looked the part and balanced the performance with good acting.

We were happy to find a vivacious, musically sound chorus providing background for the protagonists. It is a group that shows much potential.

As for the orchestra, under the direction of James Thompson, much can be said for their efforts on such short notice. There were ensemble problems and, at times, an aleatoric touch, as in the "Vesti la Giubba" aria, but in general they fulfilled their task. Thompson is to be commended for his undertaking in the midst of the hectic symphony season.

The operatic production improved as it progressed. The second act never lost dramatic tension and came to a resounding conclusion. Dr. Arturo Machuca Padín provided competent stage direction while the scenery by Rafael Ríos Rey was suited to the limited stage area. Randy Juarbe Jordán prepared the chorus and merits praise for his work.

Here is a chance for San Juan to enrich its cultural life with opera. The *Pagliacci* currently offered provides a pleasant evening's entertainment and at the same time offers opportunity to the many vocal talents in our music world. Government and industry should not let this opportunity slip away. Opera 68 deserves public support because it has shown that it can provide good quality opera and that it has the will and drive to continue doing so. If you enjoy opera, don't miss *Pagliacci*.

Mandolinist and Pianist
Give Imaginative Recital

The San Juan Star
April 16, 1970 By Francis Schwartz

Piano accompanied by a tambourine and a triangle? A pianist who sits four and a half minutes in front of the keyboard without sounding a note? Mandolin music by the Titan from Bonn, Beethoven?

Yes, it was all present Sunday afternoon at the Institute of Puerto Rican Culture in a concert presented by mandolinist Gustavo Batista and pianist Jesús María Sanromá.

The first half of this imaginative recital featured variations, two sonatinas, and an adagio by Beethoven. These works, with the exception of the adagio, are inconsequential when mirrored against the composer's catalog; but they are a lot of fun and show just how human and how capable of folly a great master can be.

The players were at a disadvantage since Mr. Batista's mandolin had been stolen during the past week and he had to readjust to an unfamiliar instrument. This probably accounted for the ensemble problems.

Also programmed were a very interesting sonata by Hummel and two waltzes for piano, triangle and tambourine by Clementi, providing an example of delectable buffoonery.

John Cage and Henry Cowell, two great American composers of the twentieth century, filled the remainder of the program. Pianist Sanromá gave excellent readings of Cowell's *Six Ings* (1922), *Friend Conversation* and *Banshee* (1930). The playing of *Banshee*, which takes place inside the piano, was truly first rate. It was one of the best realizations of the work which this listener has ever heard.

Cage's *Amores* (1943), for prepared piano, makes use of a standard grand piano with screws and rubber doorstops wedged between the strings, expanding the timbral palette of the instrument to an enormous extent. Cage's fascination with oriental music and Eastern philosophy led him to these new practices and propagated a new vocabulary in the world of music.

The final work, *Four Minutes Thirty Three Seconds*, in which the player sits immobile at the piano for the indicated length of time, opens up a new world to the listener. We are accustomed to music according to fixed definitions. Cage throws that out the window and draws on the sounds around us for his creation. The hum of the air conditioning unit, the scrape of a shoe, a deep throated cough, a whisper: all are sonoral elements of the creation. Philosophically, it proves that the old values are outworn, that what appears to be true, upon closer perusal is false.

Would not the average listener or even composer consider Cage's work a construction in silence? But we see that what is accepted as silence is not silence at all. A vast amount of sound occurs during the pianist's stay at the instrument, even his circulatory system would be audible to him were he in a soundproof chamber. Thus for the human being, silence does not exist, merely different levels of sound.

A hearty bravo for a first class concert.

A Mediocre Performance

The San Juan Star
April 17, 1970 By Francis Schwartz

The tragic state of the musical art in Puerto Rico was vividly demonstrated Wednesday night at the Tapia theater, when the Puerto Rico Symphony Orchestra, under the direction of Victor Tevah, presented a program of Handel, Gershwin and Franck.

The opening Concerto Grosso of Handel received proper treatment. The playing was vigorous; it moved ahead; and the overall sound was less ragged than in past performances by this orchestra.

Then came the F Major Piano Concerto of George Gershwin, with Jesús María Sanromá as soloist. This composition with its combination of academic and jazz elements brings to mind the world of the Roaring Twenties; F. Scott Fitzgerald, Al Jolson, Babe Ruth, Calvin Coolidge, Paul Whiteman: a dizzy, unrealistic era whose devil-may-care attitude led to the 1929 cataclysm. Gershwin premiered the concerto at the age of 27, in 1925. It is an expression of youthful dynamism using the popular elements of his era.

Sanromá knows the style very well. He performed with vigor and flexibility. His toying with certain phrases, teasingly holding then back, is interpretatively correct for this give-and-take exists as an integral part of Gershwin's music. While the playing was not technically clean (there were several bothersome passages, especially some triplet figures in the first movement) the artist created a stimulating interpretation.

Unfortunately the same cannot be said for the orchestra. They attempted to accompany in musical fashion. They failed. Tevah led in a stiff manner, doing his utmost to hold the players together. The rhythm was shaky, the violins pathetically poor, the give and take with the soloist: nonexistent. Sanromá often tried to play with a phrase and was forced to hurry back to the conductor's unsympathetic beat.

And now to the tragic part. The ovation given the soloist was richly deserved. However when the orchestra was asked to stand, the public cheered with even greater enthusiasm. Why? Has art become so meaningless? Must a disfigured version of a concerto be rewarded with praise? Are ideals to be stepped on in the interest of camaraderie?

This listener witnessed young music students applauding among the group and we wondered, what does music mean to them? If you love art fiercely then you must be equally demanding with yourself and others. To condone the mockery of music by bestowing laurels on poor performances is to institutionalize mediocrity and guarantee that the following generations will be condemned to hear similar travesties.

We have a serious problem in our music world. There is an epidemic of "superlativitis". Fantastic, greatest, brilliant, are the watchwords. Nobody makes any demands on the artists. And artists have a difficult time maintaining standards under these conditions.

In short, irresponsibility on the part of knowledgeable concertgoers as well as musicians, can be blamed for the substandard renditions we so often hear.

Until these people show a little love for music and just an iota of courage, the public of today will continue to be cheated of their due right: to hear the best available players recreating the glories of music.

Symphony Season Closes With Thud

The San Juan Star
April 28, 1970   By Francis Schwartz

    Burlesque in the hallowed halls of the University of Puerto Rico? Yes sir, in every sense of the word: Richard Strauss' *Burlesque*, for piano and orchestra and the Puerto Rico Symphony's burlesque of unified orchestral playing. Our local orchestra season ended Friday night as Victor Tevah led the seventy-five musicians through two hours of Wagner, Strauss and Dvořák.
    Elías López Sobá, piano soloist in the Strauss work, gave a technically competent performance. His playing was cool, measured, carefully calculated. Unfortunately there was little excitement generated with this approach and the music never broke out from the imposed straitjacket. The *Burlesque* begs for pliancy, for occasional bravura. López's playing lacked sufficient amount of either. The orchestra sounded like a faulty zipper: zig, zag, zip, snag. We have become accustomed to the refined ineptitude of the violins, but Friday evening the violas and brass decided to join the fun with poor entrances and exotic intonation.
    Dvořák's New World Symphony, in spite of all the flaws (and they were as numerous as dented fenders in San Juan), had spirit. There were times when we could sit back, listen to the music, and relish the Czech master's worthy ideas. These moments balsamed frayed nerves. Also programmed was Wagner's Rienzi Overture.
    And so closes a dismal chapter in the music history of Puerto Rico. The performance level this season has been poor. Within the orchestra, morale is at an all-time low. Fights have broken out between the conductor, Victor Tevah, and players. Last year's near tragedy when the plane carrying the orchestra almost crashed in Guatemala after the orchestra had protested the use of an old airplane, has made the musicians

suspicious of the administration. Undisciplined rehearsals where players crack jokes have brought the group to its very sad state.

It behooves the officials of the Festival Casals Inc. and Fomento to carefully study the present situation so that we do not duplicate the farce of 1970. If Puerto Rico is to have a good, professional orchestra, then an adequately long season must be planned with competent players.

As we have said in this column, local players should be given preference. But excellence must be a constant guide for the growth of the organization and only capable professionals who can negotiate the difficulties of the musician's task should be taken into the Puerto Rico Symphony Orchestra. Let us hope that the future will be better.

Important Musical Era Ends

The San Juan Star
May 16, 1970 By Francis Schwartz

An important musical era in Puerto Rico ended Wednesday night amid tears, embraces, laudatory speeches and music. Augusto Rodríguez, founder and director of the University of Puerto Rico chorus for thirty-six years, strode onto the stage of the UPR Theater to conduct his beloved singing group for the last time. It was a moving experience.

After receiving plaques and awards from many cultural and student organizations, Rodríguez presented a splendid program of choral music. There were compositions from many parts of the world, and Rodríguez was able to draw a full, vibrant sound from the singers.

Of course, the high point of the evening was a group of his own compositions which represent an authentic, firstclass adaptation of Puerto Rican cultural themes to the strictures of the academic music world. The "Carreteros," a musical representation of country life, vividly recreates the beginning of a day in the life of a cart driver. Using the voices with expertise, Rodríguez captured the essence of the bucolic setting.

The work is pure nostalgia since the Puerto Rico referred to has been practically obliterated by technological advances. Listening to the flowing music with coquí sounds interspersed, one thought of an era when life was not chained to the hands of a clock; a time when exhaust fumes did not asphyxiate pedestrians; when one could spend two hours at lunchtime around the family table.

The concert closed with a rousing version of the UPR Alma Mater, Rodríguez's own composition, sung by former chorus members. It was a great tribute to a man who has dedicated his life to music and to Puerto Rico.

University of Puerto Rico's legendary choral conductor Augusto Rodríguez, attending a 1978 rehearsal.

Casals Festival: Where Have The People Gone?

The San Juan Star
June 7, 1970 By Francis Schwartz

What evil force haunts the concertgoer's mind, inspiring fear of the phrase "string quartet concert?" The Friday night performance by the Guarneri String Quartet found the University of Puerto Rico Theater half empty. This afforded everyone more elbow room, but sadly confirmed the theory that a Roman Circus psychology pervades the atmosphere of the Casals Festival. The Cecil B. DeMille and Radley Metzger philosophy of art may cause the critic's combative juices to stir, but it puts the box office guardians in a euphoric state, with apparent justification.

The Guarneri Quartet is composed of violinists Arnold Steinhardt and John Dalley; Michael Tree, viola; and David Soyer, cello. Their interpretation of three Beethoven quartets revealed them to be among the best string ensembles on the international scene. The C Minor Quartet, Op. 18 No. 4 had drive, always phrased with good taste, never methodical in approach. Cellist Soyer could have used a bigger sound, for at times the lowest musical line was barely audible. The group's ensemble is exact and Steinhardt's beautiful sound enhances the overall impression. The F Major Quartet, Op. 135 was played with sensitivity and preserved the mood of each movement without resorting to "expressive" gimmickry. Lucid development best characterizes the rendition.

While the Guarneri's shadings are admirable one wishes for an expanded dynamic range. In other words, they could use more decibelic firepower. If they widened the scope of their dynamics the already colorful nuances would become more effective.

Why was the final repeat omitted in the last movement? Beethoven left it up to the players but for the sake of consistency it makes sense to repeat it. The architecture suffers no damage, and the conclusion can be more persuasive. The concert closed with the "Rasoumowsky" Quartet, Op. 59, No. 2, which received a felicitous reading much in the style of the previous works.

Again we decry the shameful absenteeism among Puerto Rico's concert public. Perhaps the administrators of the Casals Festival Inc. will have to resort to such publicity ploys as giving chamber music concerts "X" ratings, thus insuring a packed house. Or "Fanny Hill once listened to these quartets, have you?" In this year of the Beethoven bicentennial, where is Grove Press when you really need it?

Casa Blanca: Music For A Sunday Afternoon

The San Juan Star
November 4, 1970   By Francis Schwartz

The musical dollop served by the Plectrum Musica Quartet at Casa Blanca on Sunday afternoon proved nourishing though sufficiently unorthodox to provoke debate. Two mandolinists, Gustavo Batista and Jaime Camuñas; a lutenist, José Delgado; and guitarist Leonardo Egúrbida form the foursome of plucked music players.

Should works originally composed for bowed string instruments, such as the programmed Beethoven String Quartet Op. 18 No. 4, be adapted to other instruments which alter the original timbre and conception of execution? For example, the long melodic line of a slow movement is virtually impossible to achieve on a constantly plucked instrument. The resultant hurdy gurdy-like repetition makes a mockery of the composer's original intentions. A purist finds this bordering on musical licentiousness. Whether the Cotton Mathers of sound are correct in their hostility can be argued ad infinitum, but this lack of cohesive sound demonstrates the limitations of the plucked string medium. Without a satisfactory legato, the antithesis of the long bowed line, i.e. the plucked attack, will wreak havoc on most slow movements of the classical and romantic eras.

The opening Haydn Quartet, Op. 20 No. 6 received a vigorous, intelligent interpretation. The dynamics were carefully planned and the phrasing clearly outlined, but we take exception to the minuet movement, which lacked grace. Even considering the bucolic elements which often characterize Haydn's minuets, the approach was too heavy, too aggressive. First mandolinist Batista showed musical sensitivity throughout the performance, for he grasps the style well.

An excerpt from Purcell's *The Fairy Queen* followed, with soprano Annie Figueroa as soloist. While the seldom heard work showed inventiveness of programming, the interpretation suffered from unwise tempos and yo-yoesque ensemble work which found the group together only occasionally. The soprano attempted to portray the melancholy of "The Plaint," but was so hurried by the pluckers that she was forced to move on, sacrificing drama for union. With judicious pacing, this work can result very well in the future. The concert closed with the aforementioned Beethoven quartet: musically good, technically spotty.

Romantic Music Series Lacks Sense of Purpose

The San Juan Star
November 13, 1970   By Francis Schwartz

Musical romanticism suffered a devastating defeat Tuesday night at the University of Puerto Rico amphitheater, in the so-called Romantic Music Series. The soporific program confectioned by the UPR Cultural Activities Department managed to present one of the most exciting eras of music history as weak-kneed, bloodless and dawdling.

In fact, the entire series smacks of institutional prissiness, a sop to the cognoscenti, a pompous exhibition of elitist taste. What distortion of the Romantic ideal could have inspired this musical selection of Spohr and Weber? Are these works the manifestation of Novalis' "World Soul?" Do they symbolize the emotional power and sensuality of the Dionysian spirit? Of course not.

The Weber quintet is a clumsy, sprawling work which should be relegated to the scholar's reference room or performed as a musical curiosity in a musical ambience where Romanticism is a commonly known factor. But since it is the responsibility of these concerts to attract, first and foremost, university students, such esoteric presentations merely serve to drive these young people into the waiting arms of the discotheques.

We have seen the constant failure of serious music vis-à-vis the young. There exists a suspicion among members of the new generation that serious music lovers are stuffed shirts. In some cases, they are right.

So the juxtaposition of this insipid programming with the popular attraction of a Charles Aznavour concert confirms the students' opinion of serious music: that it is boring, irrelevant, and only suited for the intellectuals. How tragic!

We find missing from the Romantic series a composer you may have heard of: Chopin. The great Russian school—Tchaikovsky, Moussorgsky, Rimsky-Korsakov—doesn't rate a place on the program while there is a duplication in the case of Schubert and Brahms. And to eliminate Berlioz, one of the towering giants, is the epitome of obtuseness.

Franz Liszt, that demonic virtuoso whose pianistic wizardry entranced nineteenth-century century audiences appears in this music series as the composer of four songs. How very quaint. That's like saying that General Motors is known for its windshield wipers.

The Romantic Music Series lacks a sense of purpose. It appears to be a loosely knit concoction of works which the participating musicians happen to have in their repertoires, divorced in content from the current musical needs at our university.

If the philosophy behind this presentation is to perpetuate the "coterie concert style" then it is on the right track. If it is desirable to have 20 or 30 students attend serious music concerts out of a student body of some 25,000, then Cultural Activities should continue along the same path.

But the day will come when the musicians will be all alone, abandoned by the generation of young people who could have been their staunchest supporters.

Locally Styled *Viet-Rock* is Scathing Attack on Military

The San Juan Star
November 24, 1970 By Francis Schwartz

The Southeast Asian War, a catalyst of social change in the United States, has motivated musicians, poets, composers, moviemakers and novelists to make public their attitudes toward that bloody conflagration. Viet-Rock, a musical play currently running at the San Patricio Plaza's Ondergraun Pleijaus ("Underground Playhouse," to you) is a bitter, scathing attack on the military, on morally bankrupt politicians and on the brainwashed average citizen.

Adapted from a New York based work of the same title, the Pleijaus players molded the protest to the Puerto Rican reality. All the characters are present: the armchair generals who wage war from the safety of their senate or corporate desks; the 200 percent American whose country is always right; the young militant who menacingly warns the *blanquitos* of their impending doom; the innocent draftee who doesn't know where Viet Nam is but must serve there because that is what is expected of him.

The public was made up of young people under 25. One could feel the tension spread throughout the theater as a young recruit was taught to kill for the values proclaimed in Fourth of July speeches. And one could note the cynicism as bitter laughter drowned out the words "I love my president."

Director Jorge Pérez has managed to keep the dramatic interest at high level at all times. Imaginative use of movement and lighting makes Viet-Rock a worthwhile event; while the acting is spotty in quality, spontaneity and conviction buff over most weaknesses. Iván Figueroa's songs are pretty much run of the mill. While they serve as moments of ideological focus, musically they are bland. Also, the rug-covered theater floor allows little resonance in the vocal numbers.

If you want to be jolted by a political statement, if you want to be aware of the new generational reality, then see this play. You will leave the theater with your mind abuzz with thoughts—and not thoughts about next year's automobile.

Chamber Orchestra at Casa Blanca

The San Juan Star
December 24, 1970 By Francis Schwartz

Augusto Rodríguez burrowed deep into rarely visited regions in structuring his Sunday afternoon Casa Blanca concert. Selecting a seldom heard repertoire for the Institute of Puerto Rican Culture Chamber Orchestra, he presented three first performances in Puerto Rico of works by Mozart, Creston, and Schiassi.

The program opened with what was purported to be Mozart's first symphony. There seems to be confusion on this point, since Mozart's First Symphony is K 16. We suspect that the performed work was the D Major Quartet from 1772, which actually is a *sinfonia* in the Italian style. In any case, the grace and technical expertise demonstrated by the sixteen year old Mozart is amazing. The profound musings of the *andante* movement belie the composer's age.

The Institute's orchestra still must overcome myriad problems, including intonation, precise attacks, clean articulation and others. We do acknowledge an improvement since last month's Tapia Theater debacle, but Rodríguez will have to drill these players for a long time before any homogeneous sound can be achieved.

Accordionist Esther Eugenia Bertieaux performed the A Major Concerto by Pietro Deiro. The original orchestra part was reduced for string orchestra on this occasion. The music provides an endless string of hackneyed patterns. Fortunately Miss Bertieaux, a fine musician, managed to make this musical gruel quite palatable, while her clean touch made the running passages sparkle. And her phrase-molding gave evidence of a superior musical intelligence. We hope to hear this performer more frequently.

Also programmed were works by Creston, Geminiani, Cowell, and Schiassi.

In 1970, Puerto Rico's governor **Luis A. Ferré** chats with **Pablo Casals** during the Festival.

The Casals Festival

The San Juan Star
May 30, 1971 By Donald Thompson

STAR Music Critic Francis Schwartz has often expressed the wish, shared by many musicians and concertgoers here, that the programming of the annual Puerto Rico Casals Festival be broadened to include works by composers other than a handful of classic masters. This view may even be shared by those currently responsible for planning the festival repertory, for as Schwartz pointed out in a recent column, this year's series is to include some works which were composed in the present century. As much as I share the belief that something must be done about the festival programming, I believe that they are barking up the wrong tree where this detail is concerned.

Their error lies in their confusing the function of this brief annual series of special concerts with that of a regularly constituted symphony orchestra. In the case of a symphony orchestra, its season of activities firmly rooted in the educational and cultural needs of the populace, there can be no question; programming should cover the broadest possible range of musical periods and styles. The case of the annual Puerto Rico Casals Festival is a very different matter, as may be seen from a brief look at its origin and early history.

This festival was first conceived in 1956, to serve a number of symbolic and practical purposes. Symbolically, this was a means by which musicians and music lovers from the four corners of the world could assemble to honor don Pablo Casals and the music with which he had become very closely associated. It was also spoken of as a symbolic gesture on Casals' own part: a means by which he could honor Puerto Rico, his mother's birthplace. But legislatures are seldom moved to vote heavy appropriations by sentiment alone (we hope). On the practical level of money and politics, the prime purposes were to open a previously untapped field of tourism by placing Puerto Rico on the international music festival circuit and to improve Puerto Rico's own cultural image abroad, which would have a healthy effect on general tourism and other aspects of the island's economic development.

At first, remarkably little was said about any direct contribution which the festival might make to the island's own cultural life. Gradually, however, and in response to various pressures exerted locally, several adaptations were made. The Puerto Rico Symphony Orchestra and the Puerto Rico Conservatory of Music were created by the legislature and placed under the management of the Festival Corporation, and the programming of the festival's own brief series was broadened to include works by a greater number of composers and a wider representation of soloists and conductors. The first two innovations have been, I believe, a net gain to music in Puerto Rico, although both entities are plagued by problems which can be traced directly to their origins in the industrial development branch of government. But I believe that attempting to broaden the base of the Casals festivals themselves, by turning them into something like a standard symphony season condensed into ten or a dozen concerts, is a great error.

Pablo Casals has repeatedly expressed himself publicly on the subject of modern music; unless recent years have brought about a change of opinion, he doesn't like it. What speaks to him is the music of the classic masters, to which he has devoted a long lifetime of loving study: works by J.S. Bach, Mozart, Schubert and Beethoven. These are works to which he has applied his unique touch as performer and conductor; works to which he brings an electrifying interpretive insight; works which represent Casals himself to two generations of international festival followers. These, and especially the works of Bach, are the music upon which Casals and Alexander Schneider based the Prades festivals of the early 1950s, after which the Puerto Rico Casals Festivals were deliberately patterned.

The basic purposes of the annual Casals Festival have not, to my knowledge, changed. Why, then, should the type of repertory change which was so closely bound up with the very conception of the festival itself? I believe that to broaden the repertory can have only one result: to rob the festivals of their spiritual focus, their emotional basis: indeed, their festive nature itself. To change this would be disrespectful to the great cellist and to the conservative tradition which he so eloquently represents.

The annual Puerto Rico Casals Festival is an institution, a monument, a *fait accompli*. There are other entities, tied not to a revered individual but to the more broadly conceived cultural needs of Puerto Rico, whose nature better fits them for the exploration and dissemination of music of all styles and all periods. Among these is the Puerto Rico Symphony Orchestra. I suggest that Schwartz and others who share his opinion devote their energy to publicizing the great potential and the great needs of that organization rather than trying to refashion the foundations of an established monument. Casals Festival is (and rightly) the voice of the past; the Puerto Rico Symphony Orchestra, that of the future, and the future of music in Puerto Rico lies to a great extent in its hands.

Ferré: La Fortaleza's Best Musician

The San Juan Star
April 7, 1972   By Francis Schwartz

    Just how good a pianist is Governor Ferré? Many people were asking this question last week after the governor's appearance as piano soloist in Beethoven's *Third Piano Concerto* at a special concert for school children. The governor was then asked to perform *in camera* for the STAR's music critic, and he agreed to do so.
    As I entered the governor's office Tuesday night, I spied a man hunched over the small grand piano, diligently practicing a tricky passage for the left hand. Cellist Adolfo Odnoposoff was already tuning his instrument and the music making was about to begin. Ferré appeared tired after a heavy day of work. He had learned Beethoven's Sonata for Cello and Piano, Op. 69, as a gift for Catalan cellist Pablo Casals' 95th birthday. Ferré claimed he had neglected the sonata. I sensed a trace of nervousness, for he told me this three times before the performance began, once during the playing and two more times afterward, with Odnoposoff adding contrapuntal corroborations. As the players were about to begin I was seated next to the piano, clearly in Ferré's line of vision. That's like placing King Herod alongside the children's playpen. Whether or not this rattled the Governor I cannot say, but the first movement was less than felicitous. Ferré rushed ahead in the technically easy parts, slowing—excessively—in more difficult ones. His rhythm often went astray and even he admitted the need for counting more. As this session was informal, the commentaries during the breaks were quite jovial.
    At one point, Ferré wrestled with a difficult left-hand phrase which he could not execute properly. We suggested to him that perhaps Beethoven had written the part just to bother pianists. The Governor

exclaimed gleefully, "That's it! He did it just to bother us pianists!" He then performed the passage correctly.

For the final three movements I stood behind the Governor, turning pages occasionally while observing his hands. Ferré is quite nimble for a man of 68 who practices no more than an hour daily. His hand position is good, he uses his arms freely, and in the slow passages manages to coax a pleasant sound from the piano.

There is a slight swelling of the third finger of the right hand due to a serious accident. Ferré had slipped on a tennis court and broken the finger so badly that the upper two joints curved at a near right angle to the rest of the finger. He said that moments after the fall he had pulled the finger back into a normal position. "I only thought of one thing: my piano playing. It hurt like hell, but straightening it out saved my finger."

After the Beethoven, Ferré played the *Cantique D'amour*, by Franz Liszt. Liszt and Beethoven are the Governor's favorite composers. The *Cantique* is in an early stage of preparation and the Governor will have to dedicate much time to the triplets, which escaped him. Rhythmic correctness must be one of his main goals if he is to play well.

A short discussion about pianos and acoustics sent us downstairs to try out the new grand piano in the formal meeting room. Here he again played the Beethoven sonata, which fared much better. Then the Governor played the solo part of the first movement of Beethoven's Third Concerto. He truly enjoyed himself, proclaiming the beauty of a passage, marveling aloud about the musical development and architecture. This writer was asked to play the orchestra part from a standing position during the final measures of the movement so that the dialogue between soloist and orchestra would be fully realized.

Ferré is genuinely enthusiastic in his music making, and what he may lack in technique is made up for by a healthy love for the art. The performance closed with a charming salon waltz by Arístides Chavier, one of Ferré's childhood teachers.

Historically speaking, Governor Ferré belongs to a long tradition of political men who also tried their hand at music. Was not King David an accomplished harpist? Roy Henry, the nom-de-plume of England's King Henry the Fifth composed excellent music. And Frederick the Great struggled equally with the flute and the Austrian armies. In this century, Jan Ignaz Paderewski, the legendary pianist, was also prime minister of Poland in the years immediately following World War I. Today, Britain's prime minister Edward Heath is by far the most competent of the politician-musicians. Heath formally studied choral conducting and recently conducted the London Symphony Orchestra in a successful performance.

As we were leaving, the governor assured us that he was going to practice and would arrange another get-together so that his interpretation of the Beethoven sonata would be more representative of his capabilities. He is also to begin work on Schubert's "Arpeggione" sonata for cello and piano. Unless Jesús María Sanromá decides to run for the governorship, we can state unequivocally that Luis A. Ferré is the finest pianist ever to occupy La Fortaleza, and should have little competition for a long time to come.

Concert Honors Massacred Pilgrims

The San Juan Star
June 2, 1972   By Francis Schwartz

The spectre of death haunted the opening night of the sixteenth annual Puerto Rico Casals Festival. The leaden Wednesday night atmosphere permeated the University of Puerto Rico Theater, as the concert was dedicated to the fourteen Puerto Rican religious pilgrims who lost their lives in the vicious terrorist attack at Tel Aviv's Lod airport.

These gentle people, whose trip to the Holy Land was motivated by the same spirit which sends all people to seek peace and beauty in the realm of art, fell before the mad dog actions of self-anointed paladins. The grief brought to these shores as well as to homes around the world is immeasurable.

We hope that the advocates of violence will remember and learn from this tragic experience. Decent men everywhere are outraged by such inhuman methods and everyone who has intentionally fomented hatred as part of a plan of action must share responsibility in these deaths. The shoe fits many, many feet.

The program opened with Pablo Casals' United Nations Hymn, under the direction of Sergije Rainis. Rainis substituted for Maestro Casals, who was indisposed due to some recalcitrant cold bacteria. We wish Maestro Casals a *prestissimo* recovery. Participating in the performance were the festival orchestra and the Puerto Rico Conservatory of Music Chorus.

Argentine-Israeli pianist Daniel Barenboim, who divides his time between the conductor's podium and the keyboard, was the soloist in Brahms' majestic B Flat Piano Concerto, Op. 83. Barenboim's approach to the music is athletic and free. He attempts to draw the maximum dramatic effect from each phrase, at times holding back before slamming into an intense chord, at times caressing a poignant melodic tone. We feel that this is *rubato* playing in the best sense of the word, and there was no doubt that the pianist has his own personal view of the concerto.

Barenboim frequently stressed harmonies which are usually passed over. He also lavished care on bass lines which are secondary but very meaningful. We found the performance both emotionally and intellectually stimulating.

Leslie Parnas demonstrated exemplary musicianship in his third-movement cello solo and the rapport established between pianist and cellist later in the movement proved rewarding. Alexander Schneider led the festival orchestra in providing an uneven accompaniment. More precision, especially at the phrase endings, was needed.

After intermission, Barenboim returned to conduct the Schumann Fourth Symphony, which was placed on the opening night program at the last minute due to Casals' illness. The orchestra sounded lackluster and Barenboim never really penetrated beyond the surface level of the score. No doubt more rehearsal time would have helped. What the conductor achieved with the Schumann was a professional reading by a highly experienced and gifted orchestra. But nothing memorable occurred.

Exhilarating Verdi at Festival

The San Juan Star
June 7, 1972 By Francis Schwartz

What makes a composer write music the way he does? How can non-musical elements intrude upon and decidedly influence the sonoral world? These questions came to mind Monday evening during the Casals Festival performance of Verdi's Requiem. The well attended University of Puerto Rico Theater was the scene of some exhilarating music making with Zubin Mehta conducting the festival orchestra and the Conservatory of Music Chorus; with soprano Martina Arroyo, mezzosoprano Grace Bumbry, tenor Plácido Domingo and bass Justino Díaz as soloists.

Verdi, a fervent admirer of the great Italian novelist Alessandro Manzoni, received a crushing blow when the aged writer succumbed to injuries received due to a fall on the steps of the San Fedele Church. Verdi was so emotionally shaken that he could not attend the funeral. The composer, considering Manzoni a symbol of Italian nationalism and human integrity, decided to create a commemorative work.

The *Dies Irae* (day of wrath or judgment) motif dominates the entire composition. The apocalyptic urgency with which Verdi wrote clearly determined the length of the *Dies Irae* section of the mass, and its musical reoccurrence in the closing *Libera Me*. We are convinced that had Verdi reacted to Manzoni's death in a more resigned, controlled manner, the Requiem would have taken another form of emphasis and musical expression.

Zubin Mehta's handling of the score was excellent. He held the disparate elements in check, asserted strong musical control, and allowed the music to flow without undue exaggeration. Mehta balanced the sound with expertise and allowed the soloists enough freedom so that pliancy, not larceny, resulted. He has a truly fine concept of the work.

The soloists were quite up to the occasion. Martina Arroyo possesses a beautiful, polished voice which she put to good use. Her *Recordare* with Grace Bumbry was one of the evening's high points. Miss Arroyo's pitch flagged momentarily in the closing section of *Libera Me*, but her overall performance was lovely. Mezzosoprano Grace Bumbry sang with surety and drama, while her high musical level was consistent throughout the evening. Plácido Domingo again demonstrated that he is one of the best tenors on the international scene by his moving, vocally rich singing; and basso Justino Díaz rendered meritorious service as he infused his melodic lines with emotion and drama.

The Conservatory of Music Chorus, prepared by Sergije Rainis, conveyed the necessary excitement in their singing, although the male voices sounded thin. We found that the fugato sections of both the *Sanctus* and the *Libera Me* needed tightening, while the unison quality of the choral subdivisions was rough. Still, the overall achievement was worthy of acknowledgement.

One could cite many outstanding moments such as the perfect rhythmic pace of the *Lachrymosa* or the tonally pure unfolding of the *Agnus Dei*, but space does not allow it. We merely wish to say that this was the most rewarding concert to date of this sixteenth Casals Festival, and the music making we heard will stay cataloged in our mind's library of fine performances.

Casals Festival Applauded for New Works

The San Juan Star
June 9, 1972   By Francis Schwartz

    Who would have thought, six years ago, that a Casals Festival concert would include works of Prokofiev and Mahler, not to mention Bartók and Stravinsky (to be performed in future concerts)? Certainly there can be no doubt of our public's acceptance of these masterworks after the tumultuous applause that rocked the University of Puerto Rico Theater on Wednesday evening. This progressive, unfettered programming style can only enrich our musical experience and stimulate the exploration of more recent forms of composition. Festival planners as well as the general public should be happy with this improvement in the repertoire.

    Itzhak Perlman, the young Israeli violinist, unleashed his artistic firepower in a dazzling performance of Prokofiev's Second Violin Concerto. Perlman played brilliantly, continuously pushing the music ahead. He judiciously selected varied sound colors from his wide tonal palette, and demonstrated a profound understanding of Prokofiev's salient characteristics: percussive modernism fused with romantic lyricism.

    Zubin Mehta felicitously conducted the festival orchestra in the accompaniment, maintaining proper sectional balance and following the soloist closely.

    After the concerto, Perlman presented a lagniappe to the audience in the form of Paganini's Twenty-fourth Caprice, for solo violin.

    Itzhak Perlman, at the age of 27 years, is considered one of the great violinists in the world today. His is a unique talent. Perlman's command of the violin reminds us of the great virtuosos of bygone days. He comfortably changes styles depending on the concerto at hand and always generates enthusiasm in his performance. For this listener it was a great pleasure to hear such artistry, and we are sure that the young violinist will be one of the major world artists during the coming decades.

After intermission, Zubin Mehta led a carefully planned, dynamic performance of Gustav Mahler's First Symphony. One either likes Mahler or detests him: neutrality is difficult. His mastery of orchestration reveals incredible knowledge of the orchestra and of instrumental idiosyncrasies. Of course, Mahler was one of the great orchestral conductors of his epoch.

The First Symphony has been ferociously criticized for being simplistic and vulgar. These negative opinions miss the profound personal expression which Mahler couched in the accessible melodies. Mehta has a special feel for this type of music. Perhaps the conductor's years of study in Vienna allowed him an intimate look into this very distinct Central European style.

Festival Fizzles

The San Juan Star
June 19, 1972 (a) By Francis Schwartz

The final concert of the sixteenth annual Puerto Rico Casals Festival came to a low-keyed close Saturday evening at the University of Puerto Rico Theater. Pablo Casals' peace oratorio, *El Pessebre* (The Manger), based on the poem of Catalan poet Joan Alavedra, was politely applauded by the near capacity audience which witnessed the writhings of conductor Alexander Schneider in his attempt to lead the festival orchestra and the Conservatory of Music Chorus through the lengthy work. Only when Casals took the podium in order to conduct the final *Gloria* did the public respond with vigor.

The ovation given Maestro Casals attests to the affection and great esteem audiences have for him as a hearty, battling nonagenarian and as a proponent of world peace. As for Casals' oratorio, we have previously reviewed the work and will not reiterate our many objections from a musical viewpoint. Whether we agree or not with his compositional ideas, we can enthusiastically join our voice to his call for peace on this troubled earth. His motivation is unquestionably noble and one must respect that.

Alexander Schneider led the orchestra and chorus most unevenly. Often the orchestra sounded ragged. The entrances of instruments and voices were imprecise and the resultant ennui proved to be soporific. It is hard to remember a less satisfactory Casals Festival concert. We have heard how the festival orchestra can sound under Mehta, and to a lesser extent, Barenboim. The final performance level under Schneider's baton was depressing.

Maureen Forrester sang with conviction and aplomb. The mezzo-soprano possesses a large, golden voice which reaches the most distant cranny in the hall. Her excellent collaboration brightened the performance.

Soprano Olga Iglesias has sounded better on other occasions, for her usually pure voice had an edge to it. She also strained on the high notes, which were far too strident. Musically, Miss Iglesias knows the part intimately, for she has performed *El Pessebre* more than any other singer alive.

Once again, baritone Pablo Elvira demonstrated his artistic solidity. His voice shone in fine fashion and he continues to grow in musical stature.

We could work up little enthusiasm for tenor Paulino Saharrea, whose tone production lacked a rounded quality, and whose intonation wavered too often. Perhaps an indisposition?

Young Carlos Serrano, a baritone making his festival debut, still has a long road of study ahead. But his voice has good potential. He is timid on the stage, but experience will correct this trait. With more time and dedication Serrano could develop into an interesting singer.

So closed the sixteenth Puerto Rico Casals Festival. There were some magnificent instances of music making, and given the low median age of the soloists (Casals excepted), the emphasis was on youth. The repertoire has expanded into the present century and we hope that intelligent, imaginative programming and selection of artists will give us an even better festival next year.

As we see old acquaintances from the orchestra grow paunchier, balder, more wrinkled, we're filled with certain nostalgia. This festival, for many of us, is a gauge of time, and the years have a way of flowing past quickly. Even this writer has been accused of mellowing with age. Can you believe it?

♪

Setting the Facts Straight

The San Juan Star
June 19, 1972 (b)   By Francis Schwartz

"A little learning is a dang'rous thing . . . ," said the venerable Alexander Pope. We would add that the wrong kind of learning is equally deleterious and that those who drink at the Persian spring of knowledge should make sure that the water is not contaminated.

Every Casals Festival we are deluged by letters and calls; some favorable, some negative, but all actively concerned with some aspect of the yearly music making. Such effervescence demonstrates a commitment to cultural activity.

This year many colleagues and students have consulted me on the musico-historical commentaries which appear in the official program. The notes purportedly orient the public about the music to be performed and allow them to view the works in proper perspective. We wish to set the record straight for the public's benefit.

Writing about the Tchaikovsky First Piano Concerto, the annotator of the Casals Festival program states, "The concerto was premiered in London and the soloist was Edwin Dannreuther." This comes as a shock to us music lovers who thought that Tchaikovsky's first concerto was premiered in the United States of America. The fact is that Hans von Bülow did perform the work for the first time in Boston, in 1875, and there is ample documentary proof to substantiate this assertion.

The commentary on the Mahler First Symphony states that Mahler abhorred program notes and programmatic titles. This is correct. His first symphony was performed in Weimar with very romantic sectional titles against the wishes of the composer.

However, the following note in the program states: "One understands the indignation of Mahler, as perhaps Beethoven felt when his

Sonata Quasi Una Fantasia was entitled "Moonlight Sonata," without his knowing about it." Unless Beethoven came back from the grave, he could not have felt anything when his sonata received such a poetic title since this took place after Beethoven's death. Unless the author of these program notes is a practitioner of the occult, we fail to see how he could have had the necessary contact with Beethoven in order to be privy to the Bonn Master's indignation.

Commenting on the first movement of the Mahler, the program annotator states "... there is a theme already used in a song by Mahler and even an unmistakable passage from Lehár's *Merry Widow*." Mahler composed this symphony in 1889, revising it in 1893. Franz Lehár's *Merry Widow* did not appear until 1905, sixteen years later. If any musical "borrowing" was involved, let us get original property rights straight!

As a closing treat, we recommend to those fans who used to relish the humor of the late Eddie López's Spanglish "Candid Flowers" columns in this paper, a perusal of page 30 of the Casals Festival program book. You will find several "puttings in of the animal foot."

There is much valuable information in the program, but it behooves the Casals Festival to be more careful in publishing information which the public takes on good faith. After all, this is an international music festival.

The Future of the Casals Festival

The San Juan Star
June 20, 1972 By Francis Schwartz

    Music is alive and well in Puerto Rico. After witnessing the recent and well attended Casals Festival, nobody could doubt that the people of Puerto Rico are interested in a concert life of quality. Currently, two opera groups are preparing a promising season; the University of Puerto Rico and the Institute of Puerto Rican Culture have active music series; ballet companies are competing for the public's favor; and more musical projects are underway now that in any other period in Puerto Rico's history. Much credit goes to Casals Festival Inc. for its yearly summer music festival which brings internationally known artists to these shores.

    Casals Festival, Inc., a semi-public corporation under the wing of Fomento, also runs the Puerto Rico Conservatory of Music and the Puerto Rico Symphony Orchestra. Any student of Puerto Rican history knows that music did not begin here in 1956, when the Casals Festival was established. There were operas, concerts throughout the past century, and the idea to establish an official conservatory of music dates from the end of the nineteenth century. But of prime importance in the existence of the Casals organization is the government's commitment to music. When a budget of $1.2 million has been allotted to the musical entity and Fomento's publicity machinery continually emphasizes the prominent place which this art plays in our lives, the public impact is very great.

    First of all, the festival concerts are broadcasted on television and radio, allowing the event to enter thousands of homes around the island. Psychologically, the government's participation makes the people feel that the event is prestigious and important to the quality of life on the island. Also, publicity is sent around the world as part of the Puerto Rico

"Showcase of the Americas" image in order to attract tourists and demonstrate an amenable, sophisticated climate which might interest investors and industries. Thus the function of the Casals Festival falls into three categories: education of the public, the enrichment of artistic life here, and the utilization of the famed event for economic purposes, i.e., tourism, industries, etc.

Since the inception of the festival, people have speculated on its longevity. Would the music event continue in a post-Casals era? Was the government planning to close shop after the demise of Maestro Casals? Fortunately the Casals Festival Inc. is developing many plans of action.

As this column appears, the entire festival orchestra will be airbound to Caracas where the Puerto Rico Casals Festival will spend five days offering concerts. The government of Venezuela underwrites all expenses of the tour and, according to executive director of the Casals Festival Inc., José Franceschini, there will even be a profit left over which will be applied to local activities.

The idea of taking the festival on tour began last year with a visit to Guadalajara, Mexico. Fomento sees these trips as a means of publicizing Puerto Rico throughout the world. A tour throughout South America is currently being studied and there is even an invitation from the Kennedy Center in Washington.

"It would be excellent to present the Casals Festival Orchestra for a week in Washington, just as we are doing in Venezuela," stated Franceschini.

The Casals Festival has now branched out into new areas. Last year, the Casals organization collaborated (though not financially) with a new opera company, Opera de Puerto Rico, formed by Manuel Fernández Cortines and Alfredo Matilla. Due to the favorable public response to the two presentations, *Aida* and *Don Giovanni*, the festival agency decided to take the opera entity under its aegis. Negotiations are under way to bring internationally prominent ballet companies to Puerto Rico as part of Casals Festival Inc.'s activity, and preparations are now being made to celebrate the hundredth anniversary of Casals' birth in 1976.

"Puerto Rico will be celebrating the 200th anniversary of the United States as well as the centennial of the maestro's birth," according to Franceschini.

Plans are being made to begin the 1976 celebration in January, with concerts, operas and ballets to culminate in the summer festival.

Governments around the world will be invited to participate, sending their finest artists for the event. Thus the projections of the Casals Festival organization extend far into the future.

We envision clashes on the local scene as the Casals Festival begins to branch out into other areas. Many artists will see this expansion in monopolistic terms. There will be charges of unfair competition and conflict of interest. This is unavoidable. Also on the political front, the presence of the Casals Festival in Washington will create a turmoil among pro-independence groups. And without doubt, the linking of the U.S. bicentennial to the Casals Festival, with all the possibilities of international publicity, probably will turn the event into a battleground for you know what: the status question.

For those observers of history who also take delight in music, the coming years promise to be fascinating. And right in the thick of it will be Casals Festival Inc.

Tosca: Alive and Well in San Juan

The San Juan Star
September 27, 1972   By Francis Schwartz

In spite of the many deaths which take place in this opera, Puccini's *Tosca* is alive and well in San Juan. The Casals Festival Organization, making its full fledged debut this year as an opera impresario, has managed to stage a solid, apparently well rehearsed production of the sanguinary work.

During the Sunday night performance at the University of Puerto Rico Theater, we were haunted by the notion that perhaps this heady mixture of blood, lust, torture and betrayal was in some way the precursor of the too, too explicit Old West movies coming out of Italy these days.

Grace Bumbry, in the soprano title role, is a singer of considerable power. She activates her dramatization with vigor and enthusiasm. It is perhaps this energy which gives her voice an edgy quality, at times excessively so.

Miss Bumbry's approach avoids daintiness and exaggerated female frailty, which makes good sense. We found occasional slackening in her acting, especially when she realized that the evil Baron Scarpia was not pursuing her purse, rather her pulchritude. The discovery of her beloved's death could also have been more persuasive, though vocally it was intense.

Plácido Domingo, the Spanish tenor, acquitted himself in splendid fashion with a first class realization of the aristocratic, revolutionary painter, Mario Cavaradossi. Domingo's voice has a sumptuous quality and he handles it with consummate skill. His taste and intelligence allow him to effectively toy with the melodic lines without committing what he denominates "tenor's larceny." There are not many tenors on the world opera scene who can rival this excellent artist.

Justino Díaz began his Scarpia performance in a lowkeyed fashion allowing the villainous side of the police chief's character to build gradually. We found Díaz a bit stiff in the first act but he quickly remedied this. His second act was dramatically well planned.

Díaz showed his evil intentions without twirling his mustache in Perils-of-Pauline fashion. After all, Baron Scarpia was not evil incarnate. He was merely a counter-revolutionary police chief who tortured an artist and threatened him with death in order to possess the artist's lady. Díaz complemented his judicious theatrical pacing with solid vocal delivery. We found this view of Scarpia highly satisfying.

In the lesser roles, Gimi Beni proved to be a genial, full voiced sacristan; Iván Janer was sufficiently sycophantic as the police agent but needed more vocal projection. Toshiaki Kuni rendered yeoman service as Angelotti. Also cast were Migdalia Batiz and Carlos Serrano as the shepherd boy and the jailer, respectively.

The orchestra under the baton of Rudolf Kruger showed signs of reaching the level of adequacy. Though there were many moments of bad intonation, imprecise entrances, etc.; there were also times when one could sit back and enjoy the sounds emanating from stage AND pit. Kruger conducted very well. It is difficult to do much with the score when you are worried whether or not the instrumentalists will hold together, yet he managed very well.

We found the staging both imaginative and stimulating. Stage director Piero Faggione utilized the available areas well, never allowing any static quality to weigh down the plot. The first act procession which utilized the aisles of the theater, thus directing the dramatic flow to the stage for the climax, was successful; incense, candles, robes: all served to enliven the scene and envelop the audience in the action. The scenery, brought from Venice, was attractive and functional. We found the costumes designed by Fernando Rivero satisfactory and the lighting by Antonio Frontera usually good, though the dawn scene of Act 3 lacked subtlety.

The chorus of young adults and children performed creditably.

We consider the production enjoyable, but the work is philosophically jarring. All the main participants are removed from the realm of the living, terminated in one way or another; only the lackeys survive. Should we draw the conclusion that those who make waves will soon be swamped by them? *Tosca* is eloquently relevant these days.

Eaton Displays Art of Electronic Music

The San Juan Star
February 28, 1973   By Francis Schwartz

Electronic music filled the University of Puerto Rico General Studies Amphitheater last Saturday night as composer-performer John Eaton delighted the capacity audience with his new art. Eaton, a composer of considerable merit, brought his own equipment to Puerto Rico in order to achieve the live realization of several of his works.

Using the Synket electronic synthesizer with keyboards and pedal, the performer gave a stimulating demonstration of the instrument's possibilities. Contemporary electronic music is usually created in laboratories where the composer has ample opportunity to edit his work and rethink every sound before delivering an exactly reproduced tape version to the public through the use of tape recorders and speakers. Some creators combine traditional instruments with the fixed magnetic tape; such is the case of Mario Davidovsky, whose *Sincronismos* has been heard here on several occasions.

Eaton prefers to create his works before the audience, performing in a great virtuoso tradition of live creation/performance. Obviously it would be easier for him to prerecord every work and merely replay it in the hall. But his approach is more spontaneous, offering the excitement of instant recreation on stage as if the composition were a Bach fugue or a Brahms intermezzo.

Of the works presented, the strongest from our point of view were the prerecorded *Blind Man's Cry* and *Thoughts on Rilke*, both of which explore the endless possibilities of vocal production combined with electronic instruments. The zygotic result was quite successful.

Unfortunately the speaker system was not of greater resonance. The hall should have been bathed in sound; it was not. Also, the very subtle

Soliloquy fell flat as an opening piece. Perhaps a rearranging of the program order would solve the problem for future presentations.

John Eaton presents a lively, stimulating approach to electronic music making and he certainly must be considered an important composer. As time passes, we feel confident that live performance techniques will become standardized in electronic music as they have for all the instruments of the past, and that Eaton will occupy a niche in the pantheon of pioneers.

The famous Figueroa Quintet in 1974, on one of their many international tours. (Left to right: José, Kachiro, Narciso, Rafael and Guillermo Figueroa.)

Five Figueroas and a Varied Program

The San Juan Star
March 6, 1973 By Francis Schwartz

The Figueroa Quintet, recently returned from a European tour, offered a varied program Sunday afternoon at Casa Blanca in Old San Juan. As the Official Quintet of the Commonwealth of Puerto Rico the brothers Figueroa—José and Kachiro, violins; Guillermo, viola; Rafael, cello; and Narciso, piano—undertook a good will tour during January performing in centers in Spain, Portugal, France and Austria.

Opening with a Vivaldi Concerto in A Minor, the group needed more sparkle and energy in its approach to the Baroque score. One missed the clearly differentiated dynamic levels, which is a salient characteristic of this particular style. This reduced arrangement for a quintet can in no way compare with the original orchestral version with the violin solos. While the music is of quality, the reduced ensemble appeared anemic in both volume and color.

The Dvořák "American" Quartet, Op. 96, fared well in the Figueroas' hands, sans pianist Narciso. This composition was born in Spillville, Iowa, in 1893 when Dvořák visited this Czech colony in the U.S. Midwest. In a burst of creative energy, Dvořák completed the quartet in two weeks.

The Figueroas played with elan, shading when necessary, taking a free-breathing approach as the music unfolded. Particularly commendable was the *lento* movement with its piquant lyricism. The ensemble playing reached a high level with only occasional inexactitude. The exigencies of the recent European tour had sharpened the quintet's technique, and one hopes that they will maintain this standard in future concerts.

Walter Piston's attractive Quintet closed the program. The interpretation was intelligent and carefully delineated, which corresponds admirably to the obvious structural concern of the composer. Piston's music possesses a jocose quality which is carefully tied to a clear musical architecture. The Figueroa Quintet conveyed this idea to the letter.

As a closing word, we wish to remind our readers that the Institute of Puerto Rican Culture features a Sunday afternoon concert series, with performers offering their artistry in the beautiful surroundings of Casa Blanca. We hope that the public may take advantage of their government's cultural projects, which are designed to improve the quality of our daily lives.

The "Popularization" of WIPR

The San Juan Star
March 16, 1973   By Francis Schwartz

Recent statements by newly appointed WIPR Administrator José García landed like a bombshell on institutions which are devoted to the development of the fine arts in Puerto Rico. García commented to the press that he did not see why WIPR could not present popular singers such as Chucho Avellanet and Lucecita Benítez more frequently instead of "concerts and operas" which cater to a "culturally select group."

Coming from the person who will be responsible for programming policy over the coming years, this negativism concerning the forms of art glaringly absent from commercial stations augurs poorly for the future of the government facility. One can only wonder what concept García has of a public non-profit mass medium dedicated to educational progress irrespective of commercial appeal.

WIPR Radio-TV is the only station which attempts to link quality presentations with the task of public education. As a non-profit government entity, WIPR has access to vast film, music and videotape libraries around the world and can practice cultural xenogamy at a cost far less than commercial stations. Since WIPR does not have to satisfy the profit demands of investors or stockholders, there is an unlimited field of programming possibilities. To state that the fine arts, i.e. concerts, ballet, plays, opera, is the property of a culturally select few is not only erroneous in concept but a serious threat to quality presentations in the future. Certainly the panacea proposed by García makes little sense when we consider the number of commercial stations which flood the airwaves with "popular" material.

Precisely the opposite approach is needed in order to more effectively communicate the message of great art to an ever growing audience.

Instead of retreating before an imagined "elitist" monopoly of the arts, an idea thoroughly disproved in Sweden, Austria, the Soviet Union, Israel, Denmark and China, among other countries, what is called for is a more dynamic structuring of these very programs. One remembers when concerts at the University of Puerto Rico were sparsely attended. Now, after years of planned art education, the public flocks to concerts, films, exhibitions, etc. WIPR has the opportunity to use wisely the tremendous amount of local talent in the dissemination of art to the viewing public.

More should be done in the field of adult education. This society is badly in need of trained people, and the government station should play a major role in such preparation. Certainly there would be a place for well selected popular music events with the caliber artists mentioned by the WIPR administrator. But not at the expense of "concerts and operas," which clearly must be mainstays in the cultural philosophy of a government educational station.

No doubt García wishes to offer instructive, relevant programming to the people of Puerto Rico. In order to take the pulse of this rapidly evolving society he should create an advisory board consisting of teachers, writers, composers, trade unionists and industry representatives, which could serve as a valuable source of ideas. Only by weighing these divergent viewpoints as to the needs of our society can WIPR hope to articulate a clear policy which corresponds to Puerto Rico's educational needs.

WIPR should not lower its standards in material selection or presentation methods. Now, more than ever, a quality educational station is needed which can provide learning opportunities to the public at large and serve as an example to other stations in the mass media field.

Cathedral Acoustics Mar Concert

The San Juan Star
March 25, 1973 By Francis Schwartz

The San Juan Cathedral was buzzing with lights, people and cameras last Sunday evening as the Puerto Rico Symphony Orchestra performed a concert in honor of Cardinal Aponte. Under the baton of guest conductor Kenneth Klein the orchestra offered works by Moncayo, Griffes and Dvořák.

José Pablo Moncayo's *Huapango*, a coloristic composition based on Mexican and Spanish musical elements (see Albeniz' *Rondena*), received admirable treatment from both Klein and the orchestra. The playing was brisk and snappy, with sufficient technical solidity.

The acoustics of the cathedral place a heavy burden on any performer, and one must salute flutist Peter Kern for his excellent rendition of Griffes' Poem for Flute and Orchestra. In spite of the excessive resonance and echo, Kern's musicianship shone through. His shading and his clarity of execution, complemented by Klein's intelligent accompaniment, fashioned a truly enjoyable performance.

Dvořák's Eighth Symphony, Op. 88 closed the program. There were moments less than felicitous in the violin section. One still hears occasional microtonal playing in this section, and the horns were rather murky. However, the overall effect was of both drama and relaxed melodiousness of Dvořák's score. Especially convincing was the slow tempo chosen at the opening of the final movement. This idea created even more tension as the music progressed.

Cardinal Aponte received the musical offering with enthusiasm, as did the capacity crowd in attendance.

The Terrible Trauma
That Trapped Tristan Trimble

The San Juan Star
May 6, 1973   By Francis Schwartz

Actually, Tristan Trimble looks like Henry Kissinger as played by Peter Sellers. Or Peter Sellers played by Henry Kissinger, I haven't decided which.

After agreeing to write an orchestral work for my friends at Inter American University in San Germán, I decided to enlist the aid of some other friends in its creation. I should like to mention them. They are Ezra Pound, Jorge Borges, Juan Goytisolo, the Marquis de Sade, Richard Milhous Nixon, L. Patrick Gray, Goethe, Mighty Mouse, Suleiman the Magnificent, Moshe Dayan, Clarence Darrow, La Lupe, Cheetah, Thomas Mann, Mallarmé, Schopenhauer, Xenakis, and above all, Ivan the Terrible. Perhaps I should not mention all these influences. But I do it in order that graduate students and erudite musicologists may some day pave their way to academic fame by tracing the origins of this new work which turned out to be *The Tropical Trek of Tristan Trimble*, a venture into symphonic composition with narration and smells.

This all presupposes that anybody would want to research the background of *Tristan Trimble*. In any event it happened this way:

In March, while the piece was still in my head, I happened to be reading Jean Paul Sartre's study of the French playwright Jean Genet, in which Sartre comments, "Honesty is an eternal essence which is not dimmed by accidental lapses."

I was truly astonished by this. Here I was, a product of morning pledges of allegiance; of terrible things I had witnessed in my life. I remembered an old lady outside a church in Monterrey suckling an emaciated baby from a withered breast while begging for coins. I remembered the stench which rose from the Houston slums as I bourgeoised through the poverty. I remembered the films of Auschwitz, Dachau, Theresienstadt, which froze my pupils as they seared my psyche. And I reached out for four seconds of silence in the hope that the memories would vanish into a Lethean mist.

Theodor Adorno had the temerity to bother me with "In the history of art, late works represent catastrophes." I suppose it was then that I called upon Tristan Trimble to speak out. I was persecuted by these intellectual friends. I sought Tristan as an ally.

"I never knew how contradictory the Truth could be."

He said, "I heard the revolution preached by men who clipped the privileged coupons from their bluechip families. I saw the revolutionary artists do a Marxist Mazurka . . . for a fashionable while. I saw people who use people and use them and use them and use them. And I met fear and cowardice and more fear."

Tristan should not talk this way, I thought. It is not very politic. He should weigh his words more carefully so that he may someday become a "Gran Cocoroco" (That's a sort of Big Shot for those of you who have never read Palés Matos or heard this word flung around with regionalistic bite). But Tristan paid me no heed.

A flurry of woodwind sounds came to mind as I saw the notes dancing in a cellar in Cologne, during the Nazi scourge. The flute flutter-tongued its way over the inscription written on the wall: "I believe in the sun even when it is not shining. I believe in God even when He is silent." I had to liberate all the winds, cajoling them into a minuet of chance. Taunting them to invent: to read the inscription on the walls in the hope that they would drive away the past with an affirmation of the future.

Then I began to write down brass notes. High brass, low brass, middle: vast blocks of metallic sounds which somehow reminded me of a movie I saw in a red carpeted Loews Theater which dealt with the lives of the Pharaohs. I added percussion while listening to a dulcet voice whispering Li Po's poetry. My percussion is Chinese-inspired.

And the final crescendo—26 seconds—devilish seconds. Tristan Trimble is dead and will soon join Wagner in Valhalla. I drive the orchestral mass upward, unrelenting, always louder, trying to penetrate the very being of my listeners. I burn out their cancers with a white hot sound while holding them gently so as not to hurt them.

That is how Tristan Trimble was born. That is how he died.

I suppose that one should love one's progeny. So I will defend Tristan Trimble. As I said before, he often speaks frankly, flirts with Truth, and naturally nobody likes that. We always kill the truthsayers. And yet, for some reason, they refuse to die.

World Harmony Defeated

The San Juan Star
May 18, 1973 By Francis Schwartz

The cause of international harmony suffered a serious setback at a Saturday night World University-sponsored concert in honor of Pablo and Martita Casals. Having titled the evening, "Puerto Rico Sings to World Peace," the soporific atmosphere which pervaded the entire evening foreshadowed an era of strife rather than brotherhood.

The originally scheduled appearance of an orchestra to assist in both vocal and instrumental solos was scuttled by behind the scenes musical battles which involved competing teams of players. This organizational dissonance made the participation of an orchestra impossible.

Also the obvious lack of sufficient rehearsal created intonation and ensemble problems throughout the program.

There were occasional breaks in the musical gloom. Pianist Jesús María Sanromá performed his solo version of George Gershwin's Rhapsody in Blue, which seems to require an extra hand in order to cover all the added ideas. Sanromá will never be accused of being an overly clean pianist—he missed plenty of notes—but he certainly projected this Jazz Age score with stylistic authenticity. From an artistic viewpoint, this was the pinnacle of the concert.

Basso Justino Díaz expressively sang an aria from Verdi's *Attila*. His professional ease carried him through nicely. The final trio from Gounod's *Faust*, with Díaz, Camelia Ortiz del Rivero and Edgardo Gierbolini, also proved satisfactory in both ensemble and ease of execution.

Other composers represented were Beethoven, Strauss, Mozart, Bach, and Casals.

The evening was very disappointing, and certainly the organizational difficulties contributed to the poor quality of performance.

Also participating in the concert were Puli Toro, Héctor López, Migdalia Batiz, Aura Robledo, Luisita Rodríguez, Carlos Serrano, Iván Janer, Ángel Cruz, Luz Hutchinson, Cecilia Talavera, Sergije Rainis and the Puerto Rico Conservatory of Music Chorus.

New World Work Marks Casals Festival First

The San Juan Star
May 31, 1973								By Francis Schwartz

Geriatrics or music? That is the question which always comes to mind on opening Casals Festival nights. People flock to the University of Puerto Rico theater to see the aged Catalan cellist-conductor, Pablo Casals, take up the baton in service of the Orphean art. Casals proved beyond doubt that he was at Tuesday evening's concert for no-nonsense music making.

He led the festival orchestra in a moving, well paced reading of Mendelssohn's Hebrides Overture, Op. 26. The playing had flow, good balance, and dramatic tension.

The presentation of Heitor Villa-Lobos' First Piano Concerto (1945-46) represents a historic step for the Casals Festival. Finally, a work from the New World has made its way into the programming; this demonstrates a growing cultural awareness in Puerto Rico's most powerful musical organization.

Villa-Lobos, the Brazilian giant, has certainly composed better works than the concerto performed here by Spanish pianist Luis Galve, under the baton of Alexander Schneider. The piece is too long and most uneven. The best movements, in our opinion, are the second and the fourth. The rich folk rhythmic source of the final section is a splendid example of nationalistic writing, similar to the Tchaikovsky or Bartók piano concertos.

While the opening movement possesses a lovely G sharp minor melody which should be subtitled "Love Story on the Amazon," there is far too much unnecessary busywork. Villa-Lobos needed pruning shears in order to lop off the musical filler. Pianist Galve gave a fine, rhythmically solid performance of the work. His virtuosity in the cadenza was impressive. His often dry sound was appropriate for the percussive passages, though we would have preferred more flexibility in the lyrical sections. There were several passages which could have been cleaner as far as the orchestra is concerned.

The ice is broken. Now let us hope that in future years, the very best music of our hemisphere might find a place alongside the European masters. The time has arrived.

After intermission, Casals conducted the First Symphony of Beethoven. The slow, deliberate pace of the first movement allowed one to hear every part carefully articulated. This approach made sense. The other tempi were not particularly slow and the finale adagio opening was ideally planned. Casals occasionally asks for exaggerated accents. But this interpretation of the Beethoven symphony was generally of high quality and quite inspired.

Year after year, the Casals Festival opening night has tended to drag. This year there seems to be more adrenalin flowing. That's just fine.

Festival Program Evokes Yawns

The San Juan Star
June 9, 1973   By Francis Schwartz

The dark clouds of uninterest continued to gather over the seventeenth Puerto Rico Casals Festival as the festival orchestra played to an anemic house Thursday night at the University of Puerto Rico Theater. For the third concert in a row, hundreds of seats have gone unsold, and both musicians and festival fans are asking, "What's going on?"

One possible answer to the musical malaise can be found in the programming. After a demanding first half, which featured the Bartók Violin Concerto, the program offered, back to back, the interminable, soporific Bruckner A Major Adagio with Beethoven's *lento* movement from the String Quartet Op. 135. We don't know who concocted this mixture, but he should patent it, for it is the greatest cure for insomnia on the market. Aside from the dubious merit of making a programmatic stew from movements wrenched from their originally destined contexts, the lack of atmospheric change in the two aforementioned works almost assures an unenthusiastic reaction from the general public. Festival concerts should not be structured without taking into account the optimum impact they may produce. We are the first to ask for adventuresome, imaginative programming, but there is no need to anesthetize the audience in order to present some off the beaten track composition.

Certainly the bright spot of the evening was Pinchas Zukerman's splendid performance in Bela Bartók's Concerto for Violin and Orchestra (1938). The young violinist put his formidable technique at the service of the score and plumbed the emotional depths of this Magyar-inspired composition. Zukerman's warm, dulcet sound brought out the lyricism which permeates the concerto. The boisterous sections were crisp and stinging. Five years ago we heard Zukerman at the festival and were impressed by his technique and talent. To those qualities we can now add, artistry.

As for the concerto, in our opinion it is one of the greatest works ever composed for violin and orchestra. Bartók continues to grow in stature and his works will be among the treasures that our century leaves to future generations. The violin concerto, along with these of Prokofiev and Berg, will represent the genre at its best. We don't think the Stravinsky, Schoenberg or Barber will stand the tests of time as easily. Bartók possessed a magical sense of orchestral color, and he brilliantly fused this element with the rhythmic and melodic beauty of Magyar folk music. The results are monuments to his genius.

Alexander Schneider and the festival orchestra are to be commended for their performance. It is very difficult to prepare such a work as the Bartók in two rehearsals and the generally felicitous music making pointed out the high professional quality of these musicians.

The concert opened with a sparkling reading of the Mendelssohn Tenth Symphony, for strings. Also programmed was the fugue from the String Quartet, Op. 59 No. 3 of Beethoven.

When is a Festival Not a Festival?

The San Juan Star
June 12, 1973   By Donald Thompson

    According to normal usage, a music festival is a brief series of concerts devoted to the performance of works which display some strong unifying characteristic. Thus there have been avant-garde festivals, Renaissance festivals, rock festivals, Baroque opera festivals . . . the list is endless. Often an attractive or unusual locale, together with some unifying aesthetic principle, provides the theme: Edinburgh, Vienna, Santa Fe, Donaueschingen and Prades immediately come to mind. Rarely (in fact, I know of only one case in the entire history of music festivals) has the name of a living person been invoked to provide the basis of a festival involving more than a concert or two.

    I submit that the annual Puerto Rico Casals Festival is not a festival at all, for it no longer possesses a unifying principle. In the early years there was a reason for festivity, in the repertory. Mainly heard were works of Bach, Mozart and other pre-Romantic composers for small orchestra or chamber ensemble: music which can never appear on standard symphony orchestra series for the simple reason that it neither utilizes big symphonic forces nor appeals to symphonic audiences. It is music played by specialists for connoisseurs. The premise of the Casals Festival as a tourist event was clear: rarely heard music was being played by distinguished soloists in Puerto Rico and if you wanted to hear it you'd better get on down there. Pablo Casals provided another unifying force as conductor, as performer, and as the one who selected the repertory and invited the other participants. Theoretically, his presence was transmitted to the audience by these means even in seasons when he did not appear.

    In the past ten years, however, the June festival has lost its way. The repertory has expanded enormously, as have the orchestral forces.

Virtually the whole of the standard conservative symphonic repertory has by now been presented in Puerto Rico by festival orchestras, while whole platoons of soloists and conductors—distinguished and not so distinguished—have marched across the stage of the University Theater. But the artistic and festive losses have been great. Gone is the unity formerly provided by the handful of specialists performers, soloists all, who came to spend a couple of relaxed weeks with the master; in recent years the orchestras have consisted mainly of symphony men and freelance players, hard pressed during a tough musical season in New York and still hard pressed during a Caribbean continuation of the same. Gone is the unity formerly provided by the repertory of seldom heard works; the present repertory can be heard in Oklahoma City or Pittsburgh during the normal symphony season. Gone is the unity formerly provided by the Casals touch, which lies precisely to his extreme dedication to a limited number of jewel-like small scale classic works. The fact that music of Bartók and Stravinsky can be heard during a series of concerts connected with the Casals name is absurd, for the only public utterances which the master has made during the past twenty years concerning the music of our century have been unfavorable. Where does this leave Casals' own tastes, which provided a basic and compelling force in the early festivals?

For these reasons I maintain that the June concerts have lost their festive nature. Furthermore, I believe that the present format of the annual observance has become a burden rather than an attraction and that the time has come to make some changes.

Carlos Passalacqua, president of the Casals Festival Corporation, recently made two public statements which I believe are symptomatic of the confusion and improvisation that have marked the Corporation's endeavors in recent years. One of these statements concerned the permanent nature of the festivals. Passalacqua, on WIPR-TV during an intermission chat, observed that the Salzburg Festival and the Bayreuth Festival are permanent institutions, functioning long after the honored figures, Mozart and Wagner, have passed from the face of the earth. By the same token, he said, the Casals Festival here will be a permanent annual observance. Passalacqua's error lies in his equating Pablo Casals, a truly extraordinary instrumentalist in his time though a dabbler in composition, with two of the most profound musical creators that the world has known. Mozart and Wagner were composers of genius, and it is by their compositions that we remember them. Their celebration at annual festivals is completely justified by the enormous scope of their production and the aesthetic unity which marks the total output of each. It is this unity which gives glowing life to the Salzburg and Bayreuth Festivals, not the fact that Mozart or Wagner might have been a noted instrumentalist or a saintly person. Wagner, as is well known, was neither, and any attempt by festival promoters to create such an image for him would only inspire worldwide laughter of truly Wagnerian sonority. No, to attempt to base a permanent festival on the personal qualities or technical proficiency of a performer, as beloved or masterful as he might be, would be awkward, inappropriate, artistically untenable and of questionable service to the memory of the artist himself.

Passalacqua's second error, occurring during the same television interview, was his announcement that the broadening of the festival repertory had been the result of a reasoned educational plan to lead the musically untutored Puerto Rican public chronologically from the eighteenth century to the present, in a gargantuan music appreciation course lasting 17 years so far. I, for one, can't swallow this, for several reasons: (1) the Festival Corporation was in 1956 granted neither a franchise, nor accreditation, nor authority to make of itself a snail-paced music appreciation institute. In fact, it is unlikely that any legislature anywhere in the world would have even listened to such a hare-brained scheme. (2) The historical and biographical notes which form part of the printed concert program have been from the beginning a fantasy of misinformation, misinterpretation and historical inaccuracy. Surely, if the corporation had been serious from the beginning about public education, it would have obtained pedagogically respectable program material instead of the platitudes with which its printed programs have been burdened. (3) Finally, if the corporation had indeed had this educational goal, it would certainly have announced it at the beginning, would have made a general syllabus available, and would have developed its program in conjunction with the Department of Education or some other educational agency.

Passalacqua's remarks leave me unconvinced. Rather, I believe that the change in programming came about in direct response to falling attendance and rising complaints. His explanation, after the fact, has the empty ring of a justification, and a singularly weak one, at that. I am convinced that the Casals Festival Corporation has simply saddled itself with an increasingly unworkable formula, and is desperately improvising a solution.

A solution has been at hand for at least a decade, but the Corporation has consistently chosen not to see it. Among the agency's responsibilities, you see, is the development of the Puerto Rico Symphony Orchestra, a responsibility which it accepted from the legislature in 1958. Its record in carrying out this assignment has been less than noteworthy, for the Symphony Orchestra has been an orphan under Casals Festival auspices from the beginning: understaffed, underpaid, undertrained, unpublicized and mismanaged. During most of its fifteen years of activity, the Symphony Orchestra, fundamental to the island's musical culture in ways that no brief festival can ever be, has languished. Meanwhile, as I have pointed out, the Corporation has ironically opted to devote its energy to the presentation of standard symphonic works performed by a standard symphony orchestra, conducted by standard conductors and with soloists who, by and large, are of standard cut—but in the context of a festival format which has clearly played itself out. The solution to the Corporation's problem now becomes clear, I believe. It should finally face its broader responsibilities and invest its resources in the improvement of the island's day-to-day cultural environment through the creature which it reluctantly spawned 15 years ago: the Puerto Rico Symphony Orchestra. To do this it must of course reexamine its premises, readjust its priorities and reshuffle some of its elements.

The Puerto Rico June festival should be just that: a week of internationally publicized concerts devoted to one or another among scores of attractive themes, which could change from year to year. Among these, naturally, would be music which Pablo Casals loves, or at least music with which he can be reasonably associated in the public's mind. Other obvious possibilities are Latin American music, Puerto Rican composers, and such specific figures as Mozart, Stravinsky, Brahms, Villa-Lobos, Ginastera, etc., as anniversaries and centennials roll around. The Puerto Rico Symphony Orchestra, with appropriate financing, would then be assigned the function which has gradually been usurped by the annual festival: dealing in a normal way with normal symphonic music.

The Symphony Orchestra, or elements of it, would provide the nucleus of the annual June festival. More importantly, however, during its own long season it would take on the fundamental educational and cultural duties for which permanent symphony orchestras exist but which this one has not been allowed to assume. Suitably expanded, it would play its repertory as the composers intended, instead of in hasty arrangements necessitated by a shameful lack of important instruments and players. With adequate financial support, it would finally engage the full complement of skilled instrumentalists, here and abroad, by offering them a season long enough to justify their professional commitment. With proper planning instead of last-minute scheduling of concerts, it would develop artistically, through collaboration with the better ones among the traveling conductors and soloists who have appeared in the June festivals of recent years, among others.

It has recently been announced that PRIDCO, of which the festival corporation is a subsidiary, plans to cut back its support of the annual Casals Festival. If this occurs, the redirection of effort which I have outlined will become doubly urgent. Festivals are (or should be) extraordinary events. As such, and sad as it might be, they must be considered expendable when the pinch is really on. What is not expendable is the contribution to public education and culture which only permanent musical institutions, organically rooted in the needs of the populace, can make. The Puerto Rico Symphony Orchestra was conceived to be such an institution, and it should now be allowed to fulfill its purpose. If the Casals Festival Corporation cannot handle the task through a realistic readjustment of its priorities, perhaps some other government branch should be given the responsibility—and the means.

For the Birds

The San Juan Star
September 13, 1973   By Francis Schwartz

The evil eye works in mysterious ways. Obviously young Puerto Rican guitarist Juan Sorroche passed through the gaze of some malevolent spirit because his San Juan debut, taking place Sunday afternoon at the Caribe Hilton convention hall, was plagued by a series of mishaps. After an exaggerated delay, the concert began with the E Major Partita of J.S. Bach (originally for violin). Sorroche's playing was accompanied by the caws of caged parrots located outside the door of the hall. The aviary sounded like a scene of slow strangulation and the noisy shrieks were clearly audible in the concert hall. The guitarist seemed a bit rattled by this unexpected counterpoint and was unable to completely focus his attention on the artistic task at hand.

Sorroche programmed the very interesting Paganini Sonata in A, which again was punctuated by the cries of feathered hecklers. We abandoned the scene at intermission. It is a shame that this young artist, obviously well schooled, must return home to such an unprofessionally planned debut. It would be eminently unfair to render a critical opinion about Sorroche's playing under such circumstances. We welcome the opportunity to hear him on some future occasion, in a proper setting, where he is not distracted by roving photographers, fidgety spotlights and uninvited members of the animal kingdom.

If our readers will permit this succinct observation: this concert arrangement was strictly for the birds.

What Does a Tricycle Have to Do With Music?

The San Juan Star
October 7, 1973 by Francis Schwartz

The little girl pedaled her tricycle as the public looked on with disbelief. Eduardo Kusnir, Argentinean composer, ran his fingers over the keyboard, occasionally glancing at his partner (Francis Schwartz) performing at the other piano and at the little girl cycling around them. This world premiere of Kusnir's *Brindis* [Toast] No. 3 jolted many people who attended the San Juan Casa Blanca concert last Sunday. "What, asked one puzzled music teacher, "has a tricycle to do with the composition? Is this a joke?"

Kusnir in no way considers this unusual approach a joke. The use of a tricycle, or any other material, belongs to his musical philosophy. "Perturbations" or "interferences" are important elements in the construction of a Kusnir work. The composer intentionally uses interferences to provoke new situation, to create different ways of looking at objects. Within his *Brindis No. 3*, certain key fragments by Beethoven serve as a signal for the pianists to change from one musical pattern to another. When one pianist plays the Beethoven fragment, the other must necessarily stop, move on to another part of the composition, and eventually play the Beethoven signal which will interfere with the musical trajectory of the first pianist. A state of provocation, of tension exists as if two steel marbles were released simultaneously in a pinball machine, bouncing against each other, constantly creating new situations.

The tricycle interferes with the public. As the child pedals throughout the composition, the listener-watcher reacts differently than he would if the tricycle did not exist. "Suppose we heard a pianist perform an all Bach concert," says Kusnir, "but instead of the traditional presentation we tie a rooster to the piano leg. Certainly the audience would not perceive the music in the same way. The rooster is the "perturbation."

The Kusnir musical structure is bombarded by contradictions, by interferences, in order to avoid a strictly linear development of the music. Kusnir does not want the public to recognize a carefully balanced architecture in which at the end of the piece a melody reappears so that the listener is satisfied by this identification. He plays with the use of "chance" and allows his music to develop according to the same principles that rule daily life. The unexpected often impinges upon one's daily program. It is this way in the music of Kusnir.

The idea of play permeates Kusnir's music. He has a fascination for circuses and carnivals which stems from childhood, when he spent vacations traveling with his uncle's road show amusement park. Kusnir possesses a solid preparation in traditional music having studied piano, conducting and composition before entering the vanguard world of music at the Di Tella Institute in Buenos Aires, an internationally known center for new music activities. After two years of work at Di Tella, the composer traveled to Europe, working in electronic music laboratories in Paris, Holland and Belgium.

Kusnir, who refuses to say how old he is (he is 34), currently lives in Paris, but expresses disdain for European musical movements. He believes that the real creative activities are being done by composers of the Americas. Yet he feels that his presence in Paris is not a contradiction. "I live in a foreign environment even though the musical activity is not terribly inspiring, because as a foreigner I must define my art as clearly as possible. I must make my art as strong as possible, clarify my identity, so that I may fend off attacks. The foreigner is always vulnerable and must protect himself."

Many voices stridently objected to Kusnir's second premiere in Puerto Rico, *Brindis No. 4*, also on Sunday's program. This work finds two pianists seated at two pianos with their heads and arms protruding from huge white cubes which they wear as vests. This Beckett-like atmosphere lasted 15 minutes during which the pianists played no music. The composition is based on 12 typical gestures of pianists such as moving the head while playing or raising the eyebrows during the execution of a musical passage. Kusnir insists that it is as important to see a work as to hear it, and so developed this game of gestures between the two encubed pianists. When asked about the public's reaction he said, "The public doesn't have to look for any special symbolism, or seek out the "true" meaning. That's a lot of foolishness. I'm interested in the game; let the public react however they want. You know, the public has a terrible fear of anything that they cannot catalog or classify. They feel threatened and consequently tend to denigrate that to which they cannot relate easily."

The Argentinean composer will not defend his works. He feels the presence of an umbilical cord between him and his composition during the act of creation but once the work is completed it must stand by itself. "My compositions, once finished, are objects. Let people do what they want with them. They can use them as toothpaste or soap. It's up to them. I will not waste time protecting my music."

One of Kusnir's greatest dislikes is "The Intellectual". His contact with the musical elite in Paris proved dissatisfying. He felt that they dwelled to such an extent on the beauty of constructing a sound, either electronic or from natural noises, that they all ended up with a meaningless, bloodless preciosity. Kusnir hates to be bored. It grates upon his nerves. Unfortunately he often feels suffocated by the monotony of daily life.

As for the future, Kusnir sees life ahead as a great "Incertitude full of colors." He relishes his situation, which is also an intimate part of his musical philosophy. "I do not feel sufficiently provoked by this incertitude to find a definite planned solution to the future. I accept these perturbations and I accept the incertitude."

Whether Kusnir desires it or not, his life and his way of being are like his *Brindis*, fascinating mixtures of seriousness and refreshing playfulness.

Maestro's Favorites are Played in Homage

The San Juan Star
October 24, 1973 By Francis Schwartz

Maestro Pablo Casals, one of the twentieth century's great musical performers, was buried Tuesday at 4:00 P.M. in the Puerto Rico Memorial Cemetery in Isla Verde. The Catalan cellist was honored by musical offerings with interpretations of music by some of his favorite composers.

In a Monday night vigil at the Casals home, violinist Alexander Schneider, pianist Eugene Istomin and cellist Leslie Parnas, among others, performed works of Schubert and Mozart, composers who received remarkable treatment throughout the years from Casals.

The Tuesday morning state ceremony in the rotunda of the Capitol was complemented by a performance of Beethoven's Funeral March movement from the Third Symphony, the "Eroica." Under the baton of Victor Tevah, the Puerto Rico Symphony Orchestra gave a moving rendition of the work in an emotionally charged atmosphere. Two sections of Casals' oratorio *El Pessebre* (The Manger), the *Gloria* and the *Child Jesus' Imploration*, were sung by the Puerto Rico Conservatory of Music Chorus.

At La Piedad Church, where Luis Cardinal Aponte officiated during the pre-burial ceremony, a recording was played of Casals performing *The Song of the Birds* (El Cant dels Ocells). The simplicity and melancholy of this Catalan Christmas carol has been made world famous by Casals. As the inimitable Casals cello sound filled the church, one realized how communicative this man was through music.

But perhaps the very greatest tribute and most appropriate for this great artist and simple man, was a performance on the cemetery grounds by the Free Schools of Music Band. Young high school students stood under the scorching afternoon sun to honor a man who had dedicated his life to the noble art of music, an art which they intend to follow. As the students performed Chopin's Funeral March and Juan Morel Campos' danza *Carola*, one saw the future saluting the past.

This homage by music students assures the perpetuation of the art which filled Casals' life. Undoubtedly a most fitting farewell.

Butterfly Feebly Flutters

The San Juan Star
December 14, 1973 By Francis Schwartz

We fought the idea for two complete acts. Finally when the Star Spangled Banner motive reappeared the guffaw shot out involuntarily. In the midst of Giacomo Puccini's Italianate Nipponese, the U.S. national anthem as a leitmotive seemed jarringly incongruous.

Madama Butterfly, the 1904 opera which has gained one of the most favored places in the repertory, came to life at the University of Puerto Rico theater last Sunday afternoon under the sponsorship of World University. And while one could appreciate the effort of the company, the weaknesses of the production were too widespread to ignore.

In the title role, soprano Migdalia Batiz sang fluently and with considerable poise. Unfortunately her voice is small and often was covered by the orchestra when she moved toward the back of the stage. Dramatically, Batiz' diminutive figure and delicate gestures fitted her geisha character very well. If she had more vocal projection her performance could be most convincing. Antonio Barasorda's Pinkerton had many felicitous moments. However his lyrical voice needs more resonance and there were times when he could not be easily heard. Pablo Elvira sang splendidly as the U.S. Consul, Sharpless. But who chose his costume? He was wearing a suit and tie which we saw advertised in last week's *San Juan Star*. Elvira was supposed to be in turn of the century Nagasaki. Also, he wore the same outfit for each of the 3 acts, which encompass a three-year time span. This speaks poorly of the haberdashery awareness of the U.S. Consular Corps and possibly explains why U.S. Asian policy has foundered.

Puli Toro proved adequate as Suzuki while Norman Veve's Goro added a genuine touch of humor.

Edgardo Gierbolini staged the opera with the delicacy of a George Grosz drawing. As for the chorus, prepared by Roselín Pabón, their second act participation was very good. Yet the third act offstage singing lacked unison and quality. A mixed result.

The orchestra, under conductor Efraín Guiguí, managed to give a creditable showing until the third act, when things really went astray. Missed entrances, non-Puccinian microtonal pitches, plus an overall uneasiness pervaded the opera's close. There were so many extraneous, non-instrumental noises coming from the pit that at one point we wondered if somebody had preceded Cio Cio San in a self-immolatory act.

In general, this plot seems terribly outdated. In 1973 it is hard to believe that Madame Butterfly would kill herself because the American father of her child had wed another. Most likely she would call the local "Gengokuren" and organize a protest at the local U.S. Naval Base screaming "Off Pinkerton!"

The lighting and stage design by Antonio Frontera and Julio Biaggi were well done and the costumes proved attractive.

Symphony Concert Hits Sour Note

The San Juan Star
February 2, 1974   By Francis Schwartz

The second half of the Puerto Rico Symphony Orchestra season began on a somewhat sour note last Saturday evening at the Conservatory of Music.

This concert, supposedly the musical complement to the Third Biennial of Latin American Graphics, was scheduled in the foreboding wilds of Hato Rey, which accounts for the absence of both visiting artists and critics. It is a shame that the orchestra could not perform in the Dominican Convent in Old San Juan, where the new art works are on display.

From an aesthetic viewpoint, we saw little relationship between the featured music and the Biennial, which deals primarily with contemporary art. The two Puerto Rican composers, Rafael Aponte-Ledée and Luis Antonio Ramírez, represent the progressive and ultra-conservative schools, respectively. The other compositions, by Revueltas, Ginastera and De la Vega, have little to do with recent artistic ideas and problems. Certainly a more contemporary program would have been appropriate.

Under the baton of guest conductor Kenneth Klein, the orchestra began with Aurelio de la Vega's *Elejía*. It beggars the imagination to describe what went wrong. Slipshod playing, bad intonation, insecurity: all created what we restrainedly call a grotesque performance. *Elegía* was inadequately prepared and should not have been played in such condition.

Luis Antonio Ramírez' Suite fared well in Klein's hands. The conductor lavished considerable care on the niceties of the score and the orchestra responded. Ramírez deals with tonal ideas, simple and direct in character, with very sparse development. His music is rooted in the compositional firmament of Copland, Hindemith, etc.

The *Elejía* of Rafael Aponte-Ledée explores a wide range of sounds for string orchestra using both precisely organized and aleatory techniques. The work is most convincing in its myriad colors and constant flow. Klein and the orchestra gave a sympathetic rendition. Certain features of the performance could have been improved, such as the harmonics and the pizzicati.

Silvestre Revueltas' *Redes* received vigorous treatment. Klein feels very comfortable with this music. We consider *Redes* as Mexico's answer to *Also Sprach Zarathustra*.

With a few more performances the Puerto Rico Symphony Orchestra should be able to bring out the tremendous drama of this magnificent composition. More accuracy from strings and brass will improve the interpretation.

The concert closed with Alberto Ginastera's *Estancia* ballet suite.

Meeting of Musical Minds

The San Juan Star
June 4, 1974 By Francis Schwartz

The Puerto Rico Musical Society (Donald Thompson, presiding) celebrated its second annual convention at the Hotel Guajataca in Quebradillas last weekend. Dedicated to the serious study and dissemination of musical subjects, the Society offered several highly informative lectures by leading music figures in Puerto Rico.

María Rosa Vidal began the formal session with "The Harp in Contemporary Music," signaling the various uses of the instrument in our contemporary era. Fernando Caso (University of Puerto Rico) revealed to a surprised audience the musical compositions of Friedrich Nietzsche (yes, that's right), the renowned German philosopher. His lecture was illustrated by soprano Annie Figueroa.

The Nietzsche songs demonstrate a Schumannesque style with occasional harmonic quirks which bring to mind the modulatory daring of Franz Schubert. Taking all things into account, Nietzsche was a pretty fair composer . . . for a philosopher!

Roy Carter (Inter American University) gave a delightfully witty talk on "New Music: Present, Past, and Future." Drawing a bead on composers whose fixation with novelty leads them into a competition as to who can be more "avantgarde" than the other, the professor indicated that perhaps all this "originality" was not really so new. Carter also delivered a jeremiad on theorists who are far behind the times and whose methods of analysis are imprecise.

After the luncheon break, Luis Manuel Álvarez (University of Puerto Rico) discussed "Musicological Research in Puerto Rico," and gave examples of his research using tapes and slides. Jack Délano, composer, in his "Electronic Music in Puerto Rico: 1947-48," spoke of musical experiments conducted at the governmental Division of Community Education while making didactic films in the late 1940s. Délano worked in the most primitive fashion in those days and the result, while not exciting from a musical viewpoint, is fascinating from a musico-historical one.

Luis Antonio Ramírez (Puerto Rico Conservatory of Music) read a paper on the late, multi-faceted musician Alfredo Romero, who died several months ago. Romero's death was a serious blow to musical pedagogy in Puerto Rico and Ramírez' information carefully illustrated the life of a practical musician who could compose, perform, arrange and teach with equal ease. The vast amount of unpublished music left by the Spanish musician was previously unknown to the music world. José Daniel Martínez performed a movement from one of Romero's sonatas.

The Puerto Rico Musical Society has done an important job in the serious presentation of subjects dealing with theory, history, teaching techniques and musical aesthetics. Stimulating interchange among musicians remains one of Puerto Rico's prime needs, and the second annual convention proved a solid success in this area. Certainly this organization will play an important role in the development of music here during the coming years.

Fine Performance, Poor Attendance

The San Juan Star
June 9, 1974 By Francis Schwartz

The demons are at work. Whether it be demon or dybbuk, something is tampering with the Casals Festival chamber music concerts. The Friday night Casals Memorial chamber music event at the University of Puerto Rico Theater found the hall at least two thirds empty and the participating musicians unannounced on the program.

It is a (expletive deleted) shame that such an excellent program draws a meager public and at a Casals memorial concert, no less. If the exclusion of the performers' names in the program was an act of self-effacement or merely an assumption that everybody knows the artists, we recommend that on future occasions somebody either print an informative flyer or make an announcement. One must always assume that some members of the public are present for the first time and should be afforded the opportunity to know who is participating in the concert.

Opening with Mozart's String Quintet (K 516), the chamber group, composed of violinists Alexander Schneider and Felix Galimir; violists Walter Trampler and Jaime Laredo and cellist Leslie Parnas, gave a splendid performance. The musicians fathomed the depths of this emotionally charged score, which reflects Mozart at his most serious. The rapport achieved among the five players reached a peak in the *adagio ma non troppo* movement. This was transcendental playing. Certainly one of the best performances this listener has ever heard of the Mozart work.

Michelle Zukovsky, clarinetist, joined the string quartet (Schneider, Galimir, Trampler and Parnas) for the A Major Quintet (K 581) of Mozart. The young clarinetist possesses a lovely sound and molds phrases with the expertise of a mature, experienced artist. The ensemble work was of sterling quality, and one must admire the players' concept, which provided a wide gamut of dynamics. The tempi were ideal.

After intermission, Schubert's Quintet for Two Violins, Viola and Two Cellos added another new face to the musical event: cellist Laurence Lesser. In this composition, one of the gems of the chamber music literature, Schubert experimented with an unusual instrumental arrangement. Using two cellos instead of two violas, he was able to achieve a more resonant, full bodied sound from the string group. The ineffable quality of the musical ideas needs no comment, and one is stunned by the fact that the 33-year-old Schubert could pen such a profound composition in the year of his death. The work appears to encompass the wisdom of a long, experience-enriched life, yet it is the product of a relatively young man.

The playing remained on the high level of the previous works. Mr. Laredo had a few rough spots in the first violin chair, but these were minor detractions.

This concert emphasized youth: Mozart, Schubert, plus several of the performing instrumentalists. What a pity that so few people attended. It seems that our concert going public is still possessed by the idea that a concert must be circus-like in atmosphere with musical gladiators galore on stage, or a highly sophisticated social event where jewels, clothing styles and exclusivity take precedence over the music. Neither Mozart nor Schubert would have been welcome in such an atmosphere. What is needed here is a first-rate exorcist.

Casals Festival:
Empty Seats and Nothing Memorable

The San Juan Star
June 14, 1974 By Francis Schwartz

A myth died Tuesday night at the Casals Festival. For those optimistic souls who believed that absenteeism had been caused by the chamber music syndrome, the sea of empty seats at the University of Puerto Rico Theater for an orchestral concert with a scheduled violin soloist set the record straight.

The Casals Festival is in serious trouble and we foresee more concerts with sparse attendance. We shall analyze the problems of inept programming and administration in a future article, but the dreary atmosphere which permeates this eighteenth festival clarifies one point: the ostrich-like attitude of the Festival Casals, Inc. can no longer guarantee its future.

The fifth concert featured Víctor Tevah as guest conductor. Opening with Brahms' Tragic Overture, Op. 81, the playing alternated between moments of dramatic tension and dynamic flabbiness. The interpretation lacked sufficient tensile strength. As a musicological footnote, would it be too much to expect from the program of an international festival to consistently use opus numbers when available? From both a pedagogical and a professional viewpoint it would be most appropriate.

Bolivian violinist Jaime Laredo performed Saint-Saëns' Violin Concerto No. 3 in B Minor, Op. 61 in a fluent, technically commendable fashion. While the playing demonstrated superior musicianship, one missed the special, rarified mood which this music can create. Tevah's accompaniment was, at best, pedestrian. After intermission, the symphonic triptych Mathis der Maler (Mathis the Painter) by the twentieth-century composer Paul Hindemith received its first festival hearing. The work is taken from Hindemith's opera of the same title, completed in 1934, which was based upon the life of Matthias Grünewald, whose famous Isenheim Altar at Colmar provides a pictorial base for the symphonic work. Grünewald possessed a highly developed political conscience and it is not coincidental that Hindemith used him as an operatic character during the years 1933-34 when the Nazis were taking power.

The *Mathis* came off rather well. The violins were edgy at times but the winds and brass rendered yeoman service. Tevah worked well with the orchestra. Perhaps the final movement, "The Temptation of Saint Anthony," was a bit low keyed in temperament considering the vicissitudes of that holy man. In general, the Hindemith proved to be best part of the evening and Tevah's most successful endeavor.

Very often the test of a concert's impact is the memory one takes away from the hall. Certainly nothing musically memorable happened Tuesday night. Yet that huge open space where Puerto Rico's music lovers should have been sitting, should worry every devotee of music; especially those Casals Festival officials whose laudatory rhetoric has done little to solve very real problems.

A TV-Eye View of the Casals Festival

The San Juan Star
June 20, 1974 By Francis Schwartz

We relished the music of the Tuesday night Casals Festival concert with our shoes off. This was not a violation of decorum within the hallowed confines of the University of Puerto Rico theater, but rather our comfortable position for this year's review from the televiewer's niche. Much has been said and written regarding the quality of the Casals Festival telecasts and we decided to sit in as the public's "amicus curiae."

The program had been altered due to conductor-cellist Antonio Janigro's last-minute cancellation. Milton Katims, musical director of the Seattle Symphony Orchestra, flew in to assume conducting duties and bass Justino Díaz sang three arias to round out the program.

From the outset, one noticed the lack of proper musical orientation which should be an important part of music telecasting by the government station, WIPR, an entity under the aegis of the Department of Education. Jesús Latimer, an excellent newscaster, was put in the unenviable role of having to proffer musical commentaries which were truly inadequate for such an important cultural event. There are established techniques for music education via television which have been successfully realized by such personalities as Leonard Bernstein and Michael Tilson Thomas. WIPR-TV has even used these series on previous occasions. The Casals Festival would be an ideal moment to promote this type of solid public educational activity. Why were these public facilities not put to optimum use? Truly a missed opportunity. There are several professionally prepared educators in the music field who could have shared the wonders of the music with the viewing public and offered a sound pedagogical guide in the appreciation of the repertoire. Hopefully this will be corrected in the future.

One must praise the camera work and camera direction, for it was evident from the opening Schubert Fourth Symphony, the "Tragic" (D.V. 417), that the camera work was aware of the musical score. Since composer Jack Délano directed the program, one can understand the musical intelligence with which the cameras moved. Somebody was following the music, and kudos are deserved by the entire crew for this laudable work.

The sound on our television set was relatively clear though there were certain inexplicable fluctuations in volume unrelated to the music or the conductor's intentions. For example, in the closing work, the symphonic poem Don Juan, Op. 20 by Richard Strauss, the splendid interplay between the oboe and clarinet came through clearly. Yet the violin solo sounded so muffled, so weak, that we had to raise the volume in order to hear it properly. Could it be the direction of the microphones? Or some acoustical phenomenon? Or could it have been interference in the atmosphere? The technical experts no doubt have the answer.

Bass Justino Díaz, relaxing in Puerto Rico, was summoned to service at the last moment in order to provide a soloist for the evening. He performed two arias from Mozart's opera *The Magic Flute*: "In diesen heil'gen Hallen," and "O Isis and Osiris." Also sung were the recitative and aria "The Trumpet Shall Sound," from Handel's oratorio, *Messiah*. On television, Díaz did not sound as articulate or resonant as on previous occasions, but we must in good conscience reserve judgment since the sound in the hall may have produced another effect.

Katims also conducted Haydn's Symphony No. 88 in G. He possesses a clear technique which is much easier to observe on TV than in the hall. We look forward to his work in the next concert which we shall hear in the theater.

The embarrassingly sparse audience reported to us by attending members of the press cannot be attributed to TV coverage. The impact one receives from the televised concert is far below the level of excitement one experiences in a concert hall. We recommend that people go to the concerts so that they may experience the dynamism of live music making.

Dull Performance Concludes Festival

The San Juan Star
June 24, 1974   By Francis Schwartz

A lackluster finish to a dull festival. This year's Casals Festival broke camp Saturday night at the University of Puerto Rico Theater with the final concert dedicated to the memory of Maestro Pablo Casals.

Under the baton of Alexander Schneider, the festival orchestra performed Richard Wagner's Siegfried Idyll in a rather ponderous manner. The moments of impassioned music making were often offset by imprecise cutoffs and entrances. In short, it was rather uneven in quality. Beethoven's Third Symphony, Op. 55, the "Eroica," followed. Again, the players sounded tired and Schneider's exaggerated "milking" of the expressive elements detracted from the interpretation. Aside from the aleatory aspects of the second movement, the work progressed in a not particularly inspired fashion.

After intermission, Schubert's Symphony in B Minor, the "Unfinished" (D.V. 759), unfolded in a fluent, balanced way, with some lovely work by the wind section. This interpretation was perhaps the most satisfying of the concert.

Pablo Casals' peace oratorio *El Pessebre* (The Manger) terminated this eighteenth Casals Festival. Soprano Olga Iglesias, the Conservatory of Music Chorus and the festival orchestra, led by Schneider, gave a dull, unmelded reading. Miss Iglesias was not in good voice, the chorus sang unevenly and the result deflated the finale of the yearly event.

The eighteenth Casals Festival lacked the quality of earlier years. One remembers the exciting performances of the past: Rubinstein's piano recital, Mehta's reading of the Verdi Requiem, the Guarneri Quartet's Beethoven and Perlman's Prokofiev's Second Violin Concerto. These were great treasures in the world of art.

This year, and we are still very close to the proceedings, the few truly bright moments are heavily outweighed by a drab atmosphere caused by unimaginative programming and contracting of soloists.

We shall publish an extensive proposal as to how the Casals Festival can be rejuvenated and more fully integrated into the musical life of Puerto Rico. It is withering on the vine, and those Casals Festival officials who sincerely desire a top ranking international festival (which we did not have this year) should take action.

A Proposal to Save the Casals Festival

The San Juan Star
June 29, 1974   By Francis Schwartz

During man's long evolutionary journey from the primeval bog, he has managed to distill the workings of his passions and experiences into realities which defy the passage of time: art. Certainly the most durable of man's activities. On the planet, art should rightfully occupy an important place in the daily life of any conscientious person for it provides a touchstone with the finest moments of the human experience and serves as a means of spiritual inspiration.

In Puerto Rico during the past eighteen years, the Casals Festival has annually offered concerts with the intention of presenting and sharing musical masterpieces with the public. Now that the charismatic figure of Pablo Casals is no longer present to shore up the festival, a more imaginative approach must be sought to truly integrate this activity into the life of Puerto Rico. It is not sufficient to announce on a press release or program that the Casals Festival is a long tradition. The community must also support the institution. We have perceived many weaknesses in the Casals Festival over the past years which can seriously jeopardize its future. This valuable means of education and spiritual exploration should not be lost, but unless the government of Puerto Rico and the festival planners effectuate necessary changes, we are certain that the event will disappear in the future. We submit the following proposals for consideration by the Casals Festival officials.

Artists

For the annual celebration, the festival should invite top conductors and soloists. Such attractions are necessary if the general public is to flock to these closely scheduled concerts. With the tremendous competition of recordings within everyone's reach, the live performances must truly warrant the time and effort needed to go out to a concert. With this excellent festival orchestra, it is a waste to allow anybody but a top conductor to lead this splendid group. We need conductors such as Bernstein, Solti, Karajan, Ozawa, Leinsdorf, Maazel, Mehta and Ormandy. It is obvious to even the tyro that the music making changes in quality when a fine conductor stands before the festival orchestra. Also, the soloists must be of top caliber. With the great interest that exists in Puerto Rico for the vocal art, far more singing greats should be invited for solo roles with the orchestra, opera in concert version, lieder recitals, and solos in major oratorios or masses. The selection of instrumentalists should not exclude young new talent, but the bulk of the artistic labor should be in the hands of the world's great: Rubinstein, Horowitz, Stern, Rostropovich, Ashkenazy, Oistrakh, Gilels, Bream, Serkin, Watts, and so on. Singers such as Lear, Sills, Horne, Sutherland, Nilsson, Caballé, Domingo, Fischer-Dieskau, Pavarotti could generate far more public enthusiasm and raise the artistic level of the festival, which has foundered during the last three years. If financing this type of programming presents difficulties, then the government must make a decision. Without adequate backing for a top international festival, it will not be possible to continually attract the great aforementioned artists. Casals is no longer physically present and many people came here in the past for personal reasons. The great international stars have hurried, overloaded schedules and Puerto Rico will have to compete with the burgeoning number of excellent international summer festivals.

Length

For the Casals Festival to extend itself beyond the eight-concert formula presents both economic and attendance difficulties. Unless there is a day's rest between concerts, many members of the concertgoing public cannot summon up sufficient energy (or baby sitters) to attend. This past festival there were concerts on three successive evenings, which turned the festival into an endurance test. The attendance flagged.

Chorus

The Casals Festival should certainly present one major concert featuring an oratorio, mass or a Passion to adequately utilize the Conservatory of Music chorus. This past year's participation was depressingly skimpy. The chorus should be singing Bach Passions, Handel oratorios or other exciting works by Penderecki, Berlioz, Mahler, Orff, Prokofiev and Carrillo, among others. So many great choral works have never been performed in Puerto Rico and there exists an opportunity for both chorus members and public to make new musical acquaintances.

Chamber music

We feel that chamber music has an important role to play in the Casals Festival. However, let it be presented in the proper surroundings and with an attractive, balanced program. Why must the festival be geographically chained to the University of Puerto Rico Theater? If a chamber concert were scheduled in the interior patio of the Convento de Santo Domingo in Old San Juan, which currently houses the Institute of Puerto Rican Culture, the beautiful atmosphere of the convent plus the attraction of the old city would certainly bring out more public. It is not difficult to arrange seating at the convent. A stage and acoustical shell are available so that the performing groups would be easily audible. As for interesting chamber programming, the festival should explore works which use guitar, voice, unusual combinations, as well as the standards which we have been hearing year after year. Why has no serious Renaissance music been presented? There is a rich repertoire which could be incorporated into the present fare. And of course the great chamber works of this century should be played. We are going to celebrate the centennial of Arnold Schoenberg's birth this year. This great musical figure has magnificent art songs and string quartets, including one with soprano. Should he not be honored by a performance of one work? And the American Charles Ives, also born in 1874, was one of the original minds of the last hundred years. There are also many chamber works of his which could be included.

If we can break out of the limited repertoire in the chamber music area, more and more listeners will discover the wonders which this particular genre offers. The old stereotype label which classified chamber music as dull is rapidly disappearing.

Publicity

The publicity of the Casals Festival has been poor. Some members of the news media receive incomplete press releases at very late dates, if they receive anything at all. It is inconceivable that in the first year after

Casals' demise, the international wire services did not even receive an invitation to attend the festival. In the case of United Press International the agency made three different calls to the festival offices in order to receive information about the programs, dates, etc. After deciphering confused, contradictory replies, UPI was forced to call the Puerto Rico Information Service for help. This is rank amateurism in the realm of public relations which we hope the festival will correct. There should be a formal press conference at the beginning of each annual event and the main publicity package should be in media hands at least a month before the festival begins. This way newsmen can plan feature stories, interviews, research properly the compositions to be performed, plan space. Businessmen have constantly complained throughout the years that it is more difficult to get Casals Festival posters than a tax exemption. It should be a major project of the Casals publicity office that all of Puerto Rico be covered with festival posters, and well ahead of the opening date. Every town in Puerto Rico should have an office where information about the festival is made readily available and even ticket purchases made possible. The public schools, the city halls, the Institute of Puerto Rican Culture centers could provide space. This is how one achieves community contact. It is not sufficient to create a few TV or radio spot commercials. The physical presence of a cultural organization is absolutely necessary if it is to become part of the people's daily lives.

Education

Blocks of tickets to the Casals Festival should be provided to students throughout Puerto Rico and busing facilities provided for those living in distant areas. In this case, pre-concert orientation talks could be presented by competent professionals and meetings could be arranged between students and the festival musicians. This would provide a rewarding educational as well as human experience for all concerned. The government stations WIPR and WIPR-TV should contract educators who can present the festival repertoire in an interesting and knowledgeable manner. The concert broadcasts are supposed to be educational, but only through detailed, scientific planning can one achieve this goal. We also recommend several programs dealing with the forthcoming festival repertoire, which should be initiated two or three months before the beginning of the festival. The public would be provided insight into the music they are to hear and once again would provide a stimulus for attending the concerts. Certainly the program notes that the festival passes out during the concerts must be upgraded in quality. We recommend that a team of professional musicologists research the repertoire and offer the very best in musical information.

The Americas

The Casals Festival takes place in the Caribbean, in the heart of the Americas. Yet the Casals Festival treats New World composers with disdain. We have repeatedly opposed this cultural myopia and can only state that time has proven that the Americas have concert music worthy of performance in any festival, any time, any place. In eighteen years the Casals Festival has most reluctantly programmed two works of American composers. We recommend that a special concert be dedicated to the cultural treasures of our continents and that the works of Ginastera, Villa-Lobos, Copland, Barber, Ives, Roldán, Chávez, Campos-Parsi, Gandini, Davidovsky, Aponte-Ledée, Gershwin, Carter and Sessions, among others, be performed for the delight of public and performers. It is shameful to deny one's cultural heritage and the Casals Festival takes place in the Americas and is sustained by citizens of the Americas.

Unions

In 1928, Pablo Casals established a Workingmen's Concert Association in Barcelona. Why haven't the labor unions of Puerto Rico been actively involved in this musical event? The Casals Festival image today, in many sectors of the community, is elitist. Certainly the educational programs which many unions are currently undertaking could be enriched by some cooperation with the Casals Festival people. These union members and their families should be one of the important bulwarks of the festival, yet if one were to honestly appraise the average worker's attitude toward the festival he would probably say "that's not for me." This is ironical since it was Casals who was determined to share the joys of music with the blue-collar workers. We suggest that the Casals officials make contact with union leaders so that exploratory talks might begin.

Attitude

As a closing proposal, we urge the Casals Festival planners to end their negative attitude toward the music of our time. Good and poor music is being created in this historical period as it was in past eras. One cannot close one's mind to the artistic manifestations of the times. Rather one must seek out what is valuable, communicative and spiritually satisfying, so that the artworks of our era will take their place alongside previous works in the pantheon of art. The great contemporary composers such as Xenakis, Penderecki, Ligeti, Lutoslawski, Carter, Stockhausen, Berio, should be invited to this festival. After all, a celebration implies life and action. What better way to honor music than to include those creators who are struggling with artistic forms and techniques today, as did the composers of the past.

We offer these proposals in the most constructive spirit with the hope that some of the ideas will prove beneficial to the development of music in Puerto Rico.

A Praiseworthy *Figaro*

The San Juan Star
July 20, 1974 By Francis Schwartz

The Opera 68 production of Mozart's *The Marriage of Figaro* was given life last weekend at the University of Puerto Rico theater. The presentation was ably coordinated and while one could appreciate the solidity of this musical undertaking, it lacked sparkle.

Mozart's opera, whose libretto is based on Beaumarchais' stage work, criticized subtly and not so subtly the behavior and the lifestyle of the nobility at a time (1786) when the pillars of aristocracy were about to be shattered. When we observe the artwork today, it is intellectually possible to appreciate the thematic relevance to Mozart's contemporaries; and we can also marvel at the composer's craftsmanship and melodic inventiveness. But the combative juices no longer stir in the audience of today as they did in the earlier period. We simply are not faced with the same problems which beset Mozart and his public.

Imagine an opera which dealt with Watergate, the copper mining proposal in Puerto Rico, Caribbean superports and slot machines. The contemporaneity of the issues which affect the lives of every citizen would provoke a more dynamic reaction from the listener-viewer. This does not fault Mozart (God forbid!), who was most involved in the problems of his era; rather it points out the changing projection of an artwork throughout the continuum of time. Each generation sees and hears in a different way, conditioned by new experiences. Time becomes a filter through which the creator's work is perceived.

Robert Shiesley gave a creditable performance as Figaro; Annie Figueroa proved a most vivacious Susanna; Pablo Elvira once again demonstrated his high professionalism as Count Almaviva. In the role of Cherubino, the amorous page, Teresa Pérez Frangie opened in a slightly jittery fashion which later resolved positively. Her acting was very good.

Aura Norma Robledo acquitted herself nicely as the Countess and Pedro Morell's Doctor Bartolo complemented the dramatic action successfully. Darysabel Isales sang a very competent Marcellina. Also cast were Carlos Serrano, Marta Rosario Márquez, Miguel Rivera, Ilca Paizy, Valentín Fernández and Bertha Ramos.

Donald Thompson conducted the orchestra with expertise and the intelligent stage direction of Richard Getke kept the singers moving. One felt no static quality in the entire production. The scenery by Julio Biaggi was serviceable as were the costumes by Wayne Thomas Seitz. Alberto Zayas was the producer. In short, a praiseworthy effort.

Casals Festival: The View From The Courtyard

The San Juan Star
June 5, 1975   By Donald Thompson

It was a beautiful evening for a concert as the nineteenth Casals Festival in Puerto Rico opened in Río Piedras on Tuesday evening. Warm breezes played through the palm-lined courtyard of the University of Puerto Rico Theater and coquís warbled in the gardens as this reviewer received confirmation at the box office that there were no opening night seats reserved for the press. Austerity's horny hand had struck the Casals Festival Corporation!

As the pre-concert promenade was just beginning in the courtyard, however, I decided to turn the occasion to advantage by reviewing an aspect of the annual festival which according to reports has attained great brilliance during recent seasons: the part which takes place in front of the theater.

In women's fabrics, pastel shades of cool chiffon predominate this season, falling in delicate pleats fore and aft. Of course, for the opening concert there was an ample representation of gently draped jerseys as well, while many readers may be fascinated to learn that most of the new designs are conceived to hang either from the shoulder or from the waist. In men's fashions the butterfly or "mariposa" tie of recent seasons appears to be giving way before the nostalgic thrust of the thinline bow of the 1950s. The fashion-wise will wish to take this as a hint of future developments in festival wardrobe, although my fashion consultant believes differently. She maintains that what we saw really **WERE** thinline bows of the 1950s, dragged out from the back of a drawer. Hysterically frilled shirtfronts were very evident on Tuesday, while tuxedos ranged in subtle shades from conservative black to a paralyzing electric green number which drew favorable comment from a number of music lovers. There may be austerity backstage, but out front with the Beautiful People one gets the impression that Puerto Rico is riding a wave of great prosperity, reflected in up to the minute fashion consciousness (except maybe for those bow ties).

Toward 9 P.M., as the last of the elegant promenaders filed slowly into the theater this reviewer made his way homeward, emotionally exhausted but happy in the knowledge that he had witnessed—nay, taken part in—still another brilliant Casals Festival opening.

Perlman Shines at Festival

The San Juan Star
June 11, 1975   By Donald Thompson

Cancellations due to illness continue to cause changes in the programming of the present Casals Festival series. On Monday evening, conductor Zubin Mehta and violinist Itzhak Perlman subbed for Claudio Abbado and pianist Rudolf Serkin, with corresponding program adjustments.

Opening the concert was Anton Webern's Five Orchestral Pieces, Op. 10. This work, dating from just before the First World War, has almost nothing in common with the three centuries of Western music which preceded it, but its paternal presence hovers over virtually everything which has been conceived by the avant-garde (aleatory, serial, electronic or what have you) from the early 1950s to the present day. Sparse, atonal and extremely condensed, Webern's music always strikes conventional audiences as some kind of put-on, and this is precisely what occurred on Monday. Predictably, there were titters in the audience, and predictably, the reduced orchestra of soloists under Mehta's direction played the work a second time.

After witnessing this performance I am more eager than ever that someone explain to me the unifying artistic principle which caused Webern's pieces to be played in a Casals festival. As part of a modern music festival, certainly; on a regular symphony orchestra series, by all means at least once every two or three years; but it will take some doing to logically connect this music with an especially organized festival dedicated to the memory of Pablo Casals (if, indeed, that's what we're dealing with this year).

Violinist Perlman made his second appearance in the festival with a very fine performance of Tchaikovsky's Concerto for Violin and

Orchestra. This work, so very well known to almost everyone nowadays, is often subjected to exaggerated interpretation by violinists, perhaps in an effort to impress. Perlman knows better; his playing was fully expressive but always within the bounds of appropriateness. This is not a matter of "restraint," in the sense of holding oneself back from doing something he wants to do, but rather of basic concept. Perlman has the concept, the technique and the style to make the Tchaikovsky concerto a thoroughly pleasurable experience, which he did on Monday.

Conductor Mehta and the festival orchestra provided the soloist with especially well matched collaboration, with some excellent playing by solo winds in the second movement. The performance of Brahms' Fourth Symphony, on the other hand, seemed to this reviewer to be marred by some of the same flaws which he perceived the other evening in a Beethoven work plus some more: imprecise string playing, some questionable pitch in the winds, and an evident lack of the "long line" in Brahms' expressive melody. Mehta's conducting is marked by great vigor, but somehow the complementary quality of extended melodic flow doesn't come through, or at least it didn't reach this reviewer through the festival orchestra under Mehta's direction on Monday.

Casals Festival Questions

The San Juan Star
June 27, 1975   By Donald Thompson

The nineteenth annual Puerto Rico Casals Festival ended last Friday, leaving in its wake a mixed set of artistic impressions and some nagging questions concerning what it was about, where it is headed, and why.

No matter what the casual concertgoer might wish to think, these aspects are intimately related. Artistic results can usually be traced to administrative decisions back along the line somewhere, while these in turn can only be made within some kind of general policy concerning purpose and function. If this festival were a self sustaining operation there would be no problem, for a commercial management's only purpose is to sell tickets at a profit; the impresario's function in society is to provide entertainment in return for payment received. Here, however, the situation is quite different. The Casals Festival Corporation is not a commercial agency but a minor government branch which sometimes makes noises as if it were a ministry of culture. As a branch of government involved in the arts, it must be held accountable not only for the artistic results of its labors, but also for the long-range policies which underlie them. Let us see, then, how this recent festival shapes up artistically and as an expression of public policy.

It is no secret anymore that the quality of the festival orchestra has slipped steadily in recent years, but the reasons may not be widely known. The earlier orchestras were made up of some of New York City's finest players, who came to the festival to spend a couple of relaxed weeks with Pablo Casals in the study of a select repertory which they didn't often play in the course of a normal professional season, or to experience the unique Casals touch with more familiar music. This is no longer the case. Several of the early participants have died while others have retired; still others choose not to come simply because the festival no longer interests them. Their places have been taken by younger players whose motivations are naturally very different. Casals is no longer here; the orchestral repertory in recent years has been more or less standard fare; and the only study involved has been by younger players who may not be completely familiar even with this music. For many instrumentalists the festival has become just another brief job, but one which offers some off-season income and maybe a crack at other contract work next fall in New York. In the meantime, the ratio of rehearsal time to performances has remained fairly constant over the years. The inevitable result this year has been hastily prepared and sometimes shaky performances of standard works at an average level of quality which would not be countenanced for very long in other large cities. The high artistic quality and the exalted spirit of the once renowned Casals Festival Orchestra are simply gone, and could probably be regained (if at all) only by returning to something resembling the original Casals concept.

The two orchestral performances which most closely approximated the Casals concept this season were both for reduced orchestra, and both of works by Mozart. The first, occurring early in the series, was the Divertimento in F Major (K 138), conducted by Jorge Mester in his first festival appearance; the second was the Violin Concerto in G Major (K 216), conducted by Alexander Schneider and with the participation of that splendid violinist Isaac Stern. Other orchestral highlights were Ravel's second suite from *Daphnis and Chloe*, of which the very capable Jorge Mester made a fine performance in spite of the above-mentioned difficulties, and the orchestral half of Beethoven's powerful Emperor Concerto, also conducted by Mester.

Zubin Mehta's conducting failed to sustain the impression which his previous appearances here had created, perhaps partly because of where he was scheduled in the series. As the first conductor up, Mehta bore the responsibility of putting together an instant orchestra. By the time the familiar Tchaikovsky *Violin Concerto* came along in the fourth concert, however, things were as well in hand as they were ever going to get; the orchestra, Mehta, and soloist Itzhak Perlman provided a model performance of this work.

This year's soloists included violinists Stern, Perlman and Guillermo Figueroa; cellist Leonard Rose; pianists Eugene Istomin and Yvonne Figueroa; contralto Maureen Forrester; soprano Beverly Sills; and a spate of orchestra principals who appeared in various combinations.

The performances of Stern, Perlman, Rose and Forrester simply confirmed what we had known about them from their previous visits. These are performers who rightfully occupy high places in the world's hierarchy of honored artists. Miss Sills, in her first appearances in these festivals, also made a lasting impression through her warm and musically intelligent performance of opera and concert excerpts with Jorge Mester and the festival orchestra.

The case of Yvonne and Guillermo Figueroa is curious. That these young people show great ability and high promise is obvious from their performance of a demanding sonata by Prokofiev; they both will certainly bear watching as they continue to develop. But their inclusion in this series makes one wonder if the management really considers them equal in stature to Serkin, Stern and Perlman. At the very least it did the Figueroas no favor to program them alongside such heavyweights, while at the worst this gesture might be interpreted as a sop to the rebellious natives.

The inclusion of several final evenings of chamber music was a noble experiment which failed, although at least one of the reasons for failure (the overdue demise of the theater air conditioning system) was not the festival management's fault. Nor is it anybody's fault that among the many things the University Theater is not good for, chamber music is supreme. But most of the difficulty is a natural result of an unannounced managerial decision of several years ago to expand into the big and brilliant symphony orchestra repertory. By contrast, classical chamber music (although theoretically more in line with the nature of these festivals) can only seem bland to ears still ringing with Bartók, Stravinsky and Ravel. Placing these intimate concerts at the end of the series only dramatized a situation which had been developing for some years. This time, it was a sure guarantee of falling attendance and an accompanying letdown of enthusiasm just when it would have been expedient to whip up a grand finale.

An aspect of the festival which held up well this year was television coverage by WIPR-TV, made possible by some emergency fund raising among concerned private sources and by some eleventh-hour craftsmanship by the WIPR staff. This is a part of festival-related activities which does not always receive the attention it deserves, despite the fact that one of the festival's principal justifications in recent years has been that the concerts are broadcasted to the entire island. In this way, festival officials have often claimed, the brief event has become an institution serving all of Puerto Rico, not just the relative handful who attend the concerts. It is doubly strange, then, that this year's broadcasts took place only over the strenuous objection of the festival management itself in what became the great backstage TV wrestling match of the year. High festival officials, beginning with president Marta Montañez de Istomin herself, complained that broadcasting would jeopardize ticket sales, forgetting (until the legislature reminded them) that the island population through taxes picks up almost all of the tab for those who physically attend the concerts. The officials' position apparently represents still another change in festival policy, and one which might bear looking into as budget time rolls around again.

About the only firm conclusion that can be drawn from this year's series is that audiences (now 95 per cent local, according to the estimate of a management functionary) are thirsty for the standard symphonic repertory and reasonably pleased, on the average, with the performances of this recent festival orchestra. Who knows? Citizens might even support, through taxes, a long repertory season by an orchestra which could not only offer seven annual concerts in the UPR Theater, but also perform throughout the year in other island centers. There might be two ways to accomplish this. One would be to expand this orchestra to satisfy the technical demands of the music which it now appears destined to perform, while extending its season to a reasonable 35 or 40 weeks. The other, less costly and probably much more productive over the long run, would be for someone to create a proper Puerto Rico Symphony Orchestra. Why do you suppose nobody has thought of this during the past nineteen years?

Martínez Zarate Quartet: Four Guitars

The San Juan Star
February 6, 1976 By Donald Thompson

Subscribers to the University of Puerto Rico cultural activities series had the unusual pleasure on Tuesday evening of hearing the Martínez Zarate Quartet in concert in the University Theater. Unusual because this widely known ensemble is composed of four guitarists (a rare combination), and a pleasure because they are exceedingly good players.

The guitar possesses an amazing range of expressive qualities, but it takes a master hand to bring them out. Most of these qualities were evident in Tuesday's varied concert, which ranged from eighteenth-century dance pieces to the avant-garde.

Early times were represented by works by Pierre Attaignant, Johann Heinichen and Girolamo Frescobaldi, all figures who are normally (and unfairly) relegated to the library shelf and the music history class. In skillful transcriptions by members of the quartet, this old music attained a bounce and swing which it is rarely allowed; especially joyous were two canzonas by Frescobaldi.

One of the main problems with ensembles of similar instruments, like this guitar quartet, is that of giving the necessary prominence to melodic lines and important figures as they pass rapidly from hand to hand. More than anything else, this is a matter of the instruments' staying out of each others' way in a constantly shifting set of subtle relationships. A lesser group would have made a homogenized stew out of this early music especially, but the Martínez Zarate Quartet brought out its inherent contrasts in ways which are characteristic of the best chamber music playing.

The second half of Tuesday's concert was devoted to music of this century, including works by Ponce, Tsillicas, Piazzolla, and Martínez

Zarate himself. The Ponce quartet and the Tsillicas *Tetrafonias* demonstrated the extremes of style and means which seem natural to the guitar: the former's rhythmic yet highly melodious thrust, and the latter's constant thumping, scraping, rattling, sliding, rubbing, bumping and tweaking: in short, the whole catalogue of avant-garde musical effects applied to this venerable and resilient instrument.

The entire first half of Tuesday's concert was seriously marred by waves of late arrivals greeting their friends and groping for seats in the darkened theater. This is perhaps not so much the fault of a generation raised on movies and television as it is the error of a concert management which does not fully understand its obligation both to performers and to the public which wishes (against odds, sometimes) to hear them. It is hoped for the benefit of all that this can soon be corrected at the UPR Theater.

The Vienna Choirboys

The San Juan Star
February 12, 1976   By Donald Thompson

    Last weekend the Vienna Choirboys finished their highly successful island tour with a set of three concerts in the ballroom of the Caribe Hilton Hotel in San Juan. The group's appearances in Puerto Rico were offered for the benefit of World University and sponsored by Malta Corona.
    The Vienna Boychoir is, of course, the great granddaddy of all kiddie choruses everywhere. Despite its scrubbed and sailorsuited appearance, however, the group is no kiddie chorus but a beautifully trained and tightly disciplined company of young singers. In Puerto Rico they have nightly knocked off what would ordinarily be a full length concert of demanding choral music and thrown in a miniature opera to boot with hardly a sign of fatigue. Their training shows. The ensemble which visited Puerto Rico is only one of several traveling platoons drawn from the parent (might we say "mother?") organization in Vienna, but the impression was of musical training so complete, so secure and so unified that any one of the 25 boys could have taken his part anywhere in the world.
    The treble of unchanged boys' voices sounds cool, disembodied and otherworldly to ears accustomed to the warmth of the mature female soprano or contralto. The boy soprano has a character of its own which makes it exceedingly well suited to some types of music, less well to others and not at all for still others. The music which worked best for the boys included church music by Schütz and Croce, a set of charming but very tricky songs from the 1930s by Poulenc, and an avant-garde piece by Erich Eder de Lastra. These were successful because they are appropriate for the "white" unchanged voice. Austrian folk songs also sounded extremely well when sung by the boys, because the character of the voice

itself is not really very important in these pieces. What seems not to work very well with boys' voices is music originally conceived for the mature female voice, especially opera music or where musical characterization is involved. It was here that the boys' performance misfired, because of the inherent conflict between means and purposes. In this category was a well known trio of the Three Ladies from Mozart's *The Magic Flute*, while one of Verdi's very sensuous Hymns to the Virgin Mary fared no better. An abbreviated and considerably arranged version of Haydn's little opera *The Apothecary* fell into an almost fatal cuteness because of this disparity. Technically, these performances ranged from good to very good; in spirit, not so. Such composers as Mozart, Haydn and Verdi knew very well what they were doing; these works were conceived for mature vocal expression and they require mature voices—and mature minds—to bring them to life.

At concert's end the group's very able musical director Ewe Harrer took his bows like a gentle and paternal Gulliver among the Lilliputians. Come to think of it, the logistics of touring with a boychoir must be terrifying. What happens if an epidemic of puberty suddenly wipes out your entire company? Perhaps it's partly as insurance that the boys' management keeps another platoon or two on ice back home in Vienna.

Politics And Music:
The Proposed Casals Foundation

The San Juan Star
February 26, 1976   By Donald Thompson

    The past several weeks have seen preliminary legislative work on a bill which would have far reaching and highly unfavorable effects on the island's musical life if it were allowed to become law in anything resembling its present form. The measure is Senate Bill 1653 (House Bill 1796), which seeks to convert the Casals Festival Corporation, until now a dependency of the Puerto Rico Industrial Development Company (PRIDCO), into a Pablo Casals Musical Foundation. The bill bears the names of a great number of Popular Democratic Party senators and representatives as sponsors; nonetheless, it is very clear that the measure was drafted not in the Capitol but in the offices of the Casals Festival Corporation itself.
    The idea seems harmless enough on the face of it, for the term "foundation" lends an air of benign generosity to the title page at least. One visualizes a small staff charged with distributing to worthy cultural causes the income from a handsome endowment left by Pablo Casals, or perhaps one created in his name by his widow or close friends, in the manner of the well known philanthropic foundations. After reading the bill, however, one sees that there is no Casals endowment of any kind, nor is one expected to materialize. What is proposed is the creation of a tax-supported musical monopoly in the form of a public corporation, which would operate to the detriment of all other musical institutions in Puerto Rico without in any way providing better performances, better training, better facilities or better opportunities in music for island residents. In fact, odds are that island-wide, these would rapidly decline

under the new law. This is essentially the same bill that was prepared a year ago, then hastily withdrawn in the face of heavy opposition by an important segment of the island's musical community. The measure has since been redrafted, but it is still hopelessly marred by fundamental flaws.

Strenuous objection to the latest form of the bill has recently been expressed in public hearings held by the appropriate senate and house commissions. External objection has been directed principally against the bill's intention to duplicate in the foundation many of the functions of the Institute of Puerto Rican Culture, the Department of Public Instruction, the University of Puerto Rico, the Free Schools of Music and many other island institutions both public and private. Another source of irritation to cultural agencies here is a stipulation granting deduction from taxable income, without limitation, of donations made to the proposed public corporation by companies and individuals. As was repeatedly pointed out during the early hearings, this favored tax position would only act to the detriment of all other entities in Puerto Rico which receive donations to support their activities. If offered a choice, a patron would naturally give money where he could deduct it from his income tax; why should he donate money to Cause "A" and be taxed on it, if he can give it to the new corporation and write it all off? In these circumstances, which cause is more likely to prosper, the corporation or "A", which might be equally or more deserving of private support?

A third area of deep concern is a clause which would endow all graduates of the proposed corporation's technical training branch, the Puerto Rico Conservatory of Music, with instant certification as teachers in all of the educational institutions in Puerto Rico, public or private, which engage music teachers. This clause, if not absolutely illegal, clearly violates the long established and necessary right of educational bodies to determine the conditions of contracting their own teachers. In addition, on the level of school music teaching such an unheard of privilege would discriminate heavily against those prospective music teachers who go the whole teacher-training route: meeting university admission standards, undertaking background studies in liberal arts and humanities, successfully undergoing supervised practice teaching in the schools, and meeting state certification requirements, in addition to their technical studies as performers. As for other levels of music instruction, it is simply ludicrous to expect the island's universities to accept a conservatory diploma—or any other predetermined document—as an automatic licence to teach.

During these recent hearings, the Casals Festival Corporation found heavy opposition to its bill even within its own household. The faculty and student body of the Conservatory of Music, for example, are solidly opposed to the measure because it would strip from their institution the very slight measure of self government and the very mild gains in faculty and student rights which it has been able to wrest from the Casals Festival Corporation. In fact, the most eloquent testimony regarding this bill was presented in the legislative hearings by the conservatory faculty and students, represented by Héctor Campos-Parsi, noted composer and president of the Conservatory Teachers' Association. In a penetrating analysis of the bill and its many faults, Campos pointed out that the development of the festival corporation and its various elements during the past two decades was based on very shaky legal ground to begin with. For this reason, its conversion to the proposed new public corporation, in the manner foreseen in the bill, would probably be completely illegal.

If this bill is so clearly a bad one, why have its authors gone to such lengths—twice—to get it into the legislature? Where is the pressure originating to do something—anything—about the Casals Festival Corporation? A great part of the answer is to be found in the corporation's present administrative placement, as a subsidiary of the Puerto Rico Industrial Development Company. It has probably become obvious even to PRIDCO that the annual Casals Festival has outlived its usefulness in the promotion of industrial development, while the other two corporation branches, a symphony orchestra and a music school, have only been headaches to PRIDCO from the beginning.

It is common knowledge that Fomento Administrator Teodoro Moscoso has been trying to get the whole thing off his back for years now, and the time may be running out in which he and the Popular Democratic Party can gracefully bring this about. This would explain the urgency of getting a bill—any bill—through the legislature this session. It still doesn't explain why in this day of a much publicized plan to streamline the government, still another public corporation should be created, and one designed to duplicate the functions of existing educational and cultural institutions, at that.

The answer to this question is to be found within the Casals Festival Corporation itself. This anomaly has come into existence not through any process of responsible planning, but mainly through the shifting forces of corporate and political expediency. The three units which comprise the corporation (the annual Casals Festival, the Puerto Rico Symphony Orchestra and the Puerto Rico Conservatory of Music) are locked into a relationship which is rife with conflict, contradiction and cross-purposes. There is no good reason why they should at this late date continue under a common management, and in fact there are plenty of good reasons why they should have been separated years ago. However, the political clout of the existing corporation depends on keeping its three units together under a mystique which until now has successfully repelled all attempts at cold analysis and objective evaluation. For this reason, any "reform" law drafted within the corporation itself can only look toward its own perpetuation with all of its crippling organic weaknesses and conflicts.

It could be that the solution to PRIDCO's problem is to simply remove the Casals Festival Corporation—whole—from PRIDCO jurisdiction and drop it on someone else, as this bill proposes. It would appear more logical, however, for the legislature to pause a bit and study (for the first time) the agency's past performance and future possibilities in terms of the functions and realistic goals of its constituent parts before formulating any solutions at all. It is quite possible that other solutions, more productive for Puerto Rico's musical life, would appear. One thing is certain: almost any solution would be better than that proposed by the bill which is now before the legislature.

Variety Of Singers Adds Spice To Met Auditions

The San Juan Star
March 6, 1976   By Donald Thompson

Before a panel of three judges and a full house of well wishers in the theater of the Puerto Rico Conservatory of Music, a dozen hopeful singers competed at the second annual Puerto Rico District auditions for the Metropolitan Opera National Council.

To many, one of the most interesting aspects of the event held last Sunday was the great variety among the contestants, each of whom sang two arias. Among them were the products of San Juan's principal voice studios and musical training institutions alongside singers whose training had been gained in the U.S. or Europe. Some contestants had never been on a stage before, while others were seasoned performers. A few were pushing the upper age limit, which varied from 30 to 32 depending on the voice category, while at least one barely made it within the lower limit of eighteen years. What they all had in common was motivation and determination: the desire to sing opera and the readiness to compete in progressively tougher auditions for a chance at being admitted to one of that profession's principal centers, New York's Metropolitan Opera Company.

This year's local winners were all sopranos: Teresa Pérez Frangie (first), Mercedes Alicea (second), Zoraida López (third) and Iris Birriel Cabrera, who received the Alexander Saunderson Award for the most promising of the younger talents. Left behind this time were a baritone, a tenor, a covey of other sopranos and a brace of mezzos.

What makes a winner? This year's judges were New York critic Byron Belt and two highly regarded singers from the Metropolitan roster, Betty Allen and Justino Díaz. What rang the bell with this panel was a combination of skill and presence, the results of extensive studies and considerable experience. The first prize winner, Teresa Pérez Frangie, is a graduate of the Vienna Hochschule für Musik and the product of a couple of years in Milan on top of early studies at the Puerto Rico Conservatory of Music. In Austria she formed part of the Opera Studio of the Vienna State Opera, while in Puerto Rico she has appeared in opera (most recently in Mozart's *The Marriage of Figaro* with Opera 68), in solo recitals, and with the Puerto Rico Symphony Orchestra. Later this month she will sing the role of Desdemona in a San Juan production of Verdi's *Otello*, and she is engaged for leading roles in the Dominican Republic for next season. In short, Miss Pérez is no beginner but a seasoned and realistic singer who regards her success in these auditions as another important step in a career which is already well launched. Mercedes Alicea, in second place here, is another experienced young singer who knows very well what she's doing and what it involves. Miss Alicea is a graduate of the Manhattan School of Music and the product of further studies in Zurich and Vienna. In Puerto Rico she has appeared in concert with the Puerto Rico Symphony Orchestra and as Mimi in Opera 68's production of Puccini's *La Bohème*. She is scheduled for further work with the Puerto Rico Symphony Orchestra in May, following which she will fly to Vienna for television presentations.

Zoraida López, in third place, has a master's degree in voice and opera from the Manhattan School of Music, and has appeared in numerous studio productions in New York City.

Raymond Watson, auditions director and an enthusiastic spokesman for the district committee, explained that the two top local winners will be sent to New Orleans to compete Sunday in the Gulf Coast regional competition. From there, a single winner goes to New York for the semifinal and final judging. The final winner usually receives a contract with the Metropolitan company and other professional benefits.

Justino Díaz, a Puerto Rican who has been through the mill himself, believes that the Metropolitan auditions will help raise standards among singers here. For one thing, the auditions provide an occasion for young performers to be judged by professionals who themselves are identified with no local studio, group, or clique. As Díaz points out from his own experiences with professional auditions: "It doesn't matter who your teacher is or where you've been or whom you know; you sing or you don't."

With such objective counsel in their ears the two top local winners are off to New Orleans and perhaps farther; the rest of this year's contestants are headed for their practice rooms to prepare for next year's auditions.

Otello Takes Much Moor Than Local Casting Gives

The San Juan Star
March 21, 1976 By Donald Thompson

Another of Puerto Rico's several opera groups was heard from on Friday evening, with the first of two performances of Verdi's *Otello* in the UPR Theater. The company is Agrupación Puertorriqueña de Teatro Lírico (APTEL for short), the one which insists on doing it the hard way. The hard way by deliberately choosing one of the biggest of the big operas to put on, the hard way by recruiting the entire cast locally, and the hard way by devoting months upon endless months to putting it together.

As an exercise in courage, stamina and idealism the effort is highly laudable; however, to do artistic justice to the last Verdi operas requires much more than these admirable qualities. These works are not for home town opera companies, and unfortunate as it may be, on the scale of production required by *Otello*, Puerto Rico is still very much in the home town league.

Weaknesses which were glaringly obvious in Friday's performance would probably have passed unnoticed in a more normal, more tuneful opera. However, *Otello* is not an opera of tunes but of continuously mounting tension generated musically. If the production doesn't build through music it doesn't build at all, and not even the most skillfully designed stage action can raise it off the ground.

Friday's performance had some impressive visual scenes played within Nina Lejet's extremely effective and very simple sets. Musically, however, the work remained static, rarely attaining anything like the relentless continuity and pulse which the logic of *Otello* requires. Jesús Quiñones Ledesma makes an imposing figure of an Otello, with a voice big enough to fill the cavernous UPR theater and to spare. He makes one think of the "Golden Age" tenors, not only in some favorable aspects but also in ways which nowadays are not so admired. For example, Quiñones is much given to the grand gesture; so much, in fact, that very early on, one wishes for a little less grandeur and a little more subtlety. After all, we're going to be looking at this crazy Moor for another couple of hours, and he's going to get a lot crazier. Aura Robledo played the part of Desdemona on Friday, with a cold so bad that it damaged every scene she sang in. This particular part in this production was double cast, presumably to prevent just such calamities from occurring. With the alternate Desdemona seldom more than twenty feet away, the failure to switch sopranos on Friday is completely mystifying, and can only be attributed to a lack of responsibility to the composer, to the audience and to the rest of the cast. Héctor López performed the difficult role of Iago with great vocal skill, while among the other principals were several young singers who continue to improve with every engagement. Especially impressive in this regard was Eusebio González as Cassio.

Odón Alonso Conducts PRSO

The San Juan Star
April 7, 1976 By Donald Thompson

Odón Alonso, the Spanish conductor, completed his visit here in a pair of concerts with the Puerto Rico Symphony Orchestra in the theater of the Puerto Rico Conservatory of Music. Wednesday's soloist was pianist Harold Martina, who himself was finishing up a series of engagements here. Martina's performance of Saint-Saëns' Piano Concerto in C Minor only deepened my respect for him as a versatile and polished performer.

On the same program was *Impulsos*, by Rafael Aponte-Ledée. Aponte is one of a handful of island composers who have over the years waged bitter battles for recognition and support by the musical establishment. *Impulsos* was a highly controversial work not many years ago, and the fact that it and other compositions of the same general style are now regularly programmed here indicates that the composers' efforts have borne fruit. The management of this orchestra, a publicly funded institution, has at last begun to accept some responsibility for expanding the musical culture of the citizenry which it serves.

Impulsos, for large orchestra, is dedicated to the memory of poet Julia de Burgos. The work is completely atonal, and bears occasional resemblance to the music of Anton Webern in the more sparsely treated sections. Mainly, however, *Impulsos* is thickly scored; blocks of contrasting sonorities succeed each other in gradually increasing tension until midpoint. After an awesome percussive blast, the work falls away in receding plateaus to end bleakly with a whipcrack and a ratchet.

Alonso's second concert, on Sunday morning, featured the brief and charming Concertino for Percussion and Orchestra by Darius Milhaud. A product of the naughty '20s and early '30s in French music, this work is an exercise in percussionistic choreography for a single soloist. On Sunday, soloist Pavel Burda demonstrated a fine craftsman's skill in rapidly adapting to the work's split second changes in musical expression as he struck, beat, rattled, kicked, rubbed or otherwise caused to sound some twenty different instruments.

The big work on both of Alonso's concerts was Tchaikovsky's Sixth Symphony, the "Pathétique." Aside from the conductor's excellent work with the week's soloists, it was in this major symphony that his style and technique were most evident. Alonso is elegant, precise, clear, careful and very correct. These are all priceless virtues in a conductor, but in sum total they failed to make much of Tchaikovsky's grand symphony. I do not believe that the fault is entirely his.

This orchestra still suffers from ills which have plagued it for years, among them rhythmic imprecision, insecure entrances and faulty pitch. On the grandiose scale of the "Pathétique" symphony and similar works, these often conspire to produce less than satisfactory performances regardless of who's on the podium. What should sound luscious sounds anemic, what should soar barely walks, and what should sparkle just seems dull. This is largely a matter of scale. All else being equal, to keep a big symphony afloat is a very different matter from producing a convincing performance of a smaller work.

This was evident on Sunday, when Alonso closed his engagement here with two melodious zarzuela overtures by Ruperto Chapí. In some ways, these pieces are as technically difficult as the Tchaikovsky symphony. However, the scale is much smaller and the works are much more manageable. The orchestra's performance of these sparkling preludes was first rate, and Sunday's audience would have been happy to hear them again.

Double Bass Recital A Rare Event

The San Juan Star
May 7, 1976   By Donald Thompson

The double bass is a sort of super-violin, best known to laymen through seeing a bunch of them toward the back of symphony orchestras and through funny (?) cartoons depicting (1) a bass player trying to get on or off a bus during rush hour with his instrument, (2) the bass used as a rowboat, or (3) the bass played with a handsaw instead of a bow. That the instrument has a long tradition and considerable repertory in solo performance and chamber music often comes as a great surprise, even to people who should know better.

On Sunday afternoon a double bass recital by Federico Silva, accompanied by pianist Luz Hutchinson and other colleagues in the theater of the Puerto Rico Conservatory of Music, did little to dispel this mystery. Due to the complete absence of publicity except for the word of mouth variety, the unusual event was attended only by people who didn't need convincing: another bass player, a benign cellist or two and a few other friends.

Federico Silva is a leading member of the Puerto Rico Symphony Orchestra who brings to the concert stage the product of extensive studies and experience abroad, mainly in that hotbed of advanced double bass playing, the U.S. West Coast. His program on Sunday nicely demonstrated the instrument's capabilities on at least the more conservative side, ranging from a sonata originally written for viol by Henry Eccles (1652-1742) to a rarely performed piece of chamber music by Serge Prokofiev (1891-1953). For this listener, Silva's most impressive performances were in the slow and moderate movements of the Eccles work, where his very perceptive phrasing and eloquent tone had ample space to develop. In contrast, the faster sections of solo pieces on Sunday's program occasionally seemed hurried and forced, as often occurs with this large instrument.

For what was probably the first performance in Puerto Rico of Prokofiev's Quintet, Op. 39, Silva was joined by Susan Boni (viola), David Bourns (oboe), Kathleen Jones (clarinet) and Saul Ovcharov (violin). In many ways, this work is reminiscent of Stravinsky's *Histoire du Soldat*, dating from the same general period: icy, dissonant, occasionally jazzy and always difficult. Sunday's performance by five excellent players was completely convincing, and very nicely rounded out the afternoon's demonstration of the double bass as a solo and chamber instrument.

Glosses, Muddles, Spirited Youth At Festival

The San Juan Star
June 16, 1976 By Donald Thompson

The premiere of a new work by the celebrated Argentine composer Alberto Ginastera was featured Monday at the Casals Festival. Especially commissioned for this event, the brief work is entitled *Glosses on Themes by Pablo Casals*, and consists of musical commentaries on three Casals melodies.

The term "glosses" instead of "variations" is well chosen. Instead of using the Casals tunes as the basis of variations in the traditional way of successively altering different aspects of a theme, Ginastera retained the themes intact, but wove new material around and through them. The result is a juxtaposition of two violently opposed musical styles, Casals' and Ginastera's.

Judging from the little music by Casals which has been published or otherwise made known, he was an extremely conservative composer and one especially fond of folk and folk-like music. The Casals melodies embedded in the present work are of this type. Around them has been woven a tight web of the most advanced techniques applicable to the stringed instruments: techniques which naturally make no pretense of tonality, harmonic reference or traditional consonance. In fact, these are avoided. Ginastera probably did not expect the work to be found "pleasant," a word which seldom appears in the glossary of modern music. In those terms it simply makes no sense. It does make sense, however, as a tribute by a composer very much of today to the memory of a musician of yesterday. If any more profound message than that is sought, it might turn out to be that music is not the "universal language" which some would like it to be, but that each musical generation must find its own voice. This, though, might not be quite the symbolism that the patrons had in mind in commissioning this particular work.

The string orchestra which performed this premiere is billed as an Inter American Youth Orchestra and is conducted by Alexander Schneider. In addition to its spirited playing of the Ginastera work and of an encore composed by Pablo Casals himself, this ensemble presented three works by J.S. Bach: the Third Brandenburg Concerto, the B Minor Suite for Flute and Strings (with the eminent flutist Jean-Pierre Rampal), and the Concerto in C Major for Three Harpsichords and Strings. Both the string orchestra and Rampal are scheduled for another appearance in this series, but I may be permitted the hope that we be forever spared such brutal attacks on music as the three concert grand steamrollers which wiped out the Bach concerto on Monday.

Individually, the three soloists (Mieczyslaw Horszowski, Eugene Istomin and Rudolf Serkin) are noted pianists—in music written for their instrument. This Bach concerto was not written for pianos, and with harpsichords and skilled harpsichordists common enough nowadays, the piece is almost never played on pianos (except here). No matter who the three pianists might be, its performance in this way can only produce a dull and muddled caricature of Bach's music, bringing neither edification to audiences nor glory to managements. And as for the "Inter American Youth Orchestra," I hope that this experience is not supposed to be part of a training program of some kind, because if it is, it's roughly equivalent to learning *King Lear* through watching animated figures. No matter how fast the figures are moved about it's not Shakespeare, and that wasn't Bach on Monday, either.

Children's Choir, Rampal At Festival

The San Juan Star
June 19, 1976 By Donald Thompson

Flutist Jean-Pierre Rampal appeared again on Wednesday at the Casals Festival with the Inter American Youth Orchestra in a suite for flute and strings by Telemann. As had occurred in Monday's performance of a Bach suite, the flute was often swamped by an orchestra three to four times as large as it should have been for this music. Consequently, it was not easy on Monday to arrive at anything like a satisfactory idea of Rampal's playing.

This problem was finally and gloriously solved Wednesday when Rampal played as an encore Debussy's fascinating *Syrinx*, for unaccompanied flute. This is flute music at its best, and Rampal played it with an amazing big sound, faultless phrasing and unbelievably liquid delivery. To many, this will be remembered as the definitive performance of *Syrinx*. Also played on Wednesday were a Bach concerto for harpsichord and strings (played on the piano by Mieczyslaw Horszowski as soloist), Bartók's rhythmic Divertimento for String Orchestra and as an encore a concerto grosso by Vivaldi.

The surprise of the series for many concertgoers, including this one, has been the San Juan Children's Choir, a group which was organized only a few years ago by conductor Evy Lucío but which has already become a highly respected island institution. Consisting of 28 experienced young singers, the Children's Choir presented, from memory, a widely varied program of choral music originally written for "white" voices or skillfully adapted from other fields of choral literature. Whatever its origins this music was the real stuff, in from two to five parts and demanding the skill and concentration of trained singers, which these young people are. Their pronunciation is very clear and very correct in five or their rhythmic sense is solid as a rock and their blend is faultless. A few touches of uncertain pitch in the topmost voices may have been caused by changes which have chosen this week to turn a couple of child singers into teenage singers. If this is so, there is certainly nothing to do about it except maybe congratulate them! Best of all, these capable performers listen to each other and watch their excellent conductor like a hawk. In all, their performance on Wednesday evening can be taken as a lesson for their elders in choral discipline, choral technique and choral spirit.

Rostropovich: Knockout Performance

The San Juan Star
June 30, 1976 By Donald Thompson

    Matters took a sudden turn for the better at the Casals Festival on Sunday evening with the first appearance here of the Russian cellist and conductor Mstislav Rostropovich. A sign of things to come appeared even before Rostropovich reached the podium to greet Sunday's audience, for as he left the wings he walked into a stageful of smiling players. This is almost unheard of, for at best an orchestra's expression will usually be carefully neutral. When an orchestra actually appears glad to see a conductor, something unusual is about to happen.
    Rostropovich is an extraordinary musician. As a conductor he is certainly not elegant; for that matter he isn't even especially graceful. Nevertheless, he communicates what he wants to an orchestra in ways which many of the more "artsy" conductors might envy. On Sunday, Rostropovich provided a new look at Tchaikovsky's Fifth Symphony and the same composer's Francesca da Rimini Overture, mainly by eliminating a number of "interpretive" features which have become attached to Tchaikovsky's music by tradition (at least in the West). At the same time, he brought out countermelodies and secondary lines which are never really heard in this densely orchestrated music. Ordinarily, these secondary lines only muddy up the texture, and for that reason have earned the uncomplimentary epithet "garbage." By causing these parts to be heard, Rostropovich actually caused Tchaikovsky's music to sound crystal clear for once, a most welcome innovation for many listeners.
    As cellist, Rostropovich performed Joseph Haydn's "other" cello concerto, the one in C major, with a reduced orchestra. Here, as soloist, Rostropovich demonstrated the basis of his orchestral and conducting concept, for his playing is incredibly clean and neat, yet marked by wholly

fitting expression and contrast. One might argue with the style of his cadenzas, which appeared not completely appropriate to the eighteenth-century manner, but the overall effect of his performance was a knockout.

Rostropovich is scheduled to appear twice more in this series: this evening as conductor and on Saturday as cello soloist.

Betty Allen

The San Juan Star
July 1, 1976   By Donald Thompson

    Interviewing Betty Allen is like interviewing a runner in the San Blas Marathon during the race itself. A recent midday appointment with the noted mezzosoprano occupied most of an afternoon and covered most of metropolitan San Juan, while touching on subjects ranging from avant-garde music to home gardening.

    Ms. Allen came to Puerto Rico this time to participate in the Casals Festival performance of Beethoven's Ninth Symphony on June 19, and stayed to conduct a week of master classes for singers in a concentrated program sponsored by the Puerto Rico Conservatory of Music. This format of instruction is often found in music and dance, where an eminent outsider offers a tightly condensed series of classes, usually to professionals and advanced students regardless of their local loyalties and local commitments. Betty Allen's classes, for example, attracted singers from the University of Puerto Rico, the Conservatory of Music itself and from a number or private studios in addition to several performers whose careers are already fairly launched.

    In truth, Betty Allen is hardly an outsider in Puerto Rico, for she has been coming here off and on for years. In March, for example, she served on the jury which sent two local singers to New Orleans as part of the Metropolitan Opera auditions. Through dealing with island artists she has become well acquainted with the Latin temperament, which combines sensitivity to criticism with readiness to break into laughter. Her classes profit from this awareness, for she applies a blend of seriousness, clowning, cajoling and mimickry, depending on her unerring evaluation of each case.

For those students who have little or no English she draws upon her extensive but highly original Spanish to get the message across, and will prod and pummel a singer to get him or her to loosen up. The result is dramatic; after a pummeling by Betty Allen one sings loose. Her method consists of three phases. First, the student sings through whatever he has brought to work on, without stopping. Next, Ms. Allen takes the piece—and the singer—apart, stopping in virtually every measure to correct faulty phrasing, a misplaced breath pause, or (most frequently) an error in pronunciation. Sometimes she asks "Do you have any idea what you're singing about?" In this phase, one experienced singer was moved to tears on receiving the full impact of a text which she had sung for some time. In this second phase, Ms. Allen's extraordinary teaching skill is called into play, along with the wisdom of an experienced performer. When a student reacts to an error by shamefacedly shaking his head: "Never do that! You just told the audience that you made a mistake, and most of them would never have known it. Let them find out for themselves!"

When a student repeats the same error several times: "The next time you do that it will cost you twenty five cents!" Aside to the class with a big grin when the student sings it perfectly: "Wonderful how money works, isn't it?" She roars with laughter, carrying with her the whole class of a dozen or so, at a student's feeble excuse.

The third phase is to put it all back together again in an uninterrupted presentation of the song or aria, and here is where the improvement shows. Small voices are bigger, texts are clearly understood, uptight singers are relaxed and pitch is better all around.

Over lunch, conversation turns to how Betty Allen got that way. An only child, she was given everything she wanted, and what she wanted was music. Raised in a suburb of Youngstown, Ohio (not one of the world's most beautiful spots, she admits), she had the usual middle-class childhood piano lessons, but also an unusual exposure to symphonic music as probably the only black child in Youngstown to attend children's concerts at that time. As a student at Wilberforce University she had no intention of following a musical career, but was mainly interested in languages. Touring with the university's select group of singers, plus a change of voice from soprano to mezzo, turned her in the direction of technical vocal studies and led her to the studio of Sarah Peck More, in New York and Hartford. Here she gained a permanent respect for fundamental studies, for her teacher kept her on exercises for seven months, then two years of the old Italian repertory before permitting her to study romantic opera arias and roles.

Betty Allen's career has followed the parallel lines of opera, oratorio, symphony orchestra work and recital. Unlike many singers, however, she prefers the recital field because here the singer is less dependent on other performers. There is more freedom in recital, and at the same time much more personal responsibility—a responsibility shared only with a pianist who hopefully becomes a full partner, not simply an accompanist. She gained a solid reputation for professionalism early on, as well as invaluable experience in all fields, by accepting jobs which others didn't want— or were afraid of. While other mezzos were waiting for the "plums," Ms. Allen was deliberately seeking rare repertory and out-of-the-way performance opportunities. This professional curiosity turned her into a library buff, and some of her most rewarding repertory has come from out of print and unusual music which she has found in libraries.

In the University of Puerto Rico Music Library Ms. Allen examined some new songs by island composer Ernesto Cordero, which naturally led to a discussion of modern music and the singer. Commenting on the reluctance of many singers to tackle contemporary music, she observed that neither contemporary music nor any other music will "ruin the voice"; it depends on "how you do it." In addition, she pointed out that composers have always welcomed the counsel of performers, so singers should not hesitate to offer their recommendations to avant-garde composers. "You have to protect your instrument, of course, but no professional can foolishly reject modern music and refuse to sing it."

And what of the young singers whom she has met on visits here and through her recent master classes? She finds no lack of talent here, but a certain shyness, coupled with reluctance to explore and experiment. She believes that island singers should look into ways to create opportunities for themselves by forming groups and companies. In addition, and in keeping with her own background, she urges singers to welcome small roles, to understudy other singers, to study all kinds of music, and above all, to WORK. She has great faith in the ability of island singers, but would like to see them prepare themselves as completely as possible because the competition outside is tough.

The interview continued at an Isla Verde supermarket, where Ms. Allen picked up a few snacks for her two children (aged 7 and 9) and her husband, who had been enjoying their island visit at a beachfront hotel.

What about an artist's career and raising children? In Betty Allen's case she "has had the best of two worlds," because of a completely understanding husband (a social service executive) and relaxed children, aided by a resident mother in law who sees to the continuity of home life while the singer is away from New York on professional engagements.

Her recent engagement in Puerto Rico, aside from whatever it may have done for Ms. Allen's already flourishing career, has been beneficial to a great many others, for it has given the island's music a small but powerful push in the right direction: the direction of serious study and of professional concentration.

New Horizons For Casals Festival?

The San Juan Star
July 12, 1976   By Donald Thompson

The twentieth Casals Festival in Puerto Rico, which came to an end last Monday, was offered in honor of the first centennial of the great Catalan cellist's birth. Partly because of its commemorative nature, this year's festival was marked by a number of innovations of broad scope and deep significance. Some of these innovations may also point the way to solutions for some of the problems which have hovered over the government-sponsored event ever since Casals' death. But others may be symptomatic of new problems which are just now beginning to peek over Puerto Rico's musical horizon.

This year's first surprise was an unprecedented ambiguity over exactly when the festival was to begin: with the first concert of the Puerto Rico Symphony Orchestra on June 10 or with the first concert of the Casals Festival Orchestra on June 19. The Governor, in a solemn proclamation appearing in the program book, observed the June 19 start, as did Mrs. Marta Istomin (president of the festival corporation's musical committee) in a New York Times interview of the same date. The local officers of the festival corporation evaded the question but seemed to favor the June 10 date in some mystic and freely associated sense, and most island news outlets went along with them. WIPR-TV bought both dates, and played it right down the middle. On the air, the June 30 concert was described by one commentator (at the station) as the tenth concert, and by another (at the theater) as the sixth.

What difference does it make, anyway? It makes a great deal of difference in view of the oft-questioned future of this festival, which since Casals' death seems to just about make it from one season to the next. Viewed in this light, the ambiguity was no accident but a calculated festival corporation maneuver to hedge all its bets in an uncertain market. Depending on how the winds of expediency blow in the next few months, the festival management can claim in retrospect that (1) the 1976 festival included the Puerto Rico Symphony Orchestra and other entities, or that (2) these were only preliminary warm-up bouts, not to be confused with the "real" festival. An alternative but related explanation, rumored within the festival staff itself, is that the owners of the name "Casals Festival" would not allow its use for events which were not under their direct control, thus fixing the official beginning of the festival as June 19. The local officers, then, had to hedge mightily in order to make the preliminary events look like part of the festival without explicitly saying that they were. In any case, the inclusion of entities other than the festival regulars in the festive (or pre-festive) observances was indeed an innovation. How did they fare?

The Puerto Rico Symphony Orchestra, a local subsidiary of the Casals Festival Corporation, fared much better than even its own management had predicted, thereby raising some serious questions about that very management and its handling of the island's symphony orchestra during the past eighteen years. If the Puerto Rico Symphony Orchestra could do it in 1976, why not in 1970 or 1966, when it was in fact a better orchestra? In this connection, it must be remembered that the symphony orchestra's inclusion this year was not due to any initiative of the Casals Festival Corporation, but rather to heavy pressure brought by other island musical forces and gently but effectively transmitted through the island legislature.

Other circum-festival performances were by the very fine San Juan Children's Choir, directed by Evy Lucío; by the mixed chorus of the Puerto Rico Conservatory of Music, directed by Sergije Rainis; and by most of Alexander Schneider's New York String Orchestra.

This last, with funding by the local U.S. Bicentennial Commission and by the Casals Festival Corporation, surfaced here as an "Inter American Youth Orchestra," performing as one might expect of advanced students and young symphony orchestra players from the continent: damned well. What sticks in many throats both here and in South America, however, is that this "Inter American" ensemble of 42 included only four or five players actually selected in Latin America, and that no auditions were held in Puerto Rico despite the fact that its two concerts cost island taxpayers something on the order of $40,000. Can it be that

Puerto Rico's universities, music schools and private studios have no string students capable of even auditioning for such an ensemble? Who in the Casals Festival hierarchy could have made such a decision, and on what basis? What was the position of the local festival officers in this matter? How could such a scheme gain the approval of the Puerto Rico U.S. Bicentennial Commission, which put another $20,000 into it? These are a few of the questions which are being asked in island musical and political circles and which may lead to an investigation of the whole affair.

A milestone this year was the premiere performance of an especially commissioned work by outstanding Argentine composer Alberto Ginastera. To be sure, the extremely dissonant composition, entitled Glosses on Themes by Pablo Casals, was presented not within the festival itself but in a pre-festival concert conducted by Alexander Schneider. Still, to many concert goers the work appeared almost an affront to the memory of Casals, whose reaction to it would probably not have been entirely favorable.

Nor was Ginastera's the only modern Latin American music to be heard in this year's series. As a result of heavy pressures, the festival management programmed works by three island composers, marking its first recognition in twenty years of Puerto Rico's own musical life. The three compositions (by Jack Délano, Héctor Campos-Parsi and Amaury Veray) are not all of the highest interest, but they make one wonder what the island's composers might have contributed by now had they received this kind of official recognition fifteen or twenty years ago. But that's another chapter, and it certainly can't be rewritten now. What is important is that the ice has finally been broken, opening the way to a great number of possible future developments.

This year's festival and associated events presented a wide variety of conductors and soloists, including not only the regulars but some welcome new faces too. For the festival audience, the most welcome face of all belonged to the great Russian cellist Mstislav Rostropovich, who appeared on three climactic concerts toward the end of the series. To many concertgoers Rostropovich's concerts *were* the series, with what came before and after only filling. By the middle of the Russian's third concert, there was even some half playful discussion by government figures of changing the name of this annual event to "Rostropovich Festival," as that is what this one had in fact become. Don't knock it; the thought is not without merit as one possibility among the many ideas which have been advanced recently to provide the island's annual music festival with a solid rationale and a viable format.

In a general way, many of this year's festival innovations can also be explained as adjustments preparing the way for a fundamental change in the nature of the Casals Festival Corporation, a change which has been rumored since shortly after Casals' death. There are signs and portents that the corporation's officers are moving toward the creation of a multinational franchise operation under the Casals name, with its head in New York City and branches in as many Latin American countries as will permit their establishment. The Puerto Rico operation, which has been functioning here for two decades, would provide the ready model and probably some of the financing as well. For openers, plans are in various stages of development or have been proposed for Mexico, Venezuela and El Salvador to regularly hold Casals observances at different times of the year. With such a program fully developed and greatly expanded, the festival corporation will be able to move its own pre-packaged soloists and orchestras around from place to place with a maximum of efficiency, the advance work already done by the local office in each country. The festival formula which was tried out in Puerto Rico for the first time this year could easily be applied anywhere: the scheduling of a few native groups and native soloists before the main orchestra and the featured soloists arrive from New York. In the meantime, festival backers in the various countries will be allowed to believe that theirs is the "real" Casals event, and that the others are only incidental observances. This, too, was first tried out in Puerto Rico and has been very successful so far. In addition to this program, the agency would presumably offer to help with the organization of local musical entities in the various countries where it establishes bases, as it has in Puerto Rico with a symphony orchestra and a conservatory of music.

On the other hand, as this ITT-ization of the Casals Festival proceeds, Puerto Rico, rather than becoming simply another way station in a franchise operation, might wish to channel its musical energy and its governmental backing into a somewhat different and more flexible kind of festival. One attractive possibility would be a Music Festival of the Americas, which could again endow Puerto Rico with the musical prestige which it once enjoyed but which has been piddled away. This time, however, many islanders would hope that Puerto Rico's own music and musical institutions, instead of being ignored for twenty years, would form an integral part of the planning from the start.

This next year will probably be crucial for the future of a music festival here, with 1977 seeing a Casals Festival, or a Rostropovich Festival, or a Festival of the Americas, or all of these, . . . or none at all. We shall see.

Pianist **Rudolf Serkin**, one of the Casals Festival's most popular artists.

Casals Festival:
A Political Picnic With Incidental Music

The San Juan Star
November 13, 1977   By Donald Thompson

Following the recent settlement of the Puerto Rico Symphony Orchestra strike and the related decision of the students at the Puerto Rico Conservatory of Music to return to their lessons, an uneasy calm has again settled over the offices of their parent agency, the Casals Festival Corporation. The calm might not last for very long, but while it does it might be a good time to take a searching look at this virtually autonomous government branch, its original purposes, its history, its problems and its possible future.

In the view of many Festival Corporation watchers, this might also be a good time to consider making some sort of realistic adjustment of the corporation's elements, which have been tied together in a kind of restless and contradictory troika for two decades. The oldest of these elements is the annual Casals Festival itself, associated with the name of the late great Catalan cellist and originally of international importance. The other members of the combination are the Puerto Rico Symphony Orchestra and the Puerto Rico Conservatory of Music, which were entrusted to the Casals Festival Corporation for development.

The most recent signs of crisis in the festival agency were of course the resignation of Marta Montañez de Istomin as co-chair of the corporation's board of directors and of Elías López Sobá as president of the corporation itself. As often happens following such dramatic occurences, there was for a day or two a sense of glowing euphoria in some circles associated with the orchestra and the music school: a general feeling that all problems were now solved and that the future could only be bright.

It soon became evident to cooler heads around the shop, however, that the departure of López Sobá and Ms. Istomin will in itself bring about no great improvements. The problems of the Casals Festival Corporation lie much deeper than questions of who's up front, and the resignations of these two figures are now being recognized as symptoms of crisis rather than solutions to anything. Indeed, they may simply have been harbingers of a general exodus: the first to prudently separate themselves from a failing enterprise.

How did the Casals Festival Corporation, whose name can still evoke borrowed images of high purpose and steadfast idealism, manage to get itself into such a bind? Taking the historical view, it is becoming clear that the roots of the agency's difficulties in recent years are to be found in the origin and development of the corporation itself, complicated by a set of built in conflicts among its various subsidiaries which could not have been more divisive and destructive had they been carefully planned that way from the start.

The death of Casals himself in 1973 was naturally a mortal blow to the annual festival, which, as became embarrassingly obvious, soon began running on borrowed time. Orchestral quality declined alarmingly and audiences melted away, while artistic policy vacillated wildly, finally settling on the elimination of all connection with Pablo Casals' widely known musical convictions. Now, it is useless to even dream of regaining the musical distinction and social prestige which the festival enjoyed during its early years. The Puerto Rico Casals Festival was an idea whose time has passed—quite a while ago.

It must be remembered that for reasons now all but lost in the early years of Operation Bootstrap, the Casals Festival Corporation was created as a public relations subsidiary of PRIDCO, the commonwealth's industrial development branch. During the first years this relationship was highly favorable; in fact, the annual festival could hardly have been launched without Fomento's public relations skills and image making techniques. It made no difference that the PRIDCO officials assigned to deal with the festival knew nothing about music or the music business; most musical and administrative decisions were made in New York anyway. However, when PRIDCO began to deal with Puerto Rico's own musical life it immediately got into trouble. The Puerto Rico Symphony Orchestra was born paralyzed and has remained blighted to this day for lack of managerial knowledge of how to deal with musical matters on a day to day basis.

The Conservatory of Music, entrusted to the festival agency by the island legislature in 1958, has developed along equally warped lines if not worse. Errors built into the early relationship of the music school to an industrial development agency have perpetuated themselves into ever-deepening mires of improvised administrative patchwork. A melancholy climax of sorts was reached a couple of years ago when key festival and conservatory administrators were found by both commonwealth and federal courts to have conspired to violate the constitutional rights of conservatory teachers in the King and Aponte-Ledée cases. Indeed, a far cry from the idealism of the great cellist in whose name the administrators had been appointed to their posts.

Festival, symphony orchestra, music school: tied together by intricate administrative and fiscal bonds and apparently destined to go down together, unless some relatively healthy part can be identified, extricated and salvaged. This is no new idea, the thought having been kicked around from time to time over the past years. It is, however, a very tricky idea to implement and one with potentially treacherous political ramifications.

In this sense, the problem is not musical or cultural at all, but purely political. The original concept of a Casals Festival in Puerto Rico, like the Operation Bootstrap of which it was a symbol, enlisted the thinking of some of the best minds of the Popular Democratic Party. Twenty-odd years have brought far-reaching changes to Puerto Rico; nobody talks much about Bootstrap anymore, while the only thing left of the Casals Festival concept is the name Casals—and even that might disappear with Mrs. Istomin, Casals' widow, who in resigning threatened to take it with her. Although PDP legislators have been well aware of the decline of the annual festival and the awesome problems of its subsidiaries, they have been extremely reluctant to do anything about the situation, for two reasons. One is sentimental; after all, this thing dates back to the good years of Muñoz, Moscoso, Bootstrap and the party itself. For this reason, the annual Casals Festival has always had something of the atmosphere of an old fashioned political picnic, with incidental music.

The other reason is pure politics. No politician is eager to move on anything, regardless of its merits, unless it can do the opposition some damage at the same time. Conversely, if a potentially unpopular decision must be made, the political intuition is to wait; let the opposition make it. This, I believe, is the present situation. When their party enjoyed a legislative majority, Popular Democratic Party legislators were reluctant to do anything about the Casals Festival Corporation despite the mountainous evidence of crisis, based on professional criteria, that was brought before them. Aside from the above-mentioned sentimental factors, I believe that they were waiting for someone else to propose a change, mainly so that they might oppose it on vague "cultural" grounds while allowing it to get them off the hook themselves.

The time has come; the PDP is in the minority, and can be expected to extract every bit of mileage possible out of any move by the majority New Progressive Party to alter the Casals Festival status quo. In fact, the political maneuvers have already begun, with the rumor that the NPP is out to "kill the Casals Festival." If anyone will just stop to think about it, he will see that the Casals Festival died some time ago; what's needed now is to recognize the fact, bury the corpse with dignity (if that is still possible), and get on with the work. Artistically sound, but politically . . . will anyone take the risk?

Opera de Cámara: A New Force

The San Juan Star
December 7, 1977   By Donald Thompson

    Last weekend a new opera group moved into the Patio Theater of the Institute of Puerto Rican Culture, with four performances of Pergolesi's miniature comic opera *La Serva Padrona*.

    The company is called Opera de Cámara, or Chamber Opera, and it sees as its function the presentation of lyric theater in island towns, away from the University of Puerto Rico-Tapia Theater axis. So far, so good. There are a number of attractive operas requiring small casts which could be carried about with a minimum of grief and breakage and put on in island schools, civic clubs and cultural centers. However, these small operas bring big problems. They demand complete understanding and a unified stylistic concept on the part of everyone involved, and they are absolutely intolerant of error.

    This is partly a matter of scale. The big operas of Verdi and Puccini can absorb a certain amount of sloppiness before it begins to show very much; *La Serva Padrona* cannot. This is a very jewel of an opera, and for it to function at all, it requires jewel-like precision within a convincing concept of music, staging and style. Taken separately, many elements of Friday's performance were adequate—even praiseworthy. It was a pleasure, for example, to see how baritone Héctor López has developed both musically and dramatically over the past several years. In the comic role of the skinflint Uberto, López offered a musically convincing performance.

    Soprano Ramonita Meléndez, as Uberto's wily ward, Serpina, displayed a pleasant voice and an attractive stage presence. Heberto Ferrer Duchesne, as Serpina's non-singing accomplice, Vespone, is clearly a gifted mime. Luis Pereira's translation into Spanish seems to work very well. But these separate aspects remained just that: separate aspects.

Dramatically, it was as if one were seeing three different plays at the same time, ranging from the commedia dell'arte style of Vespone to a late Verdi Uberto, with Serpina hovering somewhere between Susanna and Leonora. Assuming a certain minimal level of acting ability on the part of the cast, this state of affairs can only have been the result of fatally faulty stage direction.

And the orchestra—Lord love us, the orchestra! Placed behind the stage action and without a conductor, there was little that the five could do to even stay together themselves, let alone help the singers or even less, contribute to a unified production of lyric theater.

Opera de Cámara's purposes are noteworthy, while something like this company is probably needed for the development of opera in Puerto Rico. I think that once its management gets its artistic concepts together, Opera de Cámara might make a valuable contribution to the island's music.

Serrano and the PRSO

The San Juan Star
December 18, 1977 By Donald Thompson

This week the Puerto Rico Symphony Orchestra has been presenting a last round of pre-Christmas events under the direction of its recently named titular conductor, Sidney Harth. Thursday evening's concert, presented at the Puerto Rico Conservatory of Music in Hato Rey, offered a varied program of Sibelius (First Symphony), Ravel *(Rapsodie Espagnole)* and Handel *(Messiah* excerpts). Soloist on Thursday was baritone Carlos Serrano, still another of the many island singers who have established successful careers abroad. Every time Serrano returns for an engagement here his continuing musical growth is more striking. Last week, his presentation of a set of excerpts from Handel's celebrated oratorio demonstrated a fine voice with excellent expressive qualities. Serrano's voice is very neat and precise—the ideal instrument, in fact, for the cantata-oratorio-recital repertories in general. Next time he appears in Puerto Rico, it would be good to hear Serrano in a different setting, perhaps a song recital.

On the musical plane the Puerto Rico Symphony Orchestra continues to lurch ahead. However, it is still dragging along some logistic and managerial features which are reminiscent of a much more primitive state of affairs: a state which was transcended decades ago in most parts of the civilized musical world. For example, the entire first half of Thursday's concert was tragically marred by the rhythmic squeaking of a tape recorder reel, part of a machine which is used to record these concerts for broadcast later. Ordinarily only visually distracting (placed as it is smack in front of the orchestra) in this instance it was aurally offensive as well: an insult to composer, orchestra, soloists, conductor and public. And, of course, the tape will faithfully reproduce for broadcast the

Mickey Mouse effect of a squeaky tape recorder, which can only further defeat the artistic purpose of these concerts.

Another type of barbarity continues to occur at these concerts, which can only contribute to any true music lover's decision to stay home and listen to records. This is permitting people to enter the hall during the performance of a work. Between movements is bad enough, but Thursday evening's audience was treated to a scene reminiscent of the neighborhood movie house: people entering the hall from beside the stage during the playing of a piece, then leisurely strolling up the aisle looking for seats. At La Cucaracha during a Saturday kiddie matinee this may be all right, but it is not all right during a symphony orchestra concert or any other live artistic presentation, and it is one of management's jobs to arrange traffic so that it cannot happen.

Pabón Lends Fresh Style

The San Juan Star
January 20, 1978   By Donald Thompson

The Puerto Rico Symphony Orchestra has expanded its activities in a number of new directions this year, while maintaining a busy schedule based on its two regular series of subscription concerts. One of the season's novelties is a set of "gala" concerts, taking place outside of the subscription series and offering a look at some of the island's own developing conductors.

The first pair of these concerts took place last weekend in the theater of the Puerto Rico Conservatory of Music, and were led by Roselín Pabón. Pabón is a young pianist and choral conductor who has had a great deal of advanced study on the orchestral conducting side as well. His work here demonstrated a number of virtues often lacking in conductors twice his age and with many times his experience.

Not the least of these virtues was the thorough knowledge of his scheduled works. When added to a solid and generally efficient baton technique, this knowledge produced very satisfying results in a varied program including the Third Symphony of Brahms, Dances From Galanta by Zoltán Kodály, and two works by island composers. Both *La Reina Tembandumba* by Jack Délano and *Oda a Cabo Rojo* by Héctor Campos-Parsi are by now thoroughly familiar to island audiences, but I doubt if they have ever been more convincingly presented than last weekend. This is not only because of orchestral familiarity, which naturally increases with each playing; the truth of it is, this music does not hang together easily no matter how often it's played. Both works are sectional in nature rather than developmental, consisting of alternating stretches of lyric and rhythmic expression rooted in one or another thread of Puerto Rican folk-popular music. A great deal of Pabón's success with these pieces, success which has eluded many other conductors, was due to his understanding of the motor force which drives the island's folk music even when it's distilled into concert forms. Other leaders have simply been baffled by these two compositions in particular; Pabón made a great deal of sense out of them by recognizing their essentially rhythmic nature and by moving them along at just the correct tempos to make this rhythmic thrust fully and enjoyably evident.

Soprano Evangelina Colón: Warmth and Clarity

The San Juan Star
February 16, 1978 (a)   By Donald Thompson

    At the risk of becoming repetitive, it is necessary to point out still again that Puerto Rico, especially during the past decade or two, has become a seething hotbed of fine voices. For whatever the reason may be —sea air, good early training, or simply the fresh pineapple juice—the island has produced successful singers out of all proportion to the expected ratios. It's a great pity that few find it possible to return and work here after their professional studies and debuts abroad, but that is a situation shared by many island instrumentalists, dancers, athletes, actors and practitioners of several other arts and professions as well. When all is said and done, you go where the work is, and there just isn't a great deal of it here for high sopranos or, for that matter, low tenors either.

    The latest in this season's long list of singing returnees is soprano Evangelina Colón, formerly a member of the University of Puerto Rico music faculty and now an active opera and recital performer in wintry northern climes. Last weekend Ms. Colón appeared on the Puerto Rico Symphony Orchestra's pair of subscription concerts with Mozart's lovely *Exsultate jubilate*, and on Sunday's concert only, Musetta's waltz from Puccini's *La Bohème*. Together, these demanding pieces amply demonstrated the versatility and warmth of the soprano's clear and flexible voice.

    Also appearing on the weekend's concerts was the Second Symphony of Tchaikovsky and Bach's Brandenburg Concerto No. 2, the latter work featuring a nicely balanced quartet of soloists drawn from the orchestra's own section heads: José Figueroa (violin), Peter Kern (flute), David Bourns (oboe), and Orlando Cora (trumpet).

The week's symphonic activities were led by composer Karel Husa. Husa clearly knows his own music and also knows how to put it together with an orchestra, as was shown by the fine performance of his Music for Prague 1968. However, and despite such obvious exceptions as Bernstein and Boulez, composers are rarely the most capable conductors of other people's music. In this Husa's work ran true to the pattern; with the glorious exception of his own composition, the weekend's offerings seemed a bit edgy and insecure on the orchestral side, falling short of the island orchestra's accustomed level of performance this season.

Husa's Music for Prague 1968 is an extremely well made example of atonal modern music which fully utilizes all of the resources of the full symphony orchestra, and for convincing musical purposes. In fact, I don't think the work really needs the descriptive title and the psychological message which are attached to it, dealing with the Czech crisis of 1968. Music is music, and this is a fine example which can stand on its own feet.

Cellist Norma Erickson: First Rate Recital

The San Juan Star
February 16, 1978 (b)   By Donald Thompson

Cellist Norma Erickson is one of a number of skilled instrumentalists who in recent years have come from outside to form part of the island's regular population of working concert musicians. At any given moment there are never very many of these hardy immigrants on the local concert scene, but their contribution, rendered mainly in the anonymity of posts within sections of the Puerto Rico Symphony Orchestra, is extremely important.

For the past several seasons Ms. Erickson has been a key member of the PRSO; her solo recital last Sunday afternoon in the Patio Theater of the Institute of Puerto Rican Culture presented the other side of her considerable abilities.

The cello as a solo instrument has attracted the attention of many composers, and those who have undertaken to write for it have gone out of their way to explore its great expressive capabilities. Sunday's program, in which Ms. Erickson was joined by accomplished pianist Mildred Bou, offered a very attractive selection of works for cello and piano.

From the standard repertory came Prokofiev's Sonata, Op. 119 and Robert Schumann's lovely Op. 102 pieces, *Stücke im Volkston*. The Prokofiev work explored the cello's more crisp and incisive side, while in the Schumann pieces Ms. Erickson beautifully brought out the instrument's singing qualities, often sought but seldom fully attained. Also appearing on Sunday's concert were *Cantos de España*, comprising four Hispanic atmosphere pieces by Joaquín Nin, and *Sonata Elegíaca*, by island composer Luis Antonio Ramírez. The Nin work shows how effectively the cello lends itself to Spanish music, for the instrument can uniquely evoke both the vigorous cantilena of Spanish song and the driving rhythm of the strummed guitar. Ramírez's composition is one of his most interesting works; bleakly melodious in an introspective and somewhat distant fashion, this *Sonata Elegíaca* incorporates double stops and other idiomatic features of the cello in a completely natural and convincing manner.

Contemporary Chamber Music

The San Juan Star
March 15, 1978 By Donald Thompson

The Patio Theater of the Institute of Puerto Rican Culture was the scene on Sunday of a very successful incursion into the world of contemporary chamber music.

Well, almost contemporary; a better designation might have been music of the twentieth century, for Sunday's offering touched many of the bases of this century's styles, beginning in 1914. Not all, of course; to do so would require not one concert but fifty concerts. However, Sunday's event again showed that there are performers and a public here for infrequently heard music. Both performers and public must be nurtured and encouraged in this, for here, friends, is where music is at (as they say) today. Unless this music—and a great deal more—becomes known and assimilated, there will simply never be a living music of tomorrow.

Sunday's able performers were Henry Hutchinson Jr. and Alan Grunfeld (violins), Francisco Figueroa (viola), Norma Erickson (cello), Kathleen Jones (clarinet) and Luz Hutchinson (piano). In various combinations this quintet presented a varied list of works by Roberto Sierra, Margarita Luna, Donald Martino, Aurelio de la Vega, Anton Webern and Douglas Moore. Some of these names are, or should be, well known. The music of Webern (1883-1945) is the granddaddy of almost all of the avant-garde musical production of the past thirty years, of whatever persuasion: serial, aleatory or what have you. For this reason it was especially gratifying to see Webern's early Three Little Pieces for Cello and Piano on Sunday's program, and very neatly played by Mss. Erickson and Hutchinson.

Another old timer represented on Sunday was Douglas Moore, a highly respected U.S. composer of the time when people still spoke seriously of an American music as contrasted to, say, a French, or a Russian, or a Brazilian. His Quintet for Clarinet and Strings (1946) contains many stylistic reminiscences of North American folk music. The brief third movement, in fact, was on Sunday a beautifully presented example of how far "American" music went before the universalist style began to predominate everywhere. Other parts of the Moore work, however, seemed tentative and lacking in flow, indicating that the ensemble might have profited from another rehearsal or two.

Of great interest was a brand new Quintet for Clarinet and Strings by island composer Roberto Sierra. Sierra is remembered here as a prize winner in an Ateneo competition a few years ago, and the present work shows how far he has progressed since those early days. His quintet is a very effective and well assembled piece which mainly contrasts the melodious aspect of the clarinet with the rhythmic side of the stringed instruments. Sierra's idiomatic use of the strings is particularly reminiscent of Bartók, with perhaps a dash of Stravinsky. The young composer has mastered at least one of the languages of twentieth-century composition, and his progress from here on out will be interesting to watch, along with the many other island talents that are loose out there.

Composer **Amaury Veray**, in 1971, a leading voice in the world of music in Puerto Rico.

Margarita Castro Offers Varied Program at UPR

The San Juan Star
April 1, 1978   By Donald Thompson

The voice of Puerto Rican soprano Margarita Castro has aroused something approaching a frenzy among island opera buffs. Ms. Castro, you see, attained the final stage of the prestigious Metropolitan Opera auditions a couple of years ago, and since that time has wisely devoted herself to the development of her impressive native gifts. On Tuesday evening, close to a thousand music lovers attended a recital of songs and opera airs which Ms. Castro and pianist Elías López Sobá presented in the UPR Theater under the sponsorship of the Puerto Rico District of the Metropolitan Opera Council.

The program was nicely varied, with a bit of Granados and Falla, a touch of Liszt and Charpentier, a couple of charming songs by UPR music teacher Ernesto Cordero, some extremely welcome Mozart, and the heavy artillery: extended and much beloved excerpts from operas by Puccini and Verdi.

There is no doubt about it: Margie Castro possesses what singers are pleased to call a glorious instrument. The voice is big, open and of generally consistent timbre throughout its entire range. In addition, it is beautifully flexible on the plane of dynamics: capable of producing the most hair raising of pianissimos as well as the anguished near shriek of a Desdemona. Finally, it also has an expressive intensity about it: an intensity which drives home the emotional thrust of what's being sung.

However, this same expressive intensity can also be treacherous, pushing the pitch off center and driving a basically good vibrato completely out of control, as occasionally occurred in Tuesday's opera excerpts. There are also some stylistic problems which the gifted Ms. Castro will have to solve somewhere along the line. For example, expressive devices which somehow don't seem out of place in the big and romantic operas of Puccini—devices known in the trade as scoops, dips, and slides—are definitely out of place in Mozart, and were bothersome on Tuesday. The complete singer develops the wisdom and the skill to use these devices subtly and tastefully; the clever singer (and there are many of these) limits his repertory to those works which suit his own stylistic bent. Ms. Castro has enormous potential, and probably a pretty good chance of achieving it. The next couple of years will probably be decisive in determining how far her gifts will take her, and which of these singer's paths will be hers.

Experimental Music

The San Juan Star
April 8, 1978   By Donald Thompson

The term "Experimental Music" has come into use during the past 25 years or so to describe a broad and diverse field of modern sonoral phenomena. This music is apt to be only loosely committed to the Western concert music tradition of the past couple of centuries, but is often associated with the electronic production of sound, or with visual effects, or theater, or improvisation, or all of these to one degree or another. One branch of experimental music, in fact, is almost indistinguishable from the "happening" of a few years back.

At best, experimental music is truly innovative; at worst it can be a paralyzing bore and a cynical cop-out. By labeling his work "experimental," a composer can happily throw half baked or worthless ideas before a public. As his commitment to his offspring is minimal, he's off the hook if the piece doesn't "work out," for it was only an experiment anyway.

The natural habitat of experimental music is the university campus rather than the concert hall, for only university campuses can offer the necessary continuous communication among artistic disciplines and because of the spirit of unbiased inquiry and enlightened curiosity which we like to believe prevails around universities.

Puerto Rico's unabashed experimental music movement is centered on the Music Department of the University of Puerto Rico. Here, an experimental music workshop, under the direction of visiting professor Eduardo Kusnir, offered on Tuesday evening the second of three concerts devoted to the presentation of new music from here and abroad.

An interesting work first presented on Tuesday is *Persona*, by Rayda Cotto. This extended piece utilizes a pair of athletes in a Karate demonstration, as well as a number of traditional musical instruments used in untraditional ways, an electronic synthesizer, and a couple of narrators delivering such timeless expressions as "I like you" and "Brush your teeth before going to bed." The composer conducts, from a position in the audience, and the result is an attractive kaleidoscope of juxtaposed visual and aural images.

Another fascinating piece on Tuesday's program was *Interphone*, by Michel Decoust. This work consists partly of a pre-recorded tape of electronic and natural sounds including the human voice. Accompanying the playing of the tape is a tremendously imaginative series of light projections designed by Carlos Sueños and consisting of lattices, blobs, shimmers, melts, blends, excrescences and like phenomena.

Musical Archaeology, Fine Talent Bring *Macías* to Life

The San Juan Star
June 7, 1978   By Donald Thompson

It was a great pleasure to see a new old opera last weekend, and one grown right here on the island, at that. The opera is, of course, *Macías*, by the Puerto Rican composer Felipe Gutiérrez (1825-1899), and the company which recently brought it out of a century's deep sleep is Opera de San Juan.

For newcomers to the island's game of opera-group watching (as distinguished from opera-watching), it should perhaps be pointed out that this company, under its original name of Opera 68, was the one which showed the others how to do it here ten, eight, six years ago. At a time when locally produced opera seemed to have about as much future here as cross-country skiing, Opera 68 took the risks, raised up a public, generated an atmosphere of confidence in advertisers and backers and began to create performance opportunities for island singers. In the subsequent decade a number of other lyric theater groups and offshoots have come into existence, and all have profited by Opera de San Juan's early spadework in what was fertile but untilled soil ten years ago.

With its resurrection of the forgotten *Macías*, Opera de San Juan has performed a number of other deeply significant services to the island's cultural life. The most obvious of these has been to bring to life an important work of Puerto Rican art of the past century. As very often occurs in a sort of chain reaction, this act, while solving one scholarly-artistic problem, has generated ten or fifteen more. These will provide fascinating grist for the research mill for many years to come, as Puerto Rico's hidden history of music becomes painstakingly elucidated. On the more immediately effective plane of public perception, a very healthy effect of the resurrection of *Macías* has been to quietly refute a misconception perpetrated here and abroad during the past two decades by the promoters of an annual music festival which takes place in Puerto Rico. According to this self serving dogma, art music arrived in Puerto Rico only with the festival management itself, the previous four centuries of benighted island history having passed without knowledge of great musical art. The falsehood of this bit of flackery has long been known to specialists, and now a considerable segment of the citizenry has seen proof that it just isn't so. And a third healthy effect of this labor of musical archaeology has been to turn main attention, if only briefly, toward a work of art itself and away from whoever happens to be performing at the moment.

How, then, is this *Macías* of Felipe Gutiérrez? First of all, and make no mistake about it, this is real opera, not zarzuela, operetta, or any other popularly conceived relative. The story, set in fifteenth-century Spain, is very characteristic of the romantic nineteenth-century opera plot. *Aida*, *Tristan* and a host of other famous works immediately come to mind, for example, in the redemption through death of a pair of doomed lovers. The dramatic and musical demands of *Macías* would be a challenge to any opera company, while the music itself is on a par with probably 85 or 90 percent of the opera music composed in nineteenth century Europe.

The music of *Macías* is securely planted in the midcentury style; so much so, in fact, that it can only be recognized as the tip of an iceberg regarding the island's musical life a century ago. For a largely self-taught local composer (and one who had not traveled abroad) to have written such a work means that Gutiérrez lived within and thoroughly absorbed the contemporaneous European tradition during the 1850s and 1860s, but here in the far Caribbean. For this to have occurred there must have been a much richer musical life in San Juan than has been documented or even surmised, and Gutiérrez would have had an important (or at least continuous) part in it.

Some of the more direct influences on Gutiérrez' work are obvious; Donizetti and Rossini, for example, can be seen rather clearly in harmony, vocal style and instrumental usage. Gutiérrez would have received these influences through acquaintance with European scores performed by visiting and native companies, but which . . . who? . . . when? . . . where? . . . how often? . . . Yet at the same time *Macías* is definitely an original work and one which deserves to become much better known both in itself and as the tip of that tantalizing iceberg.

And what, then, of the weekend's performances? In the title role of the returning knight was lyric tenor Antonio Barasorda, still another of the fine island singers who have made careers abroad. Opposite him as the tragic Elvira in Saturday's performance was powerful soprano Teresa Pérez Frangie. The excellent voice and solid acting of baritone Carlos Serrano brought the villainous Hernán convincingly to life, while bass Pedro Morell made a suitably distant and inscrutable Don Enrique de Villena. Smaller but important roles in the scheme of things were ably played by tenor Valentín Fernández and that impressively developing baritone Noel Ramírez. Gutiérrez' complex choral numbers were handsomely prepared by Rafael Ferrer, while the chorus itself provided an important positive element in the working out of the opera's plot. Musical and stage pacing were both excellent, under the direction of Odón Alonso and Pablo Cabrera, respectively, and even what some might consider the picky minutiae of opera performance—details like incidental flute, clarinet or cello solos—were handled with both precision and polish. And finally, the Opera de San Juan production profited enormously by Julio Biaggi's fine sets and Benito Gutiérrez Soto's handsome costumes.

A Musical Conversation Among Equals

The San Juan Star
June 24, 1978   By Donald Thompson

After a couple of days off, the Casals Festival moved back down to the Tapia Theater on Wednesday for another evening of chamber music. Wednesday's performers were Puerto Rican pianist Irma Luz Vallecillo and the principal members of the 1978 Casals Festival orchestra's string sections: Stuart Canin (violin), David Schwartz (viola), Peter Schekman (cello) and David Walter (double bass).

Ms. Vallecillo is a formidable pianist, and a polished artist of whom Puerto Rico is rightfully proud. Among other things, she is a splendid and widely recognized example of the ideal chamber music player. Of virtuoso skill as a soloist, she can yet blend her part with those of other and less powerful instruments to accomplish the goal of this intimate art, a musical conversation among a handful of equals.

And Ms. Vallecillo's colleagues on Wednesday were equals: first rate players with a world of experience behind them and complete familiarity with the music at hand. Yet, the group's performance was clearly not the work of a completely polished ensemble. This was most evident in the "Trout" Quintet of Schubert. A peculiarity of Schubert's music is a repeated "spinning wheel" or "shuttle" kind of accompaniment figuration, often occurring in pairs of stringed instruments. If complete unity is lacking, this kind of rhythm gets out of phase very easily; for this reason only permanent ensembles are likely to ever be really free of this and such other problems as occurred in Wednesday's performance. Another rehearsal or two might have made a great deal of difference in the performance of the Schubert work. The Quartet for Piano and Strings, Op. 25 of Brahms, however, seemed completely and triumphantly free of problems, partly because its construction is very different. Here, the texture is more orchestral and not nearly so transparent; in addition, the Brahms work depends more on the interaction and answering of melodious solo voices and less on treacherous accompanying rhythms of the Schubert type. Especially captivating on Wednesday was the work's Gypsy finale, which brought the Tapia Theater audience to its feet.

In addition to participating in the Schubert and Brahms works on Wednesday, Irma Luz Vallecillo offered a beautifully moving solo performance of three works by island composer José Enrique Pedreira (1904-1959). The Pedreira pieces are very pianistic and extremely effective. Of a somberly post-romantic cast, they also suggest something resembling the impressionism of Debussy, but with more obvious formal design than is usually associated with Debussy. The truth of it is, the Pedreira pieces are original and important works in the growing repertory of known and performed Puerto Rican music.

Opera Stars Spellbind Audience

The San Juan Star
October 14, 1978 By Donald Thompson

Pro Arte Musical has done it again, repeating on Monday evening in the University of Puerto Rico Theater a winning formula which was found so effective here last season. At that time it was the combination of soprano Mirella Freni and tenor Luciano Pavarotti which rang the bell with island music lovers; this week it was soprano Katia Ricciarelli and tenor José Carreras who held a couple of thousand people spellbound with an evening of opera arias and duos. Accompanying on both occasions was the Puerto Rico Symphony Orchestra, this time under the extremely able direction of Eugenio Marco.

Opera lovers are a strange breed; much stranger, in fact, than the average art-music buff. The closest extramusical parallel is probably with hockey fans, who develop loyalties toward their favorites which verge on religious fanaticism. Ricciarelli and Carreras have clearly formed their own followings of devoted fans, for they drew heated applause and a "bravo" or two even before opening their mouths on Monday. In the peculiar world of opera, such adulation is not always based on vocal or dramatic skill, and public acclaim is sometimes gained for all the wrong reasons. For example, a tenor's winning smile, broad gesture and continuous fortissimo can hide the fact that he really has no technique to speak of and that he hasn't a clue to the meaning of his texts. Roughly the same thing occasionally occurs with sopranos, with the necessary adjustments made for gender and vocal range, of course. Happily for all concerned, the recognition offered to Ricciarelli and Carreras these days is earned. Carreras is not your garden variety opera screamer but a highly intelligent performer who usually lets the music speak for itself. He possesses that great gift of musical expression, the "long line" of phrasing which singers occasionally compare to a fine violinist's playing but which instrumental teachers claim comes from singers. Only on a few occasions on Monday was Carreras' fine voice driven sharp, perhaps by a momentary excess of musical feeling. Otherwise, his performance was a model of musicianly control and expression; that "long line" was especially felt, and especially welcome, in an extended aria from Puccini's *Turandot*.

Katia Ricciarelli is a recent arrival on the world opera scene but has already paid her way and more by virtue of her great gifts. For one thing, her voice is enormous, filling the cavernous UPR Theater without apparent effort. But what impresses most is its unforced, "floating" quality, the result of superb control. This quality was seen at its best on Monday in excerpts from the melodious Verdi operas, most notably in the well known "Pace, Pace mio Dio" from *La Forza del Destino*.

The Puerto Rico Symphony Orchestra did not sound particularly good on Monday. This was due in great measure to the lack of any acoustical shell or other reflecting surface behind it, on a stage which desperately needs such a device. In its absence, much of the sound was drawn upward into the three stories or more of open space above the stage, or sideways into the dressing rooms. What reached the audience could only be a thin and feeble imitation of symphonic sound. A second reason is that this event, although contractually part of the orchestra's work week, was laid on in addition to an already full round of normal orchestral activities. The result was a tired orchestra playing under the pressures of last minute rehearsals, an odd sort of concert format, and an unsettling move to an unaccustomed hall. There may be good reasons for the occasional collaboration of the island's symphony orchestra with privately financed entities, but such collaboration must be managed with extreme care and foresight if it is to work for the benefit of all parties.

A Fitting Finale for Island's First Music Biennial

The San Juan Star
December 5, 1978   By Donald Thompson

The First Puerto Rico Biennial of Contemporary Music offered its twelfth and final concert on Friday evening in the Humanities Amphitheater of the University of Puerto Rico. The event was dedicated to the memory of the late British composer Benjamin Britten (1913-1976). Quite fittingly, the concert included one of Britten's compositions, a very early and very English Fantasy Quartet for Oboe and Strings. Although not yet 20 when he composed this work, Britten was well schooled in the subtleties of instrumental writing; this quartet already shows painstakingly correct stylistic characteristics of some of his music written forty years later. Friday's performance, sadly enough, suffered from the "under-rehearsal blues," an ailment which has struck some of these concerts like a recurring case of the tropical flu.

Soprano Luisita Rodríguez and pianist Pablo Boissen offered songs by island composers Amaury Veray and Jack Délano, demonstrating the great variety which exists in even this small corner of Puerto Rico's art music. The most interesting of the Veray songs offered Friday are from the late '60s, and are based on poems by David Ortiz. Here, Veray's music is a juxtaposition of long asymmetrical phrases in the vocal line against a nervous and rhythmically disjointed accompaniment. The result is a kind of expressive musical declamation: in fact, not song in the strict sense at all but something approaching recitative.

Jack Délano's *Canciones para Laura*, based on poems by Emilio Delgado, are in the highly distilled Caribbean style which the composer has so ably cultivated for the past quarter century. Délano's music is always highly rhythmical and clearly tonal, while incorporating certain characteristics of island folk music in a perfectly natural way. According to one view of things, the stylization of island folk elements through artistic expression is the only way to forge a viable Puerto Rican music (as contrasted to a Russian, or a French, or an Argentine music). If this is so, and if the question is still of interest to anyone in today's world of deliberately international styles, Délano must be reckoned among the most successful creators of a Puerto Rican art music. His compositions certainly satisfy this criterion, and in addition are both highly performable and pleasant to listen to.

Also appearing on Friday's closing Biennial concert was *Canciones y Recuerdos*, by the Argentine composer Luis Zubillaga, while to close the entire series with an impressive finale, two works by major twentieth-century composers were offered. These were Concertino, by Luciano Berio, and the Dumbarton Oaks Concerto, by Igor Stravinsky, both for small orchestra and both ably conducted by Eduardo Kusnir. Concertino dates from 1951, before Berio became one of the most controversial innovators of the avant-garde. It is thus pre-electronic, pre-aleatory, and pre-indeterminacy, in the Berio progression. As the title indicates there are solo elements, and these, mainly for clarinet and violin, are staggeringly difficult. On Friday, these solo passages were brilliantly played by Kathleen Jones and Henry Hutchinson. The Dumbarton Oaks Concerto, named after the estate of Stravinsky's patrons of the moment, is one of the composer's piquant neo-classic compositions of the 1930s. The work is scored for a small orchestra of strings and winds, and cast in the general form of an eighteenth-century concerto grosso. Yet there is a great deal of the twentieth century in it as well, mainly in harmony, rhythm, and a peculiarly Stravinskyan melodic turn. The result is a gracious miniature from the pen of one the most important and influential composers of modern times. Its performance on Friday was admirably neat and trim, providing a fitting finale for this first Puerto Rico Biennial of Contemporary Music.

Audacious, Unprecedented, Innovative and Successful

The San Juan Star
December 16, 1978   By Donald Thompson

Audacious, unprecedented, innovative, and by and large successful was the First Puerto Rico Biennial of Contemporary Music, sponsored by the small but hardy Contemporary Music Society of Puerto Rico and recently ending with an appropriate bang. Comprising a dozen concerts and a number of lectures, spread out over the San Juan metropolitan area and free to the public, the Biennial offered a full month of musical attractions. During the month, the varied events drew an ever-snowballing public of confirmed modern music buffs along with people who were curious to learn what the composers have been up to since the time of Brahms and Tchaikovsky.

FREE concerts, you say? Yes, thanks to grants and other help provided by a distinguished roster of backers. Among these were the National Foundation for the Arts, the Music Performance Trust Fund, the University of Puerto Rico Cultural Activities Office, the Institute of Puerto Rican Culture, WIPR, and many other public and private entities and individuals.

One question usually raised by such events as this biennial is what sets this music apart from "non-contemporary" music, anyway, and why should it require such special treatment? Interestingly enough, until the middle of the past century, ALL music performed was "contemporary" music. Gradually, however, the great symphony orchestras and the great opera houses came into existence as the major institutions of musical performance, supported by conservative publics who mainly wished to hear the same relative handful of certified masterpieces repeated—and again repeated. As a result, music written before or after the "repertory" period was not likely to be heard except as an occasional novelty. A circular set of causes and effects, involving both taste and economics, came into existence which even today tends to limit the performances of the musical establishment to the tried and true standard repertory. As a consequence, contemporary music, along with "ancient music," has become the province of specialized groups. Eventually, both of these kinds of music, along with their advocates and enthusiasts, found a home in that last refuge of the oddball, the university. Today, music composed prior to the middle of the eighteenth century is cultivated mainly in universities by a Collegium Musicum or other such "ancient music" ensemble, while most of today's serious composers are associated with university music departments as composers in residence or composition and theory teachers. The Contemporary Music Society of Puerto Rico is of this tradition, for most of its leaders are connected with one or another island academic institution.

The society's purpose is clear: to bring modern music to the attention of concertgoers, while hopefully creating a public for more of the same. Its task has been difficult, for the island's musical public has always been very conservative, and this conservatism has only been deepened and confirmed by the ultra-conservative course which large-scale government subsidized musical presentation has taken during the past two decades. On the other hand, a great deal of the newest music fits nicely into the improvisational aesthetic which speaks so clearly to people under thirty and to a few of their elders, as well.

The statistics concerning this recent series are interesting. Some 85 unusual compositions were presented, by about forty different composers. Of the total number of works, probably a quarter were among the most important of twentieth-century compositions. These included works by such key figures as Schoenberg, Ravel, Debussy, Webern, Berg, Stravinsky, Stockhausen, Milhaud and Berio, sprinkled among compositions by many of the century's lesser lights and relative newcomers. Most of the century's main compositional trends were represented, from the impressionism of Debussy and the bristling atonality of early Schoenberg all the way down to (are you ready?) Odormusic. This last can probably be considered the latest manifestation of the avant-garde; one young enthusiast, with unconscious humor, observed during the presentation of a smellpiece, "Man, that's a real gas!"

Puerto Rican music of all persuasions was well represented, but by no means dominated the programs. In keeping with what was observed above about the home of modern music generally, ten of the sixteen island composers represented have studied or taught in the music department of the University of Puerto Rico, while four others have been teachers in the Puerto Rico Conservatory of Music. On the whole, music by island composers held its own in the international frame of the Biennial.

Also on the whole, the selection of works for the series was very good. *Pierrot Lunaire* of Schoenberg was there, as were the Dumbarton Oaks Concerto of Stravinsky and Bartók's Sonata for Two Pianos and Percussion. These three compositions in particular are among the central accomplishments of twentieth-century music, and their presence on any concert series tends to set a high standard.

Performance? Generally high marks, with points off for under-rehearsal of some compositions. It's a great pity when this happens, for it doesn't do the cause of modern music any good. The idiom is likely to be strange to begin with, and a tentative audience needs all the help it can get in the way of accuracy and general security. Performers themselves were a highly respectable lot, comprising some of the most skilled of the island's musicians plus some first class imports. It should be possible to broaden the base of island performers engaged for future series, which could better distribute the rehearsal load. As it turned out, a couple of island sources of able performers were not tapped at all for this series. Logistic hassles provided a barrier to complete success in a few cases, such as failure to control audience traffic into and out of the hall during the performance of a work. A couple of events suffered so badly from this barbarity that they seemed more like movie matinees than live concerts. Managements here are reluctant to do anything about this, and as a consequence the situation is deteriorating fast. The Biennial concerts simply gave it another kick down the slope.

Another barrier to enjoyment during some of these concerts was the presence of photographers passing up and down aisles and even crossing between performers and audience. Their work was officially approved, of course, for a photographic record of a musical event is a valuable piece of documentation. There are, however, other ways to get it. There are few performers, for example, who would refuse to stay after a concert for a photo call. Anything else is disturbing to both performers and audience, and has no place in serious concert life.

Contrasted to these discouraging signs of managerial informality, one aspect of the series' nuts and bolts deserves high praise for its professional approach: the general program. This seventy-page book was produced by the UPR Cultural Activities Office, and provides an authoritative record of the entire series complete with photos, drawings, biographical notes and brief comment on the compositions. One might quibble over a few works described as island premieres which weren't, or the accuracy of a few biographical judgments. One, for example, allows that composer Francis Schwartz has become part of the island musical scene "despite" his North American heritage. The truth is, Schwartz has played an important part in *forming* the present island musical scene itself, heritage be damned. It is inconceivable, in fact, that this Biennial itself could have taken place without the spadework of Schwartz and a few colleagues and their students over the past decade. On the other hand, the program book's layout is attractive, the proofreading first rate, and the format very handy. The book will surely find its way into many libraries and collections both here and abroad.

The First Puerto Rico Biennial of Contemporary Music was, all in all, a highly significant contribution to the development of the arts in Puerto Rico, and certainly one of the most important musical events to take place here during the past fifteen years or so.

Sarmientos and the PRSO

The San Juan Star
March 29, 1979   By Donald Thompson

The Puerto Rico Symphony Orchestra has recently been in the capable hands of Jorge Sarmientos, the Guatemalan director who adds his bit to the cumulative contribution of a couple of years of short-term and guest conductors here.

While a situation like this—the lack of a resident conductor—can't go on for much longer, the orchestra has benefited in many ways from having a wide range of conductors wave a stick at it. Some of these wanderers have been good, some bad and some about average. Sarmientos is one of the good ones, and his work with the island orchestra has set it on a healthy course which will hopefully last until the end of the season.

The week's subscription concerts featured twentieth-century works for large orchestra. Among these was *Impulsos* by island composer Rafael Aponte-Ledée, an example of the uncompromising avant-garde of a few years ago. There is little evident order in *Impulsos* and the generation of composition which it represents, but much contrast among sections of the work which explore previously unknown realms of instrumental and vocal sound. In performance, *Impulsos* constitutes a catalogue of resources of the international orchestral music of the past couple of decades.

Also offered on the week's concerts were the Fifth Symphony of Shostakovich, by now a universally (well, almost universally) accepted masterpiece of modern music, and a new work by conductor Sarmientos himself. The Sarmientos composition is entitled *Ofrenda de Gratitud (Terremoto de 1976)* and is, like *Impulsos*, a successful if somewhat more conservative piece of contemporary music. But here the music is not the whole story. *Ofrenda* bears a whole set of extramusical "meanings," which were identified beforehand by extensive program notes (on Thursday) and by the composer himself in a brief speech from the podium (on Sunday). The extramusical references are to the great Guatemala earthquake of 1976, and here, as with all descriptive music, an aesthetic Pandora's box (not to say a can of worms) pops open.

There are three sets of problems connected with descriptive music, especially descriptive music composed nowadays. After all, one of the great accomplishments of twentieth-century music has been the "objectification" of music: the recognition that what music expresses best is music itself. It seems a step backward at this late date to expect music to carry a load of non-musical baggage, which is what this *Ofrenda* is asked to do.

One of the problems of descriptive music is that any piece which is supposed to describe such-and-such an event could just as well describe any one of a whole range of other events—and this without even going outside the extremely limited field of Western art music. Without intending the slightest disrespect to Sarmientos or to his very well made *Ofrenda*, it must be pointed out that the same music might just as well have been entitled "A Midnight Auto Trip from Río Piedras to Ponce, With a Car Wreck at the Cayey Exit."

Second, descriptive instrumental music isn't even necessary anymore. There are media much better suited to the depiction of events than orchestral music, which has its own very difficult tasks to perform. If sonoral representation is desired, why not offer, for example, ten or twelve minutes of carefully edited tape of the event itself? In other words, if the "message" of a piece of music must be painstakingly explained ahead, perhaps music was not the best medium for delivering that message in the first place.

Third, such loaded titles as "The Martyrdom of Saint Frodegunde" or "Mothers Day on the Farm" already program an audience's emotional response, virtually guaranteeing the work a sympathetic reception or at the very least a friendly suspension of judgment. Anyone who would criticize a work entitled "The Martyrdom of Saint Frodegunde" must be some kind of cynical atheist, regardless of what the piece itself is like. As a true test of audience perception, however, the same music would have to be played for a fresh audience but with such a title as "Homage to a Sweet Guy, Charlie Manson."

Leaving aside these admittedly grumpy comments on modern

program music in general, Sarmientos' composition could probably stand on its own feet as an interesting piece of modern music without its descriptive references. On those terms I wish the new work and its composer well.

Soloists' duties for the week were split between baritone Ángelo Cruz on Thursday and violinist Narciso Figueroa on Sunday. Cruz is one of the many island singers who are mainly working abroad for lack of performance opportunities here. Cruz has recently been based in New York City, but returned for this one-shot appearance in a set of French works which displayed his best lyric qualities. Especially impressive was his melodious presentation of *Don Quichotte à Dulcinée*, a group of three songs which constitute the last compositions of the incomparable Maurice Ravel.

On Sunday, young violinist Figueroa courageously offered the Tchaikovsky Violin Concerto in his first appearance here with orchestra. It is evident that Figueroa has the makings of a soloist, but for the first time out the Tchaikovsky is a bit much. This is one of the biggest of the big ones, and its successful presentation requires a level of skill and interpretive maturity far beyond the reach of most students.

Caballé: High Point of the Season

The San Juan Star
April 2, 1979   By Donald Thompson

    After soprano Montserrat Caballé's recent recital on the UPR Cultural Activities series, a music lover observed that the rest of the season can only be downhill. He may be right. Hearing this woman sing is more like a privilege than only a pleasure, and it will take some doing to top her appearance here. More; for anyone actively involved in musical performance the occasional exposure to this kind of singing should probably be a requisite for continued certification in the profession—something like the continuing education of physicians and auto mechanics.

    The first half of Mme. Caballé's program offered a batch of arias by Handel and Vivaldi. Unusual, this. It's true that a normal sort of recital will often begin with a selection or two from what used to be called the "Old Italian" repertory. But fully half of an evening's program makes unrelieved demands on any singer in two principal ways: long, sustained expression and its opposite, rapid scales, arpeggios and ornaments. Early on, Mme. Caballé showed her mastery of these and all other technical aspects of singing. In fact, this is the great lesson to be learned from her evening's work; she is in complete and calm control of every parameter of singing: pitch, inflection, and even such subtleties as the velocity and range of vibrato and trill. These last are often considered to be outside the control of the performer—and not only singers but many instrumentalists as well. Mme. Caballé has them completely within her domain, even to the point of being able to play with them for purposes of expression.

    The second half of the program was a splendid sampling of Spanish music of more recent times, including both art songs and excerpts from stage works. Here, accompanist Miguel Zanetti showed himself to be a fine artist in his own right, for much of this music depends as much on the piano as on the voice for its successful presentation. Here, too, the full range of Mme. Caballé's expressive gifts was added to the unquestionable technical skill already displayed, to make of the event a stellar occasion and perhaps, as the man said, the high point in the island's 1978-79 season.

The Collapse of a Festival[1]

The San Juan Star By Donald Thompson

I. THE BACKGROUND

May 24, 1979

With the first wave of emotional reactions starting to subside it may now be possible to begin to see the collapse of this year's Puerto Rico Casals Festival, and some of its possible consequences, in the cold light of reason. The bare facts are simple enough. The Puerto Rico Symphony Orchestra had been invited to participate in this year's Casals Festival, and its acceptance had been assumed as a foregone conclusion. In fact, the orchestra's participation was built into the programming of the festival as early as five or six months ago. Negotiations broke down last week between the Symphony Orchestra members, represented by the president of the island local of the American Federation of Musicians, and the Casals Festival Corporation, a subsidiary of the Puerto Rico Industrial Development Company (PRIDCO). Following the collapse of negotiations over the conditions of participation by the Symphony Orchestra, the festival management decided to cancel the festival entirely rather than proceed without the PRSO. This means that for the first time since 1957 a postseason music festival, bearing the name of the great Catalan cellist Pablo Casals, will not be held in Puerto Rico.

One of the most colorful of the initial reactions to the debacle was voiced by Fomento Administrator Manuel Dubón, who claimed that the Symphony Orchestra had "finally shot down the festival." The implication is that the festival was flying high under its own power until some

---

1. This series of three articles received the Overseas Press Club of Puerto Rico award for 1979 in the "Columns" category.

malign external force was finally able to destroy it with a single stealthy stroke. In the light of this festival's documented history, a more appropriate simile might have been with an apparently hearty oak tree being felled by a wisp of tropical breeze. Of course, any oak tree so easily downed must have already been hollow and ready to fall. By the same token the Casals Festival may have been about to collapse from internal ailments even without last week's events.

Indeed, historical evidence points to an accumulating burden of internal problems which have resulted from PRIDCO's handling of the festival, coupled with external changes wrought by the passing years and decades. The following are some of the symptoms, all of which were clearly evident in time to take corrective action. Sadly, no corrective measures were ever taken; the result was the situation in which the festival management found itself last week.

(1) The first subtle symptom of internal disorder occurred over a decade ago, when the annual Casals Festival began to lose contact with the purposes for which the island legislature had created it. These purposes were (a) to stimulate tourism and (b) to enhance the image of Puerto Rico as a tranquil and pleasant place for purposes of attracting investment capital for the island's industrial development program. It is for this latter reason that the management of the festival was entrusted to PRIDCO, then at the forefront of the island's economic development and, it was thought, eminently capable of handling a promotion based on a music festival as well. All well and good for the first years, until it became evident that few if any tourists were drawn here by the festival and that industrialization was losing its rosy glow as the only solution for the island's deep economic problems. But still the festival continued, now as a government-financed social event cut off from its roots. An educational function through television was vaguely claimed from time to time, but one year the management even tried to curtail television coverage so as not to jeopardize ticket sales. So much for any serious educational function. **First symptom of serious ailment: loss of purpose.**

(2) In the meantime, the average musical quality of performances declined as the budget rose. The Casals Festival orchestras, basic to the established festival formula and at first composed of some of New York City's finest symphony orchestra musicians, needed more rehearsal time but could never get it. As a result, many performances showed the unmistakable signs of having been thrown together by a harried and

unprepared orchestra. **Second symptom of serious ailment: decline in quality.**

(3) The death in 1973 of Pablo Casals eliminated the last valid reason for the festival's existence: to honor the famous cellist by offering an annual set of concerts in his name. When this last element of unity and purpose disappeared, the festival was left even more stranded than before. As was colorfully expressed by a former fan at the time of the first post-Casals event, a Casals Festival without Casals was like chicken asopao without the chicken. Instead of ending the festival gracefully and powerfully with a last memorial season, the management then embarked on five more years of increasingly pointless "Casals" festivals marked by a complete lack of artistic policy and by wildly varying degrees of performance quality. **Third symptom of serious ailment: lack of managerial policy.**

(4) A supposed managerial dedication to the high humanistic precepts of Pablo Casals, much proclaimed during the early years, went down the tube in 1974. In the celebrated cases of Frederick King and Rafael Aponte-Ledée, the festival management was found in island and federal courts to have violated the rights of teachers at a festival subsidiary, the Puerto Rico Conservatory of Music. There are few signs that the festival corporation's treatment of its professional musical staff has improved since that time. **Fourth symptom of serious ailment: abandoning the known principles of Pablo Casals, in whose name the management itself had been created.**

(5) Two years ago Mrs. Marta Istomin, Pablo Casals' widow, resigned as musical director of the festival, bringing to an end the last connection with the person of Pablo Casals. Along with her resigned Elías López Sobá, festival president, in a move which clearly demonstrated a skipper's awareness that the waves were lapping at the foredeck. **Fifth symptom of serious ailment: the abrupt resignation of the agency's two highest officers.**

All of these symptoms were and are public knowledge. Can anyone have seen them and still believe that the Casals Festival was suddenly destroyed by the Puerto Rico Symphony Orchestra, an entity which was completely irrelevant to the festival for 21 of the past 22 years? More likely, the festival was ready to fall of its own weight. Ironically, it might soon have fallen without any help from the Puerto Rico Symphony Orchestra or anyone else, and the orchestra would not have become the villain in the piece.

II. THE PUERTO RICO SYMPHONY ORCHESTRA AND HOW IT GOT THAT WAY

May 30, 1979

The Puerto Rico Symphony Orchestra is described as having played a decisive role in the events leading up to the cancellation of this year's Puerto Rico Casals Festival. What **is** this orchestra, which tends to burst into the public consciousness rarely, but spectacularly? What is its connection with the Casals Festival, anyway?

The first Puerto Rico Casals Festival took place in 1957. Organized around concepts connected with tourism and island image-making, the first festival more than fulfilled the expectations of its organizing agency, the Puerto Rico Industrial Development Company (PRIDCO). One of the direct consequences of this success, however, was an increased desire by island music lovers for a permanently established resident orchestra which might serve the cultural needs of the populace itself, and during the rest of the year. There was also an immediate reaction by the island's concert musicians, astonished and pleased by the government's sudden interest in music. Of course, there had previously been orchestras devoted to the performance of concert music in Puerto Rico, in an almost unbroken chain extending back a century. Very few of these orchestras had enjoyed any kind of government aid, but many had made fundamental contributions to the island's music. Instead of patiently building on existing institutions and traditions, however, the island legislature in 1957 chose to start from scratch, placing its faith in PRIDCO for the creation of a resident symphony orchestra. PRIDCO in turn placed *its* faith in violinist Alexander Schneider, the dynamic organizer of the Casals Festival but (as later became clear) no believer in island initiatives or island institutions in music.

The first season of the new Puerto Rico Symphony Orchestra took place in the fall of 1958, offering eleven concerts in different island centers. Conducted by Schneider himself (except for the opening concert with Pablo Casals), the orchestra consisted almost exclusively of New York players associated with one or another of Schneider's projects there. The exceptions were a few islanders, mainly in such positions as second clarinet, second and third trombone, etc. When the three-week season ended and the Puerto Rico Symphony Orchestra returned to New York the island was left in the same orchestra-less condition as before, but worse. There was now not the least interest anywhere in underwriting or aiding local initiatives in music, for now "PRIDCO was taking care of it."

Second season, five concerts. . . . Fifth season, eight concerts. Same management, same players. A talented Puerto Rican violinist, returning to the island because his family had written that there was now a resident orchestra, was told at PRIDCO that there was no information here about how to audition for the Puerto Rico Symphony Orchestra; he should see Mr. Schneider's staff in New York. No study was ever made of how the general citizenry might be brought to an interest in concert music, and no attempt was made to cultivate future generations of music lovers through well organized school and educational concerts. After six years under PRIDCO the Puerto Rico Symphony Orchestra was still a fleeting fantasy without roots in the island's musical life. By the mid 1960s it was becoming clear, in fact, that PRIDCO and its subsidiary Casals Festival Corporation were not interested in developing an island orchestra. Nor was the legislature interested in sticky musical problems anymore. If PRIDCO reported every year that the island's musical life was peachy, then peachy it was.

The relationships and attitudes established during these early years set the patterns for the entire subsequent history of the Puerto Rico Symphony Orchestra. One of the first and strongest patterns to be established was an adversary relationship between the festival management and the island-resident members of the Symphony Orchestra. This adversary relationship was due mainly to three causes. One reason for members' resentment was the fact, obvious after four or five years, that the festival corporation had no plan at all to develop a symphony orchestra in Puerto Rico, but was simply going through an annual public relations ritual. Another reason for resentment was the knowledge that the Puerto Rico Symphony Orchestra budget was merged with that of the annual Casals Festival, and that it was impossible to learn where one ended and the other began. Members suspected, and continue to suspect, that the development of the Symphony Orchestra as a permanent and vital force was sacrificed for a brief annual festival with little direct effect on the island's music.

On the management side, resentment and distrust of the symphony orchestra members were largely the product of management's own lack of knowledge and experience. Until relatively recently, the officers of the festival corporation who dealt with the Symphony Orchestra were PRIDCO executive types exclusively: sincere music lovers, perhaps, but without managerial or performing experience in the arts. In addition, contracting the annual festival in no way prepared them for dealing with a permanent orchestra. The festival was always handled through intermediary contractors who did all the dirty work, leaving the festival officers to sign the vouchers and mingle with the soloists. Dealing directly with musicians and their representatives, however, brought them unprepared and bewildered into the stark realities of backstage life as it is lived wherever there is a permanent symphony orchestra, opera company, musical theater or recording industry; in other words, wherever there is professional musical life. To management, however, it was absolutely inconceivable that any true musician could ask anything more from life than to be associated—however remotely—with the Casals Festival enterprises.

Down through the years, each side has evolved a set of responses with which to face the other side. Early on, symphony orchestra members turned to the Puerto Rico Federation of Musicians (the island local of the AFM) for guidance in labor matters and to represent them in contract negotiatons. The festival management, on the other hand, very soon discovered a couple of subtle but powerful techniques of its own. One was to incorporate another island musician or two in the annual festival orchestra when the pressure seemed to require it, and the other was to from time to time offer the Symphony Orchestra the promise that eventually—if it could only somehow get good enough—the whole orchestra just might be able to perform in the Casals Festival! Of course, it was the festival management itself which determined how fast the Symphony Orchestra improved, through its control of the orchestra budget and all other factors of development and growth. These two forces have just about kept each other in balance. With the exception of one spectacular leap forward in the length of its season, gained through the direct efforts of then governor Luis A. Ferré, most of the PRSO's material progress has been due to the classic device of organized labor: adversary negotiation, backed by the possibility of boycott or strike and the willingness to go the whole route if necessary.

There has been great improvement in the Puerto Rico Symphony Orchestra, both material and artistic, since Ferré's Great Leap Forward, and largely due to it. The orchestra season now stands at a respectable

37 weeks of concerts and other activities. Three years ago a general manager was finally engaged for the Symphony Orchestra itself, some twelve years after the desperate need for such a post was first pointed out. In recent seasons the orchestra has been directed by a great number of generally able guest conductors who have helped the orchestra attain a higher level of experience and sophistication. Many soloists with the orchestra have been of international stature, while the orchestra's capabilities of repertory are now limited mainly by the lack of players in some sections. A new and capable musical director has just been engaged, whose presence over the next years can only further solidify the orchestra's artistic gains. In addition, a responsible musical director can transmit some basic truths about music and orchestras to a governing board of laymen who would never believe the same truths if told by a mere musician.

A subtle change has occurred in the Symphony Orchestra's attitudes toward the annual Casals Festival in recent years. Formerly, the management's promise of more island participation in the festival was a powerful lever in dealing with the orchestra. When the symphony season was ten or twelve weeks long, the promise of another week or two of work, and at a considerably higher salary, was indeed attractive. In addition, participation in the Puerto Rico Casals Festival of a decade ago had an aura of professional prestige about it. However, with a season approaching forty weeks another week of work is not quite so urgent, while the gradual decline of the annual festival orchestras has naturally reduced the compelling attraction of playing in them.

There can be no doubt that the Puerto Rico Symphony Orchestra at its best has sounded better than some of the performances of the annual Casals Festival orchestras of recent years. Maybe, after all, symphony orchestra members needed the annual festival less than had previously been thought. On the other hand, it began to appear toward the end of the recent aborted negotiations that the festival needed the Symphony Orchestra much more than had ever been admitted.

III. And Now What?

June 6, 1979

Following the recent collapse of the 1979 Puerto Rico Casals Festival and even as the painful sifting of the rubble begins, attention naturally turns to the future. Can this festival be revived on the same basis as before? Should it be revived on the same basis? Should it be revived at all? What was its historical function as a government agency? Do the same economic conditions exist here now which existed in 1957, causing a music festival to be created under an industrial development branch of government? Does Puerto Rico need an annual festival of standard symphonic repertory? Would the same need exist if the island had a fully developed resident symphony orchestra with sufficient budget to hire an occasional big name soloist and now and then a glamorous guest conductor?

Could it be that the whole idea of "festivals" for local consumption needs study? Maybe what's wanted are fewer "festivals" and more well organized, well managed and well publicized "seasons." If not mainly for local consumption, perhaps there is a place for a tourism-based festival of some kind, which might even return to the basic premises of the old Casals Festival. But does anyone really know? Have there been any recent studies to determine what really attracts those elusive critters, the tourists? If so, what kind of a tourism-oriented festival should it be? Should it be a concert series based on standard repertory and the more or less normal run of guest soloists and traveling conductors? Probably not. It was this formula which came to dominate the Puerto Rico Casals Festival in recent years; it failed to attract visitors then and it would probably not attract very many in the future either.

These are a few of the questions which are being kicked around in island musical circles nowadays, with nothing resembling a consensus in sight yet. On the august level of legislative expostulations, the cooler heads are calling for a pause during which a complete study might be undertaken of the Casals Festival Corporation, its history, its purposes and its relation to its parent PRIDCO, with an eye to bringing about fundamental changes in the whole thing. And the "whole thing" reaches far beyond the scope of a brief music festival, which is how the festival agency got into trouble to begin with.

There is no dearth of possible solutions to the problems brought to light by recent events. Basic to all solutions, however, will probably be the long overdue separation of the festival agency from the Puerto Rico Symphony Orchestra. A properly founded symphony orchestra has fundamental and permanent responsibilities for a great part of a community's musical health, and requires the full time attention and support of its governing organisms. Here, the tail wags the dog, for the resident orchestra is a subsidiary of an agency whose own main purpose is much more limited: the promotion of a brief annual concert series which has no necessary connection with the permanent orchestra at all. To compound the paradox, all aspects of the development of the permanent orchestra have been tightly controlled by the festival agency: budget, publicity, the hiring of musicians, the purchase of equipment and the engaging of soloists and conductors. In many ways the various purposes of the parent festival corporation have in fact been at war with each other, creating over the years a network of internal tensions and contradictions which could only culminate sooner or later in disaster.

If not under the Puerto Rico Industrial Development Company, then, where in the island's governmental structure might the Puerto Rico Symphony Orchestra find a home? One possibility might be under the Office of Cultural Affairs at La Fortaleza, an existing high-level agency whose functions, purposes and limits have not yet become clearly defined. Why not begin with a symphony orchestra? This would certainly serve to channel (not to say galvanize) the agency's efforts, and might eventually lead to a very healthy realignment of some other wandering cultural agencies as well. On the other hand, in some countries where large scale permanent musical entities are underwritten by government, the symphony orchestras work in close connection with the state radio and television authorities, sometimes as their direct subsidiaries. This device, if applied here with WIPR and WIPR-TV, could lead to the realization of the Puerto Rico Symphony Orchestra's immense potential for public education. In addition, this would effortlessly provide one of the basic elements which the orchestra's present administrative placement has always denied it: continuous and widespread public awareness of its existence, its purposes and its program.

A new element is on the horizon now, which if properly handled will become a potent cultural force in the next few years. This is the new Arts Center now under construction in Santurce. Undetermined at this late date is who will run it, with several government agencies engaged in an elegant backstage scuffle. Some of the claimants can only cause surprise, including—yes—even Fomento, an agency which seems destined never to learn an obvious lesson about industrial development and arts management. Beyond question, however, is that the island symphony orchestra should find its permanent physical home there. Depending on what shape the management of the arts center finally takes, the PRSO could perhaps become an administrative subsidiary of the Center itself.

So much for some possible futures for the Puerto Rico Symphony Orchestra. What of the Casals Festival itself, if it should be determined that an annual music festival of this kind is needed here? It might actually be possible now for some non-governmental agency to rally new support for such an event. If this is so, the organization of an annual Puerto Rico Casals Festival could be turned over to a group of volunteer enthusiasts who would then engage whatever orchestra and whatever soloists they might consider appropriate. The officers and main supporters of such an organization could probably be quickly recruited among those island music lovers who have most enthusiastically praised the Casals Festival policies and programming during the past five years or so. Such a privately sponsored organization would be completely free to raise funds from like-minded citizens on the basis of their proposed musical programming, in a subscription arrangement. In addition, of course, the festival organization could petition the legislature annually for financial aid precisely as do the island's privately organized opera companies, concert societies, theater groups and other cultural agencies.

PRIDCO officials and Casals Festival Corporation board members used to speak in reverent tones of an Eternal Trinity which had been mystically entrusted to their stewardship: the annual festival itself, the Puerto Rico Symphony Orchestra and the Puerto Rico Conservatory of Music. Now, if it should turn out that the trinity was not so eternal after all, it will be necessary to find a new administrative placement not only for the PRSO but for its associated music school as well. This may be the simplest of the problems to solve, for this school fits a rather straightforward pattern albeit with some peculiar local variations. It should not be difficult to fit it into the governmental structure at one point or another.

According to the law which created it, the main purpose of the Conservatory is to provide musicians for the Puerto Rico Symphony Orchestra itself. In addition, by now the two institutions have become closely intertwined, with many PRSO members also serving as teachers in the conservatory. This being the case, the simplest solution might be to keep the conservatory connected to the orchestra as its training branch, moving it along to wherever the orchestra itself finds an administrative roost.

Other possible placements are suggested by the nature of the school's training program. With the impressive expansion of the conservatory's elementary and high school level offerings during recent years it is clear that to a great extent its program now runs parallel to the purposes of the government's Free Schools of Music. Its ideal placement might be, then, at the administrative center of the island-wide Free Schools network as a positive channeling force in the technical training of orchestral performers here. Still a third possible placement for the conservatory is suggested by the similarity of its philosophical goals and purposes to those of the government's School of Fine Arts, a dependency of the Institute of Puerto Rican Culture. Both schools are deeply concerned with the development of artistic talent in an appropriately conceived and highly specialized environment with considerably less concern for academic matters. An administrative and programmatic union of the two elements, one specializing in the visual arts and the other in the sonoral arts, would certainly lead to the enrichment of both.

The Casals Festival Corporation and its subsidiaries evolved into their present form over a period of years. Far from springing into perfect life from the inspired vision of Pablo Casals or anyone else, this interrelated complex of enterprises developed through the more or less normal working of political, corporate and public relations forces. It is no more eternal than any other product of human folly and wisdom, and if the time has come to end it in its present awkward form, then it must be ended. A concerned citizenry (if such there be) can only try to insist that the future of the musical entities involved in the reconstruction be better planned than their past was.

Opera de San Juan: *Don Pasquale*

The San Juan Star
July 24, 1979 By Donald Thompson

One thing Puerto Rico does not seem to lack is opera companies. At last count there were seven of them enlivening the island stage with occasional productions of melodious works ranging chronologically from *The Medium* back to *La Serva Padrona* with a lot of Verdi and Puccini in the middle plus now and again *The Merry Widow* and a zarzuela or two. Whether or not there is really a need for seven different companies is another matter; such a multiplicity of effort and fragmentation of interest may reflect more a general state of bullheadedness among opera lovers and company organizers than any realistic response to the market.

How can seven groups even hope to survive, when a prepared market for the product of even one proper company is questionable? The answer is in the term "occasional," for each of the groups can be counted on to put together one—maybe two—productions annually before exhausting its technical and financial resources and running out of theater dates. Between times what they mainly do is recuperate their energies, eye the competition and intrigue for dates in the two more or less adequate theaters which exist in San Juan: the University of Puerto Rico Theater (too big by far) and the Tapia Theater (too small by far).

There have been very healthy signs lately of the beginning of cooperation among the various groups (is it really possible?), under the umbrella of a jointly established Puerto Rico Lyric Theater Company. One can only wish this cooperative venture the best of success, in the meantime trying to sort out the field as each existing lyric company makes its annual splash.

The oldest of the bunch is Opera de San Juan, which as Opera 68 initiated the current wave of home grown opera companies in the late

1960s. Among its many accomplishments, this group has contributed heavily to the development of the island's talent in principal roles during the past decade, in addition to performing a priceless service a year or so ago in putting on the stage a valuable—and previously unknown—work of nineteenth-century Puerto Rican art: *Macías*, by Felipe Gutiérrez Espinosa. Over this past weekend, Opera de San Juan added to its high score by offering in the UPR Theater a thoroughly satisfying production of Donizetti's fluffy masterpiece *Don Pasquale*. Under the general artistic direction of company founder Camelia Ortiz del Rivero a fine cast of principals, all associated in one way or another with Puerto Rico, brought the work to sparkling life.

Antonio Barasorda possesses one of those light tenor voices which seem to float effortlessly on the air. Deceptive, of course, but perfectly suited to the romantic roles in which these envied voices are usually cast. In Saturday's opening performance, Barasorda made a fine impression as Ernesto, the young and (of course) triumphant hero of the piece. His colleague, the conspiratorial Dr. Malatesta, was solidly played by Guillermo Silva-Marín, an island singer who is much too seldom heard here. Norina, the clever heroine in the transparent plot of comic deception, was played by soprano Arlene Randazzo, whose voice took a while on Saturday to come into the light quality required by the role.

But the prize of the production was baritone Abraham Lind-Oquendo in the title role of the flummoxed Pasquale. Lind is not only a first rate singer but an astoundingly gifted actor. Himself a young man, Lind reproduced the entirely sympathetic character of a dotty old suitor without letting his characterization lapse for a second. His playing of Pasquale must certainly be one of the most successful operatic performances to be seen on the wide stage of the UPR Theater in quite some time.

The imaginative stage director of this production is Richard Getke, who has a number of previous San Juan productions to his credit, while the musical director is Rafael Ferrer, well known here as a coach and chorusmaster. Speaking of choruses, Saturday's *Don Pasquale* chorus was one of the best prepared musically and best directed stage-wise to have appeared here for a while. Instead of simply standing around as more or less neutral background, the members of this chorus took on individual and highly comic characteristics, adding greatly to the success of this latest Opera de San Juan production.

Niculescu and Elvira for Pro Arte

The San Juan Star
October 26, 1979 By Donald Thompson

Engaging stellar musical attractions is a bit like investing in next year's wheat crop. Both must be done far ahead in order to get into the market at all, but a lot can happen—and probably will—between the contract and the crop. In the case of the wheat, harvest prices and values can soar, or the bottom can fall out. By the same token, something will probably happen to either greatly raise an artist's market value or to reduce it drastically between the signing of the contract and the opening downbeat months or years later.

The Pro Arte Musical Society made a first class investment in island baritone Pablo Elvira, who appeared here on Sunday with soprano Mariana Niculescu on the venerable concert society's own series. Prior to Elvira's appearance it had become known that he had signed for a number of appearances with the Metropolitan Opera Company, and lo and behold: during the intermission it was announced that he had also accepted a commitment in Chicago. In other words, Elvira's stock is very high just now, and to all appearances can only continue to climb. And for good reason. Here is a musician's musician, a performer who has calmly and carefully built a career on the solid rock of musical intelligence, deep self knowledge and of course, an excellent set of pipes.

Consistent with Pro Arte's recent record in the realm of vocal presentations, the Niculescu-Elvira recital was limited to the most familiar excerpts from the most familiar representatives of the most familiar of all opera repertories: Leoncavallo's *I Pagliacci* and Verdi's *Rigoletto*. This anthology of old favorites certainly offered nothing new in the way of music, but it did provide a welcome opportunity to hear Pablo Elvira again.

Ms. Niculescu, on the other hand, left a mixed set of impressions of her first island visit. Her voice has a deep dramatic quality to it, but I don't think it's well suited to the particular excerpts presented here. In addition, a "covered" quality seemed to affect the clarity of her voice while obscuring her pronunciation. And finally, the constant overuse of certain vocal effects eventually canceled their effectiveness entirely. Among these was the "scoop," in which a singer begins a note somewhat low, then brings it up to pitch as a means of increasing its dramatic intensity. Once or twice in the course of an evening this can be a hair raiser, but the more predictable it becomes the less effective it is, in an inevitable progression of diminishing returns.

Yet at the same time Ms. Niculescu has a great deal going for her; despite the drawbacks which I have pointed out, the UPR Theater resounded with shouts of praise following her presentation of the famous "Caro Nome" from *Rigoletto*.

Soprano **Marta Márquez**, at the time of her 1979 debut in German opera houses.

An Amateur Endeavor

The San Juan Star
February 5, 1980   By Donald Thompson

The Institute of Puerto Rican Culture's Patio Theater provided a showcase on Sunday afternoon for a vocal presentation by XXX, M.D.[1]

Music, like sports, still-life painting, carpentry and whoring, means different things to different people. The professional practitioner will have one vision and one set of responsibilities, the appreciative spectator another, and the hobbyist still another.

Amateur work in any field is apt to be characterized by a specific set of features. First of all, of course, is enthusiasm; amateurs MUST like to do it, for most of us put an awful lot of unnecessary energy into our hobbies. Secondly, and whether it be tennis or home carpentry, amateur work tends to be inconsistent, quirky and ultimately "irresponsible"; i.e., responsible only to the hobbyist's own and perhaps foggy understanding of just what it is he's doing.

This is not to say that all amateur work is bad; in fact, amateur endeavor in many fields has often been of the highest imaginable quality, far outdistancing the average professional product. This is bound to happen once in a while, for the hobbyist's head is not on the block every single time out; he can afford to try that audacious smash, that home-concocted wood stain or that exposed high D, for his career doesn't depend on it. If it works, bravo; if it doesn't, well, it isn't really his field, you know, but he sure tried, didn't he?

The performance of music by amateurs and hobbyists is a much respected tradition going back centuries and accounting, year in and year

---

1. Due to the tenor's amateur status, marginal to the real world of music in Puerto Rico, his name has been deleted.

out, for a great deal of happy music making. Usually, however, this kind of performance takes place in the warm and friendly setting of the home musicale or in the cloistered confines of academe. Only rarely do musical hobbyists become persuaded to offer themselves up on the sacrificial altar of professional musical life, even in Puerto Rico, where the line is not always easy to draw.

The line was easy enough to draw on Sunday, however, for Dr. XXX's case (speaking clinically) displayed all of the classic symptoms of the untrained voice with little prognosis for development in any direction. There is no evident sense of musical phrasing here, while adding to the diagnostic picture is a wobbly and uncontrollable vibrato accompanied by consistently faulty intonation.

Even the basic technical equipment of the beginning singer, the ability to sing scale patterns in tune and rhythmically, is conspicuous by its absence; some mildly difficult passages of this kind on Sunday brought to mind the wail of a physician with his thumb caught in the crank on his examining table.

Maybe I'll offer the good doctor a deal: I'll stop prescribing sure cures out of my herb garden if he'll limit his musical presentations to the salon and the medical convention.

The Culture Bills

The San Juan Star   By Donald Thompson

I. Measure for Measure, for Better or Worse
June 12, 1980

Governor Romero's recent signing of legislation dealing with cultural matters marks an important point—or perhaps an omen—in the development of the arts in Puerto Rico. As usually occurs when important legislation is under consideration or in process, this package of five related bills aroused widespread interest, with the strong polarization of opinion for and against the measures. For better or for worse the culture bills are now law, with the first phases of implementation already being worked out.

The legislation was conceived as a group of five interconnected bills, designed to bring under a central administration a number of cultural ventures which had originated in different government branches and for widely differing purposes over the past quarter century. Some of these creations have outgrown their original purposes, while others have taken on exotic and unforeseen functions. The purposes for which some agencies were created have long ceased to exist, and for a few there may never have been a real need to begin with. In the meantime, new sets of cultural conditions have come into existence in Puerto Rico and no institution or agency is equipped to deal with them. Who, for example, could have foreseen today's vigorous but sporadic and unfocused activity in opera and ballet twenty five years ago? The new legislation creates mechanisms which deliberately allow great flexibility in dealing with these and other cultural manifestations both present and future, while clearly stating that such matters are of common—hence governmental—concern.

This concept is completely foreign to the view built into government on all levels in the United States, but approaches the pattern seen throughout Europe and Latin America. Thus there is irony in the spectacle of a pro-statehood government putting into law a concept of governmental responsibility in the arts which would raise blood pressures in every state legislature from Florida to Hawaii. On the other hand, such a concept would seem perfectly natural to an Austrian or an Argentine, who would only question why it wasn't done sooner and why this legislature stopped short of creating a full fledged cabinet level department of culture and fine arts.

The central bill in the present package creates an Administration for the Development (*Fomento*) of Arts and Culture, whose functions extend over a wide range of activities. These include overseeing many of the island's public libraries and museums, encouraging private ventures in the arts, and coordinating all other governmental programs in fields of arts and culture, including their physical facilities. This central administration is to be governed by a board of nine directors named by the governor of Puerto Rico, through an administrator similarly appointed.

The design is that of an autonomous authority rather than an executive branch, which supposedly removes the agency from direct political intervention while setting it on a serene and unhindered course of cultural and artistic enrichment. The activities and responsibilities of this central administration, except for a few functions dealing with libraries, museums, the channeling of funds and the organizing of literary and artistic competitions, are delegated to a quartet of subsidiary bodies. The creation of these subsidiaries occupies the rest of the new legislative package.

A number of existing governmental programs come to roost here, in a division of structure and hierarchy which was evidently designed to better serve the differing needs of competing organisms. The four subsidiaries are a Corporation of the Puerto Rico Performing Arts Center, a Corporation of the Puerto Rico Symphony Orchestra, a Corporation of the Puerto Rico Conservatory of Music and a Corporation of the Performing Arts (*Artes de la Representación*).

The four units have almost identical administrative structures. Designed as public corporations, all are governed by boards of directors through executive directors. The connections with the central Administration for the Development of Arts and Culture are watertight. The four executive directors and almost all members of the four boards of directors are to be named by the board of directors of the central administration. In addition, the four executive directors plus the head of the central administration are to form a council for the planning and execution of all aspects of the entire apparatus. Finally, the Administration for the Development of Arts and Culture retains a tight hold on all fiscal matters regarding the subsidiary agencies and their programs.

No legislative measure is ever conceived and developed as an isolated inspiration. Instead, new bills usually originate in some kind of pressure or tension, which the legislation is designed to relieve. What pressures and tensions were behind the conception and elaboration of these bills?

First, the existence of cultural entities either hooked onto government at points which made no sense or hanging by a thread of dubious function but great political clout. Some of these anomalies have been mildly embarrassing to the government for years, but no political party in power was ever quite ready to deal with them. Second was the urgency of deciding who was to run the new performing arts center in Santurce. Third was probably the intuitive political knowledge that culture, like motherhood, is usually a fine subject for attention with an election approaching. And fourth may well have been a wish on the part of the party in power to "do something" about the Institute of Puerto Rican Culture, as has been stoutly maintained by opponents of the new legislation.

Setting aside for a moment the question of the Institute of Puerto Rican Culture and its relation to the new laws, what other governmental programs are affected by the legislation?

The Performing Arts Center, a new element in the island's cultural panorama, is of prime importance, for this much needed and long awaited facility will provide the physical focus for much of Puerto Rico's activity in the performing arts. Its three halls will immediately provide relief for such overworked facilities as the UPR Theater and the venerable Tapia Theater. In addition, it will now be possible for the Puerto Rico Symphony Orchestra to move out of its completely unsuitable quarters in Hato Rey. The creation of an administrative framework for the Performing Arts Center was a necessity, and it is probably true that a broader policy base was needed for it than any existing government agency could provide.

The Puerto Rico Symphony Orchestra has long suffered from its administrative placement as a subsidiary of the Casals Festival Corporation, itself a creation of the industrial development branch of government. In fact, the wonder is not that the permanent symphony orchestra has not accomplished more in its twenty-odd years of existence, but that it has survived at all in such a disadvantageous situation. A new administrative placement had to be found for the PRSO, and this is perhaps the best solution. The orchestra's board and management will now be solely, exclusively and very visibly responsible for the development and promotion of the island's major performance entity. In its new placement the orchestra should now enter a new era of accomplishment, service and visibility.

The Puerto Rico Conservatory of Music has been another battered offspring of PRIDCO and the Casals Festival Corporation. This institution was created in the late 1950s to produce instrumentalists for the PRSO and singers for the island's opera and concert life, in much the same way that its parent industrial development program at one time generated welders for the island's construction industry. However, no studies were ever made to determine what the market might be for the music school's product, or if that product would indeed wish to participate in the island's symphonic and vocal activities. As a result of this and other conceptual and operational conditions, the Puerto Rico Conservatory of Music, like its symphonic sister, has had a checkered history as a subsidiary of the Casals Festival Corporation. This new placement might provide the stability which the school has never enjoyed in its original setting.

The fourth member of the quartet of cultural corporations is a catch-all. The Corporation of the Performing Arts includes everything that anyone could think of which was not already accounted for in the other three bills. Here, for example, appears the Compañía de Variedades Artísticas de Puerto Rico, a training school for show-biz talent which was created by the 1973 legislature. Also falling within the responsibility of this fourth public corporation will be the annual Puerto Rico Casals Festival, now shorn of its subsidiaries. Other aspects of this agency's work will be to devise an integral plan for the development of theater, music and dance in Puerto Rico, and to provide "all the aid necessary" to the island's opera, zarzuela, operetta and ballet groups.

II. A LONG LOOK AT THE
INSTITUTE OF PUERTO RICAN CULTURE

June 14, 1980

A great deal of bitter debate surrounded the conception, formulation and signing of the new culture bills, much of it centered on a fear that the new Administration for the Development of Arts and Culture would absorb functions long associated with another government branch, the Institute of Puerto Rican Culture. This concern appears to a great extent justified, for many of the areas staked out by the new bills are fields in which the Institute of Puerto Rican Culture has operated without competition or challenge during the past two decades. This is not to say that such usurpation of functions is necessarily bad; indeed, something like the expected takeover may have been inevitable sooner or later anyway.

The 1955 law which created the Institute of Puerto Rican Culture was clearly concerned with the identification and preservation of specifically Puerto Rican values and cultural manifestations. A quarter century ago there was certainly legitimate reason for such concern. Under Operation Bootstrap a predominantly rural and conservative Puerto Rico was experiencing the first wrenching dislocations of industrialization, a process which brought with it a continuous and heavy barrage of new and heady freedoms, opportunities, pleasures and models. Traditional customs, values and folkways were rapidly disappearing along with what was left of the island's tangible history in the form of archaeological and architectural objects.

It is difficult today to recall the frenzy with which much of Puerto Rico embraced the new economic marvel of industrialization while hastening to rid itself of the old "preindustrial" ways. It was in this atmosphere that the Institute of Puerto Rican Culture was conceived, and the legislation which created it clearly established the limits of its mandate.

The Institute law (June 21, 1955) speaks eloquently of the need to study and preserve the island's folklore, as well as the arts and crafts of popular tradition: "carving and engraving, weaving, embroidering, ceramics, leathercraft and other activities of like nature." A second point of concern was with the preservation of historic buildings and the regulation of construction in historic zones. Third came an interest in publication, with particular mention of Puerto Rican history and biography.

Nowhere are the performing arts mentioned or implied; the clear message is of a measure designed to preserve the tangible objects and the folk-handicraft traditions of a rapidly disappearing age of innocence.

The Institute of Puerto Rican Culture later branched out into many different fields unforeseen and unimagined by the legislature which created it. Among these ventures the most successful was a program designed to aid the island's theater movement, a movement which in the mid '50s was practically limited to activities at the University of Puerto Rico. Another successful thrust led the Institute into the sophisticated visual arts via graphics, in a sense continuing some of the valuable work of the Division of Community Education. Meanwhile, the Institute's music program called attention to the production of island composers and offered performance opportunities to island musicians during a long period when the government's more prestigious concert agencies studiously and as a matter of policy ignored the island's own music.

No one can deny that the contributions of the Institute of Puerto Rican Culture to the development of the arts have been both numerous and important. However, they have been limited by the available resources and, more importantly, by a governing concept. While expanding into new fields right and left, the Institute has, at least in its doctrine, observed one aspect of its mandate: that the focus of its efforts be recognizably Puerto Rican. Long after the original point had been made, reinforced and nailed down—that traditional island values were in dire need of documentation and preservation—the agency remained theoretically tied to the promotion of specifically island forms and styles, island works and island-born performers. Only through logic bending and verbal waffling was it possible for the Institute to justify its incursions into world art, as contrasted to native art: special international festivals of rather ordinary non-Puerto Rican theater, special series of standard Spanish and Latin American concert music, and exceptional events during which an occasional non-native performer might be more or less legitimately presented. In other words, the Institute of Puerto Rican Culture's operational programs have over the years expanded into fields which the agency has never been equipped by design or by conceptual frame to serve.

What then of the relation between the Institute of Puerto Rican Culture and the new Administration for the Development of Arts and Culture? In an attempt to calm the heated opposition to the new legislation, the culture bills underwent almost continual cobbling and patching as their preparation and debate progressed. In the final version the Institute and its programs are explicitly excluded from the authority of the new administration. In addition, the interests of the Institute of Puerto Rican Culture are supposedly protected by devices which provide close contact between the two agencies at several levels of policy and decision making.

Despite these connections, it can be expected that when push comes to shove over the funding of the competing agencies, matters of "general" culture will be favored in the Administration for Arts and Culture. Matters of specifically "indigenous" culture, on the other hand, will probably continue to get the nod within the Institute of Puerto Rican Culture. Because of these pressures the latter agency may see its functions gradually trimmed back to something resembling the specifications of its original mandate. It may also discover for itself some new ways to deepen and fortify its very real commitment to the investigation and preservation of the island's indigenous cultural heritage.

Quite apart from whatever real effect the new laws might have on the island's arts and culture, one aspect of their implementation is mind-boggling: the bureaucracy which by law must be created before the machine can even crank out a *pas-de-deux*. For openers, a total of 37 seats on the various boards of directors are to be filled by the governor of Puerto Rico or by people named by the governor. Naturally, each board will need its own secretariat and staff, while each of the top administrators created by the legislation must be provided with his own stable of assistants and office help. A personnel office (if not several) must be created as well as finance and payroll divisions. Then, provision will have to be made for transportation, entertainment and public relations activities on all administrative levels. And finally the operational levels can be staffed and some concerts and art shows organized—if there's any money left.

Many opponents of this legislation have expressed the fear that the new agencies will deliberately suppress the finest expressions of Puerto Rican values and Puerto Rican traditions in favor of some kind of "universal" values. These "universal" values, it is argued, will somehow be of greater use in perpetuating the political grip of the party in power than would be the promotion of purely "native" traditions. A thorough study of the five culture bills raises the question of whether this is really the problem. Indeed, the problem may simply be whether any culture at all can survive the massive governmental attention which is soon to be lavished upon it. Enthusiasts of the new bills envision the 1980s as the Era of the Arts in Puerto Rico. However, the coming decade might turn out to be only the Era of the Arts Bureaucracy in Puerto Rico, a very different thing.

Bravos to Alonso and Orchestra

The San Juan Star
June 22, 1980   By Francis Schwartz

"Casals Festival Strikes Back" aptly describes the Wednesday night Casals Festival concert which finally packed the University of Puerto Rico theater. After stumbling along with attendance more worthy of the Mona Island concert series than an international event, the programming of a guitar concerto plus a Tchaikovsky symphony under the baton of a well known conductor brought the general public to Río Piedras.

Spanish conductor Odón Alonso led the festival orchestra in the Roman Carnival Overture by Hector Berlioz. This exquisitely orchestrated work was given a solid, imaginatively colored interpretation. Alonso obviously inspired his colleagues and a genuine enthusiasm emanated from the orchestra. A fine opening.

Joaquín Rodrigo's Concierto de Aranjuez is undoubtedly the most popular of twentieth-century guitar concertos. Its rhythmic and melodic elements, clearly rooted in the Iberian musical past, are easily accessible to the general public since the composer shunned the more radical compositional techniques of his era.

On this occasion, the soloist was Carlos Barbosa-Lima, a Brazilian guitarist. Whoever decided to electronically amplify Barbosa's guitar in such an incompetent manner should be locked in a spaceship with Darth Vader. The distortions that belched forth from the two large speakers disastrously affected the performance. We personally favor the judicious use of contemporary electronic means to "equalize natural imbalances of sound," but how is it possible that in an international festival there were no plans to correct the potential difficulties that arise from the use of electronics in live concerts? Even amateur music makers are sensible enough to take such precautions!

We cannot know how much this comedy of errors bothered Barbosa-Lima, but it certainly must have be upsetting for him. He was obviously very tense and played unevenly. While he is a fluent, expressive performer, there were mishaps in the passage work and the sound produced was very taut and diminutive. Having heard this fine musician on previous occasions, we hope to hear him in more felicitous circumstances.

After intermission, Odón Alonso conducted an emotionally charged version of Tchaikovsky's Sixth Symphony, the "Pathétique." His feel for the big structural line and his ever present dramatic flair inspired the orchestra. The result was highly enjoyable. Bravo to him and the players.

Second Biennial at Midpoint

The San Juan Star
September 17, 1980 By Donald Thompson

Works, styles and performers proliferated richly as Puerto Rico's Second Biennial of Twentieth Century Music reached its recent midpoint. The series has continued to spread out geographically as well, extending all the way down to the Carnegie Library's pleasant Old San Juan hall for an afternoon of chamber music. Performers on this occasion were visiting oboist Germán Cáceres (to appear later in the series as a composer as well), pianist Mildred Bou and clarinetist Genesio Riboldi. In different combinations this worthy trio led a retrospective stroll down some almost forgotten twentieth-century musical byways.

Principal works were from the solid German repertory: the 1938 Sonata for Oboe and Piano by Paul Hindemith and one of Max Reger's three sonatas for clarinet and piano. Hindemith is a known quantity, and at least part of an audience today can be expected to have heard some of his music. Tidy, neat, buttoned down and beautifully crafted, this oboe sonata is a good example of Hindemith's much admired music of the period when he apparently set out to compose solo sonatas for all instruments.

Reger, on the other hand, is known mainly as a footnote in music history textbooks and as the subject of oblique references on record jackets. Consequently his music, on its rare performances, arouses great interest. When it comes it hits you like a baseball bat, for here, you feel, is the culminating point of nineteenth-century German instrumental music: Brahms carried into the twentieth century! Hindemith went farther, and in fact tipped over the edge into new territory, but Reger is the endpoint of the older line: solid, sober, expansive and with his roots in the Germanic stream from Bach on down.

A sampling of American music (South, Central, Caribbean and North) brought to the theater of the Puerto Rico Conservatory of Music a mixed bag of twentieth-century musical items ranging from the late '50s down to a week or so ago. Included were works by Luis Manuel Álvarez, Esther Alejandro, Jack Délano and Ernesto Cordero (Puerto Rico), Paul Arma (Hungary-U.S.-France), Germán Cáceres (El Salvador), Manuel Simó (Dominican Republic) and Walter Ross (U.S.). With most of the composers present in the hall, this event took on the pleasant atmosphere of a professional get together, which in fact is one of the purposes of any kind of festival . . . but that's another story.

What about the music itself? Musical composition in Puerto Rico has made great strides during the past decade, impelled almost exclusively by the same figures who have organized these two biennial observances. Island representatives in the present sampling held up well, displaying a pretty fair level of skill on the whole plus a wide range of means and purposes. Esther Alejandro's Two Songs offered an interesting alternation of recitative and song along with sometimes witty effects provided by bassoon and prepared piano. Ernesto Cordero's Three Songs and Jack Délano's Flute Sonata displayed the stylization of island folk elements in concert form which is still an important thread in Puerto Rican concert music, thankfully far removed by now from the pretentious and naive, romanticizing Latin American concert music of a few decades ago. Délano is especially skilled in this matter; his witty stylizations of island rhythms (as in the final movement of this work) remain the most successful concert usages of island folk material going.

Luis Manuel Álvarez' Three New Alvaradas, for solo guitar, carry this stylizing process a few steps farther—but in reverse. The first two Alvaradas (a term based on the composer's surname combined with *alborada*, or sunrise serenade) are completely abstract presentations of percussive sounds drawn from the guitar's sounding parts. Only in the third Alvarada are we privileged to learn the source of these rhythms: a completely conventional guitar piece composed in the melodious mountain style. Germán Cáceres and Manuel Simó were represented by string quartet music, the former by a fully developed recent three-movement work and the latter by a brief romantic movement only, extracted from a 1950 composition. Both works showed a high degree of skill in composition; Simó is of course no beginner but a widely recognized figure, while the Cáceres quartet displays solid training and good understanding of the traditional string quartet idiom. Yet the impression of both works suffered from under-rehearsal, an illness which happily has not been widespread in these concerts.

A brilliant stroke of programming (or was it, in keeping with the tenets of the avant-garde, pure chance?) placed Walter Ross' Prelude, Fugue and Big Apple at the end of the concert. For bass trombone and electronic tape, this graceful piece is an extremely imaginative demonstration of the integration of electronically and conventionally produced sound. And for the whistlers, there were even tunes to whistle on leaving the hall.

Able performers for this sampling were sopranos Aura Robledo and Diana Villafañe, flutists Peter Kern and Rubén López, guitarists Ernesto Cordero and Leonardo Egúrbida, pianists María Teresa Acevedo and Francis Schwartz, bassoonist Félix Febo, trombonist Aldo Torres, violinists Kachiro and Narciso Figueroa, violist Francisco Figueroa and cellist Joaquín Vidaechea.

Patio Theater Concerts Regain Dignity

The San Juan Star
October 5, 1980 By Donald Thompson

When a pollution problem is solved along a public beach, it is only proper that the warning signs be removed so that swimmers may know that it's now safe to enter the surf. The same principle applies to concert life, and music lovers can now be advised that the serious traffic problem has been solved at the Patio Theater of the Institute of Puerto Rican Culture. As a result, artists are no longer distracted and seated patrons' feet mashed by latecomers entering the hall and groping for seats during the playing of a composition. With this measure the Institute concerts have regained their former level of concentration and dignity, and can again be recommended for both the toe dabbler and the total immersion music lover.

Saturday's offering on the Institute series was a solo guitar recital by Ana María Rosado. Ms. Rosado is the product of first rate island training plus advanced technical work in Europe. In addition, she brings to her task the inquiring mind of a scholar; her recently completed work on the classical guitar in Puerto Rico will take its place among the most accurate and most useful sources of information on the island's music. Ms. Rosado's program included some works which she had played on the recently concluded Biennial of Twentieth Century Music, but they sounded much better in the Patio Theater than they had at the Ateneo. Of this batch, especially impressive were Falla's Homage to Debussy and a set of études by the noted Cuban composer Leo Brouwer. Brouwer is an extraordinary guitarist himself, and these six brief studies could not have been better conceived for his instrument.

Fantasías Amazónicas, by Francis Schwartz, is a programmatic sort of guitar piece which my concert companion found strikingly evocative of creepy jungly things. Nice, I suppose, if that's what you look for in music. Also offered were some selections from the more traditional guitar repertory, for example Fernando Sor's charming Variations on a Theme by Mozart.

Last Sunday afternoon's Patio Theater concert seemed like a continuation of the recent Biennial, for it consisted exclusively of twentieth-century music. Excellent performers were violinist Hans Christian Siegert and pianist Klaus Borner, who also offered from the stage some useful information on some of the unusual music presented. It's uncanny how things work out. Bartók's Sonata No. 2 for Violin and Piano was one of the key works on the Biennial; its companion, the Sonata No. 1, appeared here two weeks later in a fine performance by Siegert and Borner. Siegert played Xenakis' startling *Mikka*, for solo violin: one of the opening Biennial concerts featured a version for solo viola of the same fascinating piece. Maybe there's a message here....

Especially interesting on Sunday was a violin sonata by a young German composer, Gunter Schillings. As Siegert explained from the stage, the current generation of German composers has extended its vision far beyond the fashions of the recent avant-garde, reaching out, as it were, toward some kind of contact with the older, "expressive" modes. This well-made work is a case in point, for if it must be categorized with a specific adjective, it would have to be "neo-romantic!" Also offered were works by a West African composer, Akin Euba; by the Brazilian Claudio Santoro; and the familiar Suite of Popular Spanish Songs by Manuel de Falla.

Northerners are apt to treat Hispanic music as they do Beethoven, Sibelius, Britten and Schoenberg: quite literally and with a great deal of respect. There is nothing wrong with this approach, of course, and we often long for a little more of this literalness and respect in island performances. Still, it is unusual to hear Falla's music played so politely. It's almost as if this fine duo somehow missed the point of these gutsy pieces. Aside from this minor (and admittedly debatable) stylistic point, this Siegert-Borner recital was a valuable addition to the San Juan concert season, while its timing could not have been better.

Marina

The San Juan Star
October 9, 1980 By Donald Thompson

You say you've never heard of Spanish opera? Well, there's a favorite one playing at the Tapia Theater these weekends, so if you hurry on down to Old San Juan you might learn something and spend a pleasant evening at the same time—always a welcome combination. The work is *Marina*, by Pascual Juan Emilio Arrieta y Corera (better known as Emilio Arrieta), and its present production is by the Puerto Rican Foundation of Zarzuela and Operetta.

Spanish opera has experienced many fits and starts since the seventeenth century, each time beginning from scratch and always looking over its shoulder. Each time around, everyone involved has been painfully conscious of opera's origin and almost monopolistic development on that other peninsula a thousand miles or so to the east, and almost pathologically sensitive to comparison. Like almost everything else in Spain, native opera has from time to time become the subject of violent controversy. Some writers used to maintain that the cause itself was absurd: that Spaniards had too much good sense to accept anything so stupid as operatic recitative on the stage. Others claimed that it was simply a matter of finding the right combination of elements from high art and popular culture. Still others believed that the native zarzuela could be developed to become the Spanish equivalent of opera. And finally, around the 1860s the idea became current that all you had to do was convert the spoken scenes of a romantic zarzuela to recitative and ZAP! You'd have instant Spanish opera!

Returning to Spain from studies (and complete musical saturation) in Italy, young Emilio Arrieta fell into the middle of this shifty battle. *Marina* was first performed as a two-act zarzuela in 1855. Enlarged to three acts and with music substituted for spoken dialogue, the transmogrified work reappeared in 1871 as opera, featuring the renowned Enrico Tamberlick in the tenor role.

The problem of Spanish opera has not only never been solved, but you might say it has lost some of its burning urgency of a century ago. In fact, nobody cares much any more at all. In the meantime it is questionable whether the Arrieta work in particular benefitted from the change from zarzuela to opera, but at least it wasn't harmed by any. *Marina*, either way, is a cheerful piece of mid-century Italian lyric theater, set, costumed and languaged in Spain and presently offered here by a cast made up of the island's leading zarzuela forces.

The Tamberlick role, Jorge, is played here by Elio Rubio, whose lyric qualities suit the part very nicely. Opposite him in the title role is Migdalia Batiz, who continues to rack up performances as probably the island's most steadily working soprano. Opening night of this production found her voice a bit harsh on top, with a slight tendency to wander off pitch at climactic moments of expression. Baritone Héctor López continues to develop both as a singer and as an actor; in this work he makes a solid impression in the supporting role of Pascual. The most lasting opening night impression, however, was made by baritone Rafael Torréns as the hero's cynical buddy, Roque. This is the sort of stock role which easily slips over the edge into exaggeration and general hamminess; furthermore, the audience rather expects this. Torréns played it close to that edge, but never quite succumbed to the temptation. In addition to qualities of a good actor, Torréns also has a fine and well placed voice. An opening night dividend was the fact that of the entire cast, his were the only sung texts which were always clearly understood.

For this second offering in the brief season of the Puerto Rican Foundation of Zarzuela and Operetta, the musical director is Ramón Bastida and the stage director José Luis Marrero, while the large chorus was prepared by Bartolomé Bover.

The Indestructible *Danza*

The San Juan Star
October 29, 1980   By Donald Thompson

    The Puerto Rican *danza* is a resilient form of music which originated in the salons of mid-nineteenth-century island society. Originally dance music in the style of the contradanza, the waltz and other forms of contemporaneous social music, the *danza* soon received the romantic influence of European concert music conceived for the piano; the same forces which shaped and were in turn shaped by the music of Chopin. In no time the *danza* became stylized into an elegant small scale species of art music itself, not necessarily intended to be danced at all. The best *danzas* of all subsequent periods have retained this elegance, along with a goodly portion of musical wit and (in the ones written for piano, at any rate) a surprising level of difficulty. For islanders, this music is surrounded by an aura of associations and beliefs, not all accurate but all stoutly held. In many ways the *danza* is alive and well today.

    The University of Puerto Rico Cultural Activities office recently brought off another of its own superproductions, this time a three-part anthology of the Puerto Rican *danza*. Ordinarily, this office devotes its energy to the presentation of ready made attractions, in the form of programs by traveling performers. Rarely does this agency assume the difficult role of producer, conceiving and assembling a tailor-made product for its audience of university people and subscribers.

    Some historic examples of this occasional in-house activity were a concert version of Bernstein's *West Side Story* (1973), a production of Weill's *Threepenny Opera* combining the efforts of the UPR Music and Drama departments a few years later, and of course the mind-boggling *COSMOS* of last May, which involved everything from the UPR Brass Ensemble to the Water Ballet and a pneumatic drill.

The recent Danza Anthology drew large and enthusiastic audiences to the UPR Theater. Key elements were the fine UPR Chorus, conducted by Carmen Acevedo, an orchestra conducted by Lito Peña, pianist Pedro Rojas and several other performers and ensembles. Among the many stylistic points of view brought to bear on the *danza*, the most interesting to this listener were those of two small ensembles. One of these, a traditional guitar trio headed by Leocadio Vizcarrondo, almost made the danza sound like folk music—almost but not quite, for whatever else it might be, folk music it is not. The other, a trio of first rate musicians from the Guayacán group, offered extremely trim and sophisticated arrangements of traditional material, but with far out harmonies and a great deal of musical wit.

The big news, however, was pop singer Danny Rivera, whose wildly applauded offerings were distributed throughout the entire evening. Some of these were musically convincing, but many were not. Farthest off base and painfully inappropriate were his "interpretations" (I think that's the best term) of the nineteenth-century *danzas* of Tavárez and Morel Campos. This music is the precise and elegant expression of a particular historical period, and its presentation requires not the blues shouting style of a pop singer but the precise touch of a concert artist. Imagine Louis Armstrong belting out a Schubert song, and you'll have an idea of the stylistic conflict built into Rivera's presentation of this material.

On the other hand, the more recent and less tidy the basic material became, the more acceptable Rivera's presentations seemed. "Verde Luz," a recent commercial-pop kind of tune distantly related to the *danza*, was completely convincing, for here the style suited the material.

A narration of mixed historical and sentimental notes tied the whole thing together, delivered by actor Miguel Ángel Suárez. As for the presentation itself and the idea behind it, it proved three things: (1) it is still possible to fill the UPR Theater several nights running: (2) it is possible for Academe to put a winning act together; and (3) the Puerto Rican *danza* is quite hardy, perhaps even indestructible.

A Plenitude of Pluckers

The San Juan Star
December 14, 1980   By Donald Thompson

There were guitars and guitarists for all seasons and all reasons as the First Puerto Rico International Guitar Festival unfolded its offerings over a recent two week period. Events included the expected proportion of public solo recitals by recognized international virtuosos and established island artists. In addition, through careful planning and coordination it was possible to intersect with the schedule of the Puerto Rico Symphony Orchestra for one very successful concert, and with other island agencies for a wide variety of co-sponsored activities.

Geographically, this Guitarathon spread out from the wilds of Orocovis to the cozy confines of the Institute of Puerto Rican Culture's Patio Theater in Old San Juan, creating an ambulatory guild of guitarists and guitar enthusiasts which took on some of the characteristics of a serenade. Along the way, crusaders and others received the benefit of several stimulating lectures on one or another aspect of guitar history, three series of master classes with some of today's leading performers and an international competition for young artists.

Solo recitalists included Manuel Barrueco (Cuba-U.S.), Leonardo Egúrbida (Puerto Rico), Angel Romero (Spain) and Juan Sorroche (Puerto Rico), with a special recital by Puerto Rican mandolinist Gustavo Batista. Venezuelan virtuoso Alirio Díaz appeared with the PRSO under the direction of Roselín Pabón, offering works by Joaquín Rodrigo and Ernesto Cordero, and Ana María Rosado (Puerto Rico) provided live illustrations for an absorbing lecture by Robert Vidal (France) on the history of the guitar.

A plenitude of pluckers, you might say, and that's not the end of it. A principal attraction of this festival was a competition which drew performers from Puerto Rico, the United States, Canada and Panama. Extending over a period of three days, the competition was gradually reduced to five finalists, then two winners. Walking away (or rather flying away) with top honors and the prize money were Matt Klassen (Canada) and Stephen Pearson (U.S.), both of whom showed high promise as artists on this demanding instrument.

Lectures dealing with one or another aspect of the guitar were surprise dividends in this already full round of activities. Outstanding Puerto Rican guitar maker Manuel Velázquez spoke of the development of his craft here, and Juan Helguera (Mexico) offered information on that strange figure of the guitar world, Agustín Barrios.

Yes, there was plenty of good news coming out of this First Puerto Rico International Guitar Festival, but some bad news too. The good news resulted from the high quality of the participants and the immeasurable time and energy invested by the local organizers. The bad news resulted, as it often does here, from our chronic understaffing of the organizing and administrative forces plus the usual hazards of a pioneer enterprise. In an attempt to cover all bases of support and save a buck at the same time, the management canceled out a great deal of the artistic merit of two of its own main events. The Barrueco and Romero events, conceived as solo recitals, became trio recitals instead, the accompanists being a TV camera and its operator sharing the stage at arm's length from the soloist. Neither soloist nor audience could concentrate on the matter at hand under these circumstances, while the special lighting required to get the events on videotape made it difficult to see the performers for the glare.

Another bit of bad news was the printed program, which had skipped some phases of proofreading and correction. This is a pity, for long after this festival is forgotten, the printed programs will be lurking in libraries as reminders of the quaint ways of the concert business here in the early 1980s. There are also a few mysteries planted for future researchers in the pages of this program. Think of the months some graduate student will spend trying to identify the University of Puerto Rican Culture, an agency listed among the festival's principal benefactors.

On the whole, however, this event seems to have accomplished its purpose to a great extent: to bring together, on an international level, a number of eminent guitarists, guitar enthusiasts, guitar students and other guitar people for a couple of weeks of intense concentration on . . . what else? The guitar.

Pabón Conducts Self, Orchestra Well

The San Juan Star
January 22, 1981 (a)   By Donald Thompson

    For the past year and a half, Roselín Pabón has filled the new post of assistant conductor of the Puerto Rico Symphony Orchestra. In a way, any assistant conductor's job is like that of the Vice President of the United States. The main function of both incumbents is to simply exist; to be there and ready if needed to jump in during some dire emergency. Such an emergency, if not unthinkable, is certainly unspeakable in normal circumstances: the sudden and serious indisposition of The Man. Meanwhile, an assistant conductor, like a vice president, handles the routine and mainly invisible tasks which he is assigned, keeps himself up on things just in case, and generally maintains a low profile. This last is especially important, for in arts politics as in party politics, The Man is not likely to favor any signs of what he may perceive as uppityness (or even independent expression) on the part of Number Two. It is for this reason that assistant conductors rarely become titular conductors of their own orchestras: the prudent ones never become well enough known to their orchestra's governing boards to even be considered when a vacancy occurs up top, while the imprudent ones are already long gone and out of the running.
    Roselín Pabón, Number Two of the Puerto Rico Symphony Orchestra, is the product of early training at the Mayagüez Free School of Music, excellent university and graduate level work on the continent, and some high powered piano study with such figures as Jesús María Sanromá and Francis Schwartz. During the first part of his tenure here Pabón has conducted many educational and pops concerts, made the expected run-outs to island towns, studied new works continuously and kept up his repertory in the wings according to what is being prepared by the

PRSO. Occasionally he has had a major concert to conduct, and on these occasions has unfailingly done fine work. All considered, Pabón has calmly and efficiently gone about his business in a potentially problematical job, earning for himself a high measure of professional respect and public regard in the process.

On Saturday evening Pabón confirmed this general impression of his work, conducting the Puerto Rico Symphony Orchestra in a concert dedicated to the memory of the late Miguel Besosa. Besosa was a talented flutist who for many years fought the good musical fight as a member of the PRSO and an active participant in many other artistic ventures here. Fittingly enough, Saturday's concert was built around flute music, with the orchestra's excellent present flutists Peter Kern and Rubén López as soloists. López' vehicle was the B Minor Suite for Flute and Strings of Bach, while Kern offered a charming concerto for flute and orchestra by Jacques Ibert. This latter is a tricky and fully characteristic piece of French music from the 1930s, complete with the bittersweet harmonies and jazzy touches of that period. Both López and Kern played their solo parts with skill and grace, again demonstrating the enormous range of style and expression of which the flute is capable. Also appearing in Saturday's concert was an unusual work of Brahms, the early Serenade for Strings and Winds, which does surprisingly well, thank you, without violins. And as a memorial touch, the orchestra played a work by Miguel Besosa himself: the melodious concert danza "Pasión Eterna." To many of Besosa's friends and colleagues, this work brought to light a previously unknown and welcome facet of the late musician's talents.

Mezzo Isales, One of the Island's Finest Talents

The San Juan Star
January 22, 1981 (b)   By Donald Thompson

Mezzosoprano Darysabel Isales is one of Puerto Rico's finest musical talents, and one who has steadily expanded her professional horizons over the years. Unlike many singers, who tend to cultivate a limited repertory of sure-fire hits from the operatic or song repertory (rarely both), Ms. Isales has extended her considerable gifts into areas undreamed of by most of her colleagues. From *The Marriage of Figaro* to *Pedro Navaja*, from Mahler songs to *Il Tabarro*, from TV commercials to oratorio: whatever this artist does she does well. As a result she is one of very few singers here who can really claim to be making a career of it.

On Sunday afternoon, Ms. Isales offered a recital in the Patio Theater of the Institute of Puerto Rican Culture. About half of the program was occupied by a set of Schubert songs, where her dramatic gifts and vast stage experience contributed to a beautifully expressive but always appropriately controlled presentation. Also offered were brief works by Juan Morel Campos, Enrique Granados, Pietro Mascagni and Narciso Figueroa. These last were a suite of melodies from the island's rich store of children's songs in interesting and more or less modern harmonic garb. In Sunday's concert, Ms. Isales' work benefitted from the invaluable collaboration of pianist Cecilia Talavera, one of Puerto Rico's most able and most perceptive practitioners of the accompanist's art.

Pedro Navaja: Musical Satire Sets High Note

The San Juan Star
January 31, 1981   By Donald Thompson

It should come as news to nobody by now that *La Verdadera Historia de Pedro Navaja*, rapidly approaching its hundredth performance in the Sylvia Rexach Theater, is one of the most successful works of musical theater ever to be produced here. As a benign satire on island society, politics and mores of the 1950s (and in many ways, of today as well), *Pedro Navaja* has taken an honored place in Puerto Rican theater. Not only that, but it continues to attract a paying public week after week, many of whose members are seeing the work for the third, fourth or fifth time. The piece is, you might say, a hit.

Pedro Navaja, an original production by Teatro del Sesenta, fits into a specific line of lyric theater history stretching back more than 250 years: a line which has generated innumerable stage works while contributing directly or indirectly to the development of many types of opera and allied species over the centuries. It all began with John Gay's satirical play with music, entitled *The Beggars' Opera*, produced in London in 1728. Gay's idea, perhaps motivated by an offhand remark by the great satirist Dean Swift, was to hold up a theatrical mirror to contemporaneous London society—but to show the backside, as it were, instead of the front. The form of *The Beggars' Opera* was more or less operatic, but the plot and the personages were taken from London lowlife: thieves, whores and hustlers. Some seventy catchy musical numbers, chosen from pop tunes and dance music, were arranged for a miniature orchestra by the noted musician Johann Pepusch, with Gay's new texts to be sung by normal actors instead of the often outrageous opera singers of the period. The twin messages were very clear: (1) The conventions of the serious Italian opera of the period were ridiculously artificial, and (2) at both ends of the social scale, human motivations are apt to be the same—and equally despicable.

The Beggars' Opera ran for 63 performances, establishing a theater record in London and launching a new species of lyric theater on the world: the ballad opera. The ballad opera continued on its way, to influence the development of native forms of lyric theater all over Europe and America, while *The Beggars' Opera* itself has continued to turn up in one guise or another during the subsequent two centuries and a half. One important offshoot, the Bert Brecht-Kurt Weill *Dreigroschenoper*, appeared as a gloomy portent in Berlin in 1928, setting into motion a separate line of development entirely. This line has led to translations and adaptations in all modern languages, but mainly retaining Brecht's often foggy political message and Weill's mordant music. For example, a bland and bowdlerized English-language version has played since 1955 as *The Threepenny Opera*, while the *Opera de Dos Centavos* is widely known in Spanish America in a version which originated in Buenos Aires.

The immediate predecessor in Puerto Rico of the entirely new *Pedro Navaja* was a production of *Opera de Dos Centavos* by the UPR music and drama departments together with the same institution's office of cultural activities in 1975. Until that time only Weill's famous "Mack the Knife" tune had been known here, and at that in commercial ballad or nightclub bolero style, completely isolated from its theatrical and political context. The complete UPR production, based on the Buenos Aires version but with some local adjustments in the street language used, left a lasting impression in island theatrical (if not political) circles.

La Verdadera Historia de Pedro Navaja, then, is no isolated inspiration but a new work of island theater with an impeccable literary pedigree and rooted in an extremely important musical tradition. Instead of in Hogarth's London, with undertones of depression-wracked Berlin, the new work is set in the San Juan of the early 1950s, with the *Beggars' Opera* and *Dreigroschenoper* messages brought up to date in Pablo Cabrera's extremely witty and profoundly appropriate book. The only basic alteration, in fact, is a change in the entertainment medium satirized. The work's principal predecessors were aimed at the conventions of serious Italian opera; *Pedro Navaja* explicitly satirizes the equally absurd conventions of today's TV soap operas. All the way down the line, Cabrera's characters are the modern *barrio* equivalents of John Gay's and Bert Brecht's lowlife but thoroughly bourgeois Londoners. The *mamito* Navaja is a direct descendant of the highwayman MacHeath, while his three main sweeties are the sisters of Gay's and Brecht's females. Cabrera's secondary characters as well are the direct reincarnations of the earlier ones, while the entire work is seeded with scholarly inside jokes in text and staging which vibrate across the centuries. In this sense *Pedro Navaja* exists on two or three different levels simultaneously, and is perfectly delightful on any one of them.

Having heard that the orchestral part to the musical numbers of *Pedro Navaja* was on tape instead of rising from an orchestra pit full of living instrumentalists, I went to the theater prepared to break up a few rows of seats in protest against what I could only conceive as a shameless violation of everything that's holy in lyric theater. I was sure that the taped sound would be bad, that the singers' voices would never synchronize with the tape, that there would be terrible problems of distortion, and that a critical element of theatrical flexibility and spontaneity would be missing—to say nothing of the somehow reassuring figure of a conductor waving his arms in the pit. Well, friends, I was wrong. The taped music rolls convincingly out of a juke box on the stage, the quality of the recording and reproduction is excellent, the talented actors of *Pedro Navaja* seem to have no trouble synchronizing with the tape, and as for a conductor, . . . who needs one?

The music of *Pedro Navaja*, except for the title tune by Rubén Blades, is by Pedro Rivera Toledo. This talented musician was also responsible for the rich and varied orchestral arrangements and for getting it all on tape. In the tradition of Pepusch and Weill, Rivera Toledo has used only the most familiar styles and species of popular music, and always with the most diabolically appropriate instrumentation: the tango, bolero, mambo, cha-cha, seis and romantic ballad, for example. In the Sunday evening performance which I recently attended, the fine cast of singing actors (and acting singers) included José Félix Gómez, Darysabel Isales, Manolo González, Ruth Goa, Freddy de Arce, Roxana Badillo, Idalia Pérez Garay, José Muratti, Ramón Saldaña and a first rate group of supporting actors and dancers. In music and dance as well as in theatrical literature, Teatro del Sesenta's present production of *La Verdadera Historia de Pedro Navaja*, directed by Pablo Cabrera, establishes a very high mark in Puerto Rico's passing cultural parade.

Gary Karr, Double Bass Virtuoso

The San Juan Star
February 4, 1981 (a)   By Donald Thompson

The present musical season has made of San Juan a focus of virtuoso double bass playing, while planting the seeds of what can only be important future developments in this art. Last fall the second Puerto Rico Biennial of Twentieth Century Music presented the strikingly innovative soloist Bertram Turetzky in a series of concert and television appearances, and last week the astonishing virtuoso Gary Karr was here for a round of varied activities. The cumulative effect of such visits, added to these particular artists' generous willingness to meet and exchange ideas with their local colleagues, can only result in a higher level of skill and perceptiveness on the part of performers here, as well as greater awareness and knowledge on the part of audiences.

The main event on Karr's San Juan itinerary was an appearance as soloist with the Puerto Rico Symphony Orchestra. However, a set of seminars and demonstrations at different centers, preceding Friday's climactic concert, were extremely interesting to double bass players, composers, and students and teachers of all other musical disciplines as well. On Friday afternoon, for example, the UPR Music Department began to look like the site of an elephants' convention as bass players, mostly accompanied by their instruments, gathered for an informal and highly illuminating session of musicians' talk with Gary Karr. First, for the edification of the non-specialists present, Karr explored a bit of double bass history as it has affected the instrument's shape, tuning and playing technique. Then, after warming up with a couple of staggeringly difficult solo pieces, Karr was joined by UPR bass instructor Federico Silva for a hilarious duo of pop tunes, some of which were to turn up as encores on the Symphony Orchestra concert that evening.

Most of Karr's phenomenal success as a traveling and recording soloist is due, of course, to his absolute and almost inconceivable mastery of the double bass and everything connected with it. Playing a musical instrument even halfway decently—and especially this one—is not supposed to be easy. It may not be all that easy for Gary Karr, either, but he certainly makes it seem so; so easy, in fact, that he has energy and concentration left over for a bit of fun at the same time.

Friday evening's PRSO concert, before a full house in the theater of the Puerto Rico Conservatory of Music, was conducted by John Barnett, and featured Karr as soloist in two major works for double bass and orchestra. The first of these was a Concerto in A Major by Domenico Dragonetti (1763-1846). Dragonetti was an early virtuoso on the big fiddle himself, and wrote a great deal of music for his own appearances as a soloist. This concerto is characteristic of the species: not overburdened with purely musical merit (thematic development, imaginative orchestration, etc.) but certainly an excellent vehicle for demonstrating the capabilities of the solo instrument, to say nothing of the capabilities of the soloist. Karr made the big instrument sing through the extended range required by this music, and tossed off Dragonetti's almost insanely difficult passagework like a piece of cake. Also presented was Karr's own transcription for double bass and orchestra of the "Moses" Fantasy of Paganini. This was originally a virtuoso piece for violin based on Rossini and composed for Paganini's own use, and Karr has transferred it to the larger instrument with only minor changes. The result is awesome, but it took a bass player in Friday's audience to adequately state the position. An astounded music lover observed that Karr had made the bass sound like a violin in the Paganini work, whereupon the musician countered, "No; he made it sound like a bass, playing violin music better than most violinists can play it!"

Karr's island visit will be remembered for his splendid performance with the Puerto Rico Symphony Orchestra, but also for the great sense of humanity and professionalism which he demonstrated in sharing with island musicians his insights and experiences on the level of friendly interchange. This, too, is the sign of a great artist.

Encore: New Music

The San Juan Star
February 4, 1981 (b)   By Francis Schwartz

An interesting program of electronic and vocal-gestural music took place recently at the recital hall of the new University of Puerto Rico Music Department building in Río Piedras. In this pre-inaugural recital, Brazilian mezzosoprano Ana Maria Kieffer and Uruguayan composer-electronics performer Conrado Silva offered a stimulating panorama of contemporary art spanning the past fifteen years in Europe and South America. Kieffer and Silva are two imaginative musicians who recently participated in the Tenth Latin American Contemporary Music Course given in Santiago in the Dominican Republic. Silva, along with his compatriot Coriún Aharonian, is a co-founder of this decade-long experiment in new music pedagogy which travels to different countries throughout the Americas. The duo worked without the customary theater lighting and special wardrobe but their readings were solid, inspired and projective in quality. Particularly impressive was *Graphic Games* (1975) by Spanish composer Jesús Villarojo, written for a solo singer. Ms. Kieffer plunged dramatically into the music exploring a wide range of vocal sounds which were transformed quite often by the use of the hand as a mute, sounding surface or striker. One cannot underestimate the importance of visual impact in these theatrical music pieces. *Graphic Games*, as well as the *Maulwerke* by German composer-theologian Dieter Schnebel use a gestural code in performance which transmits powerful messages to the public; it is illusory to pretend that a "purely musical" communication is being received by the audience while the interpreters are "sending" a complex combination of both sound and gestures. Composers such as Kagel, Kusnir and Boguslaw Schaeffers have made extensive use of these elements.

The Schnebel *Maulwerke* fragment, entitled "Phonoarticulations" by the Kieffer and Silva duo, is a version made by the two musicians which blends electronics and the human voice. We found the piece to be both sensitively and sensibly illustrative of Schnebel's ideas. With appropriate lighting and make-up, the expressive features of Ms. Kieffer's face must certainly add power to the interpretation.

The magnetic tape work by Conrado Silva, *Equus* (1976), inspired by Peter Schaffer's play of the same name, possessed a haunting quality. The technical aspects of the work were handled in expert fashion. *Equus* creates an atmosphere of mood change, of Ur-experience, of primeval searches which are simultaneously present but unseizable. It is a piece we would enjoy hearing again.

Two works by young Brazilian composers bore witness to the salutary compositional activity taking place in São Paolo at this time. Both the *Estudio No. 1*, by Rodolfo Coelho de Souza, and *Dimensional No. 1*, by Aylton Escobar, were skillfully created pieces of serious professional level.

The Kieffer-Silva duo made a positive contribution to our musical scene. We need more exposure to serious New Music ideas in order to educate the public, especially in a milieu where so much mediocrity passes for serious art.

Quintón

The San Juan Star
February 4, 1981 (c)   By Donald Thompson

On Sunday, and with appropriate pomp and ceremony, the Institute of Puerto Rican Culture launched the centennial year of the birth of island composer José Ignacio Quintón.

Within recent memory it has still been fashionable to believe that Puerto Rico had had no concert life to speak of before violinist Alexander Schneider discovered the island in the mid-1950s. In fact, this concept formed part of the mystique of the government's Casals Festival Corporation, which for almost two decades held a virtual monopoly on what was played—and by whom—in Puerto Rico. During this time it was official government doctrine, expressed through news releases and related flackery, that "good" music had arrived here only with the appearance of the extraordinary Catalan cellist Pablo Casals and the concert machine which was overnight created in his name: the machine which, in fact, generated the news releases which created the mystique which further solidified the position of the machine itself.

That such a coup was possible was due in great measure to the lack of basic music research and musical documentation here, and to the almost nonexistent public awareness of Caribbean musical history and of Puerto Rico's place within it.

By the late 1950s one Puerto Rican composer of the past had attained token recognition if not complete understanding: Juan Morel Campos (1857-1896). Through the efforts of the Institute of Puerto Rican Culture an edition of Morel's melodious *danzas* for piano reached print in 1958, immediately facilitating the study and the dissemination of this talented composer's music. This publication also raised questions of biography, of the flow of interisland and international musical influences in the nineteenth century, and other interesting subjects for research.

The 1960s and 1970s saw the gradual unveiling of another important Puerto Rican composer of the past whose name, but little more, had been known: Felipe Gutiérrez y Espinosa. His work is now the subject of intensive research, which will undoubtedly reveal many surprises when its results become known.

Of course, the present knowledge of Morel Campos' and Gutiérrez' lives and music is not due to any sudden revelation from above, but to the hard work of a few specialists and serious enthusiasts. It has ever been so. Consider, for example, the case of Johann Sebastian Bach. During his own lifetime Bach was already forgotten as a composer, due to changing fashions in concert music. It was not until 75 years later that enthusiasts and specialists, among them Felix Mendelssohn and Robert Schumann, brought Bach's music out of the archive and into the concert hall, where it has since stood as an inspiration to us all.

Something similar has happened here, not only in the cases of Juan Morel Campos and Felipe Gutiérrez but also in the case of José Ignacio Quintón. In Quintón's case the "discovery" is due to the efforts of such specialists as composer Amaury Veray and pianist Nydia Font. Their work has been abetted by an active group of enthusiasts, the "Friends of José I. Quintón," headed by Ramón Rivera Bermúdez, who, in fact, delivered a biographical sketch of Quintón during Sunday's ceremony in the Patio Theater of the Institute of Puerto Rican Culture in Old San Juan. It is expected that these and similar efforts will result in the publication of some of Quintón's music under the auspices of Rivera's organization and the Institute of Puerto Rican Culture.

Naturally, Sunday's inaugural activities included a concert of Quintón's music, a function handsomely carried out by pianist Samuel Pérez. How was the music itself, then, after the centennial hoopla?

Pérez offered eleven compositions from Quintón's as yet undetermined total output, ranging from simple salon waltzes to elaborate fantasies. The first thing to strike the listener is how closely attuned all of this music was to the styles and forms cultivated by Chopin—some seventy years before. This is not to say that Quintón's music is bad, by any means. It is, however, surprisingly conservative, even for a composer who spent his entire adult life in the mountain town of Coamo, Puerto Rico. A few touches of late nineteenth-century harmony are to be found in such pieces as "Una Página de mi Vida," but Quintón's musical language was basically that of at least a half century before.

Samuel Pérez played all of this brilliant piano music with an evident affinity for the romantic nineteenth-century style. As Quintón's music unfolded, one could imagine the quiet Coamo evenings before the advent of television and air conditioning. With all windows open to the breezes, townspeople would be rocking in their sitting rooms or on their balconies, quietly chatting as down the street José Ignacio Quintón worked out the final version of another new-old mazurka or concert *danza*. A charming vision, to be sure, but one which needs further documentation, the collection of scattered manuscripts and more performances of Quintón's music to fill in the still sketchy details.

Of the Arts, Politics and Elitism

The San Juan Star
February 19, 1981 By Francis Schwartz

In the Lincoln's birthday press conference (which some reporters waggishly referred to a sop to Republicanism, in reference to a historical antecedent of the party now in power), four arts corporations heads were announced. The four directors will be the chief executive officers of the Performing Arts Corporation, which includes the Casals Festival, variety shows, ballet and opera; the Puerto Rico Symphony Orchestra; and the Fine Arts Center Corporation.

The appointments were of no surprise to those conversant with art politics in Puerto Rico. Chairman of the board of the Administration of the Development of Arts and Culture (ADAC), Jaime González Oliver, states that neither politics nor elitism will be the guidelines for the new Minillas Art Center. As well intentioned as González Oliver may be, the makeup of the newly created government agency eloquently contradicts his remarks. For example, the vice president of the ADAC board is none other than Pedro Rivera Casiano, one of the pillars of New Progressive Party militancy. He was a former aide to both Governor Romero Barceló and ex-Senate President Luis A Ferré, as well as a key strategist in the PNP's 1976 and 1980 electoral campaigns. Other figures close to the executive branch of government are Under Secretary of State Frances Morán and Carlos Chardón who occupy board positions in the new art corporations. Given the existing political climate in Puerto Rico, nobody will seriously believe that the ADAC can be free from party pressures, especially with the presence of political activists in decision making positions.

The private music organization, Pro Arte, is heavily represented in the ADAC, beginning with González Oliver, its past president. This concert promotion group, made up of industry and professional leaders, has sponsored leading international soloists in local concerts. The philosophy which guides Pro Arte is elitist. The admission charges to their concerts are beyond the means of the vast majority of the public. There are at least six key Pro Arte members in important ADAC positions which signals the distinct possibility of an elitist arts policy. While one may commend the initiative of these citizens in the private sector, their reigning philosophy could be devastating to a public agency supposedly charged with the task of the development of culture in Puerto Rico. While these are sincere art lovers, they also represent a very small segment of society which has constant access to the centers of power. They are in a position of imposing their views upon the entire community via a tax-funded entity, the ADAC.

We already have an example of interference in the professional workings of the ADAC. The inaugural concert of the Performing Arts Center, scheduled for April 9, is basically a mixed bag of opera arias by three leading Puerto Rican singers accompanied by the Puerto Rico Symphony Orchestra under John Barnett. Instead of planning a major work for such an occasion, such as the Beethoven Ninth Symphony or Bach's Saint Matthew Passion or a concert version of Gutiérrez Espinosa's *Macías*, the program is a typical opera *salcocho* (stew) designed to satisfy the Pro Arte proclivities which have been in evidence over the years. No serious music director would put together such a program, unworthy of the opening of a major art center, unless there was pressure from the board. It is hard to imagine John Barnett exhibiting the Puerto Rico Symphony in a secondary role as the program indicates.

Both the antipolitical and antielitist proclamations of the ADAC board head are easily refuted. One opponent of the appointments is Senate President Miguel Hernández Agosto who excoriated the announcement as "impertinent." He indicated that the Senate (read Popular Democratic Party) was not committed to the ADAC as currently structured. In fact, he referred to the future presentation of new legislation which would considerably alter the controversial Fine Arts Center bill, passed last June by a NPP controlled legislature. Needless to say, if the ADAC cannot win the support of the Senate, it will have a difficult time finding a budget with which to finance the enormous cultural undertaking, especially with the gloomy economic prospects for the coming year.

Composer Héctor Campos-Parsi, who was named as a consultant and troubleshooter to the Performing Arts Corporation, stated, "The Populares would be wise to give us all the funds necessary. If the Center fails because they withhold public monies, they will have to answer for it in the future."

Another element in the political culture war is the Committee for Cultural Defense (Comité pro Defensa de la Cultura) which has been active on both the local and international scenes. A united front of both pro-independence and autonomist forces, these opponents of the ADAC have staged pickets, published manifestos and have attempted to mobilize public opinion to combat what they call " . . . an attempt by annexionist forces to totally control cultural manifestations in Puerto Rico in order to pave the way for statehood."

An appeal has been made to Puerto Rican singers Justino Díaz, Antonio Barasorda and Margarita Castro-Alberty to boycott the opening concert in which they are scheduled to perform. Rumors of pickets and opening night protests are rife. Obviously, this is a serious problem for the government since the Fine Arts Center inauguration will host leading political and journalistic figures from many countries. Such a negative environment would point out the volatile situation in Puerto Rico and would be embarrassing to the current administration.

Caught up in this furor are the artists of Puerto Rico who desperately need adequate facilities in which to work and who need the encouragement of governmental institutions so that they may pursue the dictates of their imaginations without enduring economic hardships or censorship. The artists' dilemma is whether or not to be "manipulated" by political forces which attempt to "purchase" compliance by the granting of contracts, commissions, concerts; or to withhold support from a politicized government agency in order to maintain personal and intellectual independence. Most artists tend to be pragmatic about their self interests, in spite of the theatrical public postures they may assume. Much to the chagrin of the anti-ADAC ideologues, many so-called anti-ADAC artists are quietly establishing relationships with members of the new arts agency in order to protect their economic interest in the future. However, given the present division of real political power in Puerto Rico, PNP vs. PDP, the pragmatic art practitioners, the philosophical *panzistas*, may simply wait in the wings to await the outcome of the culture war.

The entire situation bodes ill for the ADAC. If art is born of social turmoil, then we should be in for a very exciting decade.

Arts Center Opening

The San Juan Star
April 12, 1981   By Donald Thompson

    Well, friends, it finally opened, with the expected pomp and ceremony, the inevitable protest in the street out front and quite naturally a concert. I am speaking, of course, of the new Performing Arts Center at Minillas in Santurce, which will now become the focus of the island's performing arts activities on many levels.
    The new structure is basically a theater complex containing three separate halls. This configuration will provide great flexibility for the programming of different types of activity attracting different sizes of audience and, of course, the simultaneous scheduling of different attractions. Such a facility has long been desperately needed here and will immediately provide relief for the traditionally overworked theaters of the San Juan metropolitan area: the Tapia, the Sylvia Rexach and the UPR Theater in Río Piedras.
    The Center's grand opening took place on Thursday evening with the action occurring mainly in the largest theater, the 2,000-seat Festival Hall. As is only appropriate, the Puerto Rico Symphony Orchestra was featured on this occasion of the greatest import to island musical affairs, with the participation of three admired island singers. All of the elements were present, you might think, for an extraordinary and unforgettable musical event. But separating the central musical function from the surrounding framework of pomp and ceremony, the question remains, how was it?
    It was both ordinary and forgettable, with the fault lying squarely with those who conceived this type of musical programming as appropriate for such a significant event. A grand occasion calls for a grand musical work: a masterpiece, a unity, an artwork to illuminate the soul, refresh

the spirit and gladden the memory for many years to come: in short, a banquet. Instead, Puerto Rico received . . . a Thursday night stew.

The formula of the "opera concert" has been worked to death here during recent years by a privately sponsored concert society which has somehow been plugged into the publicly funded Puerto Rico Symphony Orchestra. In this formula, no single artwork is ever presented, but instead only the most tuneful scraps and bits of the most stylistically accessible operas. These, in turn, represent only a handful of the representatives of a single field of operatic repertory (the romantic nineteenth-century kind), for this is the repertory which a lay management whose criteria are limited to its own limited tastes is likely to emphasize. And that is probably what we're dealing with here.

The opera concert formula is nice for an orchestra fund raiser now and then, or for a TV "spectacular" designed for a home audience of limited attention span. Aesthetically its counterparts are the humorous collage, informal readings of brief and isolated scenes from plays, such recorded insults as "The Heart of the Symphony" and, yes, the stew. If the bloom had not been taken off the opera concert through its overuse here in recent years this formula just might have been successful, at least from the public relations point of view during the glitter and zap of Thursday evening's big inauguration. However, it has little place in serious and responsible concert life, and no real place at all in the opening of a new arts center.

So then, how about the different musical and logistic aspects of Thursday's concert? The Puerto Rico Symphony Orchestra has had some fine years, but this is not one of them. For subtle reasons which have been explored elsewhere, the island orchestra's recent seasons have shown a lowering of the average level of quality up front where it counts: the concert. Thursday's concert, conducted by John Barnett, displayed many of the same ills which have been evident lately. These included faulty pitch in some sections, imprecise beginnings and endings of phrases, and especially in the violins the lack of common agreement on a number of matters of technical execution. Acoustically, at least from where I was seated in the middle of the hall, the theater seemed quite good—perhaps all *too* good sometimes.

Thursday's singers were soprano Margarita Castro, tenor Antonio Barasorda and bass Justino Díaz. Each of these artists continues to develop along lines of either growth or confirmation according to his or her place in the trajectory of a singing career. Justino Díaz is of course an accomplished and polished musician and a fine performer, unshakable and completely secure in his years of fine work. Ms. Castro's voice continues to grow in size and clarity, and by now has become what singers are pleased to call, admiringly, "a beautiful instrument." On Thursday her first couple of pieces displayed a moment or two of questionable pitch and a tendency to slide around a bit more than seems justified by the dramatic quality of her music, especially in a concert situation.

Here, incidentally, is an example of another ill of the opera concert format. Without the dramatic rhythm of a real opera's development, and without the alternation of intense action and relative inaction which this provides, a singer is thrown into the middle of a stage and immediately expected to deliver at the peak. This is the blast-off without the countdown, the pole vault without the pole, the pitch without the wind-up. And it can be counterproductive or at the very least cruel to singers, depending, of course, on the particular excerpts selected.

Antonio Barasorda is admired for the cool, light and floating quality of his lyric tenor voice. His work on Thursday profited by this quality, but also showed a tendency in repertory and style to broaden into a more dramatic sort of expression. The final result of this shift remains to be seen, but Barasorda seems well on the way to accomplishing it.

To add another ingredient to the stew and to give the singers a break, opera concerts often include a purely orchestral selection or two. On Thursday, and in addition to a couple of melodious orchestral excerpts from stage works, the PRSO offered two works of island interest. The first of these was a brief *Fanfare for Minillas* for brass and timpani by Roberto Sierra. Brief is right; lasting only seconds, the piece was really too short to develop much interest. Devoid of definition and character, it did not seem the kind of piece with which one would inaugurate a modern and functional $18,000,000 structure. It was better suited, perhaps, for a neighborhood movie house. Also offered was an overture, *La Lira*, by Juan Morel Campos in a new orchestral arrangement by Roberto Sierra.

♪

Two Island Tenors: Vázquez and Soto

The San Juan Star
April 30, 1981   By Donald Thompson

A pair of island tenors has been in the musical limelight here lately. First up was Alejandro Vázquez, who with pianist Jesús María Sanromá and sponsored by the Institute of Puerto Rican Culture has embarked on a journey of three weeks' duration through the great song cycles of Franz Schubert. The first recital was devoted to *Die Schöne Müllerin*, and took place on April 19 in the experimental theater of the Performing Arts Center. The series will close next Sunday in the same hall with the *Schwanengesang* cycle. Last Sunday found this well matched pair of musicians at midpoint in this important set of recitals with a complete presentation of the 24 Schubert songs collectively entitled *Die Winterreise*, at Minillas.

The song cycle, or group of related songs presented as a unit, appealed mightily to the nineteenth-century Germanic view of things, which tended to spin out modest concepts into grand philosophical structures. Beethoven, Brahms, Schumann and Mahler made important contributions to the song cycle, and this vehicle was ready made for the song writing genius of Schubert.

Die Winterreise is a musical setting of 24 poems by Wilhelm Müller, which on the simplest level appear to describe a journey. Explicitly, the Müller texts deal in such commonplace images as snow, ice, bare trees and bitter wind, but everyone knows (and Schubert makes it abundantly clear) that what we are really dealing with is the bleak and tragic voyage of the soul itself. Thus the pursuing crow (no. 13 of the set) is the Angel of Death in both literary and musical symbolism, while the hurdy-gurdy man of the last song in the cycle, marvelously drawn in musical terms by Schubert, is the Reaper himself.

This, as you can see, is supercharged music. To come anywhere near the mark, its presentation requires a level of skill and understanding so high that the concept of skill itself disappears (if you'll bear with a bit of Germanic metaphysics here) and all that is left is the gleaming artwork itself. In other words, to put this music across you've got to be quite good and also quite smart.

On Sunday afternoon the Vázquez-Sanromá duo displayed both of these sterling qualities. Of Jesús María Sanromá there is little to be said any more; simply, here is a performer who for more than a half century has been among the world class pianists. Of Alex Vázquez, on the other hand, there is plenty to be said. Vázquez is a Puerto Rican performer who paid his dues and then some in the insular insularities of the island's somewhat insular musical ambiance, then flew the coop to Europe. There he has established a solid career in opera while cultivating the recital field as well. Interestingly enough, in Germanic lands this latter is as highly regarded as the former, while it is recognized that proficiency in the tighter discipline of song can only aid the development of the opera singer. Vázquez has done well on both counts. His brief annual appearances here only dramatize the desirability of creating mechanisms through which he and other artists of the Puerto Rican diaspora could begin to think of spending not a week or two but a season or a career in Puerto Rico.

Meanwhile, as one island tenor returns from European successes another heads toward the same testing ground. On Saturday evening Johnny Soto offered a farewell recital before taking up an opera contract in Hagen, Germany. Soto, like Vázquez before him, has appeared in principal roles with the island's opera companies. He is especially remembered for his fine work in the premiere performances of the opera *Macías* by Felipe Gutiérrez, a century after its composition. In his farewell recital Soto displayed solid technique, very secure stage presence and those cherished prizes among prizes, correct pitch and appropriate phrasing. Another winner, it would appear.

On Saturday, Soto's recital also benefitted by the support of mezzo-soprano Darysabel Isales, pianists María del Carmen Gil and Pablo Boissen, and a group of younger singers, students of María Esther Robles.

Who knows which of these younger talents might be the next to land a contract in Europe or the U.S.? Opera lovers are like horse lovers, eager to have been among those who picked the winners early on. Well, a lot of opera lovers here missed the boat on Alejandro Vázquez and Juan Soto, and if they don't stay on their toes they're going to miss some other boats too, to judge from Saturday evening's recital by (and for) tenor Soto.

One of Puerto Rico's musical pillars, **the Hutchinson-Negrón family**. (Left to right: Luz Negrón Hutchinson, Henry Hutchinson Negrón, Henry Hutchinson, Cecilia Negrón Talavera.)

Festival Opens on Discordant Note

The San Juan Star
June 9, 1981   By Donald Thompson

Pablo Casals (1876-1973) was a great Catalan cellist who at the height of a splendid career left Spain out of disagreement with the government of Francisco Franco, which had become rigidly established at the end of the Spanish Civil War. Casals settled into a life of gentlemanly contemplation, aid to other refugees and some teaching just across the border in southern France, but was brought out of relative retirement a decade later by violinist Alexander Schneider. With other musicians and organizers, Schneider created around the cellist—and around his love for the music of Bach—the relaxed and musically significant festivals at Prades over which Casals presided in the early 1950s.

In the mid-1950s the Casals name and the Casals presence were brought to Puerto Rico and lent to a very different kind of operation: a tax financed festival carefully designed to place Puerto Rico in the most fashionable circuits of international tourism. At the same time, Casals' presence here would aid the island's industrial development program by helping to create, through mainland advertising, the impression of a tranquil, stable and cultured place: a nice place to establish a factory. Casals spent the last seventeen years of his life with Puerto Rico as his base of operations although most of his energy, up to the last years, was expended elsewhere. In the meantime the relation between the annual Casals Festival and Puerto Rico was at best tenuous. As organizer Schneider once put it in a statement never refuted by the island government or anyone else, the Casals Festival was "in" Puerto Rico but not "of" Puerto Rico. After the cellist's death there was even serious talk of the event becoming simply one element in an international franchise operation: a chain of prepackaged "Casals" festivals managed from New

York City.

The purpose of these remarks has been to remind us all that from its beginning the Casals Festival in Puerto Rico was characterized as much by the tandem expediencies of political and musical empire building as by musical values themselves, often to the detriment of the latter. It was the push and shove of these forces, in fact, which created the festival's deep artistic problems, especially after Casals' death.

There was hope that the festival's new placement, as a subsidiary of the recently created Administration for the Development of Arts and Culture, would finally free it from these shackling relationships. However, judging from Saturday evening's opening concert in this year's series, in the Festival Hall of the Performing Arts Center, the situation has not changed.

A concert, like a play or a film, has a rhythm, a logic, a development of its own, and any deliberate interruption of this flow can only be seen as a shocking violation. The natural rhythm of Saturday's concert was interrupted by a demonstration of political force over the arts the like of which had never been seen here on this scale. After the first work on the program a functionary of the Administration for the Development of Arts and Culture took the stage to deliver a politically self-congratulatory speech whose only effect could be to depressingly sidetrack the development of the event. In addition, of course, this disruptive presentation will cast serious doubt over all future musical pronouncements by this artistic management, which is now hopelessly compromised politically.

The last time I saw such a spectacle was in Barrio Dulces Labios in Mayagüez almost thirty years ago, when a concert by the town band was interrupted so that a barrio hack might deliver a plea for votes in the next election on the basis of his always having supported the town band and all other manifestations of high art and culture. Saturday's speech was no more subtle and was in fact even more offensive in context, for the interrupted event was not an informal evening on the plaza but what had been, until then, a reasonably sophisticated and musically promising occasion. The place for this kind of material is the TV commercial, or the press release or the flyer distributed outside the theater, but never the concert stage.

Saturday's concert was based on the Puerto Rico Symphony Orchestra, somewhat augmented for the occasion. Also appearing were the big chorus of the Puerto Rico Conservatory of Music; violinists Henry

Hutchinson, Wilfredo Degláns and Robert McDuffie; pianist Lee Luvisi; soprano Olga Iglesias; baritone Leslie Gunn; and two highly capable but unidentified soloists (contralto and tenor) from the chorus. Conductors were Jorge Mester and Sergije Rainis, and the works presented were by J.S. Bach and Pablo Casals.

Kudos to Two Performers

The San Juan Star
June 11, 1981 By Francis Schwartz

Historical insufficiency and interpretative excellence characterized the Casals Festival chamber music concert devoted to twentieth-century composers of the Americas. The Tuesday evening Fine Arts Center Drama theater found the well known Argentinean composer Alberto Ginastera opening the program with a half-hour talk on compositional development in our hemisphere during the past centuries, with several suggestions about the future of music in Puerto Rico.

Professor Ginastera, obviously trying to create a favorable climate for the establishment of a yearly Pan American music festival in Puerto Rico, proposed the creation of music courses, of composers meetings, of a concert series where contemporary music of American (hemispheric) composers would be played and discussed. For our distinguished colleague's information, the University of Puerto Rico Music Department has offered courses in Music of the Americas and Twentieth Century Music for many years and has a functioning electronic music laboratory. Recently, the Second Biennial of Twentieth-Century Music hosted a 17-concert series in which such outstanding creators as Roque Cordero, Jacob Druckman, Manuel Enríquez and Walter Ross, among others, supervised the presentation of their music and discussed the many problems which affect our profession.

Stating his satisfaction that the Casals Festival was presenting Music of the Americas night, Ginastera felt that this augured well for the future. We can only say that the very people who supported the reactionary programming policies of earlier years are finally coming out of the closet and are suddenly struck with the beauty and relevance of our century's oeuvres. Consummatum est!

We think the ideas of this gifted composer and educator should be seriously discussed and evaluated. Puerto Rico is no wasteland regarding twentieth-century music. Much has been done here during the past decades starting with Sanromá and continuing with Irma Isern, the Fluxus Group, the Inter-American Festival of 1966, the Biennials of Contemporary Music, the UPR Music Department's artistic and pedagogical activities, and the Institute of Puerto Rican Culture. This should never be forgotten.

The musical offering began with Chilean Domingo Santa Cruz's Five Tragic Poems, for piano (1929). These very moving works were performed here in September during the Second Biennial by the distinguished Chilean pianist Carla Hubner. Tuesday night, the brilliant Puerto Rican interpreter, Irma Luz Vallecillo, turned in a profoundly dramatic performance. This excellent artist, who has yet to disappoint us in concert, possesses a magnificent technique which is always at the service of the music. Her tone rivals that of Watteau and the intricate shadings she achieves makes her a colorist of the first order. Equally powerful in delivery were the Four Preludes (1937) of Carlos Chávez, the great Mexican composer who died two years ago. The Second Chôros (1924) of Heitor Villa-Lobos was ably executed by clarinetist Kathleen Jones and flutist Peter Kern.

However, the high point of the first half of the program was the magnificent performance by Irma Luz Vallecillo of Aaron Copland's Piano Variations (1930). This composition, one of the pillars of twentieth-century piano repertoire, is in our opinion technically and musically awe-inspiring. It is no mean feat to ably solve the many pianistic difficulties of the Variations. To make the musical content sparkle with thematic coherence is another major challenge. Ms. Vallecillo's superb playing made it all sound so easy and logical. A bravo of Brucknerian proportions to her.

After intermission, the Puerto Rican soprano Evangelina Colón gave a felicitous rendition of the *Nine Antillean Songs* by local composer Luis Antonio Ramírez. These pleasant compositions utilize the poetry of three distinguished Caribbean literati: Luis Llorens Torres (Puerto Rico), Rubén Suro (Dominican Republic) and Nicolás Guillén (Cuba). The able accompanist was Ms. Vallecillo.

Closing the program with Alberto Ginastera's Sonata for Cello and Piano, Op. 49 (1979), the cellist Aurora Natola Ginastera and

Ms. Vallecillo gave a stirring reading of the work. It is a composition of considerable imagination utilizing performance techniques of the past 30 years while exploiting certain elements of South American music of earlier eras. We found the *adagio passionato* movement to be especially poetic. It is a very successful fusion of the lyrical element with a modern technical approach. The Sonata closed with Ginastera's usual steamroller energy. Kudos to the two performers who gave an excellent performance.

Lack of Professional Input in Festival Planning

The San Juan Star
June 18, 1981 By Donald Thompson

This year's Casals Festival, taking place for the first time in the new Performing Arts Center in Santurce, ended on Tuesday evening, leaving in its wake an even more mixed set of impressions than in previous years. The closing concert was conducted by festival music director Jorge Mester, and offered the Puerto Rico Symphony Orchestra in a program of music by Dvořák, Falla and Sierra. Soloist for the Falla work, Nights in the Gardens of Spain, was brilliant island pianist Irma Luz Vallecillo, who again confirmed her growing reputation as a soloist of the highest category.

With the splendid performances of the visiting Cincinnati Symphony Orchestra still ringing in the ears, the island's own orchestra did not sound so good on Tuesday. I hasten to point out, however, that little of this fault lies with the present membership of the orchestra itself. In some ways a symphony orchestra is like a produce farm or a citrus ranch. When year after year the quality of the crop declines the real fault probably lies not in the field but in the office. Chances are, basic errors occurred months or years before in planning or policy, to say nothing of the day to day management, guidance and cultivation of the enterprise.

The PRSO's season still has a bit to go; perhaps as the end approaches during the next couple of weeks it may be possible to arrive at some idea of where it's going and why.

But back to the 1981 Puerto Rico Casals Festival; where is IT going and why? Nobody knows any more, least of all its own management. The root of the word "festival" is of course "fest," or "festive," referring to the celebration of something unusual—extraordinary—off the beaten track—worthy of special notice. There are twentieth-century music festivals, Brahms festivals, double bass festivals, folk festivals, bagpipe festivals, fife and drum festivals and rock festivals, among many others, each (in biblical terms) unto its own kind. Audiences at true festivals tend to see themselves quite correctly as pilgrims, and they experience a spiritual renewal through participation in such sharply focused and illuminating events. THAT is what makes a festival.

There was certainly nothing festive about this year's programming, which in terms of any unifying and illuminating concept (especially if the visions and convictions of Pablo Casals were to be considered) ranged from the absurd to the insulting. A few works by Casals himself were presented, to be sure. In fact it is fortunate that these were few, for the remarkable cellist was not much of a composer; a more generous sampling of his music might have brought this series to an early end. The general programming of this festival was simply a hodge-podge, a grab-bag, a gallimaufry of odds and ends of standard (and substandard) repertory. There were exceptions, of course, but the exceptions (Stravinsky's marvelous *Rite of Spring*, for example) certainly do not require a "festival" format for their presentation and least of all (in that particular case) a festival supposedly connected with the known historical figure of Pablo Casals.

The Casals Festival is one of a number of island musical agencies which were originally conceived in the halls of the Puerto Rico Industrial Development Company, during Fomento's heyday a quarter century ago. Due to this placement, the management of these agencies was for decades marked by a disastrous combination of ignorance and arrogance. The former condition resulted from the managing music lovers' knowing neither the history of music and musical institutions in Puerto Rico nor the traditions and mechanisms of concert life everywhere. The latter condition (arrogance) derived from Fomento's reputation for omniscience in the contemporaneous surge of island industrialization: a reputation which tended to spill over into other fields.

It was hoped that with the recent creation of the Administration for the Development of Arts and Culture, absorbing these musico-industrial creations into a more reasoned administrative framework, a new era of professionalism and artistic responsibility might begin in Puerto Rico. Alas, it is apparently not to be so.

Judging from the programming, implementation and documentation of this Casals Festival and surrounding phenomena, there has been little professional input or artistic responsibility at any high level. Undoubtedly well meaning but obviously uninformed lay people are still making most of the operational decisions, while the grim horsemen of ignorance and arrogance sit as firmly in the saddle as ever.

A case in point occurred last week, when the question of an Inter American Music Festival here was discussed during a scheduled festival event. Obviously, the organization and management of such a festival would be handled by the new Administration for the Development of Arts and Culture, probably in some parallel fashion to the existing Casals Festival. So far so good, if that's your thing. A foremost proponent of the idea was noted Argentine composer Alberto Ginastera, who presumably would have a key role in the festival's organization. Maestro Ginastera's presentation rather glowingly described the necessity of establishing such a festival here due to the historical absence of such activity in Puerto Rico, and urged the creation of studies in the music of the Americas as well as other means of disseminating contemporary music.

It is not known to what extent composer Ginastera is unaware of Puerto Rico's very successful contemporary music movement of the past dozen or so years, a movement which has attracted considerable international recognition and participation. He should not be unaware of it at all, for he has himself been associated with it from time to time. Or if he has forgotten this, his hosts might have provided him with the background information necessary for his speech.

Ginastera might have been told, for example, about the pioneer work of the Fluxus group of the late '60s and of the two successful Biennials organized by the Puerto Rico Society for Contemporary Music, or of the third Biennial now being planned by the Latin American Foundation for Contemporary Music. He might have been informed of the new works commissioned here in the '50s by the Division of Community Education and Ballets de San Juan and of the many recordings of contemporary Puerto Rican music released by the Institute of Puerto Rican Culture during the past couple of decades. The same agency, he might have recalled, has for many years presented an annual series of concerts of music of this hemisphere. Finally, the eminent composer might have remembered that there is in Puerto Rico a functioning electronic music laboratory, a center of research in Puerto Rican, Caribbean and Latin American music, a library of important materials for such study and a repertory of academic courses being regularly taught in all of these subjects: all on the campus of the University of Puerto Rico and not ten miles from his hotel.

Maestro Ginastera's innocence, his lack of information and his short memory can be forgiven, but it is difficult to forgive a governmental arts management which out of ignorance—or arrogance—encourages an eminent guest to climb out on a limb like that.

So, friends, the great wheel turns and there's little new under the sun regardless of who runs the Casals Festival and allied enterprises: PRIDCO for a quarter-century or these new people for—how many years, I wonder?

A Concert of Great Contrasts

The San Juan Star
June 20, 1981   By Francis Schwartz

It is hard to imagine a greater contrast in quality than the eleventh Casals Festival program, offered last Sunday evening in the Festival Hall of the Performing Arts Center. The Puerto Rico Symphony Orchestra, under the baton of John Barnett, its titular conductor, presented an all-Beethoven concert with guest soloists Ilca Paizy, soprano; Lee Luvisi, pianist; and José Ferrer, narrator.

The Fidelio Overture opened the program. Rarely have we heard the PRSO sound better. They performed with vigor and technical solidity. Barnett's concept is based on the dramatic qualities of the score and he achieved judicious sectional balance which fortified this musical view. Our orchestra is capable of such playing, of such music making. The future challenge for both Barnett and the players will be to make this level the absolute minimum standard which they will accept.

Lee Luvisi, one of the festival's outstanding performers this year, continued his winning ways by giving a beautiful rendition of Beethoven's Fourth Piano Concerto. This work was considered very radical in 1806, as it upended classical tradition by beginning with the solo piano rather than the orchestra. Also, the unacademic key relationships sent some Guardians of Musical Purity into paroxysms on hearing such avant-garde "mistaken" artistic procedures. Luvisi sculpted an interpretation of great breadth and profound introspection. The accompaniment was superbly handled by Barnett, whose expertise in this difficult area is considerable.

After intermission the musical Dow-Jones average dropped about 30 points. Festival music director Jorge Mester decided that our festival needed a narrated version of the Beethoven-Goethe collaboration,

"Egmont." In fact, Beethoven wrote the music as a complement to the theater piece of the great German author. Apparently cognizant of an Erich Leinsdorf narrated version, Mester informed John Barnett that this work was to be included on the program with a Spanish language version to be used by the narrator. Héctor Campos Parsi and Edgardo Gierbolini lent their talents to the realization of this Spanish language version.

José Ferrer, the noted actor, narrated. It is sad to say that our favorite Cyrano was simply not up to the task. He read in a halting fashion, with little emotional commitment, while appearing to be seeing his text for the first time. Obviously, Ferrer's forte is English language theater. He should prepare himself adequately, which he did not do on Sunday. Young soprano Ilca Paizy acquitted herself well in the small role accorded to her. She has made considerable progress over the past years and should do very well in the future.

The orchestra had the ungrateful task of participating in a long, tedious enterprise. There were few moments which one could relish from an aesthetic viewpoint. We were just hoping for a merciful ending, which came all too slowly. Here again was an example of poor programming and very bad casting.

Fleischer and the PRSO

The San Juan Star
September 30, 1981								By Donald Thompson

    The Puerto Rico Symphony Orchestra has continued its recently launched season in the Performing Arts Center, with a Saturday evening concert conducted by eminent pianist Leon Fleischer. In addition to performing conductorial duties in a generally admirable fashion, Fleischer offered a capital performance of Ravel's Piano Concerto for the Left Hand Alone.
    The Ravel work is a first class example of the composer's uncanny ability to spin high art out of whatever he had to work with; this concerto occupies an honored place in the long list of works by the composer of *Bolero* and *Rapsodie Espagnole*.
    And what of our symphony orchestra, whose erratic course resembles nothing so much as a television serial? Well, as they say, you win a few, you lose a few. The past couple of years have seen abrupt and wrenching transformations in the orchestra's administrative placement and in its artistic hierarchy. These transformations have now been completed; the season now in progress is the first to be completely shaped by the new forces, and will therefore be subjected to extraordinary scrutiny by many interested parties.
    A great gain has been made in the roster of soloists this season, of whom Leon Fleischer is an excellent example. The PRSO, almost entirely sustained by your taxes and mine, is the island's principal means of public education in the vital field of art music. It is therefore appropriate that the citizenry (as well as the orchestra itself) benefit from the presence of a wide variety of soloists and conductors of the highest possible category.

Another change for the better, the orchestra's move to a permanent home in the Performing Arts Center, can only contribute to the development of basic sonoral unity and general artistic solidity. And finally, the orchestra's long overdue separation from the now defunct Casals Festival Corporation, of which for decades it was a neglected stepchild, has at last enabled it to assume its own artistic identity. This is reflected in newly designed logos, symbols and program materials; this new visibility should contribute to a higher level of artistic and managerial self-consciousness and determination.

These "environmental" gains do not seem to have been accompanied yet by much progress in the only place where it really counts: up front, in the artistic quality of the product which comes across the stage. True, it takes time to bring about real change in anything as complicated as a symphony orchestra, and this one is still crippled by conditions which predate the present management. One of these conditions is an absurd salary scale, which keeps the orchestra on a semi-pro basis while (among other things) locking it into an unrealistic schedule of rehearsals and performances. Rehearsals and concerts, it is thought, must accommodate the part-timers whose main jobs and main interests are elsewhere. Naturally, this places severe limits on the hours when school concerts and other important functions can be scheduled.

Another reminder of the orchestra's early history is the deadly tradition of engaging student instrumentalists to play in this supposedly professional ensemble, even in important positions. You will understand what the inevitable cost of this practice is, in terms of sound, general security and expensive rehearsal time, to say nothing of wrong notes and false entrances.

Third, the orchestra is still saddled with a suicidal employment policy endorsed by the governing board of a few years ago and apparently never revoked. As a result of this policy (and other conditions) the orchestra has seen an annual exodus of some of its most valuable foreign-born players, who have in many cases been replaced by instrumentalists of lesser skill and lesser experience.

And finally, it is evident that orchestra training and repertory building have virtually come to a halt during the past couple of years. The result (no matter who might be conducting at the moment) is seen in a cautious, tentative and uncommitted style of playing, even in what should be the most standard and half-memorized orchestral repertory.

Still, though, the 1981-82 season is very young; as it goes along the orchestra might make a better impression, depending only partly on who's standing in front and what music is on the stands.

A Bartók Commemoration

The San Juan Star
October 1, 1981 (a)   By Donald Thompson

One of the greatest innovators in twentieth-century music was Bela Bartók (1881-1945), the brilliant Hungarian-born composer whose influence in Western art music, especially during the middle third of the century, was both profound and widespread. Naturally the centennial year of Bartók's birth has seen a great deal of worldwide centennial activity, including concerts, exhibitions, research, publications and lectures.

Puerto Rico has made a modest contribution to these proceedings, with a Bartók work or two offered on several of the island's regular concert series. The most concentrated of these observances, however, has been a set of concerts recently offered by the Latin American Foundation for Contemporary Music.

The Foundation is a new and welcome element on the island musical scene, with important connections in both North and South America. It is headed here by Rafael Aponte-Ledée, who has been a tireless driving force in the island's modern music movement since the late 1960s and who never fails to come up with something both interesting and significant.

The foundation's recent Bartók commemoration also engaged the support of the National Endowment for the Arts and of Inter American University in San Germán, where two of the three concerts took place. In fact, the IAU campus became for a few days last week a hotbed of Bartókiana, with lectures, exhibits, workshops and discussions devoted to the man and his music. A basic element in all of this was the IAU Music Department, which provided logistic and operational support as well as some important lectures on various subjects connected with Bartók.

Tuesday evening's concert was in the capable hands of the Mendelssohn Quartet and soprano Victoria Villamil. Offered were the third and fourth quartets of Bartók and that marvel of twentieth-century music, the prophetic Second String Quartet of Arnold Schoenberg—the one with voice ("I feel the air of other planets . . ."). Ms. Villamil's gifts are well known from her previous appearances here, but the splendid work of the Mendelssohn Quartet came as news to us. The rich and glorious sound of these bright, talented and well organized young performers will long be remembered.

Thursday's San Germán concert, repeated on Friday evening at the Carnegie Library in San Juan, joined soprano Villamil with New York's Continuum ensemble, also well remembered from previous island appearances. Strangely, of the five works presented only two were by Bartók himself, the rest by Arnold Schoenberg. And most of the ensemble's energy (the entire second half of the concert, in fact) went into a performance of Schoenberg's *Pierrot Lunaire*. Granted, this is one of the monuments of twentieth-century music, and its performance by Ms. Villamil and Continuum was absolutely first rate. However, (1) it was presented here a year or two ago by the same forces—although not in San Germán—and (2) it occupied, at least for this Bartók-hungry listener, a disproportionate amount of time on this already sharply limited Bartók series.

Also offered on the San Germán-San Juan Continuum concerts were a set of Schubertian four-hand pieces by the student Schoenberg (1894), his Violin and Piano Fantasy (1949) and two Bartók works: a brief set of Slovakian folk song settings for voice and piano, and the powerful Piano Sonata of 1926. Masterfully presented, this Bartók sample, but like Bartók's life, all too short.

Schwartz at the Institute

The San Juan Star
October 1, 1981 (b) By Donald Thompson

The concert devoted to the works of a single living composer is, like the one-man art show, a fine opportunity to see what the subject has (or has not) been up to during the past years or decades. Of course, for it to work the one-man format must be able to draw upon a considerable body of material in order to be able to choose only the top drawer stuff (yes, children, even Beethoven had his off days).

Island composer Francis Schwartz' catalogue of works now includes close to fifty compositions, many of them published and some regularly performed in international avant-garde circles. Four Schwartz-pieces were offered on Saturday evening on the Institute of Puerto Rican Culture's regular concert series, in visual settings generated and directed by Nelson Rivera. Together, they provided a sample of Schwartz' musical production over the past eight years.

"Musical," did you say? Well, it all depends on your point of view. The Schwartz aesthetic, shared by many thinkers during the past thirty years, claims that the term "music" had become rigidly, pretentiously and erroneously limited to a tightly circumscribed field of sonoral phenomena in Western "high culture" during the preceding several centuries. One of the main purposes of the avant-garde movement of the past three decades (and before, if you want to go back to the irreverences of Erik Satie) has been precisely to force a re-examination of the question of what IS music, always bearing in mind the derivation of that word from the Muses. We are advised not to forget that there were from three to nine of these legendary ladies, and that they were concerned not only with sound but with all that was contemplative, reasoned and beautiful. "Beautiful," you say? Well, again, it all depends on how you look at it.

One of the most recent of the Schwartz-numbers presented on Saturday was *Fantasías Amazónicas* for solo guitar (1979), played by Ana María Rosado. These brief pieces sounded much more solid than on their first presentation a year or so by the same soloist: so much more solid that I think that they could now stand on their own, simply as guitar music without the evocative (therefore limiting) title and without the spoken text which introduced each piece on Saturday.

I don't believe that good music needs the crutch of extramusical verbal associations, especially in this age of the "objectification" of art. A significant sector of the avant-garde has very successfully cut itself off from the past through its insistence that for music to be "interesting" is enough. At this late date, then, a reversion to program music or sound effects seems a fallback to a once popular (if no longer widely accepted) aesthetic position: in other words, a cop-out.

Much new music is described as "experimental." Why not experiment, then, with scraping off some of the loaded titles, presenting the works (beginning with these nice guitar pieces, perhaps) simply as music? The result of that experiment might indeed be, as they say, "interesting."

Other *Schwartzwerke* offered on Saturday included the entirely pre-taped *Caligula* (1975) and *L'oncle de Baudelaire* (1980) for solo piano. Or rather, for solo piano and highly mobile pianist. Schwartz himself (aside from it all an accomplished concert pianist, let it be known) was the soloist here, contributing gestures, groans, sighs, grunts, hisses, coughs, grimaces, scowls, snarls, smiles and tongue clicks. Is this a put-on? Mostly. But is it serious? Mostly. Come on, though; is it art? Well, as the bishop said to the duchess, you've got your problems and I've got mine, but don't knock it if you haven't tried it.

Closing Saturday's Schwartzorama was *Mis Cejas No Son Pobladas* (My Eyebrows Aren't Bushy), an oldie dating from 1972. The version presented here was that designed by Carlos Vázquez and Nelson Rivera for the II Biennial of Twentieth Century Music of 1980. Participants were a pre-recorded tape, a human being and a stageful of pianos, percussion instruments and such other artifacts of today's world as a door mirror, a projector and screen and a spray can of lavender paint. That talented mummer Sunshine Logroño kept the whole thing moving along nicely between slides and spray, pratfalls and piano pizzicatos. The ending of *Cejas* seems to suggest that it all might end with neither a bang nor a whimper, . . . but with a kiss. This is certainly the cheeriest news to be received here in a while, and if Schwartz and his oracular co-conspirators are correct they merit honor, praise and glory. Up the avant-garde!

Forrester and the PRSO

The San Juan Star
October 28, 1981 By Donald Thompson

The admired contralto Maureen Forrester was heard in the Festival Hall of the Performing Arts Center last week as one of this season's roster of fine soloists with the Puerto Rico Symphony Orchestra. Ms. Forrester is well remembered here for her appearances with the Casals Festivals of a bygone era; her present visit has helped to establish a web of good associations ("vibes," if you wish) around the new hall which will become part of the place itself.

Under the direction of John Barnett, Ms. Forrester and the PRSO offered two sets of songs from the rich and romantic nineteenth-century repertory. These were Gustav Mahler's early *Lieder eines fahrenden Gesellen* and Antonin Dvořák's *Zigeunermelodien*, Op. 55.

The Mahler songs were composed to the composer's own texts, and looked forward to his future development of the symphony with solo voice. Still, however, these four songs retain the fresh and delicate charm of the mid-century German art song. The Dvořák set, on the other hand, are from the Czech composer's maturity, and reflect his superb skill in evoking exotic images—or at least exotic to the Western European music lovers of the time. Here the images are Gypsy, settings of romantic texts by the poet Adolf Heyduk.

The language of both the Mahler and Dvořák cycles is German, and Ms. Forrester's diction is so clear that even those to whom German is a third or fourth language had little difficulty in following the texts. Of course, the visual expressiveness of her presentation aided greatly in this, for this artist has, in addition to her glorious voice, expressive line, elegant presence: STYLE.

Speaking of German, wasn't there a time when the PRSO programs included translations into Spanish of texts sung in other languages, as a matter of routine? This type of material is not difficult to obtain, and it is a great help (as well as a courtesy) to patrons. And speaking of German, Spanish and printed programs, recent ones have certainly struck a new low in information, style and proofreading. Composers' dates are wrong, names are ridiculously misspelled, words are missing and foreign language titles are hopelessly mutilated. This is a pity, for any printed program becomes an important document for the study of a particular period's musical interests, activities, personalities, and yes, its level of sophistication. Imagine the chuckles of a graduate seminar even ten or twenty years from now on examining those quaint PRSO programs from the fall 1981 season!

Opening Saturday's concert was a charming orchestral suite by Ernst von Dohnányi. Some sections of our symphony orchestra manage to retain their security and solidity year after year, particularly the woodwinds. Others, however, are presently in a period of decline, and when they will hit bottom cannot now be foreseen. For example, most of the orchestra's string sections suffer to one degree or another from specific or general musical maladies, but the violins seem to be in the worst shape of all. Evident is a disturbing lack of agreement in such basic matters as bowing, fingering, pitch, the length of phrases, the use of open strings and the precise placement of pizzicato notes. Naturally, not all of the fault lies with individual players themselves, for there are questions of leadership and direction involved, too. And such errors as over-conducting, occasionally evident on Saturday, can often do more harm than not conducting at all.

String section faults were most evident in the Dohnányi suite's third movement, marked on Saturday by a kind of shotgun approach to the pizzicato, and in many sections of the Mahler songs, where the desired blanket of soft, warm, thick and shimmering string sound simply was not there. Well, the season is still young, and it may still be possible to get it together.

Accomplished Soprano: Susan Pabón

The San Juan Star
November 18, 1981 By Donald Thompson

Susan Pabón is an accomplished soprano who has been making ever greater contributions to the island's musical life during the past several years. On Sunday afternoon she presented a pleasing program in the Institute of Puerto Rican Culture series in Old San Juan, aided by guitarist Juan Sorroche, pianist-conductor Roselín Pabón and, for the last work on the program, a stageful of able instrumentalists comprising a miniature opera orchestra.

Accompanying the entire first half of the concert was guitarist Sorroche, himself one of the island's foremost soloists but one who is all too infrequently heard these days. Offered were two charming songs by Fernando Sor, four by island composer Ernesto Cordero and five of the celebrated *tonadillas* of Enrique Granados.

Ernesto Cordero is himself a fine guitarist, and most of his production is for the guitar, either alone or in interesting combinations. His music is always melodious, always highly conservative and always well made. Sunday's songs also demonstrated his skill in writing for the voice, and Ms. Pabón's fine presentation brought out all of the virtues and all of the pleasant associations inherent in Cordero's music.

The Granados *tonadillas*, on the other hand, did not fare so well. Here is a curious case of translation of musical material from one instrumental medium to another, a practice which sometimes works and sometimes doesn't. You see, the instrumental part of the Granados songs was originally conceived for piano, but obviously with the guitar (or guitar harmony and guitar rhythm) in mind. You'd think, then, that a transcription for guitar of this guitar-like material would work very well, right?

Wrong. Even a transcription made by such a skilled guitarist as Juan Sorroche sounded empty and spineless on Sunday, seemingly leaving the singer stranded without the effervescent, rollicking and often gutsy power of the piano. It may have been this change of sonoral frame which forced Ms. Pabón into an all too solemn style of presentation, especially of the musical jest "El tra la la y el punteado."

The best qualities of Ms. Pabón's voice shone forth in the somewhat heavier material represented by three of Richard Wagner's rare songs, ably accompanied by pianist Roselín Pabón. These three ("Der Engel," "Stehe still" and "Träume) are from a set of five which Wagner composed on texts by Mathilde Wesendonck, serving as brief studies for the monumental *Tristan und Isolde*. Susan Pabón's voice is just right for this kind of music, for it possesses the required "floating" quality, a perfectly even and controlled vibrato, and that long and expressive "line," as singers like to say.

These qualities also held her in good stead in the concert's final offerings: opera excerpts by Verdi and Mozart. This last was a moving scene from *The Marriage of Figaro*, accompanied by an able but anonymous orchestra of Mozartean dimensions conducted by Roselín Pabón.

It is not often possible for a singer to assemble a program so highly varied in style and means as this one. Susan Pabón is to be both congratulated and thanked for having done so on this occasion.

PRSO: A Nicely Balanced Concert

The San Juan Star
November 25, 1981 (a)   By Donald Thompson

The Puerto Rico Symphony Orchestra has recently been in the capable hands of Associate Music Director Roselín Pabón, who is now well into his third season as Number Two in the island orchestra's artistic hierarchy. On Saturday evening Pabón conducted the orchestra's regular concert in the Performing Arts Center, with a nicely balanced program of Bach, Chopin and Hindemith.

The Bach was the First Brandenburg Concerto, which features several solo instruments against a transparent background orchestra of strings and harpsichord. A miniature wind ensemble made up of the orchestra's two oboes and first bassoon did splendid work here, with other "soloistic" participations marred by faulty intonation, bad rhythm and an occasional false or missing note.

The big orchestral work on Saturday was the Mathis der Maler Symphony by Paul Hindemith (1895-1963). Hindemith was one of the great craftsmen of twentieth-century music, whose works were among the last to successfully reconcile the thrust of modern "up for grabs" harmony with the stability of the older forms and styles of concert music. *Mathis der Maler* was a characteristically complex opera of Hindemith, and this often performed "symphony" is made up of the orchestral interludes originally associated with the opera. Like Stravinsky's Rite of Spring, Bartók's Concerto for Orchestra and almost anything by Britten, Prokofiev or Shostakovich, Mathis der Maler is a good test of what an orchestra can do. With notable exceptions (mainly in the woodwinds), Saturday's performance of the Hindemith work showed what this orchestra cannot do very well just now.

For reasons which have been explored elsewhere and which should be of the deepest concern to the orchestra's new management, there are great raw patches in the orchestral picture here, especially in the strings. Some of these are due simply to numbers; it takes a lot of fiddle players to get the sound required by the music of Mahler, Strauss, Wagner and Hindemith. Other raw patches, however, are due to lack of skill, concentration and the professional continuity required to build security, reliability and unity in string section response. This is not entirely a matter of numbers, but goes back in part to managerial policy in engaging and retaining the best available players—or in not engaging and retaining them, as it appears. String section weaknesses were glaringly evident in Saturday's Hindemith, including but not limited to faulty pitch and rhythm, with a few hairy false entrances laid on for good measure.

The picture brightened greatly after intermission, when pianist María del Carmen Gil and the PRSO offered a nice performance of the Second Piano Concerto of Chopin. Here, the orchestra's role is one of accompanying. This is not so, of course, of all piano concertos, but it is indeed the case in those of the superpianist Chopin. This particular concerto is not one of the big ones popularwise, but it is certainly a valuable and interesting one, and as much a challenge to a pianist as almost any other.

María del Carmen Gil is an accomplished musician who continues to make important contributions to the island's musical life. Her performance on Saturday was marked by clean and complete technique, providing a sparkling and liquid delivery of Chopin's music.

Conductor Pabón provided the necessary element of control and coordination between soloist and orchestra, adding greatly to the success of the Chopin performance. Pabón seems to be a very careful and accurate conductor who does his homework well. His beat is clear and understandable and he gives all of the necessary cues and entrances, which of course is basically what a conductor is for. Nor does he expend much energy dancing on the podium, which is what a lot of conductors do. Pabón's work as Number Two with the PRSO has been good, and he will bear watching as his career develops along the rocky musical road which he has chosen.

Gym Audience Sweaty but Smiling

The San Juan Star
November 25, 1981 (b) By Donald Thompson

The gymnasium of the UPR Medical Sciences Campus was the scene last week of an important event in the present San Juan musical season. On Wednesday evening the campus' cultural activities office, in collaboration with its sister agency at the Río Piedras campus, offered a program which was simply entitled "The New Music." Performers were eminent Argentine composer Alcides Lanza and the versatile actress-singer-dancer Meg Sheppard, who presented a varied sample of present and recent tendencies in musical composition of international scope.

The truth is, music today has gone far beyond its traditional sonoral province, claiming in a mystical search for artistic *Lebensraum*, as it were, territories which for centuries have either belonged to someone else or have lain unattended in an unexplored wilderness. For this reason many contemporary composers speak not of music, particularly, but of music-theater, or of mixed media, or of polyart. A given work may thus include not only sound (produced in orthodox or unorthodox ways) but also dance, mime, narration or recitation, film or slides, light play and even odors and temperature changes. Naturally, various flourishing technologies have had their hand in these developments, including electronics, the computer, sound reproduction and astounding advances in the design, recording and projection of light and film effects.

And here, in fact, is part of the problem. If the composer is not really on top of all of these technologies, or if he has not had at hand all of the means required for the realization of what he has in mind, or if some elements are lacking at the moment of "retrieval" (i.e., the concert), the product can appear amateurish or pretentious, and the result will be counterproductive.

In these circumstances anyone interested in the musical avant-garde would have done better watching the first ten minutes of some space or sci-fi movie playing nearby, for here—in the incredibly complex technology of the big time movie industry—is where all of this really comes together nowadays. I might add that in many neighborhood theaters this experience can also include mixed-media odors, aleatory temperature changes and a whole range of unusual tactile sensations as well . . . if that's what turns you on. . . .

The Lanza-Sheppard concert-in-the-gym came off rather well on the whole, with this pair of experienced troupers surmounting every challenge which the environment hurled at them. These chance factors included a rock concert downstairs, a creaking stage, not wholly adequate projection equipment and the generally uncontrollable conditions which exist in such spaces as gyms, circus tents and dirigible hangars. Offered were two mixed-media works by Lanza himself, music for piano by the noted Spanish composer Luis de Pablo, interesting pieces by Canadian composers Micheline Coulombe St. Marcoux and Serge Perron, and one of those almost forgotten precious jewels from the misty prehistory of the avant-garde movement: Bacchanale by John Cage, for prepared piano and dating from the late '30s.

Fine, but what do you do for an encore? As if to answer the frequently asked "Sure, but can you guys play any REAL music?" the Lanza-Sheppard duo offered "Send in the Clowns," from the musical play *A Little Night Music*. This tied it up nicely for Wednesday's youthful audience, which left the gym sweaty but smiling.

On the Road with the San Juan Children's Choir

The San Juan Star
December 26, 1981   By Donald Thompson

Sunday, December 20. Daybreak. Enjeeped and on the road in search of San Juan Children's Choir. Elusive group, sighted on Saturday in southwest Puerto Rico. Headed north. Hope to intercept in remote northwest corner of island. What's this San Juan Children's Choir? Muster of young musicians, splendid international tradition. Excellent training. Broadest repertory. Superprofessional self-discipline. A decade and more of fine concerts here and abroad. Not the same kids for so long, of course. Boys' voices change (we hope) and girls' do too, but in a different way.

Your correspondent deeply inspired by smashing accounts in STAR of safaris to murky island lakes, remote waterfalls, secret canyons, vine-covered auto carcasses. Tries to attain similar sense of adventure. Almost succeeds thanks to bad brakes on jeep, descending a steep and muddy road above Arecibo. Why above Arecibo? Lost. Map helps this sense of adventure, too. Shredded fragment which covers from Carolina to just beyond Manatí. Must get a new map before trying anything like this again.

Concert announced for 10:00 A.M. at Moca. Where's Moca? Employing time honored navigation aid, consult four boys on bicycle. With broad smiles, helpfully direct me due north, straight into the Atlantic. Even I know better than that. Can't be, for it puts the morning sun on my right, right? Finally find the turn, onto highway 110, I think. Last two digits covered by old political stickers. Sign "Moca" also deceptive. Watch out, travelers. Metal post twisted some 80 degrees; seems to point

CONCERT LIFE IN PUERTO RICO   361

back toward Arecibo. Moca turns out to be one of those innumerable sweet island towns. Pretty plaza, old fashioned Roman Catholic church, drowsy público drivers and cart vendors on a sunny Sunday morning.

Gain vantage point in unused choir loft of church among dusty saints and busted clockwork just as San Juan Children's Choir begins processional just below. "Silent Night" in three languages, but not all at the same time. Thirty-five talented people aged six to sixteen years. Program ranges from Spanish *villancicos* to music by Domingo Santa Cruz Wilson and Zoltán Kodály. Instruments, too: guitars, cuatros, recorders. Beautifully performed. Townspeople get the message. Complete silence during each piece, thunderous applause after. Quite right. When was the last time an early Renaissance French carol was performed with such grace and skill in the Church of Our Lady of Monserrate in Moca? Complete with stylish Landini cadences, too.

Why Moca and why 10:00 A.M.? Part of a *trulla navideña*, it turns out. Ambulatory Christmas party/serenade. San Juan Children's Choir beginning third and last grueling day of concerts in central and western Puerto Rico. But why would these seemingly normal kids do such a thing, for heaven's sake?

Dedicated founder/teacher/conductor Evy Lucío explains. Hispanic tradition of neighborhood *trulla*. Also, excellent training for choir members as troupers. Also, desire to share broad spectrum of best Christmas music performed correctly. Even so, twelve concerts in three days on the road! The mind reels.

After Moca come Isabela, Quebradillas and Camuy, I think. Blurred memory and wriggly notes due to sacrifice of customary rejuvenating siesta. Not practical in jeep. On other hand, snoozer subject to arrest or worse if found supine on the shady roadside. Nevertheless, some impressions remain. Uncompromising choral quality, for one. Regardless of surroundings, rhythm is faultless, pitch impeccable. Pronunciation in four or five languages as clear as can be. Churches the ideal acoustical setting for these voices. Vaulted ceilings, hard walls provide just enough echo when the place is full of people, without exception the case on this tour. Minimum of stagecraft necessary. Kids carry on their own instruments, sing and play from memory. Troupers indeed. Off the bus, into the church, processional, perform, bit of socializing (maybe three minutes), back on the bus and on to . . . where next?

Speaking of buses, who popped for this one? SJCC definitely a non-profit enterprise. From its own funds probably couldn't have paid for the gasoline. Gasoline. Gasoline? You got it! I look around for an angel, a sponsor, a benefactor of both SJCC and the people who hear it. Discover Ms. Teresita Bagué, vice president, no less, of Public Relations Group Inc. This firm represents Esso Standard Oil Company (Puerto Rico), which has underwritten the whole exercise: TV shots, newspaper advertising and announcements, bus, overnight accommodations . . . the works. Hardworking Ms. Bagué sees this as a valuable contribution both to the development of an important island cultural initiative (the San Juan Children's Choir) and to the joy of a lovely tradition: this musical Christmas ramble. I concur. Ms. Bagué promises me a new Esso map.

Moca, Isabela, Quebradillas, Camuy. Despite desperate physiological condition already described, your correspondent slowly becomes aware of other adults peripheral to the tour. Who are they? Turn out to be parents. Officially ignored and rigidly barred from contact with their offspring before, during and after concerts. Nonetheless, form a caravan of ten or a dozen cars following the bus from town to town. Why? What in heaven's name do they see in this racketing about the far reaches of Borinquen?

Mrs. Beddie Nemcik de Rodríguez has a nine-year-old daughter in the SJCC. She has followed this tour since it began in Utuado (how many days or weeks ago?) and intends to hang on until the end, whenever that might be. This is her second annual San Juan Children's Choir island tour, which she sees as an important educational and cultural experience for its members. Adds that the same thing goes double for the parents, who come to know the island, each other and themselves better. Have fun, too.

The tour is to end in the Cathedral, in San Juan. From Camuy I'm told it's a straight shot eastward down highway 2. Hard to get lost, right? Wrong. Decide to take a look at the beach along the way. Half hour later, finding ocean on my right and sun in my eyes, begin to wonder if I've made a wrong turn. Sure enough, headed west not east. Need that map.

San Juan Cathedral is an impressive space indeed, after modest island parish churches. Different sort of audience, too. Couple of thousand at least. Pews packed, overflow milling around the edges and all the way back to street. Impossible to see, very difficult to hear. Worried sacristan to an assistant: "Watch carefully lest someone knock over a saint or try to steal a camel. You can never tell with a mob like this." A mob maybe, but certainly an appreciative one. After final piece (Kodály), seemed ready to knock over the pews and steal the entire San Juan Children's Choir, Evy Lucío and all.

Me—I'm glad I saw the SJCC in the island churches, both for the sound and for the spirit. Too, there's no better way to launch the Christmas season than by joining such a joyful *trulla*. Next year I go the whole route, but I sure hope Ms. Bagué sends me that map.

John Cage Week

The San Juan Star
March 11, 1982   By Donald Thompson

    The Cultural Activities Office at the University of Puerto Rico came through the recent campus dislocations virtually unscratched. Without missing a beat, this important element in the island's musical life bounced back to present in quick succession one of the world's greatest pianists (Paul Badura-Skoda), an extraordinary ancient music ensemble (Music for a While) and, with the collaboration of the UPR Music Department and other agencies, a recent week of activities centered on the figure and the thought of composer John Cage.

    John Cage turns seventy this year, reaching that point in a creative life which is often marked by special observances and gentle get-togethers. Such was the nature of this UPR John Cage Week: a kind of living *Festschrift* or dedicatory anthology offered by colleagues, friends and students. A festival, you might say. . . .

    Cage was born in Los Angeles in 1912. As a young man he became widely known for his strikingly innovative views on music and art: views demonstrated in concerts which aroused public reactions ranging from amusement through bewilderment to rage. By the late 1930s Cage was established as the leader of the iconoclastic wing of the musical vanguard in the United States. A trip to Europe after WW II helped bring European composition (particularly in Germany) up to date after more than a decade of isolation.

    The principles of indeterminacy, chance and random selection in musical composition, first propounded by Cage, have been at the very center of the worldwide new music movement for a quarter century now. In fact, it is impossible to conceive of a lecture, a university course or a concert series devoted to twentieth-century music anywhere in the world which does not repeatedly invoke the name of John Cage. Simply stated, Cage is one of the great musical innovators of our time and of all time.

The John Cage Week at UPR enlisted the collaboration of international experts and specialists. From the U.S. came Cage himself plus writer/editor Richard Kostelanetz plus pianist David Tudor plus the extraordinary Merce Cunningham Dance Company. From France came singer Noemi Perugia and musicologist Daniel Charles, the latter the chairman of the Department of Music at the University of Paris VIII. Puerto Rico was well represented by actress Rosa Luisa Márquez, composers Rafael Aponte-Ledée and Francis Schwartz, and the performance ensemble Número Tres, headed by Nelson Rivera. In different combinations, these forces unfolded a panorama of activities which explored the different facets of John Cage's art and thought.

And what are some of the main facets of John Cage's art and thought? Basic to the whole Cage aesthetic, as was convincingly explained in a lecture by Richard Kostelanetz and repeatedly demonstrated throughout the week, is a tranquil, almost oriental view of the flow of things. In this flow, events are simply short lived abstractions or arbitrarily designated blocks of time-space (or better, timespace). Cage's own music, then, can be best approached as a slice out of the great sonoral timespace continuum. Ideally, such an arbitrarily selected slice would be unfocused, undirected and non-hierarchical, simply floating in the eternal "now," or as Kostelanetz so neatly put it, "between the now and the nevermore." In other words, what is, is.

This kind of thinking leads quite naturally to the breakdown of the traditional Western barriers between art forms and to new syntheses of elements formerly kept separated. This, of course, underlies the entire "mixed media" or "polyart" movement in and around the music of the past quarter century, as well as the introduction of exotic sound objects into a more traditionally conceived musical order. Thus Cage's prepared piano of the early '50s, with screws, coins and erasers between the strings; thus his famous work 4'33", in which the only performer sits through the work's carefully timed three movements without playing a note; and thus a quarter century of musical or multi-media "happenings" worldwide, most of them consciously incorporating principles first outlined by John Cage.

Of course the same kind of homogenizing impulse has been felt in other areas of the "great timespace artistic continuum" over the past half century, from typography to painting to sculpture to poetry to fiction to—you name it. A couple of Cage Week presentations focused on the history of such manifestations in Puerto Rico, with Rosa Luisa Márquez emphasizing the theater end of it and Rafael Aponte-Ledée the musical. And who better than Aponte-Ledée to describe the pioneer thrust of such island groups as Fluxus in the '60s and Soprodimus a little later, or the three astounding Biennials of Twentieth Century Music, in whose organization he played a leading role? It was mainly in these concerts and these series, in fact, that the music of John Cage first received consistent attention in Puerto Rico.

Throughout the Cage Week's panels, lectures, concerts and other events, the unifying thread was the composer himself. Cage was usually present and smiling while around and through the UPR campus flowed the great eternal timespace continuum, disturbed only by final examinations. Aside from his benign presence itself, Cage offered a couple of solo performances, as you might say. These, whether cast in the form of poetry or in more mundane prose commentary, focused the rather diffuse thought generated by surrounding Cage Week events onto the man himself. Cage's remarks revolved mainly around his affinity for the works of James Joyce, Marcel Duchamps and Erik Satie, and in fact blended into a kind of Joycean stream of consciousness scenario. Calm, clear, almost seventy-year-old voice delivering pretty close to a nonstructured, non-hierarchical slice of the eternal timespace continuum . . . right here in Río Piedras. . . .

What spectacular effects of Cage's visit will be felt here? None, for Cage's nature, presence and purposes are nonspectacular. On the other hand, he may have exercised a very healthy calming effect, if the vibrations emanating from the UPR Theater and the Music Building have in any way permeated the surrounding university community. At the very least, John Cage Week has brought to Puerto Rico a momentary focus of some of the most potent musical thought of the twentieth century. What is, is.

Yvonne Figueroa and the PRSO

The San Juan Star
April 14, 1982   By Donald Thompson

    Roselín Pabón has been the associate music director of the Puerto Rico Symphony Orchestra for the past several seasons, and as Number Two has generally done a fine job on the relatively few occasions when his work has been visible. Pabón conducted Saturday evening's regular PRSO concert in the Drama Theater of the Performing Arts Center at Minillas in a varied program including two works by Puerto Rican composers. The first was a century-old overture, *La Lira*, by admired island composer Juan Morel Campos, a piece which immediately brings to mind the most solemnly melodious music of Verdi and Donizetti.

    Frequently over the past couple of years, concertgoers have expressed bewilderment over the program notes for the PRSO concerts, which in the manner of plastic foam custard fill space without providing sustenance. The notes for Saturday's concert were about par for the course. Page 22 tells us that the Morel Campos overture (1) was obviously conceived for orchestra, that (2) it doesn't lose its autoctonous Puerto Rican character and that (3) Morel had to write it for piano because of the limitations existing at the end of the nineteenth century. Statement one is questionable for the lack of evidence presented; statement two is meaningless, and the premise of statement three is false. In the meantime we are left with an overture for piano. Whose do you suppose was the anonymous but able hand which made the sonorous and stylistically appropriate orchestration heard on Saturday? We may never know, unless the next time around someone provides some hard and useful data concerning the program to be played.

    Another island work heard on Saturday was *Ode to Cabo Rojo* by Héctor Campos-Parsi, dating from the late-flowering "nationalistic" period in Puerto Rican concert music (ca. 1960). Broadly lyrical, this work brings to mind some of the "Great Plains" music of some U.S. composers of the '30s and '40s. Here, I suppose, the reference would have to be to the Lajas Valley, but somehow this particular image doesn't travel so well. In any case, I have never considered the *Ode* to be one of Campos' best works. Completely lacking in thematic development, it gains its effect mainly through the repetition of a couple of short winded themes in different keys and with a final clattering apotheosis. On the other hand, I cannot agree with the faithful concertgoer who at intermission muttered that the composer "should have stopped in Mayagüez."

One thing must be said about Saturday's performance of the *Ode to Cabo Rojo*, however. Conductor Pabón or someone has painstakingly weeded a couple of bushels of wrong notes out of the individual orchestra parts, wrong notes which have plagued and obscured the work ever since its first performances. In fact, during the past decade or so the *Ode* was in danger of disappearing entirely as layer upon layer of ad hoc "corrections" were applied by conductors and individual players, as is common practice with ill-copied or hastily copied manuscript parts for new works. Campos' *Ode* can now be perceived clearly, perhaps for the first time.

Saturday's featured soloist was pianist Yvonne Figueroa—or is it Ivonne? The printed program has it both ways. Ms. Figueroa offered a performance of the Second Piano Concerto of Franz Liszt, an intense and powerful work which seldom lets up. And when it does let up it's only for a brief spell of somewhat less intense music, as in the lyric second section.

The Liszt concerto consists of several sections, vestiges of the separate movements of the older type of concerto design but played without pause. In the manner of the tone poem or symphonic poem so ably cultivated by the same composer, this work gains its unity and flow from a handful of melodic motives or thematic fragments which recur throughout in different contexts.

Ms. Figueroa is a skilled and powerful pianist, and she played her solo part in a powerful fashion indeed. The modern grand piano can be a formidable weapon, easily capable of wiping out a singer, a violinist or some other recital or chamber music partner. It is not often that a lone pianist unrelentingly dominates a sixty-piece symphony orchestra, but this is what happened on Saturday at Minillas: a demonstration of sheer piano power.

Here, incidentally, is another example of programming problems created by the lack of a permanent home for the Puerto Rico Symphony Orchestra. This Liszt concerto and the Seventh Symphony of Beethoven, also heard on Saturday, are appropriate not for the middle-sized Drama Theater at Minillas but for the large Festival Hall—if not, indeed, for the Sixto Escobar Stadium. If, on the other hand, the Drama Theater must be used for symphony orchestra concerts, an appropriate concerto would have been a Mozart or an early Beethoven, whose sonoral dimensions fit the space.

And speaking of Beethoven, the Seventh Symphony was frankly a disappointment on Saturday: noisy, disjointed and unsubtle. Here, Pabón's conducting was more visually dramatic than has generally been his custom; in this case needlessly dramatic and perhaps even counterproductively so. Especially at the beginning of the symphony, orchestral slippages occurred which might be attributed to a lapse of conductorial attention just when and where it was badly needed. On the other hand, the first few bars of the second movement sounded lovely, involving only the orchestra's fine viola, cello and bass sections. Generally, however, the symphony displayed the customary problems of our orchestra's upper string sections: wrong entrances, wrong notes, rhythmic inaccuracies and the promiscuous use of open strings, which in the context of this symphony's key relations stuck out like barbed wire.

Casals Opener Signals Shift in Artistic Direction

The San Juan Star
May 31, 1982   By Donald Thompson

A completely revised, rebuilt, remodeled and restructured Puerto Rico Casals Festival opened on Friday evening at the Performing Arts Center in Santurce. As is widely known by now, the sponsorship of this series has passed from the Puerto Rico Industrial Development Company to the new Representative Arts Corporation, a subsidiary of the insular government's Administration for the Development of Arts and Culture. Accompanying this change but not entirely due to it has come a complete shift in the series' artistic direction. In its previous incarnation this concert series was a Caribbean extension of violinist Alexander Schneider's New York-based musical enterprises, the legitimacy of this connection deriving from a long standing professional relationship between Schneider and the late cellist Pablo Casals. The new artistic management is focused upon conductor Jorge Mester, whose tenure as festival musical director actually began before the change in sponsorship took place. However, the present series is the first to be entirely organized under the new administrative arrangements, and will for that reason attract close scrutiny.

And what does the opening concert tell us about the new artistic directions, perceptions and preoccupations? First off, it is evident that an attempt has been made to connect this annual event (or at least the first concert) to the historical figure of Pablo Casals. As Casals approached old age, and especially during the years when Puerto Rico was his base of operations, his musical tastes became more and more conservative, as is known by his reported expressions concerning twentieth-century music.

Yet the former management of the Puerto Rico Casals Festival, in a frantic and disorganized search for audiences, broadened the repertory in ways which strained (and finally abandoned) the logic of a "Casals" festival. It is an open question just how much Casals had to say about the programming of the series in his last years. In any event, the management of the "new" Casals festival seems to have taken the great cellist's expressed views into account, at least for Friday's concert. Presented were works by composers whose music Casals was known to love and to which he devoted decades of study and performance: Mozart, Schubert and Beethoven.

Mozart was represented by the miraculous Quartet in G Minor for Piano and Strings, handsomely presented by an ad hoc ensemble formed by Elmar Oliveira (violin), Jorge Mester (viola), Lynn Harrell (cello) and André Michel Schub (piano). The same performers also filled out the rest of the evening: Schub with a fine performance of Schubert's freewheeling Wanderer Fantasy for piano, then the four (with Mester as conductor) collaborating with an expanded Puerto Rico Symphony Orchestra in Beethoven's Triple Concerto, Op. 56 for violin, cello, piano and orchestra.

This concerto is an interesting work, combining elements of the symphony, the concerto, the *symphonie concertante* of Mozart's day, and the even earlier musical stratum of the Baroque concerto grosso. Basically the idea is the contrast between the sonorities of a small ensemble (the soloists) and a big one (the orchestra) while not discarding the possibility of strictly individual activity by one or another soloist along the way. The weak point of this particular work has always been the third movement, where instead of providing a fast and exhilarating finale, as occurs in most symphonies and concertos, Beethoven employs a ponderous polonaise. It takes some doing to make this finale sparkle, but sparkle it did on Friday in the hands of these fine soloists. The Puerto Rico Symphony Orchestra has not sounded so well in a long time: the reasons for this may become clear later in the week when the island orchestra has a complete program of its own to deal with.

Impressions Following the Casals Festival

The San Juan Star
June 19, 1982 By Donald Thompson

    The most recent Puerto Rico Casals Festival (getting on toward number 30 by now, it must be) ended with a couple of big concerts bringing big forces into play. More or less settled into the hall now was the Houston Symphony Orchestra, which under the direction of its own Sergiu Comissiona (Friday) and festival musical director Jorge Mester (Saturday) provided the main emphasis, with soloists and other elements laid on to vary the fare and hopefully bring the whole thing to a stirring finale. Friday's soloist was calm young Cho-Liang Lin, who made a powerful impression with the Fifth Violin Concerto of Henri Vieuxtemps. The Vieuxtemps concertos are in the lusty tradition of works by Paganini, Sarasate, and other composers who themselves were virtuoso violinists. Frankly showpieces, such works are severe tests for any soloist as well as fine indications of performance conditions at the time of their composition. If a composer wrote such music for his own performances as a violinist, we can be sure that at least one violinist was capable of playing it: the composer himself! In Friday's performance, violinist Cho-Liang Lin tossed off the concerto with apparent ease. He also drew a standing ovation from the audience and, more significantly, warm and fraternal applause from an experienced orchestra which you can be sure has heard and seen just about everything there is in the way of traveling violinists.

    Also on Friday's program was a weighty performance of a weighty work: the D Minor Symphony (why do we insist on calling it the "D Minor" Symphony? It's the ONLY symphony) of César Franck, also conducted by the frisky Sergiu Comissiona. And opening the concert was Debussy's lovely suite *Nocturnes*, performed, as the man intended, complete with the third and final movement. This third movement, entitled "Sirens", is the problematic one, for it requires a chorus of female voices intoning liquid but textless lines. Friday's women were the Women's Chorus of the Amherst College Choir, on the island for these last Casals Festival concerts. On Friday the Amherst ladies sang well in tune and displayed good control of breath and phrasing, but sounded a bit thin, seated far upstage in the big Festival Hall of the Performing Arts Center.

In Saturday night's final concert the entire Amherst group appeared, along with the Houston Symphony Orchestra and four soloists, in the Lord Nelson Mass by Joseph Haydn. The Amherst College Choir, conducted by Prof. Bruce McInnes of that venerable Massachusetts institution, is a very fine example of a species of performance organization of which there are well over a thousand in the U.S. and a couple of good representatives in Puerto Rican universities as well. Typically, the university or college chorus is made up of students whose field of specialized study is probably not music at all, but who are interested in the study and performance of choral literature as part of the rich intellectual and artistic life which from the standpoint of participants can be found today mainly (if not almost exclusively) in universities. Part of this is purely statistical; in a population of from 1,000 to 40,000 young people representing a high average of their society's intellectual and cultural experience, you can probably find fifty or a hundred able and interested choral singers without a great deal of trouble. As I've suggested, the Amherst College Choir is an excellent representative of its species, and its performance here was a fine example of what can be attained in a propitious environment with devoted and able but not necessarily super-specialized musical performers.

Soloists for Saturday's performance of the Haydn mass were soprano Aura Robledo, mezzosoprano Shirley Close, tenor Rubén Broitman and baritone Angelo Cruz. Three of the four (Robledo, Broitman and Cruz) are to one degree or another products of island musical training and experience. Aura Robledo displayed nice warm vocal quality on Saturday, but with a sound so small that at times it was difficult to hear her over the reduced Haydnesque orchestra. Tenor Broitman, a very capable young singer, is just now smack in the middle of some technical changes being wrought by intensive off-island studies. Such transformations can be traumatic, and the best anyone can do is bear with Broitman, hoping that the completed mutations will restore the "center" and the dynamic intensity which his voice displayed before his present pilgrimage began. Baritone Cruz is a very able musician who does well in almost everything he undertakes in the general area of opera and oratorio literature. On Saturday, however, his low range lacked the force necessary to deal satisfactorily with Haydn's bass lines. Cruz' pronunciation, however, was about the best, sharing this welcome distinction with mezzosoprano Close, who made a generally very good impression in her first appearance in Puerto Rico.

Saturday's concert closed with a performance (still another here) of Brahms' Third Symphony, conducted by Jorge Mester and bringing most of the big Houston Symphony Orchestra back to the stage.

And so, what with one thing and another this diverse (not to say perverse) concert series came to a close. What impressions remain? Some very specific impressions remain of one important aspect, the program book, for this is what stays in the hand after the musical bird has flown. This year's program notes dealing with specific musical works made a giant step forward. These were obviously written by someone who had access to the necessary sources of specialized information, the knowledge of how to deal with such sources, and the ability to make interesting copy out of what is basically not very interesting material in itself: the raw data of composers' lives and the dates of composition of specific works. Also extremely helpful this year was the inclusion of translations and summaries of sung texts. On the other hand, most other program material was disastrous. Who, for example, knows of a work, presumably dealing with a lovable Italian immigrant storyteller, entitled *Los Cuentos de Papa Gino* (Tales of Papa Gino), p. 97? Figure it out, opera buffs and program advertisers. In addition, proofreading of the entire production was so bad as to place it on the level of a junior high school yearbook. Almost every page offers an uncorrected typo, or an incorrectly accented or misspelled word in Spanish, or an easily corrected error of fact (Brahms dying at the age of fourteen for example). Why is this important, anyway? It's important because long after it's been forgotten how well (or how badly) some conductor conducted some particular work, this program book will remain on the shelves of a music research library as source material indicating how seriously music was REALLY taken in the Puerto Rico of 1982.

OK, but what general MUSICAL impressions remain? No general

impressions at all, at least to this listener. However, there are a few particular memories which emerge from a generally shapeless and marathonic musical mass: the Waverly Consort's stunning presentation of medieval and renaissance music, for example. Also the style and swing of Baroque music as presented by the Musical Offering ensemble. And who can forget Elly Ameling's most recent appearances here, or the extraordinary Emerson String Quartet, both with and without pianist Lee Luvisi? Violinist Oliveira, cellist Harrell, pianists Schub, Ramos and Firkusny, cellist Rose, violist Crouse . . . but, again, I keep thinking of the Waverley's kemence, ud and goat's horn.

Quite a concert series, you might say, or was it really three of four concert series compressed into a couple of weeks? And certainly not a festival, if that honored term still refers to the celebration of some single and unique concept. At most, a third of this series' offerings could honestly be connected with the known tastes and vehemently expressed views of the known historical figure of Pablo Casals, in whose name this series took place. For example, sometime look up what Casals and Igor Stravinsky had to say about each other, and you will have an idea of how far this series has strayed from any honest relationship with the memory of the great Catalan cellist. The position, it seems to me, is clear, as well as the alternatives. If this is to be a "Casals" festival, it's clear that what is offered should have some demonstrable connection with the historic figure of Pablo Casals and his known tastes and convictions. And this, if you care to look it up, rules out an awful lot of music. On the other hand, if it's to be a catch-all Puerto Rico June Festival it should be called that: a Puerto Rico Festival, with perhaps a concert or two devoted to music which Casals is known to have loved. As festival managements have learned the hard way, it's doubtful if an island public would turn out for more than a concert or two of Casals' favorite music anyway. On the OTHER other hand (are there three?), very little was presented this time which could not have been presented, perhaps more economically, by one or another of the island's regular concert-giving agencies ranging from the Pro Arte Musical Society to a properly staffed and managed Puerto Rico Symphony Orchestra and to the various university series which invite public subscription. What no existing agency is equipped to offer, such as the Houston or the Cincinnatti Symphony Orchestras, could certainly be booked as special attractions by the Administration for the Development of Arts and Culture and without involving any special "festival" format, which in the long run has only tended to inflate (and consequently devalue) the verbal currency. So the question remains, in the manner of a TV serial after every episode: "Whither the Puerto Rico Casals Festival, and Why?"

Pianist **Jesús María Sanromá**, soprano **Olga Iglesias** and tenor **Alex Vázquez** preparing for a 1982 concert.

Operatic *Déjà Vu*

The San Juan Star
September 1, 1982   By Donald Thompson

For this reviewer, *déjà vu* is becoming the name of the game in island opera presentations. Not only do the works themselves bring back scenes from 15, 20, 25 years ago, but so do most of the producers, production staffers and island-born performers who nowadays appear—and reappear—on the ever shifting (but never really changing) island opera panorama.

Teatro de la Opera's recent short run of Rossini's *The Barber of Seville* is a case in point. The work is the first opera which I ever played as an instrumentalist in an orchestra pit. It also marked my first (albeit anonymous) performance as an instrumentalist in San Juan, in a production in the UPR Theater ca. 1955 by an ambitious but now generally forgotten company called Círculo Operático. The recent *Barber* production also brings back memories on another plane, for stage-wise it drew heavily on a 1972 production of the work by another island company. And finally, the performers themselves. Baritone Pablo Elvira, the present Figaro, I first saw with a conductor's-eye view in the pit of the Tapia Theater. Elvira was a fine trumpet player (did you know that?), whose only difficulty was in ignoring the stage action and concentrating on his own part. Later, I again saw him from the "wrong" end of a baton, in an island production of the other "Figaro" opera: Mozart's *Marriage of Figaro*. Soprano Marta Márquez' appearance as Rosina in this *Barber* production has been described as some kind of debut on the island stage. It is not, for I (for one) conducted performances here to which she added a great deal of skill and sparkle. Ms. Márquez first appeared as one of the kids in *The Sound of Music* at the Tapia, and some years later as Barberina in *The Marriage of Figaro*. In the latter piece she showed, in addition to fine talent and training, intuitive stage skill in turning an often forgotten brief part into almost a major role. In the meantime, she had appeared here as Frasquita in a production of *Carmen* by still another island company. The artistic director and main mover of this Teatro de la Opera company is tenor Antonio Barasorda. *Déjà vu?* I first saw Barasorda, and with him (ready?) august legislator and sometime singer Rony Jarabo, across the conductor's desk in a production of a zarzuela in the Tapia Theater, while skilled mezzo Darysabel Isales and I have shared several productions over the years. Rafael Ferrer, musical director for this production, is a colleague in academe and sometime lyric theater collaborator, while it was the Puerto Rico Symphony Orchestra which provided the orchestral half of the Rossini work. I was a member of that assemblage for a decade or so (can it be that it sounds no worse without me?), and several of the present members go all the way back to that misty *Barber of Seville* of the mid-'50s.

So we come full circle. In an attempt to separate "A Night at the Opera" from "Old Home Week at the Performing Arts Center," then, what can I tell you? What about this production of *The Barber of Seville*, put together by producer Manuel Fernández (still another blast from the past)? Under the skilled stage direction of Michael Temme, Thursday's performance often attained the visual sparkle and drive which are associated with this Rossini work perhaps more than with any other opera. A great part of a stage director's work is to devise interesting things for people to do, while designing the flow of traffic on the stage, and all within the unyielding frame of a musical work and a developing plot. Sounds simple, doesn't it? Well, it's not, for it must also take into account the characteristics of individual performers if the whole thing is to appear natural and unforced. Temme accomplished this: what lapses and awkwardnesses occurred in Thursday's performance were due to that bane of opera production here as elsewhere: under-rehearsal due to the pressure of time. Singer-actors? The main forces of continuity in this production were Pablo Elvira (Figaro) and Richard McKee (Bartolo). Both are solid performers and first rate singers, and the comic intensity of their shared scenes never lets up for a moment. Soprano Marta Márquez' lovely voice has attained great breadth and considerable power during her flourishing European career, and she also brought to the role of Rosina a welcome measure of youthful gaiety and charm. Tenor Luigi Alva made a convincing Count Almaviva. His voice seemed harsh in his opening serenade on Thursday evening, but it gained in warmth and security as the work progressed. Alva's dramatic gifts were evident, especially in his wildly comic appearances disguised as a soldier and as Rosina's substitute music master. Island bass Justino Díaz made one of his finest acting appearances in recent memory as Basilio, and his voice has seldom sounded better. Smaller roles were nicely developed by Darysabel Isales, Oscar de Gracia, René Torres and Carmelo Santana, and an able male chorus had been prepared for this production by Pablo Boissen.

Aside from a few moments of slippage between the stage and the pit, the musical coordination of Thursday's performance seemed satisfactory. Presumably, these and a few other disconcerting details were to be worked out by the time of Saturday's final performance.

Out of Season Offering

The San Juan Star
September 9, 1982   By Donald Thompson

The 1982-83 season of your very own Puerto Rico Symphony Orchestra has more or less slid into being, with a ballet, an opera (both on other folks' series), and an "out of season" concert. This last event took place on Saturday evening in the concert hall of the Puerto Rico Conservatory of Music in Hato Rey, and was ably conducted by Roselín Pabón, the orchestra's associate musical director.

Saturday's concert had previously been described as being devoted to Puerto Rican music, but it turned into something else when for one reason or another, works by Chabrier and Rimsky-Korsakov were also scheduled. If the concert had a unifying theme or purpose, it can only have been to again demonstrate the healthy symbiosis which exists nowadays between the concert stage and the musical wing of academe. This is true everywhere, for if you look carefully at the program credits of soloists and living composers on the world's concert circuits you will find that many of these figures teach in the music department of some university. This recent Puerto Rico Symphony Orchestra concert was a case in point. One of the featured works was a new version of Ernesto Cordero's Guitar Concerto, with the solo part handsomely played by guitarist Juan Sorroche. Both Cordero and Sorroche are members of the Music Department of the University of Puerto Rico, and both have made important additional contributions to the musical life of Puerto Rico (and beyond), as well.

The present version of Cordero's concerto represents a considerable expansion of an earlier work, and has brought several improvements to it. While retaining all of the graceful conservatism of Cordero's style, this new form of the concerto is more solid and somewhat longer, because the composer has expanded and developed his own vision of the work. What was formerly thin and crystalline is now robust; what formerly was simply presented is now developed at length. A great deal of the success of Saturday's performance of the concerto must also be attributed to Juan Sorroche's fine playing of it. This performance has again confirmed Sorroche's place in the guitar world. It also reminds us that it takes two to tango; that is, to create music requires two elements: the composer who conceives the art work and performers to put the flesh on it, producing the sound which (hopefully) is what the composer had in mind in the first place.

The same happy combination of elements was present in Saturday's performance of another island work: Jack Délano's cheerful Concertino Clásico for Trumpet and Small Orchestra. Here, the soloist was Roberto Ramírez, another member of the UPR music faculty and a leading figure among island musical specialists. Délano's concertino is probably one of his best compositions; it is certainly one of his most consistent, most highly developed, and most full of delightful surprises. The second movement may be the most successful attempt to date by any composer to incorporate elements of Puerto Rican (or generalized Antillean) folk music into the forms and styles of traditional European-based concert music. The third movement of the Concertino is a brilliant and extended fanfare, the solo part brilliantly played on Saturday by Roberto Ramírez with effective backing by timpanist José Martín in an almost soloist-level part itself.

Also played on Saturday was a set of pieces (an overture and several *danzas*) by Juan Morel Campos (1857-1896) as arranged by Lito Peña. The more I hear of modern "symphonic" arrangements of nineteenth-century Puerto Rican music, the more convinced I am that the best thing you can do with this music is simply play it as it is: the same respectful principle, in fact, which we apply to the music of Mozart. Does anyone rearrange the orchestral music of Chopin and Berlioz for the modern concert stage, although God knows some of it could do with a bit of rearranging? Of course not, nor does anyone recolor the paintings of Campeche nor rewrite the works of Alejandro Tapia. Why, then, do we encourage (and even commission) people to rescore the existing concert music of nineteenth-century Puerto Rican composers? Don't get me wrong. The careful restoration of missing orchestra parts or even of an entire set of parts, within some known stylistic frame of historical reference, is perfectly legitimate and often necessary. But such "creative" touches as altered harmonies, new countermelodies and the inclusion of completely uncharacteristic instruments (xylophone, glockenspiel, celesta and high screaming horns) only obscured the charm of Morel Campos' music on Saturday. The result, in Peña's highly skilled but fatally slick arrangements, fell somewhere between the Hollywood style of 1945 and the hotel band style of a quarter century later. Although they may have been perfectly appropriate for some kind of tropical pineapple-fantasy of a hotel show, these arrangements have absolutely no place in the programming of a symphony orchestra devoted to artistic authenticity and public cultural edification anyplace in the world. Out with them!

And while we're on the subject, also out with the sometimes funny errors which continue to plague the PRSO's printed programs. Jack Délano might be flattered to be told that he was born in 1965, but Juan Morel Campos would only have been bewildered on reading his orders to join the Spanish Batallion of "Azadores" (a nonsense word).

Well, the Puerto Rico Symphony Orchestra's own season has yet to formally begin. Maybe some of these problems can be ironed out before that day dawns upon us.

A Week of Twentieth-Century Chamber Music

The San Juan Star
October 5, 1982 By Donald Thompson

It was a week for twentieth-century chamber music. For four nights running, anyone with transportation and stamina could enjoy a sample of this century's musical composition ranging from tentative and academic essays to some of the best-founded works of modern masters.

Monday evening's event took place in the Performing Arts Center in Santurce as part of the Inter American Arts Festival now in progress there. Featured were works by five Puerto Rican composers now in their thirties and early forties performed by a batch of able young performers. Three of Monday's five composers are products of the UPR Music Department of a decade or so ago, and four of the five now teach at UPR. Thus these figures form part of the strongest center of musical composition existing in Puerto Rico today. Yet although their own early studies received the influence of such recognized figures of the international avant-garde as Francis Schwartz and Rafael Aponte-Ledée most of the music offered on Monday ranged from the conservative to the ultra-conservative. Why is this?

Part of the explanation may be found in the well known desire of youth to strike out on its own; to explore new territory; to break new ground; to leave its early influences behind. But if the influences were already as far out as Schwartz and Aponte, where is there to go but backward? Secondly, there may be in the world today a true movement toward the consolidation and reconciliation of musical styles: the sort of movement which in art as in politics often follows a period of rapid thrust and seemingly perverse iconoclasm. Evidence of this was seen in San Juan a couple of years ago, in fact, with a remarkable presentation of some contemporary German music displaying a very able kind of neo-romanticism, of all things! So maybe this conservatism is the forefront after all.

But the responsibility is great. The avant-garde of the '60s and '70s was often satisfied with the exploration and application of newly discovered methods and media: electronic music; vocal ullulations; foot scraping; key flapping; mouthpiece banging; reed squeaking and other surprising (not to say shocking) sonoral innovations. In this atmosphere it was often considered enough for music to be "interesting," without a great deal of concern for overall form or any other general principle of musical construction. If the intention is now to return to conditions before this innovative period, or to somehow incorporate its undeniable accomplishments into a broader sort of flow, a great deal is going to be required of composers. We will again find concern with form, perhaps with more standardized instrumental usages, and maybe even with (lord love us) some kind of harmony!

On Monday, the only work which offered much in the way of the free-wheeling "advanced" techniques of the '60s and '70s was *Sueños de Collores*, by Luis Manuel Álvarez. And sure enough, this piece dates from some years ago. For soprano, guitar and an interesting array of percussion instruments used in a generally abstract sort of fashion, *Sueños de Collores* can still pass for an advanced work. Perhaps more solidly in tune with today's "new-old" tendencies, on the other hand, was *La Rota Voz del Agua*, Carlos Cabrer's new group of attractive settings of texts by various poets for soprano, cello, percussion and guitar. Also presented were more or less conservative works by Carlos Vázquez, José Montalvo and Ernesto Cordero.

During the rest of the week the action centered on the Río Piedras campus of the University of Puerto Rico. Here, the fine duo of Hans-Christian Siegert and Wilfried Danner offered a marathonic three-event series sponsored by the university's cultural activities office with the close collaboration of the West German consulate in Puerto Rico. The series took place in the recital hall of the UPR Music Department, and drew surprisingly large audiences for this unaccustomed kind of programming. Siegert and Danner offered works by 17 composers, 13 of them still living and most of these under forty years of age. Much of this music was as stark and uncompromising as we have come to expect of composers who came into prominence in the 1950s and 1960s. Hans Werner

Henze's Sonata for Solo Violin, for example, has become a major work of the solo violin repertory, but I don't think it will ever attain much of what you might call a popular success. It is simply too stark, too bleak and too harsh for that. Tough, though, and convincingly played by Hans-Christian Siegert on Thursday's program.

On the other hand, most of the contemporary works presented on the Siegert-Danner UPR concerts seemed to support the view that indeed we are headed into a conservative consolidation of some kind. Wilfried Danner's own Five Silhouettes, for example, reminded me of the music of Anton Webern (1883-1945), with their extremely condensed and atomized melodies cast within a perceptible rhythmic pulse.

Interestingly enough, this consolidating force (if, indeed, it exists) extends to the use of a device which has appeared and reappeared countless times during the history of Western music: parody, or the quotation of earlier material out of context. Thus the decidedly non-violent *Violencia para Violín* of Norbert Linke (b. 1933), which offers quotations from Rimsky-Korsakov, Richard Strauss and others.

There are two main and opposed views concerning the function of art music. One is that music should simply flow soothingly around us as a kind of bland, undemanding and ultimately reassuring sonoral bath. The other is that the best music, like the best theater, the best painting and the best poetry, should make us think. Last week's offerings in chamber music, both in Santurce and in Río Piedras, have reinforced the second view. Reassuring they were not; conducive to thought they certainly were.

Ohlsson and the Bösendorfer; A Week With the PRSO

The San Juan Star
October 27, 1982   By Donald Thompson

Recent musical events in San Juan have centered upon the Puerto Rico Symphony Orchestra, now well into its 1982-83 season at the Performing Arts Center, but also with a significant excursion out to the UPR campus at Río Piedras. Soloists with the Symphony Orchestra this week have been pianist Charles Rosen and violinist Guillermo Figueroa, while it was a great pleasure to again see brilliant pianist Garrick Ohlsson in Puerto Rico.

Ohlsson was here to officiate at the inauguration of the splendid new Bösendorfer Imperial piano at the UPR Theater, and officiate he did, with great style and appropriate pomp. The Bösendorfer is the Rolls Royce of pianos, and the Imperial is the top of the Bösendorfer line. The Silver Cloud of pianos, you might say.

As was pointed out in introductory remarks by Francis Schwartz, Director of Cultural Activities at UPR, the UPR Theater has been for many decades the scene of many of Puerto Rico's most significant cultural events. A list of the figures who have appeared there reads like an international Who's Who of the century's foremost musical, literary and theatrical figures, and indeed it is. Presumably this role will continue into the foreseeable future, and the acquisition of such a fine instrument as the Bösendorfer is both a symbol and a guarantee of leadership in cultural affairs here. And why not? When you come right down to it, what are universities for, anyway?

Ohlsson put the mighty Bösendorfer through its paces with a program of Chopin, Scriabin and a touch of Mozart. Not precisely the program which I'd have chosen for this particular event, but there is certainly no faulting Ohlsson's playing of it. Here is the complete pianist, possessing everything from technique to style, class, and beyond. Probably no one could have done a better job of inaugurating the new UPR instrument, and Ohlsson's salubrious and resonant vibrations will now join those of Rubenstein, Serkin, Iturbi, Arrau, Sanromá and others in the venerable UPR Theater.

Both John Barnett and Roselín Pabón have conducted the Puerto Rico Symphony Orchestra lately. The former is the orchestra's musical director and the latter the associate musical director; that is to say, Number Two in the artistic hierarchy. Barnett's program on Oct. 16 was devoted to Schubert (the Unfinished Symphony) and Brahms, with noted scholar-pianist Charles Rosen as soloist in Brahms' First Piano Concerto.

After an unnecessarily harsh (almost brutal) introduction, the Brahms at times attained the broad lyricism which we associate with this composer's music. Rosen himself played rather on the calm and studious side of Brahms, creating a bit of a contrast with the conductor's more vigorous (not to say violent) notion of the piece. To complicate matters, in the past year or so Mr. Barnett's conducting has developed a disconcerting way of crowding the third beat in fast triple meter (the case in the first movement of the Brahms concerto), which naturally evokes a rocky and unstable response from an orchestra. And finally, some disjointedness between conductor and soloist accounted for shaky conditions in the concerto's third movement. All in all, a disappointing performance of this work.

The October 23 concert was conducted by Roselín Pabón, with violinist Guillermo Figueroa as soloist. First up was the C Major Symphony by Bizet. This youthful composition, like the Classical Symphony of Prokofiev, is a test of any orchestra. As transparent as any early Haydn symphony but four times as difficult, these works require absolutely controlled and absolutely unified playing, especially in the string sections. The violin sections of the island orchestra attained neither on Saturday, instead falling victim to their traditional faults: heavy-footed ends of phrases, rushed rhythms, ragged pizzicatos and the promiscuous jangle of open strings. An anarchic approach to position shifts, in Bizet's slow movement especially, created conflicting sets of "smears"; i.e., the supposedly expressive but easily exaggerated portamento: sliding from one note to another on the violin's fingerboard. Under these conditions, the breakneck fourth movement of the Bizet symphony became little more than an hysterical scramble for notes. And in general, much too loud for the style of the piece and the characteristics of the hall (the Drama Theater at the Performing Arts Center).

Many of these faults were also present in the anguished Death and Transfiguration of Richard Strauss. However, this work is so big and so noisy to begin with that almost anything goes; the worst thing that can happen is that the texture gets muddied up a little more. Or at least it would be so in a bigger hall. In the Drama Theater, however, the fiddlers' faults were painfully evident on Saturday.

Guillermo Figueroa, Saturday's soloist, has developed into a first rate player. He offered two brilliant works with the PRSO: *Havanaise* by Saint-Saëns and Sarasate's frequently performed Carmen Fantasy. Both are showpieces of the violin repertory, and Figueroa by now has the skill and the seasoned presence to toss them off with a casual and almost offhand air. Perhaps a little too casual. There was a certain amount of faulty marksmanship in the way of muffed harmonics and inaccurate doublestops, not always obvious in the excitement of an otherwise completely convincing performance. Also, Figueroa's youthfully masterful stage presence tends to neutralize the effect of an occasional misfire. It is always a pleasure to hear him, and indeed it was on this recent occasion.

Incidentally, some of conductor Pabón's best work occurred in the accompanying duties of the Saint-Saëns and Sarasate works. Both are tricky pieces, full of boobytraps to begin with and then requiring extremely tight coordination with the soloist on top of it. In fact, such works are in many ways the real tests of a conductor's skill, not the big symphonies which most orchestras can almost play without a conductor anyway. Pabón is doing good work as Number Two, if this recent concert can be taken as typical.

Viva Sanromá!

The San Juan Star
November 10, 1982 By Donald Thompson

Island-born pianist Jesús María Sanromá reached the venerable age of 80 years this week, and the event has been marked by the promulgation of documents, scrolls, certificates and pronouncements. Rightly so, too, for here among us is Puerto Rico's principal claim to musical recognition in this century. Sanromá has really had two full and honorable careers in music. The first took place mainly in and around Boston, where for a quarter century he held forth as pianist of the Boston Symphony Orchestra under Koussevitsky, as teacher, and as frequent recitalist. At the same time, his performances as soloist took him to 21 countries for more than 3,000 appearances with close to 150 orchestras and as many different conductors. Sanromá's work in Boston placed him at the forefront of the contemporary music movement of the 1930s and 1940s, and he offered the premiere performances of works by many of the leading composers of that period. In addition, and of great significance in the later development of music in Puerto Rico, he served as a sort of one-man musical consulate of Puerto Rico in Boston. His counsel guided a number of island musicians into studies there, for the future benefit of the island itself.

Sanromá's second career began with his return to Puerto Rico in the early 1950s. First at the University of Puerto Rico, later at the Puerto Rico Conservatory of Music, he became an honored guide, mentor and focus of musical activities. His teaching naturally continued, and by now has produced a couple of generations of able island pianists. In addition, Sanromá has taken on something of an elder statesman role in different government agencies concerned with the arts in Puerto Rico.

And he continues to play. On Saturday evening Sanromá was the featured soloist with the Puerto Rico Symphony Orchestra at the Performing Arts Center, offering what must have been his fiftieth or sixtieth performance of the A Minor Piano Concerto of Edvard Grieg. What's interesting about such statistics is that an artist like Sanromá can still find it in him to make a significant performance of such familiar (not to say over-familiar) music as this Grieg concerto. Yet he did just this on Saturday, especially in the work's slow movement. Here, I felt, is where the man's years and decades of dedication to music show: in the seasoned, calm, perhaps introspective spinning out of this lyrical music. After intermission, birthday greetings were extended to Sanromá by Mrs. Elena Martín, president of the Asociación Pro Orquesta Sinfónica. This is an organization of citizens fiercely devoted to the progress of your symphony orchestra. It displays some of the characteristics of symphony orchestra boards and orchestra leagues on the continent, but due to this orchestra's unusual status as a government subsidiary the APOS cannot directly attack some of its most pressing problems. However, the organization does a great deal in the way of very important supporting functions. On Saturday the APOS greeting took the very practical form of announcing the creation of a fund to support the summer studies of younger members of the PRSO, the donor of the initial funds being one of the island's leading banks, while the program has been conceived in honor of Sanromá himself.

Also on Saturday's program, directed by visiting Venezuelan conductor Eduardo Rahn, were *Antillas*, by island composer William Ortiz, and the First Symphony of Brahms. Arriving late I missed the Ortiz, but Rahn's work in both of the evening's larger compositions showed him to be a very capable conductor indeed. Especially nice was the warm and balanced performance of Brahms which he attained with the island orchestra. The Puerto Rico Symphony Orchestra has not often sounded so well in recent seasons. As for this Brahms performance in particular, the orchestra's principal woodwinds again led the way in clean and unified playing, especially in the symphony's second and third movements.

The Biennial: A Month of Unusual Concerts

The San Juan Star
November 13, 1982 By Donald Thompson

The Third San Juan Biennial of Twentieth Century Music is now in session at different island points, again plugging us into the international currents (not to say the shocks and tremors) of the music of our own time. The first two Biennials (1978 and 1980) were organized by the Puerto Rico Contemporary Music Society; the present one has been assembled by the Latin American Foundation for Contemporary Music. The common elements in the three series have been the energy and dedication of island composer Rafael Aponte-Ledée. In order that some of his ideas for the benefit of the island's musical awareness might reach tangible form, Aponte, who six years ago was a most un-managerial sort of fellow, has more or less been forced to become an impressario. This time, he and a small band of aides and enthusiasts have hurled themselves into the innumerable tasks required to organize a full month of unusual concerts and related activities involving (it seems) a battalion of participants from many parts of the world.

Wednesday evening's Biennial offering was a chamber music concert at the San Juan Cathedral, during which a large audience became acquainted with works by Atilano Auza León (Bolivia), Juan Orrego Salas (Chile), Jack Délano (Puerto Rico) and Gustavo Becerra-Schmidt (Chile). The Auza *Danzas Bolivianas del Ciclo 'Runas,'* for violin and piano, is a gracefully conservative suite of five movements based on Bolivian social music, nicely played on Wednesday by violinist Saul Ovcharov and pianist Samuel Pérez. Program notes describe the composer as also a violinist. This sample of Auza's music certainly displays a performer's knowledge of the instrument in the confident and skillful use of harmonics, double stops, chords across the strings and other violinistic touches.

In a way, some of the writing in this work is reminiscent of Jack Délano's use of native Puerto Rican rhythmic and melodic elements, although Délano's style is more open, more disposed toward abrupt shifts in harmony, and generally wittier. Wednesday's audience heard a version for cello and piano of Délano's viola sonata, offered by cellist Orlando Guillot and pianist Samuel Pérez. I had not heard this cello version before, but enjoyed it almost as much as I always enjoy hearing the work in its original form. Or would have, under more favorable acoustical conditions. Acoustically the San Juan Cathedral produces the same phenomenon as big hard-walled churches everywhere: the piling up of multiple slow reverberations and a resultant impenetrable muddiness of sound. Great for the deliberate echo effects of big divided choruses and brass ensembles, but hell on pianos and stringed instruments. Also presented on Wednesday were two twentieth-century string quartets, played by the newly organized Puerto Rico String Quartet. This instrumental combination adds violinist Becky Kita and violist Constance Haggard to the Ovcharov-Guillot axis; the result seems to be a well-founded ensemble which can make important contributions to the island's musical life.

Both of Wednesday's quartets were by eminent Chilean composers. First up was the First Quartet by Juan Orrego Salas.

Orrego, very active nowadays in the cause of Latin American music in the U.S., has long been a leader in the field of contemporary music generally. This quartet, dating from the mid-1950s, is a first rate example of the chamber music of our century. Like much of the chamber music of the mid-century period, it is reminiscent of the more familiar music of Bartók, in principles of construction if not especially in sound. This particular quartet of Orrego Salas consists mainly of periods of restless counterpoint and developmental excursions brought to a close and separated one from another by frequent points of repose which correspond (in the older languages of musical construction) to harmonic cadences. Carrying some of the same principles farther is Gustavo Becerra-Schmidt's Sixth String Quartet, dating from some eight years after the Orrego Salas. It shows. The Becerra work is much more liberal in its use of fierce dissonance alternating with an architectonic and pregnant sort of tense lyricism. Always logical and always consistent, this is highly systematic music, imaginatively conceived and rigorously organized. Again, it is difficult to avoid hearing analogies with the chamber music of other masters. In this case Bartók again comes to mind, as he must in almost all considerations of twentieth-century chamber music, but also Beethoven, with something of the condensed and potent motivic force of the Great Fugue.

This Third San Juan Biennial of Twentieth Century Music is still in its beginning phases, with a couple of weeks yet to run. What it promises is a varied series of well organized events, worthy of the attention of anyone interested in the broader aspects of music and musical life today.

Composer **Héctor Campos Parsi**, one of Puerto Rico's most dynamic cultural personalities.

Inaccurate View of Campos-Parsi

The San Juan Star
December 2, 1982   By Donald Thompson

Island composer Héctor Campos-Parsi recently reached the honorable age of sixty, and the Institute of Puerto Rican Culture has quite appropriately honored him with a special event featuring speeches, a concert and the laying on of official parchment. The event took place on Saturday evening in the concert hall of the Puerto Rico Conservatory of Music in Hato Rey and was based on a few of Campos' works for orchestra, presented by the Puerto Rico Symphony Orchestra conducted by Roselín Pabón.

Héctor Campos-Parsi was most active as a composer during the 1950s and 1960s. In the early '50s he returned to Puerto Rico from studies in the United States and France, the latter under the tutelage of the extraordinary musical pedagogue Nadia Boulanger. The Boulanger style was already firmly stamped on such U.S. composers as Aaron Copland, Roy Harris, Walter Piston and many more. Transferred to Puerto Rico through Campos-Parsi, the melodious, flowing, mildly spiced style of the Boulanger school contributed in very timely fashion to the first belated stirrings of a twentieth-century music in Puerto Rico.

An early Campos film score, *Modesta*, was composed for the insular government's Division of Community Education, and provided an example of how island folk material could be incorporated into music of more sophisticated intent. This was to become the principal thrust of Campos' music for a decade; his best work was accomplished, in fact, in a field of music which had already ceased to interest forward-looking composers elsewhere in the world: "nationalistic" music. Understand, please, that this is a technical term in use worldwide, and has no necessary political connotation in Puerto Rico's specific (and endless) status gavotte. The term simply refers to the conscious use of identifiable elements of unsophisticated regional music (folk music, if you wish) in concert forms. Campos did this well, in ballet scores, songs, piano music and chamber works.

Meanwhile, officialdom beckoned. For neither the first nor the last time in history, the energies of a promising creative figure became channeled into administration—deskwork—organizing—coordinating—the backstage ballet of power—ultimately, politics. First as an adviser to the Free Schools of Music, later as a key figure at the Institute of Puerto Rican Culture and still later at the new Administration for the Development of Arts and Culture, Campos took on more and more administrative responsibility, consuming time and energy which in other circumstances might have resulted in significant contributions to musical composition.

This is not to say that Campos stopped composing. A number of successful works date from the late '60s and early '70s, including *Petroglifos* (violin, cello and piano, 1966); *Columnas y Círculos* (voice and piano or voices, piano and vibraphone, 1967); and *Arawak* (cello and magnetic tape, 1970). But . . . there's no free lunch. For the past decade now, Campos-Parsi's contribution to music in Puerto Rico must be measured not in terms of timely and significant musical composition, but in terms of the mainly invisible tasks which constitute administrative work in faithful government service.

As stated above, Saturday's event in honor of Campos-Parsi was based on his orchestral music, including a pair of songs on texts by P.H. Hernández (1961), The *Dúo Trágico for Piano and Orchestra* (1965), the *Ode to Cabo Rojo* (1959) and the *Divertimento del Sur* (1953). This programming was unfortunate. With the exception of the *Divertimento*, which may be his best work, Campos' most successful compositions have not been in the orchestral field but in piano music, chamber music and songs. For this reason, Saturday's selection gave an inaccurate and most unrepresentative view of Campos' work. Much better for an homage, I should think, would have been an evening of Campos' chamber music with an additional singer or two and maybe a small chorus to explore some of that side of his work as well.

Saturday's skilled soloists were soprano Susan Pabón (the Hernández songs); pianist Jesús María Sanromá (*Dúo Trágico*); and clarinetist Kathleen Jones and flutist Peter Kern (*Divertimento del Sur*). These artists were, in fact, the best part of the event. With a printed program full of ridiculous errors and unforgivable lapses, constant traffic through the hall and orchestral performances lacking in precision and style, even this unrepresentative sample of Campos Parsi's work was not well served by the event's organizers. Better luck, Héctor, on your seventieth birthday!

Third Music Biennial

The San Juan Star
December 8, 1982   By Donald Thompson

    The Third San Juan Biennial of Twentieth Century Music has come to a close after a full month of musical events throughout the island. As in the previous Biennials (1978 and 1980), performers and groups were drawn from many parts of the world, and their offerings covered a wide variety of styles, tendencies and "schools." The Biennial's final week was devoted to concerts by Spanish performers. On Tuesday evening a hardy batch of these visitors undertook a heroic trip to Arecibo aboard an ancient bus, along with some equally hardy music critics and other folks, to see a bit of the island and lend companionable support at the solo appearance of a compatriot. The event was a recital, I guess you might say, by Catalan pianist Carle Santos at the Arecibo campus of Inter American University. Santos is an accomplished pianist, yes, but his work today is mainly devoted to "polyart," an all-encompassing sort of presentation which can call into play anything which the composer wishes to incorporate. In many cases this includes electronic sounds, light play, slides, mime, and even odors and tactile sensations. Santos' Arecibo presentation, however, was limited to the piano and to his own gestures, sounds, grimaces, and other physical manifestations.
    The musical aspect of Santos' work on Tuesday was almost shockingly conservative. Relentlessly tonal and foursquare in details of form, Santos' piano music reminded me, phrase by phrase, of the type of thing which was often heard in the "fantasy" or "improvisation" style of times long gone. Another variety of presentation was based on Santos' own moving around the stage while gesturing and producing various sounds. Here, he was able to spin whole dramatic scenes out of the rhythmic and repetitive treatment of a few nonsense syllables. I was occasionally

reminded of the "scat" singing of the bebop era in jazz, but of course now free of any underlying predetermined harmonic progression. Still another kind of *Santosmusik* consisted of the declamation of a high sounding and inspiringly delivered rhetoric of nonsense syllables. Had this been a political rally, Santos could easily have been nominated on the spot! His most convincing work, however, occurred in piano music into the middle of which were hurled vocal intrusions: sighs, gasps, clucks, screeches, wheezes and explosions, as a kind of pianist-generated vocal percussion part. Some of these effects had been seen and heard in San Juan ten or a dozen years ago in the work of island "polyartist" Francis Schwartz, but never with the intensity and driving force of Carle Santos.

After the concert Santos found himself surrounded by IAU students in the lobby for a stand-up session of questions, answers, debate and general exchange. One thing is certain: his Arecibo appearance shook a few people up, which, you must recognize, is one of the purposes of the avant-garde always and everywhere. Surely, Arecibo had never seen such a thing before, unless maybe in the incantatory manifestations of some north coast plaza guru under the spell of street-corner inspiration.

The Madrid ensemble LIM (for Laboratorio de Interpretación Musical) wrapped up this Biennial with concerts at the Puerto Rico Conservatory of Music, at UPR and at the Metropolitan Campus of Inter American University. LIM is directed by clarinetist-composer Jesús Villa Rojo and is based on a clarinet quintet, of all things, with peripheral violin, cello, piano and percussion. An odd idea, and even odder when you consider the unusual clarinets which make up the LIM nucleus: soprano (the normal one), piccolo (a third shorter), alto, bass, and the monstrous contrabass. What music, you might ask, even exists for such a strange but sonorous ensemble? Virtually none, except for an extensive repertory of works especially written for LIM itself. This means contemporary music, of course, and that in turn fits right into the format of the Biennials of Twentieth Century Music.

Characteristic of much music of the past quarter century, most of the pieces offered here by the LIM clarinets incorporate the "new" sounds and mechanical effects which are intensely cultivated by many composers today. These include, but are by no means limited to, a whole repertory of by now familiar squeaks and screeches. An interesting application is also made of the sound of fluttering clarinet keys, a formidable clatter when executed on the big flappers of the contrabass clarinet. Also present, and quite appropriate for the structure and design of the clarinet mouthpiece, is heavy breathing, both on the inhale and on the exhale. In the LIM instrumentation, this sounded at times like air escaping from the punctured tires of different motor vehicles, from the contrabass earthmover to the piccolo go-kart.

But the most thoroughly studied device of all nowadays is the use of "multiphonics," in which a clarinet (as well as some other wind instruments) can be induced to produce two different notes at the same time. The result is something like double stops on the violin, but multiphonics correspond to a completely different order of acoustical phenomena. Here, one note (the fundamental) is low to medium in pitch, the other very high, representing a high "harmonic" frequency separated from its fundamental by tricks of lip and fingers. These high notes are, of course, the same unwanted and embarrassing squeaks which every junior high school clarinetist strives mightily to eliminate from his playing. But now they have become systematized, charted and brought under control in concert music, as have been many other formerly unrecognized sounds. Among these, historically, is the violin pizzicato, which became respectable only about 350 years ago. Makes you think, doesn't it?

LIM's violin, cello, piano and percussion, added to the nucleus of clarinets, makes possible the study of an enormous repertory of music calling for different combinations of instruments, and the group's San Juan concerts included a generous offering of interesting (and in some cases, significant) compositions. Present, for example, was a quartet by Hindemith for violin, clarinet, cello and piano, as well as the startling Quartet for the End of Time of Olivier Messiaen. The latter work is an apocalyptic musical vision by this strange and mystic figure in twentieth-century music. If memory serves, the LIM presentation was the first time any of Messiaen's music has been offered here.

Earle Brown, a leading figure in the U.S. contemporary music movement, was in San Juan for the Biennial's final events and conducted some of his own music on the LIM's second concert. Brown's work has been most innovative in the field of notation, especially as applied to the proportional graphic representation of durations. His spoken comments, delivered in an informal fashion before Thursday's concert at UPR, seemed to help the audience through the thorny brevities of his music. Offered were six pieces, including Brown's experimental Four Systems (1954) as well as selections from Folio (1952-53) and a collective improvisation to boot.

The San Juan Biennials of Twentieth Century Music have resulted from the dedication and hard work of a handful of specialized enthusiasts. The first two Biennials were sponsored by the now defunct Puerto Rico Society for Contemporary Music and the third by its successor, the Latin American Foundation for Contemporary Music. Through the efforts of these organizations Puerto Rico has been systematically exposed to the music of our century in generally superior presentations involving leading performers from Europe and the Americas.

Naturally, the Biennials are not the only occasions when one may hear twentieth-century music. Over the past ten or fifteen years all of the island's official concert agencies have at least made token gestures toward contemporary music. But if you study the matter closely, you will see that in most cases this has come about only in response to the veiled pressures of specific groups. The Biennial offerings, on the other hand, have been the only regularly organized series consciously (not to say aggressively) devoted to contemporary music as a matter of principle. You will also recognize that some agencies have come around only after seeing that contemporary music really does have a place in the island's musical life, and this has occurred almost exclusively as a result of these Biennials and of similar (if less elaborate) exercises which preceded them in the misty past of a decade or so ago.

The Biennials have served an important purpose in Puerto Rican musical life. If this recent one has seemed less spectacular or less innovative than its predecessors, this is partly because the Biennials' message has been received and translated into action by other island agencies. In other words, if contemporary music is no longer the shocker it was as recently as six years ago, it's due in great measure to the San Juan Biennials of Twentieth Century Music.

Daughter of the Regiment: A Fresh Offering

The San Juan Star
January 18, 1983   By Donald Thompson

Opera de Puerto Rico is the second oldest of the island's present array of lyric theater companies. This particular group had its origin in the ferment of enthusiasm which began in the late 1960s and which led to the creation of first one, then another, then a whole batch of interconnected and overlapping cells of island opera lovers. Each group is fervently dedicated to the premise that Puerto Rico can—indeed, MUST—support an island-based opera effort: naturally, the particular opera effort promoted by that particular group. It will be an interesting task for future researchers to sort out the thrusts and counter-thrusts of opera (or rather, opera lovers) in Puerto Rico during this period. In the meantime, if opera is your thing, all you can do is try to see each production as it comes along and, as the boys say down at the meat market, take the best with the wurst.

Opera de Puerto Rico has sponsored, originated or otherwise accounted for some fifteen productions since 1971, and quite naturally has had its ups and downs. Its current production of Donizetti's *The Daughter of the Regiment* must be counted among the highest of its ups. A fresh offering here and probably an island premiere of this engaging work, *The Daughter of the Regiment* had a charming opening performance on Saturday evening in the Festival Hall of the Performing Arts Center. The second and final performance will be this evening.

Strictly speaking, *The Daughter of the Regiment* is not opera at all but *opéra comique*, a species of French lyric theater in which musical numbers alternated with dialogue scenes. Later, the opéra comique was to become transformed into true French opera, but at the time of *The Daughter of the Regiment* (1840), it was still a sister to the German

Singspiel and the Spanish zarzuela. In fact, the translation into Spanish of works like this one, often with the composition of new music by Spanish composers, accounted for a great number of zarzuelas produced in Madrid during the following period . . . but that's another story.

What the Donizetti work shares with its "dialogue opera" sisters is a fluffy plot, cheerful music, happy villagers, a benevolent aristocracy, pretty mountain scenery and a troupe of operetta soldiers. Too, the principal performers must have more going for them than pretty voices, for this curious type of theater requires considerable acting skill, in addition. And yes, excellent voices with now and then a high note or two, as we shall see.

The present production is built around the extraordinary soprano Ruth Welting in the role of Marie, the daughter (i.e. mascot) of a Napoleonic regiment in the Tyrol in, say, 1815. A tough and very interesting part, this, calling for the interplay of two or three different types of vocal and dramatic expression ranging from a uniformed ragamuffin of a tomboy to a prankish girl to a young woman about to be married. Ms. Welting was simply super in her musical and dramatic development of this role on Saturday, providing the central driving force of the entire performance.

Opposite her in this production is eminent tenor Alfredo Kraus as Tonio, the humble village lad who becomes transformed into a sparkling and splendiferous military officer. In the meantime Tonio has a great deal of singing to do, of course. On Saturday Kraus did his singing extremely well, while accomplishing absolutely the best that can be done with such an empty stereotype of a role.

Kraus' work is well known here, and naturally this appearance was preceded by a great deal of opera talk. A couple of days before the opening I was buttonholed by a notorious island opera lover, beside himself with joy because in rehearsal "Alfredo" had emitted nine high C's—and in less than a minute! This may be so, and Kraus certainly sang splendidly on Saturday. Still, I don't believe that this is what opera is about. At least I hope not, for this view reduces a complex art form to something like a question of how many pushups you can do. In other words, it transforms a device—a technique—a means toward an end into an end in itself, while viewing a superb artist like Kraus as only some kind of freaky vocal gymnast. No, opera is more than high notes, although a couple of high notes at climactic musical and dramatic moments certainly don't do any harm.

The attractive role of the Marquise is played here by skilled mezzo Muriel Costa-Greenspan while sterling baritone Spiro Malas is Sergeant Sulpice. Both dramatically and musically, these fine performers brought their important roles to life. So you see, if opera were only high C's (or D's, or other notes in particular), who would need mezzos, baritones and basses? And, for that matter, would you like to imagine a stage full of sopranos and tenors, all lined up at arm's length and bombarding each other with shotgun blasts of high notes? No, thanks. I'll take phrasing, breath control, correct pitch, correct pronunciation, quality of sound, dynamic variety and dramatic skill any day. And these qualities would have shone forth on Saturday in the work's principal performers even had they sung their parts an octave lower than written.

Smaller parts are played in this production by Miguel Ramos, Carlos Bauzá, Antonio González, José Ramón Torres, and yes, that fine actress Lillian Hurst, who I don't think has appeared here on the musical stage since a production of *Fiorello* in the early '60s. A vigorous and capable chorus shows the skilled work of chorusmasters Rafael Ferrer and Pablo Boissen, while members of the Puerto Rico Symphony Orchestra fill the pit. Stage director for this production is Irving Guttman, and the musical director is Nino Bonavolunta. With this offering, Opera de Puerto Rico has courageously and successfully presented a pleasing and unusual opera to island audiences, in a tightly organized and well rehearsed production. Congratulations are in order.

Zabaleta, A Most Welcome Visitor

The San Juan Star
February 5, 1983   By Donald Thompson

You can just about count on your thumbs the world class solo harpists there are at a given moment. Nicanor Zabaleta, one of these most favored of beings, has for decades been a most welcome visitor on Puerto Rico's various concert series, for his appearances are marked by the highest level of artistry. Zabaleta was here recently to open the second semester of events on the UPR Cultural Activities series, offering a varied program of works originally composed for harp along with a few transcriptions from other fields of music.

This matter of original music versus transcriptions is one of those issues which keep backstage debates smoldering for years (occasionally breaking into public flames) but to which audiences seem singularly indifferent in the main. Some musicians don't worry much about the medium for which a piece of music might have originally been written, as long as it sounds well on their particular instrument. Others see an important relationship between the composer's thought and the medium for which it was originally conceived, with consequences and ramifications in concepts of authenticity of means, responsibility of interpretation and a whole world of other relationships.

Zabaleta is among the latter. In fact, for many years he has been a quiet crusader in a cause which has successfully turned the harp world around. Formerly (say forty or fifty years ago), the active harp repertory was made up mostly of transcriptions of piano music, and certainly not the best piano music, at that. The harp as a solo instrument was still carrying a burden of nineteenth-century associations with the social salon, stylish hotel dining rooms, angelic choruses and the like. The fact that modern audiences are acquainted with a hearty repertory of real harp music is due in great part to Zabaleta's own efforts in reviving older music for his instrument, to his interest in original harp music in general, and to his direct responsibility for the existence of a number of works in particular.

Zabaleta's playing is noted for his absolute rhythmic security, his perfect tonal balance and his ability to make the phrasing of his instrument "breathe" in the manner of a fine singer, violinist or (more rarely) pianist. These gifts were evident to a large audience in the UPR Theater in a program ranging from Dussek and Beethoven down to Paul Hindemith (1895-1963) and Salvador Bacarisse (1898-1963). These last two works are extremely interesting examples of twentieth-century music written especially for the harp. Hindemith's, of course, is a known quantity, and his Sonata for Harp, dating from 1939, is a respected element in that long series of solo works for virtually all orchestral instruments which Hindemith undertook beginning in the 1930s. The Bacarisse Partita, composed especially for Zabaleta in 1950, is a neoclassic kind of composition, very mildly spiced with the "modern" harmonies of a couple of decades before and completely convincing as a piece of harp music.

Zabaleta's presentation of all of this material—the new, the old and the new-old, as well as a set of sparkling encores—was again a revelation of high artistry for his faithful and growing island audience.

Pro Arte: A Pillar of Culture

The San Juan Star
February 17, 1983 By Donald Thompson

The privately organized and (mainly) privately financed Puerto Rico Pro Arte Musical Society has for many decades been a pillar in the island's cultural life. A hiatus occurred in the 1960s and 1970s, when it was quite mistakenly believed that the island's diversified musical needs and interests could be best served by a single monolithic government branch. Sadly, even some of Pro Arte's own leaders fell into this trap, thereby sealing the doom of their own organization (Is there a lesson here for the 1980s?). Phoenix-like, Pro Arte arose from the island's musical ashes around 1976, and has again come to play an important role in Puerto Rico's own microcosmic music drama.

What Pro Arte does best is the presentation of individual artists, chamber ensembles and other attractions requiring no "in house" production. As an extension of this principle the organization has lately taken to the presentation of lectures on musical subjects. A potentially quite healthy development, this, for it gives laymen a chance to learn about the machinery of particular works, of particular art movements, or even of particular composers, in a pleasant and not overly formal setting. Naturally, much depends on the lecturer's knowledge of his subject and his ability to organize and communicate highly technical material on a nontechnical level. For this kind of thing to work (as, indeed, for a piano or violin recital to work, for that matter), the lecturer must be a fine and secure specialist in his subject, but with great gifts of "presence," too.

Last week, Pro Arte rang the bell with a lecture on Wagner's *Tristan and Isolde* and the Romantic Essence by noted scholar Michael Steinberg. Steinberg is a veteran of musical posts at universities, of positions in musical criticism, of battles in the symphonic world, of arts councils, and of specialized writing in musical reference works. He has seen it all, and brings to the lecture stage this vast experience, a scholar's knowledge and a serene presence. The sort of thing, in fact, that one remembers from fine university lectures in general or panoramic courses, although Steinberg could certainly bash out a semester of lectures for graduate students on the function of the 6-4 chord in symphonic music from Wagenseil to Bruckner, if it came to it. In other words, a professional.

Steinberg's Pro Arte lecture dealt with the literary, musical and mythic aspects of *Tristan and Isolde*, with emphasis on questions of how Wagner got that way. In other words, on the identifiable currents of Germany's literary and musical thought into which Wagner and this particular work fit. Naturally, much of the exposition was based on, or often returned to, that concept of death as release from the tyranny of the senses (or Schopenhauer's release from the wheel of desire) which stands very close to the center of the Romantic vision. This "sinking into endless peace," this "bliss of quitting life" is a central concern of Germanic Romantic thought, particularly. It is the main thread (indeed, virtually the only thread) in *Tristan and Isolde*, expressed in the constant examination of love, death, love-death, lovedeath, being in love with death, dying for love and related concerns. Naturally, this preoccupation with reconciling what may be the world's greatest pair of opposites contrasts sharply with the Mediterranean-Hispanic-Caribbean celebration of life (including life after death) to which we are more accustomed in Puerto Rico. Yet, Steinberg was able to make profound sense of this paradox for an audience of island laymen, successfully hooking to it Wagner's musical usages in *Tristan and Isolde* while ranging outward to refer to Liszt, Schopenhauer, Thomas Mann, Bruckner, medieval Christianity and other persons and concepts.

At one point, Steinberg referred to Wagner's insistence on the complete integration of all aspects of the creation and presentation of his works: music, libretto, the whole thing. Simply paraphrased, Wagner believed that there was more to music than pretty singing. Who knows? A few more lectures of the quality of Steinberg's, and the continuation of Pro Arte's fine record in presenting a varied program of soloists and ensembles, might even contribute to a broader awareness in Puerto Rico of this great and fundamental truth.

A New *Schwartzwerk* and a *Bassmeister*

The San Juan Star
February 19, 1983 By Donald Thompson

Schwartz has done it again. For newcomers to Puerto Rico's musical kaleidoscope I should perhaps point out that the subject is Francis Schwartz, a versatile fellow whose professional activities extend from the staid exercise of university administrative responsibilities to the composition (is that the word?) of music (ditto) which incorporates sounds, sights, temperature changes, gestures, especially compounded odors, and even unto the delicate rain of cooling mists upon the very body surfaces. Hmmm.

The most recent concert of the Puerto Rico Symphony Orchestra took place last week in the Performing Arts Center in Santurce, and featured the premiere performance of a new *Schwartzwerk* entitled *Gestos* (Gestures). Especially commissioned by one of Puerto Rico's principal banking establishments, *Gestos* can perhaps be taken as an emphatic affirmation of that same establishment's effervescently positive advertising of late: "¡SÍ!"

The aggressively affirmative *Gestos* is Schwartz' latest offering in a field of endeavor called "polyart." As indicated above, polyart deals with the combination of different . . . well, you might say . . . sensations, in hopes of attaining a significant or at least memorable result. Polyart claims relationship with the Wagnerian ideal of the *Gesamtkunstwerk* or all-encompassing art work, in which different media of expression would be called into a transcendental kind of union to together illuminate and bring to realization a single grand concept (Wagner's, naturally). But polyart seems to proceed from a vision directly opposed, calling for not the combination but the juxtaposition of different orders of phenomena, in order to see what comes out.

Polyart's immediate antecedents are to be found in several manifestations current in the 1950s and 1960s, including electronic and aleatory music, a new technology of light and visual effects and the "happening" (does anyone remember that?). I suspect that lines could also be traced back to the Dada and Futurism of a number of decades before, as well as to almost any manifestation of humorous parody and musical irreverence which you might wish to cite, from ancient times on down. *Gestos* offers seven brief movements for symphony orchestra and audience, in which both parts are asked to do unexpected things. Musically, a great portion of the orchestra's part consists of quotations from known musical works, but in strange contexts. Are you ready, for example, for the medieval "Dies Irae" with a salsa beat? Orchestra sections and individual members are called upon to stand up, sit down, click their tongues, hiss and perform other actions not usually considered part of a symphony orchestra musician's professional repertory. The audience is also invited to do unusual things, or at least unusual in the ritualistic context of a symphony orchestra concert. In an attempt to break down the accustomed musical barrier between the "doers" (an orchestra) and the "done to" (an audience), *Gestos* invites the audience to repeat some of the orchestra members' sounds and actions, with the conductor in the middle as a kind of mediator. Anyone acquainted with Schwartz' previous compositions will recognize *Gestos* as the descendant of works for piano and audience in which the pianist cues the audience to repeat some of his own sounds and gestures. The best performances of these have always been with Schwartz himself as pianist. Not only is he thoroughly familiar with his own music, of course, but he also has a sort of cherubic and conspiratorial stage presence plus a showman's sense of timing in dealing with an audience. Schwartz knows how to get an audience stirred up to a frenzied response (on one occasion almost too frenzied, as I recall), and how to draw it into the work with him, which of course is the point of such ... er ... music.

Saturday's conductor was John Barnett, music director of the PRSO. Barnett made a courageous effort with *Gestos*, but never seemed quite comfortable with such goings on. Especially in cuing the audience, he consistently seemed too ready too soon to turn back to the more familiar orchestral territory. For this reason, I think, the work failed to gain the full effect which was intended and which I think it could attain.

Gestos' seven movements are cryptically titled, and the titles as well as the . . . er . . . music are full of inside jokes and minor mysteries which may provide some fun for folks who like that sort of thing. In the meantime, *Gestos* takes its place alongside COSMOS and *Mon Oeuf* as one of the most thought-provoking compositions of Francis Schwartz.

Also performed on Saturday were Concerto Grosso by island composer Ignacio Morales Nieva and a whole bundle of pieces featuring double bass virtuoso Gary Karr.

Concerto Grosso dates from 1972, and was first performed by the PRSO. The title harks back to an eighteenth-century practice of composing music requiring a small orchestra played off against a larger one. This contemporary version of the concerto grosso stands in a fine tradition reaching from Bach, Corelli and Vivaldi through Mozart, Stamitz (who?), Brahms, Bartók, Stravinsky and many others, although the works were not always so titled. The present example is scored for flute, oboe, piano and string orchestra in the best eighteenth-century tradition, while the alternation of the small and large ensembles occurs as expected. But here the resemblance ends. Morales Nieva's Concerto Grosso is cast in a bristling twentieth-century harmonic idiom.

This composer knows his instruments and has mastered the compositional techniques of dealing with them. His work tends to be eclectic, and this particular composition sounds very much like a product of the Hindemith-German-Austrian atonal or partly tonal writing of the 1920s and 1930s, not that there's anything wrong with that.

I am (or once was) a bass player, so what can I tell you about this most recent island appearance of bassist Gary Karr as soloist with the PRSO? Just drag out the heaviest superlatives in your vocabulary and write your own review, friends, for that's the way it was. Karr is the greatest, and his playing of the big fiddle probably represents the height of double bass artistry attained up to now. We know very little (except indirectly) of the playing of his admired predecessors, particularly such early ones as Bottesini and Dragonetti, but what we can surmise from their own compositions, written for their own performances, seems to indicate that Karr plays even better than they did. His playing is marked by perfect intonation, impeccable technique and phrasing so beautiful that it brings tears to your eyes. And it is (or seems) so effortless for him that Karr has energy and concentration left over for a bit of visual humor in the way of subtle clowning.

Saturday's offerings included the Koussevitsky concerto, a well known sonata by Henry Eccles, the *Kol Nidre* of Max Bruch and a hair-raising set of variations on a tune from Bellini's *La Sonnambula*, by Bottesini. It was here, in music of a style which today almost begs for satire (aside from its staggering difficulty) that Karr laid on a bit of clownery and inside-jokery. But wait. . . . Isn't this exactly what we had in *Gestos*, by Francis Schwartz on the same program? Just so, friends; watch out if this pair ever gets together!

Ho Hum

The San Juan Star
June 23, 1983 By Donald Thompson

    Ho hum. Another Puerto Rico Casals Festival ended last weekend in the Performing Arts Center in Santurce. As I was on and off the island for one reason or another during the past month or so I attended something less than half of this recent series' offerings. Still, it was possible to get an idea of how things were going, while conducting lightning interviews with colleagues, performers and a few perceptive music lovers before and after the concerts. Taking the long view, how things are going with this publicly funded enterprise can be stated in two words: "Still downhill." Still downhill because for at least a decade this annual observance has been drifting away from its once high purposes and its once high overall level of performance, while still consuming an inordinate proportion of the island's musical budget, time and concentration. What has not changed much over the years is the rate of semantic inflation which accompanies the disappearance of audiences and the decline in the event's conceptual and artistic importance.
    The Honorable Governor of Puerto Rico still writes in the program book that this event is somehow indicative of the island's "continual musical progress." Jaime González Oliver, president of the board of directors of the festival's parent Administration for the Development of Arts and Culture (a mouthful, that), writes in the same 1983 program book that this year's performers were "distinguished international artists." Both of these officials should know better, for the evidence is before them and has been before them for many years. If this recent series was indicative of any aspect of Puerto Rico's progress it was on the fiscal side, not musical: the island government apparently has enough money now to blow a great deal of it on a handful of concerts attended by a

handful of people. As for González Oliver's "distinguished international artists"; well, some were but then again, a great many weren't. Most of this year's performers were simply folks like you and me, trying to earn an honest living at their trade, and many would probably be embarrassed if some impressionable music lover or campaigning politician were to address them as "distiguished international artists."

On the other hand, another official hit the nail right on the head. Virginia Ramírez de Arrellano is the executive director of the Corporation of Performing Arts, the immediate parent of the Puerto Rico Casals Festival and of its twin, the Puerto Rico Artistic Varieties Company. Ms. Ramírez is much closer to the real action and is thus more likely to think in practical terms than in foggy expressions of political good will and general benevolence from on high. Probably the truest words in the front of the program book are Ms. Ramírez's: that to organize an event like this costs a great deal of money. Whose money? You got it, friends; your money and mine, for most of it came directly out of our taxes.

Of course there were some fine moments during these concerts. Pianist Irma Vallecillo is indeed a world class artist, and the Waverly Consort quite rightly makes a tremendous hit wherever it performs its repertory of unusual music on unusual instruments. Both the Emerson String Quartet and cellist Lynn Harrell are well remembered here from appearances a year ago, while soprano Pilar Lorengar is a welcome new face in Puerto Rico.

Two orchestras participated in this year's series: the Puerto Rico Symphony Orchestra, which I did not hear, and the Los Angeles Chamber Orchestra, which I did. The latter group ended the series with a varied program of Wagner, Mozart and J.S. Bach. The chamber orchestra sound always comes as a relief from the rich and sometimes over-ripe sonority of the full symphony orchestra: something like a switch to gin and tonic after several rounds of cuba libres or bourbon and gingers. The Los Angeles players are a well founded group, the strings especially well unified and coordinated. Saturday's closing concert offered the Siegfried Idyll of Wagner, Mozart's lovely C Major Piano Concerto (No. 21) with pianist Lillian Kallir, and Bach's Magnificat in D Major.

The last named work is an especially felicitous setting by Bach of a favored biblical text (Luke 1:46-55), its twelve verses here set for orchestra, four vocal soloists and chorus. Bach's orchestral and vocal usage is extremely varied in this work, and always effectively tied to the text.

Some sections require the entire chamber orchestra and chorus, others only a singer and a couple of instruments and still others a vocal duo with light accompaniment. Skilled singers on Saturday were soprano Mary Burgess, mezzo D'Anna Fortunato, tenor Jon Humphrey and bass Leslie Guinn, all of whom had appeared earlier in the series. Choral tenors and basses were provided by the chorus of the New England Conservatory of Music (Lorna Cooke Varon, director); sopranos and altos by Evy Lucío's rightly celebrated San Juan Children's Choir.

An interesting disposition of voices. At Leipzig's St. Thomas Church, Bach wrote for boys' unchanged voices in soprano and contralto choral parts. Here, these parts were skillfully covered by both boys and girls from the San Juan Children's Choir, solidly prepared for this occasion by Carmen Acevedo of the University of Puerto Rico faculty. Their use, rather than the much more accessible but much too "warm" mature women's voices, provided a charming and authentic touch to the work. Conducting was Gerard Schwarz, remembered here from solo appearances some years ago with trumpet and flügelhorn. A very good musician, but on Saturday Schwarz occasionally fell victim to a temptation to overconduct. This was most evident in those sections of the Bach which in fact required minimal forces (harpsichord, English horn, bassoon and double bass, for example) but which received conductorial gestures more appropriate for the Vienna Philharmonic performing a Bruckner symphony. Nor was the Mozart piano concerto completely free of such problems. Here it was more a matter of occasional instability of rhythmic impulse brought about by the conductor's arbitrary shifts back and forth between different patterns of pulse (duple and quadruple in the first movement, for example). Still, Mozart is Mozart, and the glories of Mozart's music will shine through any performance which attains any degree of respectability at all. And the Los Angeles Chamber Orchestra, while not exactly of the "distinguished international" caliber which the management would have us believe, is certainly respectable and well worth hearing.

And while we're on the subject of management, how were the visible aspects of the managerial function? General programming? First off, there was very little connection with the known historical figure of the great Catalan cellist Pablo Casals, in whose name these annual rituals still take place. The six Brandenburg Concertos of Bach, performed by the Los Angeles Chamber Orchestra? Certainly. But it is difficult to justify, in this frame of reference, the inclusion of a transcription for clarinet and piano (neither of which even existed in Bach's time) of a Bach work for viola da gamba and harpsichord. Why not simply hire a gambist and a harpsichordist? The contracting of individual artists? OK for the day in and day out musical life of a city or an island, but, again, hardly of a stature to require the format of a special government-financed "festival." Most of the soloists, ensembles and conductors presented would have fit nicely into Puerto Rico's several regular concert series, while the few attractions which would not, could certainly have been booked into the Performng Arts Center by the same promoters who book rock concerts, popular theatrical events, musical comedies and the like; or indeed, by the Administration for the Development of Arts and Culture itself, as special events.

General administrative policy? Lousy. For openers, you may have noticed that these concerts were not televised live for home audiences. It was stated, rather vaguely, that this was because of "previous commitments" on the part of the government television authority. On the other hand, it is quite possible that this was an administrative decision based on the premise that live TV coverage would jeopardize attendance in the concert hall. The premise itself is very shaky. Attendance was so skimpy that it is difficult to believe that it could have been affected one way or the other by live television transmission. In the meantime, one of the supposed purposes of the Puerto Rico Casals Festival, to transmit these events to home audiences (the educational function) has clearly been abandoned. There is also the shocking story of the cancellation of inexpensive balcony seats in the hall when it appeared that the first floor seats might not be sold for certain concerts. Shocking (1) because inexpensive seats had long been advertised through the island press and other media and (2) because again, managerial policy obviously goes against making these concerts accessible to the great number of citizens who have already paid for them through taxes. On the other hand, one aspect of managerial decision making deserves unqualified praise. This is the incorporation of program notes by a writer who knows what he's writing about and who can say it correctly, concisely, accurately ... and interestingly. This is Ramón Arroyo Carrión of the University of Puerto Rico Music Library. Long after memory fades of who played what and who wore an ugly dress, these notes will remain as the official record of what actually took place at these concerts.

Having just returned from a visit to a number of university music departments and schools of music in the southeastern United States, I was especially interested in the final concert in this year's series. Small orchestra; four able vocal soloists; a rather odd kind of chorus; a less than super-specialized conductor. What does it remind you of? Yes, of course; the sort of musical activity which takes place regularly in from 500 to 1000 universities across the country. This being the case, you might ask why the Commonwealth government doesn't finally free itself of this awkward festival format and put some of this money and energy (read "money") into the direct support and planned improvement of Puerto Rico's several university-level institutions of musical studies? You might be surprised at what could be put together with a little help from On High.

Occasional attendance at this most recent concert series also gave rise to another train of thought. It is evident that this series has become more or less an extension of the annual season of the Puerto Rico Symphony Orchestra, with a few additional attractions laid on. This being the case, it might be advisable at this time to consider closing out this exhausted festival format, investing some of its resources in a serious redesign of the Puerto Rico Symphony Orchestra. Such a project might profitably encompass the following aspects: (1) a shorter but much more intense season, with proper promotion and publicity; (2) a retirement plan which would enable some of the now arthritic orchestra pioneers to retire gracefully from the battlefield; (3) a realistic salary scale; and coupled with it (4) an honorable plan to attract and retain skilled players, instead of the shameful and probably illegal practices currently in use. In this way (and perhaps only in this way), Puerto Rico might finally have a solid base upon which to build an attractive music festival: one which could perhaps even attract visitors from abroad, as used to occur in the now forgotten Puerto Rico Casals Festivals of the late 1950s. Remember?

Evita Enters the Electronic Age

The San Juan Star
June 27, 1983 By Donald Thompson

Whatever else might be said about the production of *Evita* now playing in Puerto Rico (and I think that plenty will be said), its Friday evening performance in the Performing Arts Center almost caused a domestic crisis in one island family: mine. You see, Madame T. is a lyric theater enthusiast to begin with, and to make things worse is also a performer. On Friday our customary debate began at intermission, continued during the trip home to suburbia, gained considerably in warmth during an after-theater snack and subsided into mutterings only as I tried to get some sleep while she, enchanted, listened to a complete recording of the piece.

Evita is a dramatized and musicalized account of the rise to great power of Eva Duarte Perón in Argentina from the late 1930s until her death in 1952. Since its origins in a 1976 recording and the London staged version in 1978, the work has been played in many parts of the world and has enjoyed great success wherever it has been offered.

The present offering is a Spanish-language production which originated in Madrid in 1980 and which is now on its way to various Latin American locations via Puerto Rico. This is the same geographical trajectory which first brought to Puerto Rico most of the operas and zarzuelas heard here from the 1830s until a few decades ago. A respectable old tradition, this, and I think that it's very healthy to receive a ready-made and ongoing theatrical production from outside from time to time. And in general I believe this particular production to be a success with its public here, despite my own reservations concerning the work itself and despite a strong protest concerning its particular form of presentation here. In other words, on Friday night a capacity audience in the Festival

Hall seemed to enjoy it (including Madame T.), but I didn't very much.

The "musical comedy" genre is not noted for dramatic development to begin with, tending instead to fall into dialogue scenes separated (or hopefully, connected) by musical numbers. There are exceptions, of course, in which dramatic development flows forward in a changing panorama of means: dialogue, songs, chorus and dance numbers, etc. *West Side Story* is still probably the outstanding example of this admired type of unified lyric theater.

Evita offers no dramatic development at all, for its design is instead based on the principle of very brief vignettes or flashes, arranged in chronological sequence following an initial flashback. This design, in today's theater, often incorporates elements of high technology in the way of instant visual changes (often within a basically unchanging and somehow symbolic stage), abrupt and surprising lighting effects, and electronically produced, altered or amplified sound. And herein lies my own protest regarding this production, but more of that later. Interestingly enough, *Evita* has very little spoken dialogue, and what little there is occurs over music. In other words, in this sense the work possesses something of the design of opera itself: theater through continuous music. For this reason, I guess, it has been called a "rock opera." "Rock" is certainly not accurate; better might be "cinematic, disco, pop, rock and shlock opera," for this is the impression which I gained of the pretentious style of Andrew Lloyd Webber's music. In fact, we can be thankful that this Spanish-language adaptation by Ignacio Artime and Jaime Azpilicueta incorporates some newly arranged pieces by Juan José García Caffi to replace stylistically absurd numbers in the original (boleros instead of tangos, for example).

Principal figures in this production are Paloma San Basilio as Evita, Julio Catania as Perón, Tony Cruz as Evita's early lover Magaldi, and Charly Falcón in a smaller but symbolically important part as Perón's displaced mistress. Pablo Abraira plays the extremely important part of Che Guevara. Who? Yes, THE "Che," whose name is used here in a symbolic way (the piece is big on symbols) to represent Evita's supposedly revolutionary conscience, to shove people about the stage and to fill the gaps with wry exhortations of one kind and another. What immediately comes to mind is the raunchy and revolutionary street singer of *The Threepenny Opera*, especially in the German original. In this case, however, the "Che" seemed to me much too mild, much too kind and much too benevolent, withal. Che, indeed!

Neither the choruses nor the dance numbers impressed me very much, attaining the general level of skill and unity (and the choreographic complexity) which you might expect of an academy rather than a professional company. On the other hand, a couple of extremely clever uses of chorus people will long stick in my memory. Particularly, I remember the men as a troop of operetta cadets, first marching up and down the stage alone and later with (or around) a mixed bunch of hilariously posed and positioned stage aristocrats.

General director for this Madrid production and still with it on the road is Jaime Azpilicueta, while appearing forlorn and lonely in the orchestra pit is the road conductor, chorusmaster Vicente Alcón. And now comes the bad news.

Electronic technology has brought to pop culture (and here is where *Evita* fits) a far-reaching revolution in the public's expectations, with regard to means. In music particularly, the expectations of a whole generation of people have been determined by a technology whose product has very little to do with the means of real life. Remember the rock bands whose fortunes were based on recordings but who could never play a real job? Theirs is a music of the studio, of the electronic synthesizer, of the mixing console and now of the computer. It is now possible to electronically create and preserve virtually any desired sound, either through electronic generation to begin with or through the prior recording and alteration of "real" sounds.

This technology has spilled over from recording, TV and the night club circuit to the theater, and offers an irresistible temptation to producers of lyric theater, particularly. It is now possible to make small voices big, to convert lousy voices into acceptable ones and to cover it all with a hard electronic gloss which defies all penetration or analysis. Too, you can save a buck by hiring only a third of the chorus which the work really needs and no orchestra at all. Recordings for home use and for miming in amateur shows? Sure, but I hate to see this electronic invasion of live theater. And this is precisely what has occurred in this *Evita* production.

Voices in *Evita* are so heavily miked that it's impossible to know what they're really like, while Maestro Alcón, in the pit, waves his arms at a pair of loudspeakers and a six man combo. The stage, you see, sings along with a previously made track or tape, and it's even impossible for an audience to know how much of the stage singing is real and how much is "enhanced," reinforced or substituted for by ghostly voices on the tape. A justification of such use of orchestral tapes, at least, is sometimes sought in the uncertainties of orchestral resources where traveling companies might play. Well, a little correspondence could have resulted in the *Evita* company having a proper orchestra in the pit in Puerto Rico at least, for this music is no more difficult than has been played here for many productions over the past twenty years, and San Juan certainly has the orchestral musicians for it.

In most countries the performers' unions take a hand in determining the contractual conditions for the orchestras of visiting (as well as domestic) lyric companies. Where, you might ask, was the island local of the American Federation of Musicians when this production was being booked here? A mystery, as are the true nature and the true quality of the electronic voices on the Festival Hall stage this week.

Die Fledermaus:
A Grand Homecoming For Island Singers

The San Juan Star
July 2, 1983   By Donald Thompson

Opera de San Juan's current production of *Die Fledermaus* at the UPR Theater has inspired some historical musings on the condition of opera production in Puerto Rico. The truth of it is, today's web of island-based companies began only in the late 1960s, with a group which in fact took its name from the year of its first efforts: Opera 68. To many observers the time did not seem right at all. There had been no home-grown opera productions here for well over a decade; the musical panorama was all but monopolized by a government branch which had no interest in island-based efforts in general and certainly no skill in opera production in particular. And anyway, few people in Puerto Rico knew how to do it anymore. There was no direct and continuous island tradition on which to draw for stage, pit, voices, public, patronage, or any other aspect of opera production. Opera 68 turned this around. Within a few years other companies split off from it or were newly created; at one time there were five or six "opera companies" in Puerto Rico, competing among themselves for works, performers, theater dates, production staffers, patrons and program advertisers. The new companies tended to offer only the biggest and most popular operas of Verdi and Puccini and to bring in most of the elements from outside, assembling them in a rehearsal or two once here. Opera 68, by now renamed Opera de San Juan, attempted to use island forces exclusively (or almost exclusively) and to develop its productions here from the start. Too, this pioneer company gradually turned away from superproductions of standard operas and toward a less worn path of attractive if less well known works. Thus its internationally important production of Felipe Gutiérrez' *Macías* in 1977, and thus its present *Fledermaus* at the UPR Theater.

Die Fledermaus is the brightest, the most popular and the most Viennese of the great operettas of Johann Strauss II. First offered in 1874, it can still evoke rich satirical associations with the aristocracy and the bureaucracy of Vienna as the hot house capital of the old Austro-Hungarian Empire. Most of the work's gentle humor is in fact based on the fluffy pretentiousness of the former and the pigheaded ceremoniousness of the latter. To really work, however, all of its elements must tick along together like parts of a Swiss watch behind a porcelain face.

Opera de San Juan's productions have often provided the occasion for a grand homecoming of island singers. Such is the case at the UPR Theater this weekend. Fine soprano Evangelina Colón is Rosalinda, while opposite her as the errant Eisenstein is tenor Guillermo Silva Marín. Silva was once a baritone, but Thursday's opening performance convinced me that he has found his true niche. Here is a big and clear tenor voice coupled with good acting ability and concentration. Silva's work has done a lot for this production. Evangelina Colón possesses a warm, versatile and powerful voice, as is again shown in Roselinda's second act "Czardas." However, I do not believe the light-headed and flirty Rosalinda to be the best sort of role for Ms. Colón's more solid and substantial style. Continuing to impress mightily in this production is tenor Rubén Broitman's big voice and comic talent, here as Alfred. Roselinda's uppity maid, Adele, is nicely played by soprano Maryann Polesinelli, whose second-act laughing song impressed on Thursday. Other principal roles are ably played by baritone Rafael Lebrón, baritone José Antonio Ruiz and tenor Valentín Fernández. A big and sonorous chorus has been prepared for this production by Rafael Ferrer and general artistic director Camelia Ortiz, while the musical director is Enriquillo Cerón.

Musically, then, this production is in pretty good shape. Thursday's only disappointment on the singing side, in fact, was Edgardo Gierbolini, who as the foppish Prince Orlovski also has a bit of singing to do. Gierbolini's serious rhythmic insecurities threatened on several occasions to tip over the entire production.

It is on the staging side that this production is really weak. Stage director is Antonio Valentín, and his contribution seems to have been limited to getting the chorus people on and off the stage. Once onstage, however, they were apparently given nothing to do. This is a great pity, for the chorus is on the stage a great deal of the time in this play, and can (indeed, must) contribute greatly to its sparkle and movement. On Thursday the chorus people mostly just stood around, while even the principals seemed to be developing their own staging and their own business in the absence of any planned design or directorial guidance.

Noted actor and director José Luis Marrero plays the hilarious part of jailor Frosch in this production. Dominating the third act, the drunken Frosch traditionally expounds a bit upon timely circumstances and local occurrences, anachronistic as his comments might be. In a production which I once saw in mildly Socialist Vienna, Frosch discovered that his eyeglasses had no lenses. "Well, what can you expect?", he asks the audience. "They're from the National Health Service!" Big laugh here. "Chavito" Marrero cleverly comments on island theater life, public figures, this production's own staff and naturally, politics. For openers, are you ready for Romerovich, Padillovsky and Cuchinstein? Too long a scene, though, and it's too much to ask one lone actor, no matter how skilled, to provide the forward motion for an entire production.

And speaking of too long, the second act of *Die Fledermaus* is a big party at Orlovsky's place. This scene is sometimes extended by the inclusion of specific "cameo" acts, in the theatrical context of entertaining Orlovsky's guests. This particular production's second act is extended—and still extended—and yet extended—by the inclusion of a number of "surprise" acts by island performers and groups. These are mainly acceptable in themselves and some quite good, in fact, but they did nothing on Thursday to liven up the slow pace of this production. If anything, they contributed to a vague sense of watching a costumed concert or some kind of staged oratorio instead of a brilliant and witty piece of lyric theater.

Hopefully, by this evening the whole thing will be tightened up a few notches at least. This production's translation to Spanish is by Antonio Valentín, adapted by Camelia Ortiz. Set design is by Julio Biaggi, costumes by Tom Seitz and makeup and wigs by veteran Chick Gable. General production coordinator is Iván Janer.

Mignon Dunn Illuminates the Best *Aida* Yet

The San Juan Star
September 17, 1983   By Donald Thompson

Verdi's grand opera *Aida* opened grandly in the Performing Arts Center on Thursday, with one performance (this evening) remaining in its short run. This is not the first production of *Aida* to be seen in Puerto Rico nor will it be the last, but it will probably be remembered as one of the best, all considered. Attractively put together by Teatro de la Opera under the general artistic direction of Antonio Barasorda, the present production offers a well working combination of island forces and invited specialists.

In the title role of the Ethiopian slave at the Egyptian court is soprano Margarita Castro, very well known here since the very beginning of her career. Ms. Castro's voice has developed great skill, flexibility and control, with a rightly admired topmost range especially. Her stage presence has also improved considerably in recent years. However, it is always clear that Ms. Castro is a gifted singer who finds herself on a stage rather than a singer-actress who is developing a role. Within the generally good pacing and movement of this production, a more convincing characterization and dramatic development on the part of Aida (after all the central character of the piece) would have contributed a great deal to what should be the work's ceaseless march toward its final tragedy.

Mignon Dunn as the Egyptian princess Amneris is another story entirely. This accomplished mezzosoprano illuminates every scene in which she appears, both musically and dramatically. A scholarly commentator on the Verdi operas once described Amneris as the female role which Verdi most loved, among his operas' many principal and secondary women. I could never make much sense out of this view until Thursday, when Ms. Dunn's rich characterization literally brought the complicated

Amneris to life for me. She provided the underlying unifying force for many scenes herself on Thursday, while the entire subtle line of Amneris' development culminated in her big fourth act solo scene, logically arrived at and breathtakingly presented.

Radames, young Egyptian general and Aida's lover, is played here by tenor William Johns. Mr. Johns possesses a good set of pipes, as we used to say in other realms of the music biz. Big sound, clear throughout its range and with a high degree of dynamic flexibility. Yet for my taste (if not, apparently, for the rest of Thursday's audience) there's a bit too much sliding around from one pitch to another. This seemed consistently to take the form of an oblique approach from below, before finally clamping onto the indicated note. A good device now and again for a sort of emotional tug, but (like all such devices) it very, very easily loses its effect in a rapid progression of diminishing returns. Once, nice; second time, hmm; third time, forget it. Another thing that bothered me on Thursday was Mr. Johns' belting out the end of Radames' aria "Celeste Aida" like an Egyptian general harranguing his headquarters staff, instead of giving it the loving pianissimo (and "dying away," at that) which Verdi, an incomparable master of music-in-theater, had carefully indicated in the score (or at least as indicated in my edition).

In terms of integrated musical and dramatic accomplishment, baritone Mario Sereni did very good work on Thursday in the key role of Amonasro, captured king of Ethiopia and Aida's father. Verdi's baritone roles are often extremely interesting (take Rigoletto, for example, to say nothing of Iago and the great Falstaff), and this one is no exception. With a degree of subtlety approaching that of Mignon Dunn herself, Mr. Sereni is a very positive force in his development of the role of Amonasro.

Distinguished island born bass-baritone Justino Díaz is an appropriately oily Ramfis, high priest in the complicated religion of this ancient priest-ridden society, while smaller parts are played by Pedro Morell (king of Egypt) and Carlos Bauzá as the messenger from the frontier who starts the whole international incident rolling. The clear and ringing voice of soprano Tamara Escribano is excellent in the walk on (or, rather, stand on) role of a chanting priestess in the grandly ceremonial first act finale.

Speaking of grandly ceremonial scenes, this opera offers a plenitude. In fact, *Aida* is probably one of the best illustrations of the fundamental operatic belief that it is possible to convincingly combine music, drama and visual spectacle in one "event." Naturally, the plot has to be right for it, and this one certainly is. It may be significant that the *Aida* plot, in whose design Verdi himself played a very important part, is one of few which were conceived as opera almost from the beginning, instead of being based on older plays or novels. Think of it: unlikely lovers, parents, nations, wars, treason (unintended, of course), religion, dancing priestesses, politics, captives entertaining their captors with dances from back home, benedictions, fireworks and an extremely simple and open plot which grinds its inexorable way toward its tragic ending in the best tradition of ancient theater. A winner.

The *Aida* choruses were prepared by Pablo Boissen. The women sounded extremely and consistently good, the men not so good on Thursday. Tenors rough on top, basses mumbly on the bottom. Simple but effective dance scenes were designed by Rosario Galán for members of the San Juan Municipal Ballet. The Puerto Rico Symphony Orchestra generally sounded very good in the pit, also providing skilled execution of Verdi's frequent passages for unusual solo instruments. The imaginative use of lighting (designed by Quique Benet) contributed greatly to the dramatic effect of scenes mainly played within open Egyptian boxes big enough to hold the great multitudes which assemble with some regularity in *Aida*. Stage director and musical director for this generally quite successful production are Franco Gratale and Anton Guadagno, respectively.

The Figueroa family, next generation in a 1983 photo. (Left to right: seated; Guillermo, violin; Yvonne, piano; standing; Rafael, cello; Narciso, violin.)

Out of Limbo But Not Out of the Woods

The San Juan Star
September 18, 1983   By Donald Thompson

    When the Puerto Rico Symphony Orchestra opened its 26th season at the Performing Arts Center, the event naturally could only bring to the minds of some old time orchestra players memories of long gone colleagues, conductors both bad and good, soloists likewise, managerial and directorial blunders and professional battles won and lost.

    So much for sentimental nostalgia. On a more objective plane, the background of this branch of the insular government is such a patchwork that when a proper history of it is written someday, the book will read like some Kafka-esque fantasy of bureaucratic bumblings in arts mismanagement. More to the point, it will be seen that many (but not all) of the orchestra's present artistic problems are rooted in decisions made or not made many years ago in the cloudy corridors of inappropriate government branches.

    For more than twenty years this orchestra was a stepchild of the Puerto Rico Casals Festival Corporation, itself a tourism and image-making subsidiary of the Puerto Rico Industrial Development Company (PRIDCO). During the early years, the PRSO's only function was to serve as a pacifier to island orchestra players and a few concerned music lovers who saw, year after year, a handsome government appropriation go up in smoke in a brief annual festival, while there was no way to get the same kind of support (read "Money") for the island's own musical life, on any level. In fact, the massive concentration of effort, funds and attention on the annual festival made it extremely difficult for any other island musical effort to survive at all. Meanwhile a common view among government functionaries and laymen alike was "Music in Puerto Rico? Sure, PRIDCO and the Casals Festival are taking care of that." The

Puerto Rico Symphony Orchestra, although a direct subsidiary of the Festival Corporation itself, suffered along with everyone else. The Festival Corporation's priorities were clear, and the PRSO was not very high on the list. Except for a great leap in the length of the concert season brought about through the direct intervention of then Governor Luis A. Ferré, the island orchestra fumbled along for a couple of decades in a kind of artistic and administrative limbo.

In 1980 a reshuffling of the government's interests in concert life brought about a new alignment. The PRSO was elevated to the status of a corporate arm of the new Administration for the Development of Arts and Culture (Spanish-language acronym: AFAC), while the annual Casals Festival was made a subsidiary of a subsidiary of the same agency. As a result, your symphony orchestra has indeed gained in relative visibility; in addition, it now occupies something approaching a symphony orchestra's proper place at the very center of a city's (or a region's) musical life.

There are still plenty of problems, both artistic and managerial. Long-term managerial problems are connected to the lack of properly established working relationships with the employees, including correct conditions of hiring, firing and retirement. Almost the only thing ever said on these subjects, incidentally, was a set of absolutely horrendous statements allegedly made before the Symphony Orchestra by its musical director a couple of years ago and never refuted or even investigated, although ample documentation was offered by the orchestra members.

Artistic problems in performance are usually the result of managerial decisions made long before the problems are perceived. Some of the artistic problems still evident at the opening of the Symphony Orchestra's 26th season go back to the time when it was decided that the island orchestra should be made up of islanders, although some of them might not play so well. Some of these pioneers are still with the orchestra and still not playing so well, but they can't afford to hang up their bows due to the lack of a retirement program. Other artistic problems result from a managerial willingness to save a buck by engaging students to fill chairs in what should by now be a fully professional ensemble. Still others result from an artistic direction which may have worn itself out. Conductors of symphony orchestras, and especially orchestras of the general level of this one, tend to move around every three years or so. This helps keep them from becoming stale on the job by being exposed to new challenges; at the same time it brings new conductorial points of view to developing orchestras. Very healthy for everyone, this game of musical chairs (or unmusical, as the case might be), and it may now be time to launch another go around at the PRSO.

The season's opening concert was conducted by John Barnett, and offered rather stodgy performances of Beethoven's mighty Coriolanus Overture, his less mighty Triple Concerto (violin, cello, piano and orchestra), and Shostakovich's melodious Fifth Symphony. The Triple Concerto has never been one of my favorite Beethoven works, mainly because of its weak finale. Curiously, Beethoven cast this third movement in the form of a moderate polonaise, rather than as a more brilliant, more appealing and more characteristic rondo. As a result the work seems to just peter out rather than end convincingly. Soloists on Saturday were pianist Jesús María Sanromá, still bashing away in his 80s, and two Figueroas some forty or fifty years his junior. These were violinist Narciso and cellist Rafael, members of the third generation of an important island musical family. Both of these Figueroas are well trained and well founded young musicians although of the two cellist Rafael seemed on Saturday to have the edge in general solidity and expressive gifts.

And finally, that marvel, the Fifth Symphony of Shostakovich. This was a key work in the great composer's on-again, off-again relation to the USSR and Communist Party arts bureaucracies, and at least some of its overall simplicity and broad lyricism must be seen as part of a musico-political tightrope act which Shostakovich performed time and time again out of the sheer necessity of survival. The Fifth Symphony was his first publicly performed work after the denunciation of his music by *Pravda* in 1936, and was duly approved in advance by the Union of Soviet Composers. It was also approved, as appropriate for performance by a state orchestra, by officers of the state itself as "a sincere manifestation of his redemption in the spirit of Socialist Realism."

Aside from the undeniable virtues of the work itself, one can't help wondering what kind of symphony Shostakovich might have written had he not been obliged to satisfy political and governmental requirements. One also wonders something else. In a tiny place like Puerto Rico, with a long-observed tendency to concentrate power in the arts (or at least in music), in government branches or in particular groups helped by government, is there any chance that acceptance for performance by the state orchestra might someday depend on approval by a political party or by a "Union of Puerto Rican Composers?" Horrible thought, as well as probably being illegal here. Still, it's the kind of thing which is mentioned here from time to time, and it's a subject which this new and relatively inexperienced management of the Puerto Rico Symphony Orchestra might wish to ponder as it makes day to day decisions that when hardened into policies will affect, for better or worse, the development of music in Puerto Rico.

Pro Arte's Fiftieth Anniversary

The San Juan Star
September 28, 1983 By Donald Thompson

  The great wheel of island cultural life continues to turn. Elections come and go; political parties rise, fall, and proliferate like sand fleas; official arts bureaucracies are created and gradually turn to stone; and somehow, despite it all, musical life goes on.
  One of the most valuable elements in Puerto Rico's musical life has been the Pro Arte Musical Society, despite occasional distractions, passing enthusiasms and transitory programmatic imbalances. Launched in 1932 by a handful of island musicians, music lovers and a UPR music teacher, this organization for almost thirty years offered for its members and friends a varied series of concerts by the world's best traveling artists as well as by island musicians. In fact, as is occasionally pointed out by concert goers with long memories, Pro Arte and the UPR Cultural Activities Series (going back almost a decade longer) had put Puerto Rico on the world's twentieth-century circuits long before the Puerto Rico Casals Festival, once highly touted in this regard by its own management, was even a gleam in Alexander Schneider's eye. Then, in 1959 Pro Arte meekly folded its tent in deference to the insular government's first great experiment in the centralized control of the arts. It was not until the mid-seventies that it began to be widely recognized that Puerto Rico's concertgoing public was being shortchanged. In the field of regular recital offerings by traveling artists, only the UPR series had maintained continuity through this period, with the Institute of Puerto Rican Culture doing what little it could for island performers particularly, down at Casa Blanca in Old San Juan.
  In 1976 Pro Arte was revived, gradually regaining its important place as a privately organized and (mainly) privately financed concert agency.

However, Puerto Rico's now blossoming habits of dependence on government (that is, on your taxes and mine) for almost everything are hard to break, and even the new Pro Arte receives a certain amount of government help in one form or another. Financially, this may perhaps be necessary, given the apparently grand intentions of this new Pro Arte, but it does tend to blur what should be the sharply distinguished profiles and purposes of different agencies, public and private, which presumably have different aims and different philosophies.

The present Pro Arte season is designed to celebrate the fiftieth anniversary of the organization's founding, and opened last weekend with a pair of concerts by the Chicago-based American Chamber Symphony Orchestra, conducted by Robert Frisbie. What, you might ask, is a Chamber Symphony Orchestra? Well, it's likely to be a bit larger than the "chamber orchestra" associated with the Bach-Corelli-Vivaldi repertory but smaller than the "symphony orchestra" of the Beethoven-Schubert-Mendelssohn-Brahms sound and so on up to Tchaikovsky, Mahler and Strauss. If you're in doubt, look at the bass fiddles. If there's one bass, call it a chamber orchestra; if there are two basses it's probably already getting on for some kind of symphony orchestra. What this really means is that here we heard a small symphony orchestra, relatively portable and capable of playing a fairly wide repertory without getting into stylistic difficulties connected with purposes and means.

Saturday evening's inaugural concert took place in the big Festival Hall at the Performing Arts Center, before an audience limited to Pro Arte's numerous members and their guests. Soloists were splendid cellist Ko Iwasaki (the C Major Concerto of Haydn) and island pianist Elías López Sobá (Mozart's dramatic D Minor Concerto, K 466). López Sobá is a regular faculty member of the Music Department of the University of Puerto Rico, and Saturday's performance marked his reemergence into active concert life after many years devoted to other pursuits. His appearances on more public occasions will certainly be noted with interest.

Sunday afternoon's Pro Arte audience, but now including purchasers of individual tickets, moved out to the concert hall of the Puerto Rico Conservatory of Music in Hato Rey. Sunday's event was a hybrid kind of animal: part cello recital and part orchestra concert. Cellist Ko Iwasaki and brilliant Swedish pianist Staffan Scheja offered a dashing performance of Rachmaninoff's G Minor Sonata, Op. 19. Characteristic of

Rachmaninoff's music, this sonata is a compendium of soulful and singable melodies cast within ripe and mellow harmonies. Iwasaki and Scheja have the complete range of expressive nuance required by this romantic music, and brought it all into play on Sunday. The rest of the event was devoted to orchestral music including a pleasant performance of Aaron Copland's ballet suite Appalachian Spring, for string orchestra plus a few winds.

After intermission, pianist Scheja returned for a rollicking performance with the American Chamber Symphony Orchestra of Shostakovich's First Piano Concerto. Actually, this is a concerto for piano and string orchestra with trumpet obbligato, for a trumpet part (here nicely played by Larry Larson) is also extremely important. Pianist Scheja is a highly recognized young performer nowadays, and for good reason. His clean, clear and vigorous playing of this grotesque and satirical Shostakovich work contributed greatly to its success with Sunday's audience.

Closing the program were Mozart's miniaturely monumental Symphony in E Flat (No. 39) and a charming encore piece: a movement from one of Vivaldi's innumerable concertos, this one for two trumpets and string orchestra. Larry Larson and Greg Fudala were the fine soloists, using tiny trumpets to reach the stratospheric heights of the trumpet parts in this interesting music.

And what, then, of the American Chamber Symphony Orchestra? By simple arithmetic it's obvious that the smaller the orchestra, the more exposed are any technical faults which might occur. In other words, the smaller the ensemble the more difficult it is to hide. The extreme, of course, is chamber music: string quartets, trios, duos and sonatas. This orchestra is characterized by a hearty and youthfully enthusiastic sound, but its performances here were not particularly marked by great accuracy in pitch nor by great unity in performance. These virtues can only result from years and years of playing—and playing together. In fact, it was interesting as well as instructive to note that many of the ailments which are frequently observed in the string sections of our own Puerto Rico Symphony Orchestra were present last weekend in the American Chamber Symphony Orchestra. Among these were a lack of uniformity in bowing, the reckless use of open strings, and (although to a lesser degree), a lack of agreement on the exact length of phrases. A few erroneous and insecure entrances didn't help much, either. Robert Frisbie seems to be a capable and careful conductor, with little needless motion on the podium and a good grasp of his repertory. He is obviously interested in seeking music for the somewhat out of the way nature of his orchestra, and is to be encouraged. May his tribe increase!

Kronos; Tevah and the PRSO

The San Juan Star
October 4, 1983 By Donald Thompson

The past week's musical life centered mainly on the Performing Arts Center, with a couple of splendid string quartet concerts in the Inter-American Festival series and a regular offering by the Puerto Rico Symphony Orchestra.

The visiting string quartet was Kronos, made up of David Harrington and John Sherba, violins; Hank Dutt, viola; and Joan Jeanrenaud, cello. Individually and together, these four young artists bring to their work an admirable level of technique coupled with an extraordinary sensitivity to the nuances and subtleties of the music being performed. The Kronos repertoire, as displayed here, ranges over the panorama of innovative twentieth-century music and earlier. "Innovative" is the operative word, for without exception the works scheduled for this pair of concerts had something new and important to say. Bartók, Britten, Shostakovich, Ravel: all of these composers are recognized as pillars of twentieth-century music.

Viktor Ullman, Steve Reich, Terry Riley and Conlon Nancarrow? For widely differing reasons their music must also be performed and heard, for when it is performed with the skill and presence of the Kronos players it broadens our perceptions of music and of life itself. Ullman was an extremely capable composer of the 1930s and a tragic victim of the Holocaust, while the other three are very important composers of today's music. The Kronos appearances here have been welcome elements at the beginning of this 1983-84 concert season.

Thursday's action was centered on the Festival Hall with the second regular concert in the present Puerto Rico Symphony Orchestra series. Victor Tevah appeared as guest conductor, reminding many, on both sides of the podium, of his many years as musical director of the orchestra. Tevah's work is always marked by vigor, precision and absolute knowledge of his scores, virtues which unfailingly contribute to the vitality of his performances. Featured soloist was Brazilian pianist Caio Pagano, who offered a first hearing in Puerto Rico of Villa-Lobos' *Mômoprecóce*. This is an extended one-movement work by the Brazilian composer which evokes different images and scenes associated with revels, parties and balls. Not one of Villa-Lobos' greatest works, I think, but a characteristic example of his more playful style, cast in a relentlessly sectional kind of form. Pianist Pagano seemed closely attuned to this colorful music by his compatriot of an earlier generation.

First island performances were also offered of the concert overture *Tiempo de Adviento* by Chilean composer Darwin Vargas Wallis (b. 1925) and Variations on a Tango Theme by the Argentine composer Luis Gianneo (1897-1968). Both of these works are well made examples of the Latin American concert music of this century. Of the two, however, the Gianneo was to me the more interesting, consisting of an imaginative evocation of the essentially melancholy (not to say tragic) nature of the tango, without ever falling into facile "folklorism" or the banalities of the "symphonic synthesis."

José Enrique Pedreira

The San Juan Star
December 3, 1983 By Donald Thompson

It may someday be possible for someone to write a proper history of music in Puerto Rico, for an understanding of the island's musical history is now gradually emerging as the works of composers of the present, recent past and distant past are studied, analyzed, compared and brought to life in performance. In some cases this occurs because of the research interests of academics: university faculty members or graduate students whose labors result in dissertations, congress papers, articles in research journals, and (we hope) stylistically authentic performances. In other cases this process of dissemination results from the efforts of special groups. Consider, for example, the public discovery of Johann Sebastian Bach's music, brought about a century after Bach's death by the coordinated efforts of a few influential musician-promoters. And, of course, the work of colleagues, students, admirers and members of the families of more recent or presently active figures can provide a mighty thrust for the dissemination of a composer's production.

In Puerto Rico during the past thirty years, conscious efforts of one kind or another have brought to public awareness or scholarly interest the work of Manuel G. Tavárez (1842-1883), Juan Morel Campos (1857-1896), José Ignacio Quintón (1881-1925) and a swarm of presently active composers now between the ages of 30 and 65 years.

Just now we may expect to see a modest wave of interest in the music of José Enrique Pedreira (1904-1959) as a result of last Saturday evening's dedicatory concert by the Puerto Rico Symphony Orchestra, sponsored by the Institute of Puerto Rican Culture at the Performing Arts Center as part of the Institute's annual celebration of Puerto Rican music. Appearing as soloists were soprano Olga Iglesias, violinist Henry

Hutchinson Negrón and pianists Jesús María Sanromá and José Raúl Ramírez.

José Enrique Pedreira was himself a fine pianist, and from the way his music "moves," it's easy to imagine him doing all of his composing at the keyboard. All of Saturday's music was brilliantly pianistic, regardless of the medium in which it was presented. The style is that of grandiose nineteenth-century piano music in an idiom bounded by Schumann, Chopin and Liszt, but without these masters' great powers of extension and development. For this reason, the most successful works presented on Saturday were miniatures: songs, violin pieces and Puerto Rican *danzas*. In fact, speaking of *danzas*, Pedreira probably came closer than any other composer to coaxing this characteristic nineteenth-century mode of expression forward into the twentieth century.

As seen on Saturday, then, Pedreira's musical designs are sectional or episodic rather than developmental, and do not lend themselves at all well to large scale composition. Offered by pianist Ramírez and the PRSO were a large Fantasy and a Piano Concerto in D Minor. Due to their episodic design, these extended compositions tended to break up into rhetorically heavy but shortwinded statements tossed back and forth between piano and orchestra but musically not going much of anywhere.

José Raúl Ramírez and Lito Peña were credited with the orchestration, arrangement and/or revision of much of Saturday's music. What these terms mean is that someone has turned something into something else: a piano piece into an orchestral work, or a sketch into an extensive composition, or a modest song into something like a section of a big nineteenth-century oratorio. While this practice is often necessary for the restoration of musical fragments to performable condition, it must be done carefully and with a specialist's professional attention to stylistic authenticity. Too, whether or not to change the performance medium of a particular work must be considered within the composer's known production and the purpose of the particular exercise.

I think that since very little of Pedreira's music is known just now, it would have been better to first present it in its original form, where it could have been better perceived and enjoyed. In other words, Saturday's performances interposed arrangers, orchestrators and revisers between Pedreira and the audience, and I, for one, resent it. I went down there to hear Pedreira's music, not that of Lito Peña and José Raúl Ramírez.

Jesús María Sanromá, Olga Iglesias, Henry Hutchinson Negrón and

Roselín Pabón (associate musical director of the PRSO, conducting on Saturday) are very well known and highly regarded performers hereabouts. José Raúl Ramírez, on the other hand, has never been very active as a pianist on the island's concert circuits, being fully occupied with other aspects of the music biz. It was for this reason a great pleasure to hear him on Saturday, occupying in fact the central position in the program. Ramírez obviously has an affinity for the expressive style of Pedreira's piano music, as well as the technical skill to bring it to a successful realization. The special demands of performing with symphony orchestra created some problems for him (mainly solved by the quick responses of conductor Pabón and the PRSO), but Ramírez alone was responsible for bringing to glowing life a whole batch of Pedreira's solo pieces.

Painfully lacking on Saturday was any kind of program material dealing with Pedreira, his music or the significance of this particular occasion. A pity, for the concert was an important event in the continuing documentation of Puerto Rican concert music. True, pianist Sanromá offered a few informal notes on the subject from the stage before the concert began, but these were more in the way of a colleague's appreciation. There is very little information concerning Pedreira in print, aside from some very sketchy and completely undocumented data published by the Institute of Puerto Rican Culture's "Center for Musical Research and Publication" in a 1981 booklet. Saturday's audience would certainly have appreciated having even this limited material, reprinted right out of the Institute's own book.

Memorable Concert Best Forgotten

The San Juan Star
December 14, 1983   By Donald Thompson

Saturday evening's Puerto Rico Symphony Orchestra concert was certainly a memorable occasion, but mainly for the wrong reasons.

First off, there were not nearly enough printed programs for the audience, an audience which was by no means big enough to exhaust a normal supply of programs. This lack may have been of no concern to concertgoers who customarily study up on what's going to be played. I, however, prefer to arrive at a concert in virgin but receptive state: unprejudiced, completely open minded and favorably disposed toward whatever may have been prepared for my musical edification. In other words, as I walk into the place everyone has an "A." Nevertheless, as I take my seat I do like to learn what's going to be played and who's going to play it. No program on Saturday? Ten points off!

First piece . . . for somewhat reduced orchestra . . . Rossini style . . . the Secret Marriage Overture by Cimarosa! Well played in the winds and the lower strings, but the violins grieved me with ragged spiccato (a fast bouncing bow figuration but no big deal in fiddle playing) and jangling open strings. Ten points off.

The overture was also hopelessly marred by an ailment which had once been thought cured in the big Festival Hall at Minillas. This is the practice of permitting entry to the hall of latecomers during the performance of a work to stomp the toes, obstruct the vision and shatter the concentration of those patrons who have somehow managed to get there on time, to say nothing of the concentration of the orchestra. Bad, bad. Sixty points off.

Next work up was Bela Bartók's miraculous Concerto for Orchestra, a challenge for any orchestra and one fairly well met on Saturday by your

PRSO under the direction of John Barnett. The "concerto" aspect of this, Bartók's last symphonic work (1943) lies in its glorious use of individual instruments and other groupings as soloists. The PRSO is blessed with very good woodwind and brass sections just now, headed by a really fine set of principal players in the main. Generally, it was these principals who brought force and life to the concerto on Saturday. The high strings, on the other hand, displayed their customary ills, complicated and magnified in such music as this by a lack of numbers and lack of sonority. These string sections are simply not big enough or solid enough to balance the winds required by large works of Bartók, Stravinsky, Wagner, Mahler, Tchaikovsky, some Brahms and a half dozen other composers whose music is scheduled here with some regularity. Ten points off.

Still without a program, I learned during intermission that the great pianist Claudio Arrau was scheduled for the Emperor Concerto of Beethoven after the break. Nice planning, I thought. A gradual building up of intensity through Cimarosa and Bartók, with great expectation and attention focused on the figure of Claudio Arrau just after intermission. Right?

Wrong! First came a long speech by Jaime González Oliver, president of the board of directors of the Administration for the Development of Arts and Culture, which effectively shot the concert down just as it was reaching its logical culmination. A good idea, basically: the presentation of a plaque to the PRSO for having survived 25 years. But why not do it in an office or a TV studio with four or five senior orchestra members present, or better yet, at an orchestra party instead of before fifteen hundred grumbling concertgoers trapped in the hall and an entire symphony orchestra trapped on the stage? This situation was worse for the orchestra than for the audience, because the orchestra members couldn't grumble, scrape their feet or shift around in their seats. And as a final ludicrous touch, the speaker's lectern was left out to dominate the stage until conductor Barnett, already at the podium, requested its removal. Gross, as the kids say. Eighty five points off.

And finally, at last, Beethoven and Arrau, but now as if beginning a concert from scratch. Claudio Arrau is one of the great ones, a pillar among twentieth-century pianists. His many performances in Puerto Rico have earned him a large and faithful following over the decades, a following which seldom has been disappointed. His performance on Saturday was subtle, flexible and subdued, even perhaps introspective.

Unfortunately, the work's expansive second movement—the kind of music which Arrau plays better than anyone else—became derailed and bumped along indecisively for a while (seemingly a couple of weeks) before being put back on the tracks. Whatever the cause may have been (and there are a number of possible causes), the incident shook the concert (or what was left of it) very badly. Twenty points off.

Let's see, then. No printed program: ten points off. Painful fiddle playing: ten points off. Stomped feet, backsides in my face and ruined concentration: sixty points off. Orchestral numerical imbalance (no fault of the orchestra, of course): ten points. JGO's speech: eighty five points. Beethoven breakdown: twenty points. Hmmm. Minus 195 points, from a perfect plus 100 at 8:15 P.M. It's going to take some doing for the PRSO, but especially for its present management, to balance this out before the great end-of-season reckoning takes place up there in Mozartlandia.

A Musical Homecoming

The San Juan Star
January 3, 1984 By Donald Thompson

A special concert by the Puerto Rico Symphony Orchestra recently provided the occasion for a homecoming celebration by four young island musicians. The featured performers are products of advanced university musical studies on the mainland, and aside from their high level of individual accomplishment, they offered on Thursday an eloquent demonstration of the potential product of this characteristically U.S. marriage of academe and the arts.

Conducting were Kerlinda Degláns (University of Houston and SUNY Stony Brook) and Roberto González (Inter American University of Puerto Rico and Ball State University); piano soloist was José Luis Cáceres (University of Maryland) and trombone soloist Carlos Alicea (Indiana University). Fine academic pedigrees, these, and by and large a fine concert on Thursday.

First up was Ms. Degláns, conducting two purely orchestral compositions and an odd sort of trombone concerto. First of the orchestral works was the Rossini Semiramide Overture, a sparkling example of the Italian master's most brilliant music. Both in the Rossini and in the expansive *Les Préludes* of Franz Liszt, Ms. Degláns demonstrated complete knowledge of the works and conducting technique perfectly adequate to put them together. However, she seems given to overconducting, a common enough fault among young conductors (and let me tell you, among some not-so-young conductors as well). Much of her scheduled music on Saturday (most of the Rossini, for example) almost plays itself, and anything more than an occasional conductorial gesture or two can easily become counterproductive by evoking an exaggerated response. Or, as they used to say down home (rather, up home), "If it's not busted don't fix it." The Liszt sounded good: that musical contemplation of nothing less than the meaning of life itself, according to the gloomy poem of Lamartine which is associated with it. Perhaps a bit loud for the midsize Drama Theater at Minillas, but with good flow and contrast.

Trombonist Carlos Alicea displayed the results of good training (with Antonio Salcedo here and Keith Brown at Bloomington) in a nice performance of a trombone concerto by the Danish composer Launy Grondahl (1886-1960). The concerto is a mild and anachronistic piece dating from 1924 but in a style of many years before. Alicea's good phrasing showed it to be an attractive addition to the extremely limited repertory of trombone concertos. And Ms. Degláns' work in accompanying really demonstrated her conducting skills at their best, as very often occurs.

Conductor Roberto González did excellent work with a couple of demanding compositions, the Richard Strauss Burleske for Piano and Orchestra and a suite drawn from Stravinsky's ballet The Firebird. Strauss' dense orchestral texture, complicated by his use of the piano within it, creates great problems of line, clarity and coordination for all orchestra players, for the pianist and for the conductor. And to make things even trickier, Strauss wrote a timpani part, of all things, which itself occupies the place of a second solo part. Together with fine pianist José Luis Cáceres and timpanist José Martín and aided by a very high level of orchestral concentration, conductor González put together a completely convincing performance of Burleske.

The concert closed with a lovely performance of Stravinsky's great and evocative Firebird Suite. This is dreamland music, but behind that sonoral fantasy is music which requires a conductor of thorough knowledge and high skill. González has both attributes in addition to others of equal importance. He is a well founded and highly talented conductor who can contribute a great deal to the world's music.

The Verdi Requiem

The San Juan Star
February 1, 1984   By Donald Thompson

More than 200 people were squeezed onto the stage of the Festival Hall at Minillas on Saturday evening for a performance of the Verdi Requiem on the Puerto Rico Symphony Orchestra series. These big forces included the PRSO itself, the visiting Amherst College Chorus (Bruce McInnes, director) and four vocal soloists. These were soprano Evelyn Brunner, contralto Fredda Rakusin, tenor Carlos Montané and bass Dimiter Petkov. Conducting the whole assemblage was John Barnett, musical director of the PRSO, with a brief offstage assist by Roselín Pabón, the orchestra's associate musical director.

As a musical form with a greater or lesser degree of liturgical application, the Requiem Mass has been cultivated by composers from the fifteenth century on down. The Requiem, or Mass for the Dead, is naturally solemn music, and as a musico-sociological source provides many clues to contemporaneous views on the "meaning" of music at the time a particular work was composed. The Requiem text would be set very differently by Mozart, by Berlioz and by Verdi, and the use of certain instruments or the appearance of certain types of musical phraseology at particular moments can be significant. Mozart's use of the solo trombone, Berlioz' heavy percussion and Verdi's bass drum solos all tell us something about the sounds which in the respective composers' times and places were expected to evoke or sustain particular emotional states or responses. And the truth of it is, Verdi's bass drum solos on Saturday could still evoke a cataclysmic vision of a great Day of Wrath.

Verdi's Requiem is basically opera music, as are the *Stabat Mater* of Pergolesi and *Messiah*, by Handel. That is to say, composers have made little real attempt to differentiate in their own work between a theater style and a religious style. Certainly, religious music is apt to include many more choral sections than is theater music, while slow tempos are likely to be more numerous than fast lively ones. But beyond that a composer's style at a given moment is pretty much his style, and it's only natural that a great deal of this work should sound like *Aida* or *Otello*, the two Verdi operas which historically frame the Requiem.

Still, there will be subtle technical differences in the execution of the two types of music. This especially affects the soloists. Verdi's operas permit—indeed, invite—the use of any type of vocal expressive device which will increase the dramatic effect of the music, for the singers are actors in a play. Not so in the churchly or oratorio branch of performance, which expects soloists to hew pretty close to the written line. In general, Saturday's soloists performed their parts skillfully, decorously, and well within the frame of solemn churchly music. Soprano Evelyn Brunner displayed a clear and open voice, always within the appropriate range of expression. Fredda Rakusin's rich contralto sounded fine throughout its big range, but at times and in certain combinations of text and pitches, seemed "covered," as singers say. Dimiter Petkov is a solid and steady bass, with very good dynamic contrast. Tenor Carlos Montané, on the other hand, seemed unable to abandon the vocal tricks and devices of opera life for the straightforward and unadorned expression of the concert stage. His performance displayed the scoops, slides, dips and other alterations which are tolerated and indeed praised (if kept within bounds) in such roles as the duke (in *Rigoletto*) and Alfred (in *La Traviata*). They are not right, however, in this Requiem. In addition, Montané's failure to accommodate his voice to the pitch and volume of his soloist colleagues' voices led on more than one occasion to the derailing of Verdi's rich and subtle harmonic modulations, in passages virtually unsupported by the orchestra.

The big Amherst College Chorus sounded very good in this difficult music. Director McInnes has forged a fine ensemble up there in the wintry wastes of Massachusetts, and one of well-nigh staggering dimensions. By simple arithmetic, it should be clear that the bigger the group the less precise it will be. This is, in fact, one difference between a performance by a string quartet and one by a great symphony orchestra. It's a trade-off. The smaller, the more precise (maybe); the larger, the more impressive, commanding and grand. Still, a big chorus should be able to sing very softly when asked to do so, and as indeed sang the Amherst forces on Saturday. Too breathy a sound quality here, for my taste, but demonstrating a splendid ability to stay on pitch (all 130 of them) in several long passages unsupported by the orchestra.

The matter of size versus precision started to raise its ugly head a couple of times when the big chorus sang in long note values against rapid figurations in fast tempo in the orchestra. Some singers kept up; others fell behind as if enamored of a beautiful note and reluctant to move on to the next. A common failing, and not only in choruses. The symphony orchestra repertory is full of famous booby-traps for cellos and basses, who tend to linger over each indescribably beautiful long note while the upper strings and the winds have long since gone their inexorable way.

And as for the Puerto Rico Symphony Orchestra itself; well, it sounded all right this time. Some very weak playing (violin solos, for example), balanced by some fine and expressive orchestral playing of Verdi's romantically conceived religious music. Remembered are some nicely turned passages in the first woodwind chairs, and that beautifully tuned C Major chord in the brass which brought the whole thing to a close. And of course the bass drum, which in fact this work of Verdi converted into a solo instrument. On Saturday it was right on the nose every time, and every time a reminder that the stroke of doom—the final blow of fate—the hollow knock of earthly destiny—awaits us all alike, be we chorus, tenor, conductor, public, . . . or critic.

A Winning Team

The San Juan Star
March 14, 1984   By Donald Thompson

Luz Hutchinson and Cecilia Talavera have been among the island's musical mainstays for more years than you'd like to shake a baton at. Sisters and pianists, these two performers account for almost all of the recital accompanying that gets done in Puerto Rico, most of the accompanying for the preparation of opera choruses, and a great deal of the chamber music playing and two-piano work. They are among the steadiest, quickest and most reliable performers in Puerto Rico and it is only correct that from time to time they appear as a team on the island's principal concert series: that of the Puerto Rico Symphony Orchestra.

On Saturday evening in the Festival Hall at Minillas, Doña Luz and Doña Ceci were the featured soloists in the Concerto for Two Pianos, Percussion and Orchestra by Bela Bartók with the PRSO, a first performance here of the concerto version and a very nice job all around. The Bartók work dates from 1938 in its original form as a sonata for two pianos and percussion. In that form it has been presented several times in Puerto Rico, notably in the Biennials of Twentieth Century music organized by the Puerto Rico Society for Contemporary Music. The team of Luz Hutchinson and Cecilia Talavera has always been the basic element whenever the work has been performed here. It is for this reason that their performance on Saturday was marked by great authority and by the security which comes from the luxury of repeated performances. Other featured players on Saturday were timpanist José Martín and percussionists José Torres, Manuel García and Luis Torres.

Saturday's concert was ably conducted by Roselín Pabón, associate musical director of the PRSO, and also included Beethoven's Leonora Overture No. 3 and Dvořák's expansive New World Symphony. Here, the orchestra's fine woodwind section did impressive work, with the second movement's English horn solo beautifully played by Gloria Navarro.

Composer **Francis Schwartz** at the time of his Pompidou Center Premiere in Paris.

Grimaces

The San Juan Star
April 22, 1984   By Donald Thompson

"Actually, it was a sort of intercontinental interfusion of good will (for a change), incorporating advanced techniques of music, communications and mass improvisation. And the result was most satisfying: four or five thousand people moving about on a university campus at 8 o'clock of a tropical evening, all smiling, all taking part, and each one growing a bit as a result of the experience. And this, we hope, it what art is all about."

Speaking is Francis Schwartz, the leading exponent of avant-garde music in Puerto Rico, of the premiere performance of his COSMOS at the University of Puerto Rico campus in 1980. The present interview is taking place beneath a stunted but hopeful mango tree in one of San Juan's far suburbs, with the 5 o'clock traffic snarling just out of sight beyond a row of hills.

DT: Francis, the last time we talked about your music you had just returned from doctoral studies in Paris and a number of successful performances of your works in Europe (STAR, 28 August 1979). This COSMOS, produced seven or eight months later, was a milestone both for you and for the avant-garde in Puerto Rico, I gather, for it enabled you to pull together and apply here a number of ideas current in international circles. Am I correct?

FS: Absolutely. Stockhausen in Germany, Juan Blanco in Cuba, Murray Schafer in Canada; the "musicalization of space" was very much the new wave four or five years ago and even before, and I am very glad that we were able to be part of it.

DT: What have you done since? Was COSMOS the end of the line, or have you continued the same line of experimentation in other compositions?

FS: Very much the latter, but not on the same scale of performance. For example, my *Baudelaire's Uncle*, also from 1980, requires only a pianist, but this pianist must be a performer capable of inspiring the audience's participation, much in the same way that the audience participates in COSMOS. This is a matter of scale, after all. COSMOS at the UPR involved perhaps 200 scheduled participants (university bands, choruses, brass ensembles, athletes, construction workers, etc.) and 4,000 or so unscheduled participants (the public). You can be sure that in a piano recital at least twenty "casual" performers from the audience will be drawn into a performance of *Baudelaire's Uncle*. Same proportion, more or less. Incidentally, it was pianist Eduardo Kusnir who first performed *Baudelaire's Uncle*, during the Museum of Modern Art Polyart Festival in Paris in 1980.

DT: You might say, then, that audience participation has become an important part of your way of looking at music during recent years.

FS: Definitely. And furthermore, I believe that the public concurs. For example, consider *Gestos*, first performed by the Puerto Rico Symphony Orchestra in February 1983. This, I think, has been one of my most successful compositions, precisely because it enlists the active participation of the public.

I recently attended a performance of the Puerto Rico Symphony Orchestra in which performers were planted in the audience. A number of people later told me that this aspect of the performance (participation from this side of the stage) reminded them of *Gestos*, and that they looked forward to more of the same. The public wants to participate, perhaps because they're tired of canned (and unreal) music, canned (and unreal) theater, and canned (and unreal) life. Participation in concert music may be one of the last healthful escapes available for a public otherwise encased in sterile plastic foam as victims of entertainment high-tech. In this sense I am sure that I am on the right track.

DT: Has *Gestos* been performed anywhere else, or is it destined to become one of your "world dernières," as referred to a couple of years ago by a STAR reader?

FS: *Gestos* is scheduled for presentation in Miami next October as part of the Inter American Festival, performed by the American Symphony Orchestra. In addition, there is considerable interest in performing it in other parts of the world. A "world dernière" it is not!

DT: Something else of yours, also incorporating the participation of the public, was recently performed in New York, wasn't it?

FS: Yes. This was *A Festive Smile*, written in 1981 as a commission by the city of Juvisy, France. The New York performance, by the Brooklyn Philharmonic under the direction of Tania León, was the first in the U.S. As a result of its success there, the Brooklyn orchestra will take *A Festive Smile* on its next tour. It has not been performed in Puerto Rico.

DT: Speaking of performances of your orchestral works in Puerto Rico, the most recent appears to have been the *Gestos* premiere, more than a year ago. What plans are there for future performances?

FS: None at all. No work of mine is scheduled for the present season of the Puerto Rico Symphony Orchestra, and none is scheduled for the 1984-85 season either.

DT: Strange. To what do you attribute this, in view of your obvious and widely recognized contributions to the knowledge of the island's musical production abroad?

FS: There is a very unusual situation here. We like to think that the Puerto Rico Symphony Orchestra functions like a regular symphony orchestra; that is, the musical director would make the decisions as to what music is to be played. Of course, he may consult whomever he wishes, but the final decisions are the musical director's, as well as the responsibility. This is basic procedure almost everywhere in the world. However, it is not the case in Puerto Rico. Here, the president of the board of directors of the Administration for the Development of Arts and Culture (the parent administration of the PRSO) has signed an agreement with a specific group of self-identified island composers. According to this agreement, the National Association of Composers, as they call themselves, must be consulted in the selection of island works to be programmed by the Puerto Rico Symphony Orchestra. I myself am not a member of this association (as a number of other island composers are not), and I see no need to submit my music for the approval of this special interest group for performance by our publicly supported orchestra. Therefore, I guess, my works cannot be played by the Puerto Rico Symphony Orchestra, along with music by other island composers whose works regularly represent Puerto Rican music abroad but who are not members of any National Association of Composers: Rafael Aponte-Ledée and Roberto Sierra. Strange, indeed.

DT: Do you see same similarity, then, with the situation in countries in which artistic determinations concerning the officially supported performance institutions are made on the basis of political considerations or convenient deals?

FS: Sadly, yes. Closed shop, government censorship, or government sell-out: call it what you will, we have it here.

DT: Is this general gossip and backstage noise, or has some particular work of yours been involved?

FS: A specific work of mine has indeed been involved, and in fact has brought the whole thing to a head. I have long had the idea of writing a special orchestral work for the 1985 tricentennial of the birth of Bach and Handel. Through the generosity of private sources it was possible to obtain a commission to underwrite the composition. The projected work, based on music by Bach and Handel and entitled *Barroquísimo*, was proposed to John Barnett, musical director of the Puerto Rico Symphony Orchestra, for the 1984-85 season. Barnett was delighted with the idea and told me that such a work was a natural for an important tricentennial celebration. However, he told me that his approval would have to be conditioned pending the approval of the National Association of Composers, according to the terms of the restrictive arrangement which had been made over his head. For this reason *Barroquísimo* will not be premiered next season by the Puerto Rico Symphony Orchestra. I am certainly not going to submit it for the approval of anyone but the musical director of any orchestra, anywhere in the world.

The Institute of Puerto Rican Culture, on the other hand, is not bound by any such deals, and has produced a recording of my music, which is scheduled for release soon. It will offer a representative sample of my music of the past several years. Included, for example, are *Caligula*, for electronic tape; *Fronteras*, for solo guitar; *Baudelaire's Uncle*, for pianist; and *Paz en la Tierra*, for mixed chorus.

DT: In the way of new works and live performances, what do you have coming up now that *Barroquísimo* is on ice?

FS: Next is the premiere of *Grimaces*, to take place in the Georges Pompidou Center in Paris on April 18.

DT: Tell me about it.

FS: *Grimaces* resulted from a commission by the French Ministry of Culture, and I must say it's an honor for me to receive such a commission. *Grimaces* is rooted in the literary work of five distinguished writers, and is intended to break down the traditional barriers between concert music, literature and the public, which usually occupies a passive role in such things. The "done to," you might say, as opposed to the "doers" who occupy the stage.

DT: What writers provided the inspiration for *Grimaces*?

FS: Julio Cortázar (Argentina), Robert Merle (France), Edgardo Rodríguez Juliá (Puerto Rico), Georg Trakl (Austria) and Herman Melville (U.S.).

DT: An interesting and far reaching variety of sources, no?

FS: Yes, providing precisely the variation of motivation and force which I favor in music, reflecting today's all-encompassing and restless fluctuations of spirit.

DT: What's called for in the way of performers?

FS: Flute, saxophone, guitar, voice, percussion, double bass and pre-recorded electronic tape. Performing in the premiere will be the contemporary music ensemble 2E2M, one of the finest in Europe, and of course the audience will also join the ranks of the "doers" during the eighteen-minute work.

DT: So you are still interested in "polyart," or the combination of traditionally separate phenomena?

FS: Definitely. This is of course an ancient dream: the creation of art works which enlist different orders of sensation and so appeal to the entire sentient body. Wagner was headed this way as were Scriabin and many others, each in his own way. Do you remember my *Mon Oeuf*, produced in Paris in 1979, in which the public (one person at a time) climbed into a large ovoid structure to receive sonoral, visual, tactile and olfactory stimuli?

DT: Yes, indeed; described as an *eggs*traordinary *eggs*perience.

FS: *Eggs*actly: Well, *Grimaces* carries the same ideas further, with the added interest of live performance and the direct participation of the public. Indeed, part of the point is the elimination of the arbitrary distinction between the "performers" and the "public."

DT: You use "olfactory stimuli," you say?

FS: Why not? The sense of smell is one of our most powerful connections to the world outside our own skins, and it should certainly be brought within the range of artistic interest and analysis. Polyart does this, which is why it transcends the traditional boundaries of music, theater, light-play, etc.

DT: There were lots of jokes some years back about "smellies" and "feelies" when movie technology made a tremendous leap forward.

Wouldn't it be ironic if this somewhat mystical union of sensorial stimulations were now to take place not in the incredibly advanced technology of the movies but in the hopelessly low-tech world of concert life?

FS: Don't knock it. Your low-tech world of concert life may be the last field of the performing arts where a bit of human interaction is still possible, through the application of the principles of polyart. As I said earlier, *Grimaces* and others of my works are deliberately conceived to break the traditional but completely arbitrary barriers between fields of artistic expression.

DT: What do you expect to see at the premiere of *Grimaces* in Paris next month?

FS: Judging from past experience with this type of composition in Paris as well as in Puerto Rico and elsewhere, I think that the work will be successful. *Grimaces* will also be quite "portable," due to the relatively small number of scheduled participants. There is already a great deal of interest in performing the work in many other places in Europe and the Americas. Who knows? Perhaps there can even be more performances of my works (especially the larger ones, incorporating orchestra), here in Puerto Rico . . . someday . . . someday.

Camerata Caribe

The San Juan Star
May 4, 1984   By Donald Thompson

The Latin American Foundation for Contemporary Music had its roots in the Puerto Rican Society for Contemporary Music back in the mid-70s. From the beginning, this organization has been a prime force in the island's contemporary music movement. Its regular contribution takes the form of a Biennial of Twentieth Century Music, while between times it gets together interesting concerts of contemporary music by resident and visiting groups.

The most recent of these took place at musicians' daybreak (11:00 A.M.) last Sunday at the Puerto Rico Conservatory of Music in Hato Rey, and called upon that fine quintet of performers who comprise the Camerata Caribe. These are Peter Kern (flute), David Bourns (oboe), Kathleen Jones (clarinet), Alan Brown (bassoon) and Vanessa Vassallo (piano). These names are very familiar, of course. The first four named are the principal woodwinds (and the anchor) of the Puerto Rico Symphony Orchestra, while Ms. Vassallo is one of the most accomplished pianists active in Puerto Rico today.

Sunday's program offered polished and seamless performances of works by composers of the U.S. (Elliott Carter), Curaçao (Kim Daniel Vlaum), Venezuela (Federico Ruiz), Brazil (Heitor Villa-Lobos) and Puerto Rico (Rafael Aponte-Ledée and Narciso Figueroa). Especially interesting was a Villa-Lobos *Fantasia Concertante* for clarinet, bassoon and piano, dating from 1953. We tend to associate Villa-Lobos with a freewheeling kind of folk influence in concert music, which certainly does exist in a great deal of his music. This *Fantasia*, on the other hand, seems like an extension of the modern-romantic music of . . . Rachmaninoff! This Villa-Lobos was the most substantial piece on Sunday's program, but followed closely by Elliott Carter's set of brief and tightly woven pieces for woodwind quartet. Carter was one of the most accomplished U.S. composers of the 1940s and 1950s, and his writing displays complete mastery of whatever medium he tackled. This suite is typical of his work; Carter never asks the instruments to do anything which is not completely characteristic of them, but he never lets them off easy, either. The *Suite Antiyano* by young Kim Daniel Vlaun (b. 1955) for woodwind quartet is a witty evocation of the spirit of Antillean (i.e., Dutch Antillean) music. In movements entitled Mazurka, Wals, Dansa and Tumba, Vlaun pours sparkling new wine into old bottles of folk-popular and commercial-popular music which also turn out to have connections with Puerto Rican music. Surprise! Puerto Rico is part of the Caribbean, a fact which is all too often forgotten.

Narciso Figueroa's *El Diario de Teresita*, for piano and woodwinds, is a charming suite of four movements which evoke particular moments in a child's day, from daybreak to finally falling asleep at night. A clever idea and very cleverly carried out, somewhat in the manner of Ravel, Debussy or Prokofiev. Narciso Figueroa is himself an accomplished pianist, and if these miniatures have a fault it is that they sound like piano music still, with parts simply copied off the staff for the woodwinds. Still, they are quite witty and effective pieces, and could probably be used, I think, as ballet music. All in all, Sunday's concert (despite the hour) was a fine and welcome event, offered by a fine ensemble. Camerata Caribe and the Latin American Foundation for Contemporary Music are both to be commended.

This is a Festival?

The San Juan Star
June 5, 1984   By Donald Thompson

Getting off to a raunchy start on Saturday evening in the big hall at Minillas was this year's Puerto Rico Casals Festival. What can I tell you? With a substandard program on the racks, a substandard conductor on the podium and your very own Puerto Rico Symphony Orchestra on the stage, the event resembled nothing so much as some particularly deadly midseason concert on the PRSO's own series. In fact, had it not been for the absolutely incomparable solo playing of cellist Janos Starker in Boccherini's B Flat Major Concerto before intermission, Saturday's concert would have been better forgotten even before it began.

First up on Saturday was an orchestration by Lukas Foss of pieces by the seventeenth-century composer Salomone Rossi. In one form or another this "updating" of music of the past, utilizing the means of the present, has been going on for a long time. Think of Mozart's revision of Handel, or Stokowski's of Bach, or countless other examples. There was even a wild plan by Julián Carrillo, at the turn of the century, to keep the symphonies of Beethoven fresh for future audiences by arithmetically reducing all of their melodic and harmonic intervals, measure by measure, into the scope of quartertones!

Much has been said of this kind of modernizing effort, both pro and con, and I don't really expect to add much to the discussion in a couple of lines of text. Let me only say that in a general way I favor authenticity of means in dealing with the art of the past, insofar as it can be conveniently attained in real life today. In other words, I see no need to add sound tracks to silent movies, nor to repaint the works of Manet with vibrant Day Glo, nor to play Bach's keyboard music on monstrous concert grand pianos in public. If Salomone Rossi's music is worth performing today, it deserves the respect of performances which at least within reason, present it more or less authentically. Foss' treatment of Rossi's modest material is interesting as an orchestration exercise, but (exactly as in the case of Bach on the Steinway) its place is the teaching studio or the end-of-semester academic in-house concert, not a serious public event supposedly devoted to serious public edification.

Also appearing on Saturday were some "symphonic extracts" from Wagner's *Parsifal*, again resulting from Lukas Foss' handling of music by a composer whose stuff could probably have been trusted to speak well enough for itself. And finally, Wagner's own music in the form of the Meistersinger Overture.

Conducting on Saturday was Lukas Foss himself. Foss is a distinguished composer in his own right as well as a highly competent pianist. However, in front of an orchestra his work is that of a mime—or, yes, a dancer—rather than that of a conductor, if by conducting is still meant the economical transmission of operative signals to an orchestra for the purpose of coordinating a performance. Foss' gesture is relentlessly jerky and brusque, and lacks any kind of regular pulse, flow, continuity or logic. In no way can it be helpful to an orchestra, and in fact it can only bring out an orchestra's worst qualities despite players' attempts to ignore what's happening up front and get on with their job to the best of their abilities. Before such an onslaught any orchestra will soon become exhausted, discouraged and defeated, finally giving the man what he seems to want. Such occurred on Saturday with the PRSO, for Foss' performance toward the end of the concert brought forth some of the noisiest, roughest and nastiest playing heard here in years.

This is a festival? If you believe so, kindly tell me just what it is you think we're celebrating in this most depressing fashion.

Electronic Shlockburger

The San Juan Star
August 25, 1984 By Donald Thompson

Thirty-eight piece orchestra, sixteen-member chorus: where were these forces on Thursday evening at the Tapia, as announced in the STAR as participating in the opening performance of a "musical memoir" by Premier Maldonado and others entitled *Fela*? Most of them on tape, I'm afraid, as electronic fakery continues to invade musical theater in the fashion of some crackling and humming poisonous plastic foam from outer space. One thing is for damned sure: there were no oboes, harps, cellos or fiddles in the Tapia pit on Thursday, although their disembodied and overamplified sonorities rolled fruitily out of the loudspeakers.

Evita was bad enough a couple of years ago at the Performing Arts Center, with symphonic instrumentation and a big chorus on tape (plus really now, how many of the solo voices?), but I think that this production beats even *Evita* for electronic deception.

Apparently representing some new kind of entertainment, this work is so fakey that it defies classification; its nearest relative is not music theater at all, but the night club show in which comics mime to records. Records? Sure enough, a commercial recording of this thing was made weeks ago, and it may actually have been that recording which we heard on Thursday in the Tapia with stage people running through a sad and silent act.

Fela recreates in nostalgic fashion some episodes from the life of Felisa Rincón, colorful mayor of San Juan from 1946 to 1969 and a beloved figure in island life and politics. Still very much with us at the age of 87, Doña Fela was present at Thursday's opening, an event graced by more lace fans, bow ties and wing collars in the audience than had been seen here since the Popular Democratic Party rallies of the early fifties.

Visually, there were some nice scenes on Thursday, especially a couple of big dance numbers—mambos and cha-chas—in the second act. Very, very effective to my way of thinking is the acting of Jossie de Guzmán, who condenses into a couple of hours of playing time a lifetime of character development. She even walks like Doña Fela, and has the smile —the hand movements—the turn of the head all down perfectly and without exaggeration.

I think I would vote for Jossie de Guzmán for mayor on anybody's ticket. A splendid actress. Good work also in this regard, it seemed to me, by Marian Pabón as Felisa's sister Fini Rincón. And, of course, any appearance by Justino Díaz is worth a trip across town. Here, Díaz makes a brief and completely convincing appearance as Luis Muñoz Marín himself.

The music? Attributed to Premier Maldonado, the author of the piece, "with the assistance of others." Maldonado is unlettered musically, and the music of *Fela* displays all of the signs of a very weak amateur product almost saved by the sweat and skill of professionals. Almost, because even the aid of the tremendously skilled and talented Pedro Rivera Toledo and the collaboration of other professionals couldn't do much with Maldonado's vapid songs. The type of teamwork represented by the music of *Fela* usually involves a "composer" who bangs out tunes on the piano with one finger or mumbles them into a tape recorder, then turns his inspirations over to hired hands who provide the correct rhythms, harmony, range, countermelodies, instrumentation and notation. I think that in this case, Rivera Toledo and his colleagues have done the best that could be done with what they were given to work with.

The voices? Again, this production is so plagued by electronic fakery that it's hard to tell. That could have been Jossie de Guzmán herself singing for me on Thursday evening, or it could have been her pre-recorded self, or for that matter, some other pre-recorded self. Same goes for Marian Pabón, Justino Díaz, Rafael Torréns, Carlos Camacho and all other actors whose voices we thought we heard. There is simply no way to know about stage voices anymore, nor for that matter about anything else connected with the music of the electronic stage.

As for classifying *Fela* among the genres and forms of music, I think I have it. Why not a new species for a new age: the Electronic Shlockburger?

Turandot: An Exotic Fantasy

The San Juan Star
September 1, 1984   By Donald Thompson

    Despite the wishful thinking of realists, verists and other doctrinary theorists of twentieth-century lyric theater, opera is and always has been a province of Fantasyland. And Puccini's *Turandot*, which opened its short run in the Performing Arts Center on Thursday evening, is one of the foremost examples of opera fantasy in existence. In the world of more or less traditional opera, only some of Rimsky-Korsakov's fairy-tale operas, among them *The Snow Maiden* and *Sadko*, surpass *Turandot* in sheer exotic fancy. When well put together, *Turandot* is an escape into a dream world of musical chinoisie depicting no China ever known but one which still appeals mightily to the Western imagination.

    The present *Turandot* is a production of Teatro de la Opera Inc. and is very well put together indeed. The Puccini opera is the ninth offering by Puerto Rico's newest opera group, which was founded only a couple of years ago. Under the artistic direction and general management of Antonio Barasorda, Teatro de la Opera has made a real effort to present not only the war horses which are guaranteed to fill the house, but also some of the masterpieces which are virtually guaranteed not to. This is the only correct policy, I believe, for any privately organized entity which receives government support, for in this way it explicitly accepts and recognizes its responsibility in the edification of the citizenry.

    But what about this *Turandot*? First of all, a tight production, with few loose ends and slack moments. Good work by stage director Franco Gratale and musical director Bruno Rigacci, who respectively provided interesting and highly stylized stage pictures and kept the production moving along very nicely. Impressively exotic costumes and scenery had been provided by the experienced house of Stivanello & Co., with equally exotic makeup (the Western fantasy again), by the Charles Elsen Studio.

The plot of the piece is a one-liner: frozen princess melted by mysterious stranger. An interesting juxtaposition of stereotypes here: the cold and inscrutable Eastern princess, but then she's human after all, requiring only some attention from a good tenor to bring her around. The Princess Turandot is here played by soprano Olivia Stapp, who musically and dramatically fills the bill splendidly on both sides of her role. The good tenor is Maurice Stern, subbing for the originally announced William Johns in the role of Calaf. Musically, the role of Calaf at times approaches the style of the German *Heldentenor*, particularly in Calaf's big second act scene. Stern certainly looks heroic, and on Thursday his voice held up well through most of the work, appearing to tire and lose security a bit toward the end. Soprano Margarita Castro is in excellent voice these days as the slave Li, and the same can be said of Angelo Cruz, Adolfo Llorca and Alex Vázquez who, in addition, are fine actors in the problematic roles of Ping, Pang and Pong (sorry, but I didn't write the libretto). I have never heard Noel Ramírez or Valentín Fernández sing better (respectively, Timur and Altoum in this production), and Oscar de Gracia does a good job in the role of a Mandarin. A big chorus had been prepared by Pablo Boissen, and sang right on pitch right up until the work's final cadence, when suddenly an epidemic of exhaustion struck the entire ensemble. Throughout the opera, the choral sound and unity were good once each section was securely launched, but entrances were occasionally tentative. No wonder, the way opera must be put together nowadays in San Juan with only a couple of final rehearsals, if that.

The opening performance of *Turandot* was marred by a couple of managerial lapses which I'm beginning to believe are firmly woven into the texture of musical and theatrical life here. One was the admission of latecomers into the hall to stomp toes and stumble into their seats a full half hour into the first act, and the other was the clanking of camera shutters during the performance. The latter was apparently authorized (if not actually commissioned) by Teatro de la Opera, for sure enough, the long lens of at least one camera was protruding from the sound booth at the rear of the hall. This could maybe have been done at the dress rehearsal, or at a photo call? For a general audience to really become absorbed in anything as strange as opera is difficult enough already, without the distractions of stomped toes and banging camera shutters.

On the other hand, this Teatro de la Opera is one of the few entities here which make any effort at all to start their performances on time. For this, as well as for other aspects of this particular production, the company is to be congratulated.

Homage to Ginastera

The San Juan Star
October 2, 1984   By Donald Thompson

As an offering on the Inter American Arts Festival now in session at the Performing Arts Center in Santurce, the Puerto Rico Symphony Orchestra presented a concert on Thursday evening, half of which was devoted to works by the late great Argentine composer Alberto Ginastera. Ginastera was a frequent visitor to Puerto Rico toward the end of his life, and this concert can be viewed as a much deserved homage.

First up was Ginastera's *Variaciones Concertantes*, dating from 1953 and representing the first full flowering of the composer's mature style. Left behind is the folklorizing which Ginastera and many other Latin American composers cultivated for a while in a late approach to a nationalistic movement in concert music. Ginastera's *Variaciones Concertantes* are very similar in spirit to Benjamin Britten's great Variations on a Theme by Purcell, offering excellent opportunities for virtually every orchestral section and every section principal to shine. Especially striking was Ginastera's imaginative use of the solo double bass toward the end of the work and equally striking was principal bassist Federico Silva's fine playing of this extended solo on Thursday.

Colombian pianist Blanca Uribe was the soloist in a brilliant performance of Ginastera's bristling Piano Concerto No. 1. The concerto dates from a somewhat later period than the *Variaciones*, and represents a further stylization of Ginastera's always evolving way of looking at things. Dissonant and rhythmic, the work received a splendid performance at the hands of the PRSO, pianist Uribe and Guatemalan conductor Jorge Sarmientos, who had also very ably conducted the Ginastera *Variaciones*.

Sarmientos has previously conducted in Puerto Rico, and his work is well remembered here. He is also a widely recognized composer, and as on his previous visit he brought some of his own music along. This time it was his *RESPONSO (Homenaje II)*, which according to Sarmiento's own program notes is connected to a particular vision, in the manner of descriptive or "program" music. Frankly, I'm glad I didn't read the notes until after hearing the work, for I don't think I would have liked the piece half so much had I known what it was "about," or indeed had I known that it was "about" anything at all.

Music is "about" music, regardless of the associations which you, I or anyone else might have with a particular work. If you stop to think about it, you will have to agree that this view of music relieves the listener of a heavy and solemn burden: having to worry about what's "behind" the music itself. At the same time, however, it recognizes the listener's great responsibility in the matter: to think about music for a while, and not about oversimplified literary outlines which in themselves might be perfectly all right—but they're not music. I think I agree with the position of the composer who when asked what that beautiful piece of his was about, answered: "About twelve minutes."

But I'm off the track. Yes, *RESPONSO* is an interesting and varied work, exploring many of the orchestral devices in use by composers worldwide during the past twenty years or so. Also conducted by Jorge Sarmientos on Thursday was *In Memoriam para Orquesta*, by Marlos Nobre. Nobre is a distinguished Brazilian composer whose music has not received the "exposure" which it deserves in Puerto Rico. His *In Memoriam* is a powerful compendium of the moderate avant-garde of its time (a decade or so ago), calling for a big orchestra including piano, guitar and plenty of percussion. The work is atonal, but with sections built upon specific notes as "centers of gravity" in the absence of tonality. Among the orchestral devices appearing in *In Memoriam* are percussive pizzicatos in the stringed instruments, glassy harmonics in the fiddles, burbling brasses and windy woods. The effects are well balanced, though, and what is heard is clearly what's meant to be heard; that is, Nobre knows his instruments, their capabilities and their effective combinations and he makes very good use of them.

Also presented on Thursday was *Sinfonía a Ginastera* by Colombian composer Blas Emilio Atehortúa, conducted by the composer himself. The work, according to program notes by the composer, was commissioned by the Organization of American States for premiere presentation on this occasion. The title refers to the idea of a symphony only in the sense of Stravinsky's Symphonies for Wind Instruments, for example, in which the term looks back many centuries to the primordial sense of simply "sounding together." And "sound together" the instruments and sections certainly do here, in the alternation of tightly organized and freely floating sections. The former are tonal, phrasal and periodic (that is, very traditional) in construction, rather in the spirit of nineteenth-century music. The latter, however, are untrammeled episodes of aleatory and improvisatory music.

Throughout the work are woven references to Ginastera's name (the names of vowels therein, transformed into the names of solfège syllables), thus providing a musical homage to the deceased master.

Atehortúa is a capable composer, but I think his conducting falls short of the mark in the way of precise and economical transmission of unmistakable signals to orchestra players. There seems to be too much elbow, too much unfocused chopping and waving of the hands, too few cues, and all too much weaving and bending. This sort of action, taking place within an unchanging frame of visual reference, sends confusing signals, tires people out, consumes inordinate amounts of valuable rehearsal time and produces shaky results. Echoing Berlioz, who certainly learned the hard way, one might counsel all composers to learn to conduct themselves, yes, but conduct themselves well (get it?). Otherwise, it's usually better to simply hire a conductor and send him the score a couple of months ahead.

Sanromá

The San Juan Star
October 13, 1984   By Donald Thompson

Jesús María Sanromá was Puerto Rico's principal claim to musical recognition on the international level, and the loss of this honored pianist is a heavy loss to music in Puerto Rico and in the world. Born in Carolina, Puerto Rico in 1902, Sanromá early demonstrated a high level of musical talent. At the age of fifteen he was sent by the insular government for specialized studies at the New England Conservatory in Boston. Graduating in 1920, the young musician went to Europe where he became a student of Alfred Cortot in Paris and Artur Schnabel in Berlin. From 1926 until 1944 Sanromá was the official pianist of the Boston Symphony Orchestra under Serge Koussevitzky, while also developing a formidable career as a soloist in his own right. During his years as a traveling virtuoso he appeared in more than 3,000 performances in 21 countries, with close to 150 orchestras and conductors.

It was during this period that Sanromá made fundamental contributions to the cause of modern music, performing in the world premieres of works by such composers as Paul Hindemith, Walter Piston, Vladimir Dukelsky, Ferde Grofé and Edward Burlingame Hill. U.S. premieres in which Sanromá performed included works by Igor Stravinsky, Maurice Ravel, Francis Poulenc, Ernst Krenek, Arthur Honegger and others. With Boston as his base and while traveling the world's concert circuits, Sanromá maintained a lively interest in the musical life of Puerto Rico. He regularly appeared here during the 1930s and 1940s, often with colleagues from the Boston Symphony Orchestra. At the same time, he opened doors in Boston for a number of young island musicians wishing to undertake advanced studies there. For years, Sanromá provided an anchor in a cold, cold northern sea for young Puerto Rican musicians who are now established in careers.

Sanromá returned to Puerto Rico in the early 1950s, taking a very active part in the island's musical life. First at the University of Puerto Rico as an advisor to chancellor Jaime Benítez and later at the new Puerto Rico Conservatory of Music, Sanromá saw his ideas take shape in the implementation of musical activities and musical studies here. He was a prime mover in the Conservatory of Music itself, in the Puerto Rico Symphony Orchestra, in the Institute of Puerto Rican Culture and in the early Puerto Rico Casals Festivals.

Any musician who was privileged to work with Sanromá received lessons beyond value in repertoire, style, technique and artistic responsibility, to say nothing of an endless repertory of historical notes, professional anecdotes and musical jokes. He had an insatiable curiosity, a peerless memory for details of all kinds, and to back it up, painstakingly detailed written notes. Sanromá was, among many other things, a walking musical encyclopedia.

A splendid musician, splendid teacher, splendid man and splendid colleague, Sanromá will be sorely missed by the very many who knew him and by the very many more who were influenced by his presence.

Antidogma

The San Juan Star
April 13, 1985 By Donald Thompson

Antidogma, an Italian chamber ensemble of skilled young instrumentalists, appeared in Puerto Rico on Wednesday under the auspices of the University of Puerto Rico Cultural Activities Series, with an assist by the Italian government. Government sponsorship of presentations abroad by national performance groups is by now a common pattern; when teamed with such local nonprofit cultural entities as university concert series, these efforts can have important results.

The group offered a rather conservative program of twentieth-century music, perhaps to be expected on a concert tour into unknown lands and unknown levels of musical sophistication. Thanks in great measure to the offerings of the UPR Cultural Activities Series itself during the past four or five years, San Juan audiences can now take almost anything in stride. In this context, Wednesday's concert offered very little in the way of novelty but a great deal in the way of consolidation and even a bit of retrospective nostalgia.

Nostalgia was evoked by a very fine performance of Arnold Schoenberg's monumental *Kammersymphonie*, Op. 9 (1906) in a version conceived by his colleague and disciple Anton Webern. The original version required 15 solo instruments; Webern's condenses Schoenberg's already intense thought into five instrumental parts: flute, clarinet, violin, cello and piano. A marvelous work in any form, the *Kammersymphonie* was Schoenberg's final farewell to traditional modes of musical thought before leaping off the edge into unexplored sonoral territory and the formulation of startling new musical concepts. The new concepts formulated by Schoenberg and his school were then to underlie much of the restless musical exploration of the following 75 years. And there's no going back to before the *Kammersymphonie*. What's busted is busted forever.

Also offered were works by Niccolò Castiglioni (a contemporary Italian composer active in the U.S.); Schoenberg's sometime student Aldo Clementi (b. 1925): Costin Miereanu, himself well known through visits to Puerto Rico; and Enrico Correggia, a member of the Antidogma group itself. Of these offerings, I believe the most interesting to have been Clementi's *Duetto*, a piece of tranquil "space music" which calls for a pair of players (flute and clarinet) on the stage and another pair of players (violin and cello) behind the audience. Aldo Brizzi conducted the ensemble with gestures firm, clear and unobtrusive, contributing to a successful evening of twentieth-century music.

Bravo *Figaro*

The San Juan Star
April 21, 1985   By Donald Thompson

With the exception of theater critics, who seem to be drawn from the ranks of masochists and martyrs, reviewers generally avoid community productions, amateur productions and school productions. In the case of reviewers with a professional background, this is partly because critics see as one of their functions the offering of a responsible and fraternal opinion to colleagues who, for now, happen to be on the other end of the baton or the other side of the footlights. Amateurs and community activists, on the other hand, are not apt to find much relevance in a critic's opinions ("But we're only doing it for FUN"), while school productions are usually classroom exercises proudly (if sometimes recklessly) exposed to public view. Presumably, the students' teachers are fully capable of judging their pupils' work, so at this time the opinions of critics are neither appropriate nor welcome.

I decided to set aside this honored tradition Friday evening to attend a workshop production of Mozart's comic opera *The Marriage of Figaro*, at the Conservatory of Music in Hato Rey. One reason was that the production drew upon the skills of so many seasoned professionals that it transcended by far the bounds of the traditional school production. The other reason was pure nostalgic reminiscence; the last time this work was offered in Puerto Rico, some ten years ago, I was involved in it along with a number of the professionals who provided the flesh and the foundation for this recent production. On this level and in these terms, it was a great pleasure to see this marvelous work again.

The artistic director of the Puerto Rico Conservatory of Music Opera Workshop is soprano María Esther Robles, who has for the past thirty years given of herself generously and tirelessly for the cause of music in

Puerto Rico. Associated with her in this production are such heavyweights as stage director Pablo Cabrera, musical director Roselín Pabón, costume designer Gloria Sáez, set designer Checo Cuevas, rehearsal pianist and harpsichordist Pablo Boissen, chorusmaster Myles Hernández and soprano Susan Pabón as an all-around production person. How could things go wrong? As if this weren't enough, on stage were bass-baritone Justino Díaz as Figaro, mezzosoprano Darysabel Isales as Marcellina and baritone Oscar de Gracia, who recently attracted a great deal of attention in the Met auditions, as Count Almaviva. These solid figures provided the firm axle around which the performance turned; especially, of course, Díaz himself. Díaz, like the secure and seasoned pro that he is, fitted himself into the frame of reference required by voices and acting talents still in the phases of study and development.

The cast of younger voices was headed by soprano Virginia Gutiérrez as Susanna. Here is definitely one to watch as her vocal and acting skills develop. Soprano Aixa Cruz was the Countess, Evelyn Quilinchini appeared as Cherubino, and Jennie Carmona was Barbarina. Male roles were covered by Noel Allende as Doctor Bartolo, Samuel Pérez as Antonio, Joaquín Sánchez as Curzio and Julio García as a last minute sub for an ailing workshop member in the key role of Basilio.

While not completely without professional reinforcements, Friday's pit orchestra contained a much higher percentage of students than the stage. Consequently, the instrumentalists' work was considerably less secure on the whole than that of the singers, all of whom (let's face it) drifted off the beat at one time or another themselves. Withal, conductor Pabón was kept very busy for a few hours on Friday. Thanks in great measure to his own skill and quick reflexes, both stage and pit got through a very difficult work in highly respectable fashion in a most unhandy theater. Congratulations are due.

Iannelli and Martínez, Two Welcome Soloists

The San Juan Star
April 26, 1985   By Donald Thompson

There is all too little solo recital playing in Puerto Rico's day to day musical life. To be sure, such agencies as Pro Arte Musical and the UPR Cultural Activities office regularly book traveling soloists, and of course the various institutions of musical instruction regularly schedule student concerts and faculty recitals. But "on the street" there just isn't very much. This shortage was relieved somewhat on Sunday afternoon when cellist Rosalyn Iannelli and pianist José Daniel Martínez offered an interesting joint recital at the Temple Beth Shalom on Santurce's Near North Side.

Rosalyn Iannelli is one of a great number of highly skilled orchestral musicians, born and trained off island, who have settled in Puerto Rico during the past couple of decades. Originally contracted to contribute to the development of the Puerto Rico Symphony Orchestra specifically, many of these valuable performers have in addition enriched the island's musical life through other means. Among these means are teaching in schools and private studios, playing in especially contracted orchestras of one kind and another, organizing chamber ensembles and offering an occasional public recital. In other words, this recent group of musical imports have made their positive mark in Puerto Rico's musical life just as their professional predecessors were doing a century ago. Ms. Iannelli is a fine representative of this tradition.

José Daniel Martínez, on the other hand, is an island-born pianist and composer with impeccable academic credentials from the Eastman School of Music. At present he is a member of the faculty of the Music Department of Inter American University in San Germán, where his frequent appearances enrich the musical scene over on that side of the island. Iannelli and Martínez made a well matched pair in Sunday's concert, which included works by Ernest Bloch, Francisco Calés-Otero and Samuel Barber.

The most extensive of Sunday's offerings was Barber's Sonata for Cello and Piano, Op. 6. A very early work by this foremost U.S. composer (1910-1981), the three-movement sonata already demonstrates mastery of the craft of composition—by a 22-year old! In addition to his own instrument, the piano, Barber also understood the cello, for the work is demanding yet idiomatic for both instruments in the best style of chamber music. The slow movement of the sonata, as well as the two brief pieces by Ernest Bloch which opened the recital (*Prayer* and *Meditation Hebraïque*) demonstrated Iannelli's rich tone, steady vibrato and general security of technique; virtues gained through an active musical life where most instrumental music has always been lived: behind a music stand in an orchestra.

Pianist Martínez' solo offering was a set of brief pieces by the Spanish composer Francisco Calés-Otero (b. 1925). Entitled Five Sephardic Songs, these are harmonizations of traditional Sephardic melodies in a more or less neo-impressionistic style reminiscent not so much of Debussy as of Griffes. Martínez' work was not helped by a piano of less than concert category; however, it was not difficult to perceive both his own considerable ability and the charm of the Calés pieces on Sunday.

A Privileged Voice

The San Juan Star
May 4, 1985   By Donald Thompson

Puerto Rico recently experienced the pleasure of hearing one of today's most privileged voices, as soprano Kiri Te Kanawa appeared as soloist in a special concert by the Puerto Rico Symphony Orchestra. Conducted by John Barnett, this extraordinary event took place last Saturday evening in the Festival Hall of the Performing Arts Center, attracting a sizable audience to what might well be Te Kanawa's only appearance here, at least for a long time.

As is well known, Kiri Te Kanawa's operatic career began its meteoric ascent with Mozart, and particularly with the role of Countess Almaviva in *The Marriage of Figaro*. Her first offering on Saturday was in fact a sequence of the Countess' two *Figaro* arias ("Porgi Amor" and "Dove Sono," plus the recitative which precedes the latter ("E Susanna Non Vien?"). A marvelous voice, yes, I thought, even if slightly affected by slides which many consider foreign to the best Mozart style in concert presentation. Second was a set of sunny songs by Marie-Joseph Canteloube de Malaret, a very conservative twentieth-century composer much given to the collection and arrangement of folk songs for concert performance. The four pieces comprising his *Chants d'Auvergne* (1923-30) are charming settings for voice and orchestra, charmingly presented by Kiri Te Kanawa. But there was still little demonstration, I thought, of what has been described as the completely exceptional gift of this performer.

All changed after intermission, when the program turned to a heavier repertory representing romantic Italian grand opera where, yes, a dramatically gifted singer has some room to expand. Not that the admired Te Kanawa line and phrasing were absent from the Mozart and Canteloube; these qualities simply find more room for development in Bellini,

Boito and Puccini than in concert presentations of Mozart arias. Particularly in a moving excerpt from Boito's *Mefistofele* and in an encore drawn from Puccini's *La Rondine*, the Te Kanawa voice displayed its full and extreme range of expressive qualities. Here, her appearance became an occasion to remember in the unfolding panorama of Puerto Rico's concert life.

Doña Francisquita: Still a Winner

The San Juan Star
May 23, 1985 By Donald Thompson

The romantic Spanish zarzuela, after serving out a natural lifetime of some six decades as a vital form of lyric theater (roughly 1850-1910), lost the interest of its public to more titillating products arriving from Paris. However, it was yet to experience a brief revival at the hands of a last generation of able theater composers, teamed with eminent librettists who could breathe new life—for a while—into this fondly remembered species of Madrid show business.

Doña Francisquita, by the noted composer Amadeo Vives and equally noted librettists Federico Romero and Guillermo Fernández Shaw, is probably the finest existing example of this late blooming and nostalgic variety of zarzuela. *Doña Francisquita* offers everything: a plot of impeccable literary pedigree (traceable back through Lope de Vega as far as Boccaccio), bright music by one of Spain's most accomplished composers, plenty of dancing and partying, and a stageful of traditional character types from the Spanish spoken theater who now sing, too!

Composed and first offered in 1923, the work has received well over 4,000 performances in Spain alone, with another couple of thousand in Latin America by now. It has been given in French, German and English, and has provided the subject of at least one Ph.D. dissertation. *Doña Francisquita* is a winner.

Offered during the past two weekends at the Performing Arts Center by the Puerto Rican Foundation for Zarzuela and Operetta, *Doña Francisquita* was given a pretty fair showing, despite production difficulties which would bring almost any company to the edge of collapse. The level attained here was probably well above the average for those thousands and thousands of performances worldwide. The production represented a noteworthy and courageous undertaking by the Puerto Rican Foundation for Zarzuela and Operetta, which during the past several years has become an important element in San Juan's theatrical life.

The cast which I saw on Friday evening was headed by soprano Elaine Arandes as Francisquita; veteran mezzo Darysabel Isales as her dotty mama, Francisca; tenor Ulises Espaillat subbing for the ailing Antonio Barasorda as the romantic Fernando; splendid actor Herman O'Neill as Fernando's sidekick Cardona, mezzo Evelina Quilinchini as Aurora the temptress, and another fine actor, Pedro Juan Texidor, as Fernando's gullible papa, don Matías. Other named figures in the large cast filled small parts in a list as long as your arm, beginning with Humberto González in the important secondary role of Aurora's sometime sweetie, Lorenzo Pérez.

Among this multitude of stagefolk, some of the names are established figures and known quantities on the San Juan stage, and we take their high skill for granted wherever they appear. These is little new to say, for example, of the wit, grace and skill of a Darysabel Isales or a Herman O'Neill. I myself believe that the "gracioso" role represented by the character of Cardona (O'Neill's role) in this work should be played raunchier and with less attempt at accurate singing, for example (as sort of a dirty young man, you might say), but that is a matter of taste. And after all, the production profited by the stage direction of veteran Manuel Codeso, who certainly knows what he's about.

The same, I believe, goes for Aurora. Aurora Beltrán is an actress, a racy and reprehensible element in the stuffy stratum of Madrid society depicted by *Doña Francisquita*, and she must establish herself as a bad one the first time out. Otherwise, what's the scandal? Evelina Quilinchini started out too much the lady by half, although by the middle of the second act she was hurling herself around the stage quite convincingly. The Quilinchini voice is developing very nicely indeed. It will probably never possess the gutsy quality which we associate with the actresses (not singers) who usually play such roles as this one, nor do I believe that any "straight" singer should try to develop this "belting" style. Ms. Quillichini, I believe, is headed in another direction. Her sure sense of pitch, her good diction, her fine phrasing and her general musical intelligence, shown in this production and on other recent occasions, will hold her in good stead in what we like to think of as more "serious" realms of music.

For soprano Elaine Arandes, the Francisquita role simply adds another accomplishment to her growing list of roles and performances. This role fits her well; it lies high in the voice, it consistently requires the type of agile coloratura which seems most natural to her, and it fits her into a slot of acting and movement which also seems perfectly natural. Her Friday performance was a success in every way. Tenor Espaillat, as noted above, was plugged into a running production as a short notice substitute. These are not the best of circumstances, but I believe Espaillat made the best of them in Friday's performance. He has a nice clear voice with the general lyric qualities required for the role of Fernando in this work, although his acting was necessarily tentative on Friday. I'd like to see him in a more secure situation sometime.

Musical director for this production was Rubén Malán, who as a very capable pianist does a lot besides conduct the pit orchestra in the preparation of these works. He had prepared the big and complicated choruses, for example, as well as working with the singers and sticking the whole thing together musically. Unfortunately, for one reason or another such productions as this can rarely contract the orchestral forces required for a really solid foundation in the pit, which is where the whole structure rests. The *Doña Francisquita* orchestra was about par for the course, its lapses occasionally detracting from a generally satisfactory production. Pity. Maybe another quarter century will see us with enough orchestra work in San Juan to support a second line of professional players for just such occasions as this.

Bright and vigorous choreography was by Zayda Varas and an able *rondalla*, or strolling ensemble of guitars and other instruments, had been assembled by Raúl Rodríguez Morales for this production. The set design was Julio Biaggi's, and the show was costumed by Wardrobe Research and Design.

A Fitting Performance

The San Juan Star
May 29, 1985   By Donald Thompson

The B Minor Mass of Johann Sebastian Bach represents a historic watershed in the development of that branch of Christian church music which utilizes orchestras, choruses and soloists. Such works composed before the period of the B Minor Mass (1738) are sometimes studied in order to trace some kind of trajectory leading toward the composition of this great work, while everything of its species composed during the following 250 years is often studied in relation to the great progenitor itself. Its performance on Saturday evening as the final concert on the 1984-85 season of the Puerto Rico Symphony Orchestra was superbly fitting, in view of this widely celebrated tri-centennial year of the composer's birth.

Several other occurrences were being observed as well on Saturday evening, not the least of which was the combination of elements selected from two of the San Juan metropolitan area's principal choruses in a single grand undertaking. These were the venerable chorus of the University of Puerto Rico, in recent years handsomely revived and presently conducted by Carmen Acevedo, and the Chorus of the Puerto Rico Conservatory of Music, conducted by Myles Hernández. And finally, Friday's performance marked the end of John Barnett's six year tenure as musical director of the PRSO.

However it may be considered liturgically, on the musical plane the B Minor Mass is a big work for chorus and orchestra, with occasional solo sections for specific voices and specific instruments. Able vocal soloists on Saturday were soprano Elaine Arandes, mezzosoprano Linn Maxwell, tenor John Daniecki and bass Thomas Paul. In the context of this particular choral work, the brief performances of these artists, while pleasing enough in themselves, in the logistics of the thing served mainly to give the chorus a break. Tenor Daniecki seemed occasionally to slip over the thin line between the concert style and the opera style, introducing mild scoops, slides and portamentos which are often very effective on the opera stage but which in concert can be bothersome. Otherwise, the soloists' work on Saturday was correct, expressive and decorous. The orchestra's function in this work, characteristic of its historical period, is generally limited to accompanying the singers, except for an occasional instrumental solo of hair-raising difficulty which seems to pop up out of nowhere. On Saturday, solos by the PRSO's principal players included extended passages for oboe, flute, trumpet and horn (all very nicely played), and violin (not so nicely played). Organist Roberto González laid down the kind of part which helps everyone else without itself becoming obtrusive . . . or without even being consciously heard, in the main. Only in such lightly scored sections as part of the chorus "Et incarnatus est" and the tenor aria "Benedictus qui venit" did the organ part rise to a subtle level of prominence on its own.

A choral work, yes, indeed. And the especially formed chorus for this B Minor Mass performed in the main with satisfactory unity, clarity, dynamic subtlety and force. A passage of especially well modulated choral volume occurred at the end of the "Crucifixus," as the choral sound virtually disappeared only to address the following "Et resurrexit" at full and stirring volume. On the other hand, the strident voice of some overenthusiastic soprano would occasionally damage the ensemble, while Bach's murderous high lying choral parts on more than one occasion led to a general sagging of pitch in the soprano section especially. Too, you've got to recognize that Bach expected singers and wind instrument players to behave like organ pipes, with an inexhaustible supply of air coming from . . . where? Nobody knows, and it's certainly not Bach's problem any more, but the chorus conductors'.

So, then, the choral performance was sometimes tentative . . . sometimes uneven . . . and so sometimes the sopranos sagged. An often remarked characteristic of island perceptions is that we easily forget where we are and what our resources really are. Raised on phonograph records, many of us expect to hear on the concert or opera stage an exact replica of what we have heard—and again heard—on some beloved disk whose conditions of hi-tech production may have had absolutely nothing to do with real musical life anywhere in this world. Me, I'll take reality over electronics any day, and Saturday's performance of Bach's B Minor Mass was certainly as good a performance of this difficult work as could realistically be organized in Puerto Rico (and many other places) today.

Orchestra conductors tend to move around from job to job in the fashion of football coaches. Both conductors and coaches are often engaged in the first place to solve some particular problem or to bring to bear some particular field of expertise. When the problem is solved or the man's contribution has been made, coach and conductor move on. Such is the case with John Barnett and the Puerto Rico Symphony Orchestra. When Barnett was engaged in 1979, the PRSO had never enjoyed (if that's the word) the stabilizing influence of a fully resident conductor. There had been titular heads, of course, including such figures as Alexander Schneider, Juan José Castro, Victor Tevah and Sidney Harth, but none of these conductors had been able to really spend much time with the PRSO due to the pressure (or the temptation) of other engagements. It was believed that the orchestra's dramatically extended season now needed a resident leader, and John Barnett was the man chosen. The great wheel turns in orchestra land as everyplace else, and it may now be time to again enlarge the orchestra's experience through working with guest conductors, each of whom will bring a particular insight or a particular point of view. This will also launch a kind of slow courtship gavotte in which conductors, management, orchestra and public circle about while sizing each other up with an eye to making a new match after a season or two. And then the cycle will begin again with the naming of a new musical director, hopefully for the benefit of the orchestra, of the music which it is called upon to perform, and of the citizenry which supports it.

Festival Long Ago Ceased to Serve Its Purpose

The San Juan Star
June 26, 1985 By Donald Thompson

As The Detroit Symphony Orchestra, the Minnesota Chorale, the University of Puerto Rico Chorus and the San Juan Children's Choir were packing up Saturday night after the final concert of the 1985 Puerto Rico Casals Festival, festival goers were trying to figure out just what they had witnessed this year in this almost entirely tax supported enterprise—and why. While they were driving home Saturday night, citizens may well have let their memories range back over the entire series of 28 annual festivals and asked themselves what had happened to turn a brilliant international musical event into an annual set of rather ordinary concerts, always saved at the last minute by the arrival of a big and impressive orchestra and by a final week of spectacular (if ill-attended) concerts.

Old timers remember that the first Puerto Rico Casals Festivals were organized around the admired figure of Catalan cellist Pablo Casals, who in the mid-1950s was persuaded to establish the base of his revitalized international activities in Puerto Rico. Around him gathered colleagues and friends who devoted their attention to the study of a select musical repertory: a repertory which could convincingly be identified with Casals' elevated tastes and which required little or no on-site rehearsal. The Casals Festival was at that time a subsidiary of the Puerto Rico Industrial Development Company (PRIDCO). PRIDCO's clearly defined justification for investing public funds in a scheme as extraordinary as a music festival were (1) to present a tranquil and positive image of Puerto Rico to potential sources of off-island industrial development capital, and (2) to attract to Puerto Rico the kind of world class festival goers who in the 1950s were still seeking unusual artistic experiences in out of the way places. To see Pablo Casals was certainly unusual, while Puerto

Rico was still considered an exotic place.

The first festivals served these purposes admirably, except that their function as a tourist attraction soon disappeared. In the face of disappearing audiences, first visitors and then islanders, the festival management hopefully began to expand the concert repertory and to enlarge the especially assembled festival orchestras accordingly. Quality slipped badly. By the end of the 1960s, the festival orchestras were little more than casual ensembles hastily recruited among the players available in New York City, while the repertory might be heard on any regular Thursday evening concert in Kansas City or Tulsa. Since the death of Pablo Casals in 1973 there has really been no reason to continue the festival at all, and by now even the original industrial promotion purpose of the festival has disappeared. Little industrial development is going on anywhere, and the public relations image of a pleasant place and a cultured populace no longer carries much of a message to industrialists. The bottom line is now read in terms of wages, costs of transportation and electricity, political stability and tax exemption.

A new festival management, centered on conductor Jorge Mester as musical director, has tried its best during recent years to find a purpose for the Casals Festival, but has only succeeded in further diluting whatever thin stream of continuity might still have existed with those significant musical events of a forgotten quarter-century ago. Recent years have seen the development of a new format, marked by the climactic appearance on the scene of a big mainland orchestra performing representative and very well solidified works from its own repertory, as well as a premiere or two of compositions by island musicians. Soloists, by and large, are today's comers, some of whom have appeared in Puerto Rico already and who offer only the most familiar repertory pieces. And the final shot, the performance of a major work which fills the stage with orchestra, chorus, soloists—the works—is expected to leave observers with the conviction that something important and festive has taken place.

Observant music lovers with an analytic bent universally agree that something important has indeed taken place, with the presentation of the Pittsburgh, Houston, Cincinnati and Detroit orchestras and with the participation of big and impressive choruses. But impressive single performances, preceded by a couple of weeks of ill-attended and completely unfocused offerings, do not make a festival. They do, however, cost money: a million dollars annually, give or take a couple of hundred thousand. One possible solution to this festival's dilemma, occasionally discussed among thinking music lovers, would be to divide the million into two separate appropriations. One would be earmarked for the occasional presentation of visiting orchestras and chamber groups as a significant investment of public funds for educational and cultural purposes. The other appropriation would go for the improvement of the island's own orchestra, the Puerto Rico Symphony Orchestra, along several lines which are occasionally pointed out with some urgency. This latter use, especially, would again honor the name and the mission in Puerto Rico of Pablo Casals. Part of the Casals mission, as some music lovers still recall, was to inspire the solid growth of island musical institutions. The annual Casals Festival is at a conceptual dead end, having long ago ceased to serve the purposes for which it was created and which no longer even exist. On the other hand, the Puerto Rico Symphony Orchestra has not yet been able to assume the fundamental roles which a symphony orchestra (especially one financed by public funds) absolutely must assume.

Rosado with Style and Zeal

The San Juan Star
September 15, 1985   By Donald Thompson

Sacred Heart University in Upper Santurce is not one of the island's major sites of elaborate musical events, but year in and year out it does offer its students and the general public a nicely varied set of activities. This year's cultural activities series is dedicated to the tricentennial observance of the birth of Johann Sebastian Bach, and appropriately enough it opened on Thursday evening with a musical event.

Featured was island guitarist Ana María Rosado, whose announced "polyartistic tryptich" turned out to be a recital with commentaries delivered from the stage by the artist herself. This is a tricky format, and one better avoided, in the main. Performers usually have enough to worry about just getting the notes right, without having to worry about data, diction and dry throats. My usual reaction to comments from the stage is "What happened? Didn't they have time to get the program notes together?"

It takes a cool and well prepared performer to handle a recital with commentary, but Ana María Rosado is both cool and well prepared. Her comments on Thursday were short, accurate and to the point, in addition helping to break the ice of the always problematic ritual of the unaccompanied solo recital.

The first half of the concert was devoted to music of the distant past, in terms of the stylistic evolution of Western music. Three works by masters of the great age of Spanish music, the sixteenth century (Milán, Narváez and Mudarra) demonstrate the contrapuntal capability of the guitar, while three movements from a lute suite by J.S. Bach demonstrated the technical and interpretive ability of the guitarist. Ms. Rosado played this vigorous music with great style and zeal. The force and drive of Bach's music were evident in her playing, but also the polish and flexibility of an accomplished soloist.

The second half of the program was devoted to music of Latin American provenance: works by Jorge Gómez Crespo, Edmundo Vásquez, Heitor Villa-Lobos, Francis Schwartz and Antonio Lauro. These works ranged from the folkloristic conservatism of Gómez Crespo's *Norteo* to the—my goodness, what would you call it?—of Francis Schwartz's *Bato*. *Bato*, according to Ms. Rosado's illuminating explanation, is inspired by an old indigenous Antillean Indian ball game (of which much is surmised but very little known), in the sense of physical movement, tension and relaxation, stress and release, and perhaps a bit of ying and yang and this and that. *Bato*, in the fashion of the characteristic Schwartz work, incorporates percussive sounds, bent pitches, thumpings, scrapings, vocal utterances, belly-bangings (the instrument's belly, not the player's) and other sonoral surprises. Ana María Rosado is one of Puerto Rico's most successful interpreters of contemporary music, and on Thursday she unveiled Schwartz's guitaristic innovations with skill, grace and security.

What IS a Puerto Rican Work?

The San Juan Star
September 21, 1985 By Donald Thompson

    The Puerto Rico Symphony Orchestra offered the second concert of its regular season on Thursday evening at the Performing Arts Center in Santurce, continuing an established practice of from time to time presenting the premiere performance of a Puerto Rican work.
    What is a "Puerto Rican work," anyway? A theory of Puerto Rican music might prescribe any one of a number of criteria, none of them very satisfactory. For example, one criterion might be that the work have been composed here. On the other hand, could a Repertory Screening Board ever be absolutely sure that the composer hadn't sneaked in a few measures on the plane coming back from vacation? Or even worse, that the whole piece hadn't been written while the composer was fishing in Scotland? Or gambling in Monaco? Or studying in Kansas?
    Another criterion might be that the work be conceived in the style of Puerto Rican music. But here is a real can of worms, for strain as we might, there is absolutely no way in this world that a Puerto Rican style in concert music can be identified or defined, except in some kind of circular exercise in non-logic: The music of X, Y and Z, composed (presumably in Puerto Rico) at around the same time, seems to share certain very obvious characteristics, perhaps the incorporation of *plena* rhythms or the use of maracas. Therefore, to be Puerto Rican, music must sound like the work of X, Y, and Z, complete with *plena* rhythms and maracas. And, of course, there is the matter of the adjectival designation "Puerto Rican" applied not to the music but to the composer. Very risky, this one, for some immigrants have certainly incorporated folk elements as ably as anyone born here (if Puerto Rican means folkloristic), while there are island-born composers (if that's the criterion) to whom *plena* rhythms and maracas are simply not of interest in concert music.

Yes, it's a conundrum, and I sympathize with anyone who has to serve on the PRSO's Puerto Rican Music Repertory Screening Board in this age of shifting conceptual frontiers, momentarily expedient criteria and federal grant guidelines.

All of the above went through my mind on Thursday evening as I listened to the concert opener, a short work by Mayagüez-born José Montalvo which in fact represents a commission by the management of the Puerto Rico Symphony Orchestra. Montalvo's contribution, entitled *Espejos*, is a rather conservative exercise in contrasting sonorities, in the fashion of much orchestral music composed during the past thirty years. Glissandos in the strings, percussive pizzicatos, abrupt changes in dynamic level: they're all there. But the design of the piece is itself an improvement over much music of this same general type, for the work is divided into sections most of which are short enough to maintain an audience's attention. Only the last section of *Espejos* seemed to unduly stretch the possibilities of the material on which it was based. Montalvo has a very good grasp of traditional instrumentation and, as indicated above, a good sense of a general public's sensibilities and tolerances.

Soloist for the evening was brilliant violinist Elmar Oliveira, offering a stirring performance of the Dvořák D Minor Violin Concerto. Especially gratifying was the work's lyric second movement, played with clear and beautifully modulated sound.

The PRSO, under the direction of guest conductor Bernard Rubenstein, sounded a little better than it had a couple of weeks ago, but still rough, unresponsive and rhythmically uncertain. Rubenstein appears to be a good straightforward conductor who knows his scores and plans his work carefully, but the PRSO just doesn't offer him a lot to work with, at the moment.

Thursday's concert closed with the bleak and twisted First Symphony of Dmitri Shostakovich, which in happier days this orchestra (or an orchestra bearing the same noble name) has played much better. Some solo playing was very good on Thursday, while some was very bad, but the general level of orchestral performance was set, inevitably, by the mass of strings. And here the general level was the same fogbound plateau which has often been noted—worse, of late. However, in addition to the widely known catalog of PRSO string section faults, Thursday's fiddle sections sounded desperately under-rehearsed. Is the orchestra's valuable rehearsal time again being unwisely sacrificed in the preparation of events outside its own calendar?

Foundation Keeps the Flame Burning

The San Juan Star
October 2, 1985   By Donald Thompson

    The Latin American Foundation for Contemporary Music, based in San Juan, goes back a number of years now as a prime element, if not perhaps the only continuous element, in the island's contemporary music movement. Every couple of years the foundation puts together an ambitious celebration of mainly significant works performed by mainly significant performers and ensembles. In between, it keeps the flame burning with occasional concerts and other activities assembled by the tireless Rafael Aponte-Ledée, the organization's musical director and a composer who came into concert management by the back door. Simply, nobody wanted to do a job which had to be done, and the unlikely Aponte-Ledée sort of volunteered. In the aggregate, the Foundation's contribution over the years, guided by Aponte-Ledée and a handful of stalwart colleagues, has been extremely important.

    One thing that the Foundation does not do well, however, is let people know of its activities. A subsidiary of no governmental or educational institution, this agency must really scrounge for publicity. In fact, precisely because it represents no institutional power base the Foundation is something of a black sheep; it seems difficult to get much word of mouth publicity, while many people who could learn from its offerings seem to avoid them, perhaps because the organization is completely neutral politically and therefore suspect. Nothing can be politically neutral and expect to survive very long in Puerto Rico.

    On Sunday afternoon a sparse-to-middling audience attended a Foundation concert in the theater of the Puerto Rico Conservatory of Music in Hato Rey, and those who attended received the benefit of a good presentation of several monuments of twentieth-century music plus a couple of dividends. Sunday's concert was based on the wind ensemble Aulos, which has been together long enough now (since 1981 or so) to develop a strong base of unity and security. Added to Aulos' flute, oboe, clarinet, horn and bassoon on Sunday were other instruments necessary to cover the sometimes peculiar instrumentation required by the works offered.

The monuments, mentioned above, were The Soldier's Tale by Igor Stravinsky (1918) and Octandre, by Edgard Varèse (1924). Neither work had been heard in Puerto Rico for a long, long time, and who better to present them than the Latin American Foundation for Contemporary Music?

Octandre, for flute/piccolo, oboe, bassoon, clarinet, horn, trumpet, trombone and double bass, is still capable of raising a few wigs, although its shockingly innovative techniques have long since been incorporated into the flow of new music. In fact, the composition itself is an example of how everything new builds upon previous accomplishments, for rhythmic occurrences toward the end of the work definitely look back to Stravinsky's great Rite of Spring of 1913. But then what work composed during the past 70 years doesn't look back to The Rite of Spring? Stravinsky's The Soldier's Tale is an old friend to anyone who is at all acquainted with the music of the twentieth century. Itself a cornerstone of modern music, it requires the highest degree of skill and concentration on everyone's part to even come close to attaining a satisfactory presentation. To speak of only one aspect of this challenging work, Stravinsky's notation of the rhythms is extremely complicated—perhaps needlessly so. Yet that's the way it is, and that's what players and conductors have to deal with. Sunday's players and Sunday's conductor dealt with the work in a completely convincing way.

Conducting on Sunday was Tania León, a gifted musician who has visited Puerto Rico on several occasions, engaged by one or another of the island's musical institutions. She had Sunday's difficult music well under control, with a tight crisp beat and no waste motion. In terms of sports, both the Varèse and the Stravinsky are "sudden death" events; either you survive or you don't. And it was largely due to Ms. León's abilities that Sunday's ensemble survived very nicely. She is not only a gifted conductor, but a composer and pianist as well, as was demonstrated by her performance of her own interesting Momentum for piano solo, dating from 1984. Her work in Puerto Rico has always pleased mightily; on this recent occasion it has also impressed mightily, which is not necessarily the same thing at all.

Present Evokes Past

The San Juan Star
October 8, 1985 By Donald Thompson

Last Friday the "Asociación Nacional de Compositores" offered a concert entitled "Contemporary Puerto Rican Music" as part of the Inter American Arts Festival now in progress at the Performing Arts Center.

What, I wondered, might an "Asociación Nacional de Compositores" be? Perhaps an island chapter of the American Composers Alliance, I figured, or maybe a branch of the venerable National Music Center. With a name like that could it be a strictly local effort? I found no help in the printed program: no names of officers, no paragraph of organizational history; only the information that the efforts of the "Asociación Nacional de Compositores" were being supported in part by a tobacco company. This being the case, and in the absence of clarifying information, I naturally began to fear the worst: a nationalist attack by a band of hairy middle-aged musical terrorists, spraying the audience with wrong notes from behind a smoke screen of aromatic Virginia!

I needn't have worried. Friday's performers were all young and clean cut, while most of the evening's music evoked nostalgia, not fear; in fact, few works even evoked much curiosity after a minute or two. There was considerable straining for "contemporary" effects in some of Friday's offerings, but these efforts simply resulted, in the main, in internal disparity of style. One work even followed a promising exercise in abstract sonorities with a repeated—and repeated—and again repeated—and still repeated—fragment of completely tonal, completely conservative mountain music. Was the composer serious, or having said what he had to say, was he constrained to fill up a certain amount of time with whatever he might find knocking about in his memory? And that wasn't much.

The most convincing music on Friday's program was by two composers who have never made any claim to modernity, but who simply continue to produce well-made music which could have been written from 30 to 130 years ago. These are Ernesto Cordero and Narciso Figueroa, whose music for solo guitar and for voice and piano, respectively, lightened Friday's atmosphere considerably. Both Cordero and Figueroa are accomplished performers themselves, and the security of performers shows in their music. I should be very pleased to hear Cordero's *Descarga* and *Piezas Afrocubanas*, and Figueroa's *Impresiones Boriquenses* again, but I think not on a solemnly entitled "contemporary music" concert, thanks. Also of interest, but hardly representative of today's music, was José Rodríguez Alvira's well-crafted *Árboles*, for the very unusual combination of voice, oboe and bassoon. This, too, I should like to hear again.

Friday's able and well prepared performers were soprano Virginia Gutiérrez, pianists José Daniel Martínez and Rafael Sueiras, guitarist Eladio Scharrón, oboist Harry Rosario and bassoonist Roberto López.

Quintet of the Americas

The San Juan Star
October 10, 1985 By Donald Thompson

Concert life at the Inter American Arts Festival took a happy turn on Sunday afternoon with an appearance of the Quintet of the Americas, or Quinteto de las Américas, at the Experimental Theater of the Performing Arts Center. This able quintet is a wind ensemble, based in New York but with historical connections in Latin America and with a repertory which nicely spans the Western Hemisphere. From what was heard on Sunday, the group's members, its repertory, its itinerary and its prospects are very well matched. A happy turn, indeed!

The existing repertory for the instrumentation of flute, oboe, clarinet, bassoon and horn is vast, and Sunday's concert offered a selection from the moderate to light end of the spectrum. This may perhaps have been a deliberate adaptation to what seems to be the prevailing wish of the festival management to keep things light for the general public which it hopes to attract. This is OK, I guess, but I think the people who turned out for a wind quintet concert on the third day of a tropical deluge would have done so anyway, especially as the titles of many of the works programmed and the names of their composers were not familiar even to specialists. So how could the announced program have been a factor in attracting a tentative audience?

No matter, after the event. The program was varied, it was attractive and the ensemble played very well, attaining a very high degree of precision and unified phrasing. And wonder of wonders, they even attained a high level of unified pitch among five very, very different instruments.

The heaviest work in Sunday's concert was a Partita for Wind Quintet by U.S. composer Irving Fine, dating from 1948. Melodious and sparkling in the style of much concert music (especially in the U.S.) just before the avant-garde struck its first mighty blows, this set of five movements very nicely explores the contrasting sonorities of the five winds, in a constantly changing palette of colors and textures. Sunday's other major work was *Salsa para Vientos*, that brash and evocative three-movement quintet by island composer Roberto Sierra which has had quite a bit of play here recently.

Other offerings on Sunday included Alberto Ginastera's interesting Duet for Flute and Oboe (also heard here a couple of times recently; nobody's fault, but just one of those things . . .) and one of those innumerable and always fascinating works of Villa-Lobos for all conceivable combinations of instruments, this time a nicely played *Chôros No. 2* for flute and clarinet.

The whipped cream on Sunday's cake was provided by a number of very skilled arrangements for wind quintet by Ronald Tucker. These included two Colombian dances by Jorge Olaya Muñoz and several pieces by nineteenth-century U.S. pianist and composer Louis Moreau Gottschalk, who himself has a pleasant historical connection with Puerto Rico. Gottschalk was here for part of 1857 and 1858 accompanying the teen-aged soprano Adelina Patti, meeting and working with the best island musicians while he incorporated island tunes and rhythms into his own compositions. One of these island-inspired pieces, originally conceived for Gottschalk's own performances as a virtuoso pianist, is his *Souvenir de Porto Rico: Marche des Gibaros*, based on a tune still known to every three-year-old in Puerto Rico today. And sure enough, Gottschalk's *Souvenir* turned up in a very nice arrangement for wind quintet on Sunday, nicely played by this *Quinteto de las Américas*.

Latin Pops

The San Juan Star
October 16, 1985　　　　　　　　　　　　By Donald Thompson

　　Arturo Somohano was a piano playing and song writing bon vivant of a man who, working out of a much frequented home in Miramar, organized orchestras for whatever occasion might arise during a very slack time in the concert business here, the early 1950s. The nucleus of the Somohano forces was provided by a dozen or so scarred veterans of governmental attempts to establish stable orchestras, going back to the thirties and before. Additional instrumentalists were recruited from among younger professionals out of work, gentlemen amateurs, music students and a fiddle playing housewife or two. Never quite able to pay the union minimum scale, Somohano managed to keep his people working (working very part time, that is) with an occasional park concert, government reception or TV shot. At a time when *Eine Kleine Nachtmusik* was considered heavy fare here, Somohano's efforts helped keep a very old orchestral tradition alive in Puerto Rico during a difficult time.

　　Whether or not Somohano "rescued the Puerto Rican musical tradition," as was freely claimed, is debatable. For many players, however, it was a chance to drag out the fiddle and the tux again, or to pick up a few bucks after work, or simply to hang around with the few orchestra players who still existed here, as for sure nothing else was going on with orchestras in Puerto Rico.

　　The repertory of the Puerto Rico Philharmonic Orchestra, as Somohano rather pretentiously called his floating ensemble, was mainly Latin pops, with emphasis on Cuban tunes, Rafael Hernández in big-band style, maybe a Caribbean Rhapsody of Somohano's own design, and a touch of Leroy Anderson. For really formal occasions there was, yes, the first movement of *Eine Kleine Nachtmusik,* complete with added piano and wind instrument parts. This repertory never changed, which is why Somohano was always able to put something together on seemingly a half hour's notice. As every musician in San Juan knew the book from memory it was seldom necessary to rehearse, only when the occasion required *Eine Kleine Nachtmusik*. Usually, one simply turned up at the job, tuxed and with instrument.

Then things slowly began to pick up. Serious orchestral activities began in a small way at the Ateneo and on the UPR campus, followed in the due course of events by the establishment of the present Puerto Rico Symphony Orchestra. Within a few years there was really little need for the Somohano orchestras, as the old timers, part-timers and students were gradually fitted into the UPR group or the PRSO itself. Even the Latin Pops repertory and Leroy Anderson tunes eventually began to appear on the PRSO park concerts. But that, of course, is another story.

Somohano is gone, but his orchestra, now the Arturo Somohano Philharmonic Orchestra, lives on, an anachronism but one capable of drawing a nostalgic crowd (a full house, in fact) to the Drama Hall of the Performing Arts Center for a concert last Saturday evening as part of the Inter American Arts Festival now in progress. Now conducted by Gualberto Rivera Capdeville, himself a veteran of the early Somohano orchestras, the orchestra is still made up largely of students and part-timers, but now with a few PRSO members on an evening off and . . . can it be? . . . a *retired* PRSO member or two! The repertory hasn't changed much since the 50s, nor has the casual and seemingly unrehearsed style of playing. Neither, for that matter, has the audience changed much; folks are now thirty years older and bring their grandchildren, but they display pretty much the same faces.

Saturday's concert was short on precision but long on nostalgia. Featured were several of Somohano's own arrangements, still sounding like soundtrack music for some old "South of the Border" movie, as well as more recent arrangements in the studio orchestra style by such skilled craftsmen as Enriquillo Cerón, Lito Peña and Mandy Vizoso. Leroy Anderson was represented, of course, while a nice surprise came in the form of soprano Migdalia Batiz offering a set of songs including one by herself. Batiz' pleasant voice was overamplified to the point of cracking the fillings in my teeth, but she looked well and, except when the amplification rose to painful levels, sang well. She is a trouper and a valued member of the island music-theater scene, especially.

In the old days of the Puerto Rico Philharmonic Orchestra (otherwise known as the Miramar Experience), no great occasion was complete without a master of ceremonies announcing the pieces (never mind the printed program), a speech or two, maybe a plaque and if possible, a cake. Saturday's concert incorporated all of these elements, to the great joy of the audience. Just like 1954 again. Maybe my Uncle Charlie was right: the more things change the more they remain the same.

Ringing Out the Old: 1985 in Music

The San Juan Star
January 6, 1986 By Donald Thompson

Much of Puerto Rico's daily concert life has been controlled directly by government branches since the 1950s. Naturally, such centralization of concept and effort has a profound effect on the music presented as well as how and by whom it will be presented during the annual cycle of activities which powers the island's musical microcosm. Let's see how the government's own musical efforts fared in 1985, then take a look at the broader panorama of the year's general musical accomplishments and disappointments, extending outward in ripple fashion from the central (and centralizing) force of two government agencies.

The major governmental force in the island's music today is the Musical Arts Corporation (Spanish-language acronym: CAM), which was born in the political shifts and tremors that followed the 1984 elections and which inherited most of the turf formerly controlled by the short-lived Administration for the Development of Arts and Culture. This latter agency (Spanish-language acronym: AFAC) was itself a direct descendant of the Casals Festival Corporation, with a few other subsidiaries thrown into the basket as AFAC came into existence in 1980. And the Puerto Rico Casals Festival Corporation, you may recall, had itself originated in the mid-fifties as an unnatural musical subsidiary of the government's Puerto Rico Industrial Development Company (PRIDCO).

What has this to do with music in 1985? Plenty, in the backstage offices where gears are meshed, deals are done and fundamental decisions are made concerning the island's music. Patterns of planning, of staffing, of decision making and of communication were established thirty years ago according to modes appropriate not for the arts but for industrial development promotion, and no matter how earnestly each new group of postelection functionaries tries to redesign the shop, underlying it all are the same old industrializing patterns of 1956. Ironically, the movers and planners themselves can't see it, for they have always come not from the arts but from business, management, politics, administration: everywhere but from music. Old patterns persist. More than a year after the most recent hopeful elections there is still no visible and administratively responsible musical input in the CAM's decision processes. A knowledge gap exists in Puerto Rico's musical officialdom, and it operated to the detriment of the island's music making in 1985.

What did the new CAM bring us in 1985? The central element in the CAM array (and indeed, the very heart of Puerto Rico's musical life) is the Puerto Rico Symphony Orchestra. The PRSO is frankly in a quiescent state, a dormant phase, a holding pattern just now. The island's major musical force finds itself between musical directors, for the most recent one completed his contract last May and the next one has not been named yet. Consequently there is little thrust to orchestral affairs, little visible planning, little continuity of effort, little hoopla; only a marking of orchestral time while the future prepares itself backstage—we hope. Associate Music Director Roselín Pabón has done a good soldier's job since May as the only more or less permanent conductor in sight, but even Pabón's recent work has suffered from an apparent lack of force and will. And little wonder; he's working in a vacuum.

The orchestra's best work in 1985 came in May when it performed the great B Minor Mass of Bach with combined island choral forces. The present season, on the other hand, started in a drab and uncertain fashion in September and has still not managed to get fully cranked up despite the participation of a long roster of soloists and guest conductors. Your symphony orchestra ran on momentum during a great part of 1985.

Another CAM subsidiary is an odd sort of Inter American Arts Festival, inherited from the AFAC, which had created it. I say odd, because this agency has never had any kind of distinguishing character; in attempting to cover all the bases it has really covered none at all. The musical level of the most recent festival (September-October) was set by popular-commercial singer Danny Rivera and also featured a nostalgic pops concert by the Arturo Somohano Philharmonic Orchestra, reminiscent of a simpler and more charitable era in the island's music. But also appearing was the Quintet of the Americas, a very able wind quintet of the art music persuasion which was an anomaly in this context, albeit a welcome one. It had simply been booked for the wrong series.

The programming of the 1985 Puerto Rico Casals Festival, still another agency now under the control of CAM, had been planned by AFAC. Recent festivals have been based on a redundant series of ill-attended concerts of more or less standard repertory with an exception or two, followed by the sudden materialization of a splendid orchestra, big and interesting works and the climactic presentation of some grand composition calling for orchestra, chorus, soloists: the works. The 1985 festival's climactic forces included the Detroit Symphony Orchestra, conductor Gunther Herbig, the Minnesota Chorale, the San Juan Children's Choir, the UPR Chorus and able soloists, in a resounding performance of Berlioz' staggering The Damnation of Faust. Grand and impressive, yes, but my goodness, couldn't the management have simply offered the Detroit orchestra (for example) as a special presentation on a long weekend during the regular musical season, forgetting the devaluated and costly "festival" format altogether? Maybe the new folks at CAM will have the courage to do something like this in 1986. Nobody else has ever dared to do it, although the once important festival has by now slipped irretrievably away.

The other government branch which has a stake in music is the Institute of Puerto Rican Culture. This agency was established in the 1950s, with a mandated responsibility in such fields as folk crafts, island history, research, publication and architectural restoration. Later moving into the performing arts and other fields as well, the IPRC became an important force in theater and dance, while also establishing a solid but conceptually problematical place for itself in art music. The Institute is currently experiencing a period of deep travail (if not, indeed, a fatal meltdown), and the music office seems to be especially afflicted. In fact, the course of the present IPRC season may provide a convincing argument *against* naming specialists to high administrative posts, for the agency, now headed by a musician, appears completely unable to get its musical act together. Marked by amateurish and utterly inept concert management and promotion, the Institute's musical work during much of 1985 is best forgotten.

Well, then; outside of officialdom, how did the island's music fare in 1985? Understand, please, that almost everyone receives at least a little help from the government anyway: the use of rehearsal space, perhaps the invaluable participation of the PRSO at less than cost, etc. But we still like to speak of independent musical activity as if such a thing were really possible today.

The Pro Arte Musical Society came through again with an interesting series of activities. Recovering from the temporary dependence on opera stars which hampered its efforts for a while, Pro Arte has reclaimed its historic role in the presentation of varied artists and ensembles. Especially remembered from 1985 are a fine concert in March by the Beaux Arts Trio and a splendid recital in November by violinist Aaron Rosand and pianist John Covelli. Among other attractions, Pro Arte's imaginative lecture series offered an illustrated lecture on jazz as a classic form by flutist Nancy Janoson and a swinging ensemble.

The UPR Cultural Activities Series is, of course, a quasi-governmental agency itself, although its programming is as completely independent as Pro Arte's. Interestingly enough, during their best periods these two agencies have historically run more or less parallel, with one serving a population of direct subscribers plus other smart concertgoers, the other mainly a population of academics plus equally smart concertgoers. UPR's major musical offerings during 1985 included such stellar attractions as flutist Pierre-Yves Artaud, the Juilliard Chamber Symphony Orchestra, the Kronos String Quartet, the Siegert-Danner Duo, pianist David Bar-Illan and the Free Flight jazz group.

Opera and zarzuela maintained their traditional importance in Puerto Rico, with two companies alternating in the presentation of big works. Opera de Puerto Rico continued to offer such favorites as *Tosca* with Plácido Domingo and other worthy artists in April, following the more daring Teatro de la Opera's production in January and February of Donizetti's *Norma*. Teatro de la Opera then took to the stage again in August with a big production of Verdi's *La Forza del Destino*, especially remembered for the fine work of mezzo Mignon Dunn and baritone Pablo Elvira. Zarzuela kept rolling along, with an especially remembered and very ambitious production of Amadeo Vives' *Doña Francisquita* in May by the Puerto Rican Foundation for Zarzuela and Operetta. But I think that in the long (and I mean LONG) run the most significant lyric theater production of 1985 may turn out to have been *Little Red Riding Hood* at the Tapia Theater in August, put together by the fresh and feisty Opera de Cámara company, a group which happily takes on jobs that nobody else wants to bother with.

Opera de Cámara represents an entirely different league from the island's other opera companies, of course. This is why the true significance of its efforts will be perceived in the long run: in the creation of audiences for the production here of operas of Verdi and Puccini (and maybe even Berg) in the opening decades of the next century.

The list of able island soloists who appeared in 1985 is as long as your arm. Chamber music also held its own very well with such skilled groups as Tocata, Camerata Caribe and Aulos making regular contributions. The last named group, a very able wind ensemble, appeared in October on a series sponsored by the Latin American Foundation for Contemporary Music, itself guided by composer Rafael Aponte-Ledée. Talk about independent! Downright rebellious, I should say, is the valuable Latin American Foundation for Contemporary Music!

The noted Figueroa family, now consisting of somewhere close to a dozen active string players and pianists, offered a series of chamber music concerts toward the end of the year as the Official Quintet of the Commonwealth of Puerto Rico in groups of from two players upward, under the auspices of the Institute of Puerto Rican Culture. Hmmm. We're back to the government again with an Official Quintet, no less. What will they think of next? Why not an Official Music Critic?

Yet there are independent musical forces at work in Puerto Rico in addition to Rafael Aponte-Ledée. Among the most persistent are a couple of ensembles conceived, coaxed into existence and conducted by the persevering James Rawie: the Puerto Rico Chamber Orchestra and the Puerto Rico Symphonic Chorus. The latter is based down around San Germán, where it contributed to a highly regarded Mostly Mozart series last summer, abetted by the former ensemble, itself a more or less ad hoc group created anew for each occasion. The Rawie legions accounted for some ambitious music making in 1985, including Bach's St. Matthew Passion in March (with the New England Youth Symphony Orchestra) and the sublime Requiem of Mozart more recently.

San Juan's Union Church launched a promising series of professional music matinees in 1985, and according to reports the Puerto Rico Guitar Society had a fine series going. But for independence (not to say stubbornness) coupled with the highest level of choral skill you can't beat the San Juan Children's Choir, which always ends the year with a profound message of musical hope for all.

The island's music was well represented abroad in 1985 by composers and performers. New compositions by Roberto Sierra and Francis

Schwartz enjoyed premiere performances abroad, the former at Carnegie Recital Hall with island mezzo Puli Toro and the Quintet of the Americas and the latter at Radio France and the Pompidou Center in Paris. And of course there were probably close to fifty island performers, composers and conductors dispersed throughout Europe and the Americas singing, playing, composing and waving their arms for the greater glory of Puerto Rican music in 1985.

The future? Well, it will belong to today's youth someday. And Puerto Rico's musical youth made a pretty good showing in 1985. The young and you might say maturing performers who made a bit of a splash last year included soprano Elaine Arandes and baritone Oscar de Gracia (both recently off to Europe), other singers Virginia Gutiérrez, Evelina Quilinchini, Noel Allende, Julio García, Magda Nieves and Adolfo Llorca; pianist Erwin Solivan and clarinetist George Morales, among many, many other promising talents. The thought of musical youth brings us around to institutions of higher learning, which is where most of today's musical youth hangs out. Some fine work was done in 1985 by university and conservatory ensembles, notably at Inter American University in San Germán, at UPR in Río Piedras (especially by its venerable and now revitalized chorus) and at the Puerto Rico Conservatory of Music, most splendidly represented by its Opera Workshop.

With a little help from government branches and educational institutions and guided by wise, modest, skilled, professional, responsible and well informed stewards, may the island's music continue its erratic but generally ascending spiral in 1986 and long thereafter.

Tocata

The San Juan Star
January 29, 1986   By Donald Thompson

    As was promised, the chamber ensemble Tocata offered the second and final concert of its present series in the recital hall of the Puerto Rico Conservatory of Music on Sunday afternoon. The Tocata group is based here in San Juan, and during the past few years has become an extremely important element in the island's expanding musical life, especially valuable not only for the high level of skill represented by the individual members but also for the imaginative approach to the programming of works which the group has consistently demonstrated. Every Tocata concert is different, and every Tocata concert has something unusual to offer.

    Can you believe that a Haydn quartet is unusual? Unless I'm mistaken, it's been a while since such a work has been prepared and presented here by a resident ensemble, and the appearance on Sunday of the first of Haydn's Op. 76 quartets, written in the composer's advanced age and in his absolute musical maturity, was indeed a blessing in a Puerto Rico currently somewhat deprived of chamber music for strings.

    This Haydn is real string quartet music, conceived by one of the inventors of the string quartet itself, and for public performance you don't fool around with it. Either your group can play it or it can't. Tocata can and did on Sunday. Especially impressive was the unified phrasing attained by the group, as well as the clear movement of inner voices (second violin and viola), both of which can only have resulted from long rehearsal and debate by intelligent and responsible performers.

    The same virtues were evident in the first performance here in recent memory of the Trout Quintet by Schubert, a marvelous extended expression of song in the Schubert mode, but for instruments not voice. But in Sunday's concert the voice was represented too, in the very

Schubert song which in fact gave the Trout Quintet its name: "Die Forelle," for voice and piano, upon which is based a set of variations incorporated in the Trout Quintet. A nice touch, this, the presentation on the same concert of two closely related works for such different performance media. Susan Pabón's privileged soprano was Sunday's voice, as clear as the limpid brook wherein swam and disported the playful and immortalized Schubertian trout itself.

But . . . unusual . . . you say unusual? For unusual, try to beat a Grand Spectacular Romantic Expressive Fingerbreaker Duo for Violin and Double Bass with the Earnest Collaboration of a Skilled Pianist, the likes of Which had Not been Heard in The Antilles for At Least the Last Thirty Years (and Indeed Probably Never), by Giovanni Bottesini and Quite Correctly Entitled *Grand Duo Concertant*.

Giovanni Bottesini (1821-1889) was himself a double bass virtuoso; one of the greatest of this tribe, in fact, in addition to having been a conductor (of, for example, the first performance ever of Verdi's *Aida*) and a highly regarded composer in his own right. Aside from that, what can I tell you about the unlimited virtues of bass players, having once been one myself? Sunday's performance of the Bottesini *Grand Duo Concertant* displayed a sometime kittenish and always excruciatingly difficult interplay between violin and bass, calling into play all of the resources of these solo instruments as they were known a century ago. Sunday's soloists (Hutchinson and Groninger) were beautifully matched, not only in technical ability but also in imagination, fantasy, caprice.

Tocata's able performers on Sunday were violins Henry Hutchinson and Enrique Collazo, viola Francisco Figueroa, cello Mary Ann Campbell, double bass Mik Groninger, soprano Susan Pabón and pianist María del Carmen Gil. May they prosper.

Poles: A Unified Ensemble

The San Juan Star
February 10, 1986 By Donald Thompson

It's not often that you see a full house in the UPR Theater these days of a dispersed university community, especially on a Wednesday evening and especially for anything which strays very far off the popular music circuit. Well, last Wednesday there was close to a full house for a concert by the touring Polish Chamber Orchestra, appearing on the University's own vigorous Cultural Activities series.

The Polish Chamber Orchestra is a unified ensemble of somewhere around twenty stringed instruments plus harpsichord. This is the ideal ensemble for an enormous quantity of music from around the time of Bach and Handel, a smattering of works of the period from Mozart to Wagner, and then a respectable repertory again from the twentieth century, including music by such pillars as Stravinsky, Bartók, Hindemith, Vaughan Williams, and in the New World Carlos Chávez and who knows who all else? In fact, the revival of this type of orchestral ensemble in modern times resulted from a hankering of composers for an orchestral medium of tighter, neater, cleaner sonority than that of the monstrous symphony orchestra of the end of the past century; the resulting "neo-classic" sound indeed provided the frame for a great deal of twentieth-century music, at least up until the explosion of the avant-garde in the 1950s and 1960s.

Wednesday's program emphasized the eighteenth-century repertory almost exclusively, with offerings by Corelli, Vivaldi and Telemann occupying almost the entire evening. Corelli was represented by the Christmas Concerto, Op. 6 No. 8, an admired work cast in the "concerto grosso" format with two violins and a cello as a small solo ensemble played off against the larger string body. Beautifully played, but it's a pity the soloists must remain anonymous for lack of identification in the program. Also offered was the curious Don Quixote Suite of Telemann, a piece of Baroque program music which was designed to evoke some of the images suggested in titles from Cervantes: Quixote's attack on the windmills, the galloping of the Don's horse and of Sancho's mule, and others. I don't know . . . I have never been much of an admirer of program music, whether from the sixteenth, the eighteenth, the nineteenth or the twentieth century, believing that music has its own tasks to perform and that it tends to suffer when it's tied too closely to other modes of imagery. Or, you might say, "If you want a picture, hire a photographer." But this use of music as sound effects has certainly attracted the attention of some of the world's greatest composers, while audiences sometimes seem to believe that this is what ALL music is "about."

Cervantes and the Quixote aside, the Telemann was very nicely played on Wednesday, as was Vivaldi's WHOLE set of four violin concertos collectively known as The Seasons. Yes, friends, Baroque program music again, this time evoking the seasons of the year through the use of such devices as trills and cuckoo calls (birds), tremolos and rapid scales (storm), plaintive violin melody (a shepherd weeps), more scales, now crisscross (lightning), pizzicato (raindrops), more trills (chills), slithery phrases (walking on ice), etc. What's ironic in this particular set of concertos is that they sound just fine even if you don't know the references. Vivaldi was a wildly experimental kind of composer anyway, and many of the odd things which occur in these works also occur in his other works and without programmatic intent, or at least so far as we know today. Wednesday's skilled soloist was Jan Stanienda, concertmaster of the Polish Chamber Orchestra and obviously a fine performer in his own right.

The only more or less modern work on Wednesday's program was a Concerto for String Orchestra by the Polish composer Grazuna Bacewicz, dating from 1948 and sounding like a very able synthesis of European styles of composition of its period and perhaps the previous fifteen years. The Concerto for Orchestra idea reminds one of Bartók, whose great formulation dates from the same general period and which also views the orchestra, orchestra sections and individuals within the orchestra as soloists in turn: again, a neo-classic revival of the concerto grosso scheme. Its application to the string orchestra in the Bacewicz work nicely ties up a number of historical threads in an interesting work. The Polish Chamber Orchestra, directed by Volker Schmidt Gertenbach, played very well on Wednesday. It would be a pleasure to hear them again if they ever again find themselves in this part of the world.

Homage to Pepito

The San Juan Star
February 11, 1986   By Donald Thompson

One of the island's leading musical figures received a highly deserved expression of homage and recognition on Saturday evening. This was José ("Pepito") Figueroa, now in his eighth decade of life, his seventh decade as a violinist and probably well on his way to his two thousandth concert played. For many years, especially since the 1950s, Pepito Figueroa and the late pianist Jesús María Sanromá were the two indispensable focal points of instrumental music making in Puerto Rico. With Sanromá gone this leaves Pepito, and it is difficult to imagine an event involving chamber music or orchestral music here which does not include him at the first violin chair. Service well rendered indeed, and fully worthy of solemn and ceremonial recognition.

Saturday's event took place at the UPR Theater in Río Piedras, and was jointly sponsored by the UPR Cultural Activities office and the Puerto Rico Symphony Orchestra. Quite fitting, this, for Pepito Figueroa has served the present PRSO as concertmaster since the orchestra's creation almost thirty years ago, and he taught at UPR for a while during the same early period. Saturday's concert was not particularly based on violin music, violin playing or music teaching, but it did offer a pleasant opportunity for this kind of friendly observance and a bit of that symbolic speech making which seems highly appropriate for university campuses particularly.

The PRSO was neatly and economically conducted by associate musical director Roselín Pabón, offering works by Bach, Mozart, Tchaikovsky and Glinka. Tchaikovsky and Glinka, represented respectively by the Romeo and Juliet Overture-Fantasy and the Ruslan and Ludmila Overture, are no big surprise at the PRSO, but Bach and Mozart are something else. If memory serves, it had been a while since works by either composer had been programmed by the island orchestra, and it was certainly a pleasure to hear Bach's Third Brandenburg Concerto and Mozart's G Minor Symphony so convincingly played. Well, sure, the performances were marred by the same old violin section faults which seem built in by now: mainly the lazy use of jangling open strings, a practice which can scuttle the most sonorous of Mozart's melodies or derail the sleekest of Bach's scalewise passages. And so easily corrected, too, with a word from up front. . . . But many of the PRSO fiddles do this in all other music, too, so why has the orchestra programming avoided Bach and Mozart, to say nothing of Haydn, during the past few years? Difficult it can be for everybody certainly, but avoiding a certain repertory because it's difficult could soon put the PRSO back on the unrelenting level of Paralyzing Pops, which is where it was for a while. Better to play the real symphonic repertory, but work at solving the orchestra's problems meanwhile. Within its known and by now traditional frame of problems, then, the PRSO played a quite satisfactory concert on Saturday.

A word on the preservation on videotape of such events as Saturday's, nowadays more and more frequently perceived as necessary. For the sake of discussion let's assume that it is desirable to have on tape a record of every open string sounded, every scratch and grimace of each player, and every exalted adjective emitted by each inspired speaker during Saturday's ceremony. The microphones mounted around and above the stage and the three cameras occupying fixed places in the auditorium offended nobody. But the camera operators roving the stage certainly did, providing a constant distraction to the audience and canceling out a great deal of the significance of the event. I can see no need for ever having roving cameras on the stage of an orchestral or theatrical event, but if the UPR TV Division and similar agencies think differently, there is a simple way to make this practice palatable (indeed, probably invisible) to 95% of an average audience. Simply dress the operators in black suits and bow ties (not a white shirt and a red sweater, for Pete's sake), keep them well toward the back of the stage and have them change position only between movements. If they're seen at all they'll be conceptually absorbed into that population of percussionists and other musicians who quite correctly move about the stage during a concert. Otherwise, the concentration—and the regard—of at least a part of any audience and a good portion of any orchestra will be lost, and at least one music reviewer will be infuriated.

Continuum: In Honor of Berg

The San Juan Star
Feb. 13, 1986 By Donald Thompson

Alban Berg (1885-1935) was one of those great musical innovators of the early twentieth century whose formulations created new worlds of sound and new worlds of musical thought. Through Berg's work and that of his colleague Anton Webern and their teacher Arnold Schoenberg, new channels were opened which are still being explored and which still lead away, in a kind of supergalactic explosion, from the modes of musical composition which prevailed before the advent of this Second Viennese School.

Sponsored by the University of Puerto Rico Cultural Activities office, the exemplary chamber ensemble Continuum is offering a pair of concerts this week in honor of Berg's work and thought, at the Julia de Burgos Amphitheater on the Río Piedras campus. Continuum has been in Puerto Rico on a number of other occasions, and always brings something both interesting and significant. The present series, judging from Tuesday's concert and from the announced program of today's event, is another of Continuum's important contributions to the knowledge and enjoyment of modern music in Puerto Rico.

Berg himself was represented by four of the Seven Early Songs, performed by soprano Victoria Villamil and pianist Joel Sachs, as well as Four Pieces for Clarinet, with clarinetist David Krakauer and pianist Sachs. Nothing less than hair-raising was the contrast demonstrated by Berg's settings of the same song text, "Schliesse mir die Augen beide," at two very different stages in his development as a composer: first as a youngster in 1900 and then as a mature member of a musical vanguard a quarter century later. The truth of it is, in 1925, and a quarter century after that, and even another quarter century after that, many people were still writing songs in the same style as the fifteen-year-old Alban Berg in 1900.

Pianist Cheryl Seltzer, flutist Jayn Rosenfeld, violinist Mia Wu and cellist Beverly Lauridsen then took turn about with their Continuum colleagues on Tuesday with a series of works by twentieth-century composers of more recent decades, including Vivian Fine, Leon Kirchner, Mario Davidovsky (himself remembered from a visit to Puerto Rico in the early '70s), Howard Roviks and Conlon Nancarrow.

The music of Conlon Nancarrow cuts completely across anything conceived by any group, school, tendency or clique in this or any other century. Related to jazz and ragtime (but sometimes distantly) Nancarrow's music is conceived for, and laboriously punched into, piano rolls of all things, and in its original form can only be played by a player piano. In this way Nancarrow can attain rhythmic and harmonic combinations which are simply beyond the reach of human performers. To put Nancarrow's music into more or less normal musical notation is a gigantic feat in itself, while to then perform it on a normal piano with normal ten-fingered pianists is still another gigantic task. Continuum's Cheryl Seltzer and Joel Sachs performed this task with skill and grace on Tuesday, again adding greatly to an island audience's understanding of still another aspect of twentieth-century music.

Bravos for APOS

The San Juan Star
February 18, 1986   By Donald Thompson

APOS is the Spanish-language acronym of a vital volunteer force for good in the island's musical life: the Asociación Pro Orquesta Sinfónica, a kind of booster group for the Puerto Rico Symphony Orchestra. APOS organizes a number of activities for the benefit of the orchestra during the year, as well as activities for the benefit of concert goers and music lovers. Among these latter are lectures and chats on matters connected with the orchestra's concert calendar, events which regularly attract sizable audiences of people interested in knowing more about what's going on here in music.

One of the main events in the APOS' own calendar is an annual chamber music concert whose proceeds, augmented by important corporate and individual grants as well, go to a fund which helps to underwrite the continued studies of Puerto Rico Symphony Orchestra members. The scholarships so generated are named after the late Puerto Rican pianist Jesús María Sanromá, and the plan's first three years have benefitted seven young PRSO members in as many different academic and professional programs abroad. In the long run the orchestra itself benefits from this steady and cumulative improvement in its individual members, and that, of course, is the whole point of the exercise.

As a very nice touch, the performers on each year's Sanromá Scholarship concert are players who have themselves been recipients of the grants. Thus each year's concert includes more players and a wider variety of works; in fact it's becoming a pleasant challenge to the players to come up with works composed for the strange combinations which can result from the addition of each year's new harvest of Sanromá Scholarship colleagues.

The Third Annual APOS Sanromá Scholarships Chamber Music Concert took place on Sunday afternoon before a large audience in the auditorium of the Puerto Rico Conservatory of Music. Performers included flutist Rubén López (the pioneer); cellist Mary Ann Campbell, clarinet Kathleen Jones and trumpet Roberto Ramírez from the second year; and Robert Donehew (violin), Francisco Figueroa (viola) and Roberto Rivera (horn), who were awarded grants to study last summer.

What kind of a concert can you put together with that crazy instrumentation? Well, the seven put their heads together and came up with a winning program for a very pleasant afternoon of chamber music. Violin, viola and cello were nicely taken care of by an early Beethoven trio conceived for this uncommon combination, while in somebody's cabinet of unplayed and probably never to be played music appeared a serenade for Flute, Clarinet, Trumpet and Cello by the contemporary Argentine composer Augusto Rattenbach. Every musician accumulates this kind of curiosity because they are curiosities involving one's own instrument, and anyway, you never can tell. . . . This Rattenbach is a pleasant and eclectic suite of five movements framed by wry marches and offering in the middle, as a nod to the Homeland, a clever movement entitled "Milonga," in which that traditional Argentine rhythm is all but stylized right out of existence.

After intermission the only still missing instrument of the Sanromá Seven, the horn, was placed in a Sextet for Violin, Viola, Cello, Clarinet, Horn and Piano by the Hungarian-U.S. composer Ernst von Dohnányi (1877-1960). Completely unknown to all of those polled in Sunday's audience and previously unknown even to the performers themselves, this work turned out to be a very melodious, harmonically complex, technically challenging and completely welcome addition to the known world of chamber music hereabouts. Pianist for the Dohnányi was that always helpful and always superprepared pillar of Puerto Rican pianism, Luz Hutchinson, who like skilled program annotator Ramón Arroyo Carrión has never been a Sanromá Scholar but was just along to help out.

APOS has created a unique place for itself in the island's musical affairs on the highest level, and one of the organization's most important activities is its sponsorship of these Sanromá scholarships and of the annual concert associated with them. In the interest of perpetuating the marvelously unusual programming which resulted this year, I should like to propose that a particular stipulation be incorporated in the implementation of each scholarship granted. According to the Thompson Stipulation, each scholarship winner would be expected to locate and bring back as his contribution to the following year's concert several attractive chamber works involving his instrument in unusual combinations and not heard in Puerto Rico for at least 25 years—preferably, never before. In this way APOS could add still another distinction to its growing catalog, and would also very directly recognize and institutionalize the gleeful and almost obsessive interest in unusual music which was characteristic of Jesús María Sanromá himself.

The Organ at UPR

The San Juan Star
March 3, 1986 By Donald Thompson

After thirty years of bewilderment, I have finally discovered what the cavernous UPR Theater in Río Piedras is good for. It's good for organ recitals! On Wednesday evening, masterful organist Roberto González offered a full program of splendid organ music at the UPR Theater, sponsored by the UPR Cultural Activities office and utilizing the still new Allen instrument whose normal habitat is down in Santurce at the Performing Arts Center.

This particular instrument was once aptly described as an electronic marvel: a cross between the main computer at the Pentagon and the central switching facility on the California Grid. Of course all big organs are complicated, whether of the electronic or of the historical but now disappearing pneumatic variety, and anyone who can control such a monster is easily cast in the role of a superhuman wizard creating sounds to shake the earth. Well, Roberto González didn't shake the earth, but he did cause the UPR Theater to resonate as if it were part of the instrument itself. And that is, indeed, the ideal of organ playing: if the instrument wasn't especially designed for and built into the structure which houses it, the organist must make it seem so.

Wednesday's program included a number of compositions from the first great period of organ music, around and before the time of Bach: works seldom if ever heard in Puerto Rico by Buxtehude, Couperin, Bach himself and other composers. Very nicely played, displaying appropriate stylistic judgment, high technical skill, and (not always observed in organists) excellent digital and pedal marksmanship. The second half of Wednesday's program offered music from the twentieth century, including an interesting and evocative exploration of the instrument's possibilities in the realm of purely sensuous sound by the French composer Louis Vierne (1870-1937). From Tomás Marco of the Spanish avant-garde came a relatively benign piece of space music entitled *Astrolabio*, and the rest of the evening was occupied by a jolly kind of suite for organ and narrator by William Albright, entitled The King of Instruments. The suite's thirteen short movements present as many different aspects of the modern organ's capabilities, from a solo for pedals to the display of the instrument's most brilliant sonorities. The narration, read on Wednesday by island composer Francis Schwartz, introduces each section with a wry comment or two in the style of Ogden Nash: "The flues: blues," for example, or "The clarion needs marryin'; the faggott does not." A section devoted to the gamba ("Have you ever heard a gamba do a red hot Latin samba?") was terminated only by a timely squirt of mosquito spray directed at the organist himself. And so on. The Albright suite is good clean fun and a splendid introduction to the glories of the instrument. In addition, it provided a fine ending to Wednesday's highly successful recital of unusual music. And a bouquet of tulips, gracing the instrument during the second half of Wednesday's recital, didn't do any harm either, as a symbolic recognition of the organ's growing importance today.

♪

Baritone and Pianist in Song Cycle

The San Juan Star
April 29, 1986 By Donald Thompson

    The art song is one of the major species of concert music, and has been cultivated in most parts of the Western world at one time or another with varying degrees of intensity and with varying degrees of skill. To many, the German art song tradition represents the finest flower of this development, but here there is disagreement over the significance of one figure in particular: Franz Schubert, and whether he represented the end of one splendid line of song composers or the beginning of another. There is no disagreement, however, over the importance of Schubert himself as a song composer. His more than 600 songs, composed on poems by Goethe, Schiller and other celebrated German poets, are the main pillar of the song repertory, and the works with which all other song composers' production is inevitably compared.

    An interesting province of the art song is the song cycle, a group of songs by a single composer and deliberately grouping a set of related poems. This is basically a German contribution itself, and among those who cultivated it are found Brahms, Beethoven, Schumann and Schubert. In dimensions, a song cycle is on the order of a symphony or a big sonata, and can even occupy an entire recital program or at least a good portion of one. On Wednesday evening baritone Angelo Cruz and pianist José Daniel Martínez presented one of the big German song cycles, Schubert's great *Die Winterreise*, on the UPR Cultural Activities series. Cruz is still another of the present generation of island singers now established abroad but who from time to time let us see how they're getting along. Cruz is getting along just fine, judging from Wednesday's performance. His voice is rich and resonant with plenty of expressive flexibility, teaming nicely with skilled pianist Martínez in exploring the many realms of musical and poetic symbolism embodied in the Schubert cycle.

A "winter journey," indeed, but a journey of the soul through that bleak and forbidding passage which we all traverse. A journey toward death, replete with those wintry symbols so beloved by the German poets of the past century: icy winds; hail; tears freezing on the cheeks or falling on the snow, futile dreams of spring; loneliness; the rejected wanderer; the cemetery as guest house. It required Wagner's heroic dreams of Teutonic grandeur to finally shake them out of it! But that's another story.

On Wednesday evening Cruz and Martínez brought Schubert's wintry visions alive with skill and concentration, for the edification of an audience in a tropical milieu worlds removed from their original chill setting: the Central Europe of almost 160 years ago.

Play it Again, Mónica!

The San Juan Star
May 9, 1986 By Donald Thompson

The UPR Cultural Activities Series closed out its second semester of activities on Tuesday evening with a brilliant concert of harpsichord music offered by Puerto Rico's resident harpsichordist, Mónica Rivera.

The harpsichord was the expected keyboard instrument for most purposes in the seventeenth and early eighteenth centuries, and became one of the immediate predecessors and close relatives of the upstart pianoforte. It virtually disappeared during Mozart's time due to the greater volume and broader sonoral seductiveness of the piano, but reappeared in the early twentieth century when a few ancient-music freaks began to wonder what the music of Bach and his forgotten contemporaries had really sounded like. Then composers began to take it up, in the spirit of neoclassicism which has guided much of the new music from the twenties on down. And finally, the bright sound of the harpsichord was found useful in the composition of jingles for commercial advertising, and soon became incorporated in the formidable sonoral array of the modern electronic keyboard. The harpsichord sound (or rather an electronic approximation thereof) is no longer much of a surprise, but an evening of real music performed on a real harpsichord by a real harpsichordist certainly is, and Tuesday's audience received a treat indeed.

Any capable pianist can do a fair to middling job in the workaday world of harpsichord playing, involving such tasks as providing the harmonic filler in Baroque orchestra music. But the instruments are really very different, and it takes a specialist to make the harpsichord really sing. Mónica Rivera does this. The product of studies at the University of Puerto Rico and the Vienna Music Academy, she has mastered the subtleties of the harpsichord and uses its own peculiarities to bring to life the music which was written for it. The result on Tuesday was a triumphant confirmation of the view of some crusty hardnosed purists, myself included, that music usually sounds best when played on the instrument for which it was conceived! Generally speaking, just play piano music on the piano, organ music on the organ, guitar music on the guitar and harpsichord music on the harpsichord, and we'll all be happy.

Tuesday's recital offered music by Bach, Handel, Scarlatti, Vincent Persichetti and Gyorgy Ligeti. Harpsichord music has a lot of notes, mainly because no note produced on the harpsichord is going to hang in the air very long, and another one must soon take its place. Extremely interesting is the way such leading contemporary composers as Persichetti (b. 1915) and Ligeti (b. 1923) have applied this ancient principle to their own definitely contemporary vision of musical construction. The result is a fascinating fusion of the old and the new, and was a revelation to Tuesday's audience.

Mónica Rivera is a fine performer on a noble instrument, and it would be a great pleasure to hear more from her; maybe a recital every two weeks would not be too much to ask?

The Fauré Requiem

The San Juan Star
May 17, 1986   By Donald Thompson

The Requiem Mass of Gabriel Fauré is certainly not one of the world's most awesome examples of that musical form; think of the Brahms and the Berlioz, (even Mozart), to say nothing of the thunderous whack of that bass drum of Verdi's. THAT is awesome! But the Fauré has its great and subtle virtues; the trouble is that it takes a really fine chorus to bring them out. Such a chorus is the University of Puerto Rico Chorus just now, under the skilled direction of Carmen Acevedo. This ensemble offered its annual spring concert on Wednesday evening in the UPR Theater in Río Piedras, beginning rather courageously with the Fauré work and then leading into more familiar styles.

The virtues of the Fauré are to be found on the contemplative side rather than the apocalyptic, and they find expression in finely detailed melodic phrasing, subtle harmonic movement and carefully plotted dynamic contrast. For this reason its successful realization requires a perfectly trained chorus and intelligent direction; anything less and you simply have a dull piece. Wednesday's performance was at no moment dull; in fact it was highly moving in both a musical and a spiritual sense due to the application of choral skill and directorial intelligence. The performance of the Fauré Requiem was greatly aided by the presence of soloists Zoraida López (soprano) and Angelo Cruz (baritone) in sections conceived for solo voice, and of organist José Daniel Flores throughout.

The more I listen to choruses the more convinced I am that the key to choral success is correct breathing, for without enough breath (and uniform breathing) there can be no uniform phrasing, no correct pitch and no security at all. Lately, the performances of the UPR Chorus have seemingly transcended all of these worries, for the music simply rolls out in completely natural fashion. Such were my thoughts during the Fauré work and in fact throughout most of Wednesday's concert.

Also offered on Wednesday was Jack Délano's witty evocation of island rhythms and melodic turns in his choral suite *Me Voy a Ponce*. Not one of Délano's major works, this is a very nice one nonetheless, and deserves hearing. On Wednesday its presentation was preceded by the placement of clever road signs and by a tape of highway noises, as costume changes and other major adjustments took place backstage.

Besides singing well, the UPR Chorus plans its staging very nicely. Stage effects were also cleverly used during the last part of Wednesday's concert, devoted to lighter music. This was offered as a reminder of the group's recent trip to Venezuela in the continuing revival of an ancient tradition of tours abroad in representation of the institution and of Puerto Rico. Can you think of any better way to represent Puerto Rico than to send this fine university ensemble around and about?

A Memorable Guitar Recital

The San Juan Star
July 2, 1986 By Donald Thompson

Well, sir, your everyday garden variety solo guitar recital is quite likely to begin with music of Luis de Narváez or one of his contemporaries in the great flowering of Spanish music of the sixteenth century, move on down to a transcription or two of music by J.S. Bach or Domenico Scarlatti, have a crack at something by Fernando Sor or Francisco Tórrega, and end with some pieces by Villa-Lobos, these last offered as a nod to the music of the twentieth century.

Island guitarist Ana María Rosado tends to take up where her colleagues leave off. On Sunday afternoon and before a large audience in the theater of the Conservatory of Music in Hato Rey, this gifted performer offered a rarity hereabouts: an entire program of twentieth-century guitar music. Sunday's recital was sponsored, logically enough, by the irrepressible Latin American Foundation for Contemporary Music, an island-based agency which has racked up far more than anyone's statistical quota of unusual and significant musical events over the years.

Villa-Lobos was present, certainly, in his *Estudio No. 1* and his *Preludio No. 1*, the latter, at least, a seemingly required offering on every guitar recital nowadays. But the rest of Sunday's music was much less familiar—a blessing in a land where guitar recitals are almost as frequent and as ritualized as traffic jams. Several threads and tendencies of twentieth-century music were represented and, in this context, the conservative wing held its own. A cradle song of Leo Brouwer (Cuba), a *Chôros de Saudade* by Agustín Barrios (Paraguay), the lyrical *Norteña* by Jorge Gómez Crespo (Argentina) and a sweetly contrapuntal *Créole et Lontaine* by Edmundo Vásquez of Chile: all demonstrated the continuity of the art music of the present century with that of earlier periods and with simpler modes of expression, and all displayed the lyric potentialities of the guitar in the hands of such a versatile performer as Ana María Rosado.

But the modern stuff—where's the modern stuff? This was represented too on Sunday, and very well represented at that. For example, it's hard to beat the music of Roque Cordero for honest, craftsmanlike, interesting music in the modern idiom, and one of Cordero's most recent works was conceived, in fact, with Ana María Rosado and other specific guitarists in mind. This is his *Cinco Mensajes para Cuatro Amigos*, which was given its world premiere performance here a couple of years ago by Rosado and again offered on Sunday's recital. Atonal, rhythmic and vigorous, the *Cinco Mensajes* is a welcome addition to the modern repertory of extended guitar works, and was securely and expressively played on Sunday.

It's difficult to imagine a concert of contemporary music in Puerto Rico which does not include something by Francis Schwartz, who for some fifteen years or more has been one of the island's main movers in this previously neglected field. And so it was on Sunday, with the presentation of one of Schwartz's most attractive new short works. Entitled We've Got (Poly)rhythm, the piece is a kind of homage to George Gershwin, calling upon a number of unorthodox guitar techniques along the way as well as other Schwartzian curiosities. Schwartz has steadily gained security and confidence with his catalog of compositional oddments during recent years, and by now can pretty well calculate the tolerances, durations, intensities and expectations of the concert situation, coming up with satisfying results more often than not.

We've Got (Poly)rhythm explores, more than any earlier *Schwartzwerk*, strange realms of vocal sounds and facial expressions, to be executed by the performer. It is for this reason that the piece could in no way be performed by a clarinetist or a trombonist: the performer must constantly be grimacing, sighing, or otherwise using the facial musculature while making the instrument sound. Try that on your kazoo! Among other features, We've Got (Poly)rhythm calls for the vocal imitation of the jazz drummer's hi-hat cymbal played by brushes, for footstomps, finger snaps, an evocative text ("pocketapocketa," mainly), a bit of audience participation (unnecessary, I think), and some remote but accurate reminiscences of the compositional style of George Gershwin. I think that of all the performers and ensembles who have been called upon to deal with the music of Schwartz, Rosado comes closest to bringing it to life for a general audience; at least she certainly did so with this recent work on Sunday.

And by golly, Sunday's concert, consistent with the spirit of the Latin American Foundation for Contemporary Music, offered the world premiere of a new work: *Paisanos Semos* by the Cuban born composer-conductor Tania León. Ms. León is very active in New York City just now, and is remembered in Puerto Rico from a number of very successful appearances here as a conductor mainly, but not exclusively, of contemporary music. She is a valuable resource, and her new work for solo guitar is evidence of a high degree of talent and dedication. According to the composer herself, *Paisanos Semos* is emotionally connected to her interest in the eternal processes of creation and renewal (seeding, birth and death) which unite us all. As expressed in guitar music, these concepts take form in an attractive suite of three brief connected sections. On Sunday, *Paisanos Semos* was played twice, the second time after a brief description of the work and its associations, offered by the composer herself. And speaking of valuable resources, Rosado is herself a most valuable resource, especially in the context of the general conservatism of guitar performance which prevails in Puerto Rico today. Academic and technical preparation, musical curiosity and a scholar's dedication combine to make of such events as Sunday's, memorable occasions in island musical life.

The Good, the Bad and the Thoughtful

The San Juan Star
September 16, 1986 By Donald Thompson

One of the welcome innovations of the present Puerto Rico Symphony Orchestra season is a set of concerts offered at the University of Puerto Rico Río Piedras Campus as a joint undertaking with the UPR Cultural Activities office. The idea is not an entirely new one; if memory serves, something like the same arrangement was made maybe a decade or so ago. However, unlike the previous effort, whose concert programming ranged from the tedious to the soporific, the present one obviously represents the result of a great deal of thought. Much of this thought originated with Odón Alonso, the PRSO's new musical director and one of the very few of the orchestra's titular conductors over the years whose thinking has risen much above the level of getting enough rehearsal time, grinding down the players and throwing the audience a nice profile from time to time.

Alonso is himself a university person, and his vision of the university as a community of people capable of thought, while not common nowadays, is refreshingly positive. In basic terms, this kind of vision asks why we must keep teaching young adults things which they should already know, with a concomitant belief that if they don't already know it, maybe they should be encouraged to pick it up someplace else.

Applied to musical programming, this means an end to the Nutcracker Suite as regular fare on university concert series, and the presentation of some meatier and less hackneyed fare from time to time. If the PRSO series at the UPR makes some people think a little, all the better. That's what the people are there for, we like to believe.

Well, now; after all that I must point out that there was a bit of standard repertory on Saturday evening's concert too: the warhorse *Les*

Préludes of Franz Liszt, which threatens nobody and with which everyone can be comfortable. This too is good programming, for it teaches people that there will be a bit of variance between what they've learned from some beloved recording and what they'll find in real musical life anywhere in the world: tempos slightly different, orchestral balance which may bring into prominence instruments which are barely heard on the recording; who knows, maybe even a wrong note or two. This is also characteristic of real life, but certainly not of the high-tech electronified computerized fantasy product which you buy in a record store. In these terms, *Les Préludes* sounded fine on Saturday (wrong notes and all), except for some details to be mentioned below which were not the fault of the PRSO or its management.

What Saturday's concert was really about was a pair of Spanish works of the twentieth century, both of which resonate with university associations. First was *Para un Códice Salmantina* by Joaquín Rodrigo on a text by Miguel de Unamuno. The Unamuno text is a brief ode to the University of Salamanca, where the distinguished author served as teacher and rector during the opening years of the century. Of uncertain literary merit, the Unamuno text nevertheless serves as an attractive evocation of some dimly remembered virtues of university life, among them "the maturation of the harvest of tranquil thought." How does that idea grab you in 1986?

Joaquín Rodrigo (b. 1901), the medievalizing composer of the Salamanca music, has his own connection with universities, among them the University of Puerto Rico, where he served as visiting professor during the birth of the UPR Music Department some decades ago. Small world, isn't it? Saturday's other Spanish work was a setting by Casablanca-born Maurice Ohana (b. 1914) of what is considered one of Federico García Lorca's most significant poems. This is a grim elegy entitled *Llanto por Ignacio Sánchez Mejías*, inspired by the death by goring of the bullfighter, Lorca's friend, in 1934. Ohana's setting dates from 1950, and starkly, almost brutally, underlines the emotion of the Lorca poem. The university connection? Lorca's early studies at the University of Granada and his later immersion in the cultural life of the University of Madrid, itself the center of Spain's intellectual and literary activity in the early 1920s. Too, this year marks the fiftieth anniversary of Lorca's death, an occasion worthy of note in universities worldwide.

Baritone Angelo Cruz and the University of Puerto Rico Chorus

(Carmen Acevedo, director) participated nobly and clearly in the realization of the Unamuno-Rodrigo Salamanca music, while the bleak *Llanto* of Lorca-Ohana again called upon baritone Cruz, along with a secure unison choir of women's voices from the UPR Chorus and narrator Pedro Zervigón.

All of the above can be taken as the good news of Saturday's concert. Now for the bad news. The UPR Theater is a noisy sort of place to begin with, starting with seats which creak and groan at every opportunity. Hard walls and harder floor faithfully amplify these noises, as well as every snuffle, sneeze and cough from the audience. At this late date there's probably little that can be done about these built-in hazards short of still another remodeling job. But the major fault of the place is the apparent impossibility of keeping the doors closed between the hall and the lobby after a concert has begun. Consequently, the pregnant opening bars of the Liszt work (the part which tells you what the work is about, in fact) were inaudible on Saturday, as latecomers sought seats, coughed, muttered, rattled their programs and greeted friends throughout the hall. At one time this traffic in the UPR Theater was handled better as a matter of routine, with the inner lobby becoming a sort of holding tank for latecomers, allowing the first work on the program to play in conditions approaching Unamuno's "maturation of the harvest of tranquil thought."

Secondly, if Saturday's concert was blessed and ennobled by rich university associations, it was cursed and blighted by a handout of program notes the likes of which would earn an F in a high school music appreciation course anywhere in the civilized world. Marked by ridiculous spelling errors, extremely superficial and questionable information and an inane and breathless style, this production has no place within miles of a university campus or a symphony orchestra concert. I hasten to add that the notes were not a product of the PRSO management but of the other partner in the concert's sponsorship. Let the literary axe fall where it will, although it might not fall at all. Perhaps there's too much "tranquil" and not enough "thought" in Río Piedras these days, at least in the office where those abominable notes were hatched.

Three Premieres

The San Juan Star
October 10, 1986   By Donald Thompson

As part of the Inter American Arts Festival now in progress, the National Association of Composers (that is, national of Puerto Rico) offered a varied program of new music on Thursday evening at the Performing Arts Center in Santurce. A full house in the Experimental Theater greeted three premiere performances and two near-premieres, presented by a wind quintet (Aulos), a pianist (Teresa Acevedo), a soprano (Tamara Escribano) and a bass (Noel Allende).

Amaury Veray's A *Portrait of Juliet*, one of Thursday's premieres, is a setting for soprano and piano of five Shakespeare texts in a style which according to the program notes should in a general way remind one of Renaissance music. It did not remind me of Renaissance music in the least, or of any other specific music for that matter, but it did seem to me a nicely rhythmic polytonal and almost-tonal accompaniment to Veray's arched vocal phrases. One of the five Shakespeare texts is not sung but recited, which I think is a mistake. This device requires an abrupt change in both the singer's technique of vocal production and the audience's mode of perception, and is received as an intrusion in what has until then been an ongoing musical process. Thursday's performance also brought other problems into play. For example, Tamara Escribano has often been admired for her clear and correct pronunciation of sung texts in any language with which she deals. But as any singer knows, singing is very different from speech, and what works nicely in the former cannot necessarily be expected to work in the latter. Shakespeare's recited English suffered on Thursday, but not only for this reason do I believe that the composer should consider setting that fourth text in song also.

José Montalvo offered a premiere performance of a new Study for Wind Quintet, ably performed by the resident Aulos group. This Study is an interesting exercise in dissolving unisons and vanishing themes, designed to explore the sonoral combinations possible among a handful of instruments within a kaleidoscopically changing rhythmic frame. Like the Veray songs, this work sometimes seemed ready to acknowledge an old fashioned tonal center—which it finally did, but only in the very last chord of the piece. This may be a stylistic blunder; the ending is so different from the expectation generated by the restless flow of the remainder of the suite that it shocks by its very blandness-but that is perhaps the desired reaction. On the other hand, another reaction was expressed by a music lover seated near me: "Well, he finally found his chord!"

Another premiere was *Apariencias*, a three-movement suite for wind quintet by Alfonso Fuentes, cleverly expanded to incorporate the related resources of piccolo, English horn and bass clarinet, without increasing the number of players. This device brings into play a whole set of new sonoral dimensions and instrumental contrasts. Piccolo and bass clarinet make an especially effective combination, as do flute and English horn within the context of an otherwise traditional quintet instrumentation. Of the youngest island composers active today, Fuentes may possess the highest level of skill in the art of instrumentation, as well as the ability, uncommon nowadays, to generate extended musical statements. Perhaps this ability is basically the tenacity required to start a musical idea and then keep it rolling for a while instead of losing courage and grasping at something else. In any case, the Fuentes work made a good impression on Thursday.

The rest of Thursday's concert was occupied by new music by old timers, not to say pioneers, in the island's musical revelations of the past forty years or so. Jack Délano was represented by two songs for voice and piano on poems by Luis Muñoz Marín, here performed by bass Noel Allende and pianist Teresa Acevedo. The Muñoz texts are strong indeed, dating from a time when the young author was more a rebellious poet than anything else, finding his way toward what would eventually become a world view and then a political platform. Délano's attempt at a monumental style in these songs, entitled "Escúchanos" and "Panfleto," is very different from most of his previous work, where a light touch prevails. He is a master at that light touch, and has provided a great deal of extremely attractive music for the Puerto Rican repertory. But despite their literary and symbolic significance, the Muñoz songs are not among Délano's most successful works, seeming at times pretentious rather than poetically or musically meaningful.

Thursday's final premiere offered five sixths of a new work by Héctor Campos-Parsi for voice and wind quintet entitled *Sonetos Sagrados* and based on old Spanish poems of religious devotion. This was by far the most extended work on the program and I think the most successful, all considered. I believe that Campos in his mature wisdom has decided to steer clear of today's musical fads and fashions (even if it were possible to find out what they are) and simply write some music. Campos knows and respects the human voice, and his songs are in fact among his most engaging works. Here, he skillfully combines the voice with wind ensemble, and the result is a gracious if by no means easy addition to his extensive and varied catalogue of compositions. I look forward to hearing the completed work, especially if it is again sung by that fine performer Tamara Escribano.

A New Ensemble Emerges

The San Juan Star
October 15, 1986   By Donald Thompson

It has often been noted that among other priceless benefits, the presence of a symphony orchestra with a long season tends to generate spinoffs in the form of stable chamber music ensembles and ad hoc chamber music events. This enables players to regain some of the sense of individuality which they sacrifice in orchestra work and also to exercise a somewhat different order of skills from those which are drawn upon by most orchestra playing. The Puerto Rico Symphony Orchestra has begotten three stable chamber ensembles during the past decade, and last week a fourth orchestra-based group made its appearance on the island's musical scene with a concert sponsored by the Inter American Arts Festival. The new ensemble is called Solistas de Puerto Rico, and percussionist José Alicea is its musical director.

Solistas de Puerto Rico, in its inaugural appearance in the Drama Hall of the Performing Arts Center, presented a dozen players, mainly members of the PRSO, in various combinations and in an extremely varied program of twentieth-century music. First up was a set of witty variations for piano on the "surprise" theme which forms the basis of the second movement of Haydn's Symphony No. 94. The present set, composed and here played by pianist Víctor Meléndez, displayed a great deal of subtle humor in the way of parody: parody of the styles of Chopin, Liszt, Brahms, Beethoven, Debussy, Albéniz and other identifiable composers, in settings which were not all easy, by any means. This would be a fine piece, I think, as a cheerful encore on any pianist's recital program.

Akira Yumaha's Divertimento for Alto Saxophone and Marimba is a strange piece, dating from 1968, which on Friday brought soloists Robert Handschuh and José Alicea to the stage. A strange piece because the two parts don't really seem to connect very often, although each is in itself quite interesting. In a general way the harmonic style of the work is reminiscent of "big city" movie music of the '50s, while its design is that of a generalized rondo with alternating vigorous and lyric sections.

From among the innumerable follies, fancies and bagatelles composed by Darius Milhaud (1892-1974), the trio of Harry Rosario (oboe), Jorge Morales (clarinet) and Roberto López (bassoon) offered a sweet suite of eight very brief neoclassic pieces "after Correte" and incorporating the designs of the eighteenth-century dance suite. A bit of froth, like much of Milhaud's music, but well worth an occasional hearing.

"Concert jazz" also made its appearance on Friday, in the form of three movements from Claude Bolling's gentle Suite for Flute and Jazz Piano, well known here from the regular use of several of its sections as filler music by island radio stations. Performing were Rubén López (flute), Víctor Meléndez (piano), Federico Silva (bass) and Tony Sánchez (drums). This kind of jazz (if that's what it is) certainly won't shock anyone but it can be a painless introduction, for those who may need it, to both concert life and to the styles of marginally commercial pop music of a few decades ago.

Ah, but the prize of the concert, and indeed perhaps the very reason for the existence of such groups as Solistas de Puerto Rico, occupied the entire second half of Friday's event. This was Stravinsky's suite from his miniature stage work *The Soldier's Tale*, which was first performed in 1918 and which launched an entire line of twentieth-century composition among several generations of admirers. The work is tightly condensed in both style and means, requiring only seven players who nonetheless work overtime in skill and concentration. The Stravinsky work has been presented here a number of times within memory, both with and without the recitation and mime which are rightly part of it. I do not think that it has been played any better here, though; especially memorable from Friday's performance was the extraordinary playing of violinist Cheryl Trace, who attained just the right degree of languid meanness to evoke Stravinsky's diabolical fiddler. Especially notable in this regard was her playing of the fiendish "Tango, Waltz and Ragtime" section. Harry Rosario conducted the Stravinsky work, with a clean and precise gesture which provided exactly what was necessary that the ensemble might bring the challenging work to life.

More Surprises in Music Biennial

The San Juan Star
November 11, 1986   By Donald Thompson

The Latin American Foundation for Contemporary music is one of Puerto Rico's most pertinacious musical entities, having survived a decade and more of successful activities without a great deal of support (indeed, almost none) from the island's musical Establishment. One of the Foundation's principal activities is the organization every two years of a San Juan Biennial of Twentieth Century Music, which regularly unfolds for island audiences the glories and near-glories of almost a century now of advanced music.

The 1986 Biennial is currently in progress, with a series of concerts and seminars at different points in the San Juan metropolitan area. On Sunday afternoon a fair-sized audience of the musically aware and the intelligently curious attended a piano recital by Evelyne Crochet at the Puerto Rico Conservatory of Music, offered as part of this Fifth Biennial of Twentieth Century Music.

Evelyne Crochet is a formidable pianist, who has in her fingers not only the technique needed for the realization of the music of recognized masters (Ravel, Stravinsky, Falla) but also the stylistic flexibility required by the new and still unfamiliar music of more recent composers. Sunday's recital, consistent with the goals and purposes of the Biennials of Twentieth Century Music, offered a bit of both.

The music of Ravel and Manuel de Falla offers few surprises, except now and again in a specific presentation: such was the case on Sunday, when Ms. Crochet made an indelible impression through the sheer brilliance and force of her playing of Ravel's *Gaspard de Nuit* and Falla's *Fantasía Bética*. This is repertory stuff, but neither work is often presented anywhere with the authority, accuracy, contrast and polish of

Ms. Crochet's performance on Sunday. Igor Stravinky's Tango is a bit of fluff dating from the time of the great composer's flirtation with the popular music of the New World: 1939-45, when he was assuming his third nationality and also his third (or was it the fourth?) change of musical style. His Tango is not completely successful as a stylization in concert music of popular styles, but it does indicate an essential point of similarity among at least three modes of popular expression with which many islanders are familiar today: the Argentine tango itself; ragtime, as exemplified in the recently celebrated music of Scott Joplin; and . . . the Puerto Rican *danza*! The similarity lies in the incorporation in the three species of a particular type of rhythm, present in an impressive range of popular music styles of the Americas, most of which have developed more or less independently of the others. What was the common root? Try West Africa.

Other surprises on Sunday's concert came in the form of works by Toru Takemitsu (Japan, b. 1930), Heinz Holliger (Switzerland, b. 1939), and Jarg Wyttenbach (Switzerland, b. 1935). A quarter century has now passed since the first self-conscious fanfares of the musical avant-garde of the sixties, one of whose tenets was the espousal of a "minimalist" kind of music reminiscent of the cerebrations of Webern a half century before. The works by Takemitsu, Holliger and Wyttenbach offered on Sunday are all from the sixties and all are of the angular minimalist style cultivated at that time, but displaying important differences, too. Undisturbed Rest by Takemitsu (1962) makes extremely clever and extremely precise use of an often underestimated resource of the piano, the sustaining pedal; *Elis* by Holliger (1961) and Three Pieces for Piano by Wyttenbach (1969) explore such resources as strumming, plucking or striking the piano strings directly. These devices were as expected in the piano music of the sixties as garlic in a Dracula movie, but they were not always handled as neatly as in these works. The second of the Wyttenbach pieces also makes important structural use of the piano's sustaining pedal as a device in causing the controlled production of overtones or harmonics. This acoustical phenomenon results from the generation of secondary and clearly audible frequencies in a sounding string. Heavy acoustics, perhaps, but the device has been recognized for a couple of centuries although its use has seldom been so carefully plotted as in the Wyttenbach music.

First of the Super-Pops

The San Juan Star
November 15, 1986 By Donald Thompson

Your very own Puerto Rico Symphony Orchestra is offering a surprising variety of activities this season. These include the orchestra's regular subscription series and a February Grand Gala at the Performing Arts Center plus several sets of activities scheduled at the UPR campus in Río Piedras. These last range from a well attended series co-sponsored by the UPR Cultural Activities office to a group of special concerts and even a pair of "Super-Pops" events. The first of the Super-Pops concerts took place on Saturday evening, drawing a big audience of the young and the not so young to the venerable hall for an extremely attractive program directed by Odón Alonso.

Alonso is now in his first promising season as the PRSO's music director, and Saturday's concert can be taken as a sign of the diversified programming and broadening appeal of the island orchestra as it enters its second quarter-century of activities.

Featured on Saturday was the Billy Taylor Jazz Trio, consisting of Taylor himself (piano), Victor Gaskin (bass) and Curtis Boyd (drums). Aside from his creative accomplishments in the world of jazz, reaching back in an unbroken line to the 1940s, William (Billy) Taylor is a leading figure in jazz education, with an earned doctorate, a long string of academic honors, and numerous publications to his credit. Taylor's own playing and that of his groups is always clean, precise and imaginative. It never fails to revive the spirits of jazz enthusiasts, who usually feel oppressed by the brainless commercial rock-disco-pop-shlock which has contaminated the atmosphere and corrupted the musical sensibilities of the citizenry for a couple of decades now. In addition, Taylor's presentations can usually be counted on to attract at least a few converts to the true cause from a populace which is too young to remember the days when jazz was a widely known and widely experienced musical phenomenon instead of the museum art which it has mainly become today.

The trio's appearance was in the way of something resembling the concertino, or solo ensemble, playing against a larger orchestra in an eighteenth-century concerto grosso. This attractive idea appealed not only to Vivaldi and his contemporaries but also to a long line of composers reaching down to the present. And why not a jazz concerto grosso? Featured on Saturday were two of Taylor's own compositions, a two-movement Impromptu and a more ambitious Jazz Suite for Piano and Orchestra, the latter work dedicated to the memory of pianist Art Tatum. In both works, and true to the concerto grosso idea, sections played exclusively by the trio or lightly accompanied were introduced and framed by orchestral passages. The trio playing was completely convincing and was even certainly improvised in great measure in the best jazz tradition, although I couldn't help wondering how many times the Billy Taylor Jazz Trio had played these particular works and reflecting on how easily one's fingers follow well established patterns which have been found to work nicely before. The orchestral writing was usually imaginative and subtle, except in the big climaxes which reminded me of nothing so much as the pretentious closing music for many movies of the fifties and early sixties. I think that on balance the Taylor jazz concertos are successful, but I have no doubt at all that their successful realization requires the participation of the Billy Taylor Jazz Trio itself.

Also on Saturday's concert were a suite from the ballet *Estancia* by Alberto Ginastera, George Gershwin's Cuban Overture and Silvestre Revueltas'striking *Sensemayá*. These important brief works of Latin American music (well, "fruity hat" Latin American, in the Gershwin case) were very nicely and very vigorously played by the PRSO with only a few rhythmic stumbles in the Revueltas work, which for reasons connected to its notation is a beast. Maestro Alonso conducted the jazzy Billy Taylor music with the same aplomb and poise that he applied to the familiar Gershwin, Ginastera and Revueltas works or that he would to a Schubert symphony. This again illustrates the great truth that it's all music; when you get right down to it, it all comes from the same bag. Except, of course, for that brainless commercial rock-disco-pop-shlock . . . (see above, and repeat ad libitum).

♪

Canadians Bring a Mixed Bag of Music

The San Juan Star
January 20, 1987   By Donald Thompson

At midseason in its annual cycle of offerings, San Juan's Pro Arte Musical Society has continued its encouraging policy of reaching beyond the world of star singers and piano soloists to bring to Puerto Rico a wider variety of attractions. This is a very healthy policy indeed for any agency, public or private, which sees itself as an instrument of public cultural edification. Let's hear it for the New Pro Arte!

Friday's event was a concert by the very able Canadian Chamber Ensemble, a group based around Kitchener (Ontario), where the players are also active in the region's resident orchestra and other musical enterprises. The concert was conducted by Raffi Armenian, the regular conductor for the Kitchener-Waterloo Orchestra itself, and featured works by Kuleska and Haydn (very successful) and by Bach, Debussy, Johann Strauss II and Stravinsky (all unsuccessful to one degree or another).

Gary Kuleska's Chamber Concerto, opening Friday's concert, is a recent piece for winds and percussion which nicely illustrates the workings of musical neoclassicism within a convincing contemporary musical language. The titles of Kuleska's three movements tell the story: "Prelude," "Passacaglia" and "Rondo." These are ancient bottles indeed, into which the composer has poured the new wine of his own time as Hindemith, Bartók, Stravinsky, and countless others have done since the beginning of the present century. The combination of centuries-old designs and modern harmonic procedures always fascinates—if it's done well. And Kuleska's brief orchestral concerto is very well done. It was also well played on Friday by the skilled Canadian players.

A Cassation in F Major by Joseph Haydn was next up on Friday, requiring an ensemble of violin, viola, cello, double bass, oboe, bassoon and two horns. What is a cassation and how does one cassate, anyway? Nobody knows anymore, for the title "Cassation" was apparently used very freely during Haydn's time for almost any loosely hung together suite of bright and melodious movements designed as "useful music": informal music, background music; yes, "wallpaper music," you might say: music designed to be played but not really heard during aristocratic receptions, fashionable garden parties and other such non-events. Logistically the "cassation" seems to occupy a middle ground between orchestra music and chamber music, and can be convincingly played either way, depending on how many string players you want to hire for the job. Friday's reduced forces sounded just right in this cheerful suite of five movements, despite some questionable pitch in the violin. Oh, that we might have such charming background music as this Haydn "cassation" for today's garden parties, receptions and department store openings! What do we get instead? Plastic Disco.

Reduced strings seemed successful enough in the Haydn, but not so successful in J.S. Bach's A Minor Violin Concerto, in which violinist Victor Danchenko played the solo part. Why not? I think that aside from the fact that we're simply accustomed to hearing more sound from the orchestral strings in this and similar works, a fuller string sound in the orchestra gives the soloist something to "play against," which is after all what a solo concerto is for. Without this contrast, the solo part itself loses character and tends to disappear in the general smoosh of an unbalanced sextet. In addition, a bigger string body gives a conductor something to do. In the context of Friday's performance of the Bach concerto, conductor Armenian's work was simply superfluous.

What was wrong, then, with the Debussy, Strauss and Stravinsky? Different things. With Debussy's luxuriant Prelude to the Afternoon of a Faun and Strauss' regal Emperor Waltz it was a matter of ridiculous arrangements, obviously designed to reduce these orchestral masterpieces to the dimensions of this particular ensemble for use on the road. Can you imagine that juicy symphonic work of Debussy played by squeaky solo strings, thin and noodling winds and NO HARPS AT ALL? Or that noble Strauss introduction without horns? Shameful! The impression was of an informal family musicale on a dusty Sunday afternoon, with everyone playing whatever instrument might be at hand while Uncle Clyde bangs out the missing parts on the parlor upright. This is in fact a very pleasant kind of musical game, but it's frankly not the sort of thing that one does in public. What about The Soldier's Tale of Stravinsky? Well, at least the master's instrumentation was respected (and the piece was really rather well played), but what Friday's audience got was a truncated 60% or 70% of what Stravinsky wrote, and with a hokey ending which I'll bet a dollar Stravinsky neither wrote nor endorsed.

Where does the blame lie for such artistic blunders? About 98% of its lies with the artistic management of the Canadian Chamber Ensemble itself, which clearly has no qualms about carving up the very flesh of musical artworks. What occurred on Friday is roughly equivalent to the management of an art museum displaying pale photo reproductions of Goyas and Picassos as the real thing, or sawing off the arm of a statue so that it might fit some assigned space in the gallery. This practice would not be tolerated in art, literature, theater or architecture; why then, is it calmly accepted in music? A vast repertory of splendid music exists, composed originally for the very combinations which were seen on Friday evening at the Performing Arts Center. There is absolutely no need for anyone to resort to shabby arrangements and reductions of symphonic music for such occasions. Too, some of Friday's problems may have been due to a breakdown in communication between the tour management and the local sponsorship. Somebody in Pro Arte would certainly have asked about the group's tour instrumentation, and what exactly it planned to play with those forces. At the same time, it could have been made clear that The Soldier's Tale of Stravinsky is very well known here from perhaps four (complete) performances during the past few years; maybe an alternative work could have been programmed instead.

All of this having been said for the record and while also lamenting that some fine solo players must remain anonymous and herein unpraised due to the lack of a list of members of the Canadian Chamber Ensemble, I do wish to congratulate the Pro Arte organization for its vision in programming a wide variety of attractions lately. The fine tuning of some artistic details may now be in order.

Tocata: A Sunday Treat

The San Juan Star
February 3, 1987 By Donald Thompson

    A music lover observed on Sunday that it is a great treat to be able to spend an afternoon listening to chamber music live and well played, right here in Puerto Rico. I can only agree, although it takes one out of the usual Sunday rut of the beach or tennis—or perhaps precisely because it takes one out of the usual Sunday rut.
    The operative expression, of course, is "well played," and well played it was on Sunday by San Juan's own Tocata ensemble at the Puerto Rico Conservatory of Music theater. Tocata, made up of some of Puerto Rico's most talented and active instrumentalists, has in a few short years become one of the island's most steadfast and reliable musical institutions. This has not come about by accident, of course, but through the careful selection of regular members and guest artists, the wise choice of repertory, and plenty of hard and continuous rehearsal. As a result, concert-goers can be sure of an authoritative, pleasing and well balanced concert every time Tocata takes the stage.
    On Sunday, Tocata offered a worthy sample of the music that exists for ensembles of solo stringed instruments, both with and without piano. First came a Prelude and Fugue in D Minor for violin, viola and cello by J.S. Bach and W.A. Mozart, representing not some crazy musical time warp but a prelude by Mozart followed by his own transcription of a fugue from Bach's Well Tempered Clavier, transposed from the unholy key of D Sharp Minor and the parts simple copied out for the stringed instruments instead of keyboard. Although such arranging is frowned upon by purists in today's environment of hopeful stylistic authenticity, it was freely practiced in earlier times. Mozart himself was responsible for one of the known and regularly performed "improved versions" of

Handel's *Messiah*. It is difficult, though, to knock Mozart; his prelude was revealed on Sunday as a typical example of his late harmonic style perfectly conceived for the three instruments. The Bach fugue in transcription? Well, any sophomore music student could have done the transcribing job as well and in fact it would have sounded the same: after all, this was Bach speaking, not Mozart, but Bach in an unaccustomed setting and one which he himself would not have employed. Tocata also offered quartets for piano and strings by Mozart and Brahms, a specific pair of works that in fact lie at the very center of the world of chamber music. The Mozart was the G Minor Quartet for violin, viola, cello and piano, the first of his two essays in this form, while the Brahms was the great C Minor Quartet, conceived for the same instrumentation but about ninety years later. What a difference a century can make in essentially the same sort of phenomenon: the same means, but by no means the same language! Where Mozart is clear, Brahms is ambiguous; where Mozart is brief, Brahms is expansive: where Mozart writes for solo voices and with no doubt about it, Brahms seems to be asking for a symphony orchestra of four people!

On Sunday, Tocata displayed the best of both worlds, with the performers' modes of expression finely adjusted to the stylistic demands of each. Sunday's performers were Henry Hutchinson (violin), Francisco Figueroa (viola), Mary Ann Campbell (cello) and María del Carmen Gil (piano).

Tocata, consisting of six skilled performers who rotate the duty for specific works and specific concerts, is solidly rooted in Puerto Rico's day to day musical life and is among the principal movers thereof. This being the case, and in view of other musical initiatives which have been taken by the island legislature, it would, I believe, be perfectly correct for the lawmakers to designate this group the Official Sextet of Puerto Rico, to represent the island on those occasions where a musical ensemble of six players is appropriate. Official Sextet, Official Quintet, Official Trio; following the logic of the thing the august legislators might end up with an Official Soloist and of course an Official Music Critic, to keep it all straight both here and abroad!

Otello is Best on Stage

The San Juan Star
February 11, 1987   By Donald Thompson

    Juaco, who lives just down the street, is my ancient, and if you've forgotten what that means you might wish to look it up because a little later we may be talking about Shakespeare. Juaco is also a veteran viola player who has put in untold hours in the orchestra pit while some of the world's greatest opera singers, as well as some of the world's least opera singers, have thundered out the Puccini, the Gounod and the Verdi, unseen, just above his head. Juaco was curious about Saturday evening's Tapia Theater presentation of an opera movie which I had attended, so I enlightened him while profiting from his own deep musical wisdom during our daily brisk walk around the barrio, at daybreak on Sunday. Our conversation went more or less as follows:
    J: You mean to tell me that people actually paid $35 or more to see a movie?
    DT: Well, yes, but you've got to understand that it was a most unusual movie to begin with. And anyway, the donation was not really for the film, but to help launch the activities of a new organization, Culturarte de Puerto Rico Inc., which promises to bring not only musical attractions to Puerto Rico but also ballet, theater, and who knows what all else. I'm for Culturarte de Puerto Rico Inc. and for all other similar battalions of volunteer soldiers in the Great Ongoing Culture Crusade. Right on, lads!
    J: From what I saw in the papers the movie was based on Verdi's *Otello*, with Plácido Domingo, Katia Ricciarelli and Justino Díaz in the principal roles, no?
    DT: Yes, and these voices were in absolutely top shape. The same can be said for Petra Malakova, Urbano Barberini and others, but their

musical appearances were unfortunately too short to really create anything but a very general impression.

J: What do you mean, too short? Do you mean that those roles in *Otello* are too short (which is not the case, as I recall) or that somebody cut the piece?

DT: Well, the opera had obviously been cut rather violently, probably to fit it into whatever playing time is necessary in movie houses nowadays to get one bunch of popcorn crunching bag rattlers out and the next bunch in. And in fact the cutting bothered me considerably, because eliminating so much material can only weaken the dramatic flow of any work as tightly organized as Verdi's *Otello*. What's left after the cuts absolutely could not stand as opera on any real stage.

J: So what was cut? Any really important stuff or only the kind of filler whose purpose is to get someone on or off the stage?

DT: Would you believe the soprano's "O Salce! Salce!" from Shakespeare's "O Willow, Willow," a cornerstone of both the Shakespeare and Boito-Verdi works?

J: I see what you mean. A pity. But what about today's international movie high-tech and the particular aesthetic of film itself, as opposed to the stage? Didn't these things compensate for what otherwise seems to have been a Violated Verdi?

DT: Not for me. Sure, director Franco Zeffirelli or someone on his staff has an absolute genius for visual angles and spaces; shapes and textures; objects and views; colors and shades; objective realism and misty impressions; the restless prowling of the camera eye; and everything else that is held sacred in the world of flicks. The camera makes possible a whole galaxy of subscenes and ancillary developments: flashbacks, distant visions and even whole episodes planted in Otello's head by the vile Iago but certainly unknown to Shakespeare and Boito. And this is to say nothing of a topless Plácido Domingo performing a pagan ritual of expiation right there in the Holy Chapel! Some of the scenes of this movie are absolutely breathtaking visually, but not all of the breathtaking scenes are justified by the lurching progress of what's left of Boito's libretto, nor do they always manage to fill the gaps with "psychological" plot development, no matter how visually seductive they might be. As consistently convincing as the acting is in this movie, motivations are not always clear due to the lack of explanation in the missing texts. But of course there's no time for those texts in a movie of normal length. The audience for the next showing is right out there in the lobby, milling restlessly around and mumbling resentfully as it cracks the next carton of popcorn!

And as for the high-tech, we are still at the stage of first recording the music, voices and all, then rehearsing and finally fitting the action to the pre-recorded tape for the camera. This is an extremely primitive, painful and slippery process, but it is still the only way to put it all together in any fashion which even begins to make use of the peculiar virtues of the film medium. But sometimes the high-tech fails to come together in the hall, just as in real opera you might have a capricious spotlight or a chorus tenor with a cough to spoil the whole thing. On Saturday, the first reel of film (how quaint an expression today!) displayed a disjuncture between the video and the audio, causing a fatal mismatch between facial expressions (and even the movements of crowds) on one hand and the corresponding sounds on the other. At such a moment all the high-tech in the world can't save the production, and we're back forty years to shaky Saturday afternoon kiddie cartoons at the neighborhood flick, for a dime.

J: You're obviously bothered by the movie, but I think I can help. The way you describe it, I think that what you saw wasn't a movie of an opera at all, but a completely new cinematic construction by Franco Zeffirelli based on ideas of plot that go back at least to Giraldi and his crazy sixteenth-century Moor of Venice, with a lot of Verdi's music, some of Boito's opera libretto, and a few elements of Shakespeare's very complicated story still evident. You'd probably feel a lot better if you could see it this way, and realize that this kind of thing doesn't belong to our world of music and opera at all but rather to the world of moviegoers, which has its own set of strange rules and curious values. And I know, because I've been thinking about these matters ever since I played fiddle for the silent films in Caguas. I learned very soon to stop in the middle of a phrase of Tchaikovsky not because there was any musical reason to stop but because that's where the scene changed. Unlike in opera, in the world of movies the screen controls the score, whether newly made as movie scores should be or using someone else's music for new purposes.

For example, if you want to know what the strange world of the flicks really takes seriously, try to remember the closing credits for Saturday's show. You know: the names that are scrolled on the screen at the end of the film, in a final rite of productorial self-congratulation. What did you see?

DT: Well, there were accountants, clerks, dressers, electricians, microphone boom handlers, sweepers, grips, gaffers, gofers. . . .

J: How about assistant conductors? The orchestra personnel manager and his staff? Rehearsal pianists? Coaches? Copyists? Piano tuners? The orchestra librarian? The concertmaster? Other section leaders? The oboe player who played that marvelous solo, unless it was cut for the movie music? The chorus' conducting staff, administration, section leaders and pianists?

DT: Well, no.

J: Of course not. Those final credits, together with the cuts which you say were permitted in the Verdi score, should tell you that still again, the musical art has simply been used in someone else's game for someone else's purposes, purposes which have almost nothing to do with music itself or even opera, for that matter. And the name of this particular game, friend, is MOTION PICTURES. Musically, we're back again to the silent films in Caguas when I was a kid, and that's a fact. You see, we're not really talking about opera at all, but about something else entirely. So tell me, do you feel any better about Saturday's movie now that you've had a chance to talk it all out?

DT: Not much, Juaco, not much. I would certainly be interested in seeing a proper high-tech cinematic *Otello*, especially conceived for the movies from the very start and with new music especially commissioned for a new text, but in the meantime I'll take Verdi's *Otello* on the stage any day. And for drama in the movies, I still think it's hard to beat *Casablanca* and *High Noon*!

David Krakauer, Clarinetist

The San Juan Star
February 16, 1987   By Donald Thompson

Off the beaten concert track but highly successful all the same is a series of very special concerts which from time to time flower in Puerto Rico.

The Cultural Activities office of the University of Puerto Rico, working with the New York-based Affiliate Artists organization and with the generous help of the General Electric Foundation, has during recent years arranged the appearance in Puerto Rico of five individual performers on this special series of residencies. The events take place mainly in such places as schools, hospitals, retirement homes, facilities for the blind and rehabilitation agencies. Performers, all recognized artists in their own right, offer up to eighteen concerts during a typical two-week stay; resident artists here have included two guitarists, a mime, a dancer, and just now a clarinetist.

Presently going the rounds is clarinetist David Krakauer, remembered here for his appearances on such other series as that of the Latin American Foundation for Contemporary Music, the regular UPR Cultural Activities series and others. The Affiliated Artists tour also includes, naturally enough, an appearance on the sponsoring agency's own turf; accordingly, on Thursday evening Krakauer appeared at the UPR itself, along with masterly pianist Elizabeth Rodgers. Krakauer is the Compleat Clarinetist, and his UPR recital was beautifully balanced among the repertories of standard items, advanced middle ground and far out. This is very wise programming, for it can please all concert tastes while demonstrating just what the clarinet can do as a solo instrument; it also nicely answers a senseless complaint which can still sometimes be heard after concerts of avant-garde music. "Well," you hear, "Anyone can play that junk, but can they play REAL music?" Yes, Krakauer and Rodgers can play both "old" real music and "new" real music, and they do it with the same professional skill and dedication.

The traditional repertory brought Brahms, Schumann and Debussy, played with great precision and with a sound which filled the hall but which could also retain its full rich quality at the level of a whisper. Accompanists are often grateful for this kind of soloist, for they, too, can then play out at a comfortable level without dominating the partner. In this regard Krakauer and Rodgers are a well matched team. More modern music, by Anthony Coleman, Sidney Bechet (yes, the great Sidney Bechet of jazz) and Krakauer himself explored some less familiar aspects of clarinet playing. Krakauer's own Improvisation No. 1, as explained in the program notes, consists of freely improvised sections framed by composed and unchanging pillars. There are frequent reminiscences of early and middle jazz in the work, as well as the use of the clarinet techniques of the avant-garde. These techniques include multiphonics (the production of more than one note at a time), bent tones of one kind or another and even the squawks and fuzzy sounds that beginning clarinetists endeavor mightily to overcome. The work seems to condense into a few minutes of playing the entire history of the clarinet, even at times suggesting the screech of a hollow stick with a loose splinter at the business end which may have been the primitive great granddaddy of all clarinets everywhere.

Food for such deliberative conjecture was also offered by Anthony Coleman's The Kaspar in Me. This work is spun from a handful of recurring notes and patterns rather calmly presented, while all around, hell breaks loose, usually in the piano but occasionally in the clarinet itself. Intense and bleak it is: "Is there hope?" it may ask. "Probably not," it answers, "But just maybe . . ."; "But then on the other hand . . . , probably not."

PRSO Pension Gala Raises Retirement Funds

The San Juan Star
February 18, 1987 By Donald Thompson

A solid concert was offered for a good cause on Saturday, on the occasion of the Puerto Rico Symphony Orchestra's more or less annual Gala Pension Fund Concert in the big Festival Hall at the Performing Arts Center. Understand, please, that the PRSO pension fund is not in any sense a gala matter itself, but that the Pension Fund Concert usually is. The orchestra's pension fund in its present state is not only not gala; it is operationally nonexistent, and the reasons for this go back to the orchestra's strange beginnings almost thirty years ago.

When the PRSO was launched in 1958 by PRIDCO (the Commonwealth government's brilliantly successful Puerto Rico Industrial Development Company), it was not with any idea of establishing a permanent island-based symphony orchestra. The intention was simply to quiet the mutterings of island musicians and a few music lovers who had fought the good fight for the creation of stable orchestras here in a line going back a century and more. These figures, including some very capable musicians, were now seeing undreamed of sums of tax money going for the annual contracting in New York City of a special orchestra of superstars (and believe me, the Casals Festival orchestras of the earliest years were indeed composed mainly of superstars) who left the island after a couple of weeks of resplendent concerts. What hurt was that the festival orchestras took with them all hope of arousing any official interest at all in the creation of a solid island-based orchestra, to say nothing of the rich secondary cultural benefits which could flow therefrom.

In order to get off the hook, PRIDCO simply applied to island instrumentalists the same formula which seemed to work for the festival orchestras: the temporary hiring of players for a very short engagement without any commitment to orchestra growth or to the development of a responsible corps of instrumentalists or even, for that matter, to the development of an audience for art music. These matters are of the deepest concern to all properly motivated and properly organized orchestra managements, but they were not even imagined by PRIDCO industrial planners.

As the PRSO started to develop into a serious enterprise with serious purposes, beginning around 1972, it also began to display the organizational and administrative needs—the need for infrastructure—of serious orchestras everywhere, including a reasoned plan to attract and hold good players and to enable members to gracefully leave the battlefield after making a professional commitment spanning several decades. In other words, a retirement plan. But managerial concepts formed back in the days of short PRIDCO contracts survived long after the orchestra gained its own administrative structure. And when a more responsible view finally began to prevail it was discovered that for technical reasons the PRSO staff could not be fitted into the existing Commonwealth government retirement plans. So, no pension plan. However, recent managements have brought to their task not only a greater understanding of the purposes of the whole enterprise, but also the desire to do something about some of the inherited problems which had their origin almost thirty years ago.

The Pension Fund Gala Concerts are part of this effort, and in a few short years have amassed over $200,000 toward a fund whose product might make possible a reasonable pension plan, which after all is just the other face of a reasonable recruitment plan. Actuarial studies are now in progress which are expected to generate some figures which can provide the objective basis for a program.

But why is this important? Don't orchestral musicians play simply for the love of it? For the glory of playing the music of Beethoven? For the joy of wearing a tux and a bow tie? Well, not entirely. Too, lungs wear out and fingers slow down, while the eyesight begins to go after a while and even the ear can lose its edge, which brings us to Saturday's concert.

The concert was conducted by Odón Alonso, now about halfway through his first year as the PRSO's music director, and appearing as soloist was violinist Itzhak Perlman, perhaps Mr. Number One in the world today. Together, Alonso, Perlman and the PRSO offered a good look at some of the music of Johannes Brahms, to whose music the present

PRSO season is in fact in a general way dedicated.

How did Perlman do, you ask? What can I tell you? Here is one of today's great ones, and he tossed off the familiar Brahms concerto as if it were an ice cream cone, which it most certainly is not. Perlman's presence simply added a touch of crowning glory to an already significant event.

But what about our orchestra? Well, one of the things Brahms is noted for is the use of parallel octaves between the first and second violins in orchestral music. On Saturday, some of our fiddlers' fingers didn't fall precisely where they should have, creating some excruciating almost-octaves. On the other hand, Odón Alonso has clearly attained in a few short months with this orchestra something which very few conductors —visiting or "permanent"—have been able to attain here: a general feeling of solid orchestral rhythmic security and an extremely satisfying sense of dynamic contrast.

Beaux Arts Trio

The San Juan Star
March 11, 1987 (a)   By Donald Thompson

San Juan's stalwart Pro Arte Musical Society brought its 1986-87 season to a close on Sunday afternoon with an elegant program in the Festival Hall at the Performing Arts Center. The very idea of a Pro Arte concert in the afternoon had thrown me completely out of orbit; consequently I missed the first third of the concert by arriving twenty minutes late for a 4:00 P.M. start instead of (as I had thought) a safe ten minutes early for a 4:30 start.

On the stage was the celebrated Beaux Arts Trio, well remembered in Puerto Rico from other presentations during past decades and again offering a varied and solid program. The Beaux Arts is composed of Menahem Pressler (piano), Isidore Cohen (violin) and Bernard Greenhouse (cello), all seasoned veterans in the world of chamber music who together form a rightly honored team. I had missed the scheduled Trio in C Major (K 548) of Mozart, the concert opener, but the music that I heard was well worth the trip, even on a Sunday afternoon. This included a new trio by George Rochberg, especially written for the Beaux Arts Trio and premiered only a year ago, and the interesting Trio in B Major, Op. 8, of Johannes Brahms. The trio is interesting because this is one of the very few examples of Brahms' production which he allowed to exist in two versions. Brahms was much more given to simply discarding earlier versions of a work, allowing only the latest one to survive officially. The two versions of the Op. 8 trio have thus provided generations of scholars with grist for the Brahms-studies mill, and chamber music players with some fascinating comparisons.

George Rochberg is a distinguished U.S. composer with a long list of compositions for all performance media and a long record of teaching and publication; a fine representative of the scholarly line of musical composition which has continued in the U.S. during the past thirty or forty years. This second of Rochberg's trios consolidates many of the more important threads of musical compositions of the present century in a thoroughly absorbing fashion. It is not difficult to perceive reminiscences of styles associated specifically with Bartók, for example, or Berg, but there is no question about it: this is Rochberg speaking, and speaking a convincing twentieth-century musical language which has developed naturally from past modes.

The Beaux Arts Trio? Well, this splendid ensemble gave us all a profound lesson in technical skill and unity, chamber music concentration and expressive musical phrasing: the subtle "breathing" of each phrase as it contributes to the reconstruction of a musical edifice: be it designed by a Mozart, a Rochberg, a Brahms, or as in the trim encore from the "Dumky" Trio of Dvořák.

Sunday's concert was a thoroughly enjoyable musical experience, and one which again confirms the historically significant role of the Pro Arte organization in the cultural life of Puerto Rico.

Melody Reigns Supreme

The San Juan Star
March 11, 1987 (b) By Donald Thompson

Melody reigned supreme at the Festival Hall of the Performing Arts Center on Sunday evening as Opera de Puerto Rico, now well into its second decade as a force in the island's music, offered an opera concert in the grand tradition. With the Puerto Rico Symphony Orchestra on the stage, Sunday's opera concert was based on the presence of mezzo-soprano Agnes Baltsa and tenor José Carreras, with Edoardo Müller conducting.

The Opera Concert format is opera without scenery, opera without plots, opera without costumes, opera without special makeup, opera without stage directors or chorus people; only the part which turns most self-confessed opera fans into mango paste: THE TUNES! And tunes there were aplenty on Sunday but within a limited historical and stylistic range, from Rossini through Mascagni and Cilea: all representative of the mellifluous Italian (and a bit of French) repertory to be sure, but excluding Handel, Mozart, Gounod, Weber, Donizetti, Wagner, Strauss and a few others who might have been included in a proper anthology of opera airs and duos.

Ah, but that's the problem, you see. With a mezzo and a tenor engaged for the date, you have to tailor the program to what the tenor and mezzo want to sing, and even more, to what they can sing together at least once or twice during the evening.

Don't get me wrong. This is certainly not to knock the proven skill of a José Carreras, already well known in Puerto Rico, or the fresh presence here of Agnes Baltsa, but maybe, sometime, someone will make up an opera duo concert observing the same ground rules that seem to apply to solo and duo recitals with piano, including the honored criterion

Concert Life In Puerto Rico

of historical and stylistic variety.

Well, then, how about this Carreras and this Baltsa? Very fine singers they are, as was shown in solo arias and a couple of carefully chosen duos. Carreras is definitely a lyric-dramatic tenor, and his selections were wisely chosen to show off this aspect of the tenor's craft instead of the shotgun blasts of unrelieved high notes which others might have programmed. First rate. Mezzosoprano Agnes Baltsa had also chosen very well, depending heavily on pieces that would show her considerable coloratura gifts: Rossini and Bizet, particularly. However, and despite an absolutely staggering ability in the characteristic rapid work of this virtuoso repertory, the Baltsa voice displayed a disturbing harshness in the middle of its range which made me wonder: maybe the lady's not a mezzo at all, but, a soprano, of all things!

Granted, Baltsa would make a knockout operatic Carmen, as indeed she reportedly does, because this harshness in the middle range is suited to the character of an operatic Carmen. But in front of a symphony orchestra during a concert is something else entirely. Other realms of expression are called for.

Sunday's duos were carefully chosen and also very effective. Again, Bizet's *Carmen* set the pace, with a long scene from the opera providing in fact the evening's climactic offering, with the two soloists displaying the best of their well matched abilities. Too, an excerpt from Verdi's *Aida* will long be remembered, which became not a duo at all but quite correctly a Verdian trio of mezzo, tenor and bass clarinet, with orchestral accompaniment. Here, the third voice was carried by Robert Handschuh, a veteran member of the PRSO and an important figure in the island's music.

Conductor Edoardo Müller and the Puerto Rico Symphony Orchestra? Very good, with Müller an enthusiastic and knowledgeable leader, if not perhaps a very efficient one.

All considered, Sunday's opera concert speaks well of the intentions of the Opera de Puerto Rico group.

♪

The renowned University of Puerto Rico chorus, conducted by Carmen Acevedo in a 1987 TV concert.

UPR Chorus Celebrates First Fifty Years

The San Juan Star
March 21, 1987 By Donald Thompson

Some 2,600 ecstatic concertgoers greeted the University of Puerto Rico Chorus as it presented its fiftieth anniversary concert on Wednesday evening at the UPR Theater in Río Piedras. And rightly so, for reasons nostalgic, sentimental, symbolic and musical.

Naturally, Wednesday's concert was dedicated to the figure who launched the UPR Chorus back in the 1930s and who for years occupied a key place in the island's musical life in composition and choral arranging, in the correct but premature vision of what might constitute a proper music department at the UPR, in the formation of professional concert orchestras in an extremely difficult period, in exploring the history of the island's music, and even in the creation here of a musicians' union long before its time: the fiery Augusto Rodríguez.

As in all things here below, nothing is created out of thin air, and of course the Augusto Rodríguez UPR Chorus of the thirties had its precursors and predecessors, including, for the record, a university choral ensemble conducted by the fondly remembered UPR music pioneer and talented researcher, Monserrate Deliz. And I wouldn't be at all surprised to find that choral activities also took place at the Normal School, which at the turn of the century was the beginning of the present University of Puerto Rico.

Conceived and conducted by Carmen Acevedo, the present director of the UPR Chorus, Wednesday's fiftieth anniversary concert incorporated a great number of former chorus members going back to the early days, and an inspiring sight (and sound) it was, as well over a hundred old timers (and some not so old, I hasten to add), added their voices to those of the 75 or so young people who regularly constitute the UPR Chorus.

Significantly, very few concessions were made in the program for tired lungs, creaky vocal cords and the half-remembered repertory of thirty or forty years ago; this was most emphatically not a sentimental reunion, but a concert of real choral music in the Carmen Acevedo fashion. This means a varied program, a technically demanding program (here, perhaps, a bit of a concession in Wednesday's planning), a superbly prepared program and an interestingly staged program. What more can one ask for a fiftieth anniversary concert, or any concert, for that matter?

The work of the UPR choral program, as it has been developed during recent years by Professor Acevedo and the UPR music department, is marked by solid technique, absolute rhythmic security, excellent breath control, faultless pronunciation and beautifully expressive phrasing: choral virtues which are guaranteed to produce a splendid result whether twenty or 200 singers are involved. And so it was on Wednesday, with a program which included some Beethoven, some Palestrina, some Mozart, some Bruckner and Bizet, and an extremely powerful performance of Francis Schwartz' *Paz en la Tierra* of a few years ago. This work bears absolutely no relation to what most choruses spend most of their time doing, but calls upon new and unheard of techniques of choral sound, as well as the chorus dissolving and spreading out into the audience to offer individual messages of peace on earth. A powerful message indeed, when offered by over 200 people apparently operating individually but in truth tightly coordinated under the faultless timing of Carmen Acevedo.

The older UPR Chorus repertory was certainly represented as well, including vivid performances of a number of Augusto Rodríguez' own compositions and arrangements and naturally of the UPR hymn itself, composed by Rodríguez on a text by distinguished island playwright Francisco Arriví, himself present to receive merited recognition as a pioneer member of the UPR Chorus of the thirties. Wednesday's concert was a symbolically moving, historically important and musically significant event, and many of the participants and audience are already looking forward to the UPR Chorus' 75th Anniversary Concert, scheduled for the year 2012!

Special

The San Juan Star
March 25, 1987   By Donald Thompson

In recent seasons, the work of the Puerto Rico Symphony Orchestra has blossomed out into a proliferation of regular series, special series, superpops series, concert series at the UPR in Río Piedras, educational concerts, and, of course, the annual and extremely important Pension Fund Gala Concert. This kind of calendar is in fact rather typical of what symphony orchestras do with their time, especially those that have long seasons under contract or are on their way to becoming full time enterprises. Your PRSO is both, and such a breadth of activities can only solidify its already fundamental position in the island's music.

One of the most popular of the PRSO's present series has been that of the special concerts at UPR. On Saturday evening the orchestra, conducted by its regular music director Odón Alonso, offered an interesting concert of music by Vivaldi, Joaquín Rodrigo and Manuel de Falla. The concert was programmed around the stellar figure of guitarist Narciso Yepes as soloist in the Vivaldi and Rodrigo works, and I suppose the thinking was "Well, as we've got Rodrigo's music for the soloist in the first half, why not go the rest of the way with Spanish music and get up some Falla for after the intermission?" Fine with me, and the complete Three-Cornered Hat music was very nicely played, with the two brief vocal sections cleanly sung by island light mezzosoprano Evelina Quilinchini, now based in Boston but a welcome returnee.

Writers of program notes don't always do their homework, or perhaps the ample program material dealing with soloist Yepes came ready-made from Spain. In any case, it would have been nice for Saturday's audience to know that Yepes has played in Puerto Rico several times before, and that one of his most significant performances here took place in the same hall some quarter century ago in a program devoted entirely to the music of Joaquín Rodrigo, who was then a visiting professor in the UPR Music Department.

On that occasion Yepes made a brilliant impression with the Spanish composer's *Fantasía para un gentilhombre* for guitar and small orchestra, an impression that has been confirmed on his subsequent visits and again confirmed on Saturday with Rodrigo's *Concierto de Aranjuez* and a Concerto in D Major for guitar by Antonio Vivaldi. Yepes' playing has always been marked by technical mastery and stylistic grace, both amply demonstrated on this occasion.

At intermission, a couple of friends in the orchestra sought me out with a complaint, perhaps laboring under some harmless misconception regarding the power of the press as applied to real life musical affairs. I certainly have no illusions about this subject, but I do share my colleagues' concern, and don't mind airing it again myself. It deals with a combination of factors, some of which are seen regularly at other concert halls, but which seem to form a conspiracy of concert crudeness every time the PRSO plays at the UPR Theater. These involve latecomers stomping toes and arguing over seats as the orchestra begins the first piece or waits in embarrassed silence along with soloist and conductor as occurred on Saturday; the distracting use of flash cameras during the performance; illicit recording; and now the intrusion and use of bulky video cameras, the operators freely moving about during the concert. Barbaric, barbaric. An irate violinist pointed out that to get into a rock concert at the Coliseo you are likely to be searched for weapons. Cameras and tape recorders are lethal weapons at symphony orchestra concerts, she reasons, and perhaps the same logic could be applied here, as well as closing and guarding the doors ten minutes before the baton comes down. Right on, I say, but I don't think it's going to happen. Managements would certainly be reluctant to impose and enforce such drastic measures, and a couple of generations raised on movies, TV and shlock concerts simply don't know any better. It's a barbaric world out there, kiddies, and the message may simply be that the gentle world of concert music as we have known it is going the way of the scribe, the blacksmith and the candlemaker. Something else will take its place, certainly, but I'm not sure that I want to know what it is.

♪

Friend of Music

The San Juan Star
March 30, 1987 By Donald Thompson

Roberto Ferdman, a resident of Puerto Rico for many fruitful years who died in Houston last week following heart surgery, represented the best type of professional person fully committed to the improvement of the cultural life of his community, completely apart from the honorable exercise of his specialized professional skills. Roberto was an engineer and builder and a very successful one, having created a flourishing practice starting from nothing and knowing nobody, in a matter of a dozen years or so. But more to the present point he was a patron of the arts, in the best sense: in the sense of not only buying paintings and sculptures and subscribing to every concert series in sight, but of doing a great deal of the dogwork involved in keeping these currents flowing in Puerto Rico and in the world.

Roberto Ferdman was a key figure in the revival of Puerto Rico's venerable Pro Arte Musical Society, which had been inactive for a number of years prior to 1976. Such a revival appeared to many (including myself) a futile exercise, in view of the iron grip then held on the island's music by Big Government. Well, we were wrong. The grip was finally broken thanks in great measure to the courage of the new Pro Arte, itself inspired in great measure by the reason, the calm determination, the patient diplomacy and simply the hard work of Roberto Ferdman. The success of the reborn Pro Arte is partly due precisely to these virtues, virtues which I'm not at all sure Roberto even knew that he possessed. At the time of his death, he was for the second time, and in the same spirit of selflessness, serving as president of Puerto Rico's principal privately-sponsored agency of musical betterment.

Roberto was also very, very perceptive when it came to hidden language and inside references in the music business. He soon learned that among working musicians (and occasionally even among writers on musical subjects) the term "music lover" can have certain mild connotations of amused condescension, referring to the naive and childlike acceptance of the momentarily fashionable by an impressionable lay public. This implied adversary relation between "musicians" and "music lovers" greatly bothered Roberto, for he understood the context and the semantic intent of the expression. With his characteristic diplomacy and profound understanding, he once proposed the introduction of a third term, which might be applied to a category of lay people who sincerely wished to see beyond the immediately fashionable, and to perceive the true purposes and the true needs of the musical art. Roberto's proposed term was "friend of music," which when you think about it fills the bill perfectly. Not only does it fill the bill for a necessary expression in the lexicon of writing about music and musical life, but it also perfectly describes Roberto Ferdman himself. I shall remember him as a true personal friend, and also as a true friend of music.

Lucia: Italian Opera At Its Sweetest

The San Juan Star
April 25, 1987 By Donald Thompson

The sweetest of sweet music gently draped on a simple and sentimental plot which slowly makes its way toward a grim and tearful ending: this is Italian serious opera of the early nineteenth century, before Verdi began to twist its tail. It is also a direct ancestor of today's TV serials, a relation which in part explains its continuing appeal for today's opera audiences. Donizetti's *Lucia di Lammermoor* is a prime example of the species, which, I hasten to add, is also characterized by a great deal of the kind of singing which has opera lovers counting high notes and debating matters of tessitura and vowel shadings in the lobby at intermission. The Donizetti work is now playing in a series of two performances at the Festival Hall of the Performing Arts Center, and offers a fine opportunity to hear some spectacular singing and a lot of nice music in a highly respectable presentation by San Juan's own Teatro de la Opera company.

Lucia is no stranger to Puerto Rico, for its first performances here go back to 1842, when the piece was only seven years old and in fact a year before it was first seen in New York City. *Lucia* was one of the required offerings in the repertories of the Italian companies which tirelessly traveled the world a century ago and which often crossed paths in the hills between San Juan and Humacao or between Ponce and Cabo Rojo. In fact there appear to have been times toward the end of the century when *Lucia* was being offered on both sides of the island by rival Italian companies locked in a sort of tenors' duel to the death of one company or the other, the losing group to be reborn in Havana or Caracas the following season.

What do you suppose those performances were really like, of such works as *Lucia, Norma, Rigoletto* or *Aida*? There is of course no way to know except by reading the reviews in the papers of the time, and everyone knows how fundamentally untrustworthy music critics are.

The present production features a nice mixture of island-based singers and first time visitors, under the musical direction of Joseph Rescigno, subbing for the scheduled John Barnett, and the stage direction of Franco Gratale, whose work is well known here. The tragic Lucia is brilliantly played by soprano Masako Deguci, the tragic Edgardo very solidly played by tenor Enrico di Giuseppe, the tragic Enrico (yes, there are a lot of tragic roles in this piece) played like a rock (as always) by baritone Pablo Elvira; Raimondo by bass-baritone Noel Ramírez, whose voice and presence continue to improve mightily; Alisa by Darysabel Isales, one of Puerto Rico's most versatile and most indispensable performers; Normanno by tenor René Torres, a new and welcome force in the island's music; and the tragic Arturo (what did I tell you about tragic roles?) by valuable tenor Juan Soto.

Without simply reeling off a catalogue of the first lines of arias and ensembles, it would be difficult to say much about the generally high level of singing in this production, once it pulled itself together after a shaky start on Thursday. Soprano Deguci, for example, started weak, but developed into a strong player as her role grew. Lucia's third-act mad scene is as much a landmark in Italian opera as the "Hallelujah Chorus" of Handel's *Messiah* or the restroom at the Ponce McDonald's during an island excursion; everyone is watching for it, waiting for it, reassured by its appearance and renewed (not to say relieved) by having experienced it. If there were any doubts about soprano Deguci's technical and expressive gifts on Thursday evening they were brilliantly dispelled in the third act. The work's other major landmark is the second act sextet, which combines the thoughts and the modes of expression of the six principal figures in a classic case of the necessary theatrical suspension of disbelief, but a potentially beautiful musical experience nonetheless. And such it was on Thursday, with the main voices of this production.

Chorusmaster for this Teatro de la Opera production is Pablo Boissen; choreographer, Rosario Galán; able dancers are provided by the San Juan Municipal Ballet, and the Puerto Rico Symphony Orchestra occupies the orchestra pit.

Raunchy Zarzuela

The San Juan Star
April 29, 1987   By Donald Thompson

During most of its life as a fresh and vital form of lyric theater (say, from around 1860 to the 1890s), Spanish zarzuela plots offered about as much sexual innuendo as a Doris Day movie. Then the lighter branch especially, the *género chico*, became heavily influenced by the French music hall style, and a number of new types came into a fleeting and ephemeral kind of existence, including the Jolly Zarzuela, the Can-Can Zarzuela, the Topical Revue Zarzuela and what can only be called the Really Raunchy Zarzuela. The appearance in Madrid of such disreputable cousins must have had the worthy fathers of the grand zarzuela turning in their graves, but they at least helped the Spanish lyric theater to stumble along for another couple of decades.

An especially well made example of the Really Raunchy Zarzuela is *La Corte de Faraón*, or "Pharaoh's Court," with music by Vicente Lleo and libretto by Guillermo Perrín and Antonio Palacios, dating from 1910. There is absolutely nothing to be taken seriously in this Egyptian romp, and even the work's subtitle of theatrical designation, "A Biblical Operetta," is a gag. Also consistent with a general spirit of irreverence, satire and parody to be seen in the Madrid theater at the turn of the century and occasionally applied to the sacred cows of Italian opera, is the Egyptian setting of the work itself, to say nothing of some episodes of the plot. It is difficult, in fact, not to see in *La Corte de Faraón* a parody of —lord preserve us—Verdi's *Aida*.

The Puerto Rican Foundation of Zarzuela and Operetta has again assembled a good cast of principal actors for their production of this work, which opened on Saturday evening at the Performing Arts Center. Among these are Herman O'Neill and Marian Pabón as a perfectly matched pair of comics; the veteran Manolo Codeso, so skilled that the raising of an eyebrow can cause waves of laughter in the house and bring the play to a stop; and operatic soprano Teresa Pérez Frangie, who gradually becomes completely convincing in a very unusual type of comic role for her. Excellent work is done by Ana del Pilar Pérez, Marisol Calero and Luis Raúl (I'd like to see a libretto of the work from 1910, for I wonder how much of THAT role is original); as well as in some smaller parts by occasional entrants. In fact, among the principal figures only Rafael José, an import from the world of commercial-popular music, seemed to me really inappropriate in both acting and voice on Saturday, even for this most forgiving of stage forms.

Opening night jitters caused some uncertainties both among chorus-folks and in the orchestra pit, while I felt that many scenes could have done with a bit more detailed and imaginative stage direction, especially in a type of very specialized theater which actually verges on the burlesque. Not for the likes of O'Neill, Pabón and Codeso, of course, for these talents could have improvised an evening of convincing business all by themselves. But I'm thinking of the general flow of the thing, which at times on Saturday didn't seem to flow at all. Choreography for an attractive corps of dancers is by Zaida Varas; the extremely witty sets (*Aida*, indeed!) were designed by Julio Biaggi; chorusmaster is Héctor Vega Drouet; stage director, Antonio García del Toro, and musical director, Rafael Ferrer.

Alonso Overcomes

The San Juan Star
May 29, 1987
By Donald Thompson

Maestro Odón Alonso has ended his first season as musical director of the Puerto Rico Symphony Orchestra, with encouraging gains in orchestral development to show for it. As has been noted with every change in the orchestra's musical direction over the years, some of the PRSO's problems are seated very deeply and are becoming worse as the years and decades pass, while no conductor can do much about them. For example, no conductor can do anything at all about creaky fingers and slipping eye-hand coordination among players who might like to retire but can't hang up their bows yet because the PRSO, in existence a quarter of a century and more, still has no retirement plan. I assure you that retiring a dozen exhausted players and replacing them with young and hungry tigers would improve the quality of the PRSO string sections thirty percent overnight, regardless of who happens to occupy the podium at the moment. This is because it is not the conductor who sets the basic conditions of orchestral employment but the management: in this case the Musical Arts Corporation, and behind the MAC the island legislature and behind the legislature the citizens who through their taxes provide most of the operating budget of the Puerto Rico Symphony Orchestra. So, you see, the general level of individual skill in the PRSO is not under the musical director's control at all, although ironically it will profoundly affect his work.

Odón Alonso has done very well this year with what he was given to work with, and has maintained throughout the season an average level of performance which I believe to be much higher than that attained by any previous titular musical director of the PRSO. Alonso has also broadened the orchestra's repertory and has designed, for this honeymoon season at least, an interesting and varied set of programs.

Last Saturday's featured soloist was island-born cellist Rafael Figueroa. Figueroa is a rapidly maturing artist, gaining international recognition at a startling rate and establishing a solid name for himself as a soloist. He is laying the groundwork for what could become a fine solo career, and judging from his performance on Saturday he might have a pretty fair crack at it. With the PRSO, Figueroa offered a calm and serene performance of the A Minor Cello Concerto of Robert Schumann. This is not one of the big and spectacular works of the solo cello repertory to be sure, and in fact the composer had no intention of writing simply another vehicle for instrumental calisthenics. For this reason it requires a little more expressive contrast on the soloist's part, even perhaps (horrors!) a bit of exaggeration of Schumann's written instructions to really bring out the concerto's beauty. This is called "interpretation," the extremely limited field of individual initiative which legitimately exists for the performer. Figueroa's performance, while technically absolutely faultless, seemed to lack, for my taste, this extra edge of seasoned and expansive interpretation.

The major work on Saturday's program, and indeed a climactic accomplishment for the season (if not for the past decade), was Prometheus: Poem of Fire. As the "funny music" began to sound, as the programmed smoke began to roll from the stage and as the intense beams of colored light began to penetrate the murky space above the orchestra, a concertgoer consulted his program, muttering "Francis Schwartz strikes again," referring of course to the exotic concepts of this imaginative island composer. But Prometheus: Poem of Fire is not by Francis Schwartz but by Alexander Scriabin (1872-1915), and dates, if you can believe it, from 1911! Prometheus: Poem of Fire was conceived by Scriabin as one of many attempts during this past century and a half or so to bridge the perceived gaps between music and movement, music and fiction, music and biography, music and poetry, music and painting, music and philosophical thought, music and light, music and temperature changes, music and odors, music and bio-rhythms, music and intestinal occurrences, and music and who knows what all else. Me, I tend to think that music has enough of its own problems to worry about without getting involved in these matters, but that's another story. Saturday's performance involved, in a grand artistic 1911 "let it all hang out," the PRSO, organ, celeste, smoke generators, very effective light effects conceived by the technicians of the Performing Arts Center, and the excellent University of Puerto Rico Chorus (Carmen Acevedo, Director), which filed from the foyer like friendly and faintly fluorescent flitting festive fairy fireflies . . . well, if you weren't there you won't understand it anyway. For the record, let it stand that the 1986-87 season of the Puerto Rico Symphony Orchestra, conducted by Odón Alonso, ended well.

Monteverdi Vespers

The San Juan Star
June 17, 1987   By Donald Thompson

. . . Or did the 1987 Casals Festival really begin on June 13? Now THAT was festive! Six skilled vocal soloists, an organ or two, the Spanish National Chorus of some 110 voices, a specialized Baroque instrumental ensemble ("Zarabanda"), the distinguished San Juan Children's Choir, and the especially bifurcated Puerto Rico Symphony Orchestra: all rather successfully united under the direction of Odón Alonso in the presentation of a big and brilliant work previously unknown in Puerto Rico. Yes, colorful and festive indeed, and it took some doing to get it all together.

The work offered was Claudio Monteverdi's sprawling Vespers for the Holy Virgin, itself an anthology—a compendium—a collection of pieces in different styles and conceived for different combinations of things. The pieces originally formed part of an even more sprawling collection entitled *Sanctissimae virgini missa senis vocibus ad ecclesiarum choros ac Vespere pluribus decantandae—cum nonnulis sacris concentibus ad sacella sive principum cubicula accommodata*, which Monteverdi had presented to Pope Paul V in 1610 and which was published shortly thereafter. The whole apparatus represented not a "work," in the sense of an individual composition, but rather the sort of package that a composer would assemble as a ceremonial offering or a representative portfolio, very much in the spirit of Bach's Brandenburg Concertos of a later period.

As was pointed out in the concert program book in excellent notes written by Ramón Arroyo Carrión, little is known of the actual performance condition of a great deal of early music. In fact, questions of the "best" way to edit early music for modern performance have destroyed marriages, broken up publishing houses and generated bitterness which can last generations, finding outlet in decades of nasty attacks and counterattacks in specialized journals. Of this Monteverdi work in particular, known familiarly in the trade as the Monteverdi Vespers, no "score," in the modern sense, ever existed; only a set of sketchy partbooks which can tell a lot about Monteverdi's harmony and something about his text setting practices but very little about how these Vespers, probably never performed in the composer's lifetime, should be presented: even unto which and how many instruments should be used.

Most of the technical details of making a "work" out of such a catalogue of oddments, then, plus generating a set of performance materials which musicians can use to bring it to life, is left to a modern editor. And here is the rub. An edition will depend on the editor's historical knowledge, on the views prevailing at the time regarding "authenticity" in performance, and on other transient factors of taste and skill. I have been unable to determine the edition used on Saturday, but the performance was probably based on G.P. Malipiero's contributions to the Monteverdi Collected Works edition, dating from around 1940 (that very volume was missing from the library whose holdings I consulted. Hmmm.), with some local amendments and accretions. The result involved grandiose forces that Monteverdi could not have envisioned in his wildest dreams and for that reason was rather short on historical authenticity, but it was long on spirit and good will, which counts for a lot. In other words, you wouldn't expect to see such a performance at a Monteverdi Festival or an Early Baroque Music Festival, but in Santurce on a Saturday night in June, why not?

In that spirit, then, a word or two about the general level of Saturday's performance. The chorus (Carmen Helena Téllez, director)? So big as to obscure the subtleties of much of its own music, while usually overbalancing the contribution of all other vocal forces. A third that many would have been about right. In addition, a few overenthusiastic individuals, mainly in the sopranos, occasionally allowed their parts to attain an obtrusive level; i.e., they stuck out. The Puerto Rico Symphony Orchestra? Also too big, but much better controlled dynamically than the chorus. Some excellent solo playing by PRSO oboes David Bourns and Harry Rosario, as well as by other occasional soloists. The Zarabanda ensemble (Alvaro Marías, director)? Like that of many such groups, Zarabanda's work seems to be damaged by out of tune playing in the winds. Granted, playing the old types of wind instruments requires special skills, but they can be developed. Otherwise, the Zarabanda Contribution was usually difficult to perceive in the general sonoral blend. Not at all difficult to perceive, however, was the fine solo playing of Zarabanda violinist Isabel Serrano and, seated beside her, PRSO violinist Henry Hutchinson, the latter borrowed for the occasion. The San Juan Children's Choir (Myrna Díaz Feliciano, Director)? Solid as a rock as always, lining out the psalm tones in the clean, strong and precise delivery of the cool veterans which they are. The soloists, from sopranos Judith Nelson and Julianne Baird down to baritone Luis Álvarez, with tenors Nigel Rogers, Patrick Romano and Luis Félix in the middle? Very good, and especially memorable was the delivery of the exotic, complicated and today completely foreign vocal ornaments, to my semispecialized ear perfectly applied on Saturday.

Island Composers Featured

The San Juan Star
October 3, 1987 By Donald Thompson

As part of the Inter American Arts Festival now in progress, Puerto Rico's National Association of Composers offered a concert on Friday evening devoted to music written by a specific group of island composers, at the Experimental Theater of the Performing Arts Center, with the music performed by members of the Solistas de Puerto Rico ensemble.

The concert was supposedly devoted to contemporary music, but it offered very little of contemporary (1980s) stylistic relevance, although some of the pieces were in fact being performed for the first time. The most convincing of Friday's new works in old styles was a dramatic cantata cast in recitative and aria form and entitled *Medea*, by Ignacio Morales Nieva. It was intensely dramatic indeed, and very ably presented by soprano Susan Pabón and pianist Victor Meléndez. This work by Morales Nieva, dating from 1974, recalls the German expressionism of sixty years ago, in a kind of free-floating tonality with occasional excursions outside the boundary of the harmonic world as it was then known. Tying the work together, also reminiscent of the time when composers were still interested in such things, is the skilled application of a "motivic" kind of construction utilizing the recurrence of brief melodic "cells."

José Daniel Martínez's Sonata for Violoncello and Piano, also given its premiere performance on Friday, provided another glimpse of the musical world of the rapidly receding past, but now displaying some stylistic characteristics of an historical French style, a style often referred to as "Impressionist." The Martínez sonata is mainly tonal but incorporates a few tonal escapes in the way of whole-tone scales; bent pitches, clouds of high harmonics in the cello and pianistic waterfalls. There is considerable use of internal thematic reference rather in the manner of the classical sonata forms, which again makes the listener think of a return to the musical ways of yesterday. The Martínez sonata was presented by cellist Rosalyn Iannelli with the composer as pianist.

William Ortiz, recently re-established in Puerto Rico, has cultivated the stylization of urban street music as a viable species of concert music, mainly for small and middle sized ensembles. An Ortiz work offered on Friday is in fact entitled Street Music, and utilizes flute/piccolo, trombone and percussion to evoke the tension and stress—and perhaps a bit of the humor—of street corner life among barrio Blacks and Latinos in New York City. Ortiz has been very successful at this kind of evocation, although he has been more successful, I believe, in some other and rather wilder pieces than in Friday's offering.

For a while this general kind of urban evocation (in music and elsewhere) was described as being "committed," or as constituting some kind of "statement." Well, I don't know about that, but I do know that Ortiz' music is always fresh, potent and interesting. Without calling his work derivative, I do see a relevant connection with some past music which in its day indicated a very promising line of development but one which I do not believe was taken up at the time: a line indicated in some of the dance numbers particularly of Leonard Bernstein's *West Side Story*. Is this what Ortiz' street music goes back to? One could do a lot worse.

Also offered were a Toccata for Piano by Amaury Veray and Two Pieces for Clarinet by Carlos Vázquez. Both seemed to me more appropriate perhaps as ballet music than as concert music, needing a visual counterpart of some kind to maintain attention, for without such a counterpart the music seemed vague and shapeless. I am seldom given to the elaboration of extramusical pictures while music is going on right in front of me, but on Friday these works had me choreographing my own mental ballet company to music by Vázquez and Veray.

And opening the concert were *Three Antillean Songs* by Victor Meléndez, performed by soprano Pabón and the composer himself. These songs fit into a very attractive tradition of Antillean songs as written by numerous composers over the decades on texts by Caribbean poets and usually incorporating a bit of Caribbean rhythmic and harmonic spice. The Meléndez songs are based on texts by Manuel Joglar Cacho and Nicolás Guillén, and join other examples by Jack Délano, Héctor Campos-Parsi and other island composers in a steadily growing literature. Again, however, by no stretch of the imagination can the Meléndez songs be considered "contemporary" music; even if written on Friday morning they, along with most of the other pieces offered on Friday, would have to be considered as simply representative of one or another trend (some of them, long gone) in the music of our century.

Aside from the performers already mentioned, Friday's Solistas de Puerto Rico ensemble included Rubén López (flute), George Morales (clarinet), José Pérez Ayala (trombone), Vanessa Vassallo (piano) and percussionists Orlando Toro and Luis Cotto.

Caballé: Memorable Recital

The San Juan Star
October 23, 1987   By Donald Thompson

One of the most privileged voices of our time has again appeared in Puerto Rico, borne by the incomparable soprano Montserrat Caballé. On Tuesday evening the great Caballé offered a recital of known and unknown music before a large audience in the Festival Hall of the Performing Arts Center, sponsored by the Opera de Puerto Rico company.

The first half of Tuesday's recital (the half which I heard; see below) was devoted to an historical unfolding of Italian opera excerpts representing the first flowering of the species, from Vivaldi through Donizetti and Rossini. This is of course the period which saw the rise of bel canto in opera, first as cultivated by male sopranos and later applied by all opera singers but particularly sopranos and tenors. Caballé does it very well, in a style which probably approaches the ideals of bel canto very closely, although there is no way to really know at this late date. But the elements are all there: an even tone throughout the full range, fine legato phrasing (resulting from the complete mastery of breath control), agility in florid passages and skill in the high range. In other words, if this is not the bel canto of late eighteenth-century Italy, it's plenty close enough for me.

These virtues were most consistently demonstrated on Tuesday in works from the early period: arias by Gasparini, Paisiello, Giordani, Vivaldi and Marcello. Much of this music in modern performance calls for the addition of ornamentation and embroidery to the solo line, for the notation as it has come down to us is skeletal: a kind of melodic shorthand. Singers today devote a great deal of time to the study of ornamentation in early opera music (or have it done for them by specialists), and as a result we can better appreciate the beauties of this music today than was possible a few decades ago. Among other virtues, Caballé's work on Tuesday was distinguished by the perfectly appropriate and beautifully executed ornamentation of the vocal line in this early repertory.

Arias from the later period included pieces by Bellini, Donizetti and Rossini, which simply brought Caballé's impressive interpretive gifts forward by a half century. It was here that her great stage experience became evident, in the application of a splendid sense of tempo and timing. Caballé knows just when to push a phrase, when to understate a line and when to hold back a bit in the name of dramatic flow. This gift was especially evident in an aria from *Sancia di Castiglia*, by Donizetti, where this reasoned flexibility added greatly to the dramatic effect of the music itself. Throughout, Caballé's work was beautifully supported by the subtle and flexible collaboration of pianist Miguel Zanetti.

Pity that I missed the second half, devoted to melodious Spanish music of the stage and concert hall, but I had given up the battle at intermission. You see, seated toward the back of the hall, I had shared with several rows of paying patrons the dismaying and concentration-wrecking phenomenon of a slow and clanking camera shutter just over our shoulder and firing regularly throughout the entire first half of the concert. One irritated concertgoer likened the camera's sound to that of an amplified coffee grinder. Granted, a few photos were probably needed for publicity purposes or simply for the Opera de Puerto Rico archives, but an institution already exists for this purpose which puts no strain on audiences and maintains the serene artistic dignity of the presentations themselves. This institution is called the "photo session," wherein after the job the performers again take their places on the stage and run through a piece or two for the photographic record. The performers wouldn't like it, you say? They might dislike it less than you think, especially if they were expecting it, and in the meantime audiences, which as you might recall support the enterprise, would be allowed to enjoy the event without coffee grinders over the shoulder.

A Nineteenth-Century Ponce Home Musicale

The San Juan Star
October 30, 1987 By Donald Thompson

A Wednesday evening musical event sponsored by the Ponce Historical Society at the Tapia Theater in Old San Juan became a relaxed exercise in time travel, as it gradually shed the characteristics of today's uptight concert life and took on the style of a gentle nineteenth-century Ponce home musicale.

Entitled "A Tribute to Our Danza" and featuring concert pianist Samuel Pérez and gentleman pianist Luis A. Ferré, the event was scheduled to begin at 8 P.M. As 8 P.M. came and went it became clear that nothing would begin anywhere near that hour for lack of performers, audience and printed programs. Did it bother anyone? Only a music critic, and by 8:30 even he began to slip into a fantasy of a genteel but now cushioned and air-conditioned past, induced by the hypnotizing study of the Tapia's handsomely restored wooden ceiling.

Beginning at 8:45, but with the program announced from the stage (still no printed programs), gifted and powerful island pianist Samuel Pérez, fresh from concerts on the continent, offered a glimpse of what might have been played in Ponce toward the end of the past century (without, I'm sure, having intended through his programming to contribute to a time warp): Franz Liszt, Juan Morel Campos and Manuel Tavárez. Pérez is especially sympathetic toward this expansive repertory, and has become quite successful in its secure and subtle interpretation. Pérez also offered a version for solo piano of Gershwin's Rhapsody in Blue in a brilliant performance but one which for a while shattered the otherwise successful Ponce time warp.

Meanwhile, other aspects of Wednesday's event continued to evoke not a formal concert but a home musicale, including the seating of latecomers down front during the performance, pleasant speeches, a long and relaxed intermission, the formal recognition from the stage of persons in the audience, and the unveiling of a painting by a young and talented (but otherwise unidentified) artist with the unveiling's own attendant speeches, recognitions and expressions of appreciation. Although the printed programs had arrived hot from the press at intermission, the program was still announced from the stage, somewhat redundantly and at the cost of audience concentration. Did all of this bother anyone? Only a music critic, who by this time had been so lulled by the speeches, the Morel Campos and the Tapia ceiling that the only thing that really pestered him a little was curiosity about the identity of the young and talented painter.

There can be no ignoring the fundamental contributions which Luis A. Ferré has made to the island's music. In private life, he has been virtually the only representative here (during any period) of the respected European tradition of individual private patronage in the arts, as contrasted to the recent development of corporate patronage through gifts to institutions and government agencies. Ferré's initiatives as governor of Puerto Rico resulted in a dramatic overnight leap in the length of the season of the Puerto Rico Symphony Orchestra, enabling that ensemble to finally begin its long and painful transformation from a melancholy catch-all of students, part timers and struggling professionals to the very anchor of the island's musical life. Memory (especially where politics is concerned) is sometimes very short in Puerto Rico, but Ferré will be remembered in music here by virtue of a number of living monuments, not the least of which is the present PRSO.

Perhaps more to the point of Wednesday's musicale is Ferré's long activity as a performer. Again in a European tradition but one which has also been known in Puerto Rico, here is an extremely busy man who has for decades faithfully cultivated music as an active and serious hobby, with all that is implied in the way of regular study, practice and the exploration of new repertory. An avid chamber music player, Ferré has always sought partners to share this pleasant pastime with him, and here is where the duo of Pérez and Ferré fitted into Wednesday's musicale. Together they offered a set of original four-hand danzas by Morel Campos, in yet another evocation of times past. Before movies, the automobile and television began to affect family life, such activities as playing four-hand piano music were common in many homes, and would certainly have been present at a musicale at many island homes at the turn of the century.

Still lulled into a mildly euphoric state by the contemplation of the Tapia ceiling and the illusion of past glories, the now fully tranquilized music critic left the theater expecting to find his carriage drawn up and waiting outside.... But what's this? A police van rounding the corner on two wheels, siren wailing? Three swingers in a tiny car parked across the street, the radio volume full on and the salsa bass threatening to bring down the Columbus statue? No carriage but only the same old klunker, with a newly bashed fender and a missing radio? Back it is a full century to the late 1980s, then, and the sobering realization that despite the most earnest efforts of the august Ponce Historical Society there is no return, and anyway (now trying to start the klunker), if you take back the cushioned seats and the air conditioning from the remodeled Tapia Theater, maybe those days weren't really so great either.

Old Vivaldi Was Right

The San Juan Star
November 10, 1987   By Donald Thompson

The Fifth Puerto Rico International Guitar Festival closed on Saturday evening with a climactic concert in collaboration with the Puerto Rico Symphony Orchestra. Taking place in the University of Puerto Rico Theater in Río Piedras, Saturday's event brought to the stage not only the PRSO itself but also the eminent Venezuelan guitarist Alirio Díaz and two island soloists in a varied offering before a large audience.

Saturday's islanders were versatile guitarists Miguel Cubano and José González, who have established a secure place for themselves in Puerto Rico's day to day musical life through the imaginative programming of a broad repertory embracing several styles of music and several different instruments. Here they appeared with the cuatro, a smaller relative of the guitar and an instrument which is closely associated with Puerto Rican folk music of the interior mountains and valleys. The cuatro is a most celebrated instrument in that context, but its possibilities as a concert instrument have not as yet been explored. In fact it is high time that someone write a proper concerto and maybe a bunch of solo sonatas for the instrument, as well as some chamber music. In this sense I'm thinking of Paul Hindemith, who did precisely that in breaking new ground with solo pieces for all sorts of unusual instruments. Are you ready, for example, for a trio incorporating the Heckelphone? Hindemith wrote one, and perhaps we're ready for an Hatillo Hindemith who will tackle the cuatro as a solo instrument in the concert tradition.

Impatient with the lack of a proper concert repertory for the cuatro, then, Cubano and González have been led to jump the gun with performances on cuatros of a Vivaldi concerto for two mandolins and orchestra. Hmmm. This use of mandolin music would be excellent as a studio exercise for teaching the cuatro, I'm sure, but I say that if Vivaldi wrote it for two mandolins it should be played on two mandolins and not two cuatros or two anything else. And sure enough: when in doubt and as a last resort you should trust the composer, for Saturday's performance showed that old Vivaldi knew exactly what he was doing. Despite the undoubted technical mastery of the soloists, completely lacking in their work was the steely "bite" of the mandolin sonority which Vivaldi had in mind. It is simply not in the cuatro, at least in the range of the instrument which was used on Saturday. I don't believe that this kind of performance does any good: not to Vivaldi, nor to the mandolin, nor to the cuatro itself. Let's hear it for idiomatic music for all instruments as soloists, and especially for an authentic concert repertory for the cuatro!

A perfect example of what I mean by idiomatic solo music was offered on Saturday in the form of the Third Concerto for Guitar and Orchestra of Mauro Giuliani, masterfully presented by Alirio Díaz with the accompaniment of an appropriately reduced PRSO conducted by Odón Alonso. Giuliani was himself an acclaimed guitar virtuoso of the early nineteenth century, and published more than 200 works for the guitar. Stylistically, Giuliani's music might be that of a bland and placid Beethoven, but it certainly provides a stage for demonstrating what only the guitar can do, in the guitar's own technical language. In other words, Giuliani's guitar music is completely and triumphantly idiomatic. It is tailored specifically for the guitar, and for that reason it is not likely to fit any other instrument very well. Díaz played the concerto with the calm security of a world-class virtuoso (which he is), bringing honor to his instrument, to Giuliani's music, to Saturday's event, and to himself.

Also offered on Saturday, now by the full PRSO under the direction of music director Odón Alonso, was a spirited performance of Dvořák's New World Symphony. Spirited, yes, but not particularly accurate, especially in the high strings. Maybe for some purposes the UPR Theater's new and resonant concert shell reflects all TOO faithfully! The famous English horn solo in the symphony's second movement was beautifully played by one of the many skilled but unsung and mainly anonymous mainstays of the PRSO: oboist Gloria Navarro.

An Ivesian Cheer for Harold Lewin and the LAFCM

The San Juan Star
November 11, 1987 By Donald Thompson

The Latin American Foundation for Contemporary Music, based in San Juan, has for years been a strong positive force in the island's musical life. The brainchild of composer Rafael Aponte-Ledée, the Foundation through its sharply focused biennial concert series has brought significant twentieth-century works and distinguished performers to Puerto Rico, many (works and performers alike) for the first time. Between biennials, the Foundation manages to keep things stirred up with an occasional event devoted to the music of our century.

The Foundation did it again on Sunday afternoon in the hall of the Puerto Rico Conservatory of Music, with a solo recital by pianist Harold Lewin. Well, not really a solo recital, for Lewin shared the stage with a tape deck and a pair of loudspeakers which in two works emitted prerecorded sounds, synchronized with the pianist's work at the piano keyboard. In fact, the first work on Sunday's program was one of Mario Davidovsky's series of pioneer works from the 1960s and 1970s entitled Synchronisms. In Davidovsky's Synchronisms, live performers are teamed with taped sounds in what at the time represented a "re-humanizing" of electronic music by composers. It is probable that this "live-electronic" movement actually saved electronic music after the first great wave of "pure" electronic music, at first shocking and exciting, became simply boring. For example, how many hours are you willing to spend staring at naked loudspeakers on the stage without a human being in sight?

Davidovsky's Synchronism No. 6, played on Sunday by Lewin and tape, is from around 1970, and as Lewin himself explained from the stage, the taped part resulted from the application of the now classic (not to say primitive) techniques of that medium: essentially, recording and altering electronically produced sounds, then cutting and pasting together bits of tape. On the other hand, the taped part of Dexter Morrill's Fantasy-Quintet for Piano and Computer, dating from some eight years later than the Davidovsky, resulted from the use of that now indispensable implement of modern high-tech life, the computer. No cutting, no pasting, no yards of tape unlabeled and crackling underfoot: a very clean and neat studio process. The Morrill work sounds very much like a traditional (well, more or less traditional) wind ensemble with piano soloist, with a great deal of humor in the way of the strange harmonic turn (yes, kiddies, harmony!) or the unexpected rhythmic twist.

Without the helpful program notes and Lewin's also helpful comments form the stage, it would have been difficult if not impossible to recognize the technical differences in the two works. In the rarified atmosphere of the shadowy world of electronic music, influences and techniques promiscuously cross, interact, separate and recombine. Davidovsky's work sometimes sounded as if it might have been generated on the computer, while Morrill's often sounded like old fashioned electronic music, even (who now remembers?) "musique concrète," of real sounds recorded, altered, cut and pasted.

Also appearing on Sunday was a monument of twentieth-century music and one not previously heard in Puerto Rico: the First Piano Sonata of Charles Ives. What was heard here some years ago is Ives' Second Sonata, subtitled "Concord, Massachusetts, 1840-1860," and Sunday's performance provided a noble companion to that previous Ives landmark. Ives was a most remarkable and most original figure in U.S. music of the early part of the century, working in isolation from the world's great currents of musical composition but strangely anticipating a number of important developments. The centennial observance of Ives' birth generated a frenzy of musicological excitement around 1974, and brilliant careers in musical research were launched and maintained for a few years on questions of Ives' harmony, Ives' rhythms, Ives' melodies, Ives' orchestration, Ives' home life, Ives' insurance business and every other aspect of the man's life and work. By now, a decade and more later, things have relaxed considerably on the Ives front, and we can now enjoy the performance of an Ives work in a refreshing atmosphere of calm serenity.

The First Sonata is a sprawling fantasy, lasting some 35 minute of cranky rhythms, ornery harmony, spiky melodies and finger-busting technical problems. Ives was himself a demonic improviser, and on a first hearing the sonata displays the beauties and also some of the faults of a 35-minute improvisation. For example, themes there are, of course, but mainly fragmented, juxtaposed and tortured. And the staggering scope of the work does not facilitate the perception of its shape and internal design. What it means, I'm afraid, is a trip to the music library and a couple of hours studying the music. Why didn't I do it last week? But maybe this is the function of a performance of Ives' music: to goad the listener into thought and action, a function I'm sure the crusty Ives would have endorsed.

Sunday's concert was followed by a period of general discussion by and with the hardy Lewin, as well as the performance of another, unscheduled, work: Remembrance II by Elias Tannenbaum, based on a Charlie Parker tune. What? You don't know who Charlie Parker was? Then it's down to the music library for you, too. Meanwhile, an Ivesian cheer for pianist Lewin and the Latin American Foundation for Contemporary Music!

Symphony Orchestra Launches UPR Concerts

The San Juan Star
January 19, 1988 By Donald Thompson

The Puerto Rico Symphony Orchestra, after a few weeks of midseason "pops" concerts and similar functions, is cranked up and running again with a full program of more formal concert activities. Among the scheduled events for this second half of the season is a tightly organized set of activities at the main campus of the University of Puerto Rico in Río Piedras during January and February, which includes lectures, seminars and chamber music events as well as full orchestra concerts. Jointly sponsored by the UPR Office of Cultural and Recreational Activities, these events are open to the general public for a small admission charge, and promise to be among the most interesting offerings of the 1987-88 PRSO season.

The UPR concerts were launched on Saturday evening with the PRSO on the stage of the UPR Theater and under the direction of the orchestra's music director, Odón Alonso. Presumably, part of the purpose of the UPR concerts is didactic; if this is the case Saturday's programming, limited to two extremely contrasting works, served the purpose very well. Before intermission, a reduced orchestra presented the First Brandenburg Concerto of J.S. Bach, utilizing a group of instrumentalists drawn from the orchestra itself to make up the featured solo group within the ensemble, in the fashion of the eighteenth-century concerto grosso. In the main the playing of this "concertino" group was very good, calling upon a brace of well matched oboes, a pair of horns successfully negotiating their stratospheric and difficult parts, and a solid but flexible solo bassoon. Only the solo violin seemed out of his depth on Saturday, in a disparity which might be taken as symbolic of the PRSO's traditional disbalances in skill and presence between its string and wind sections, of course disregarding a number of exceptional individual cases among string players. In an intramural musical olympic event by sections, my money would be on the PRSO winds every time.

The other work on Saturday's program was the staggeringly vast Seventh Symphony of Dmitri Shostakovich. With a playing time of well over an hour, the Shostakovich work is a test of the endurance of orchestras and audiences alike, and its success will depend largely on the conductor's ability to keep it rolling within such an enormous frame of musical reference, contrast and tension. This is especially so in sections of this curious work (such as most of the first movement) which depend not on the development of themes but on the sheer piling up of forces in a design calling for the interminable repetition of a single simple tune, each time almost imperceptibly louder. Many composers have used this device (Rossini and Ravel immediately come to mind), but few have called upon it so heavily, not to say mercilessly, as Shostakovich in this work. The basic device of the first movement, this procedure returns again in the fourth in approaching what is described as the symphony's triumphant finale, representing, one is told, the inevitable victory of the great Soviet People over the Nazi Invader. Hmmmm.

To me this simplistic type of musical construction always brings movie music to mind; fine for its purpose, of course, but in the almost complete absence of musical development it is necessarily dependent on two of the least interesting aspects of traditional musical composition: repetition and getting louder. In these terms the Seventh Symphony of Shostakovich was a winner on its first presentations in the Soviet Union in 1942, and that success has followed it ever since. But the program book should really explain the significance of that dumb "Nazi" tune in the first movement for the edification of students and the general public as well.

Saturday's performance was brilliant in the percussion and winds (augmented by some ten or a dozen brass players to serve the necessities of the score), but weak in the strings. This is not right, trying to balance that concert band of winds, especially when backed up against the UPR Theater's new acoustical shell, with the PRSO's traditionally understaffed and sometimes shaky string sections. Still, such enormous works must be played in the name of the orchestra's artistic and didactic responsibility toward the population which through the government supports it. I wonder sometimes, though, how well this responsibility is being served through the presentation of unbalanced (hence mutilated?) works due to local weaknesses in what represents every orchestra's main body: the string sections.

Piano and Violin

The San Juan Star
February 28, 1988   By Donald Thompson

Music lovers courageous enough to brave the perpetual weekend San Juan traffic jams enjoyed a fine recital by violinist Henry Hutchinson and pianist Luz Negrón Hutchinson up at the Institute of Puerto Rican Culture on Sunday afternoon.

Hutchinson is part of a distinguished family of island musicians and is very active in many phases of Puerto Rico's day to day musical life. He is a principal member of the Puerto Rico Symphony Orchestra and has been a founder of several island chamber music ensembles, while carrying on as much of a solo career as other duties permit. Hutchinson's solo appearances are always well planned and well played, and have the curious effect of inducing several hundred normally sane people to fight the San Juan traffic to hear him instead of calmly spending the afternoon at the beach or in the mountains. So it was on Sunday, as a capacity audience jammed the Institute's Patio Theater for an interesting and varied program including works by Mozart, Mendelssohn, Stravinsky and Ravel laid out in something approaching a chronological sequence.

First up was the delightful Sonata No. 3 (K 306) of Mozart. The young Mozart was skilled both as a violinist and as a pianist, and the layout of this work seems to imply a greater sense of equality between the partners than sometimes prevails in the sonatas of the period, as if the young composer didn't know (and didn't care) which part he would be playing. It even offers in the last movement a written out cadenza for the two players, a most unusual symbol of equality. Chronologically moving down some 60 years then, the Hutchinson/Negrón duo offered a bravura Sonata in F Major by Felix Mendelssohn, where especially in the expansive second movement the duo's expressive gifts were emphasized.

This is not to say that technical mastery is not also required; the Mendelssohn's final movement, a breakneck *assai vivace*, contains a bit of the composer's deceptive "fairy music," light, lethal and faultlessly played on Sunday.

Igor Stravinsky's Duo Concertant, dating from 1923, opened the second half of Sunday's recital, in the "neoclassic" style cultivated by the crafty composer during the 1930s and 1940s especially. The Duo Concertant is a severe test for any violin-piano duo, for even making sense of its musical designs is a challenge. In fact, it sometimes sounds more like a trio than a duo, because for a great deal of time the violin is playing in double stops, providing two simultaneous lines. Especially enjoyable on Sunday was the sparkling "gigue" movement, where a persistent left hand pizzicato, right out of Paganini, takes on the character of some peasant joke, very typical of the witty Stravinsky.

Ravel's *Tzigane* is a fiery fingerbreaker which most fiddlers would rather avoid but which all violin soloists must master. It contains every challenge conceived by the diabolical Paganini himself, and then a few more. Cast within a scheme suggesting stylized Gypsy music, the Ravel work is complicated by harmonies never dreamed of by Gypsies or by Paganini either, for that matter. The *Tzigane* is, in short, a beast. Closing Sunday's recital with it, the Hutchinson-Negrón duo racked up still another enormously successful recital and through skilled and subtle playing, a real contribution to the island's music.

Forum Draws Caribbean Composers

The San Juan Star
5 March 1988   By Donald Thompson

    The First Caribbean Composers Forum took place last week on the University of Puerto Rico Río Piedras Campus, sponsored by that institution's Office of Cultural and Recreational Activities with a very strong logistic assist from the UPR Music Department. Four days of activities drew together figures from Venezuela, Mexico, Cuba, the Dominican Republic and Puerto Rico, joined in fraternal conclave to learn about the composer's lot in the various Caribbean lands, swap gossip and cassettes, engage in power-base maneuverings for future forums, eat some mofongo, drink some beer and maybe hear some music.

    Representation had been drawn from each country's active group of composers and music scholars, with the significant exception of Puerto Rico itself, whose representation the organizers had entrusted to a non-musician—a sociologist, in fact. One of Puerto Rico's leading composers observed, following the sociologist's presentation, that it would be fully appropriate now to have the island represented in some future international sociological congress by a musician: indeed, perhaps one or another of Puerto Rico's most active composers who were not invited to participate in this event.

    A great deal of time was spent during the week examining the state of music in the lands of the various participants, and it soon became evident that wide differences exist in the region; in some places it is extremely difficult to obtain the most basic materials of study, teaching and work: scores, books, records and pianos, to say nothing of the high-tech equipment now considered indispensable and taken for granted elsewhere.

    Composers in some places still seem to be spinning their wheels in the morass of "national expression," while most other lands successfully surmounted that crisis forty and fifty years ago. In this regard a Mexican delegate told the story of a tenor who, no longer able to hit the high and climactic notes at the end of pieces, maintained a brilliant career in his homeland by simply shouting "Viva Méjico" instead. Is this the nationalistic composer's final cop-out?

Considerable time was also spent exploring the matter of the relation between individual expression and the obligation apparently felt by some (although it was never clear just who had imposed the burden) of transmitting some great and unique message to a needy and eagerly waiting constituency. Again, a witty participant observed that for his part, he feels no such weighty duty but is extremely pleased if he simply learns that one of his compositions has been favorably received by persons, perhaps on the other side of the world, whose opinion he values. In the meantime, he sees no need for any composer anywhere to break his skull over any supposed missionary calling.

As sometimes occurs at international conclaves there was also a certain amount of political sniping. Here, this took the form of occasional reference to "Puerto Rico's present colonial status," made by island figures who perhaps embrace the Statehood Persuasion, a position which is fervently devoted to ending what is perceived as a colonial situation in Puerto Rico. What this political question might have to do with music and the composition and performance thereof, however, was not made clear during the forum.

Naturally, a composers' conclave would include a certain amount of music, presented both as illustrative matter during presentations and during special concerts scheduled as part of the congress activities. This First Caribbean Composers Forum ended with a concert in the recital hall of the UPR Music Department on Thursday evening, offering a sampling of the music composed during recent decades in the countries represented in the forum. It is difficult to believe, however, that most of the works presented are in way representative of their countries' best recent music. With the exception of Alfredo del Mónaco's fine Syntagma A, for trombone and tape and dating from the early 1970s, most of Thursday's pieces could have been written in the '30s and '40s.

Judging from this closing concert and from some of the concerns expressed and confessions uttered during the week, "Caribbean Music" (if indeed such an animal exists) is at least a half century behind "World

Music" and probably needlessly so, given today's means of instant communication and rapid travel. On the other hand I think I would agree, at least for the moment, with an often cited precept which again found expression here at least once last week: that there is really no art music, folk music, commercial music or regional music, only good music and bad music. And Lord love us, alongside some of the former there is also plenty of the latter, even right here in the Caribbean.

Elvira Exhibits Craft in PRSO Appearance

The San Juan Star
April 13, 1988   By Donald Thompson

Stellar baritone Pablo Elvira's orbits through the celestial reaches of the international concert and opera world again brought him to Puerto Rico last week for an appearance with the Puerto Rico Symphony Orchestra. Elvira is one of the growing roster of island-born singers who have forged successful careers in the bigger world; a few of these careers, like Elvira's own, have attained very high levels. Elvira's success has resulted from a combination of innate talent, solid early musical training and experience, an unusual degree of self knowledge, and the careful cultivation of his gift through regular study and through the reasoned development of roles and repertories. Elvira has never seemed to be in a rush to get there; consequently his arrival has been gradual, seemingly unhurried and perfectly logical. Looking back now, it's hard to see how his career could have taken any other course.

Among works scheduled for performance by Elvira and the PRSO on Saturday were four of the *Rückert Songs* composed by the great Gustav Mahler in the first years of the present century, but due to a mix-up regarding the rented orchestra materials only two could be performed. A tempting sample, this, for these songs show Mahler at the height of his powers and in a mystical mode of thought approaching that of his younger contemporary Alexander Scriabin. The two songs offered on Saturday were fascinating in another sense as well, for unlike the grandiose instrumentations required by much of Mahler's orchestral music, these two pieces called for sharply reduced wind sections in a context approaching that of the chamber orchestra. Vocally, they placed the solo baritone voice in a subdued and contemplative mode not often experienced in the operatic repertory which we associate with Pablo Elvira's work. Filling in for the two deleted *Rückert Songs* were two admired arias from Mozart's *The Marriage of Figaro,* the second of which, the Count's aria, is well remembered here from Elvira's own splendid work with an island-based opera company more years ago now than anyone would like to remember.

The truth of it is, I think Saturday's audience was just as pleased by these arias as it would have been by the rest of the Mahler songs, for the Mozart pieces prepared the way for the extensive opera excerpts which provided the rest of Elvira's scheduled appearance.

Saturday's concert was much better planned than the usual concert of opera arias and instrumental excerpts, for in several cases it very nicely combined an instrumental section with an aria from the same work. Take for example the Prologue from Leoncavallo's *I Pagliacci,* in which the orchestral overture leads quite naturally to the first vocal presentation by the baritone himself. Or take the orchestral music to the ballet scene and the masterful "Credo" in Verdi's *Otello,* sung on the opera stage by the vile Iago. In these integrated presentations, as well as in extended recitative and aria from Bellini's *I Puritani,* Elvira's voice and presence worked very well alongside the PRSO—and why not? Elvira is a superb master of the operatic craft, and gets steadily better at it all the time.

On Saturday, his singing was marked by complete ease and secure and open expression, with his dramatic gifts evident in every small gesture. The hand raised an inch or two, a glance sideways, a raised eyebrow: enough to convincingly underline the dramatic significance of what he was singing, but not enough to distract attention from the music itself.

In addition to its support of baritone Elvira and to the orchestral excerpts already noted, the PRSO offered as a concert opener a generally successful presentation of Tchaikovsky's grand orchestral fantasy *Francesca da Rimini.* Inspired by the gloomy story of Francesca and Paolo from Dante's *The Divine Comedy,* the Tchaikovsky work outlines the main details of the tale through the identification of themes and the use of certain conventional orchestral devices if you have recently re-read your Dante and know the devices. If not, well, old *Francesca* can still be stirring music and in some measure was on Saturday, especially in the unsurpassable solo playing of PRSO first clarinet Kathleen Jones.

In the role of guest conductor on Saturday was Theo Alcántara, whose work seemed efficient but not especially noteworthy, failing to attain with the PRSO any particularly distinguished level of unity or precision.

Los Gavilanes Offers
a Good Idea of the Zarzuela

The San Juan Star
May 18, 1988 By Donald Thompson

Zarzuela, that beloved Spanish form of lyric theater, is a most ornery and problematical animal indeed. The type of zarzuela which is most widely known today, dating say from the period 1870-1930, will have a sentimental plot in which young love triumphs; will offer plenty of opportunity for healthy and happy operetta-villagers to dance and sing; and will call for some real singing of operatic caliber on the part of the principals figures. Curiously, the performance tradition of the romantic zarzuela also provides latitude for the development of improvised comedy by some standard roles which will sooner or later appear in the work, as inexorably as the mirror in a Dracula movie. And finally, but with some most distinguished exceptions to the rule, zarzuela music is apt to be extremely uneven, with the same work displaying some imaginative piece the equal of anything written by Donizetti, followed by a fourth rate music hall tune. The zarzuela tradition is strong in Puerto Rico, with the average performance level of the San Juan companies probably surpassing that of Spain itself.

The island-based Puerto Rican Foundation for Zarzuela and Operetta has a production running at the Performing Arts Center right now, offering a pretty good idea of the zarzuela species in general and also offering an evening of pleasant music in particular. With another weekend to run is the foundation's production of *Los Gavilanes*, by the noted zarzuela composer Jacinto Guerrero (1895-1951) and dating from 1923. Featured soprano is Evangelina Colón, on a zarzuela break from opera jobs in Europe to play the maternal role of Adriana with a voice which continues to grow impressively in size, flexibility and dramatic intensity. Alongside soprano Colón, and by one of those twists of show biz fate, is her own daughter, soprano Ana María Martínez in the role of Adriana's daughter Rosaura.

And let me tell you: completely aside from the maternal and filial quirks of show biz, the third act scene between Adriana and Rosaura was one of the very few moments which raised Sunday's matinee performance of *Los Gavilanes* out of the world of theater busywork and into the realm of musical theater. The Martínez voice is extremely interesting and extremely promising, sounding in its light and clear marksmanshp for all the world like her mama's not long ago!

Tenor Efrén Puig appears as Rosaura's sweetie Gustavo, with an especially impressive performance on Sunday of the demanding song "Flor roja," while it was a pleasure to see how bass Noel Ramírez continues to develop both vocally and dramatically. Ramírez has in recent years become a very versatile and very flexible performer, as the variety of his occasional island appearances demonstrates in recent years. Experienced actors Esther Mari, Genie Montalvo and Santiago García Ortega provide the solidity and skilled timing of the spoken theater, while the comic contributions of veterans Manuel Codeso and Ricardo Fábregues never let up.

Speaking of improvised laughs as a traditional element of comic relief in the sentimental zarzuela, are you ready for references to Pepsi Cola, miniskirts and contemporary Puerto Rican politics in a story taking place in the north of Spain in 1845? Try it; you might like it!

Musical director for this production of *Los Gavilanes* is Rafael Ferrer; stage director is Myrna Casas; choreography is by Zaida Varas; imaginative sets were designed by José Llompart; and a resonant chorus had been prepared by Héctor Vega Drouet.

Casals Festival Off To Splendid Start

The San Juan Star
June 7, 1988   By Francis Schwartz

It's Casals Festival time! And we have returned to the critic's column after seven years of wandering through the world of arts administration, concerts and musical composition. This will probably gladden some hearts . . . and constrict others. Ah well, that's democracy.

For the thirty-second year, the government of Puerto Rico has underwritten with public monies its most expensive musical event, which during two warm weeks in June offers a dozen or so concerts to the people of Puerto Rico and a small slice of the tourist trade. The organizers of this yearly event proclaim it to be of top international quality. This subject as well as observations regarding programming, choice of soloists and other related matters will be discussed in a future article. One thing is certain: judging from the opening night audience that packed the Performing Arts Center Festival Hall for the Verdi Requiem, there is considerable public interest in cultural promotion.

The selection of a requiem mass for the annual Casals kickoff reveals a curious philosophical approach to a festive event which supposedly celebrates life and creativity. Opening with a large work for orchestra and chorus with stellar soloists makes sense because it draws large numbers of family and friends of the many participants. Also, the opportunity to hear a major composition with such massive forces appeals to the spectacular inclinations in all of us. But why a requiem?

Hyper-imaginative analysts of the politico-cultural scene and other practitioners of the occult will possibly find some special significance here. Are there 1992 quarter notes in the "Libera Me" section which will have a particular effect on us? We're going to ask our astrologist. Everyone else is doing it.

The Requiem Mass, by the great nineteenth-century Italian composer Giuseppe Verdi (1813-1901) was an impassioned expression of personal admiration for the writer Alessandro Manzoni, who died in May 1873. Verdi venerated the distinguished literary figure, whose patriotic ideas coincided with Verdi's own commitment to the unification and development of Italy. The Requiem was premiered in Milan in 1874 with resounding success and has subsequently taken its place in the repertory alongside similar works by Mozart and Berlioz. As Verdi's great gift lay in opera, it would be surprising not to find his splendid theatricality in this religious work. Using the Roman Catholic Mass for the Dead, Verdi created a mesmerizing, emotionally charged work which transcends the more disciplined atmosphere of a church service. We are in the presence of unstaged (costumes, scenery) Romantic musical theater of a special type.

Maestro Odón Alonso, Casals Festival music director, led the Puerto Rico Symphony Orchestra with a quartet of soloists composed of Awilda Verdejo, soprano; Florence Quivar, mezzosoprano; Neil Wilson, tenor; and bass Justino Díaz. The gigantic choral forces consisted of the Temple University Chorus under Alan Harler; the Puerto Rico Conservatory of Music Chorus prepared by Susan Pabón; the Mendelssohn Club Chorus under Tamara Brooks and the Coral Bel Canto, led by William Rivera Ortiz. Alonso, conducting from memory, fashioned an interpretation of strength and breadth. His sensitivity to the rhythmic pace as well as to the dramatic content was ideally suited to this major composition. The orchestra performed with general competence.

As for the soloists, mezzosoprano Florence Quivar was truly impressive. She used her full, rich voice with extraordinary skill in her powerful artistic projection. One recalls her vibrancy during the "Liber Scriptus" and the ethereal "Lux Aeterna." Justino Díaz, that "young old pro," had some splendid moments. The stark drama he achieved in the "Mors Stupebit" confirmed once again that he is a master of timing: of the poetic pause which infuses a text with poignancy. Tenor Neil Wilson was a most satisfying interpreter whose pleasant, lyrical voice demonstrated solid technique and musical intelligence. Soprano Awilda Verdejo possesses a voice of considerable power. While she experienced some difficulties with control and clipped phrase endings, the impression received was of a singer of merit who should fare well in her profession.

Congratulations to the chorus, which rendered yeoman service. This is not an easy score and they managed to execute the musical exigencies with ability. The power of their "Dies Irae" must have jarred a few sinners in the audience into thoughts of repentance.

And while we're on the subject of sin, let it be said that those people who insist on bringing electronic beepers and tinkly wristwatch alarms to the concert hall should desist immediately from such antisocial practices. In deference to Puerto Rico's recent and sudden rediscovery of the Spanish motherland, all we can say is "Where is Torquemada when you really need him?"

Stykhira: From Russia with Love

The San Juan Star
June 17, 1988   By Francis Schwartz

These are fascinating times. Dominating the news today are stories about *glasnost*, of "enemies of the Soviet state" being rehabilitated (in reputation, naturally) and of new cultural freedom in the U.S.S.R. Even that prominent Thespian-on-the-Potomac has ceased to rail against the "evil empire." Could it be that a great resurgence of humanism and artistic creativity will burst forth from the vast regions of the Soviet Union? Given the rich tradition of Russian (now Soviet) history, we are probably at the beginning of an important epoch.

Taking the podium at Tuesday evening's Casals Festival concert at the Performing Arts Center was Mstislav Rostropovich, the famed Russian cellist. Conducting the National Symphony Orchestra of Washington, D.C. (of which he is director), this famous Soviet exile chose a work by the contemporary Soviet composer Rodion Schedrin to open the program. One is struck by the significance of an artist forced to leave his homeland due to matters of conscience presenting the artistic product of a society in which he was honored and then vilified by officialdom. Rostropovich's programming of *Stykhira* is a noble gesture toward the creators of the Soviet Union.

Simultaneously, this composition, which commemorates the millennium of the acceptance of Christianity in Russia, obviously does not follow Communist Party strictures of an earlier, more intolerant era. Schedrin, who composed the work for Rostropovich, can now do artistically what would have been disastrous for him professionally, and possibly, physically only a few short years ago.

Stykhira is a well constructed piece which imaginatively utilizes Russian liturgical melodic elements within the context of modern orchestral writing. Schedrin effectively employs the instrumental resources in his quest to recreate an atmosphere of a past historical epoch. His poignant use of bells and gongs added a special coloristic dimension to the sectional alternations. The profound spirituality of *Stykhira* is present throughout the work; we are pleased that the public had the opportunity to encounter this example of contemporary Soviet music.

The development of a society's cultural consciousness cannot be divorced from the creative forces of the moment. As we have stated doggedly for the past 23 years, the Casals Festival should present twentieth-century works of different styles and formations in an appropriate balance with the rest of the historical repertoire. Why not invite Xenakis or Dutilleux or Ligeti to create new compositions for the festival? It would add new energies to the musical atmosphere and increase the international projection of the yearly event. Perhaps our readers (the younger ones) do not recall when it was necessary to do public battle for the inclusion in the Casals Festival of such composers as—are you ready?—Mahler, Tschaikovsky, Verdi, Ravel, etc., etc. But time flows on, minds grow and yesterday's anathema becomes today's vogue. We trust that our cultural administrators will reflect upon these ideas.

Substituting for the ailing German violinist Ann Sophie Mutter, Rostropovich was soloist in Haydn's C Major Cello Concerto. Conducting from the soloist's position, the exuberant maestro performed splendidly. His total immersion in the work created an interpretation of stunning expressivity. We recall with great satisfaction the transcendental *adagio* and of course, the whirlwind pace of the final movement which left everyone breathless. In short, it was an exhilarating experience. Bravo!

After intermission, the National Symphony Orchestra, under the baton of Rostropovich, performed Tchaikovsky's Fifth Symphony, Op. 64. The musical spirit and energy that pervaded the four movements could be admired; however, there were some problems in balance which were disconcerting. Especially noticeable was the first movement where the brass practically smothered the strings. Also, there was an occasional edginess to the violin section sound. The National Symphony is a good orchestra. No doubt about it. Since they were not scheduled to perform the Tchaikovsky, we will not pick nits. OK?

The Three C's at the Casals Festival

The San Juan Star
June 18, 1988   By Francis Schwartz

You've heard of the Three B's of Music: Bach, Beethoven and Brahms? Well, the Casals Festival came up with the Three C's last Thursday night: chaos, confusion and cop-out. The chamber music concert, presented in the Drama Hall of the Performing Arts Center by members of the National Symphony Orchestra, was free to the public. Yet due to a confused ticket distribution policy many people were forced to line up at the theater entrance and wait a considerable amount of time before being allowed to enter. There were many protests and though the attending administrators courteously attempted to assuage the public ire, we must strongly recommend that a new, unequivocal system be established to avoid such unfortunate incidents. One must respect the public's rights. After all, it is the public treasury which underwrites this yearly event and no politically appointed public official should ever forget this fact.

The program was a mixed bag of musical fare. The printed program represented an unusual foray into the world of chance; of Cagean indeterminacy. We were allowed to guess which of the three listed violinists performed in the three works using that marvelous instrument. Since one of the three wore a gown and earrings, we assumed that this person corresponded to the female name on the list. To avoid confusion and for historical accuracy, we suggest that the performers' names appear with the works they are to play on a program where there are so many interpreters involved. To simply sprinkle a bunch of names on the program heading is reminiscent of a high school matching quiz.

Opening with only the first movement of Tchaikovsky's A Minor Trio, Op. 50, one of the male violinists, one of the male cellists and pianist Lambert Orkis gave a correct if not terribly inspired reading of this composition. The violinist had some pitch problems and the sound quality was often gritty. The subsequent piece of musical fluff, the humorous Sonata for Trumpet, Horn and Trombone by Francis Poulenc, was well played by Edwin C. Theayer, Steven Hendrickson and Milton Stevens. This was relaxed, easy going music making. Bartók's magnificent *Contrasts*, for clarinet, violin and piano was superbly performed by Loren Kitt, Elizabeth Adkins and Lambert Orkis. Without question this was the high point of the entire concert. The expert ensemble playing, the effective projection of mood change and an overall buoyant quality drew resounding applause from the audience. Adkins was most impressive in her chamber role and we would welcome the opportunity to hear her as a soloist.

David Ott's *Dodecacelli*, for a cellistic dozen scattered around the stage, was conducted by a thirteenth cellist, Mstislav Rostropovich. This modern, conservative styled exploration of the sonoral possibilities of a small cello ensemble proved to be a well crafted piece. Ott obviously knows the instrumental possibilities and had an excellent ensemble to present his ideas. *Dodecacelli* would make a good training piece for advanced student players.

After intermission, Schubert's A Major Quintet (D.V. 667), known as "The Trout," was performed by a male violinist, violist Denise Wilkonson, a male cellist, bassist Harold H. Robinson and pianist Lambert Orkis. The playing was of competent professional quality, sans magic.

Casals Festival: Lightweight Programming

The San Juan Star
June 22, 1988   By Francis Schwartz

The 32nd Casals Festival ended Saturday night on a carnavalesque note. The Performing Arts Center Festival Hall was replete with beautifully clad pulchritudinous ladies and stylishly bedecked representatives of contemporary manhood.

At the outset of the festival we received many complaints because the Verdi Requiem had no intermission in which the attending public might socialize and exhibit and observe the latest in clothing styles. This faux pas was corrected in the final concert when the cognoscenti were able to participate joyfully in the visual festival of fashion that traditionally accompanies the sonoral one. Coco Chanel, smile on us, please.

Conducting the National Symphony Orchestra in its final 1988 appearance, Mstislav Rostropovich led a vigorous, well balanced version of Berlioz's Roman Carnival Overture. The entrances were precise and clean with excellent contrasts at all times. This was the best the visiting orchestra sounded during the festival. Following on the program was Haydn's Symphony in G, No. 100, the "Military." Rostropovich proved to be a far better conductor than he had previously demonstrated. The interpretation had charm, there was athleticism when required, moments of humor and no small measure of bubbly enthusiasm. Haydn's clever use of the percussion instruments was poignantly emphasized. Very enjoyable.

Pianist Eugene Istomin, spouse of Festival Artistic Advisor Marta Istomin, performed as soloist in the Beethoven Fourth Piano Concerto, Op. 58. Istomin demonstrated his competent pianism, which is rooted in solid musicianship and good taste, although we found his interpretation on the emotionally cool side. There were some very special moments in the *andante con moto* second movement.

Regarding the National Symphony Orchestra's participation in this festival, we can only give it moderate praise because of its lightweight programming. Maestro Rostropovich, with all due respect for his musical stature as a cellist and his gracious camaraderie, must bear the ultimate responsibility as the orchestra's music director. To bring a large symphony orchestra to the festival in Puerto Rico in order to accompany operatic arias and perform several pops concert compositions, offer a second-rate chamber music concert and even a sub-standard soloist, is not the type of contribution that will improve the standards of the yearly event. Without question, the Puerto Rico Symphony Orchestra, with all of its instrumental limitations, offered a far superior program with the performance of the Verdi Requiem, the Mahler Third Symphony and the Brahms Fourth Symphony.

We are pleased to have heard the National Symphony Orchestra but feel it is time for the Casals Festival to invite another symphonic ensemble here. There are several excellent candidates and all that is needed is professional expertise on the part of the Casals organizers so that plans can be made for the future. Planning far in advance must be the watchword. That is how we can attract the great soloists that this festival so badly needs and also plan musically exciting projects such as centennial celebrations of great composers' births or deaths. Finally, the current administration has returned to the tokenism of the past regarding Puerto Rico's composers. With all the bluster about cultural promotion, there was only one Puerto Rican work in this 1988 festival. There used to be three local compositions presented.

See you next year.

♪

Stormy PRSO Opening

The San Juan Star
September 14, 1988   By Donald Thompson

    A stormy Saturday evening at the Performing Arts Center in Santurce marked the opening of the 30th season of the Puerto Rico Symphony Orchestra. There were storms outside, with Hurricane Gilbert passing to the south of the island, and also storms inside, with stormy music by Gustav Mahler and Roberto Sierra, and even a bit of a tempest in an eighteenth-century Turkish teacup by the incomparable Wolfgang Amadeus Mozart (the Abduction from the Seraglio Overture).

    Yes, friends, thirty seasons, more or less, of your own government-sponsored, tax-financed symphony orchestra. A priceless boon, you might say, right up there in citizens' benefits with public schools, museums, libraries, public health facilities, highways and utilities. In fact, considering the panorama of such government programs in Puerto Rico over the past three decades, the record of the PRSO looks pretty good. This may be because there has never been a great deal of money, party politics, inept bureaucracy or naked hype connected with this agency. Some, of course (except for the money). For example, the existence of a big staff of able musicians on the government payroll is a temptation difficult to pass up when it comes time to glorify the party in power with a cocktail party or two. Too, old timers will recall that the PRSO's natural development was obstructed for a long time by surely one of the most confused and most inappropriate arts managements imaginable. But that, of course, is another story, and I mention it here only for the record. The point is that the PRSO survived for a couple of decades in spite of the agency to which its development had been entrusted—but it survived. NOW it comes out of the closet, and an analogy might be possible with some hardy and potentially lovely plant buried for years beneath a pile of

... never mind. And the result is really not all that lovely yet, either, but judging from recent seasons there is considerable hope, just as there has lately been considerable progress.

The hope is due to changes in the PRSO's administrative and contractual conditions, which just might permit a healthy renewal of personnel by providing—after thirty years, OK?—a viable retirement plan. The progress has been not only artistic, but I believe of equal importance, conceptual. For a long time the PRSO was the cinderella, the ugly duckling, the black sheep, the unmentioned relative of another musical agency but one with considerable clout; any suggestion that the island orchestra itself might assume an important role in cultural affairs was guaranteed to get a laugh. But now I think it is generally understood that in real terms of a central and permanent contribution to the musical arts in Puerto Rico, the PRSO is about all there is, and that if the musical arts are to improve here you'd better start with the resident symphony orchestra and surrounding conditions. This I believe explains the belated drafting of a pension plan, the contracting of more important soloists, the creation a few years ago of the post of associate music director, the existence of pops and school concerts, and even talk of a separate Symphony Hall that would improve the orchestra's rehearsal conditions and general musical accomplishment by some 300 percent.

But what of Saturday's concert, which launched a significant season as well as this present flow of heavy musico-political analysis? Conducted by PRSO Music Director Odón Alonso, the orchestra showed itself to be in about the same place as a year ago, carrying a burden of past sins which inevitably affect present performance. Among these sins, in addition to the one implied above in the context of retirement plans (no fault of the players, of course), a certain amount of inaccuracy of marksmanship affected the intonation, striking even the woodwinds of all people, a section which is normally the very pillar of security in this orchestra. Pitch problems were truly bothersome in the performance of the First Symphony of Mahler, and not only in the woodwinds. This condition may have resulted from the way in which the orchestra was expanded to cover the heavy instrumentation of the Mahler work, which lies beyond the regular PRSO forces.

As announced from the stage, the orchestra was augmented by a great number of younger players, who "at some future time might become regular PRSO members." Although the intention may have been laudable (to give the young folks a crack at the Mahler—or maybe to save the taxpayers a dollar or two in professional extras), the result was predictable. You see, this is like having apprentices fix your Lamborghini or perform heart surgery on your Rottweiler: it might work, but it probably won't. And it didn't work very well on Saturday, in terms of pitch, unity of expression and general orchestral security.

Roberto Sierra is one of the island's most capable and most active composers, with a long list of successful compositions to his credit and a long and continuous record of performances worldwide. He certainly knows his business when it comes to the effects which orchestral instruments can produce, effects which have been very deliberately explored for some decades now by composers but which are somewhat off the main paths traced by their predecessors from Bach to Stravinsky. In short, today's living music inhabits worlds undreamed of not long ago . . . but then so do today's painting, sculpture, poetry, literature, even architecture. What else is new?

A new work by Sierra, entitled *Descarga* and in fact commissioned by the PRSO management, was given its premiere performance on Saturday. It displayed Sierra's known skill in dealing with the orchestral possibilities, but to my ear at least, seemingly without much goal or purpose. Like much of Sierra's music, *Descarga* contains many subtle references to Caribbean music, often so skillfully woven into the orchestral texture that they pass almost unnoticed.

Descarga even builds to an expected (indeed, almost inevitable) sonoral culmination in the best tradition of orchestral music since The Rite of Spring. In other words, the effects are all there, and they are extremely well handled. What's missing, I think, is the substance . . . unless, heaven help us, the effects ARE the substance? In the words of a by now classic tune, "Is that all there is?"

César Hernández, one of Puerto Rico's outstanding tenors.

Into the Realm of Bel Canto Opera

The San Juan Star
September 17, 1988 By Donald Thompson

Teatro de la Opera is that group of courageous island opera patrons which dares to wander off the safe and familiar path of popular opera to explore realms of large scale lyric theater which should, some believe, be known at first hand. It is Teatro de la Opera which has successfully produced here such risky ventures as A *Masked Ball*, *Macbeth*, *La Forza del Destino* and *Turandot*, and it is Teatro de la Opera whose present production of Bellini's *I Puritani* has another evening to run (tonight, in fact) at the Performing Arts Center in Santurce.

I Puritani (The Puritans) is a prime example of that curious branch of opera known as "bel canto opera." What, first off, is "bel canto"? Well, basically it refers to a particular singing style developed in (you guessed it) Italy, which stressed technical brilliance and sheer beauty of sound, probably at the cost of dramatic expression and everything else.

Nobody living today can really say what, in performance, was and was not bel canto, thereby perhaps helping to reproduce it in a living human throat. However, from what was written about it and from evidence found in the music itself, it is generally agreed that bel canto singing must have produced a clear, agile, effortless, flexible, floating, seemingly disembodied sound. The operas, then, might be expected to be full of music which would emphasize this kind of singing. Too, they would have skeletal plots and librettos, just enough to move the singers on and off the stage and provide them with some texts full of vowels on which to vocalize. Finally, stage action would be minimal, because this kind of singing you can't do while running around the stage. And the orchestra? Despite the already considerable richness of instrumental combinations available in the orchestra pit by the early nineteenth century, the orchestral role would be reduced to accompanying the singers, with extremely little to do otherwise. In other words, bel canto opera would be the ideal, the ultimate, the transcendental concert-in-costume.

I think this must have been the concept which guided scholarly stage director Pablo Cabrera's staging of the present production of Bellini's *I Puritani*, and he may be on fairly solid historical ground. For periods of seemingly a half hour or more, nobody appears to move; the stage simply becomes a tableau out of which rise voices: now the chorus, now an ensemble of principal singers, now a soloist or a duo. Or very often, the voices don't rise from the static stage at all but from backstage, contributing greatly to a mystical sense of musical disembodiment to be sure, but contributing very little, I'm afraid, to the technical coordination of the various elements. Even so, such visual immobility could be justified within the concept of a concert-in costume if all voices (and I mean all) were attuned to what we think of as bel canto performance. In this production they are not.

Principal singers include soprano Masako Deguci, tenor Aldo Bertolo, baritone Pablo Elvira, bass Noel Ramírez, bass Carlos Conde, mezzosoprano Puli Toro and tenor César Hernández. As might be expected, most of the work in this piece falls to the soprano and the principal tenor. On Thursday almost all principals started weak but began to open up along about the middle of the second act. Baritone Elvira and soprano Deguci led the way in this unfolding of forces, with Deguci's clear, agile and even voice offering some of the most difficult music ever written for soprano. Until near the end of the opera tenor Bertolo displayed a good voice and fair control of it in the middle range, but his occasional high passages stung like birdshot.

Finally, however, things came together; the third act performance of Deguci and Bertolo justified in musical terms (or rather, bel canto terms) the snail-paced development of the opera itself. Bass Carlos Conde, let it be said, is an impressive recent recruit to the island's lyric stage; he has the musical equipment to accomplish a great deal as he gets a few more years on him. But it must be pointed out that on Thursday evening it was usually Pablo Elvira's entrances which awakened a somnolescent performance. Bel canto or no bel canto, on Thursday Elvira consistently maintained the long line, the extended phrase, the musical arch which is basic to vocal expression and which can bring this kind of opera to life for today's audiences if anything can.

Musical director for this production is Paul Nadler; production director, Manuel Fernández; artistic director, Antonio Barasorda; chorus director, Rafael Ferrer. Austere sets and puritanical costumes are by Sormani (Milan), and the Puerto Rico Symphony Orchestra occupies the orchestra pit.

A Festival?

The San Juan Star
October 5, 1988   By Donald Thompson

The seventh annual Inter American Arts Festival is currently in session at the Performing Arts Center in Santurce. This series involves concert music, dance, lyric theater, children's theater and other assorted forms of expression and entertainment. It results from the efforts of the Musical Arts Corporation (CAM), a government agency, and specifically the efforts of a CAM subsidiary, the Corporation of the Musico-Scenic Arts. Also acknowledged is sponsorship by the R.J. Reynolds Tobacco Co. and the Puerto Rican Commission for the Celebration of the Fifth Centennial of the Discovery of Puerto Rico and America. With such very heavy governmental and commercial artillery behind it you might think that this present Inter American Arts Festival would be a sure winner, right?

Wrong. On the musical side, at least, attendance has been extremely scanty, promotion in the island press has been almost nonexistent, and the awareness of the island citizenry is at about the level of .005%. Why is this? Well, on the island level at least, maybe the arts are really of daily interest to only about .005% of the population anyway. This is OK in itself, except that this event, like many others taking place in Puerto Rico during the past quarter century or so, has been announced as a "festival," which may have hopefully been intended to attract a new and broader audience but which in itself brings into play a whole new array of qualitative and programmatic expectations.

I myself think that the citizens are staying away from these events because they have had it with "festivals" offering little more than standard repertory performed by standard ensembles: events which if simply offered as concerts on somebody's series (WHICH series doesn't really matter) would draw the expected part of the .005% of the population that is already interested in such matters. In other words, a devaluation of the semantic currency has taken place here, specifically involving the concept of "festival" as festive, extraordinary, something to celebrate and something worth spending the taxpayers' money on.

The present series, in these terms, is simply no festival at all. On the international level, where you might think the term "festival" could still have some meaning, this one (like other "festivals" sponsored annually by the government of Puerto Rico) is completely unknown. Unknown in world listings of festivals, unknown in reference sources, unknown in travel literature and unknown in the international musical press. No pilgrim music lovers in sight, you say? Then the attendance at the official music festivals in Puerto Rico must depend exclusively on local audiences (see above), which seems to suggest a sort of vicious circle of insular cause and effect, and I mean "insular" in the geographic, governmental and cognitive senses.

What, then, of recent concerts in this series? Well, I attended one on Saturday evening in the cavernous Festival Hall (yes, it's actually called that) at the Performing Arts Center. On the stage was the Puerto Rico Symphony Orchestra conducted by Juan Pablo Izquierdo and offering some very weak music as well as some very strong music, all by South American composers (little INTER-Americanism here) and featuring noted guitarist Carlos Barbosa Lima. In the hall were so few music lovers that ushers had been instructed to empty the balcony so that the first floor, at least, might present something like an audience. Festival, indeed!

One of the very weak pieces was a guitar concerto by Heitor Villa-Lobos; surprising, until you remember that the incredibly prolific Brazilian composed more than 2,000 works. Among 2,000 compositions there must be some very weak ones, which a composer with more discipline would pitch. This guitar concerto is marked by Villa-Lobos' stylistic traits of melodiousness, harmonic simplicity and a continuous temptation to break into a tropical bolero, but with very little of the composer's incisive bite. Villa-Lobos certainly knew the guitar, though, and the concerto is so guitaristic that it would be impossible to imagine it adapted for any other instrument. On Saturday the work was saved, in fact, by soloist Barbosa Lima's fine playing, with his gifts most evident in the second movement's long cadenza, which in his hands became an imaginative fantasy for solo guitar.

Even weaker musically than the Villa-Lobos work was a watery piece by Antonio Carlos Jobim entitled *Saudades do Brasil* and also calling upon solo guitar and chamber orchestra. This work would also be thrown out by a more disciplined composer, I think. It displays only the simplest of harmonies, the most elementary principles of musical composition, and the most repetitive of procedures. For me, *Saudades do Brasil* ruined one of the most attractive devices of traditional composition, for it will be a long time before I will want to hear another four-measure repeated harmonic sequence, even by the sublime Mozart!

Saturday's strong music was a *Suite Introspectiva* by Juan José Castro and a First Symphony by Juan Orrego Salas. The Argentine Castro and the Chilean Orrego have been among the most distinguished Latin American composers of this century, and their music can hold its own against anybody's. Especially impressive was the Orrego symphony, an extended work which brings to mind the great skill and musical vision of Paul Hindemith of an earlier generation.

The Puerto Rico Symphony Orchestra sounded at its best on Saturday, except for some tragically flawed incidental solos for violin. A pity.

Spanish Guitarist's Gifts Have Deepened

The San Juan Star
October 9, 1988   By Donald Thompson

    About a quarter-century ago, this correspondent had the pleasure of preparing and conducting an entire concert of orchestral music by Joaquín Rodrigo. The concert had been organized in honor of that distinguished Spanish composer, then a visiting professor in the University of Puerto Rico Music Department, and caused a bit of a stir at the time. The event took place in the UPR Theater with the composer present and occasionally frowning but more often smiling. Among the featured soloists on that concert was Spanish guitarist Narciso Yepes, who was already forging a very impressive record as a soloist on the international circuits. Yepes had been booked for a solo recital at UPR, but graciously threw in his lot with the local forces for a significant event which is still remembered here by a handful of performers and music lovers.
    On that occasion Yepes played the Rodrigo *Fantasía para un gentilhombre* with the small orchestra which had been especially formed, impressing me and everyone else with his great technical mastery, digital facility and speed. The result of this combination of gifts was a greatly fluid and seemingly effortless performance of this melodious music. And if I'm not mistaken, this very performance by Yepes was influential in turning a few budding island guitarists toward the serious study of their instrument as a medium of concert expression.
    But so much for the passing island music scene of a quarter century ago. What brought on this attack of nostalgia was the appearance of Narciso Yepes as featured soloist with the Puerto Rico Symphony Orchestra and conductor Odón Alonso on Saturday evening. On this occasion Yepes offered a full house of music lovers in the big hall of the Performing Arts Center in Santurce the same *Fantasía para un gentilhombre* (you

guessed it) as well as Joaquín Rodrigo's equally melodious but more expansive *Concierto de Aranjuez*. If anything, Yepes' gifts of a quarter century ago have broadened and deepened, taking on a contemplative dimension as well but without sacrificing anything of his remembered technical facility and clarity. Especially impressive on Saturday were the several cadenzas and cadenza-like sections which are woven into the Rodrigo works, allowing ample space for the display of the soloist's skill. Yepes has many admirers in Puerto Rico, and several thousand of them were present on Saturday to greet him warmly, both before and after his two appearances with the PRSO.

Also offered on Saturday was nothing less than a cornucopia of orchestra soloists in works by Mozart and Rimsky-Korsakov, not to speak of the many incidental passages which occur for principal orchestra players in the two Rodrigo works. The Mozart was an early divertimento ("amusement," you might say), for oboe, two horns and string orchestra. The horns were not specifically identified in the program, but they did an excellent job along with their colleague, oboist Harry Rosario, who was appropriately identified. Rosario is a mainstay of the Music Department of the University of Puerto Rico, a regular member of the PRSO, and a versatile performer who will bear watching as his career continues to develop.

The Rimsky-Korsakov was the *Capriccio Espagnol*, subbing for the originally programmed Ravel *Rapsodie Espagnole*. The Rimsky-Korsakov work, a sort of Andalusian *Scheherazade*, is a kind of Iberian concerto for orchestra in the fashion of a Bartók, with challenging solos for violin, flute, clarinet, harp, cello and other principal players. On Saturday these duties were discharged with varying degrees of success, from the clarinet (super-extraordinary) down to shaky (not to say embarrassing) performances in the solo fiddle.

It's Refreshing to See a Maverick Thrive

The San Juan Star
November 30, 1988   By Donald Thompson

    The Latin American Foundation for Contemporary Music is one of the island's principal pillars of privately sponsored concert activity. Well, privately sponsored in the main, for this organization, like many similar ones active in the arts here, receives a bit of legislative help from time to time. Still, it's refreshing to see a maverick concert agency apparently thrive in a land where the tune is mainly called by one or another government branch directly. That the LAFCM survives is largely due to the bullheadedness of its musical director, composer Rafael Aponte-Ledée, who along with a handful of like spirits began to see some twenty years ago that the island musical establishment (at that time solidly bunkered in government) was shortchanging its constituents, the taxpayers, by completely ignoring the music of recent decades and in fact, all music which diverged from the beaten concert track and the most traditional of repertories. The official picture has changed somewhat in the meantime, indeed due in great measure to the presence of such perennial irritants as Aponte-Ledée himself, but a perceived need still exists for an occasional focused look at twentieth-century music, and here is where this organization fits in.
    One of the foundation's regular contributions is a series of especially planned and organized concerts taking place every couple of years and mainly devoted to music of this century. The present series, the Sixth San Juan Biennial, is now in session at various points in Puerto Rico, having begun with a concert by the Puerto Rico Symphony Orchestra in the UPR Theater on Saturday evening. Intersecting with its own season now in progress, the PRSO offered an interesting glance at some music

conceived in our time, although not all of it was representative of our time's principal musical trends and movements by any means.

First up was a curious work by Luciano Berio, entitled *Quattro versioni originali della 'Ritirata notturna di Madrid' di Luigi Boccherini*. Berio, born in 1925, is one of the very baddest of the bad boys of contemporary music, yet in 1975 he took time off from shocking the concert-goers to assemble these bland variations on a bland tune by the bland Italian contemporary of Haydn. These Boccherini variations have absolutely nothing to do with contemporary music—unless they were conceived a mild put-on?

But wait—do you mean to suggest that composers, Solemn Vessels of the Divine Gift, can be guilty of perpetrating put-ons? Well, friends, you might be surprised at how much concert music of the past half century, some of it hatched quite close to home, floats on flimsy footings of the jest, the wisecrack and the gag. This is of course another story, but it is the only explanation I have found for Berio's variations on Boccherini: a mild sort of joke or maybe a resurrected undergraduate orchestration exercise.

Also offered on Saturday was Lament in Memory of the Victims of Hiroshima by Krzysztof Penderecki. Penderecki, born in 1933, is a great and widely imitated innovator in the field of effects produced on the usual orchestral instruments but in unusual ways. Thus the thumps, squeals, hums, buzzes, knocks, slides and grumbles which proliferate in Penderecki's Lament as well as in untold hundreds of other orchestral works conceived in the past thirty years or so. No joking in the Lament to be sure, but a high level of sonoral and emotional tension created by the interplay of these seemingly otherworldly forces—and, of course, with the title of the piece always in mind....

As I said, these orchestral effects have been around for a while now, and you'd think that they would be known and serenely accepted by today's audiences. But then I realize that there is a whole new generation of potential concert goers alive today whose musical perceptions have been shaped by movie scores, disco-shlock and the last sad sighs of rock 'n' roll. A bit of Mendelssohn these younger folk might be able to manage, but Penderecki is strong medicine. This was demonstrated on Saturday evening by a certain amount of muffled snickering which occasionally rippled across the University of Puerto Rico Theater audience. If the San Juan Biennials of 20th Century Music help to shake island audiences up a bit and perhaps arouse some curiosity about the very big and very real world of concert music that exists out there, I'm for the Biennials!

Then there is island composer Francis Schwartz, whose Liberty Fantasy substituted on Saturday for an originally scheduled work by Cristóbal Halffter. It was Schwartz who, along with Rafael Aponte-Ledée, helped plug Puerto Rico's modest but influential avant-garde music movement into the international mainstream some twenty years ago. Lately, Schwartz' own music has often incorporated audience participation, in an avowed effort to break down what the composer perceives as artificial barriers between those who perform and those who are performed at. To what extent the barriers are undesirable is, as you and I know, debatable (after all, who wants to go cheek to cheek with a dancing bear?) but that's what happens in the Liberty Fantasy along with quotations from "God Save the King," which I believe has another set of words, too. No, not the dancing bear, I mean, but audience participation, here in the form of foot stomping, more or less to the same obsessive beat but which I believe would be more appropriate if the piece were instead entitled, say, "Nuremberg Fantasy". The Schwartz work also features the orchestral string sections passing their bows above the strings as if playing, but producing no sound at all. A wag observed in a stage whisper, "That's the best the PRSO strings have sounded all season." On the next downbeat I naturally stomped his foot as a gesture of solidarity with the PRSO, then applied a bony elbow to the trachea as an impromptu cadenza in the best spirit of Schwartzean concert improvisation.

Also presented on Saturday, perhaps as a first performance in Puerto Rico although it was not so noted in the program, was the short Antigone Symphony of the eminent Mexican composer Carlos Chávez (1899-1978). And as a cheerful antidote to all of these serious goings-on (serious with the possible exceptions of the works of Berio and—I hesitate to suggest it—Schwartz) was offered the always welcome *Divertimento del Sur* by Héctor Campos-Parsi. If Schwartz and Aponte placed Puerto Rico in contact with the aggressive international avant-garde of the late 1960s, Campos was the point of contact with a more benign line of melodious concert music a decade and a half before. His production of that period brings to mind some of the expansive theater music of Aaron Copland, for example, a far cry indeed from the Berios, the Pendereckis and the

Stockhausens. Campos' *Divertimento del Sur* is scored for flute, clarinet and string orchestra. Saturday's performance featured flutist Peter Kern and clarinetist Kathleen Jones, who along with reduced PRSO string sections gave an appropriately light and evocative reading. Saturday's able conductor was guest José Ramón Encinar.

Tribute to Vázquez

The San Juan Star
December 23, 1988   By Donald Thompson

Alejandro Vázquez was one of the astonishing number of Puerto Rican singers, out of all proportion to the island's own population, who during recent decades have increasingly peopled the world's concert and opera stages. During the years when he made his home in Europe, Alex would return to the island more or less regularly to offer an occasional recital or to take part in an opera production, thereby maintaining family and professional contacts here while sharing with island audiences his continual artistic growth. Two years ago he again established himself in San Juan, as director of the music program of the Institute of Puerto Rican Culture.

Alex died in September after a long illness, whereupon a concert which had been planned by his friends and colleagues as a fund raiser for his own medical treatments became rescheduled as a memorial concert. The money raised would then be used in his name and in support of other causes concerning worthy performers, of whom Puerto Rico certainly has no scarcity.

The rescheduled Alex Vázquez concert took place on Thursday evening in the Performing Arts Center, enlisting a stellar roster of performers and before an audience of Alex's friends in life. Necessarily using performers who were to be in Puerto Rico for the date or who could arrange to get here, Thursday's programming was eclectic but no less interesting for all of that.

As might be expected, the concert was dominated by vocal music, including a set of Schubert songs, representing a field of music in which Vázquez himself excelled. Here, Vázquez's own Spanish translation of a number of the *Schöne Müllerin* songs served as a narrated introduction to the pieces themselves. Performing were baritone Rafael Lebrón and pianist Joel Sachs, with the Spanish-language interludes delivered by Idalia Pérez Garay and with choreographic impressions by Gilda Navarra executed by dancer Roberto Rodríguez. Other vocal offerings, now from the melodious field of opera also cultivated by Alex Vázquez, were by soprano Evangelina Colón and bass-baritone Justino Díaz, accompanied by pianist Luz Hutchinson with her customary high level of skill and dedication.

The purely instrumental side of Thursday's varied memorial concert presented one of Luigi Boccherini's mellifluous quintets for guitar and string quartet, this one featuring a fandango finale whose hypnotic harmonic tonic-dominant seesaw was relieved somewhat by the contribution of offstage castanets making, technically, a sextet out of it, I suppose. Able performers were Henry Hutchinson and Mayra Urdaz, violins; Martin Goldman, viola; Rosalyn Iannelli, cello; Luis Enrique Juliá, guitar; and the anonymous off-stage castanetist.

And of course, always present in everyone's mind was tenor Alex Vázquez, who himself had made many important contributions to the island's music and in whose worthy memory this event had been organized.

♪

P.D.Q. Bach: A Rich World of Musical Parody

The San Juan Star
January 25, 1989 By Donald Thompson

The University of Puerto Rico Theater in Río Piedras was the scene of astonishing revelations last week as the distinguished (extinguished?) musicolologist (his word, not mine) Peter Schickele exposed in Puerto Rico his greatest professional resources: the life and works of the rightfully neglected composer P.D.Q. Bach.

"THIS is a life?," you might properly ask. "THESE are works?" P.D.Q. Bach and his leaden progress in the muddy field of musical decomposition are the great discovery of Schickele himself, who has brought to the stage, to recordings and to his *Definitive Biography of P.D.Q. Bach* a rich world of musical, linguistic and historical parody and humor. In Saturday's concert were to be found every sight gag that has ever occurred to irreverent orchestra players and many more; a thesaurus of musical puns and verbal twists across several languages; and a thematic catalogue of musical blunders, botches and bungles.

Nothing is sacred in Schickele's presentations right from the top, for his formal manner of professorial delivery is that suffered in every conclave of musical scholars as participants bring to light still another facet of some unexplored (and in most cases perhaps better left undisturbed) musical past. His behavior as piano soloist in the P.D.Q. Bach Concerto for Piano vs. Orchestra exposes every affectation and pose of pianists since their instrument was invented. And his appearance as a specialist in odd instruments in the P.D.Q. Bach Gross Concerto brought to mind every performance ever experienced of ancient instrument ensembles where performers juggle a variety of strange and strange-sounding instruments.

The P.D.Q. Bach music itself offers very learned and very successful satires on specific historical styles and forms, with reference also to specific instrumental usages, players' problems and orchestral situations. In this, P.D.Q.'s music is in a direct line of descent from Mozart's A Musical Joke. The main difference is that the inside jokes in the Mozart piece are so obscure and so subtle that they make sense only to specialists. Too, it may have been very difficult for Mozart to write bad music at all, whereas it apparently came perfectly naturally to P.D.Q. Bach.

The Shleptet in E Flat mimics composers' usages in chamber music and has a horn player faint as he runs out of air; the Gross Concerto is a wicked catalogue of the orchestral clichés of Antonio Vivaldi; the Concerto for Piano vs. Orchestra has the conductor lost in the score and the soloist being revived like a boxer between rounds. Attributed to Schickele himself is *Eine Kleine Nichtsmusik* (A Little Nothing-Music), which superimposes on the familiar Mozart work a stunning overlay of musical quotations ranging from nursery rhymes and "Yankee Doodle" to Tchaikovsky, Beethoven, Brahms, Grieg, Dvořák, Rossini, Verdi, a couple of Strausses, Stephen Foster . . . you name it. Only missing from this medley of familiar tunes from the concert and operatic world, I believe, is the medieval "Dies Irae," beloved of musical quoters for a couple of centuries now.

Despite his having had his occasional way with religious music (for example in the Half Nelson Mass and the *Missa Hilarious*), P.D.Q. Bach was, according to Schickele, a deeply secular composer as well as a deeply lazy one. Here is a suggestion for a new line research which could, as lines of research have a way of doing if properly cultivated and properly funded, generate countless other lines of research and so on into future centuries of P.D.Q. Bach studies: What did these jerks have against the "Dies Irae?" If it was good enough for Berlioz, Liszt, Saint-Saëns and F.A.O. Schwartz, why wasn't the "Dies Irae" good enough for P.D.Q. Bach and Peter Schickele?

Conspiring with Schickele in the exposure of P.D.Q.'s greatest glories on Saturday evening were the Puerto Rico Symphony Orchestra, conductor Roselín Pabón and Schickele's sidekick stage manager William Walters, whose ballet with music stands is guaranteed to strike home with anyone who has ever had to deal with the damned things, certainly the most unhandy implement ever devised by mankind. Also to be applauded is whoever conceived a short staged number dealing with translation, in which an intermediary was supposedly conveying to Saturday's audience the gist of Schickele's commentary in line-by-line Spanish, but was instead maligning the gullible and smiling "musicolologist" to his face.

Schwartz's Long History of New Ideas

The San Juan Star
April 5, 1989 By Donald Thompson

"Yes, the work was first performed at the Centre Pompidou shortly after our last chat (STAR, April 22, 1984) and enjoyed great success, with the concert recorded and later broadcast by Radio France. It was performed by a leading new music ensemble, the 2E2M of Paris, and employed two conductors. . . ." Thus, Francis Schwartz, leading exponent of the musical avant-garde in Puerto Rico, described the premiere performance of his *Grimaces* (Paris, 1984). This interview was conducted in the composer's pleasant apartment in the University of Puerto Rico Faculty Residences in Río Piedras, for in addition to his international activities Schwartz has been for almost a quarter century a leading figure in the cultural life of the island's principal university and indeed of Puerto Rico itself. The immediate reason for the conversation is a concert of Schwartz' music to be offered this evening by the University of Puerto Rico Cultural and Recreational Activities Program.

DT: As you have indicated, every now and again over the years and decades we have discussed your work, your plans and the state of new music in the world generally. The first of these conversations took place almost ten years ago (STAR, August 28, 1979), and through them we've been able to trace the evolution of your views while noting several phases of technological advancement in the broader world of music. Tell me first about two conductors, please. Many of our friends in symphony orchestras around the world would maintain that one conductor at a time is bad enough; why are two required for your *Grimaces*?

FS: One for the instrumentalists and one for the audience, because the work involves audience participation as a basic element.

DT: How are the two conductors deployed in such a work? Would you say belly to belly, or cheek to cheek, or what? And what about that audience participation? Tell the readers about THAT.

FS: The two conductors are back to back, naturally, and as for audience participation, this is nothing new in my music. I have long felt, along with John Cage and other experimenters, that the traditional separation of performers from audiences in Western concert music is completely artificial and counterproductive. Much healthier is the non-Western view: that art is life and that everyone possesses some degree of artistic ability, therefore being capable of participating in the unfolding of the art work. My own experience has convinced me that audiences yearn to participate more directly in concerts, and a great deal of my music is conceived to make this possible. A great number of my works composed during the past fifteen years incorporate the participation of the audience, which then becomes a collaborator rather than simply a passive "target" or consumer, you might say.

DT: What else have you been up to during the past few years?

FS: Among other things, I've had some works premiered in important places, thereby bearing the message abroad and certainly not doing any harm to the understanding abroad of Puerto Rico's musical movement, either. Among these were Let There be Peace: Homage to Segovia (New York, 1987), in a performance which the great guitarist himself attended not long before his death. Just recently, then, my The Haunted Palace was premiered at the Library of Congress in Washington by the Arioso Trio, a splendid chamber music ensemble.

DT: What about your recent compositions? How would you describe their style?

FS: Well, I never thought it would happen, but I've reached a new stage in my development which I can only refer to as conservative! I find myself utilizing techniques that go back to my student days, resulting in music which reminds some listeners of works of Alban Berg, Bela Bartók and other early twentieth-century composers.

DT: Have you given up such things as audience participation, aromas and computer generated sound, which identified your music of eight or ten years ago?

FS: By no means. These things still appeal to me, but now I find myself using other elements too, in perhaps a more consolidated way. For example, I still have instrumentalists do things during the work which are not traditionally asked of instrumentalists—on the job, at any rate.

DT: Such as?

FS: Such as in Daimon II: El Velorio, which was premiered by the Continuum ensemble at Lincoln Center in 1985. Here, the instrumentalists in addition to playing their instruments are directed to execute some steps reminiscent of Flamenco dance. And why not? The sound of the heels on the floor is certainly musical, while the movement of the instrumentalists' bodies adds an important visual effect, making of the work a "music theater" piece.

DT: Traditionally, instrumentalists have been hired on the basis of their playing skill alone; this has been at least theoretically true if not always observed in practice. Do you think that the time may come when instrumentalists applying for certain jobs will be asked to dance and sing as well?

FS: Why not? Something similar has happened in opera in recent decades due the influence of television and the movies. The opera public is much more conscious of physical appearance than it was fifty years ago. The voice is still supreme in opera, but you can be sure that there won't be any more 300 pound, 60 year old Salomes. Today's sopranos and tenors in youthful roles have to look and move like young people. And in my music theater pieces as well in a lot of other new music, instrumentalists must be able to move around a bit and do other things besides play their instruments.

DT: What have you done about computers?

FS: I use computers in two ways, as do most composers today. First is computer-generated sound, which was big news a few years ago. You'd go to a concert and face a pair of speakers on the stage emitting computer-generated sounds without a human being in sight. Fortunately, this phase didn't last very long, and composers soon began to incorporate computer music with "real time" human performers on the stage. This is what I've done, again in the way of integration or consolidation of resources. Second, the music writing programs that are now available have been a lifesaver to me; combined with interface software they enable a composer to play music at a keyboard, see it notated on the screen, make changes visibly and immediately, and even print out conductor's scores and instrumental parts. In both ways, I use computer technology frequently.

DT: Let's talk about audiences. Are there audiences for your . . . umm . . . consolidation of traditional instrumental and vocal usages, computer sound, aromas, audience participation and other manifestations, the whole rather reminiscent—you must admit—of the "happening" of two decades ago?

FS: Yes. When the sophisticated Alice Tully Hall audience at Lincoln Center applauds wildly at the end of Daimon II and asks for more of the same, you can be sure that there is an audience. When several hundred people from off the street joyfully take part in my *Mon Oeuf* (Paris, 1979), you can be sure that there is an audience. And when regular concertgoers in Puerto Rico still stop me on the street to ask me when the Puerto Rico Symphony Orchestra will perform another work like my *Gestos* (1983), you can be sure that there is an audience.

DT: So OK, OK, you've convinced me. An audience you have. Tell me something about your plans.

FS: First up is a commission for a double bass concerto for the great Gary Karr, a collaboration which I find tremendously exciting. As you know, Gary is a great showman in addition to being probably the world's finest double bass soloist. He appeared on the same PRSO concert as my *Gestos* in 1983, and felt that he simply had to have a *Schwartzwerk* in his repertory; the result will be this concerto, which he will premiere with one of the world's major orchestras. I also have cooking a song cycle entitled *Songs of the Americas*, for voice, flute and piano, commissioned by the Latin American Foundation for Contemporary Music and scheduled for first performance here in November 1989. Too, the management of the Puerto Rico Symphony Orchestra has commissioned a new work from me after well over a decade of my exclusion from this type of direct public support. The new work, entitled Christopher Columbus Fantasy, will appear on the final concert of the PRSO season, on April 29.

DT: I think that this just about brings us up to date regarding your activities during the past five years. Now tell me about tonight's concert. What is this *Caligula: Twenty Years of Music Theater by Francis Schwartz*?

FS: Well, *Caligula* is a reference to the titles of two works of mine. First, to My Name's Caligula; What's Yours?, which caused a bit of a stir when it was first presented in the mid-1970s. That piece incorporated most of the elements which were to characterize my compositions for the following fifteen years or so: musical instruments used in unusual ways, odors, performers moving about the stage, "music theater," etc. The title, then, suggests a sort of "field" which characterizes my work during this period. Secondly, *Caligula* is the title of a more recent work, for electronic sounds and dancer, which will be presented this evening. In fact, a total of seven representative pieces will be performed on this concert, by such fine performers as Sunshine Logroño, Awilda Sterling, Rafael Ferrer, Harry Rosario and Roberto Ramírez. Included will be the premiere performance of a new song of mine, "La hora del alma," inspired by a text by Eugenio María de Hostos and sung by soprano Melissa Santana Frasqueri. And too, music scholars will find plenty to think about in matters related to the elusive Rinsuk family, members of which may have had important connections with the musical life of Puerto Rico in the nineteenth century.

DT: Rinsuk, Rinsuk . . . ? I don't know that name! Forget Caligula and the stinks; I'll be there this evening to see what I can learn about this hitherto unknown aspect of nineteenth-century Puerto Rican music!

Soprano Colón Superb in *Luisa Fernanda*

The San Juan Star
April 20, 1989   By Donald Thompson

Zarzuela is a peculiarly Spanish form of light lyric theater which has enjoyed a fervent following in Puerto Rico ever since its introduction here some 135 years ago. The manufacture of new zarzuelas to supply Spain and the rest of the Hispanic world with mildly spiced musical entertainment was one of Madrid's principal industries for some decades before and immediately following the beginning of the present century, but the pressure of newer and more flexible forms of entertainment has brought the Madrid zarzuela mill to a halt. Attention is now focused upon a repertory of maybe thirty beloved favorites, a number distilled from a total production of thousands of works.

Playing over the weekend in the Festival Hall at the Performing Arts Center was one of San Juan's favorite zarzuelas, *Luisa Fernanda*, by Federico Moreno Torroba on a script by the proprietors of Madrid's foremost libretto factory, Federico Romero and Guillermo Fernández Shaw. The production was mounted by the venerable Elsa Rivera Salgado Lyric Theater Foundation, with Enriquillo Cerón as musical director, the gifted Myrna Casas as stage director, simple but effective settings by José Llompart and a large chorus prepared by Héctor Vega Drouet. Several very effective dance numbers had been staged by Zaida Varas, while the design of costumes was credited to San Juan's own Wardrobe Research & Design, Inc.

Luisa Fernanda dates from 1932, representing the last nostalgic gasp of the dying species and hopefully incorporating all of the features which had marked the heyday of the romantic zarzuela, forty years before. Among these are a sentimental plot centered on a love triangle, itself involving exalted sentiments of duty, loyalty and honor. Too, the work involves an historical angle: here, the popular restlessness marking the end of the reign of Queen Isabel II, a chorus of happy (or angry) peasants and villagers, an exotic setting which justifies some colorful dance numbers, and of course a bit of singing and acting.

The exalted foreground of this recent production was occupied by soprano Evangelina Colón in the title role, baritone Rafael Torréns as the wealthy but ultimately unsuccessful suitor Vidal, and tenor Rodolfo Acosta as the successful suitor (successful for no reason that I could perceive, dramatically or vocally). Skilled soprano Migdalia Batiz provided the wild card, the unsettling factor in the dramatic equation. And it must be pointed out that veteran actress Isabel Sánchez, here cast in the comic role of Marina, displayed considerable vocal skill, too. Jaime Figueroa played the role of Aníbal and Danilo Soto, that of Jeromo.

Island soprano Evangelina Colón is now settled in Europe, where she is carrying forward a very successful singing career. Her performances here as Luisa Fernanda demonstrated her continued growth both vocally and dramatically; the latter was noted especially in dialogue scenes toward the end of the zarzuela, where she really grabbed hold of the character whom she represented. At these moments Colón gave the work the only real dramatic thrust forward which it inherently offers. Baritone Torréns, a known and admired quantity vocally, has also gained in dramatic intensity lately, while his excellent sense of timing contributed to the success of his dialogue scenes. Tenor Acosta, on the other hand, has a promising voice, but his work in *Luisa Fernanda* displayed uncertain pitch and questionable technique. Acosta's acting seemed wooden in the Saturday performance which I witnessed (perhaps because of the Chocolate Soldier costume which he had to wear most of the time), and it would also be a good idea for him to take some dancing lessons sometime.

Dancing . . . dancing? Yes, Zaida Varas' excellent work as choreographer, as well as a fine dance troupe, saved an otherwise soporific third act on Saturday, while also to be highly commended is the work of veteran actors Jorge Rechani and Ricardo Fábregues, along with that of Jaime Figueroa as the comic Amílcar.

Freni In Top Form

The San Juan Star
April 25, 1989   By Donald Thompson

  The Puerto Rico Symphony Orchestra is the cornerstone of the island's musical life, for its activities and those of its individual members generate a field of energy which sooner or later affects all other aspects of music in Puerto Rico. Some aspects of music beyond Puerto Rico as well, you might say, for many works commissioned for and first performed by the PRSO later turn up in other places as a matter of course, while you can be sure that soloists, conductors and section members who have performed with the PRSO will carry the word (be it good or bad) abroad with them.

  I think it can be said without exaggeration, then, that what's good for the PRSO is good for music in Puerto Rico and, yes, even for that coveted international image whose often misdirected pursuit consumes so much governmental energy year in and year out. In other words, a step forward for the PRSO is a step forward for a number of fine causes.

  An event devoted to aiding in the PRSO's progress is the annual PRSO Pension Fund Gala Concert. How, you might ask, can such a mundane and unromantic thing as a pension fund aid in orchestral progress? Simply by enabling the orchestral roster to become periodically refreshed through a reasoned program of renewal through retirement, which itself is really only the other face of the golden coin of recruitment. Without the former the latter can never occur, and although many of us would prefer to believe differently, when it comes right down to arthritis, failing eyesight and general weariness, the orchestral profession is neither less mundane nor more romantic than any other. The PRSO Pension Fund Gala Concerts have taken a regular place in Puerto Rico's annual parade of musical rites and rituals, and have in recent years attained a level of glitter formerly reserved for events of a more self-consciously proclaimed "international" character. Too, these concerts have regularly engaged the participation of first rate musical attractions as soloists; immediate memory offers such winners as Alicia de Larrocha and Itzhak Perlman, among others.

The 1989 PRSO Pension Fund Gala Concert, jointly sponsored by Culturarte de Puerto Rico, Inc., took place on Saturday evening before a large audience in the Festival Hall of the Performing Arts Center. It may be, however, that what attracted some concertgoers was not the philosophical attraction of a noble cause, but the aesthetic attraction of a great voice: that of soprano soloist Mirella Freni, no less! Freni had last been heard here some ten or so years ago, and to my ear her gifts have not declined one whit in the meantime. This wise performer chooses her repertory very carefully, doing only what she does best and applying a level of professional discipline not always found among star singers. Consequently, Freni's presentation on Saturday emphasized the broadly expressive and lyric gift for which she is noted. Most impressive to my ears were the great dramatism, vast dynamic range, flexible expression and generally clear, open singing displayed in a moving excerpt from Verdi's grim opera *Don Carlo*. Other selections ranged from Puccini through Bizet ("Micaela's Aria"), Boito and Cilea, in a grand display of familiar and beloved opera music delivered in the illuminating Freni style.

The Puerto Rico Symphony Orchestra itself shared the stage with Freni, under the direction of the PRSO's regular conductor, Odón Alonso. In addition to accompanying the flexible Freni with efficient skill, Alonso led his forces in a number of orchestral excerpts and other instrumental selections, extending from two pieces from the hereabouts unknown *Le Villi* by Puccini to a hereabouts deadly familiar orchestral suite drawn from Bizet's *Carmen*.

The fifth row of a hall, where I was seated on Saturday, is not, to my way of thinking, the best place in which to experience a concert. At this distance, one sees and hears some things which are perhaps better left unseen and unheard. On the other hand, my concert consort, herself a singer, greatly enjoyed her proximity to the soloist, while I was pleased to witness at the distance of a mere nose-tweak, as you might say, some fine playing by the PRSO cello section in an extended Verdi excerpt.

♪

Symphony Orchestra Sounds Final Notes of UPR Series

The San Juan Star
May 17, 1989 By Donald Thompson

The Puerto Rico Symphony Orchestra's end of season activities brought the whole ensemble back to the University of Puerto Rico Theater in Río Piedras on Saturday evening for the last of its six concerts in that venerable hall. Jointly sponsored by the UPR Office of Cultural and Recreational Activities, Saturday's concert was conducted by the PRSO's own associate conductor Roselín Pabón, and featured the varied kind of programming which has characterized this interesting series.

First up on Saturday was a big work by island composer Jack Délano. Entitled *La Reina Tembandumba*, the Délano work dates from 1966 and evokes the spirit of the Afro-Caribbean poetry of Puerto Rican writer Luis Palés Matos. *La Reina Tembandumba* is thus getting on for a quarter century of life but seems to be surviving very well, considering all of the styles, modes and fads which have affected (or perhaps "infected") musical composition in Puerto Rico since the 1960s. I believe, in fact, that this is one of Délano's most successful compositions, and wish it another quarter century of performances.

I also believe that Roselín Pabón has more success with *La Reina Tembandumba* than any other conductor, mainly because he perceives better than anyone else the relationships which exist among the tempos of the composition's various sections and keeps the work rolling by convincingly connecting them.

Saturday's soloist was flutist Rubén López, a regular member of the PRSO and a very capable soloist indeed. I had wondered why I had never heard the Pastoral Concerto for Flute and Orchestra by Joaquín Rodrigo, the work which featured López as soloist. Well, there are two reasons, as I now see. One is that the work is extremely difficult for the soloist, and anyone who dares play it must have a great set of chops and a lot of courage besides. The other reason is that the work is wearisome junk, a real drag, man, which is certainly not worthy of Joaquín Rodrigo and which should be stowed at the very back of the cabinet, carefully lost together with Beethoven's Choral Fantasy and the same composer's dippy Wellington's Victory. No, I'll take that back, partly. Like the embarrassing Beethoven works, the Pastoral Concerto should be played once every twenty years or so, in order that apprentice music lovers might see that composers are human too, just that some of them have very little taste when it comes to their own music.

This work of Rodrigo's is mainly characterized by the mindless repetition of pointless phrases, and perhaps even by a bit of extramusical suggestion in the way of program music. You know how some composers, and even some people who should know better, encourage us to seek extramusical correspondences in musical sounds, in the fortuitous manner of radio sound effects? Thus, a timpani roll can remind some listeners of thunder; a trill high in the flute a cute birdie; a low trill in the same instrument a flowing brook; certain guitar effects, creepy-crawlies in the jungle; busy-busy woodwinds, scurrying furry creatures; etc. Well, maybe crafty Joaquín Rodrigo had something of this sort up his sleeve for us in the last movement of this Pastoral Concerto: a spastic chicken, no less. Be it understood that none of this grumbling is intended to detract a whit from Rubén López' skilled playing of the Rodrigo work, nor from the patience which conductor Pabón and the PRSO had bestowed upon its preparation. But for me, if I hear the piece again in twenty years it'll be too soon.

Closing Saturday's concert was one of the confusingly renumbered symphonies of Antonin Dvořák: the one now called No. 7 in D Minor (1884-85), but not to be confused with the one now known as No. 4, also in D Minor but dating from some ten years earlier. In any case, most of our Dvořák symphony of Saturday could easily have been written not by Dvořák at all but by Brahms, so consistently did Dvořák utilize the rhythmic and harmonic resources which we associate more with the German composer.

Saturday's performance of the Dvořák symphony was satisfying in every way. Pabón conducted with a firm and clear beat, drawing good dynamic contrast and nicely shaped phrases from the PRSO. Throughout the work, incidental solo passages displayed the skill of the orchestra's principal horn, clarinet, flute and other prized PRSO members.

♪

A World Far From Tense Concert Atmosphere

The San Juan Star
June 13, 1989   By Donald Thompson

    Distinguished guitarist Narciso Yepes provided the fourth concert in the Casals Festival series, attracting a large audience to the main hall at the Performing Arts Center on Friday evening. Yepes is well known and widely admired here; his most recent island appearance had occurred only seven months before, in fact, in the same hall but as soloist with the Puerto Rico Symphony Orchestra in November. On Friday, Yepes displayed the other side of his great skill and his extensive repertory: as solo recitalist in a richly varied program of music for the solo guitar. Following the generally historical scheme favored by most recital soloists, Yepes unfolded a fine variety of works and styles reaching from the thirteenth century down to music composed in recent years.

    Historically, most music for solo guitar has been written by guitarists, much in the same way that pianists themselves have generated most solo piano music. This being the case, guitar recitals usually offer a goodly percentage of music composed by guitarists, and usually a goodly percentage of the music presented is very, very familiar. Such was the case on Friday, with Fernando Sor, Regino Sainz de la Maza and Leo Brouwer all represented and represented very well. Heitor Villa-Lobos, also represented on Friday, was also a guitarist, although we do not often think of him in this connection, for his importance as a composer far outweights whatever contribution he might have made as an instrumentalist. Of this selection from the "It takes one to know one" segment of Friday's recital, I was most impressed by Yepes' performance of the Brouwer *Tarantos*, a fully convincing piece of contemporary guitar music conceived, according to useful notes in the program book, especially for Narciso Yepes and for the resources offered by his ten-string guitar.

The dedicatory piece is a nicely evocative genre of concert music, and it too was present on Friday, with Manuel de Falla's *Pour le Tombeau de Claude Debussy* and Joaquín Rodrigo's *Invocación y Danza (Homenaje a Manuel de Falla)*. The Rodrigo work is one of the Spanish composer's meatier compositions. Posthumous homage music is often evocative of the person in whose memory the music is offered, and this is certainly the case in the Falla and Rodrigo pieces offered on Friday: the former evocative of Debussy and the latter of Falla himself.

Part of the repertory of guitarists regularly consists of music originally conceived for other media of performance, and sometimes this practice of adaptation works while other times it doesn't work very well. Friday's transcriptions from other fields of music included a creampuff from the piano repertory, Xavier Montsalvatge's well known *Habanera*, as well as more serious and more successful transcriptions from keyboard music composed originally by Domenico Scarlatti and violin music by J.S. Bach (the latter's awesome D Major Chaconne). For this reviewer, however, the most welcomed music on Friday's recital was music apparently conceived for no particular instrument at all, but which has been retrieved from one of the great and venerable treasures of European poetry, art and music. This treasure is the thirteenth-century *Cantigas de Santa María*, associated with the figure of King Alfonso X of Castile and León and itself the source of some 400 poems of inestimable cultural and historical value. On Friday, Yepes presented a suite of some eight or ten of the *Cantigas*, melodies which seem apt for a plucked-string instrument, opening a window on a scene far from the often tense and strained world of today's concert music.

Márquez Performance a Reunion

The San Juan Star
June 17, 1989   By Donald Thompson

Soprano Marta Márquez was the featured soloist Thursday in the eighth concert of the Casals Festival. Very active in Europe these days, Ms. Márquez is of island birth and early training; for this reason, her concert appearances in Puerto Rico offer not only the glory of first rate musical presentations but also the joy of family reunions.

Faultlessly accompanied by pianist Hannelott Weigelt, the soprano presented a well chosen selection of more or less familiar German songs, beautifully balanced by a solo cantata by G.F. Handel, previously unknown here.

The Handel cantata is entitled *Lucrecia*. Of tragic intensity and demanding technical requirement, this is a challenging concert opener for anyone, for it gives the soloist extremely little time to get cranked up and running not only technically but in the expressive realm as well. The Márquez performance was marked by absolute technical skill and control as well as by completely convincing emotional communication of this woeful work.

The rest of Thursday's recital ranged across the field of German song from Mozart through Mendelssohn and down to that great master, Hugo Wolf. Most of the Mozart songs offered on Thursday sounded like . . . well, like Mozart opera arias. And rightly, for Mozart's deep theatrical sense permeated all of his music, even, some would say, his great symphonies. And Ms. Márquez sang them like opera arias, with beautifully appropriate hand gestures and facial expressions moderated somewhat, to be sure, for the concert stage.

The six Mendelssohn songs explored depths of emotion not usually associated with the music of this composer, whose production is often considered facile, superficial, lightweight. But as is nicely pointed out in program notes by Ramón Arroyo Carrión, Mendelssohn's songs suffer in this regard only when compared to those of his great contemporaries Schubert and Schumann. On their own terms, however, they are completely successful.

Ah, but Hugo Wolf: THERE was a song composer. Wolf's sophisticated settings, fitted hand in glove to their poetic texts, brought the great nineteenth-century German song tradition to its culminating point. Thursday's eight songs displayed the entire possible gamut of text and music as combined in this intimate art: kittenish, demure, contemplative, angry, coquettish; all perfectly brought to life by the incomparable team of soprano Marta Márquez and pianist Hannelott Weigelt.

TV's Drawbacks

The San Juan Star
June 18, 1989 By Donald Thompson

Noted mezzosoprano Frederica von Stade made her first appearance at the Casals Festival on Friday evening, alongside the National Symphony Orchestra under the direction of Mstislav Rostropovich. It took quite a while for the event to settle down into the major kind of concert which these evenings are supposed to represent, for it began in the spirit of an afternoon pops concert, or maybe of activities connected with the inauguration of a shopping mall. Not that I have anything against pops concerts or the appearance of symphony orchestras at shopping mall inaugurations, naturally. These activities, in fact, are an important part of the real life of many symphony orchestras on their home turf. But to consume the very limited time of a powerful visiting orchestra during a festival which is supposedly devoted to higher matters, in the performance of "encore music?" Come on, please.

The von Stade voice was most wisely used on Friday in the performance of Maurice Ravel's subtle cycle of *Shéhérazade* songs. Composed in the very early years of the present century, these songs perfectly evoke the perfumed, exotic, not to say decadent verses of "Tristan Klingsor" (Leon Leclerk). The von Stade mezzo is admirably suited to their performance: flexible, open and with a complete range of subtle expression.

The National Symphony Orchestra certainly gets a good sound, as well it might with those big string sections, and Mstislav Rostropovich is, as everyone knows, an incomparable instrumentalist. Still, there were times on Friday when a disjunction among forces would cause a moment's uncertainty. This occurred, for example, during the last of the Ravel songs and during an excerpt from Offenbach's operetta, The Grand Duchess of Gerolstein, when sections of the orchestra were uncertain whether to follow the singer or stay behind with the boss. Most members prudently opted for the latter alternative.

Realizing at intermission that we had not yet shared the joys of home television viewers during the present series, my concert consort and I hastened to our suburban nest, cranked up the TV and sat before it in full concert costume and at full concert attention for the second half of Friday's event. This would also give us an idea of how WIPR, the government's television authority, is faring under its new management in realms of live concert coverage. What did we see? We saw one of the best possible applications of television, as the camera continuously placed one or another performer or section right up close to us. Maybe all too close at times depending on what a momentarily unoccupied instrumentalist might have been doing just at the time the camera focused on him or her. . . . But the reward is worth the risk, for matters belabored in the classroom by generations of music appreciation teachers and diligently studied by technically minded music lovers can now become brilliantly clear, as the camera puts the viewer nose to nose with the second oboe or with the conductor himself.

And what did we hear? Having just come from the concert hall we were immediately conscious of the great deficiency in the transmitted sound, as delivered both by a three-year-old television set and by a separate and brand new AM/FM receiver. A complicating factor was what must have been disastrous microphone placement in the hall and/or subsequent mixing and adjustment during the transmission process, for the instrumental imbalance was extreme, with winds consistently overpowering the strings to a grotesque extent far beyond any possibility of any concert hall. Consequently, it was not possible for us to gain much of an idea of the musical values of this performance, which represented still another presentation here of the Second Symphony of Johannes Brahms.

On balance, then, and on the basis of this recent experience, I believe television to be an extremely valuable visual tool of public education in such fields as orchestral music, auto mechanics, brain surgery and anything else involving tools, process, dexterity and concentration. And this is probably why WIPR was first placed within the cabinet-level Department of Education. We'll see now how it fares under the Puerto Rico Telephone Company. In any case, video-wise, what we experienced on Friday was a winner. Audio-wise, the process wants some improvement before I, for one, can take it very seriously as a substitute for the concert hall.

Gabrieli Does Its Namesake Proud

The San Juan Star
June 27, 1989 By Donald Thompson

Much has been written, in these pages and elsewhere, about the additional benefits which a properly constituted symphony orchestra can generate in a community, painlessly and almost automatically. These benefits usually include the creation of chamber ensembles by instrumentalists connected with the orchestra who wish to explore other performance possibilities as well. Our Puerto Rico Symphony Orchestra is no exception; its members have formed several fine chamber ensembles and continue to do so, both for their own pleasure and for the enlightenment of island audiences.

Recently joining this family of orchestra-based chamber groups in San Juan has been Gabrieli; not "The Gabrieli" or "Johnny Gabrieli and Friends" but simply . . . Gabrieli. Named for the great Italian composer of polyphonic and polychoral instrumental music, our present Gabrieli comprises a brass quintet of standard instrumentation: two trumpets, French horn, trombone and tuba. Members are, respectively, Roberto Ramírez and Roberto Gándara; Javier Gándara; Jaime Morales Matos; and Rubén Ramírez. All of these worthy instrumentalists are or have been associated with the PRSO, and all bring to their task the benefits of excellent training and solid professional experience.

Gabrieli is just now attached to an international conclave of young orchestra players in progress here, as teachers of their instruments and as a resident professional ensemble. This association brought the group to the Puerto Rico Conservatory of Music on Friday evening for a fine concert of brass quintet music which spanned the ages and the continents. In honor of old Giovanni Gabrieli himself, the ensemble offered one of the master's brief *Canzone per Sonare*, which represent a generalized

Renaissance/Baroque ancestor of the later fugue, concerto, sonata and other forms of instrumental music. Sunday's *canzona* was brilliantly and vigorously played, with its tricky changes in meter and pulse very nicely executed. A major work on Friday was a subtle three-movement quintet by the contemporary British composer Malcolm Arnold. The Arnold work is handsomely tailored for the brass quintet medium, for it regularly calls into play the specific resources of each of the five instruments: everyone is a soloist. This, in fact, is why chamber music appeals so strongly to good orchestra players, who can in this way hear themselves as individuals instead of as more or less anonymous contributors to a vast sonoral enterprise.

Also offered on Friday were attractive original works and arrangements of music by Morley Calvert, Ludwig Maurer, Emmanuel Chabrier, Leonard Bernstein, Puerto Rico's own Luis R. Miranda, and a wildly humorous arrangement of a "Moto Perpetuo" of Johann Strauss. Speaking of arrangements, it would help a great deal if Gabrieli's printed material could include a little more information about the pieces to be played. Program notes would be ideal, of course, but in their absence at least the dates of composers and the identification of arrangers could help audiences (to say nothing of reviewers) to better place the works in historical and geographical context.

The Gabrieli ensemble played Sunday's concert with absolute rhythmic security, an amazing dynamic range and perfectly adjusted intonation, right there on the razor's edge all the time. This group constitutes a very serious addition to the island's world of chamber music, and will bear watching as it continues to develop.

A Stirring Rendition of Prokofiev Cantata

The San Juan Star
November 14, 1989 By Donald Thompson

The Puerto Rico Symphony Orchestra and its able conductor Odón Alonso were on the road again on Friday, bringing an interesting evening concert of choral/orchestral music out to the University of Puerto Rico Río Piedras Campus. Don't laugh at the expression "on the road"; it wasn't many years ago that Río Piedras was a remote and sleepy village a half day's travel and a world away from bustling and sophisticated San Juan. Well, it's again becoming a half day's job to get from San Juan to Río Piedras, but the UPR campus has become simply another metropolitan convergence of convenience (or inconvenience) for thousands of people who, once having reached home in Caguas, Fajardo or Vega Baja on a hassled Friday afternoon, are not about to turn around and fight the potholes and the crazies back to Río Piedras again, not even for Brahms, Prokofiev and the Puerto Rico Symphony Orchestra.

This is probably partly why the big UPR Theater was nowhere near full on Friday evening. Times have changed, and along with them the nature, the expectations and the priorities of potential concert audiences, including university students, university faculties and other residents of this sprawling metropolitan area. The understanding of these sociological changes and of their effects on concert life is a matter of great importance, but it is not one to be approached in a music review, right? Still, I hope someone's doing some research and serious planning in connection with the future of concert music in Puerto Rico and with the fundamental role in it of the PRSO, a branch of the government of the Commonwealth of Puerto Rico.

Opening Friday's concert was the Rhapsody for Contralto, Male Chorus and Orchestra, Op. 53, by Johannes Brahms. More familiarly known as the "Alto Rhapsody," this expansive work is a companion piece to the same composer's masterful Requiem, successfully performed here by the PRSO a couple of years ago. The excellent Coral Filarmónica (Philharmonic Chorus) shared the stage with the PRSO on Friday as it had in the performance of the Requiem, and was again rehearsed for this occasion by its expert director, Carmen Acevedo. The new element in Friday's formula was soloist Birgit Finnilae, whose warm contralto contrasted nicely with the dark sonority of Brahms' writing for male chorus.

Following intermission occurred what may have been a premiere performance in Puerto Rico of Prokofiev's heroic cantata *Alexander Nevsky*. This work had its origins in a film conceived and directed by the great Sergei Eisenstein, based on an historical event, the successful defense by Russian forces during a thirteenth-century invasion by a Swedish army. Conceived at the height of Russian consolidation of the resources of the Soviet Union during the late 1930s, the film and its music drew heavily on broad themes of folk, unity and fatherland, somewhat simplified in the name of politicizing and nationalizing culture for the cause, but quite characteristic of a great deal of music composed in the thirties, and not only in the Soviet Union. For Prokofiev, one of the world's most innovative composers of abstract music, some of the popularizing may have been heavy going, but in 1939 it earned the film one of the Soviet Union's highest awards, the Lenin Prize. As things went, Prokofiev's later music was severely condemned on grounds of "decadent formalism" by the Central Committee of the All-Union Communist Party in 1948, but that's another story.

The seven-movement cantata which Prokofiev extracted from the 1938 *Alexander Nevsky* film music stands today as an interesting choral work if not a particularly profound one. It also stands as a monument to the practice of defensive composition for the glorification of the fatherland (or whatever) through the mollification of the Central Committee, wherever it may be found and whatever it might be called. Friday's performance of this big work was probably as stirring and as musically convincing as anyone can make it, as offered by the Puerto Rico Symphony Orchestra, the Coral Filarmónica and contralto soloist Birgit Finnilae.

Starker's Unforgettable Subtlety

The San Juan Star
November 22, 1989 (a)   By Donald Thompson

Renowned cellist Janos Starker was the featured soloist with the Puerto Rico Symphony Orchestra on Saturday, with a faultless performance of the B Minor Cello Concerto of Antonín Dvořák. Here is a supreme master of his instrument, for Starker ranks among the leading cellists of the twentieth century. And not only that, but he has also exercised a great and far reaching influence on cello playing in his own time, as a teacher in the very powerful School of Music of Indiana University. It is always a supreme pleasure to hear him.

Starker's playing of the Dvořák concerto was a revelation of skill and subtlety, although his skill and subtlety were not always matched on the orchestral side. Our orchestra principals held up their end beautifully in duo passages involving the soloist and flute, clarinet, oboe and violin, but their colleagues back in the sections sometimes fell into one or another of the many orchestral boobytraps which lurk in this work. Also, a moment's disunity would occasionally mar a big orchestral entrance following a solo passage, or blur an accompaniment figure.

"Why can't this orchestra ever play *dolce?*," asks a music lover at intermission. Others have frequently asked in exasperation why the string sound is thin or why some other chronic condition affects the orchestra's work season after season. Well, friends, the PRSO is not the Philadelphia or the Chicago or even, bless us, the ever hopeful National of Washington. The subtlety attained by the Chicago and Philadelphia orchestras results from big string sections, fine instruments, long seasons and an average level of individual skill (read "salary") which is utterly irrelevant in Puerto Rico now and for a long time to come—probably forever. Quality requires money, planning and maintenance in symphony orchestras as in highway systems, libraries and public schools. Looking at it this way, I place the PRSO, with all of its problems, among the more successful efforts of the Commonwealth government just now, and yes, perhaps for a long time to come.

But how did we get onto this subject? Oh yes, Starker's extremely subtle and flexible playing, long to be remembered. Other works on Saturday's program included a set of Dvořák's sparkling Slavonic Dances as the opener and Tchaikovsky's monumental Sixth Symphony, the "Pathétique," as the closer. This Tchaikovsky is big music and, again, requires big and flexible forces for an ideal realization. Saturday's realization was by no means ideal, although I believe that the orchestra and conductor Odón Alonso gave it their very best shot. Tchaikovsky's heavy winds tended to overbalance the rachitic PRSO string sections when push really came to shove, while a wrong note or two resulted from apparent overenthusiasm here and there in the orchestra as Tchaikovsky's grandiose phrases really got up and marched. My concert consort was thrilled by it all; as for me, well, I don't like that piece much anyway, and all the way home I tried to clean out my memory with phrases recalled from Mozart string quartets.

Pre-National Universality

The San Juan Star
November 22, 1989 (b)   By Donald Thompson

    The Latin American Foundation for Contemporary Music is certainly the least predictable of Puerto Rico's established concert forces, but year in and year out it presents a series of attractive and extremely varied concerts. The Foundations's major commitment is to far-reaching and imaginative biennial presentations of international contemporary music, yet between times it keeps us on our toes with other events ranging from medieval music to popular-commercial music of the 1930s. On Sunday evening in the Experimental Hall of the Performing Arts Center, the Foundation offered a thought-provoking concert of old music associated with the Iberian peninsula, presented by the sterling ensemble Alhambra. Alhambra, based in New York City, consists of three scholarly and versatile performers: Isabelle Ganz, Martha McGaughey and George Mgrdichian. Among them the three perform a number of instrumental duties, with Isabelle Ganz also taking the vocal parts of an extremely interesting repertory.
    Sunday's concert included selections from the important thirteenth-century *Cantigas de Santa María* and from the fourteenth-century *Llibre Vermell*. Bits and pieces of the *Cantigas de Santa María* have been heard here three or four times already this year in widely varied settings, for the sources themselves are no help in details of instrumentation and other technical aspects. The Alhambra group's selection and performance were among the most attractive and most lively of these presentations, while the *Llibre Vermell* music was certainly a first performance here. The geographical provenance of these pieces is significant. Preserved in medieval Catalonia and associated with the diversions of religious pilgrims, they display the characteristic French designs of ballade

and virelai, illustrating the international (rather, "pre-national") character, the universality of much Western music up to the Renaissance.

Sunday's audience was most moved, I believe, by a skilled and animated presentation of nine pieces originating in the music of Sephardic Jews: the Jewish population expelled eastward from Mother Spain just as the nostalgically exalted glories of the Age of Discovery were getting their fumbling start in the opposite direction. Sung mainly in Ladino, the lingua franca of the Expulsion, Sunday's Sephardic pieces covered the ground from Spain all the way to Turkey, while displaying a fundamental unity in many technical details. These included some fascinating practices of melodic ornamentation, both in the marvelously expressive voice of Isabelle Ganz and in the staggering dexterity of George Mgrdichian, performing on the oud or ud, the Eastern ancestor of the European lute. Meanwhile, Martha McGaughey solidly held the middle ground with a couple of medieval fiddles known from music history textbooks but rarely seen in real life during the past seven centuries or so: the slender kemence and the more sturdy vielle.

Morton Gould at UPR

The San Juan Star
March 6, 1990   By Donald Thompson

The present season of the Puerto Rico Symphony Orchestra includes a number of concerts on the University of Puerto Rico Río Piedras Campus. Offered in the spacious UPR Theater and generally attracting fair-sized audiences, these concerts have introduced some novelties to the island's musical life, and last Saturday's concert was no exception. Saturday's novelties were several compositions by Morton Gould, veteran composer of "symphonic pops" music, who himself conducted the PRSO in their presentation.

Gould is today the venerable dean of U.S. craftsman composers. Trained on early network radio musical shows, he became (to quote a leading work of musico-biographical reference) "pregnant with the fertile sperm of musical Americana," and developed a great talent for composing singable, playable and enjoyable light pieces. Well, sez I, and based on Saturday's offerings as well as on previous performing experience with some of Gould's music, playable they surely are; enjoyable any more I'm not so sure.

Offered on Saturday's symphonic pops event were Gould's melodious ballet suite Fall River Legend (1948), his Latin American Symphonette (1940) and the piece which had brought most of Saturday's audience to the UPR Theater, his Concerto for Tap Dancer and Orchestra (1952).

The Fall River Legend suite is rather typical of most ballet music over the centuries, allowing for such exceptions as Bartók's only ballet, some of Copland, some very colorful Tchaikovsky and the early Stravinsky. Most ballet music cries out for the ballet, just as most movie scores cry out for the movies for which they were composed, for this kind of music is usually designed not to be very interesting in itself. You see, if it's too interesting musically it will distract attention from the main event taking place on the stage or on the screen, and no producer wants that! In other words, ballet music without the ballet is likely to be dull. I found the Fall River Legend music dull: so dull that I found myself designing costumes and choreography to bring it alive at least inside my own head. It helped, and I discovered creative gifts in choreography which I never thought I had, too.

The Latin American Symphonette dates from the days immediately preceding the Second World War, when the United States first became aware of the vast countries lying south of the border and of the urgency of cultivating some of their populations (or rather, their governments). Panamericanism was born, and a number of U.S. composers embraced its cause. This Latin American Symphonette is a product of that movement, but a rather silly one. Comprising a tango, a guaracha and a conga as seen from midtown Manhattan, it seems to represent a "fruity hat" approach to concert music (does any of you remember Carmen Miranda?). The piece probably pleased U.S. "pops" audiences in the forties, but it certainly bears no relation to "symphonic-folk" works by Chávez, Revueltas, Ginastera, Villa-Lobos or even Copland. Compared to even the lightest music of these masters, Gould's Panamerican offering is . . . well, airmusic.

OK, then, what about that Concerto for Tap Dancer and Orchestra? Well, you may know that there have been concertos for such oddments as harmonica, accordion, jew's harp and pantaleon, as well as a short concert piece for typewriter and orchestra. In addition, as far back as the time of Mozart's daddy people thought it cute to see toy instruments used in symphonic works. So why not a tap dance concerto? A clever idea, and certainly nobody could have done it better than Morton Gould. You see, the tap shoes are the featured instruments instead of a piano or a violin, and they are played by the soloist's feet instead of his hands.

So far, so good, and the Gould concerto generally treats the solo instrument with respect and seriousness. But tap dancing is also associated with a happy-carefree-wistful-pensive kind of show biz, and the temptation to draw upon this association can probably not be completely avoided. The work's second movement thus becomes a cute kind of miniature ballet scene which I guess might be all right too, but it does tend to mix up the artistic turfs. But wait—can this be the "mixed media" which some contemporary figures cultivate so carefully but in the main rather more solemnly? If so, they might wish to look to Morton Gould as some kind of precursor, way back in the early fifties. Me, I find it completely appropriate that there be a concerto for tap dancer and orchestra—once.

Saturday's soloist was dancer Fred Strickler. As for me, although I've become a great behind-the-eyelids choreographer my dancing skill is limited to the wedding reception waltz, and at that I must watch carefully so as not to trip over my own feet. I can in no way comment technically on Strickler's work, but can only agree with the intermission observer who said it seemed that Strickler's feet never touched the floor, although those machine-gun rhythms had to come from somewhere. Awesome.

Also offered on Saturday were two works by Leonard Bernstein: the sparkling Candide Overture and a set of dance numbers drawn from *West Side Story*. The overture sounded fine to me, but the dances, well known here from seemingly semiannual performances by the PRSO, seemed lacking in the subtleties of expression recalled from other performances: for example the nasty threat of the "Rumble," the innocence of "Somewhere" and the tightly controlled rhythmic thrust of the "Mambo." Nor did conductor Gould give all of the cues which would have been helpful; consequently a few section entrances were sloppy and a few players fell into notorious *West Side Story* booby-traps.

Talented Cast Makes *Merry Widow* a Success

The San Juan Star
March 29, 1990   By Donald Thompson

Die lustige Witwe, as I first knew it in Vienna but aka *The Merry Widow* and by seven or eight other titles according to your language of preference, is an elegant example of the Viennese operetta, and it received an elegant production over the weekend in the big hall at the Performing Arts Center in Santurce. By Franz Lehár, composer of some 25 other successful works of the same general kind, *The Merry Widow* carried into the twentieth century the same tradition represented by the admired *Die Fledermaus* by the younger Johann Strauss. There are also connections with other kinds of vernacular "dialogue-opera" cultivated throughout Europe a century ago, but the Viennese form is unique: a little more relaxed, a little less sentimental, a little more witty, a little less melodramatic; a little more satirical of the society in which it existed: in short . . . well, more *elegant*.

The weekend's production, offered in Spanish as *La Viuda Alegre*, was mounted by the Puerto Rican Foundation of Zarzuela and Operetta with Rafael Ferrer as musical director, Myrna Casas as stage director and a cast of principals fully worthy of the work itself.

This matter of a worthy cast is not always encountered in lyric theater productions here, and of course the works themselves invariably suffer from shortcuts often taken. The Puerto Rican Foundation of Zarzuela and Operetta clearly intended to go all the way in an effort to do it right this time, and is to be commended for its commitment.

Heading the cast as the Merry Widow herself was soprano Rosario Andrade, whose secure operatic experience helped set the style for this present production. Opposite her as the dissolute but redeemable Count Danilo was experienced island baritone Rafael Torréns, fully up to the vocal demands of the role as well as characteristically super-solid as an actor. Soprano Hilda Ramos and tenor César Hernández provided the secondary romantic interest as Valencienne and Camille. Hernández has been seen here in increasingly important opera roles and is doing fine work abroad just now; soprano Ramos' work as Valencienne demonstrated how very fast she is developing as both a singing and an acting talent. The point of all this is that it's easy for producers to underestimate the level of vocal skill appropriate for principal roles in operetta, zarzuela, and for that matter musical comedy, and they are often tempted to take the easy way out by engaging lesser singers and hoping for the best. But there's no free lunch in lyric theater, either, and short cuts usually result in weak productions. Clearly, this production wasn't looking for short-cuts (on the stage, at least), and the result was a thoroughly successful effort vocally as well in almost all other ways.

The extraordinary talent of Manuel Codeso was enlisted for the key comic role of the Pontevidrinian Ambassador, setting the tone in this regard as did soprano Andrade vocally. Ably supporting Codeso on the mainly non-singing side were solid actors Herman O'Neill, Elsa Román, Genie Montalvo, Glenn Zayas, Rocky Venegas and a platoon of other skilled figures down the line. Further evidence of the producers' seriousness in this production was offered by the presence of a fine dance group prepared by choreographer Zaida Varas. The brightly folksy scene which opened the second act with Pontevidrinian dances and the awesome can-can of the third act will long be remembered. Here, the bright talent of Marian Pabón was recruited for a brief presentation. Classy stylized sets by Julio Biaggi contributed greatly to the success of the production, as did fantasy-Pontevidrinian costumes designed by Carmelo Santana and constructed by Wardrobe Research and Design. For example, I think that Santana's hilarious military and diplomatic costumes were an important element in the success of a second-act male ensemble devoted to puzzlement over women's ways.

Turning things around a bit, *The Merry Widow* can also be seen as simply an anthology of beloved and extremely well made tunes by Franz Lehár, with a pleasant play to hang them on. In this regard a large chorus, prepared by Héctor Vega Drouet, helped a great deal too. I believe that director Casas did the right thing in staging the chorus in rather static fashion; by moving less a chorus can concentrate more on its singing—always assuming that something else is happening for the audience to look at. And in the staging of the big chorus scenes this was definitely the case. Contributing to the success of the biggest chorus scene of all, the opening of the second act, was another example of seriousness on the part of the decision makers of this production: the incorporation of an able ensemble of plucked strings directed by Jorge Cintrón. Mandolins and guitars very nicely underlined the *ost-europäisch* character of the Pontevidrinian (I like that word) music.

Speaking of music and of the fundamental elements of lyric theater production, only in the orchestra did I perceive a cut corner or two. Thursday evening's performance was marred by uncertainties in the strings, affecting even some incidental solos. However, as Thompson's Rule states, if for any reason the orchestra's part doesn't fully come off the entire production suffers and that's all there is to it. In other words it's a pity to make all that commitment (read "spend all that money") to ensure good work on the stage and even a reserve, then cut corners in the orchestra. For whether everyone likes it or not, friends, the orchestra pit is where all lyric theater begins and the orchestra pit is what ultimately holds it all together.

Puerto Rico to be Included in Spanish Music Encyclopedia

The San Juan Star
April 28, 1990 By Donald Thompson

    MADRID, SPAIN. According to recent developments here, Puerto Rico will be well represented in a new and highly specialized encyclopedia devoted exclusively to music in Spain and Spanish America. Meeting in Madrid for a week of deliberations are some twenty musicologists from South America, Central America, Mexico, Spain and the formerly Spanish Antilles, who are working out the technical details of the new encyclopedia and coordinating the contributions of some 500 other writers selected throughout the region. Most of the almost 9,000 entries for the first volume have been completed, covering the letters A to C, and work is in progress for the many thousands of further entries which will be required to complete the work. Entitled *Diccionario de la música española e hispanoamericana*, the new work will probably extend to ten or twelve volumes when completed, and will represent the state of the art in musical lexicography, both in content and in production details.
    The project is sponsored by the Spanish Ministry of Culture and the national authors' society (the Sociedad General de Autores de España), with the support of the Spanish Commission for the Fifth Centennial of the Discovery of America. Puerto Rico will be represented by from 150 to 200 entries dealing with musical organizations, concert life, folk music, folk dance, ballet, musical research and educational institutions, as well as with outstanding individual composers and performers both past and present. In this way the island's musical life will for the first time be internationally seen in the context of its close cultural ties to the rest of Hispanic America and to Spain itself.

In addition to daily sessions of intense work on this encyclopedic project, participants have delivered brief formal presentations dealing with the state of archival resources for music research in their respective lands. My own offering, dealing with Puerto Rico, emphasized the collection of approximately 5,000 musical works held by the Puerto Rico General Archive at Puerta de Tierra and the holdings of the UPR Music Library in Río Piedras, as well as other smaller collections and depositories which exist in Puerto Rico. This transatlantic musicological conclave has been completely successful in every way: hopefully, a portent of success for this staggering project which has brought the participants together in a unique and far reaching venture.

PRSO Presents Lyrical Spanish Music

The San Juan Star
May 23, 1990 By Donald Thompson

The Puerto Rico Symphony Orchestra offered an evening of familiar and unfamiliar Spanish music in the University of Puerto Rico Theater on Saturday evening. The last of a set of special concerts on the UPR campus this season, Saturday's concert was conducted by Odón Alonso, the PRSO's own musical director. Alonso is completely familiar with this music and with its performance traditions, and this complete familiarity made of Saturday's concert a comfortable and mainly pleasant event. No hesitation, no hassle: Alonso and the PRSO simply laid out Saturday's melodious offerings for the relaxed enjoyment of a sizable audience.

A great deal of Saturday's music was frankly lightweight: tuneful orchestral excerpts from popular works of the Madrid lyric theater. For that matter, much of the known and frequently performed Spanish music of the past century and a half is precisely of this lightweight character. Why is this, do you suppose? Well, one theory is that the potential Madrid public for concert music was so addicted to the lyric theater, lyric theater personalities, lyric theater innovations and lyric theater scandal that little time or concentration was left for concert music. And anyway, nineteenth-century concert music, as cultivated in the rest of Europe, was much too heavy, too long and too . . . well, too German for the tastes of Madrid. Not so for Barcelona, but that's another story. But to what extent Barcelona is part of Spain is open to question anyway; ask a Catalan sometime.

In any case, most of Saturday's music was colorful, bright and fast moving in the best Madrid tradition. Familiar excerpts from stage works by Chapí, Granados and Guridi filled most of the first half, with a great part of the audience ready to sing along. Also in the first half appeared an interesting work, hitherto unknown to me, by Joaquín Turina (1882-1949) entitled *Sinfonía Sevillana*, or the equally alliterative "A Symphony of Seville." Dating from 1920, the Turina work is certainly not a symphony in the classic Germanic tradition (what did I tell you?), but rather a symphonic suite or symphonic poem sounding occasionally like Puccini, occasionally like Ravel, and occasionally like Gershwin. Also occasionally, it is right on the edge of salon music, while at other times it is simply noisy. No Manuel de Falla to be sure, yet Turina had a great deal of skill in orchestration especially, and in many ways his music is a cut or two above that of most of his contemporaries.

Saturday's performance had some very good moments and some very bad ones, the latter caused by some completely unacceptable solo fiddle playing. This is a pity, because such work immediately drops an otherwise good orchestral performance back to the level of . . . well, never mind. This particular subject is (or certainly should be) a matter of some concern to the management of our PRSO just now but it's not likely that anything you or I might say about it would make much difference as the slowly turning wheels of government grind, and grind, and ineffectually grind some more.

But Manuel de Falla: now *there's* a Spanish composer who had something to say! Once the preliminary bouts were gotten out of the way on Saturday, two of his works were featured. Falla's Nights in The Gardens of Spain, the first one up, is sort of a piano concerto, except that the piano part is rather more tightly integrated into the orchestral texture than is common in concertos. Probably the best way to look at the work is as a set of symphonic impressions (the composer's own term, uttered on some occasion and often quoted) for piano and orchestra. The three movements are certainly evocative, very much in the manner of the "Spanish" music of Debussy and Ravel (with both of whom Falla was acquainted), and were well played on Saturday with the collaboration of pianist Félix Rivera Guzmán. Rivera Guzmán is a young island musician who after early studies here attended the Juilliard School and the University of Miami, where he is well along the way toward a doctorate in his field.

The *Nights* of Falla is not exactly a pianist's dream of a spectacular vehicle for technical display, but it is a very good test of general pianistic skill and of the ability to mesh an exposed and difficult part with the work of a conductor and an orchestra. Judging from Saturday's performance, Rivera Guzmán is ready for anything, and I look forward to hearing him with the PRSO in one of the really big piano concertos.

Closing Saturday's concert was a familiar set of excerpts from Falla's ballet The Three-Cornered Hat. This music is so very familiar here, in fact, that I felt that nobody on the stage was taking it very seriously. Not that there were any major slips, you understand, but only that a general lack of concentration seemed to produce a complacent and pedestrian performance completely devoid of tension and spark. Maybe the work should be retired from the PRSO repertory for five or six years and then hauled out again, refreshed. I think that Falla's fine Three-Cornered Hat music deserves no less.

PRSO: Retirees and a Rite of Passage

The San Juan Star
June 2, 1990   By Donald Thompson

A large audience witnessed an important rite of musical passage in the big hall at the Performing Arts Center on Tuesday evening, as the Puerto Rico Symphony Orchestra honored a few of its own. The occasion was the retirement of eleven PRSO members, the first batch to profit from the orchestra's pension plan now operative after many years of wishful thinking, exploration, struggle and finally, planning. A rite of passage for the retirees, yes, who total some 260 years of service among them.

Holy Mother of God, can you imagine 260 years of the Choral Fantasy of Beethoven? The mind reels at the thought, but that's another story. The point is, the hardiest of Tuesday's stalwarts go all the way back to the PRSO's foggy beginnings in the late 1950s, and a few had fought the island's orchestral battles for some decades before that. All honor to these colleagues! My own retirement from the PRSO took place under other circumstances, and that is *really* another story. . . .

But Tuesday's event was a rite of passage in another sense, too. I'm thinking of the orchestra's own belated passage to the state of an officially recognized entity with someone accepting the responsibility for its continuing development; the best sign of this is precisely the existence of a pension plan. A pension plan not only permits the toilworn and weary to honorably leave the battlefield when their hitch is up; the other side of the coin is the orchestral renewal which is possible in no other way. It is this dual process, in fact, which distinguishes an established, responsible and ongoing orchestra from a pick-up band. But, you say, wasn't all this foreseen and organized by the benevolent planners who launched the Puerto Rico Symphony Orchestra back in 1957? Well no, children, and in fact the farthest thing from the minds of the original planners was that someday there might be a properly constituted island-based symphony orchestra. Managerial folklore and political flackery to the contrary, the PRSO came into being as an improvised governmental response to justified grumbling by island instrumentalists, some of them highly skilled and fully capable of holding down full time orchestra jobs. The trouble was that there was no full time orchestra here and little prospect of there ever being one. To these performers it was painful to see great sums of tax money committed to a brief annual festival which began in 1957; lasting only a couple of weeks, this event annually exhausted the interest and the concentration of island music lovers, both within and out of government, for the next eleven months. Festivals are fine, reasoned island instrumentalists and a few clear headed music lovers, but what happens to the island's music after the festival gets back on the plane?

Representative Ernesto Ramos Antonini, introducing the original PRSO legislation in 1957, was himself a musician and was fully conscious of the problem. However, a wrong solution was hit upon as the development of an island-based orchestra was entrusted to the New York-based festival agency. Talk about putting the fox to guard the chickens! You got it: for six years the PRSO, contracted from and in New York as a pick-up orchestra, contained maybe a dozen token island players, mainly in secondary positions and some having had to audition in New York, at that, for an unvarying "season" of some eight concerts.

Then some belated changes began to take place, again beginning with a strong initiative (read "strike") by the handful of island-resident members of the PRSO. A great leap in the length of the orchestra season was later brought about by the direct action of Luis A. Ferré, an enthusiastic amateur pianist, an incomparable leader in arts patronage in Puerto Rico and at the time, governor of Puerto Rico. An island office for the orchestra was belatedly opened, and in 1975 (eighteen years after the original orchestra legislation was passed) the post of orchestra manager was created. The season and the function of the orchestra continued to grow, and the existence of a resident symphony orchestra in Puerto Rico has finally, within the past eight or ten years, seemed assured. In this sense the implementation of a pension plan is simply the final touch in the establishment—the hard way—of an institution which is now the anchor of the island's musical life. The hard way, indeed; don't let anyone beguile you with pleasant stories about a PRSO created out of someone's dream or someone's great benevolence!

Tuesday's event, then, was less a formal concert than an informal musicale organized in recognition of the hard work of some old friends. For oldtimers both on the stage and in the audience, there were many other levels of significance as well.

Casals Festival Opening Night: A Revelation

The San Juan Star
June 12, 1990
By Donald Thompson

About a third of the way through the opening concert of this year's Casals Festival on Saturday evening at the Performing Arts Center, I felt a great burden lift from my soul as I experienced one of those moments of staggering revelation, of vast and blinding vision, of . . . well, of spiritual rebirth, you might say. You see, for decades now I had been grappling with questions regarding the purpose of this annual event, its goals; its early history; and its philosophical, artistic and economic justification in the light of a steadily deteriorating concept of musical programming and a steadily rising level of flackery based on a crackpot vision of "international significance." To my old self, the crowning absurdity was attributed in recent press notices to a festival functionary who wistfully regretted the cancellation of a scheduled visit this year by an international political figure. It had been hoped that this visit, like the visit last year by violinist Alexander Schneider, would lend us a bit of international significance for a day or two. Well, I *sez to meself*, if they're depending on that kind of thing to make a music festival for them, we're in even worse shape than I'd thought!

My old self had also tried to ferret out any possible connection which Saturday's opener, Jack Délano's evocative fantasy-overture *La Reina Tembandumba*, might have with the admired and rather conservative musical tastes of cellist Casals, in whose honored name these concerts are organized. No connection could I perceive, although I must point out that to many island music lovers this matter of Casals' known views should not be a consideration at all in these "Casals" Festivals. Some, in fact, consider it perfectly natural and desirable that works by contemporary island composers be included as a showcase for festival visitors from abroad (if such wanderers there still be), and are only dismayed that it seems so difficult for an island composer to find a niche in the programming nowadays. One such partisan of the "native craft show" theory even surmised at intermission that to get programmed nowadays maybe a composer must have some connection on the Board of Directors!

But back to my moment of revelation, which occurred during an uncharacteristically clumsy modulation in Verdi's almost unknown overture to *Aida*, an extremely interesting piece in itself, but more of that later. My revelation came in the blinding realization that no matter how much I or anyone else might grieve and hassle over questions of purpose, philosophical basis, economic factors and the forgotten historical figure of Pablo Casals, it is not going to make a bit of difference to whatever elves are doing the festival programming nowadays. They will continue to do their work on the basis of . . . well, I don't know what basis, exactly, for this has not been revealed to us. But as for me, from now on I take it piece by piece as I would in any neighborhood concert regardless of what it's for and who's putting it on, even if it's with my tax money.

On the stage on Saturday was our regular Puerto Rico Symphony Orchestra, directed by its regular musical director Odón Alonso and featuring island singer Justino Díaz in an example of the familiar "opera concert" format. In this format a singer offers a set of opera excerpts and the orchestra, in order to give the singer a break and also provide some sonoral variety, plays a couple of opera overtures or other instrumental pieces extracted from operas. Oops, I forgot the Délano work, whose presence on Saturday's concert is now even harder to understand, in the context of an opera concert.

In any case, the much admired Justino Díaz is apparently shifting gears just now, in a painful process of acquiring a new repertory, a new musical mentality and a new set of musical responses. You see, Díaz has made a fine career as a lyric sort of opera bass, specializing in roles which fit his sound and his vocal range. I, among many other observers, have often felt over the years that he was really more a bass-baritone than a true bass, and apparently he has decided to give it a try, but now extending his study even up into the lyric baritone range. His work on Saturday was in fact mainly based on examples from the baritone repertory, with, I believe, mixed results. Most successful to my ear was a long excerpt from the opera *Die Walküre* of Richard Wagner, a composer whose music I, for one, should be very pleased to hear more frequently on our concert and opera stages. Well, as it turns out, the role of Wotan, of which Díaz' contribution on Saturday is part, was conceived for a bass-baritone voice. It fit the Díaz voice very nicely, both in sonority and style. Less successful, I believe, were baritone excerpts from Verdi's *Rigoletto* and *Don Carlo*. Here, Díaz seemed to be straining a bit, with even his normally phenomenally steady pitch wandering upward at times. Too, the use of music on a stand inhibited his gestures and movements, which even on the concert stage are an important if subtle element in vocal expression, especially in opera excerpts. In addition, opera is theater after all, and frankly, I had trouble visualizing Díaz in the role of Rigoletto on the stage. Not to fear, counseled my constant concert consort; Justino is such a fine actor that if he wants to do Rigoletto he can certainly make a fine acting job of it. She's probably right; me, I only hope he can successfully negotiate the shoals and reefs awaiting him in the shift of voice which he has apparently taken on.

The PRSO is still to launch the renewal heralded by the recent retirement of eleven of its honored members; accordingly, its complement on Saturday was still that of the past season. For the Wagner excerpts the wind sections were considerably augmented, enriching the sound but often creating an imbalance with the strings, not so favored. Yes, I'd like to hear more Wagner here, but maybe it will have to await the next stage of orchestral improvement which should be the expansion of the string sections.

As for the Verdi Aida Overture, this oddment turned out to be a fascinating study in overture-making based on tunes from the opera itself. Musicologically it is a prize, a curiosity which should occasionally be played on orchestral concerts (maybe once every fifteen years); musically, it's about on the level of overtures stitched together out of tunes from Broadway musicals an hour before the final rehearsal. Verdi was wise in leaving it in his desk drawer after all.

Gabrieli Significance

The San Juan Star
June 17, 1990   By Donald Thompson

Foggy fanfares of official pronouncement regarding "international significance" tend to cloud the island's musical environment, particularly at this time of year. Nevertheless, an island-based chamber ensemble has quietly gone about establishing some international significance for us, and pretty much on its own at that.

I'm speaking of the Gabrieli, a brass quintet which was launched here a couple of years ago and which has not let up for a minute in a program of steadily broadening its repertory while deepening its musical perceptions, sharpening its chamber music skills, and seeking opportunities to test itself abroad: that is to say, internationally. The members of the Gabrieli ensemble are connected with the Puerto Rico Symphony Orchestra or with circum-symphonic enterprises here, thus attaining a level of stability not enjoyed by groups which only come together from time to time to play a job. No, the Gabrieli has a solid program and is sticking to it, for the benefit of audiences wherever they play. And they have played here and there indeed; their work has already taken them to Miami, to New York City and to Hungary, in addition to an impressive record of concerts and other functions taking place at many points in Puerto Rico.

On Thursday evening the Gabrieli players offered a formal concert at the Puerto Rico Conservatory of Music, following close on the heels of a "pops" concert at the Tapia Theater a week ago and looking forward to a whole series of other widely varied events between now and December.

Thursday's concert featured two major works for brass ensemble plus some oddments. The major works were a "sinfonía" by the Russian composer Victor Ewald (1860-1935) and a sonatina by the French composer Eugène Bozza (b. 1905). Both of these works are completely idiomatic for the brass instruments, and provide plenty of opportunity for exposed solo passages for everyone in the best chamber music tradition. Too, the witty Bozza work offered a few jazzy touches, stylistically consistent with a great deal of the French music composed during the period following the First World War. These major works displayed the virtues of the Gabrieli ensemble: excellent individual control of pitch, complete unanimity of entrance and tempo, a splendid curve of the phrase, a finely tuned concept of dynamic contrast, and a performance presence free of tension and strain.

One of Thursday's oddments was Fantastic Polka, a trombone solo number composed by the extraordinary turn of the century U.S. trombonist Arthur Pryor, subtly played here by Gabrieli's Jaime Morales and hilarious in its reminders of the melodramatic band music of a century ago. The other oddment was Morales' own arrangement for brass quintet of Rossini's Barber of Seville Overture. This was a tough piece indeed, as you can imagine, and especially tough (not to say suicidal) as a concert opener. How to bring all of Rossini's finger-breaking string section music under the secure control of five brass instrument players?

To my mind the Rossini was the least successful part of Thursday's concert, for despite the excellent playing of the Gabrieli ensemble once it got properly warmed up, I could not help thinking that such a major effort was misapplied. Better, I think, would have been . . . well, a work by old Gabrieli himself, or some other music more directly associated with brass instruments.

Thursday's concert closed with a piece by Gabrieli's trombonist and skilled arranger, Jaime Morales. Cast in the form of the traditional Puerto Rican *danza*, Morales' "Para ti" was both evocative of the sweet music of the Caribbean past and fully satisfying as brass quintet music. All success to the Gabrieli ensemble; I only hope that as they continue to build a concert repertory they might also build a file of program notes for the benefit of their fans, of music lovers generally, and of lazy concert reviewers.

Bach Provides Splendid Festival Fare

The San Juan Star
June 19, 1990   By Donald Thompson

    To many concertgoers on Saturday evening, the fifth concert in this year's Casals Festival series was a reminder of almost forgotten glories. To a number of citizens, in fact, this is exactly what these concerts should be about. Not to belabor the point, but think about it: significant music, music which can easily be associated with the great cellist Pablo Casals himself, and music interestingly presented. Good heavens, you ask, what was Saturday's marvel, which can get even this crusty observer excited? Nothing less than the great St. Matthew Passion of Johann Sebastian Bach: splendidly proper fare, it seems to me, for this particular concert series. On the stage in the big hall at the Performing Arts Center on Saturday were the Puerto Rico Symphony Orchestra, the San Juan Philharmonic Chorus (Carmen Acevedo, director), the San Juan Children's Choir (prepared for this occasion by Sandra Morales), an assortment of specialized players of instruments associated with the music of Bach's time and a roster of able vocal soloists. The manner of presentation was by way of a stereophonically divided chorus (with the children's choir in the middle) and a PRSO split into two small orchestras at port and starboard with two other small instrumental groups fore and aft, you might say. At the tiller, pulling it all together and keeping it all afloat (extending the nautical image, if you will) was Odón Alonso, skipper of the Puerto Rico Symphony Orchestra itself.

    The trial and crucifixion of Jesus Christ, as described by the four Evangelists, has inspired the imagination of innumerable composers from the middle ages on down, and continues to do so today. By Bach's time the concept had already been around the track a couple of times, and his musical versions of the St. John and St. Matthew accounts (his only preserved Passion oratorios) represented a return to sobriety after a period of sentimental, indeed operatic, excesses. Sobriety, yes, but not dullness. His setting of Matthew, extended by new poetic texts and paraphrases for certain sections, became a series of cantatas, each closing with a chorale: that beloved four-square expression of the piety of the people. Between each pair of chorale pillers unfolds a series of recitatives and arias, with now and again a duet or two and enlivened by some extremely imaginative instrumental solo writing. Yes, the parishioners of the Lutheran Thomaskirche of Leipzig were paragons of piety and endurance, but they were also present at the birthing of some of the world's greatest music. Parenthetically, it makes you think: what birthings are we missing, these days?

Saturday's skilled soloists included soprano Jennifer Smith, countertenor Charles Brett, tenors Nigel Rogers and Patrick Romano and basses Ruud van der Meer, Kevin McMillan and Carlos Conde. On the instrumental side, very impressive work was done by soloists Laurie Ann Macleod (viola da gamba), Peter Kern (flute), Henry Hutchinson (violin), David Dyer and Cheryl Trace (recorders) and a quartet of oboists on resurrected eighteenth-century types of instruments: David Bourns, Harry Rosario, Gloria Navarro and Doris Caraballo.

Yes, I believe, the music of J.S. Bach is just the ticket for this particular concert series, for many reasons. Now for next year, lads, let's have the Bach orchestra suites, the Brandenburg concertos, two or three Bach cantatas, some of his works for organ, harpsichord, violin and flute as soloists and of course the solo cello suites, which would provide a natural and absolutely painless connection with the memory of Pablo Casals himself. Do you see how easy it is? I've just done next year's programming for them, and I'm not charging the government a cent!

Restored Tapes of an Amazing Time

The San Juan Star
June 21, 1990   By Donald Thompson

    A scattering of pilgrims made their way to the Theater Hall of the Performing Arts Center on Monday evening for a fascinating event offered as part of this year's Casals Festival but with no orchestra, no chorus, no chamber ensemble—not even a conductor—on the stage. The occasion was the showing of some restored videotapes of Casals Festival concerts taking place in the UPR Theater in the old days beginning almost 30 years ago. I might add the *good* old days, for once you're past 35, almost any obscure film or garbled recording of an event which one remembers from more than fifteen years ago takes on a significance far beyond that of the subject itself, objectively considered. In addition to which, I hasten to point out that the early Casals Festivals in Puerto Rico really *were* significant events in anybody's musical almanac.

    After a brief and fascinating description of some of the problems encountered in restoring the old tapes, delivered by Peter Hollander, the principal consultant on the restoration project, we went straight to the tapes themselves. These began with one of Pablo Casals conducting a movement of the Beethoven Sixth Symphony with one of those unbelievable early Casals Festival orchestras. I was reminded that Casals was not really so much a conductor as an inspirer to those orchestras which didn't exist in real musical life and which didn't need a conductor anyway, for the repertory presented. I was also reminded that the early orchestras were made up of a generation of instrumentalists many of whom had played with Casals in his post-WW II festivals in Prades and all of whom were honored to be engaged to join him here in the transplanted festival. It is for this reason that it is absolutely futile to even think of restoring the sound, the style, the subtlety and the significance of those orchestras in today's annual concert series in Puerto Rico no matter what these series might be called. Many of the early instrumentalists, seen again on Monday after a lapse of several decades, have died and the rest have retired from active professional work or are at the point of doing so. And of course Casals himself, the center of the whole thing, has not been with us for some seventeen years now.

Other tapes shown on Monday evening only reinforced the nostalgia, while also impressing specialists with their value simply as documentation. In a chamber music performance with violinist Alexander Schneider and pianist Rudolf Serkin, for example, some excellent shots of the fingers of Casals' left hand on the cello fingerboard and his right hand on the bow are gold mines for anyone interested in the details of Casals' instrumental technique, which in its time was nothing less than revolutionary. This is to say nothing of the concepts of chamber music playing embodied in the work of Casals, Serkin and Schneider together: concepts basically belonging to the nineteenth century, to be sure, but for all of that even more valuable as documentation.

Tchaikovsky Loud and Disorderly

The San Juan Star
June 22, 1990　　　　　　　　　　　　　By Donald Thompson

Tuesday evening was Tchaikovsky time at the Performing Arts Center as the National Symphony Orchestra of Washington made the first of its four scheduled appearances in the current Casals Festival series. For this listener one complete evening of Tchaikovsky every ten years or so is quite enough, and Tuesday's concert even included some Tchaikovsky which I wouldn't mind never hearing again. I'm speaking of the Hamlet Overture-Fantasy, cast in the successful mold of the Romeo and Juliet but without a fraction of that familiar work's interest. Also on Tuesday's program were the Francesca da Rimini Fantasy and the brooding Sixth Symphony, nicknamed the "Pathétique" for the feeling of sadness and distress which it seems to inspire in many listeners.

On the podium was Mstislav Rostropovich, musical director of the Washington orchestra and, according to the printed program, himself largely responsible for the planning and programming of the present Casals Festival. Enough has probably been said about that subject already; I do wish, however, that maestro Rostropovich or some other festival planner would tell us what this concert series is about.

We are, of course, extremely familiar with the National Symphony Orchestra of Washington, which has occupied for the past few years the place which was for a while occupied by a different orchestra each year in an enlightening sequence of different repertories, different orchestral styles and different conductors. Very healthy for Puerto Rico's musical life, we thought, and there are recent rumors that there may be a return to that planned and pleasant pattern of programatic presentations. In the meantime, how is the National Symphony Orchestra of Washington faring? What did it sound like on Tuesday? Well, the big string sections certainly provided a warm sound for Tchaikovsky's meanderings, but my nerve endings were occasionally cauterized by what I perceived as a brass section on the very edge of selfdestruct, even when their voices were not the main business of the moment. Sure, all of the parts in Tchaikovsky are written loud in places, but implicit in the orchestral concept is an idea of sonoral balance. Well, maybe those string sections should be a third bigger yet, if that's the way the man wants to play Tchaikovsky.

I'm speaking of the conductor, naturally. Mstislav Rostropovich is of course a phenomenal cellist, and his performances as an instrumentalist are unparalleled. I have never felt the same about his conducting, however, feeling that he tends to go for the grand gesture (and there's plenty of temptation in Tchaikovsky) at the cost of line, phrase and precision. As a result, Tuesday's performance was marked by minor inaccuracies of attack and blurrings of effect in all sections: just enough to take the bloom off of what I think that orchestra can probably do when at its best.

Speaking of the Sixth Symphony of Tchaikovsky, this performance reminded me of a recent contribution dealing with the island's musical life which appeared in another San Juan publication. The author, a notorious music lover, claimed that in San Juan we have some of the most destructive music reviews on this side of the Atlantic. Of course he was not speaking of MY work, but that's not the point.... The point is that in the view of the distinguished music critic of the Boston Evening Transcript, writing in 1898, this very symphony of Tchaikovsky "threads all the foul ditches and sewers of human despair; it is as unclean as music well can be.... That unspeakable second theme [of the first movement] may tell of the impotent senile remembrance of calf love." Now THAT is criticism, alongside which the most virulent Puerto Rican product pales into benevolence and praise! Me, I don't think the Sixth Symphony is foul and unclean, simply occasionally loud and disorderly, as played on Tuesday.

♪

Pro Arte Lírico and *Rosa la China*

The San Juan Star
August 22, 1990					By Donald Thompson

Ernesto Lecuona (1896-1963) was a gifted Cuban composer of popular songs, several of which attained world hit status. Among these were "Siboney," "Malagueña" and "Two Hearts That Pass in the Night." Lecuona occasionally ventured into broader fields of musical composition, composing dance suites for piano as well as turning his hand to the lyric theater, represented by the topical and tropical operetta.

This kind of theater is derived from the sentimental and comic Spanish zarzuela, which as living theater spread all over Latin America within a few years of its taking definite form in Madrid about 130 years ago. By the end of the past century, not only the Spanish form but twenty or more local variants throughout the Western Hemisphere had become incurably infected by the French operetta, the French revue and other kinds of popular lyric theater, mainly French. And here is where Lecuona's *Rosa la China* fits. Cuban light lyric theater, you might say, with Spanish and French ancestors.

Over the past weekend *Rosa la China* was offered by San Juan's Pro Arte Lírico company in the big hall of the Performing Arts Center in Santurce. The production was presented as a premiere in Puerto Rico, and it probably was. At best, orchestra parts and other production materials for Spanish-language music theater are very difficult to secure, and for Cuban works . . . forget it. In fact, the present production was made possible only by a painstaking and mainly successful job of musical archeology: the reconstruction of an orchestral score and parts from an old recording, by musical director Enriquillo Cerón.

The plots of most operettas, zarzuelas, *Singspiele*, musical comedies, what have you, can be reduced to "Boy loves girl; boy loses girl; boy gets girl." Well, here it's a little different: "Boy loses girl," and that's all there is to be said about it. Still, if you can forget about this non-plot, the piece provides a framework for some nice tunes and some good jokes both visual and verbal, as put together by skilled stage director José Luis Marrero and assiduous conductor Cerón.

In Puerto Rico as well as in the rest of Latin America there are some really depressing traditions connected with the production of zarzuelas and operettas. One of them is a strong tendency toward the use of amateurs and enthusiasts on stage; there is even a long history of zarzuela presentations by companies of little kids, coming up to relatively recent times. Cute, yes, but it gives real show biz a bad name.

Well, you've got to give this Pro Arte Lírico company a lot of credit for carefully engaging fully professional talent not only in principal roles but pretty far down the line as well. This recent production featured singing actress Ana del Pilar Pérez and seasoned baritone Rafael Torréns in the leading romantic roles, along with the very solid and versatile acting talents of such other figures as Marisol Calero, Héctor Travieso, Julio Axel Landrón, Alba Raquel Barros, Mercedes Sicardó, Ofelia Dacosta and "Chavito" Marrero himself. Especially interesting to me are some of the younger but fully professional names on this list: The work of Barros, Landrón and Calero will long be remembered.

In fact, it seemed to me that these secondary singing and acting roles did a lot more than the principals to keep Saturday's performance rolling. One thing for sure: they were more secure rhythmically, causing fewer headaches in the orchestra pit and fewer skipped heartbeats in the critics' corner. The only painful exception to this production's high level of professionalism in the stage talent was a bunch of mainly little girls who formed a carnival procession, endlessly parading and pointlessly extending the playing time. Somebody sold the company a package with that number.

A key figure in this production was super veteran Santiago García Ortega, on the stage but not in the play, as it were, as the Parisian Gentleman, a philosophizing observer somewhat in the manner of the street singer in *Threepenny Opera*, the stage manager in *Our Town* or the Gallo, as I recall, in *The Fantasticks*. The Parisian Gentleman's nostalgic reciting of Havana place names drew an immediate response from Saturday evening's audience, as did Lecuona's boleros, danzones and guarachas.

In use for this production was an updated libretto by Mario Martin and Miguel de Grandy. Chorusmaster was Rafael Ferrer, very effective choreography was by Marcelino Alcalá, sets had been designed by director Marrero and Eduardo Hernández while costumes had been designed by Sylvia Lamar.

The patient reader will suffer me a final comment, referring to a situation which has already begun to change the very nature of theater as we have known it and a situation of which I was frequently reminded on Saturday. I refer to the amplification of individual stage voices, which is only a step away from the pre-recording of vocal music with the actors merely mouthing the words.

I do not wish to suggest that this pre-recorded scam may have been practiced in this recent operetta production, but the amplification of individual voices was obvious, capricious and bad. Producers everywhere, beware the wrath of the deceived, for they shall turn against you and not buy tickets anymore.

Castro's Music Shines With the PRSO

The San Juan Star
October 11, 1990   By Donald Thompson

The Puerto Rico Symphony Orchestra continued its series of regular concerts at the Performing Arts Center on Saturday evening under the direction of guest conductor Pedro I. Calderón. Offered was a diversity of works, each important for one reason or another in the island's musical life.

First up was *El llanto de las sierras*, by Argentine composer-conductor Juan José Castro. Castro was for a time very closely connected with Puerto Rico's musical fortunes, as dean of studies in the Puerto Rico Conservatory of Music and the first regular conductor of the PRSO itself. In this latter capacity he did a great deal to expand the nascent orchestra's repertory and to impress upon its reluctant management the seriousness of the task which it had taken on. He is remembered as a significant and positive force at a critical time in the island's music. Although Castro had long since made his name as a composer of importance in this hemisphere especially, he avoided the temptation to force his own works on his audience or on his orchestra. Consequently, his music is probably less well known here than in many other parts of the world. A pity.

Castro's *El llanto de las sierras* was composed in 1947 in posthumous homage to the great Spanish composer Manuel de Falla, who had recently died in Argentina. Rather somber in the manner of most such works, *El llanto de las sierras* nonetheless displays considerable contrast among its various sections, as well as reminding us of Castro's skill as a composer and of his valuable work in Puerto Rico.

Also featured on Saturday was island-born clarinet soloist Ricardo Morales, who played two demanding works with the PRSO. First was

Debussy's First Rhapsody for Clarinet and Orchestra, followed by the nicely contrasting Clarinet Concerto in E Flat by Carl Maria von Weber. The Debussy is what you might call "cool and clean" music, in the best tradition of the "impressionistic" thought of its composer. Morales certainly played it cool and clean on Saturday, without a lapse in pitch, general phrasing or technique. On the other hand, I for one missed some of the subtlety experienced in the minute details of expression and recalled from other performances here by more experienced (or perhaps only more battle-worn) clarinetists. Perhaps this order of subtlety can come only with the years, of which Morales has not seen very many yet. On the other hand, Morales' performance of the Weber concerto was a knockout in every way. Concertos by Weber, Paganini and their ilk make little pretense of musical depth, symphonic thought or profound expression; they are showcases pure and simple, and make it their main business to test the soloist and amaze the audience through the inclusion of every finger-breaking trick known to players or imagined by composers. In this sense this Weber concerto is fiendish, for it calls upon all of the soloist's technical resources in a setting of musical clarity and bright good humor. Morales passed the test brilliantly on Saturday, in a performance marked by dazzling interplay with the orchestra and staggering dexterity in the soloist's own fingers. Tempos set by conductor Calderón seemed right on the nose from the very first measures on down. Nice going, all the way around.

The main point of significance to Puerto Rico of the music of Anton Bruckner is that it isn't heard here very often. I'm not going to look it up, but I would be very surprised to learn that there have been three performances of Bruckner's music here in as many decades. But is Bruckner's music all that important? I think so, and I think audiences should be allowed to experience it in the concert hall, even though the specific performance conditions might be less than ideal. Such, indeed, were the performance conditions as our PRSO offered the Fourth Symphony of Bruckner as the second half of Saturday's concert. Less than ideal, for example, in the PRSO's imbalance of string and wind forces when it comes to the real heavyweights of orchestral music, and believe me, Bruckner's writing for winds is heavyweight. For this music, as well as for much of Mahler, Wagner and Richard Strauss, an increase of 30 percent in this orchestra's string sections would ease everybody's burden a great deal while providing that great "pillow" of string sound which we associate with this grandiose and almost mystical mode of musical thought.

On Saturday and because of this imbalance, the winds found it necessary to hold back artificially, while the strings often sounded shrill because they were called upon the produce more than their numbers could reasonably provide. Conditions may have been less than ideal also in the conductor's preparation; I often felt that he was conducting the work for the first time and missing many opportunities to help the performance by providing reassuring cues to wind instrument players who after not playing for many minutes were called upon to enter in some unlikely context. Still it was a good idea to program the work, I think, perhaps as a sign of hope for future developments in the PRSO as well as a healthful experience for San Juan concertgoers.

Forum's Final Concerts

The San Juan Star
October 30, 1990   By Donald Thompson

The Third Annual Caribbean Composers Forum offered a final concert on Friday evening before a sizable audience in the Reception Center of the Puerto Rico State Department at Plaza Colón in Old San Juan. Friday's event combined more or less successfully the functions of a concert with those of a ceremonial presentation, as due honor was rendered to forum organizers, participants and sponsors in brief speeches during breaks in the concerts itself. Well, that's OK, I guess, especially given the open invitation to rhetoric which is extended by that baroque and echoing hall itself. One thing for sure: a proper recital hall it isn't.

On stage on Friday between the speeches were a handful of San Juan's most solid performers including soprano Susan Pabón, pianist Samuel Pérez, guitarists Leonardo Egúrbida and José Rodríguez Alvira, violist Francisco Figueroa, cellist Rosalyn Iannelli and percusionist Manuel García. Individually and in small groups, these stalwarts offered a variety of works originating in and around the Caribbean and mainly dating from recent times. To my mind the most effective were Carlos Cabrer's *La rota voz del agua* for soprano and instrumental ensemble and Germán Cáceres' two-movement Viola Sonata. Music by Cáceres (of El Salvador) has occasionally been heard here before, and has usually made a good impression. This performance of the viola sonata profited by the steady work of violist Figueroa and pianist Pérez, while I have never heard soprano Pabón sing better than on Friday. Other works on Friday's climactic concert were by Alfonso Fuentes, Leo Brouwer, Alejandro Cardona and Carlos Vázquez.

Leading up to Friday's culminating event was naturally a whole series of evening offerings, of which Thursday's was a particularly significant event. Taking place with audience and performers on the stage of the UPR Theater in Río Piedras, Thursday's concert featured the University of Puerto Rico Concert Choir, which has very nicely survived one of those profound traumas which sooner or later affect every chorus in the world. This is a change of director, and there is nothing like it for sheer unsettling distress anywhere else in the life of organizations. The regular director of the UPR choruses is away on study leave, and her place has been taken by Clark Mallory, a skilled musician with a fine record of contributions to the island's music. The Concert Choir is a small and specialized unit of the UPR Choral Program and is the sort of group which is often devoted to the study of unusual or especially demanding music for special occasions. Thursday's concert qualified on both counts; the occasion was special, as part of this Third Caribbean Composers Forum, and some of the music was certainly unusual and demanding.

What's clear about contemporary choral music is that choristers can no longer expect to sing along by ear. In fact, they are required to behave like instrumentalists and to possess a whole range of skills lying far beyond the scope of traditional choral singing. This is not to say that instrumentalists are never guilty of playing along by ear, but only that the traditional expectations are somewhat different in the two fields.

Take, for example, *Paz en la Tierra*, a classic piece of contemporary choral music by Francis Schwartz, powerfully presented on Thursday by the UPR Concert Choir. Premiered by the large UPR Chorus in 1972 and now known in many parts of the world, *Paz en la Tierra* requires choral hisses, hums, mumbles, wavers and grunts derived from the work's title, as well as individual chorus members symbolically carrying a message of peace to the world as they wander about among the audience. Or take *Tempus fugit*, by José Rodríguez Alvira on texts by F. José Ramos. Here, sliding voices negotiate some extremely unaccustomed rhythms, slippery harmonies and wrenching dissonances in the realization of evocative texts. Other works in more customary styles, by Harold Gramatges, Margarita Luna, Electo Silva and Jack Délano were also given successful presentations on Thursday by the UPR Concert Choir under the direction of Clark Mallory.

Composers Forum: More Than Music

The San Juan Star
October 31, 1990   By Donald Thompson

    To those interested in the erratic course of the arts, especially in this part of the world, the recent Third Annual Caribbean Composers Forum had a lot to offer besides concerts. In fact, matters of perhaps more immediate interest to composers and hopeful composers were aired not in the evening concerts at all, but in morning and afternoon sessions devoted to oral presentations, demonstrations, a master class in composition and debates. Participating were composers and other specialists from Puerto Rico, the United States, Cuba, Mexico, Costa Rica, Venezuela, the Dominican Republic, El Salvador and Panama.
    Most of these events took place in the recital hall of the UPR Music Department in Río Piedras, while serving as principal speakers during the week were two world class heavyweights in the field of Latin American music research and publication: Gerard Béhague of the University of Texas and Robert Stevenson of UCLA. Each offered two presentations devoted to fields of his particular interest: Stevenson's dealt with concert music of the European tradition in the Caribbean during colonial times, and Béhague's with questions of national identity and political reality in the region's contemporary art music. Predictably, Stevenson's presentations provided a gold mine of historical data as well as an open invitation for more research in an attractive and almost unexplored field. Also predictably, Béhague's presentation inspired some debate on matters which can still evoke a Pavlovian reaction by a few composers and doctrinaire thinkers in the region, mainly younger ones solemnly engaged in reinventing the wheel. "National identity" is a cyclically returning buzzword in the art music of the Western hemisphere, but each time around it evokes a weaker reaction. Although the eminent Alberto

Ginastera convincingly buried "folkloric nationalism" almost thirty years ago, the concept still appeals to hopefuls who in the absence of an authentic voice of their own seek some cause, preferably one which might provide them with some exalted crusade vis-à-vis "The People."

Well, there was a certain amount of this soul searching during the week, but I perceived much less interest in these questions than was evident during the First Caribbean Composers Forum held here two years ago. At that time one neophyte got so carried away as to fervently proclaim a messianic musical mission to his countrymen, themselves of course oblivious to him and indeed to the whole question. This year, my impression was that the assembly paid some ritual attention to the subject of national identity as if acknowledging some old symbolic debt, then got on with the main matters at hand: renewing old acquaintances, talking musical politics, hearing some music and exploring performance possibilities. The general tone of much discourse during the breaks was "What's happening over at your place? You got any festivals going?"

Sessions were devoted to a demonstration of the musical applications of Steven Jobs' incredible NExT computer by Alejandro José; an interesting and provocative speech by Carlos Vázquez on the art song in Puerto Rico; a master class in composition by distinguished composer Roque Cordero over at the Puerto Rico Conservatory of Music; and in the same hall a fascinating presentation by Juan Blanco, celebrated Cuban musicalizer of vast spaces and thus a sonoral confederate of Puerto Rico's own Francis "COSMOS" Schwartz. Friday's final plenary session was devoted to procedural matters and to the nuts and bolts of the composer's world: the hopeful flow of commissions, the practical conditions of performance here and there, the reactions of concert audiences to new music, the question of international communication among specialists and the production and circulation of scores and recordings.

Too, a certain amount of procedural infighting took place for the edification of participants and observers alike, but of course this occurs everywhere and in all professions. Try the Bar Association if you don't believe me, to say nothing of the Puerto Rico Legislature. And just as happens after the lawyers' brawls and the legislative fistfights, when Friday's musical scrappers calmed down they all went out to lunch together. Nothing personal in any of it, of course. . . .

This Third Caribbean Composers Forum was put together by a hardworking team headed by Carlos Vázquez and Carlos Cabrer, two teachers in the UPR Music Department, with the direct collaboration or indirect sponsorship of numerous other agencies including the UPR Institute of Caribbean Studies, many other UPR offices and a number of Commonwealth agencies beginning with the State Department itself. All agencies and all hands are to be congratulated. For future developments I would first recommend that an attempt be made to make the forums really Caribbean in scope, with representation from the historically French, Dutch and English regions as well; second, that written program notes be provided for the concerts instead of the improvised comments of sometimes startled and not fully articulate composers; and third, that a greater effort be made to seek out and engage the most professionally secure performers available for the presentation of the forums' music.

Camerata Caribe Honors Memory of Sanromá

The San Juan Star
November 7, 1990 By Donald Thompson

Among the annual cycle of activities at the Puerto Rico Conservatory of Music is a week of observances designed to honor the memory of late pianist Jesús María Sanromá (1902-1984). Sanromá, among his innumerable other accomplishments, served as orchestra pianist with the Boston Symphony Orchestra for almost twenty years; returning to Puerto Rico in the early 1950s he became a whirlwind of musical and organizational activity including participation in the creation of the Puerto Rico Conservatory of Music itself. The Annual Sanromá Week is the right thing to do, and this year's started off in the right way: with a concert on Sunday afternoon by one of Puerto Rico's principal chamber ensembles.

On the stage of the Sanromá Hall of the Conservatory of Music was Camerata Caribe, a quintet formed by Peter Kern (flute), David Bourns (oboe), Kathleen Jones (clarinet), Alan Brown (bassoon) and Vanessa Vassallo (piano). These names might be familiar to you, and rightly so. The woodwind players are the proficient principals of their sections in the Puerto Rico Symphony Orchestra; together with pianist Vassallo they are also among the leading teachers at the Conservatory of Music itself.

The Camerata Caribe ensemble has been together for some seven or eight years now, and is an example of what a few dedicated professionals can accomplish if they set their minds to it. Their work is marked by individual artistry, by excellent ensemble work and by the constant exploration of new repertory. All of these valuable attributes were evident during Sunday's brief and varied program.

Offered were works by Johann Joaquim Quantz, Felix Mendelssohn, William Ortiz and Paul Harvey (who?). Mr. Harvey, it turns out, is a skilled contemporary English composer and a woodwind player himself.

His six Green Island Sonnets, offered on Sunday, are not only extremely attractive pieces in themselves, but (according to information smuggled to me backstage in the absence of program notes) are actually in the form of sonnets. Now *that's* a nice literary touch for a Sunday morning, what? In addition, according to my sneaky informant, they were dedicated to the Camerata Caribe ensemble itself and premiered in Puerto Rico about a year and a half ago.

This is one of the things which serious chamber ensembles do: they get new music composed for them or dedicated to them. Such was the case of another recent work on Sunday's concert: *Caribe Urbano*, by William Ortiz. Ortiz is one of Puerto Rico's most active and most original composers, and this new work represents a commission by Camerata Caribe under the auspices of the Puerto Rico Foundation and the National Endowment for the Arts. A great deal of Ortiz' previous work has been almost obsessively rhythmic and percussive, much of it deliberately evocative of the mean streets and the bitter life of New York's *barrio*. This present "urban Caribbean" music projects a much milder kind of vision: rather than rumbles it projects boleros, with perhaps a distant echo of some imagined Precolumbian dance on the now thoroughly urbanized Isla Verde beachfront.

A delicious Concert Piece No. 1 for clarinet, bassoon and piano by Mendelssohn was offered by Camerata members Jones, Brown and Vassallo. A virtuoso piece for the winds, the work gave the pianist quite a bit to do as well.

The only beef I have with Sunday's program was the use of piano instead of the much more appropriate harpsichord in Quantz' Trio Sonata in C Minor. Still, Ms. Vassallo's playing of the harmonic filler keyboard part was so subtle and so discreet that I think only a pedantic curmudgeon could object to it. Well, if the shoe fits I'll wear it. Sunday's concert ended with a beloved Puerto Rican *danza*, "Impromptu," in a witty arrangement by José Daniel Martínez.

A Revelation in Castanets

The San Juan Star
November 28, 1990   By Donald Thompson

    The Puerto Rico Symphony Orchestra offered one of its infrequent concerts in the University of Puerto Rico Theater on Sunday afternoon, attracting a big audience to a pleasing program of Spanish music. This (Spanish music, that is) is one of the things which Odón Alonso, PRSO music director, does best. With Alonso off the island due to a family emergency the concert was conducted by the PRSO's associate music director, Roselín Pabón, who did it pretty well himself on Sunday.
    A pleasing program of Spanish music, yes, but to me a learning experience as well. And a learning experience is always welcome, especially on a Sunday afternoon, right?
    What did I learn, then? I learned something about castanets played not as a clacking adjunct to Spanish dancing, but as a musical instrument in their own right. How did I learn this? From the work of Lucero Tena, appearing as castanet soloist with the PRSO. And between what I learned at the theater and what I learned by looking up a few things when I got home, I feel like a new man, castanetically speaking.
    The main work was a Concerto for Castanets and Orchestra, no less, by Spanish composer Enrique Llacer. Written for soloist Lucero Tena herself and given its world premiere performance on Sunday, the one-movement composition is laid out like a modern (well, almost modern) concerto for solo instrument and symphony orchestra. It's all there: the orchestral introduction, the accompanying role of the orchestra in solo passages, the alternation of soloist and orchestra in "trading licks" (as we used to say in the world of jazz) and even a couple of cadenzas which give the soloist some free time in which to demonstrate technical ability and expressive skills.

In Ms. Tena's hands (rather, fingers) the castanets display many of the qualities of better known solo instruments, principally lacking only the ability to move up and down over a range of pitches and/or to play chords. And by varying the point of contact and by means of other subtle adjustments, Tena even approximates these. Her dynamic range extends from a whisper to a roar, while her repertory of sounds goes far beyond the familiar drum-like castanet roll. Her rhythmic control was astounding on Sunday, particularly in passages which she shared or alternated with one or another orchestral section. Right on the nose every time.

Another work originally composed for soloist Tena and appearing on Sunday was part of a suite for castanets and orchestra written by Joaquín Rodrigo and dating from 1970. This piece impressed me as better than average Rodrigo, right up there with his honored works for guitar and orchestra. I look forward to hearing the rest of the suite when Ms. Tena comes this way again.

Also offered on Sunday were arrangements for big orchestra and castanets of modest eighteenth-century keyboard pieces by Padre Antonio Soler and Domenico Scarlatti, as well as by Mateo Albéniz of a little later. If these engorged arrangements were offered free-standing at a regular symphony orchestra concert I'd probably break up a few rows of seats in protest, but I must grudgingly concede that they worked well as accompaniments for the castanet soloist.

Music by Pablo Sarasate, Manuel de Falla, Joaquín Turina and Jerónimo Jiménez was also offered on Sunday, with suites from Falla's *El Amor Brujo* and Turina's *Danzas Fantásticas* serving as orchestral showpieces and giving the soloist an offstage break. The orchestra sounded fine, with plenty of solo work to go around and nicely coordinated by conductor Pabón.

Weighing the entire experience carefully, and while welcoming the castanets as a solo instrument played by a stand-still performer (as in such works as the Llacer concerto), I must confess that the most absorbing parts of the afternoon were those works in which Lucero Tena, a formidable dancer, combined the castanets with dance in the more familiar mode of performance. These were selections from the music of Falla (from *La Vida Breve*) and Jiménez (from *La Boda de Luis Alonso*), which respectively closed the two halves of the concert. Perhaps a great part of the audience agreed with me (not always the case, by any means), for orchestra and soloist had to repeat the last section of the Jiménez before the audience would allow the concert to end.

The concert ended but the occasion did not, for several institutions honored violinist José ("Pepito") Figueroa for his decades of contributions to civilized life in Puerto Rico, in a post-concert ceremony. True, Figueroa taught at UPR for a couple of years back in the late fifties, but his major contribution was as concertmaster of the Puerto Rico Symphony Orchestra itself from the orchestra's earliest days until his recent retirement. All honor to him for it!

Chamber Music at the Casa del Libro

The San Juan Star
February 2, 1991   By Donald Thompson

    La Casa del Libro is an internationally significant island institution whose origins go back to the times when distinguished bibliophile Elmer Adler saw San Juan as the appropriate site for a museum of the book and book arts. Adler's work was continued by the late David "Jack" McWilliams, no slouch himself when it came to knowing and ferreting out significant books and important editions. Housed in two beautifully restored buildings in Old San Juan which are owned and maintained by the Institute of Puerto Rican Culture, La Casa del Libro is now in the skilled and loving hands of John Blackley, who with the aid of a dedicated staff and an equally dedicated support group of friends is rapidly leading the institution into still wider and deeper spirals of service and influence.

    One of these spirals has led to the sponsorship of a concert series, taking place in the institution's handsome quarters and generally devoted to music which you would not likely come across in the normal course of concert life here or anywhere else. Now in its second season of concerts, Casa del Libro has presented ancient instrument ensembles, soprano soloists, guitarists, a jazz quartet and several other oddments. Lately the institution has established a "residence" relationship with a newly formed string quartet, whereby the quartet has a regular home for its presentations as well as a ready-made public: the many fans and followers of the Casa del Libro itself. These book museum groupies hear some interesting music while music lovers become interested in the extremely valuable work of the Casa del Libro, and still another spiral is launched. See how it works?

It was a new Puerto Rico String Quartet, La Casa del Libro's resident ensemble, which drew me back to Cristo Street on Tuesday evening for the first time in many years. I suspected that the quartet would be good, as it is made up of some of the Puerto Rico Symphony Orchestra's most valuable players: David Dyer and Cheryl Trace (violins), Min Hui Luo (viola) and Mary Ann Campbell (cello). Working together for only a few months now in chamber music, these solid performers are well on the way to providing another significant chamber ensemble for the island's musical life.

Tuesday's concert by the Puerto Rico String Quartet offered three works which among them covered a lot of territory. First was a quartet by island based composer Jack Délano, dating from some five years ago and representing, to my way of thinking, some of his best work to date. Délano has been active over the years across a whole spectrum of work and expression in the arts, ranging from photography to film and television direction to graphics to book illustration and on to musical composition. In music, most of his work has been marked by fine attention to detail, by practical playability and singability, and by the incorporation of elements of Puerto Rican folk music, both in rhythms and in recognizable melodic contours. At its best, Délano's music is completely respectable and at the same time enjoyable; at worst it can tend toward cuteness.

Well, friends, there is nothing cute about this string quartet and extremely little folksy. The general impression is of a powerful and well made piece of chamber music which fits nicely into the currents of twentieth-century traditions out there in a greater world of music which, believe it or not, exists beyond these tropical shores.

Also impressively performed on Tuesday were a melodious quartet by Luigi Boccherini, bridging the stylistic gap between the sons of Bach and the quartets of Haydn; and the meaty String Quartet No. 8, Op. 110 of Dmitri Shostakovich. Now *here* is a test for any ensemble, and particularly for any quartet which dares to program it on anything less than ten years of study and rehearsal. To my ear, the performance of the Shostakovich was the most successful of all on Tuesday, which says a lot for the Puerto Rico String Quartet.

Of course there are a few things that this ensemble can work on, things which are known to all string players but which are sometimes forgotten in the heat of performance. Among these are the tuning of passages in parallel octaves between the fiddles, a favorite device with composers who want the quartet to sound like an orchestra, and the exaggeration of indicated dynamic levels. This means that when the composer writes "soft" you play double soft, so that the next change will raise the audience right out of their chairs. Well, as I say, every string player knows these things; it's only a matter of rehearsing them until they become automatic.

As for me, my trip down to Cristo Street provided an unexpected dividend: finding the original 1516 edition of a book which I had recently chased as far as Berkeley, California—in hot pursuit of a lousy nineteenth-century translation, at that. For important books as well as important music, you can't beat La Casa del Libro.

Mezzo Bartoli at the Tapia

The San Juan Star
February 21, 1991   By Donald Thompson

 The San Juan Municipal Theater, officially named after the nineteenth-century literary figure Alejandro Tapia in 1937 and familiarly known as "The Tapia," opened for use as a concert hall precisely 159 years ago next week. What opened it in 1832 was a voice recital, and as I attended a voice recital in the Tapia on Sunday evening I envisioned a tableau populated by the generations of singers who have graced its stage, to say nothing of the jugglers, magicians, opera companies, pigeon acts and assorted comics who have performed there. Although most of San Juan's concert life has moved elsewhere during recent years, the restored Tapia can still be a potent force in the island's music.
 So it was on Sunday, when mezzosoprano Cecilia Bartoli and pianist Martin Katz presented a nicely conceived recital. This was the opening shot in a series of five events to be offered this year by forces representing a combination of the Teatro de la Opera group and the more recently formed Culturarte de Puerto Rico, and bodes well for the rest of the series.
 The virtuoso coloratura-mezzo is not common today (if indeed such voices were ever very common), so a full evening of such music is to be savored and remembered. This is especially the case when it is presented with the skill and style of a Cecilia Bartoli. Organized along the traditional lines of most voice recitals, Sunday's began with music from the early decades of opera: music by pioneers Caccini and Cesti, then on to Caldara, Paisiello and Alessandro Scarlatti. This programming allows both the voice and the audience to warm up with smoothly flowing music without great technical demands but displaying the singer's qualities of phrasing and expression. My feeling on Sunday was that Bartoli's

performance of this music was honest, correct and in every way praiseworthy, but with the exception of a moving aria by Vivaldi and some challenging variations by Paisiello, not extraordinary.

Ah, but then came an excerpt from Mozart's *Lucio Silla*, and from there on the evening became an unfolding of coloratura exuberance which never let up. Much of this exuberance was centered on Rossini, and specifically on some of his less familiar music. To my mind the evening's most interesting offering was a set of three songs describing a Venetian boat race—from the viewpoint of a competing gondolier's sweetheart! There is a great amount of very unusual music in Rossini, much of it in a collection of more than 150 pieces entitled *Sins of Old Age* and dating from long after he stopped composing operas at the age of 37. Such music certainly rewards exploration but not all singers wish to explore it, what with so much familiar operatic Rossini to sing and most of it already memorized anyway.

Rossini's regatta suite, considered along with four others of his songs and topped by a staggeringly difficult aria from *La Cenerentola*, displayed Bartoli's technical and expressive gifts to their best advantage, as well as a repertory of gestures and facial expressions which could only add to the audience's pleasure.

Still with energy left after this demanding program, Bartoli and fine pianist Katz performed a couple of equally strenuous encores even involving a bit of visual play. Their work has added another line to the long list of significant performances delivered from the stage of the Tapia Theater during the past century and a half.

Soloists Save the Day

The San Juan Star
March 12, 1991   By Donald Thompson

Power Opera hit the target Thursday evening as Culturarte de Puerto Rico and the Teatro de la Opera group teamed up again for a stellar presentation in the Festival Hall of the Performing Arts Center. Thursday's opera concert was the second in a series of jointly sponsored events which began in the Tapia Theater a couple of weeks ago. Stellar indeed: do you remember that incomparable coloratura-mezzo, Cecilia Bartoli? These events, so promisingly launched, will extend into November in a series which is described as an opera festival. Well, maybe so, *sez* I, but the concept of a festival usually includes some idea of joyous concentration within a temporal frame marked by chronological proximity, and five events within ten months does seem to stretch that chronological proximity a bit. This is not to knock the effort, you understand; by me they can call it a festival or a farm auction, as long as this confabulation of opera lovers continues to engage such performers as we have seen thus far in the series.

Saturday's featured performers were soprano June Anderson and tenor Alfredo Kraus, sharing the stage with the Puerto Rico Symphony Orchestra and an especially organized male chorus, the whole assemblage conducted by PRSO music director Odón Alonso.

Alfredo Kraus is no newcomer to Puerto Rico, having performed here on a number of occasions and having generated a big and faithful following. Especially memorable was his appearance as Tonio in Donizetti's *The Daughter of the Regiment* some seven years ago. Well, the famed Kraus lyric tenor is still holding its own internationally, and even seemed to me on Thursday to have gained in flexibility, subtlety and dynamic control since I last heard him. I think that his most impressive work on Thursday was in that "Ah! mes amis," from *The Daughter of the Regiment*, which the tenor shares with the chorus. Here, Kraus' very highest range was seen at its best; the chorus, prepared by Randolfo Juarbe, made a brief and completely satisfactory presentation in this excerpt.

June Anderson is well established as a gifted and versatile soprano whose accomplishments fall into the lyric coloratura category. Her major contribution to the first half of Thursday's concert came in Lucia's foreboding entrance aria, "Regnava nel silenzio" from Donizetti's *Lucia di Lammermoor*. Here were displayed her great coloratura skills, especially her effortless negotiation of trills, ornamented lines, arpeggios and rapid scales. Deeply moving was her presentation of "Et maintenant ecoutez ma chanson" from Thomas' *Hamlet* in the second half of the concert, including a rare case of operatic ululation, symbolizing Ophelia's madness. For nineteenth-century opera lovers, only Arabs and crazies ever ululated.

Anderson and Kraus joined forces, as you might expect, in a bouquet of opera duos. To me, the most impressive of these was a scene drawn from the end of the first act of *Lucia* and ending in the moving "Verranno a te." French opera provided a pair of flexible and melodious duos in the second half of the concert, in excerpts from Massenet's *Manon* and Gounod's *Roméo et Juliette*. Here, the emphasis was on line, phrase and expression, and this fine team made a lasting impression.

Let's face it: what saved Thursday's performance (and very nicely, too) was the solid work of Anderson and Kraus, seconded briefly by the male chorus. There was, however, a lot of surprisingly tentative orchestral playing, which communicated a kind of quiet panic: a "walking on ice" character which to me spoke eloquently of a desperately under-rehearsed performance. Why, I wonder? Is the PRSO short of rehearsal time lately? Again, why? What caused a complete paralysis of conductor and orchestra and a couple of very close calls during the second half? The momentary paralysis was so profound that it took a physical shove from soprano Anderson to get the machine going again. A bad business, friends, and whatever caused these conductorial and orchestral maladies must be corrected.

Sala Casals

The San Juan Star
March 14, 1991 By Donald Thompson

High in the hills behind San Juan is a place which in the past ten years has become an important center of musical activity. This center is known as the Sala Casals and is located in a house in the Monterrey section of Río Piedras which was the last earthly home of celebrated Catalan cellist Pablo Casals (1876-1973). Puerto Rico was Casals' base of operations during the last 17 years of his long life, and his name was associated with a Commonwealth government agency out of which grew three musical institutions: the Puerto Rico Symphony Orchestra, the Puerto Rico Conservatory of Music and the annual Puerto Rico Casals Festival.

The house now belongs to Dr. Alan Rapoport and his wife Marilú Alvarado, who have equipped the spacious drawing room, where Casals practiced and composed daily, as an occasional recital hall for soloists and chamber ensembles. Marilú Alvarado is a professional musician, and having been through it herself saw in the Casals house an excellent stage for young artists and new or unusual ensembles, as well as a site for other activities associated with concert music.

During the past decade the Rapoports, with recent help from a leading commercial patron of musical events in Puerto Rico, have presented a long list of island and visiting performers in the Sala Casals as well as an occasional lecture, musical chat or act of musical homage or recognition. Relaxed in format, the events are yet likely to be as artistically rigorous as anything you would see in the concert hall.

In observance of the tenth anniversary of its founding, Sala Casals resonated on Sunday evening to the music of one of Puerto Rico's sterling chamber ensembles, the San Juan Consort. Directed by the versatile David Dyer, this group devotes its energies to the study and presentation of music dating from the Renaissance and Baroque periods: very roughly, the two centuries preceding the death of J.S. Bach in 1750. There's a great deal of very interesting music there, but extremely little of it has found its way into today's regular concert life, mainly due to the rise of a "standard" concert repertory during the past century. With most of today's concert fare limited to this standard repertory, it is useless to expect Leclair or Couperin (to say nothing of Gesualdo and Schein) to elbow a place alongside Mendelssohn, Liszt, Schubert and Brahms. Therefore, specialized groups exist to bring its beauties before the public in specialized presentations. And nowadays (unlike even thirty years ago) a public exists for this fresh and attractive music; witness the success which visiting "ancient music" ensembles have enjoyed in San Juan's more conspicuous concert halls during the past few years.

The San Juan Consort makes an attempt to approximate the authentic sonority of older music through the application of known principles of appropriate interpretation (ornamentation, dynamic contrast and the like) as well as the use of historically appropriate instrumental usages. Their violins have shorter necks; gut strings are used instead of the screeching steel of modern times; the curvature of bows goes the "wrong" way, imparting a gentler stroke to vibrating strings; recorders and keyless flutes appear. The viola da gamba, that six-stringed and fretted early relative of the modern violoncello, is used as the fundamental bass. Even the unique sound of the Baroque harpsichord is closely approximated in a carefully controlled high-tech electronic keyboard.

Sunday's uniformly successful offerings included works mainly by early contemporaries of J.S. Bach: Johann Joaquim, François Couperin and Jean-Marie Leclair, as well as that incredibly prolific Georg Phillip Telemann.

For reasons of space, the Sala Casals concerts are limited by invitation to a mailing list of persons who have expressed serious interest in these unusual events and who remember how to deal with an RSVP when the invitation arrives.

♪

Guitar Trio Delivers

The San Juan Star
March 22, 1991   By Donald Thompson

In Puerto Rico the mention of guitar trios usually brings to mind the traditional ensembles of the rural byways and the recordings of melodious boleros which come rolling out of jukeboxes in the Yauco/Cabo Rojo/Mayagüez quadrant. Well, there is another kind of guitar trio now active in Puerto Rico, comprised of three guitarists trained in concert music, who bring to the concert stage an extensive repertory for music composed or arranged for their medium of performance.

The ensemble is called the Tavárez Classical Trio, after the nineteenth-century island composer, and is made up of three of the island's most active guitarists and teachers: Leonardo Egúrbida, José Rodríguez Alvira and Luis Enrique Juliá. On Sunday afternoon this group offered a concert at the Casa del Libro in Old San Juan, attracting a full house to an interesting and varied presentation.

Trapped in the great aunt of all traffic jams and having taken two hours to get from Plaza Carolina to Cristo Street, your correspondent missed the opening third of the concert (Vivaldi and Franck) but arrived in time for the end of a fine trio arrangement of a work which should be much better known here than it is. This is *Souvenir de Porto Rico*, composed by the eminent pianist/composer Louis Moreau Gottschalk in commemoration of almost a year's happy visit here in 1857-1858 with the adolescent but promising soprano Adelina Patti.

The reason that this piano music works pretty well on multiple guitars is that a lot of it is contrapuntal. The guitar certainly lends itself to contrapuntal music, in which melodies and fragments thereof chase each other around the performing medium. Ensembles of two or more guitars virtually demand this kind of music.

I am not a great believer in arrangements, believing that music can sound at its best only when performed by the medium for which it was conceived. However, if you wish to form an ensemble for which little or no original music has been composed, you obviously have to go with arrangements a lot of the time. But you've got to be very careful what kind of music you choose and how you go about adapting it to the peculiarities of its new setting. In this connection I received a very pleasant surprise on Sunday in the form of an Alpine Suite, previously unknown to me, by that incomparable English composer Benjamin Britten.

The musical evocation of a ski trip to Zermatt, several movements of this brief work evoke images of a Swiss clock, the beginners' ski slope, a frigid Alpine scene, perpetual motion down the advanced slope and a sentimental departure. Well, Britten's music seemed so perfectly suited to this guitar trio that I was ready to accept it as a work originally conceived for this medium, and that crafty Britten was certainly capable of perpetrating such an oddment. But lo; it turns out to have been composed for a trio of recorders, that Renaissance instrument which has enjoyed a revival in our time. The guitar trio simply played from the recorder parts, now and then adding a note or two or a proper guitar chord to beef it up.

Original works by Egúrbida and guitarist Juan Sorroche also seemed to fit this format very well, but to me the weakest work on the program was one by the composer for whom the ensemble is named: Manuel Gregorio Tavárez (1842-1883). This was Tavárez' grand march *Redención*, which as an orchestral work was associated with the Ponce Exposition of 1882. Here, I think, is a good example of a composition which really requires its original performance medium to sound well: the full orchestra, or perhaps—just perhaps—a piano or two. This is because with the exception of a very brief section the work is not of contrapuntal nature at all, but rather melody-and-accompaniment, in the style of countless nineteenth-century grand marches. Without the varied instrumental voices of the big orchestra, called into play to contrast a work's different sections as they occur, this music falls too easily into empty oom-pah figures, not at all native to the guitar and symptomatic of a less than successful arrangement.

Withal, Sunday's appearance of the Tavárez Classical Trio pleased the Casa del Libro audience, which still has a couple of concerts to look forward to in the present series.

Schola Antiqua Digs Deep For Repertory

The San Juan Star
May 22, 1991 By Donald Thompson

Before heading for a specialized "older music" conclave in Germany this week, the San Juan-based Schola Antiqua ensemble offered a concert of most unusual music at that hotbed of most unusual bibliophilic and artistic behavior, the Casa del Libro. Taking place in the Casa's light and airy headquarters in Old San Juan, Sunday afternoon's concert was based on European music from as early as the tenth century and as late as the fourteenth.

You ask if there was really music that long before Bellini? Well yes, indeed there was, but it has little in common with the music which developed in Europe in the nineteenth century and which forms the bulk of the art music heard in today's regular opera and concert world.

To bring this old music to life today requires great dedication, as well as the application of fields of knowledge which do not always form part of today's regular musical training. For one thing, you've got to know what you're looking for: music which might be representative of the musical activity of a certain court, a certain monastery, a certain composer whose name might be spelled in a half dozen different ways, or a certain cathedral at a certain time in history. Then you've got to know the sources: in what archive, in what manuscript, in what obscure catalog, guide or dissertation might we find a trail to the music we're seeking? And that's not all: once you find your music you've got to be able to read it, and I assure you, friends, medieval music doesn't look at all like a nice printed edition of the Beethoven piano sonatas!

Schola Antiqua knows what it's about. Sunday's music was drawn from sources most of whose titles are known to every graduate student in musicology: the Las Huelgas Codex of thirteenth-century Spain, the

Codex Calixtinus of a century earlier and others, as well as a couple of strange ones. But memorizing some titles and dates for an exam is a very different thing from dancing barefoot in the music itself (if you can pardon the expression), and that's what Schola Antiqua does.

By so doing, this fine ensemble has disclosed to us some fascinating branches of our musical genealogy, while revealing the beauties of this older music simply taken on its terms as music. On Sunday, Schola Antiqua forces included Susan Pabón and Ellen Oak, sopranos, with the former displaying unsuspected talents in medieval percussion as well; David Dyer, viola da gamba/recorder, and John Blackley, singer/chanter/leader. Carefully prepared program notes added immeasurably to the audience's pleasure and understanding.

My own belief is that no music lover who attends such a concert as Sunday's will ever be quite the same again, nor can such a person continue to believe that music began with Verdi and ended with Puccini, or Bach and Brahms respectively, or Vivaldi and Wagner. In other words, the great world of music is full of marvels which stretch the mind and bring light to the soul (could this be what music is for?), and Sunday's concert by the Schola Antiqua only brought this idea home again in full force.

The 1991 Casals Festival

The San Juan Star
June 25, 1991   By Donald Thompson

This year's Casals Festival ended on Saturday night in the Festival Hall of Santurce's Performing Arts Center. In some ways the event reminded Saturday's audience of Casals festivals of the now distant past, with a small symphony orchestra and a fine cello soloist on the stage.

Saturday's orchestra was an ensemble based in Poland whose name has been given in English as the Warsaw Symphonic Chamber Orchestra. What in heaven's name is a symphonic chamber orchestra, you wanted to know last week but were hesitant to ask? Well, I see it as an invented term which enables you to give your orchestra a distinctive name. "Chamber orchestra" was itself an invented term a few decades ago, applied to small orchestras formed to play music of Bach, Vivaldi and Corelli and maybe up to some Haydn and Mozart, but not much. In addition, "chamber orchestras" could economically play some twentieth-century music which had been specifically and refreshingly composed for smaller groups instead of the monster symphony orchestra that had fascinated composers and audiences since the time of Strauss, Mahler and others of the grandiose persuasion. "Symphonic chamber orchestra," then, seems to be an expanded "chamber orchestra" but now abandoning Bach and Vivaldi for music of composers who were writing in the period of "symphonic" expansion. In other words, we're back again to the "symphony orchestra" of moderate size and modest repertory, but under a new and catchy name. Isn't language wonderful?

The Warsaw ensemble played well on Saturday, as directed by composer Krzysztof Penderecki. Its general size was right for the concert opener, Rossini's effervescent overture to the opera *L'Italiana in Algeri*, which sounded neat and trim with some nice solo woodwind playing.

Also on the program were the "Italian" Symphony of Mendelssohn and Tchaikovsky's attractive Variations on a Rococo Theme for cello and orchestra. However, throughout the concert I was bothered by an imbalance in the string sections, an imbalance which might have resulted from a basic semantic conflict back in Warsaw. I found the orchestral sound top heavy, with the fiddle sections of a size perhaps adequate for the music of Mendelssohn and marginally so for Tchaikovsky, but with the lower sections (cellos and basses) understaffed in proportion. This may have been a managerial nod to some perceived "chamber orchestra" specification for these sections, but it left blank spots in some of the vigorous and fully symphonic developments of the Mendelssohn symphony and even the Rossini overture. Maybe you can't have it both ways; perhaps you can have either a chamber orchestra and its very specialized repertory, or an honest and forthright symphony orchestra to perform the music which is appropriate for its size and instrumentation. But aside from this imbalance (no fault of the players, of course), this Warsaw ensemble displayed a fine level of individual skill and orchestral unity, particularly noted in the realm of dynamic contrast.

Featured in the Tchaikovsky variations on Saturday was cellist Rafael Figueroa, whose occasional solo appearances here are always met with expectation and joy. Audiences are never disappointed, for Figueroa has rightly become an internationally recognized soloist: a steady performer who has completely mastered the technical and interpretive demands of his repertory. He is now in the process of acquiring that profound depth of perspective and the touches of individual subtlety which can only be acquired during years on the road. Figueroa is doing very well, and to all appearances he will continue to do very well indeed.

But, you ask, what about this recent series as a whole? What ABOUT this Casals Festival in Puerto Rico?

Has anyone ever asked your opinion, as an informed and concerned music lover and taxpayer? More or less muffled and unfocused expressions of dissatisfaction are heard annually (and depending upon which political party is in power), mainly regarding the choice of ensembles and soloists, the selection of music to be presented, artistic lapses traceable to a lack of specialized and responsible knowledge among the decision makers, the steadily dwindling concert attendance and the complete lack of interest abroad in what for a few years in the late 1950s was an international attraction.

It was this last which justified the governmental expense (that is, your expense and my expense) of the early Casals festivals: the international attention which was drawn to the island as a classy tourist haven and a safe, stable, cultured place to establish a factory. Well, friends, it has all changed, beginning with the stage. The performers who illuminated the early festivals are no longer active, many of them having joined the great cellist Pablo Casals in that great concert hall in the sky. So forget about bringing back Johnny Barrows, Eli Carmen, the Budapest String Quartet and the rest of that long list of musical glories of the early years. Nor is there anything festive about the music offered in these events any more; by broadening the repertory, the festival planners (the *what?*) lost contact with the unique character of the early festivals as well as with the figure and the musical convictions of Pablo Casals himself.

Audiences? Well, island music lovers now have the Puerto Rico Symphony Orchestra and a couple of other concert series for the regular presentation of regular repertory, thereby removing still another justification for the Casals festival as it was (wrongly, I believe) allowed to develop, especially following Casals' death in 1973. During the first period of the festival's life there was no properly constituted orchestra here to play Mendelssohn symphonies and Tchaikovsky variations for us, so one was assembled annually in New York City and brought to Puerto Rico for a couple of weeks every June. Now there is a stable orchestra in Puerto Rico, and the sooner it is recognized, supported and developed as Puerto Rico's only real claim to notice in the realm of large scale music making, the better it will be for all of us.

An unprecedented event occurred last week when Juan Albors, president of the board of directors of the festival's parent agency, the Musical Arts Corporation, publicly expressed concern over the festival and where it's going. At a news conference called to announce the next season of the Puerto Rico Symphony Orchestra, attention turned to the present Casals festival, which is under the same general management. Festival officials have traditionally been extremely tight lipped about the agency, limiting their public comments to expressions of joy, admiration and pride. Well, Albors announced that there is great concern this year over the light attendance at festival concerts, and indicated that a serious examination might be in order of the festival's nature, its programming, the time of year during which it takes place and other factors which to some observers appear to be mainly of minor and cosmetic significance in the long run.

We can only hope that Albors' serious examiners might finally grab the bull by the horns and begin at the beginning: a determination of what the festival's basic mission was, is and might still become in a musical, touristic and industrial world very different from the world of 1957. Only then, and only within a carefully designed conceptual framework, might it make sense to talk of programming, scheduling, engaging soloists and the other nuts and bolts of organizing a festival.

But don't forget that this is a government agency, and things don't move very fast or very well in government agencies here. As was predicted by a colleague in the pages of this very paper a couple of weeks ago, 2056, the tri-centennial year of the birth of Mozart, will probably find the legislature adjourning after a stimulating debate on the closing law to attend a Casals festival concert similar to those we've witnessed during the past fifteen years or so—but, I predict, in a big and empty hall.

San Juan Pops

The San Juan Star
August 20, 1991 By Donald Thompson

A new orchestral force has recently made its debut here. Called the San Juan Pops, the new ensemble seeks to carve a niche for itself in the island's musical life somewhere in the territory between the old-time park concert and the lighter end of the symphonic repertory. On Saturday evening the new orchestra repeated an earlier program at the Performing Arts Center, drawing a fair sized audience to a concert of tuneful pieces guaranteed to make no heavy demands on anyone on either side of the footlights. Summer fare, you might say, although that term, like "summer reading," loses some of its force here in the land of blue skies and eternal summer.

Such programs as Saturday's offer a touch of concert life during the off season, when the resident symphony orchestra is on vacation and the relative rigors of formal concert programming are relaxed. In the case of the new San Juan Pops, some familiar faces are seen on the stage as a few regular members of the PRSO pick up some off season work in a pattern seen in all mainland cities which are so fortunate as to have resident orchestras and some off season initiatives.

In addition to allowing supporting players in the PRSO to exercise the responsibility of occupying principal chairs for a while, the San Juan Pops as seen on Saturday also provides some good experience to players of the second line: young and able instrumentalists who do not occupy positions in the PRSO, the island's main musical enterprise, mainly because all of the positions are filled. As for me, I say we should be thankful for this second line of instrumentalists and wish them every possible success; it wasn't many years ago that there wasn't even much of a *first* line of able orchestral musicians in Puerto Rico.

The San Juan Pops is directed by Roselín Pabón, who during the regular season serves as the associate music director of the Puerto Rico Symphony Orchestra itself. On Saturday, Pabón brought to the Performing Arts Center a program as sweet as the summer breeze, and every bit as fleeting.

Much of Saturday's music originated in brief and basically simple pieces from the island itself, but heard here in pompous arrangements reminiscent of Hollywood extravaganzas of the 1950s, complete with clanking xylophones and ominous timpani. Heavy-handed arrangements of the simple music of Eladio Torres, Antonio Cabán Vale, Felipe Rosario Goyco and Rafael Hernández produced the same effect as a bowl of okra sherbet with redeye gravy, converting what should have been a moment's delight into a case of acute indigestion.

On the other hand, a couple of arrangements by Enriquillo Cerón and Guillermo Figueroa of pieces by Pedro Flores and José A. Monrouzeau were to my ear perfectly honest, perfectly appropriate and perfectly pleasing. This is because the arrangers exercised some musical discipline and some historical sense, resisting the great temptation to bury this simple music under exotic harmonies, florid countermelodies and instrumental effects which were not dreamed of when the original pieces were composed. You think I exaggerate? A concert public expresses its pleasure through the simple device of banging one hand against the other. Saturday's public was audibly moved by the simple and straightforward presentation of the music of Flores and Monrouzeau, but seemed dazed and immobilized by the extremely able but stupefying arrangements referred to above.

Saturday's major work was Ernesto Cordero's *Concierto Criollo*, for cuatro and orchestra, which a few years ago brought the native cuatro into the world of solo concert instruments. This concerto is not one of my favorite compositions among the works of island composers, but audiences here and abroad seem to like it very much. Saturday's soloist was cuatro whiz Edwin Colón Zayas, equally at home in the concerto's written-out passages as in the sections which call for improvisation, "trading licks" with a bongo player from the orchestra.

Following the Cordero work, Colón Zayas was joined by a pair of orchestra percussionists for a presentation of a very funny set of variations by Pedro Rivera Toledo on Rimsky-Korsakov's "Flight of the Bumblebee." The piece features the finger-busting cuatro part but also calls on the percussionists and the entire orchestra in a kind of lighthearted concerto grosso of the fields and byways.

Also offered on Saturday were a Verdian overture by Juan Morel Campos (*La Lira*) as arranged by Roberto Sierra, a set of dances from Bernstein's *West Side Story* and an opening fanfare from Paul Dukas' symphonic poem *La Peri*.

There is probably a place in the island's music for such an orchestra as this San Juan Pops, which could perhaps find a function not only off season but also somehow woven into the regular concert season as well. Best wishes to the new orchestra and to its pioneer supporters.

Ana María Martínez

The San Juan Star
September 6, 1991   By Donald Thompson

Still another one of the fine young voices produced in Puerto Rico and loose on the world recently checked in for an appearance on the home courts. This time it was soprano Ana María Martínez, who on Saturday evening joined veteran pianist Luz Hutchinson in a recital up on the hill in Ponce.

Up on the hill indeed, at the Serrallés Castle on Ponce's northern skyline. The castle has recently been restored, now offering a handsome Ponce landmark as well as a pleasant small recital hall built into what was reportedly at one time an enormous cistern for collecting rainwater. You can perhaps imagine some of the splashy musical puns, well Handeled and delivered with liquid tone, which resulted from that archeological revelation.

Saturday's recital was sponsored by the Art and Culture Committee of the Society of Wives of Physicians of the South, and drew a goodly public for the Martínez-Hutchinson event.

The recital was nicely balanced, with groups of songs and opera excerpts alternating with solo piano pieces. Opera excerpts included selections from Mozart and Puccini, the former especially demonstrating the clarity and agility of the Martínez voice. Especially memorable in this regard was "Deh vieni, non tardar," from *The Marriage of Figaro*. A couple of arias from Puccini's *Gianni Schicchi* and *La Bohème* also displayed Martínez' breadth of expression and volume of sound.

I think Ms. Martínez might wish to work some on achieving the long and floating line of expression especially appropriate for Puccini and for the kind of music nicely represented by three songs by Fauré, but she certainly has most of the problems of musical expression well on their way to solution. And for the technique, don't worry about it; she already has it and to spare.

The Seven Popular Spanish Songs of Manuel de Falla put it all together as the last of Saturday's scheduled offerings, for in one or another of these songs all of a soprano's skills are inevitably called into play. And so it was, for from the nocturnal coloring of "Asturiana" to the fireworks of the final "Polo," Ms. Martínez covered all the bases of both technique and expression.

Pianist Hutchinson, herself well known to Ponce audiences, contributed a Chopinesque *danza* by Juan Morel Campos and a delicate performance of Debussy's *Clair de Lune*, exhibiting, as well as a soloist's high skill, the concentration of a seasoned artist. You see, during the most delicate part of the Debussy work the recital hall door burst open to admit what turned out to be not a Steinway highjacking but six or eight concertgoers claiming admission during the performance of a work, an unpardonable offense in concert life. Not only that, but two invaders calmly crossed between the soloist and her attentive audience while seeking seats. A lesser artist might have fallen off the piano bench in shocked disbelief, but veteran Hutchinson just kept rolling out the Debussy. Me, I think that the good ladies of the SWIPOS might wish to organize a few lectures on concert etiquette as their important cultural program unfolds down there in Ponce.

Principal Singers Come Through in *Tosca*

The San Juan Star
September 14, 1991   By Donald Thompson

Puccini's tragic opera *Tosca* was called "that shabby little shocker" by one of today's foremost musical scholars. I think I would differ, if mainly to point out that productions of this work are seldom little anymore while not much shock value remains in this tale of deceit and tragedy for today's audiences, hardened by international thuggery and carport murders. Shabby? I don't think so. Some of it is musically derivative, to be sure, with much of the first act sounding like *La Bohème* played backward. But "shabby" is too strong. Call it "irregular" or "inconsistent" and I would agree.

Some of the criticism directed at *Tosca* is on dramatic grounds. The plot is rather thin, you must admit, while many of the elements which liven up the stage picture are frankly patches stuck on; take the first act kiddie scene and final procession, for example. These scenes have nothing to do with plot and everything to do with providing some variety on stage while giving the principal singers a bit of a breather backstage. I will say this, however: to make a convincing production out of this opera takes some doing, with most of the hard.work falling right on the shoulders of the three principals who play the roles of Tosca, Cavaradossi and Scarpia.

The present production of *Tosca*, brought to us by Opera de Puerto Rico and concluding its run at the Performing Arts Center tomorrow evening, rests on the very solid work of soprano Eva Marton, tenor Giacomo Aragall and baritone Pablo Elvira. Musically these three artists were in top form as Thursday's opening performance unfolded, while the acting of Marton and Elvira could make a gripping drama out of anything. Tenor Aragall is a fine actor too, but the role of Cavaradossi simply doesn't require him to do much in the way of dramatization aside from the drama which is inherent in his music.

Cavaradossi does have to sing well, however, and once Aragall's voice got cranked up and running on Thursday he made a fine impression indeed. For my money, his best solo contribution was in the third act's "E lucevan le stelle," while the big duo which follows it allowed both Aragall and Marton plenty of space for vocal display.

Speaking of acting, I was especially impressed by Marton's work in the first act; from her very first entrance she generated enough dramatic tension to move the play forward during a long time when nothing else of importance was happening. And Pablo Elvira: now *there* is a piece of work! We have seen physically attractive Scarpias here, attractive enough and smooth enough to make you wonder if Tosca isn't making a big mistake by sticking with the tenor. Well, there is absolutely nothing attractive about Elvira's Scarpia, for he very subtly plays it ugly, mean and completely despicable. In fact, Elvira is so very despicable as Scarpia that we can even occasionally overlook the seamless melodious qualities of his voice. Maybe another level of role analysis is suggested here: with a voice like that, can Scarpia really be so bad down deep?

Supporting roles are very ably played in this production by tenor José Ramón Torres as Spoletta, bass Noel Ramírez doubling as Angelotti and the jailor, and bass Antonio González Géigel as Sciarrone. The role of the sacristan in *Tosca* occupies a special category, for it can come close to dominating the scene depending on how big the singer is encouraged (or allowed) to play it. Here, the sacristan is played by gifted bass-baritone Richard McKee, who never lets it get away from him despite plenty of opportunity to do so.

Musical director of this production is Alfredo Silipigni, whose work is well known here; stage director is Matthew Lata, a newcomer to the island stage. Members of the St. John's School Children's Chorus, directed by Marilyn Carrión, provide the rebellious first-act acolytes, while chorus director Susan Pabón's fine work was especially evident on Thursday in an off-stage second act chorus. The Puerto Rico Symphony Orchestra provides the foundation down there in the orchestra pit, and the efforts of some of the island's most skilled backstage folk, including costume coordinator Gloria Sáez and makeup person Rosie Badillo, contribute greatly to the success of the production. General director of the present *Tosca* is José Gilberto Molinari.

Brain Drain Affecting the PRSO?

The San Juan Star
September 25, 1991By Donald Thompson

The Puerto Rico Symphony Orchestra has again taken up its role as the anchor of the island's concert life, with its 1991-1992 season now moving into its third week.

This year's start was a rough one, with contract negotiations coming right down to the wire, accompanied by the expected tensions and uncertainties. In addition, the orchestra has recently lost a number of fine players as around ten percent of the regular PRSO members have gone on study leave or, I suspect in some cases, have left in search of better working conditions.

Much has been written about Puerto Rico's "brain drain," a flight of skill and talent which especially seems to affect the engineering and health care professions. Well, it also affects many other professions, and we may be seeing a bit of it in our very own PRSO. I hope I'm wrong, and that all of the valuable players now missing from the orchestra will return. Their substitutes have some pretty big shoes to fill, and it is not clear yet that they are uniformly up to the task.

Sunday's concert, the second of the new season, was conducted by Odón Alonso, the orchestra's music director and principal conductor. As quite correctly occurs with some regularity nowadays, the orchestra offered the premiere performance of some new music by an island composer. Saturday's composer was William Ortiz, and the new work, commissioned by the Musical Arts Corporation (the PRSO's parent agency) is entitled *Suspensión de Soledad en Tres Tiempos*.

Ortiz, born in Puerto Rico and mainly raised in New York City, has found some very interesting things to say musically, linked chiefly to his vision of music as the distillation of experience. And the experiences which he has chosen to distill are those mainly associated with the mean streets of New York's Latino sections. Ortiz has spoken and written of the influences in his work of the rhythms, harmonies, cries and noises—the sonoral graffiti—of New York street corner hangouts.

These ideas have been successfully explored in Ortiz' music for small groups, music often based on percussion instruments and/or incorporating musical styles associated with "Street Music" (one of his titles). Here, an improvisatory style of performance can be very convincingly suggested, while a small group of performers can successfully evoke the joys, tensions, conflicts and schemes of a bunch of young people hanging loose on some street corner.

Suspensión de Soledad en Tres Tiempos, on the other hand, is conceived for symphony orchestra. Here, Ortiz again evokes the urban scene, but the canvas is larger and the message more diffuse. Its three sections are entitled (here, translated) "Bilingual Harmony," "March" and "Beat Box," with each section contributing to the development of a unified vision of the urban condition; what ties it all together is rhythm. But I don't know; the canvas might be too big for the subject. While I found the Ortiz work technically well made and orchestrally valid, I still keep thinking of those street corner pieces for small groups as more representative of the composer's best work.

Also offered on Saturday was a work by the contemporary Spanish composer Tomás Marco (b. 1942). Saturday's program book offered no biographical information concerning the composer at all except for the year of his birth, but a bit of sleuthing in the music library reveals that Marco was born in Madrid, that the present performance missed his birthday by about a week, and that he is an enthusiastic member of what is loosely called the international avant-garde. Saturday's work was Marco's Triple Concerto for violin, cello, piano and orchestra, and called upon the participation of guest artists, the Mompou Trio, also of Madrid, in the performance of the solo parts.

The Marco concerto at times very neatly combines a traditional sort of melody with avant-garde techniques, as occurs near the beginning of the one-movement work as glissandos in the orchestral strings accompany the solo cello. Too, a perfectly traditional orchestral chord occasionally closes some section otherwise marked by the perhaps overly generous repetition of a particular figure or technical device. However, much of the work seems to consist of wandering figures across the orchestra and among the soloists, directed toward no perceivable end, going nowhere, painfully repetitive and demonstrating nothing in particular, not even the sonoral and dynamic contrasts historically associated with the concerto idea or the superior level of technical display expected of soloists in a concerto situation. Nor did the Marco Triple Concerto give the Mompou Trio much opportunity to display their skills as a chamber ensemble: a selfstanding trio of presumably skilled chamber music players. And finally, speak softly when you speak of triple concertos; Beethoven was there 187 years ago and left a mark which has yet to be even approached.

Speaking of Beethoven, Saturday's concert closed with a performance of his Third Symphony, the great "Eroica" (not "Erotica", as students tend to write on exams nowadays). To some music lovers, not completely convinced by Ortiz' sonoral graffiti and absolutely turned off by Marcos' wandering redundancies, the Beethoven "saved the concert."

Well, I don't know about that, but this was a nice performance of a work favored by many music lovers worldwide. I noted some ragged chords in the first movement, and I do wish that someone could persuade the PRSO fiddles to stay off the jangling open "E" string in scale passages, for that sound loosens the fillings in my teeth. On the other hand, many incidental woodwind solos were well played throughout the symphony, and especially the oboe solos of the second movement's funeral march.

A Curious Concert

The San Juan Star
November 22, 1991 By Donald Thompson

The 1991-1992 season of the Puerto Rico Symphony Orchestra continued on Saturday with a curious kind of concert offered in commemoration of the discovery of Puerto Rico. Curious because it was a kind of mixed bag of a concert to begin with, and it became curiouser and curiouser as the evening progressed. Scheduled were a whole bunch of minor works, a bouquet of mainly concert openers and encore pieces you might say, with nary a Brahms or Beethoven in sight.

First up was *La Lira*, a concert overture by island composer Juan Morel Campos (1857-1896) which had been skillfully reconstructed by Roberto Sierra from a manuscript version (perhaps Morel's) for solo piano. The overture sounds like Verdi, and why not? By 1882, when *La Lira* won a prize at the Ponce Exposition, the Verdi operas were well known here through performance, and Morel Campos, then in his twenties, had certainly taken part in their presentation. He could have had worse models than Verdi!

In any case, it is always a pleasure to hear Sierra's instrumentally expanded but stylistically honest reconstruction of *La Lira*, what with the island's air contaminated nowadays by the clever but stylistically absurd "symphonic" modernizations of nineteenth-century Puerto Rican pieces which appear with solemn and pretentious regularity.

The major work on Saturday's concert was a piano concerto (rather, a suite for piano and orchestra) by island pianist Narciso Figueroa. The new work represents a $10,000 commission extended by the Puerto Rico Commission for the Celebration of the Fifth Centennial of the Discovery of Puerto Rico and America together with the Musical Arts Corporation, and marks a rare effort of pianist Figueroa in the field of orchestral composition.

So unusual a commission was it for him, in fact, that he turned to composer Germán Cáceres to orchestrate the work for him. Now there's really nothing terribly wrong with this kind of collaborative effort, and it's been observed half in jest that Rimsky-Korsakov and that bunch of Russians all composed or at least orchestrated all of each other's music anyway. But in truth, the orchestral thinking involved in a musical work determines much of that work's basic character, and in most concert music this process is an integral and determinant part of the original creative act of composing.

Regardless of what might be common practice in musical comedy and other marginal phenomena, in concert life orchestration is not a matter to be left to anonymous hacks. In any case, Germán Cáceres is no hack but a skilled and recognized composer, and his essential contribution to Figueroa's concerto merits the highest recognition both on the program page and in the notes. It received neither.

So then, how did the Figueroa/Cáceres piano suite fare on Saturday, with Figueroa himself rolling out the piano part? The piano part is both interesting and quite respectable. Figueroa has been a fine pianist in his time, and much of his known music gives the impression of imaginative keyboard improvisation later written down. So it was here; the music is absolutely pianistic, laid out ready-made for a good pianist's fingers. Figueroa's harmony is again traditional, but spiced with an occasional progression borrowed from the world of sophisticated show tunes of the 1930s, and bordering on blues. Present throughout the four-movement work are references to Puerto Rico's own music, from the country *seis* to a phrase or two from "La Borinqueña," the Commonwealth anthem. As a whole, the work lies in a territory bounded by the music of Manuel de Falla, Joaquín Rodrigo and Ferde Grofé, with a touch of the "Happy Latin" music of the 1940s laid on. I expect this Figueroa/Cáceres suite to find a place in the regular repertory of Puerto Rican concert music, along with works by Héctor Campos-Parsi, Jack Délano and a couple of other representatives. It made a big hit with Saturday's audience.

Also on Saturday's program, ably conducted by Roselín Pabón, were brief works by Isaac Albéniz, Aaron Copland and (subbing for a scheduled Ginastera work) Jack Délano's *La Reina Tembandumba*. Helping to make Saturday's concert progressively more curious were a couple of speeches delivered from the stage just after intermission, destroying the natural rhythm of a symphony orchestra concert, and a demonstration of photographic choreography as a video photographer mounted the stage apron and twice crossed between the stage itself and the attentive public. This sort of thing sets concert life back three or four decades every time it happens, and places it in the same category as weddings and other supposedly solemn observances controlled by photographers. I don't think it's done in concert life anywhere except in Puerto Rico. Why should we be so lucky?

Children's Choir: Artistic Excellence

The San Juan Star
December 28, 1991 By Donald Thompson

In Puerto Rico's somewhat unsteady panorama of musical forces, the San Juan Children's Choir stands as a rock of responsibility; a solid pillar of musical training; an anchor of artistic excellence.

Established 25 years ago by Evy Lucío, the SJCC has developed into a music school based on the choral arts and incorporating such integrated aspects as music reading, instrumental skills, languages, diction and general musical discipline. The product, which now consists of three or four choruses and associated instrumental groups all running at the same time, has attained a level of international recognition which might be envied by some noisier, better connected, better publicized and better financed island musical organizations.

This past weekend the San Juan Children's Choir, in a master stroke of coordination and logistics, concluded a marathon of island concerts with three interconnected events taking place in the Drama Hall of the Performing Arts Center in Santurce. A concert marathon in itself, this series provided a showcase for the various SJCC choruses in the first half of each concert. Thus at one time or another during the weekend the preparatory, elementary, intermediate and advanced groups were heard from as well as former members: a showcase indeed, of a quarter century of musical accomplishment.

Evy Lucío has a masterful grasp of international choral music appropriate for young voices, and what doesn't exist she composes or arranges herself. Thus the weekend's three marathon concerts were made up of interesting and varied music which was absolutely correct for the voices and for each ensemble's particular level of training. This careful matching of means and purposes is called professionalism, and that is why I don't hesitate to refer to the work of the San Juan Children's Choir as professional. Professional it has been for many years now, and professional is what it was last weekend.

Any concert involving young people and taking place between the end of November and the middle of January has to be a Christmas concert, right? Right, but the SJCC presentations go far beyond the realm of cutesy Christmas, and these recent ones were no exceptions. In fact, I believe that this group of interconnected activities set new marks in musical programming, preparation, rehearsal, staging, concert logic and general flow.

The second half of each concert provided a constant factor in the form of a beautifully staged nativity pageant involving the intermediate and advanced choruses, some chorus parents, some former members, some very effective dancing by members of the Ballets de San Juan School . . . everything but a partridge in a pear tree. Oh, yes, even a bit of audience participation and the fine singing voice of Evy Lucío as a soloist. Maybe *she* was the partridge in a pear tree!

The pageant depicted events before, during and after the Nativity, and drew on figures ranging from Old Testament prophets down to symbolic characters bringing gifts from the four corners of the world in an apotheosis of peace and good will. A great part of the success of this ever-mounting accumulation of bright pageantry was due, I believe, to superb costume designs attributed to wizard Tom Seitz. Animal skins, indeed, and right there in the Drama Hall!

Musically, the pageant utilized a splendid selection from Gregorian chant through Handel and on down to the island's own José Ignacio Quintón and more modern music composed in Puerto Rico. The power of Handel and Victoria notwithstanding, to me the pageant's most powerful music was an extended section composed and arranged by Evy Lucío herself, bridging the time of Mary's travail and the birth of Jesus.

To be again congratulated for one of the classiest musical acts now going in Puerto Rico—maybe *the* classiest—are founder Lucío, her professional staff of teachers and administrators who help put these ambitious events together, the commercial firms which back the effort, and of course the people on the firing line: the young members of the San Juan Children's Choir ensembles.

Concerto Fills Musical Niche

The San Juan Star
February 5, 1992 By Donald Thompson

A new orchestral force has made its appearance in the island's music: a chamber orchestra named Concerto. Comprised of some sixteen stringed instrument players mainly associated with the Puerto Rico Symphony Orchestra, the ensemble is now in the middle of a set of concerts at different island centers, polishing its performance and improving its style as it goes along.

Ensembles of this size are very useful in Puerto Rico's geographical microcosm of a musical world, for sixteen or eighteen players can easily be transported anywhere on the island and can be fairly well accommodated on small stages. A "portable" orchestra can thus perform where a symphony orchestra could never go, in this way exercising important educational functions and, we hope, generating audiences for concert music.

Concerto is conducted by Henry Hutchinson, concertmaster of the Puerto Rico Symphony Orchestra. On Sunday Hutchinson sometimes led with baton and at other times from the concertmaster's position, violin in hand, as the ensemble offered a program of works by island composers on the "Family Concerts" series at the Puerto Rico Conservatory of Music in Hato Rey.

Rather on the light side, Sunday's concert was clearly the same program which had been designed for performance in less sophisticated island centers. OK for openers, of course, but it will be nice to hear the group play some Bach, Handel, Corelli and Vivaldi, maybe some Hindemith (all rather neglected just now in Puerto Rico) as Concerto gets itself and its repertory together.

First up on Sunday was a playful set of four pieces by Javier de la

Torre, entitled *Pequeña Suite Popular*. Except for an overextended second movement entitled "Rumbón," de la Torre's work is rather in the style of "youth concert music," probably fine for this orchestra's work in remote corners of the island. Some orchestral imbalance in the first movement resulted in the overpowering of solos for violin and particularly viola, perhaps due to the composer's miscalculation of forces or perhaps to a generally too loud orchestral level. Too, the basses became detached rhythmically from the upper voices for a minute or two, causing a brief discomfort in the region of the solar plexus *(my* solar plexus, that is). To me, the best part of the de la Torre work, both in composition and in performance, was the third movement, a song without words which evoked the popular romantic songs of Puerto Rico's yesteryear.

From eighty years ago came three movements of José Ignacio Quintón's locally celebrated String Quartet, a melodious and skillfully made cornerstone of Puerto Rican concert music which can tell us a great deal about the history of the island's musical life. This music sounds for all the world like a mixture of Schubert and Mendelssohn but dates from 1913, the year of Rite of Spring, of *Elektra*, of Webern's Five Orchestral Pieces and of the "cubist" Prokofiev's shocking Second Piano Concerto. Not that there's anything wrong with writing like Schubert and Mendelssohn, you understand (I'd like to have composed that "Italian" Symphony *meself*), but the fact that one of the island's most talented composers was writing like that in the twentieth century shows us how far the island's music has come in only 80 years (or *has* it?).

The orchestral doubling up of Quintón's solo parts seemed to work all right on Sunday, but I could see nothing wrong with possibly adding a discreet bass part to give the work some depth; once you start messing around with string quartet music you might as well go a little farther and make it truly orchestral. Think of the Adagio for Strings by Samuel Barber, which started out as string quartet music but is now widely known as a string orchestra piece.

The rest of Sunday's concert was made up of short pieces by Jack Délano, Nicky Aponte, Jesús María Escobar, José Monrouzeau, Juan Morel Campos and Rafael Hernández, the first two presumably composed originally for string orchestra, the rest arranged for this instrumentation.

On Sunday the Concerto forces were arranged on stage in a fashion which we have seen a couple of times in recent years, but in which I see no advantage. This is with the members playing standing up (except for the cellos, of course), perhaps to suggest a group of stand-up soloists all. This is fine for individual soloists, for standing up provides plenty of space for free physical movement, expressive body language and other features which soloists find helpful and audiences find attractive. But when a whole orchestra plays standing up the members certainly gain no great freedom of movement, and they lose the anchored backside while jeopardizing section unity and even, I think, sacrificing good visual contact across the orchestra.

Well, think about it, Concerto, or maybe, as a kid seated nearby suggested, it's just that somebody forgot to get out the chairs. . . .

This new Concerto orchestra fills a vacancy in the island's musical life, and can make a real contribution as its very able players blend into a true ensemble through continual rehearsal, concentrated work and a lot of concerts. And for me, the sooner we get some Vivaldi, the better.

As for the logistics of Sunday's concert, one element was especially pleasing to this concertgoer: doorkeepers admitted people to the hall only between works, not during their performance. This is a bit of simple, correct and civilized procedure which is not always observed in Puerto Rico but which when encountered brings relief to performers, joy to the hearts of concertgoers and praise to concert managements.

A Refreshing Sample of Modern Music

The San Juan Star
February 15, 1992   By Donald Thompson

    The Latin American Foundation for Contemporary Music, based in San Juan, has again brought us a refreshing and instructive sample of modern music with a concert on Sunday afternoon at the Puerto Rico Conservatory of Music in Hato Rey.
    Sunday's concert featured the visiting Arioso ensemble, augmented for a couple of works by island percussionist José Alicea and clarinetist Mareia Quintero Rivera. The regular Arioso forces are soprano Rachel Rosales, pianist Harold Lewin and percussionist William Trigg. All are distinguished performers in their own right, while Lewin's work is well remembered from previous appearances here. This trio makes a formidable combination, and Sunday's performance showed the result of skill, dedication and serious study.
    From ancient times, according to the calendar of musical developments nowadays, came works by John Cage (b. 1912) and Luigi Dallapiccola (1904-1975). Both were important innovators in their day, with the completely unpredictable Cage a key figure in almost everything new that has happened in concert music, for better or for worse, since the 1940s. Dallapiccola was a more doctrinaire and academic modernist, and the works offered on Sunday well represent their creators.
    Cage's Forever and Sunsmell, for voice and two percussionists (1942) mainly explored new possibilities in the realm of sound: the piece is essentially a chant, with the accompanying percussion providing an interesting and innovative "envelope." From Dallapiccola came four songs on texts by Antonio Machado for soprano and piano, dating from 1948.
    Representing more modern times were pieces by Bruce Stark (for vibraphone and piano) and Somei Satoh (for voice, piano and percussion).

The Stark work, entitled Farewell Song, is an "atmosphere" piece based on the repetition of chords and rhythms, whose effect is gained through a gradually rising then falling of intensity. Unfortunately, this atmosphere was destroyed on Sunday by a procession of post-intermission latecomers—but more of that later.

Somei Satoh's The Heavenly Spheres Are Illuminated by Lights is a spell-inducing and peace-bringing kind of music. The voice part, from a Buddhist text, is extremely demanding, requiring the long vocal line, steady expression and secure control of the experienced concert artist. Some powerful sounds were generated on Sunday by the combination of low rolling tremolos in the marimba and piano, supporting the soprano's finely controlled chant.

No fewer than three of Sunday's works had been composed with the fifth centennial year of Christopher Columbus' westward wanderings in mind. Probably the first such works to be offered here this season, they will almost certainly not be the last, so brace yourselves, friends. 1992 is just beginning, and then we'll still have 1993 to go, when the fifth centennial of the first sighting by Europeans of Borikén, the modern Puerto Rico, gets cranked up.

Homage to Christopher Columbus, by the Finnish composer Erik Bergstrom, is a very recent piece for solo piano. On Sunday, pianist Lewin explained from the stage that the work brings to his mind the anxieties and uncertainties of Columbus' first Atlantic crossing and his subsequent discoveries.

The first movement, entitled "Santa Maria," makes him think of Columbus' fragile fleet at mid-Atlantic experiencing the anxiety of facing the unknown; the second movement, "Guanahan," makes him think of the anxiety attending the fearful encounter of the old and the new: the clash of European and indigenous American forces. As for me, the percussive repetition of rhythmic figures and the repetitive running of chords and their inversions made me think not of Columbus at all but of George Gershwin, and of what his solo piano music might have sounded like had he lived another fifteen or twenty years.

Also composed with this fifth centennial in mind was 1492 for Piano and Percussion, by Judith Shatin and indeed given its premiere performance on Sunday. Composer Shatin was present to offer some notes on its genesis for the edification of the world premiere audience. The work, as she explained it, conveys her sense of the tensions and struggles of the period; not only was 1492 the year of Columbus' first westward voyage, but it was also the year of the expulsion of Spanish Jews from their own country. Well, there was plenty of tension there, all right, and there was plenty of tension in this new work, too, often developed through percussive passages some of whose rhythms were rather reminiscent of *West Side Story*. Other sections introduced such (to me) really novel effects as causing vibraphone bars to emit hollow and ghostly sounds by rubbing them with a double bass bow.

The third "Columbus Quincentenary" work on Sunday's concert was the second of two songs by Francis Schwartz. The first *Schwartzlied*, "Canción Hemisférica," dates from 1989, and is more expansive, more relaxed and more solid than much of this island composer's work is remembered to be. "Canción Hemisférica," on a text by Octavio Paz, calls upon clarinet as well as soprano and piano (shades of Schubert's shepherd!), and here a word of explanation might be welcomed by recent arrivals to the music of our own time. Those strange and fuzzy clarinet sounds were not evidence of lack of skill on the part of clarinetist Quintero Rivera but quite the opposite: skill in the execution of certain technical devices, instrumentalists' tricks, which are part of the equipment of every concert clarinetist today but which can still cause some unrest among uninitiated concertgoers.

The second Schwartzpiece offered on Sunday was a quincentenary tour-de-force: a Schwartzrap; a rap piece in street-corner pop style but requiring the skill of concert performers. Although offering a more or less balanced account of the consequences of the Conquest, the Schwartz-text lays on some heavy guilt as it goes along, for example: "LET'S not praise the MEANies or perPETuate the MYTH (thump); they DID some very BAD things, no ANDS or buts or IFS (thump). CHRIStopher ColUMbus and his MOT-ley CREW (thump) GAVE the local CUL-tures a SCREWing through and THROUGH."

In this time of solemn praise and equally solemn rejection of the idea of the "Discovery of America," Schwartz' new "Canción del Nuevo Mundo" comes as a welcome relief, an antidote, a bit of healthy irreverence, a third force, and will certainly attain wide circulation as both the homage and the anti-homage get thicker and heavier during 1992.

The driving force behind the Latin American Foundation for Contemporary Music is composer Rafael Aponte-Ledée, who must certainly be praised for the consistently high level and healthy variety of the

LAFCM presentations. Yet a couple of logistic considerations did serious damage to Sunday's concert, a few times absolutely nullifying its value. First off, audiences need texts in the hand to fully understand the words of songs, and most especially in unusual styles or unfamiliar languages. A lot of the point of several works was simply lost, and even most of the humor of the Schwartzrap went by the board, and that's a pity. Too, Rachel Rosales is a fine and expressive singer to be sure, but exactly what text was she expressing, anyway?

Secondly, and this is the killer, the lack of a doorkeeper permitted late arrivals to enter the hall during the performance of works, thereby destroying the performers' concentration and the audience's pleasure.

The whole point of Bruce Stark's Farewell Song was lost, for example, when a platoon of latecomers banged the door just at the work's final moment. Same thing happened to the Dallapiccola work, while several of composer Shatin's informative comments were shaken by invaders.

Recent experience in the same theater showed that latecomers will cheerfully wait outside a few minutes while the performance of a work is completed, but concert organizers have to put someone there to advise them. This is a simple device and one seen throughout the world, but it is not consistently applied here. Why not?

A Schwartz Cantata and the Puerto Rico Youth Choir

The San Juan Star
April 24, 1992 By Donald Thompson

Francis Schwartz, Puerto Rico's most innovative composer today and the one whose music most often represents Puerto Rico in off-island performance, has done it again. On Wednesday a large and receptive audience took part in the premiere presentation of a new Schwartz work at the University of Puerto Rico Theater in Río Piedras.

Entitled *Cantata Juvenil del Nuevo Mundo*, the new work is indeed a youthful cantata, featuring children's voices in the main and based on a fresh and original text by Schwartz himself, a composer whose outlook remains encouragingly youthful even after several decades on the musical firing line.

The text is as timely as tomorrow, for while pleading for world peace (a favorite theme of Schwartz), it also refers to events which are very present in the western world's consciousness just now: Christopher Columbus' wanderings at the end of the fifteenth century on his way to China and some of the consequences of the Admiral's stumbling upon new continents and unsuspected populations.

This is an idea which Schwartz recently explored in a new and very successful rap-piece for soprano, piano and drum set; the present composition retains the good humor and timely mode of presentation of that work, while expanding the idea logistically to include children's chorus, tenor soloist, electronic keyboards, a couple of black-jacketed rappers, an imaginative stage setting, musical costumes (yes, the costumes themselves sound when scratched, rubbed or thumped) and a great deal of choreographed stage action.

Most of the stage action is by the children themselves, who run, jiggle, squirm, fall down, get up, kneel, squat, jog and flow in beautifully disciplined groups, squads and platoons. In addition they sing, for the cantata calls for some rather straightforward choral work from time to time in addition to hisses, groans and other vocal sounds from the established Schwartz repertory.

Wednesday's chorus was the Puerto Rico Youth Choir (Coro Juvenil de Puerto Rico), now in its third year of activity under the direction of founder Jennie Carmona. Director Carmona in fact conducted this premiere performance, skillfully holding it together from a position down in front of the stage and occasionally entering into the choreography herself. Wednesday's tenor soloist was Edgardo Zayas, now making a career in Europe; keyboardist was Fritz Kersting; the set was designed by Melquíades Rosario and the costumes by Gloria Sáez, while the really splendid choreography was by Waldo González.

Let me tell you what I thought of as Wednesday's premiere performance of this sparkling and timely work unfolded at the University of Puerto Rico. I thought of the Seville Exposition just recently opened with the Governor of Puerto Rico himself on hand for the inauguration of the much discussed Puerto Rico pavilion. I then thought of the relentless flood of salsa music which is scheduled to represent Puerto Rico in Europe for the next six months through ceaseless performances at the Puerto Rico pavilion of a kind of music which is not even specific to Puerto Rico. And then I thought of this *Cantata Juvenil del Nuevo Mundo* as the ideal counterweight to that deluge of commercial shlock: a work which is timely, serious in intent, logistically manageable and extremely appealing. In addition it is definitely associated with Puerto Rico in both concept and realization; in short, it is the perfect work for the Puerto Rico pavilion in Seville.

I urge the geniuses who have bought six months of salsa to save their faces (and ours) before the great world of music by sending Jennie Carmona, Edgardo Zayas, Fritz Kersting, Waldo González, the Puerto Rico Youth Choir and the rest of Wednesday's performance apparatus to Seville for a month or so if not for a six months run. It just might work, although the scheduled salsa is already pretty deep along the banks of the Guadalquivir.

Opening Wednesday's event was the Puerto Rico Youth Choir in a more traditional kind of performance, featuring an international repertory of pleasant pieces in arrangements for treble voices. Jennie Carmona conducted her ensemble with a sure hand, while the varied offerings also called upon guitars, recorders, panpipes, accordion, piano, bongos, tambora and other instruments in bringing this attractive music to life in a generally satisfactory manner. I should like to have seen a little more identification of the pieces in the printed program, as a matter both of documentation and of professional courtesy. I knew that I had heard some of those choral arrangements before, but the arrangers were unidentified.

And filling the middle ground between the Youth Choir and the Schwartz premiere was a choreographic dividend: a performance by San Juan Municipal Ballet dancers Vanessa Millán and José Antonio Ramos of a three-part *Canto a la Tierra* choreographed by the same gifted Waldo González whose work would be seen after intermission in the Schwartz cantata.

The *Canto a la Tierra* music turned me off absolutely, as representing the worst of today's most pretentious pop-shlock two-chord music. However, by stoppering up my ears I could enjoy choreographer González' designs in silent glory, faultlessly executed by the skilled and supple Millán and Ramos.

Wednesday's very significant concert was sponsored by the University of Puerto Rico Cultural Activities Office and the same institution's Department of Music, with the Schwartz cantata also benefitting from a commission from the Puerto Rico Commission for the Commemoration of the Fifth Centennial of the Discovery of Puerto Rico and America. And finally, the cover of Wednesday's classy program was designed by the same Melquíades Rosario whose stage set contributed to the success of the Schwartz premiere.

Opera Concert Soars With Valente and Golden

The San Juan Star
May 2, 1992 By Donald Thompson

The Puerto Rico Symphony Orchestra joined forces with the Teatro de la Opera organization on Saturday evening to present an extraordinary concert. An extraordinary concert, indeed; taking place at the Performing Arts Canter in Santurce and based on the music of only two composers, the event was a true feast for the ear.

Why a feast for the ear? Well, for one thing it enlisted the participation of distinguished soprano Benita Valente and stellar mezzosoprano Emily Golden in an evening of opera excerpts tailor made for their voices singly and in combination. And for another thing, look at the composers represented: Mozart and Richard Strauss. How could anything go wrong?

Conducting was PRSO music director Odón Alonso in one of his final concerts before his tenure with this orchestra ends. Opinions differ, but I have always believed that Alonso has been quite effective in finding interesting things for the orchestra to bring to the attention of its growing public, and this combination of Mozart and Strauss was to my mind an excellent example of imaginative programming.

Benita Valente is one of those valuable singers who seem equally at home in opera, oratorio, solo recital and everything else which singers are called upon to do nowadays; the difference is that Valente is not only equally at home but also equally skilled in all of these fields. Emily Golden, on the other hand, has specialized in unusual operas and strange combinations of things. This can easily happen to mezzosopranos, for their type of voice leads them rather naturally into the byways and singularities of the musical art. Roles in *Wozzeck* and *Lulu* of Berg, Shostakovich's *Lady Macbeth*, *Carmen* of course and "pants roles" in a number of more usual works: this is the portfolio of Emily Golden, who had been called upon to substitute for the originally scheduled Tatiana Troyanos on Saturday.

The sublime music of Mozart filled the first half of the concert, as orchestral offerings alternated with solo and duo performances up front by Valente and Golden. The overtures from *Idomeneo*, *La Clemenza di Tito* and *Così fan Tutte* had the reduced PRSO playing as well as I had ever heard it, with fine tonal balance and that sense of elegant tension which is appropriate for Mozart. The singers offered excerpts from the same operas, performing with ease, comfort and apparent enjoyment. Emily Golden's elegant performance of "Parto, parto" from *La Clemenza di Tito* will long be remembered, along with clarinetist George Morales' keen participation in the work's extended solo passages for his instrument.

The complete PRSO filled the stage after intermission and then some, with instruments added to meet the orchestral demands of Richard Strauss' *Der Rosenkavalier*. Extended excerpts from this masterwork filled the concert's second half, performed without pause and again calling upon soprano Valente and mezzo Golden in brilliant duo. *Der Rosenkavalier* is nostalgic, elegant, dignified and exquisitely crafted, while its relation to the music of Mozart is evident at all times. What? Mozart with this enormous orchestra? Mozart with those screaming dissonances and ungainly tuba solos? Yes, Mozart, and I can easily believe that Mozart might have composed like this had he lived at the beginning of the twentieth century. In this sense Saturday's programming was perfect, for it displayed two sides of a "classical" vision of music, seen from points a little more than a century apart in time.

Here again the beautifully matched voices of Valente and Golden contributed to the audience's own vision of glorious music, carefully prepared and fervently presented. Encores added to the pleasure of Saturday's audience: Valente with Puccini, Golden with Bizet (from *Carmen*, what else?) and both with Mozart and Offenbach.

Alonso Enriched PRSO and Its Audience As Well

The San Juan Star
May 13, 1992   By Donald Thompson

The Puerto Rico Symphony Orchestra closed its 1991-1992 season on Saturday evening at the Performing Arts Center in Santurce, while marking the end of conductor Odón Alonso's six-year tenure as the orchestra's music director. The event had several additional levels of significance as well, as we shall see.

Programmed were three works by island composers, works which had in fact been prepared for the PRSO's projected appearance in the Puerto Rico pavilion at the Seville Expo 92. Well, that deal fell through and other kinds of music and other kinds of groups were sent which some genius thought represented Puerto Rico: international commercial salsa, if you can believe it.

First up on Saturday was Raymond Torres' *Canción de las Antillas*, a three-movement work inspired by the poetry of Luis Lloréns Torres, which through extremely able orchestration and other stylistic means evokes images of a gentler Caribbean than the one to which we are accustomed today. Torres is a very successful film and "atmosphere" composer with an absolutely faultless sense of timing in addition to other gifts. Consider the first movement of this work, which we are advised by the program is associated with the arrival in the Antilles of the first Spaniards. By golly, you can actually see the ships approaching as those string chords creep up onto the beach, with a crescendo roll on the cymbal just a split second before one would think "OK, that's enough murmuring surf already. Give us a big wave or something!" Now that's timing!

Second was a work by Roberto Sierra for piano and orchestra entitled

Glosas para Piano y Orquesta. Here the operational word is "glosas," or glosses, comments, variants. Explored are variants of scales, intervals and rhythms, with the piano part serving as a kind of anchor to keep things from flying completely apart. I'm not speaking of performance here, but of the musical designs themselves; the neat and trim performance was at no time in the slightest danger of flying apart.

Sierra employs Antillean touches too, but in a way that is unique to him. Other composers have incorporated them in rather direct quotation, while Sierra presents only their essence, in a highly abstract and stylized manner. Sunday's very solid pianist was José Ramos Santana, to whom the work was originally dedicated.

And after intermission came Jack Délano's big *Burundanga*, bringing to the stage an augmented PRSO; the San Juan Philharmonic Choir, prepared for this occasion by Amarilis Pagán-Vila; soprano Margarita Castro Alberty; tenor César Hernández and bass-baritone Justino Díaz. This work, based on poetry by the admired Luis Palés Matos, represents still a third kind of Antillean vision. Torres' is rather serene, Sierra's cerebral, Délano's gutsy. However, Saturday's performance of *Burundanga* seemed rather on the cerebral side itself, much less loose and swinging than in the 1990 premiere performance. Saturday's chorus and soloists played it rather like some prim and prudish oratorio job, I thought, with the additional problem of solo soprano and solo bass parts which often seemed to lie too low for these particular soloists. I also think that the work's expression needs a different kind of soprano character to begin with, maybe a Carmenesque kind of gutsy mezzo which Margarita Castro, despite her other gifts, most definitely is not. As always, the San Juan Philharmonic Choir is to be congratulated on its excellent pronunciation and faultless pitch.

Yes, Saturday's concert bade farewell to Odón Alonso as PRSO music director. Symphony Orchestra music directors are something like U.S. university head football coaches. These superspecialists are hired to bring new spark, new ideas, new ways of doing things, a new face on the local social scene, new professional connections and a new repertory of plays (in football) or music (in the orchestra world). The first season is a honeymoon, the second and third a time of consolidation and from then on down it's mainly a matter of holding on to what's been gained; to gain any more is going to be very much an uphill battle. The time eventually comes when neither coach nor conductor can do much more with what he or she is given, people get worn down, relationships settle into routine and concentration wanders: for all parties it's time to begin the cycle again.

I believe that Odón Alonso accomplished a great deal in his six years with the island orchestra, and I don't believe that his concentration wandered very much. He certainly introduced some new and interesting repertory, including the Third Symphony of Mahler, Prokofiev's *Ivan the Terrible* and that crazy Prometheus: Poem of Fire by Scriabin. He made a greater effort than any of his predecessors to present works by island composers (some eighteen or twenty premieres, in fact), and to work with island soloists (more than forty, I believe). In all, more than fifty works were new to the PRSO during Alonso's tenure, which says a great deal about his interest in broadening the experience of both orchestra and public.

Musically, I think Alonso got some very good sounds out of the PRSO, and of course that's what a lot of it is about. More than once in recent years I have found myself admiring some orchestra captured in the middle of a broadcast on one of the island's institutional radio stations, only to learn that it was a tape of our very own PRSO, made during some performance.

Finally, and don't knock it, Alonso makes an attractive figure on the podium. To many music lovers, the figure of the tail-coated conductor seems to symbolize the entire mystique of the music world, as vague concepts of "authority," "interpretation," "control," "innovation" and "tradition" pass through their minds while the Tchaikovsky flows warmly around them. There are many less elegant symbols of the music world than Odón Alonso mounting the world's podiums these days, and we may see a few of them next season as the PRSO again plays host to a procession of guest conductors. For me, I think that Alonso's work with the Puerto Rico Symphony Orchestra will long be favorably remembered, both technically and symbolically.

♪

MUSICOLOGICAL SCHOLARS **ANNIE** AND **DONALD THOMPSON**
IN A 1992 PRESENTATION OF THE SEMINAL BIBLIOGRAPHICAL TOME
"MUSIC AND DANCE IN PUERTO RICO: FROM THE AGE OF COLUMBUS
TO MODERN TIMES: AN ANNOTATED BIBLIOGRAPHY."

Donald Thompson, Man of Notes

The San Juan Star
July 5, 1992   By Francis Schwartz

Sitting under the swaying tropical palms at the University of Puerto Rico faculty residences, bearded Donald Thompson, looking like a balder and thinner version of the mature Ernest Hemingway, answered our questions regarding his musical activities. Thompson, who has been retired from the university since 1985, for many years served as senior music critic for the *San Juan Star*. His collaboration with the head of the University of Puerto Rico Graduate School of Library and Information Science, his wife Annie Figueroa Thompson, has produced a major reference book which has just been published.

FS: On several occasions you have interviewed me in your capacity as STAR senior music critic and I now have the opportunity to submit you to the same type of grilling. I am intrigued by your latest oeuvre which you and your distinguished spouse, Annie Figueroa Thompson, have just published. It is an annotated bibliography on music and dance in Puerto Rico. Why a bibliography?

DT: While Annie (my constant concert consort) was director of the University of Puerto Rico Music Library during the 1960s and 1970s she constantly received inquiries from scholars in the United States and abroad concerning research sources for music in Puerto Rico. To provide this information she assembled a 300-item bibliography, published by the Music Library Association in 1975. Meanwhile, my own research in Puerto Rican and Caribbean music continued to turn up valuable sources, many previously unknown or forgotten. I also learned that very little is known about the history of music in Puerto Rico although a great deal is surmised. Obviously, having better access to sources would help colleagues here and abroad formulate a proper history of music in Puerto

Rico, someday in the future.

FS: Scarecrow Press is a prestigious publisher of reference works and other specialized books. You must be pleased that such a publisher has chosen your bibliography.

DT: It was a happy coincidence that Scarecrow was about to launch a series dealing with Latin American music under the editorship of Dr. Malena Kuss. Our bibliography was a natural. Of course we are delighted, as the book will receive worldwide distribution and promotion.

FS: Both you and Annie started as performers, Annie as a soprano and you as a double bassist and conductor. How did you get into this somewhat rarified area of music bibliography?

DT: Performers all the way, but university-trained performers. This places technical study within the context of serious higher education which entails historical, theoretical and cultural studies. This in turn encourages versatility across fields and the cultivation of intellectual curiosity which of course is the itch which research is supposed to cure but merely inflames. It provides a broad type of professional vision; we saw the need for a bibliography of music and dance in Puerto Rico and simply went about compiling one.

FS: Where did you study?

DT: Annie studied at Baylor and at the University of Southern California, then completed her Ph.D. at Florida State University. My work was done at the University of Missouri, the Eastman School of Music, the University of Vienna, the Vienna Music Academy and finally the University of Iowa for the doctorate.

FS: You were both active performers here around fifteen years ago. In fact, I recall you thumping, bowing, plucking and even cursing that noble instrument, the double bass, in the string section of the Puerto Rico Symphony Orchestra.

DT: Yes, indeed. Annie performed in operas, in recitals, and as soloist with the PRSO. I was a member of the PRSO for some ten years and also did a lot of conducting of special concerts, educational TV, ballet, opera, zarzuelas and musical comedy.

FS: There are those of us who believe that there are aspects of musical comedy in ANY musical presentation. . . . However, could you expand on your work in this particular area? That is, musical comedy?

DT: Yes, of course. One of the first I directed here was *Bye, Bye, Birdie*, which featured Raul Juliá in what certainly was one of his first appearances on the lyric stage. Others included *West Side Story*, *The King and I*, *The Sound of Music* and *Man of La Mancha*, this last with the formidable José Ferrer. A lot of talented young performers were in these productions and received some of their earliest and most valuable training there. Some went on to become important figures both here and abroad in theater, opera and show business in general. They include Camille Carrión, Johanna Rosaly, Alex Vázquez, Marta Márquez, Roy Brown and José Molinari, among others.

FS: You mentioned ballet. Any noteworthy productions?

DT: I did some conducting for Ballets de San Juan around 1958, with premiere performances of ballets by Amaury Veray, Héctor Campos-Parsi and Jack Délano, plus some interesting music by Paul Hindemith, Edvard Grieg and other composers.

FS: But the ballet orchestra didn't last long, did it?

DT: No. So that the ballet company wouldn't have to form a special orchestra and engage a special music director every season, the Institute of Puerto Rican Culture put an orchestra on salary for them: the IPRC Chamber Orchestra. However, I don't think that relationship lasted very long ... although the chamber orchestra certainly did.

FS: You recently conducted the world premiere of Robert Milano's Christmas opera, *Bethlehem's Inn*, at Inter American University with considerable success. With IAU becoming increasingly more prominent on the local culture scene, do you believe that universities should be directly involved with training and production in the areas of music, theater and dance?

DT: Absolutely! Only in a university environment can theory, performance technique, history and interdisciplinary enrichment develop naturally. You see, the age of the humble and illiterate village fiddler or juggler is long past. Today's and tomorrow's musicians and dancers and actors must be complete citizens, possessing the broadest and deepest professional and cultural knowledge possible. This has been the great contribution that such U.S. universities as UC Berkeley, UCLA, Texas at Austin, Indiana, Illinois, Northwestern, Iowa, Kansas and many others have made. Universities have performance ensembles, recitals, dance productions and other activities which interconnect among departments and enrich the experience of all participants, to say nothing of the university environment.

FS: Let's go back to research. You speak almost mystically about university life (I can see you have been away from the UPR for some time).... How does research connect with classroom reality?

DT: Very simply and very directly. The best example for university students in any field is provided by professionally active faculty, and music departments provide endless opportunity for professional activity. Thus composers teach, compose and seek performances for their music; musicologists teach, conduct research and publish the results; music theorists teach, study the ever-changing panorama of music theory and publish textbooks, manuals and guides; while performers teach, study, perform and prepare teaching materials. See how simple it is?

FS: Yes, you HAVE been away from the university for a while.... Speaking of results, what have you done lately in the area of research?

DT: I have in the process of publication a study of the early life of Manuel Gregorio Tavárez which may change some of the conventionally held beliefs concerning this island composer. And ready to go to press are two long articles, one on the musical aspects of the Fourth Centennial of the Discovery of Puerto Rico (1893) and the other, an investigation of what the early Spanish chroniclers really said about music and dance among the aborigenes of the Greater Antilles. This last work is based on a presentation I made last April in Madrid at the International Musicological Society congress.

FS: Speaking of Madrid, you have been active in a major editorial project there involving Spain and Puerto Rico.

DT: Yes, I am the editorial coordinator for Puerto Rico of an ambitious project, an encyclopedia of music in Spain and Spanish America, no less. This work will eventually grow to some ten or twelve volumes covering composers, institutions, performers, organizations, libraries, folk music and many other subjects. Puerto Rico will have around 150 entries with contributions made by some twenty specialists from here. The first volume will hopefully be published to coincide with the Fifth Centennial of the Discovery of the Americas, or whatever it is now being called.

FS: Have you done any other editorial work in the past?

DT: Yes, on a couple of occasions. For six years I was the editor of a series of scholarly indexes and bibliographies published by the Music Library Association, and a few years ago I helped put together a couple of numbers of the *Revista/Review Interamericana*, published by Inter American University, which dealt with music, theater and dance in the Caribbean. These experiences taught me to respect authors, who, after all, presumably know what they are writing about.

FS: Obviously your retirement from the UPR has provided you more time for your research penchant, or could we say . . . research vice? Any books in the making?

DT: Vice? Vice, indeed! I thought you'd never ask. Annie is working on an index to all musical references in Puerto Rican newspapers of the nineteenth century, and I am editing an anthology of articles about music in Puerto Rico in my own translations to English and with extensive historical and editorial comment. Both books will be published in the Latin American Music series of Scarecrow Press.

FS: You have discovered errors in the research of colleagues both past and present. Does that make their contributions valueless?

DT: No, definitely not. Every effort to unearth information about musical life is valuable where so little is known: a concert date, a printed program, an anecdote about social mores. All of these things focus attention on the subject; then other procedures are called into play to validate and incorporate the information. A minor slip or two, if corrected, make no great difference over the long run.

FS: In one of your pungent music reviews in the STAR you questioned the veracity of a report that a Russian music teacher named Agamemnon Rinsuk came to Puerto Rico in the nineteenth century and was murdered near Utuado, in the center of the island. Any comment on this?

DT: [Deep silence and a dirty look]

FS: At this point our subject left, making his way down the street to pump some iron at a neighborhood gymnasium.

Index

Indexed are the names of orchestras, choruses, chamber ensembles and their members, conductors, composers whose works are specifically identified in the reviews, sponsoring organizations, soloists, featured members of orchestras and choruses, and lyric theater music directors, stage directors, chorusmasters, choreographers, featured singers, actors and dancers. References to subjects of consistent concern to one or the other reviewer are also indexed: for example, the quality of program notes and problems of traffic control and promiscuous photography during performances. Titles of works as given in the index do not always correspond exactly to titles of works appearing in the reviews, as reviewers were not bound by standard titles at the moment of writing. For example, Beethoven's third symphony might appear in the reviews as the Eroica Symphony, Symphony No. 3, Symphony in E Flat Major, Symphony Op. 55 or in some combination of these identifiers.

Acevedo, Carmen. 29 Oct. 80, 23 June 83, 29 May 85, 17 May 86, 16 Sept. 86, 21 Mar. 87, 29 May 87, 14 Nov. 89, 19 June 90.

Acevedo, María Teresa. 17 Sept. 80, 10 Oct. 86.

Acosta, Rodolfo. 20 Apr. 89.

Adkins, Elizabeth. 18 June 88.

Administration for the Development of Arts and Culture, ADAC (Administración para el Fomento de las Artes y Cultura, AFAC). 12 June 80, 19 Feb. 81, 14 Dec. 83, 6 Jan. 86.

Agrupación Puertorriqueña de Teatro Lírico, APTEL. 21 Mar. 76.

Albright, William
   The King of Instruments. 3 Mar. 86.
Alcalá, Marcelino. 22 Aug. 90.
Alcántara, Theo. 13 Apr. 88.
Alcón, Vicente. 27 June 83.
Alejandro, Esther
   Two Songs. 17 Sept. 80.
Alhambra. 22 Nov. 89 (b).
Alicea, Carlos. 3 Jan. 84.
Alicea, José. 15 Oct. 86, 15 Feb. 92.
Alicea, Mercedes. 6 Mar. 76.
Allen, Betty. 1 July 76.
Allende, Noel. 21 Apr. 85, 10 Oct. 86.
Alonso, Odón. 7 Apr. 76, 7 June 78, 22 June 80, 16 Sept. 86, 15 Nov. 86, 25 Mar. 87, 29 May 87, 10 Nov. 87, 19 Jan. 88, 7 June 88, 14 Sept. 88, 9 Oct. 88, 29 Apr. 89, 14 Nov. 89, 22 Nov. 89 (a), 23 May 90, 19 June 90, 25 Sept. 91, 2 May 92, 13 May 92.
Alva, Luigi. 30 Aug. 82.
Alvarado, Marilú. 14 Mar. 91.
Álvarez, Luis. 17 June 87.
Álvarez, Luis Manuel. 4 June 74.
   Sueños de Collores. 5 Oct. 82.
   Three New Alvaradas. 17 Sept. 80.
American Chamber Symphony Orchestra. 28 Sept. 83.
Amherst College Chorus. 19 June 82, 1 Feb. 84.
Amplification and pre-recording of stage music. 22 June 80, 31 Jan. 81, 27 June 83, 22 Aug. 90.
Anderson, June. 12 Mar. 91.
Andrade, Rosario. 29 Mar. 90.
Antidogma. 13 Ap 85.
Aponte-Ledée, Rafael. 11 Mar. 82, 13 Nov. 82, 2 Oct. 85, 11 Nov. 87, 30 Nov. 88.

    Elejía. 2 Feb. 74.
    Impulsos. 7 Apr. 76, 29 Mar. 79.
    Presagio de Pájaros Muertos. 21 Sept. 67.
Aragall, Giacomo. 14 Sept. 91.
Arandes, Elaine. 23 May 85, 29 May 85.
Arce, Freddy de. 31 Jan. 81.
Arel, Bulent. 28 Mar. 66.
Arioso. 15 Feb. 92.
Armenian, Raffi. 20 Jan. 87.
Arnold, Malcolm
    Brass Quintet. 27 June 89.
Arrau, Claudio. 14 Dec. 83.
Arrieta, Emilio
    Marina. 9 Oct. 80.
Arriví, Francisco. 21 Mar. 87.
Arroyo, Martina. 7 June 72.
Arroyo Carrión, Ramón. 23 June 83, 18 Feb. 86, 17 June 87.
Artime, Ignacio. 27 June 83.
Arturo Somohano Philharmonic Orchestra. 16 Oct. 85.
Asociación Pro Orquesta Sinfónica, APOS. 10 Nov. 82, 18 Feb. 86.
Atehortúa, Blas Emilio. 2 Oct. 84.
    Sinfonía a Ginastera. 2 Oct. 84.
Aulos. 2 Oct. 85, 10 Oct. 86.
Auza León, Atilano
    Danzas Bolivianas del Ciclo 'Runas.' 13 Nov. 82.
Azpilicueta, Jaime. 27 June 83.
Babbitt, Milton
    Vision and Prayer. 28 Mar. 66.
Bacarisse, Salvador
    Partita. 5 Feb. 83.
Bacewicz, Grazuna
    Concerto for String Orchestra. 10 Feb. 86.

Bach, Johann Sebastian.
    Air (Third Suite for Orchestra). 8 June 67.
    B Minor Mass. 29 May 85.
    Brandenburg Concerto No. 1. 25 Nov. 81 (a), 19 Jan. 88.
    Brandenburg Concerto No. 2. 16 Feb. 78 (a).
    Brandenburg Concerto No. 3. 16 June 76, 11 Feb. 86.
    Brandenburg Concertos. 23 June 83.
    Concerto in C Major for Three Harpsichords. 16 June 76.
    Concerto for Harpsichord. 19 June 76.
    Concerto in A Minor for Violin. 20 Jan. 87.
    Concerto in D for Violin. 15 Feb. 67.
    D Minor Chaconne (Second Violin Partita). 8 June 67, 13 June 89.
    Magnificat in D Major. 23 June 83.
    Partita in E Major. 13 Sept. 73.
    The Passion According to St. Matthew. 17 June 63, 19 June 90.
    Suite No. 1 in C Major. June 57.
    Suite in B Minor for Flute and Strings. 16 June 76, 22 Jan. 81 (a).
Bach, P.D.Q.
    Concerto for Piano vs. Orchestra. 25 Jan. 89.
    Shleptet. 25 Jan. 89.
Badillo, Roxana. 31 Jan. 81.
Baird, Julianne. 17 June 87.
Baltsa, Agnes. 11 Mar. 87 (b).
Barasorda, Antonio. 14 Dec. 73, 7 June 78, 24 July 79, 12 Apr. 81, 30 Aug. 82.
Barber, Samuel
    Sonata for Cello and Piano, Op. 6. 26 Apr. 85.
Barberini, Urbano. 11 Feb. 87.
Barbosa-Lima, Carlos. 22 June 80, 5 Oct. 88.
Barenboim, Daniel. 2 June 72.
Barnett, John. 4 Feb. 81 (a), 12 Apr. 81, 20 June 81, 28 Oct. 81, 27 Oct. 82, 19 Feb. 83, 18 Sept. 83, 14 Dec. 83, 1 Feb. 84, 4 May 85, 29 May 85.

Barrios, Agustín. 14 Dec. 80.
    Chôros de Saudade. 2 July 86.
Barros, Alba Raquel. 22 Aug. 90.
Barrueco, Manuel. 14 Dec. 80.
Bartók, Bela
    Concerto for Orchestra. 14 Dec. 83.
    Concerto for Two Pianos and Orchestra. 14 Mar. 84.
    Concerto for Violin and Orchestra. 9 June 73.
    Piano Sonata. 1 Oct. 81 (a).
    Rumanian Dances. 15 Feb. 67.
    Slovakian folk song settings. 1 Oct. 81.
    Sonata No. 1 for Violin and Piano. 5 Oct. 80.
    String Quartet No. 2. 10 Feb. 68.
    String Quartet No. 3. 5 Feb. 67.
Bartoli, Cecilia. 21 Feb. 91.
Bastida, Ramón. 9 Oct. 80.
Batista, Gustavo. 16 May 60, 16 Apr. 70, 4 Nov. 70, 14 Dec. 80.
Batiz, Migdalia. 27 Sept. 72, 14 Dec. 73, 9 Oct. 80, 20 Apr. 89.
Bauzá, Carlos. 18 Jan. 83, 17 Sept. 80.
Beaux Arts Trio. 11 Mar. 87 (a).
Becerra-Schmidt, Gustavo
    String Quartet No. 6. 13 Nov. 82.
Beethoven, Ludwig van
    Concerto for Violin and Orchestra. 8 June 67.
    Concerto No. 4 for Piano and Orchestra. 20 June 81, 22 June 88.
    Concerto No. 5 for Piano and Orchestra, "The Emperor." 14 Dec. 83.
    Coriolanus. 18 Sept. 83 (overture).
    Egmont. 20 June 81 (narrated), 8 June 67 (overture).
    Fidelio. 20 June 81 (overture).
    Leonora Overture No. 3. 14 Mar. 84.
    Quintet for Piano and Strings, Op. 34. 5 Apr. 69.
    Sonata for Cello and Piano, Op. 69. 7 Apr. 72.
    String Quartet in C Minor, Op. 18 No. 4. 7 June 70.

  String Quartet in F Major, Op. 135. 7 June 70, 9 June 73 ("Lento").
  String Quartet, Op. 18 No. 4. 4 Nov. 70.
  String Quartet, Op. 59 No. 2, "Rasoumowsky." 7 June 70.
  String Quartet, Op. 59 No. 3. 9 June 73 (fugue).
  Symphony No. 1 in C Major. 31 May 73.
  Symphony No. 3 in E Flat Major. 24 Oct. 73 ("Funeral March"), 24 June 74, 25 Sept. 91.
  Symphony No. 5 in C Minor. 10 June 66.
  Symphony No. 7 in A Major. 13 June 60, 18 June 66, 14 Apr. 82.
  Trio (violin, viola, cello). 18 Feb. 86.
  Triple Concerto, Op. 56. 31 May 82, 18 Sept. 83.
  Works for mandolin. 16 Apr. 70.

Béhague, Gerard. 31 Oct. 90.

Bellini, Vincenzo
  Concerto for Oboe and Strings. 21 Feb. 67.
  I Puritani. 13 Apr. 88 (excerpt), 17 Sept. 88.
  La Sonnambula (arias). 10 Feb. 70.

Beni, Gimi. 27 Sept. 72.

Berberian, Ara. 17 June 63.

Berg, Alban
  Four Pieces for Clarinet. 13 Feb. 86.
  Seven Early Songs. 13 Feb. 86.

Bergstrom, Erik
  Homage to Christopher Columbus. 15 Feb. 92.

Berio, Luciano
  Concertino. 5 Dec. 78.
  Quattro Versioni Originali della 'Ritirata Notturna di Madrid' de Luigi Boccherini. 30 Nov. 88.

Berlioz, Hector
  Roman Carnival Overture. 22 June 80, 22 June 88.

Bernstein, Leonard
  Candide. 6 Mar. 90 (overture).
  Symphonic Dances from West Side Story. 6 Mar. 90, 20 Aug. 91.

Bertieaux, Esther Eugenia. 24 Dec. 70.

Bertolo, Aldo. 17 Sept. 88.

Besosa, Miguel. 26 July 60, 22 Jan. 81 (a).
    "Pasión Eterna." 22 Jan. 81 (a).

Biennials of Contemporary Music (Biennials of Twentieth-Century Music). 5 Dec. 78, 16 Dec. 78, 17 Sept. 80, 13 Nov. 82, 8 Dec. 82, 11 Nov. 86, 30 Nov. 88.

Billy Taylor Jazz Trio. 15 Nov. 86.

Birriel Cabrera, Iris. 6 Mar. 76.

Bizet, Georges
    Carmen. 11 Mar. 87 (b) (excerpt), 29 Apr. 89 (aria).
    Symphony in C Major. 27 Oct. 82.

Blades, Rubén. 31 Jan. 81.

Bloch, Ernest
    Meditation Hebraïque. 26 Apr. 85.
    Prayer. 26 Apr. 85.

Boccherini, Luigi
    Concerto in B Flat for Cello and Orchestra. 5 June 84.
    Quintet in D Major for Guitar and Strings. 23 Dec. 88.

Boissen, Pablo. 5 Dec. 78, 30 Apr. 81, 30 Aug. 82, 18 Jan. 83, 17 Sept. 83, 25 Apr. 87.

Boito, Arrigo
    Mefistofele. 4 May 85 (excerpt).

Bolling, Claude
    Suite for Flute and Jazz Piano. 15 Oct. 86.

Bonavolunta, Nino. 18 Jan. 83.

Boni, Susan. 7 May 76.

Borner, Klaus. 5 Oct. 80.

Bottesini, Giovanni
    Variations. 19 Feb. 83.
    Grand Duo Concertante. 29 Jan. 86.

Bou, Mildred. 16 Feb. 78 (b), 17 Sept. 80.

Bourns, David. 7 May 76, 16 Feb. 78 (a), 4 May 84, 19 June 90, 7 Nov. 90.

Bover, Bartolomé. 9 Oct. 80.

Boyd, Curtis. 15 Nov. 86.

Bozza, Eugène
    Sonatina. 17 June 90.

Brahms, Johannes
    Concerto for Violin and Orchestra. 10 June 66.
    Concerto No. 1 for Piano and Orchestra. 3 June 63, 27 Oct. 82.
    Concerto No. 2 for Piano and Orchestra. 2 June 72.
    Lieder. 10 Feb. 70.
    Rhapsody for Contralto, Male Chorus and Orchestra. 14 Nov. 89.
    Sonata (clarinet). 11 May 60.
    Sonata (cello). 11 Oct. 68.
    Quartet for Piano and Strings, Op. 25. 13 June 60, 24 June 78, 3 Feb. 87.
    Serenade for Strings and Winds. 22 Jan. 81 (a).
    Symphony No. 1. 3 June 63, 10 Nov. 82.
    Symphony No. 2. 18 June 89.
    Symphony No. 3. 20 Jan. 78, 19 June 82.
    Symphony No. 4. 11 June 75.
    Tragic Overture. 14 June 74.
    Trio in B Major, Op. 8. 11 Mar. 87 (a).
    Zigeunerlieder. 4 Apr. 70.

Brett, Charles. 19 June 90.

Brevig, Per. 21 Sept. 67.

Britten, Benjamin
    Alpine Suite. 22 Mar. 91.
    Fantasy Quartet for Oboe and Strings. 5 Dec. 78.

Brizzi, Aldo. 13 Apr. 85.

Broitman, Rubén. 19 June 82, 2 July 83.

Brooks, Tamara. 7 June 88.

Brouwer, Leo
    Cradle song. 2 July 86.
    Estudios. 5 Oct. 80.
    Tarantos. 13 June 89.

Brown, Alan. 4 May 84, 7 Nov. 90.

Brown, Earle
    Collective improvisation. 8 Dec. 82.
    Folio. 8 Dec. 82 (excerpts).
    Four Systems. 8 Dec. 82.

Bruch, Max
    Concerto in G Minor for Violin and Orchestra. 21 Dec. 59.
    Kol Nidre. 19 Feb. 83.

Bruckner, Anton
    Adagio in A Minor. 9 June 73.
    Symphony No. 4. 11 Oct. 90.

Brunner, Evelyn. 1 Feb. 84.

Bumbry, Grace. 7 June 72, 27 Sept. 72.

Burgess, Mary. 23 June 83.

Caballé, Montserrat. 2 Apr. 79, 23 Oct. 87.

[Cabán Vale, Antonio]
    "Verde Luz." 29 Oct. 80.

Cabrer, Carlos
    La Rota Voz del Agua. 5 Oct. 82, 30 Oct. 90.

Cabrera, Pablo. 7 June 78, 31 Jan. 81, 21 Apr. 85, 17 Sept. 88.

Cáceres, Germán. 17 Sept. 80, 22 Nov. 91.
    Sonata for Viola and Piano. 30 Oct. 90.
    String Quartet. 17 Sept. 80.

Cáceres, José Luis. 3 Jan. 84.

Cadman, Charles Wakefield
    American Suite. 17 Oct. 69.

Cage, John
    Amores. 16 Apr. 70.
    Bacchanale. 25 Nov. 81 (b).
    Forever and Sunsmell. 15 Feb. 92.
    Four Minutes Thirty-Three Seconds. 16 Apr. 70.
    John Cage Week. 11 Mar. 82.

Calderón, Pedro I. 11 Oct. 90.

Calero, Marisol. 29 Apr. 87, 22 Aug. 90.

Calés-Otero, Francisco
    Five Sephardic Songs. 26 Apr. 85.
Camacho, Carlos. 25 Aug. 84.
Camerata Caribe. 4 May 84, 7 Nov. 90.
Campbell, Mary Ann. 29 Jan. 86, 18 Feb. 86, 3 Feb. 87, 2 Feb. 91.
Campos-Parsi, Héctor. 19 Feb. 81, 2 Dec. 82
    Divertimento del Sur. 26 July 60, 2 Dec. 82, 30 Nov. 88.
    Dúo Trágico for Piano and Orchestra. 2 Dec. 82.
    Oda a Cabo Rojo. 21 Dec. 59, 20 Jan. 78, 14 Apr. 82, 2 Dec. 82.
    Petroglifos. 17 May 67.
    Sonetos Sagrados. 10 Oct. 86.
    Songs. 2 Dec. 82.
Camuñas, Jaime. 16 May 60, 4 Nov. 70.
Canadian Chamber Ensemble. 20 Jan. 87.
Canin, Stuart. 24 June 78.
Canteloube de Malaret, Marie-Joseph
    Chants d'Auvergne. 4 May 85.
Cantigas de Santa María. 13 June 89, 22 Nov. 89 (b).
Caraballo, Doris. 19 June 90.
Caribbean Composers Forum. 5 Mar. 88, 30 Oct. 90, 31 Oct. 90.
Carmona, Jennie. 21 Apr. 85, 24 Apr. 92.
Carreras, José. 14 Oct. 78, 11 Mar. 87 (b).
Carrión, Marilyn. 14 Sept. 91.
Carter, Elliott
    Eight Etudes and a Fantasy. 4 May 84.
Carter, Roy. 4 June 74.
Casa del Libro. 2 Feb. 91, 22 Mar. 91, 22 May 91.
Casals, Pablo. June 57, 13 June 60, 16 June 60, 3 June 63, 17 June 63, 10 June 66, 8 June 67, 19 June 72 (a), 31 May 73, 24 Oct. 73.
    El Pessebre. 19 June 72 (a), 24 Oct. 73 ("Gloria;" "Child Jesus' Imploration"), 24 June 74.
    Prelude. 25 Apr. 60.
    The Song of the Birds. 24 Oct. 73.

United Nations Hymn. 2 June 72.

Casas, Myrna. 18 May 88, 20 Apr. 89, 29 Mar. 90.

Casey, Edith. 28 Mar. 66.

Caso, Fernando. 4 June 74.

Castro, Juan José. 13 June 60
    El llanto de las sierras. 11 Oct. 90.
    Suite introspectiva. 5 Oct. 88.

Castro Alberty, Margarita. 1 Apr. 78, 12 Apr. 81, 17 Sept. 83, 1 Sept. 84, 13 May 92.

Catania, Julio. 27 June 83.

Cerón, Enriquillo. 2 July 83, 20 Apr. 89, 22 Aug. 90.

Cervetti, Sergio
    Cinco Episodios. 17 May 67.

Charles, Daniel. 11 Mar. 82.

Chávez, Carlos
    Antigone Symphony. 30 Nov. 88.
    Concerto for Violin and Orchestra. 2 Apr. 66.
    Four Preludes. 11 June 81.

Chavier, Arístides
    Waltz. 7 Apr. 72.

Chopin, Frédéric
    Concerto No. 2 for Piano and Orchestra. 25 Nov. 81 (a).
    Funeral March. 24 Oct. 73 (arr.).

Cimarosa, Domenico
    Secret Marriage Overture. 14 Dec. 83.

Claremont String Quartet. 5 Feb. 67.

Clementi, Aldo
    Duetto. 13 Apr. 85.

Clementi, Muzio
    Waltzes for piano, triangle and tambourine. 16 Apr. 70.

Cleveland Orchestra Chorus (Robert Shaw, Director). 17 June 63.

Close, Shirley. 19 June 82.

Codeso, Manuel (Manolo). 23 May 85, 29 Apr. 87, 18 May 88, 29 Mar. 90.

Coelho de Souza, Rodolfo
    Estudio No. 1. 4 Feb. 81 (b).

Cohen, Isidore. 11 Mar. 87 (a).

Coleman, Anthony
    The Kasper in Me. 16 Feb. 87.

Collazo, Enrique. 29 Jan. 86.

Colón, Evangelina. 16 Feb. 78 (a), 11 June 81, 2 July 83, 18 May 88, 23 Dec. 88, 20 Apr. 89, 20 Apr. 89.

Colón Zayas, Edwin. 20 Aug. 91.

Comissiona, Sergiu. 19 June 82.

Composers Group for International Performance. 21 Sept. 67.

Concerto. 5 Feb. 92.

Conde, Carlos. 17 Sept. 88, 19 June 90.

Continuum. 1 Oct. 81 (a), 13 Feb. 86.

Copland, Aaron
    Appalachian Spring Suite. 28 Sept. 83.
    Piano Variations. 11 June 81.

Cora, Orlando. 16 Feb. 78 (a).

Coral Bel Canto. 7 June 88.

Cordero, Ernesto. 17 Sept. 80, 5 Oct. 82.
    Concerto for Guitar and Orchestra. 9 Sept. 82.
    Concierto Criollo for Cuatro and Orchestra. 20 Aug. 91.
    Descarga. 8 Oct. 85.
    Piezas Afrocubanas. 8 Oct. 85.
    Songs. 18 Nov. 81.
    Three Songs. 17 Sept. 80.

Cordero, Federico. 5 Apr. 69.

Cordero, Roque
    Symphony No. 2. 2 Apr. 66.
    Cinco Mensajes para Cuatro Amigos. 2 July 86.

Corelli, Arcangelo
    Concerto Grosso Op. 6 No. 1. 13 June 60.
    Concerto Grosso Op. 6 No. 8 ("Christmas"). 10 Feb. 86.
Costa-Greenspan, Muriel. 18 Jan. 83.
Cotto, Luis. 3 Oct. 87.
Cotto, Rayda
    Persona. 8 Apr. 78.
Cowell, Henry
    Banshee. 16 Apr. 70.
    Friend Conversation. 16 Apr. 70.
    Six Ings. 16 Apr. 70.
Crochet, Evelyne. 11 Nov. 86.
Cruz, Aixa. 21 Apr. 85.
Cruz, Angelo. 29 Mar. 79, 19 June 82, 1 Sept. 84, 29 Apr. 86, 17 May 86, 16 Sept. 86.
Cruz, Tony. 27 June 83.
Cubano, Miguel. 10 Nov. 87.
Culturarte de Puerto Rico. 11 Feb. 87, 29 Apr. 89, 12 Mar. 91.
Dacosta, Ofelia. 22 Aug. 90.
Dallapiccola, Luigi
    Songs. 15 Feb. 92.
Dalley, John. 7 June 70.
Danchenko, Victor. 20 Jan. 87.
Daniecki, John. 29 May 85.
Danner, Wilfried. 5 Oct. 82
    Five Silhouettes. 5 Oct. 82.
Danza puertorriqueña. 29 Oct. 80.
Davidovsky, Mario.
    Syncronismos 1, 3. 28 Mar. 66.
    Syncronismo No. 2. 5 Apr. 69.
    Syncronismo No. 6. 11 Nov. 87.
Dawes, Andrew. 10 Feb. 68.

Debussy, Claude
  Claire de Lune. 6 Sept. 91.
  First Rhapsody for Clarinet and Orchestra. 11 Oct. 90.
  Nocturnes. 19 June 82.
  Prelude to the Afternoon of a Faun. 20 Jan. 87.
  Syrinx. 19 June 76.
Decoust, Michel
  Interphone. 8 Apr. 78.
Degláns, Kerlinda. 3 Jan. 84.
Degláns, Wilfredo. 9 June 81.
Deguci, Masako. 25 Apr. 87, 17 Sept. 88.
Délano, Jack. 4 June 74.
  Burundanga. 13 May 92.
  Canciones para Laura. 5 Dec. 78.
  Concertino Clásico for Trumpet and Orchestra. 9 Sept. 82.
  "Escúchanos." 10 Oct. 86.
  Flute Sonata. 17 Sept. 80.
  Me Voy a Ponce. 17 May 86.
  "Panfleto." 10 Oct. 86.
  La Reina Tembandumba. 20 Jan. 78, 17 May 89, 12 June 90, 22 Nov. 91.
  String Quartet. 2 Feb. 90.
  Viola Sonata. 13 Nov. 82.
Deiro, Pietro
  Concerto in A Major. 24 Dec. 70.
Delgado, José. 4 Nov. 70.
Díaz, Alirio. 10 Nov. 87.
Díaz, Justino. 10 Feb. 70, 7 June 72, 27 Sept. 72, 18 May 73, 20 June 74, 12 Apr. 81, 17 Sept. 83, 25 Aug. 84, 21 Apr. 85, 11 Feb. 87, 7 June 88, 23 Dec. 88, 12 June 90, 13 May 92.
Díaz Feliciano, Myrna. 17 June 87.
Diccionario de la música española e hispanoamericana. 28 Apr. 90.
Dohnányi, Ernst von
  Orchestral suite. 28 Oct. 81.

Sextet (violin, viola, cello, clarinet, horn, piano). 18 Feb. 86.

Domingo, Plácido. 7 June 72, 27 Sept. 72, 11 Feb. 87.

Donehew, Robert. 18 Feb. 86.

Donizetti, Gaetano
  The Daughter of the Regiment. 18 Jan. 83, 12 Mar. 91 (aria).
  Don Pasquale. 24 July 79.
  Lucia di Lammermoor. 25 Apr. 87, 12 Mar. 91 (aria, scene).
  Sancia di Castiglia. 23 Oct. 87 (aria).

Dragonetti, Domenico
  Concerto in A Major for Double Bass and Orchestra. 4 Feb. 81 (a).

Druckman, Jacob
  Animus. 21 Sept. 67.

Dukas, Paul
  La Peri. 20 Aug. 91 (Fanfare).

Dunn, Mignon. 17 Sept. 83.

Dutt, Hank. 4 Oct. 83.

Dvořák, Antonin
  Concerto in D Minor for Violin and Orchestra. 21 Sept. 85.
  Concerto for Violoncello and Orchestra. 16 June 60, 22 Nov. 89 (a).
  "Dumky" Trio (excerpt). 11 Mar. 87 (a).
  Romanze for Violin and Orchestra. 8 June 67.
  Slavonic Dances. 22 Nov. 89 (a).
  String Quartet, Op. 96, "American." 12 July 60, 6 Mar. 73.
  Symphony No. 5, "From the New World." 20 June 60, 9 Apr. 70, 14 Mar. 84, 10 Nov. 87.
  Symphony No. 7 in D Minor. 17 May 89.
  Symphony No. 8, Op. 88. 25 Mar. 73.
  Zigeunermelodien, Op. 55. 28 Oct. 81.

Dyer, David. 19 June 90, 2 Feb. 90, 14 Mar. 91.

Eaton, John
  Blind Man's Cry. 28 Feb. 73.
  Soliloquy. 28 Feb. 73.
  Thoughts on Rilke. 28 Feb. 73.

Eccles, Henry
  Sonata. 7 May 76, 19 Feb. 83.
Egúrbida, Leonardo. 4 Nov. 70, 17 Sept. 80, 14 Dec. 80, 30 Oct. 90, 22 Mar. 90.
Elsa Rivera Salgado Lyric Theater Foundation. 20 Apr. 89.
Elvira, Pablo. 4 Apr. 70, 19 June 72 (a), 14 Dec. 73, 20 July 74, 26 Oct. 79, 30 Aug. 82, 25 Apr. 87, 13 Apr. 88, 17 Sept. 88, 14 Sept. 91.
Emerson String Quartet. 23 June 83.
Erickson, Norma. 16 Feb. 78 (b), 15 Mar. 78.
Escobar, Aylton
  Dimensional No. 1. 4 Feb. 81 (b).
Escribano, Tamara. 10 Oct. 86.
Espaillat, Ulises. 23 May 85.
Ewald, Victor. 17 June 90.
Fábregues, Ricardo. 18 May 88, 20 Apr. 89.
Faggione, Piero. 27 Sept. 72.
Falcón, Charly. 27 June 83.
Falla, Manuel de
  El Amor Brujo. 28 Nov. 90.
  Fantasía Bética. 11 Nov. 86.
  Homage to Debussy. 5 Oct. 80.
  Nights in the Gardens of Spain. 18 June 81, 23 May 90.
  Pour le Tombeau de Couperin. 13 June 89.
  Seven Popular Spanish Songs. 5 Oct. 80, 6 Sept. 91.
  The Three-Cornered Hat. 25 Mar. 87, 23 May 90.
  La Vida Breve. 28 Nov. 90 (excerpts).
Fauré, Gabriel
  Requiem. 17 May 86.
  Songs. 10 Feb. 70, 6 Sept. 91.
Febo, Félix. 17 Sept. 80.
Félix, Luis. 17 June 87.
Ferdman, Roberto. 30 Mar. 87.
Fernández, Valentín. 20 July 74, 7 June 78, 2 July 83, 1 Sept. 84.

Ferré, Luis A. 7 Apr. 72, 30 Oct. 87.

Ferrer, José. 20 June 81.

Ferrer, Rafael. 7 June 78, 24 July 79, 30 Aug. 82, 18 Jan. 83, 2 July 83, 29 Apr. 87, 18 May 88, 29 Mar. 90, 22 Aug. 90.

Ferrer Duchesne, Heberto. 7 Dec. 77.

Festival of Puerto Rican Music. 23 Nov. 68.

Figueroa, Annie. 4 Nov. 70, 4 June 74, 20 July 74. Also see Thompson, Annie Figueroa de.

Figueroa, Francisco. 15 Mar. 78, 17 Sept. 80, 18 Feb. 86, 3 Feb. 87, 30 Oct. 90.

Figueroa, Guillermo (I, violist/violinist). 21 Feb. 67, 30 Jan. 69, 6 Mar. 73.

Figueroa, Guillermo (II, violinist). 23 Feb. 70, 27 Oct. 82.

Figueroa, Jaime ("Kachiro", violinist). 21 Feb. 67, 30 Jan. 69, 6 Mar. 73, 17 Sept. 80.

Figueroa, Jaime (actor). 20 Apr. 89.

Figueroa, José ("Pepito"). 21 Feb. 67, 17 May 67, 30 Jan. 69, 6 Mar. 73, 16 Feb. 78 (a), 11 Feb. 86, 28 Nov. 90.

Figueroa, Narciso (pianist). 30 Jan. 69, 6 Mar. 73
    Concerto for Piano and Orchestra. 22 Nov. 91.
    El Diario de Teresita. 4 May 84.
    Impresiones Boriquenses. 8 Oct. 85.

Figueroa, Narciso (violinist). 29 Mar. 79, 17 Sept. 80, 18 Sept. 83.

Figueroa, Rafael (cellist 1). 30 Jan. 69, 5 Apr. 69, 6 Mar. 73.

Figueroa, Rafael (cellist 2). 18 Sept. 83, 29 May 87, 25 June 91.

Figueroa, Yvonne. 14 Apr. 82.

Figueroa Quartet. 12 July 60, 5 Apr. 69.

Figueroa Quintet. 30 Jan. 69, 6 Mar. 73.

Fine, Irving
    Partita for Wind Quintet. 10 Oct. 85.

Finnelae, Birgit. 14 Nov. 89.

Fleischer, Leon. 30 Sept. 81.

Flores, José Daniel. 17 May 86.

Flores, Pedro
    Pieces. 20 Aug. 91.
Forrester, Maureen. 17 June 63, 19 June 72 (a), 28 Oct. 81.
Fortunato, D'Anna. 23 June 83.
Foss, Lucas. 5 June 84.
Franck, César
    Symphony in D Minor. 19 June 82.
Frasca-Colombier, Monique. 15 Feb. 67.
Freni, Mirella. 29 Apr. 89.
Frescobaldi, Girolamo
    Air and Variations. 20 June 60.
Frisbie, Robert. 28 Sept. 83.
Fudala, Greg. 28 Sept. 83.
Fuentes, Alfonso
    Apariencias. 10 Oct. 86.
Gabrieli (brass ensemble). 27 June 89, 17 June 90.
Gabrieli, Giovanni
    Canzona per Sonare. 27 June 89.
Galán, Rosario. 17 Sept. 83, 25 Apr. 87.
Galimir, Felix. 9 June 74.
Galván, Ventura
    Obertura Española. 17 Oct. 79.
Galve, Luis. 31 May 73.
Gándara, Javier. 27 June 89.
Gándara, Roberto. 27 June 89.
Gandini, Gerardo
    Música Nocturna. 23 Feb. 70.
Ganz, Isabelle. 22 Nov. 89 (b).
García, Julio. 21 Apr. 85.
García, Manuel. 14 Mar. 84, 30 Oct. 90.
García Caffi, Juan José. 27 June 83.
García del Toro, Antonio. 29 Apr. 87.

García Ortega, Santiago. 18 May 88, 22 Aug. 90.
Gaskin, Victor. 15 Nov. 86.
Gershwin, George
    Cuban Overture. 15 Nov. 86.
    Piano Concerto in F. 17 Apr. 70.
    Rhapsody in Blue. 18 May 73 (arr.), 30 Oct. 87 (arr.).
Gertenbach, Volker Schmidt. 10 Feb. 86.
Getke, Richard. 20 July 74, 24 July 79.
Gianneo, Luis
    Variations on a Tango Theme. 4 Oct. 83.
Gierbolini, Edgardo. 18 May 73, 14 Dec. 73, 2 July 83.
Gil, María del Carmen. 30 Apr. 81, 25 Nov. 81 (a), 29 Jan. 86, 3 Feb. 87.
Gilbert, David. 21 Sept. 67.
Ginastera, Alberto. 11 June 81.
    Concerto No. 1 for Piano and Orchestra. 2 Oct. 84.
    Duet for Flute and Oboe. 10 Oct. 85.
    Estancia. 2 Feb. 74, 15 Nov. 86.
    Glosses on Themes by Pablo Casals. 16 June 76.
    Sonata for Cello and Piano, Op 49. 11 June 81.
    Variaciones Concertantes. 2 Oct. 84.
Giuliani, Mauro
    Concerto No. 3 for Guitar and Orchestra. 10 Nov. 87.
Giuseppe, Enrico de. 25 Apr. 87.
Glinka, Mikhail
    Ruslan and Ludmila. 11 Feb. 86 (overture).
Goa, Ruth. 31 Jan. 81.
Golden, Emily. 2 May 92.
Goldman, Martin. 23 Dec. 88.
Gómez, José Félix. 31 Jan. 81.
Gómez Crespo, Jorge
    Norteña. 2 July 86.
    Norteo. 15 Sept. 85.
González, Antonio. 18 Jan. 83.

González, Eusebio. 21 Mar. 76.

González, Humberto. 23 May 85.

González, José. 10 Nov. 87.

González, Manolo. 31 Jan. 81.

González, Roberto. 3 Jan. 84, 3 Mar. 86.

González, Waldo. 24 Apr. 92.

González Géigel, Antonio. 14 Sept. 91.

González Oliver, Jaime. 19 Feb. 81, 14 Dec. 83.

Gottlieb, Victor. 13 June 60.

Gottschalk, Louis Moreau
    Pieces (arr.). 10 Oct. 85.
    Souvenir de Porto Rico: Marche des Gibaros (arr.). 10 Oct. 85, 22 Mar. 91.

Gould, Morton. 6 Mar. 90.
    Concerto for Tap Dancer and Orchestra. 6 Mar. 90.
    Fall River Legend. 6 Mar. 90.
    Latin American Symphonette. 6 Mar. 90.

Gounod, Charles
    Faust. 10 Feb. 70 (arias); 18 May 73 (trio).
    Roméo et Juliette. 12 Mar. 91 (excerpt).

Gracia, Oscar de. 30 Aug. 82, 1 Sept. 84, 21 Apr. 85.

Granados, Enrique
    Tonadillas. 18 Nov. 81.

Gratale, Franco. 17 Sept. 83, 1 Sept. 84.

Greenhouse, Bernard. 11 Mar. 87 (a).

Grieg, Edvard
    Concerto in A Minor for Piano and Orchestra. 10 Nov. 82.

Griffes, Charles T.
    Poem for Flute and Orchestra. 25 Mar. 73.

Grondahl, Launy
    Concerto for Trombone and Orchestra. 3 Jan. 84.

Groninger, Mik. 29 Jan. 86.

Grunfeld, Alan. 15 Mar. 78.
Guadagno, Anton. 17 Sept. 83.
Guarneri String Quartet. 7 June 70.
Guayacán. 29 Oct. 80.
Guerrero, Jacinto
    Los Gavilanes. 18 May 88.
Guiguí, Efraín. 21 Sept. 67, 5 Apr. 69, 14 Dec. 73.
Guillot, Orlando. 13 Nov. 82.
Guinn, Leslie. 23 June 83.
Gutiérrez, Virginia. 21 Apr. 85, 8 Oct. 85.
Gutiérrez Espinosa, Felipe
    Macías. 7 June 78.
Guttman, Irving. 18 Jan. 83.
Guzmán, Jossie de. 25 Aug. 84.
Haeflinger, Ernst. 17 June 63.
Haggard, Constance. 13 Nov. 82.
Handel, George Frideric.
    No Se Emendará Jamás. 5 Apr. 69.
    "Care Selve." 13 June 60.
    Concerto Grosso. 17 Apr. 70.
    Dalla Guerra Amorosa. 10 Feb. 70.
    Lucrecia. 17 June 89.
    Messiah. 20 June 74 (excerpts), 18 Dec. 77 (excerpts).
Handschuh, Robert. 15 Oct. 86, 11 Mar. 87 (b).
Harler, Alan. 7 June 88.
Harrell, Lynn. 31 May 82, 23 June 83.
Harrington, David. 4 Oct. 83.
Harris, Johana. 26 July 60.
Harris, Roy. 26 July 60.
Harth, Sidney. 13 June 60, 18 Dec. 77.
Harvey, Paul
    Green Island Sonnets. 7 Nov. 90.

Haydn, Joseph
    The Apothecary. 12 Feb. 76.
    Cassation in F Major. 20 Jan. 87.
    Concerto in C Major for Cello and Orchestra. 30 June 76, 28 Sept. 83, 17 June 88.
    Lord Nelson Mass. 19 June 82.
    Quartet Op. 54 No. 1. 10 Feb. 68.
    Quartet Op. 76 No. 1. 29 Jan. 86.
    Symphony No. 88 in G Major. 20 June 74.
    Symphony 100 in G Major, "Military." 22 June 88.

Helguera, Juan. 14 Dec. 80.

Helmer, Terence. 10 Feb. 68.

Hendrickson, Steven. 18 June 88.

Henze, Hans Werner
    Sonata for Solo Violin. 5 Oct. 82.

Hernández, César. 17 Sept. 88, 29 Mar. 90, 13 May 92.

Hernández, Myles. 21 Apr. 85, 29 May 85.

Hindemith, Paul
    Five Pieces for String Orchestra. 29 July 69.
    Mathis der Maler Symphony. 14 June 74, 25 Nov. 81 (a).
    Sonata for Harp. 5 Feb. 83.
    Sonata for Oboe and Piano. 17 Sept. 80.
    Violin Sonata, Op. 31 No. 1. 23 Feb. 70.

Holliger, Heinz
    Elis. 11 Nov. 86.

Horszowski, Mieczyslaw. 13 June 60, 16 June 76, 19 June 76.

Houston Symphony Orchestra. 19 June 82.

Hubner, Carla. 21 Sept. 67.

Hummel, Johann N.
    Sonata. 16 Apr. 70.

Humphrey, Jon. 23 June 83.

Hurst, Lillian. 18 Jan. 83.

Husa, Karel. 16 Feb. 78 (a).

Music for Prague 1968. 16 Feb. 78 (a).

Hutchinson, Henry (I). 21 Dec. 59, 21 Feb. 67.

Hutchinson, Henry (II; Henry Hutchinson Negrón). 15 Mar. 78, 5 Dec. 78, 9 June 81, 3 Dec. 1983, 29 Jan. 86, 3 Feb. 87, 17 June 87, 28 Feb. 88, 23 Dec. 88, 19 June 90, 5 Feb. 92.

Hutchinson, Luz Negrón de. 15 Mar. 78, 14 Mar. 84, 18 Feb. 86, 28 Feb. 88, 23 Dec. 88, 6 Sept. 91.

Iannelli, Rosalyn. 26 Apr. 85, 3 Oct. 87, 23 Dec. 88, 30 Oct. 90.

Ibert, Jacques
Concerto for Flute and Orchestra. 22 Jan. 81 (a).

Iglesias, Olga. 17 June 63, 19 June 72 (a), 24 June 74, 9 June 81, 3 Dec. 83.

Institute of Puerto Rican Culture (Instituto de Cultura Puertorriqueña). 14 June 80, 5 Oct. 80 (Patio Theater), 6 Jan. 86, 28 Feb. 88.

Institute of Puerto Rican Culture Chamber Orchestra. 21 Feb. 67, 29 July 69, 17 Oct. 69, 24 Dec. 70.

Inter American Arts Festival. 5 Oct. 82, 4 Oct. 83, 2 Oct. 84, 10 Oct. 85, 16 Oct. 85, 6 Jan. 86, 10 Oct. 86, 15 Oct. 86, 3 Oct. 87, 5 Oct. 88.

Inter American University. 6 Jan. 86.

Inter American Youth Orchestra. 16 June 76.

International String Congress. 26 July 60.

Isales, Darysabel. 20 July 74, 22 Jan. 81 (b), 31 Jan. 81, 30 Apr. 81, 30 Aug. 82, 21 Apr. 85, 23 May 85, 25 Apr. 87.

Istomin, Eugene. 16 June 76, 22 June 88.

Ives, Charles
Piano Sonata No. 1. 11 Nov. 87.

Iwasaki, Ko. 28 Sept. 83.

Izquierdo, Juan Pablo. 5 Oct. 88.

Janer, Iván. 27 Sept. 72.

Jeanrenaud, Joan. 4 Oct. 83.

Jiménez, Jerónimo
La Boda de Luis Alonso. 28 Nov. 90 (excerpts).

Jobim, Antonio Carlos
   Saudades do Brasil. 5 Oct. 88.
Johns, William. 17 Sept. 83.
Jones, Kathleen. 7 May 76, 15 Mar. 78, 5 Dec. 78, 11 June 81, 2 Dec. 82, 4 May 84, 18 Feb. 86, 30 Nov. 88, 7 Nov. 90.
José, Alejandro. 30 Oct. 90.
José, Rafael. 29 Apr. 87.
Juarbe Jordán, Randolfo (Randy). 9 Apr. 70, 12 Mar. 91.
Juliá, Luis Enrigue. 23 Dec. 88, 22 Mar. 91.
Kallir, Lillian. 23 June 83.
Karr, Gary. 4 Feb. 81, 19 Feb. 83.
Katims, Milton. 20 June 74.
Katz, Martin. 21 Feb. 91.
Kelly, Robert. 9 Apr. 70.
Kern, Peter. 25 Mar. 73, 16 Feb. 78 (a), 17 Sept. 80, 22 Jan. 81 (a), 11 June 81, 2 Dec. 82, 4 May 84, 30 Nov. 88, 19 June 90, 7 Nov. 90.
Kersting, Fritz. 23 Ap 92.
Kieffer, Ana Maria. 4 Feb. 81 (b).
King, Frederick. 2 Mar. 69.
Kita, Becky. 13 Nov. 82.
Kitt, Loren. 18 June 88.
Klassen, Mark. 14 Dec. 80.
Klein, Kenneth. 25 Mar. 73, 2 Feb. 74.
Kodály, Zoltán
   Dances From Galanta. 20 Jan. 78.
Kostelanetz, Richard. 11 Mar. 82.
Koussevitsky, Serge
   Concerto for Double Bass and Orchestra. 19 Feb. 83.
Krakauer, David. 16 Feb. 87
   Improvisation No. 1. 16 Feb. 87.
Kraus, Alfredo. 18 Jan. 83, 12 Mar. 91.
Kronos Quartet. 4 Oct. 83.

Kruger, Rudolf. 27 Sept. 72.

Kuleska, Gary
   Chamber Concerto. 20 Jan. 87.

Kuni, Toshiaki. 27 Sept. 72.

Kusnir, Eduardo. 7 Oct. 73, 8 Apr. 78, 5 Dec. 78.
   Brindis No. 3. 7 Oct. 73.
   Brindis No. 4. 7 Oct. 73.

Landrón, Julio Axel. 22 Aug. 90.

Lanza, Alcides. 21 Sept. 67, 25 Nov. 81 (b).

Laredo, Jaime. 9 June 74.

Larson, Larry. 28 Sept. 83.

Lata, Matthew. 14 Sept. 91.

Late arrivals seated during performances. See Traffic control in theaters.

Latin American Foundation for Contemporary Music. 1 Oct. 81 (a), 13 Nov. 82, 4 May 84, 2 Oct. 85, 2 July 86, 11 Nov. 86, 11 Nov. 87, 30 Nov. 88, 22 Nov. 89 (b), 15 Feb. 92.

Lauridsen, Beverley. 13 Feb. 86.

Lebrón, Rafael. 2 July 83, 23 Dec. 88.

Lecuona, Ernesto
   Rosa la China. 22 Aug. 90.

Lehár, Franz
   The Merry Widow. 29 Mar. 90.

León, Tania. 2 Oct. 85.
   Momentum. 2 Oct. 85.
   Paisanos Semos. 2 July 86.

Leoncavallo, Ruggero
   I Pagliacci. 9 Apr. 70, 26 Oct. 79 (excerpts), 13 Apr. 88 (excerpts).

Lesser, Laurence. 9 June 74.

Lewin, Harold. 11 Nov. 87, 15 Feb. 92.

LIM (Laboratorio de Interpretación Musical). 8 Dec. 82.

Lin, Cho-Liang. 19 June 82.

Lind Oquendo, Abraham. 9 Apr. 70, 24 July 79.

Linke, Norbert. 5 Oct. 82.

Liszt, Franz
    Cantique D'Amour. 7 Apr. 72.
    Concerto No. 2 for Piano and Orchestra. 14 Apr. 82.
    Les Préludes. 3 Jan. 84, 16 Sept. 86.
    Songs. 13 Nov. 70.

A *Little Night Music* ("Send in the Clowns"). 25 Nov. 81 (b).

Llacer, Enrique
    Concerto for Castanets and Orchestra. 28 Nov. 90.

Lleo, Vicente
    La Corte de Faraón. 29 Apr. 87.

Llibre Vermell. 22 Nov. 89 (b).

Llorca, Adolfo. 1 Sept. 84.

López, Héctor. 21 Mar. 76, 7 Dec. 77, 9 Oct. 80.

López, Roberto. 8 Oct. 85, 15 Oct. 86.

López, Rubén. 17 Sept. 80, 22 Jan. 81 (a), 18 Feb. 86, 15 Oct. 86, 3 Oct. 87, 17 May 89.

López, Zoraida. 6 Mar. 76, 17 May 86.

López Sobá, Elías. 2 Apr. 66, 17 May 67, 9 Apr. 70, 1 Apr. 78, 28 Sept. 83.

Lorengar, Pilar. 23 June 83.

Los Angeles Chamber Orchestra. 23 June 83.

Lucío, Evy. 19 June 76, 23 June 83, 28 Dec. 91.

Luo, Min Hui. 2 Feb. 91.

Luvisi, Lee. 9 June 81, 20 June 81.

Machuca Padín, Arturo. 9 Apr. 70.

McDuffie, Robert. 9 June 81.

McGaughey, Martha. 22 Nov. 89 (b).

McInnes, Bruce. 19 June 82, 1 Feb. 84.

McKee, Richard. 30 Aug. 82, 14 Sept. 91.

Macleod, Laurie Ann. 19 June 90.

McMillan, Kevin. 19 June 90.

Madrigalists of Puerto Rico. 30 Nov. 69.

Mahler, Gustav
    Lieder eines fahrenden Gesellen. 28 Oct. 81.
    Rückert Songs. 13 Apr. 88.
    Symphony No. 1. 9 June 72, 14 Sept. 88.

Malakova, Petra. 11 Feb. 87.

Malán, Rubén. 23 May 85.

Malas, Spiro. 18 Jan. 83.

Maldonado, Premier
    Fela. 25 Aug. 84.

Mallory, Clark. 30 Oct. 90.

Marcello, Benedetto
    Concerto for Oboe and Strings. 21 Feb. 67.

Marco, Eugenio. 14 Oct. 78.

Marco, Tomás
    Astrolabio. 3 Mar. 86.
    Concerto for Violin, Cello, Piano and Orchestra. 25 Sept. 91.

Mari, Esther. 18 May 88.

Marías, Alvaro. 17 June 87.

Márquez, Marta Rosario. 20 July 74, 30 Aug. 82, 17 June 89.

Márquez, Rosa Luisa. 11 Mar. 82.

Marrero, José Luis. 9 Oct. 80, 2 July 83, 22 Aug. 90.

Martín, José. 9 Sept. 82, 3 Jan. 84, 14 Mar. 84.

Martina, Harold. 7 Apr. 76.

Martínez, Ana María. 18 May 88, 6 Sept. 91.

Martínez, José Daniel. 4 June 74, 26 Apr. 85, 8 Oct. 85, 29 Apr. 86, 3 Oct. 87.
    Sonata for Cello and Piano. 3 Oct. 87.

Martínez, Roger. 11 May 60.

Martínez Zarate Quartet. 6 Feb. 76.

Marton, Eva. 14 Sept. 91.

Massenet, Jules
    Manon. 12 Mar. 91 (excerpt).

Maxwell, Linn. 29 May 85.

Meer, Ruud van der. 19 June 90.

Mehta, Zubin. 7 June 72, 9 June 72, 11 June 75.

Meléndez, Ramonita. 7 Dec. 77.

Meléndez, Victor. 15 Oct. 86, 3 Oct. 87.
    Three Antillean Songs. 3 Oct. 87.
    Variations on a Theme by Haydn. 15 Oct. 86.

Mendelssohn, Felix
    Concert Piece No. 1. 7 Nov. 90.
    Hebrides Overture. 31 May 73.
    Sonata in F Major for Violin and Piano. 28 Feb. 88.
    String Quartet in A Minor, Op. 13. 10 Feb. 68.
    Symphony No. 4 in A Major, "Italian." 21 Dec. 59, 25 June 91.
    Symphony No. 5 in D Minor, "Reformation." 18 June 66.
    Symphony No. 10 (strings). 9 June 73.

Mendelssohn Club Chorus. 7 June 88.

Mendelssohn Quartet. 1 Oct. 81 (a).

Merce Cunningham Dance Company. 11 Mar. 82.

Messiaen, Olivier
    Quartet for the End of Time. 8 Dec. 82.

Mester, Jorge. 9 June 81, 18 June 81, 31 May 82, 19 June 82.

Metropolitan Opera Company District Auditions. 6 Mar. 76.

Mgrdichian, George. 22 Nov. 89 (b).

Milhaud, Darius
    Concertino for Percussion and Orchestra. 7 Apr. 76.
    Suite after Correte. 15 Oct. 86.

Millán, Vanessa. 24 Apr. 92.

Mompou Trio. 25 Sept. 91.

Mónaco, Alfredo del.
    Syntagma A. 5 Mar. 88.

Moncayo, José Pablo
    Huapango. 25 Mar. 73.

Monrouzeau, José. A.
   Pieces. 13 May 91.
Montalvo, Genie. 18 May 88, 29 Mar. 90.
Montalvo, José.
   Espejos. 21 Sept. 85.
   Study for Wind Quintet. 10 Oct. 86.
Montané, Carlos. 1 Feb. 84.
Monteverdi, Claudio
   Vespers for the Holy Virgin. 17 June 87.
Montsalvatge, Xavier
   Habanera. 13 June 89.
   Songs. 10 Feb. 70.
Moore, Douglas
   Quintet for Clarinet and Strings. 15 Mar. 78.
Morales, Jorge (George). 15 Oct. 86, 3 Oct. 87, 2 May 92.
Morales, Ricardo. 11 Oct. 90.
Morales, Sandra. 19 June 90.
Morales Matos, Jaime. 27 June 89.
   "Para Ti." 17 June 90.
Morales Nieva, Ignacio
   Concerto Grosso. 19 Feb. 83.
   Medea. 3 Oct. 87.
Morel Campos, Juan.
   Carola. 24 Oct. 73.
   Danza. 16 May 60, 6 Sept. 91.
   Danzas. 29 Oct. 80, 9 Sept. 82, 30 Oct. 87.
   La Lira Overture. 12 Apr. 81, 14 Ap 82, 9 Sept. 82, 20 Aug. 90, 22 Nov. 91.
Morell, Pedro. 20 July 74, 7 June 78.
Moreno Torroba, Federico
   Luisa Fernanda. 20 Apr. 89.
Morrill, Dexter
   Fantasy-Quintet for Piano and Computer. 11 Nov. 87.

Mozart, Wolfgang Amadeus
  The Abduction from the Seraglio. 14 Sept. 88 (overture).
  Adagio and Fugue (K 546). 20 June 60.
  La Clemenza di Tito. 2 May 92 (overture).
  Concerto for Two Pianos and Orchestra (K 365). 3 June 63
  Concerto in A Major for Piano and Orchestra (K 414). 3 June 63.
  Concerto in C Major (No. 21) for Piano and Orchestra. 23 June 83.
  Concerto in D Major for Flute and Orchestra. 10 June 66.
  Concerto in D Major for Piano and Orchestra (K 451). 3 June 63.
  Concerto in D Minor for Piano and Orchestra (K 466). 28 Sept. 83.
  Concerto in G Major for Piano and Orchestra (K 453). 13 June 60.
  Così fan Tutte. 2 May 92 (overture).
  Divertimento. 9 Oct. 88.
  Exsultate, Jubilate. 16 Feb. 78 (a).
  Idomeneo. 2 May 92 (overture, aria).
  Lucio Silla. 21 Feb. 91 (excerpt).
  The Magic Flute. 20 June 74 (arias), 12 Feb. 76 (excerpt).
  The Marriage of Figaro. 10 June 66 (overture), 4 Apr. 70 (arias), 20 July 74, 18 Nov. 81 (excerpt), 21 Apr. 85, 4 May 85 (arias), 13 Apr. 88 (arias), 6 Sept. 91 (aria).
  Prelude and Fugue in D Minor. 3 Feb. 87.
  Quartet for Oboe and Strings (K 370). 5 Feb. 67.
  Quartet in G Minor for Piano and Strings. 31 May 82, 3 Feb. 87.
  Quintet for Clarinet and Strings (K 581). 9 June 74.
  Serenade (K 239). 15 Feb. 67.
  Sonata No. 3 for Violin and Piano (K 306). 28 Feb. 88.
  String Quartet in B Flat Major (K 458). 12 July 60.
  String Quintet (K 516). 9 June 74.
  Symphony No. 1 (Quartet in D Major?). 24 Dec. 70.
  Symphony in E Flat, No. 39. 28 Sept. 83.
  Symphony in G Minor, No. 40. 11 Feb. 86.
  Trio in C Major (K 548). 11 Mar. 87 (a).
Müller, Edoardo. 11 Mar. 87 (b).
Muratti, José. 31 Jan. 81.

Murcell, Raymond. 17 June 63.

Musical Arts Corporation, MAC (Corporación de las Artes Musicales, CAM). 6 Jan. 86, 5 Oct. 88.

Musical composition in Puerto Rico. 24 Sept. 66.

Musical predictions. 2 Nov. 69.

Nancarrow, Conlon. 4 Oct. 83, 13 Feb. 86.

National Composers Association (Asociación Nacional de Compositores, ANCO). 10 Oct. 80, 8 Oct. 85, 3 Oct. 87.

National Symphony Orchestra of Washington. 17 June 88, 18 June 88, 22 June 88, 18 June 89, 22 June 90.

Natola-Ginastera, Aurora. 11 June 81.

Navarra, Gilda. 23 Dec. 88.

Navarro, Gloria. 14 Mar. 84, 10 Nov. 87, 19 June 90.

Nelson, Judith. 17 June 87.

New England Conservatory of Music Chorus. 23 June 83.

Niculescu, Mariana. 26 Oct. 79.

Nietzsche, Friedrich
    Songs. 4 June 74.

Nin, Joaquín
    Cantos de España. 16 Feb. 78 (b).

Nobre, Marlos
    In Memoriam para Orquesta. 2 Oct. 84.

Nold, Donald. 10 Feb. 70.

Número Tres. 11 Mar. 82.

Odnoposoff, Adolfo. 28 Mar. 66, 17 May 67, 11 Oct. 68, 30 Nov. 69, 7 Apr. 72.

Offenbach, Jacques
    The Grand Duchess of Gerolstein. 18 June 89 (excerpt).

Ohana, Maurice
    Llanto por Ignacio Sánchez Mejías. 16 Sept. 86.

Ohlsson, Garrick. 27 Oct. 82.

Oistrakh, Igor. 10 June 66.

Olaya Muñoz, Jorge
    Colombian dances (arr.). 10 Oct. 85.
Oliveira, Elmar. 31 May 82, 21 Sept. 85.
O'Neill, Herman. 23 May 85, 29 Apr. 87, 29 Mar. 90.
Open strings. 28 Oct. 81, 14 Apr. 82, 27 Oct. 82, 28 Sept. 83, 14 Dec. 83, 11 Feb. 86.
Opera de Cámara. 7 Dec. 77, 6 Jan. 86.
Opera de Puerto Rico. 18 Jan. 83, 11 Mar. 87 (b), 23 Oct. 87, 14 Sept. 91.
Opera de San Juan. 7 June 78, 24 July 79, 2 July 83. Also See Opera 68.
Opera 68. 9 Apr. 70, 20 July 74. Also see Opera de San Juan.
Orford String Quartet. 10 Feb. 68.
Orkis, Lambert. 18 June 88.
Ormandy, Eugene. 18 June 66.
Orrego Salas, Juan
    Piano Concerto. 2 Apr. 66.
    String Quartet No. 1. 13 Nov. 82.
    Symphony No. 1. 5 Oct. 88.
    Trio, Op. 58. 17 May 67.
Ortiz, William
    Antillas. 10 Nov. 82.
    Caribe Urbano. 7 Nov. 90.
    Street Music. 3 Oct. 87.
    Suspensión de Soledad en Tres Tiempos. 25 Sept. 91.
Ortiz del Rivero, Camelia. 5 Apr. 69, 9 Apr. 70, 18 May 73, 24 July 79, 2 July 83.
Ott, David
    Dodecacelli. 18 June 88.
Ovcharov, Saul. 7 May 76, 13 Nov. 82.
Pablo, Luis de.
    Piano music. 25 Nov. 81 (b).
Pablo Casals Musical Foundation. 26 Feb. 76.
Pabón, Marian. 25 Aug. 84, 29 Apr. 87, 29 Mar. 90.

Pabón, Roselín. 14 Dec. 73, 20 Jan. 78, 14 Dec. 80, 22 Jan. 81 (a), 18 Nov. 81, 25 Nov. 81 (a), 14 Apr. 82, 9 Sept. 82, 27 Oct. 82, 2 Dec. 82, 1 Feb. 84, 14 Mar. 84, 21 Apr. 85, 11 Feb. 86, 25 Jan. 89, 17 May 89, 28 Nov. 90, 20 Aug. 91, 22 Nov. 91.

Pabón, Susan. 18 Nov. 81, 2 Dec. 82, 3 Dec. 83, 21 Apr. 85, 29 Jan. 86, 3 Oct. 87, 7 June 88, 30 Oct. 90, 14 Sept. 91.

Pagán-Vila, Amarilis. 13 May 92.

Paganini, Niccolò
  Caprice No. 24. 9 June 72.
  "Moses" Fantasy (arr). 4 Feb. 81 (a).

Pagano, Caio. 4 Oct. 83.

Paizy, Ilca. 20 July 74, 20 June 81.

Palacios, Antonio. 29 Apr. 87.

Paris Chamber Orchestra. 15 Feb. 67.

Parnas, Leslie. 2 June 72.

Paul, Thomas. 29 May 85.

Pearson, Stephen. 14 Dec. 80.

Pedreira, José Enrique. 3 Dec. 83.
  Concerto For Piano and Orchestra. 3 Dec. 83.
  Danzas. 3 Dec. 83.
  Fantasy. 3 Dec. 83.
  Piano pieces. 24 June 78.
  Songs. 3 Dec. 83.
  Violin and piano pieces. 3 Dec. 83.

Penderecki, Krzysztof. 25 June 91.
  Lament in Memory of the Victims of Hiroshima. 30 Nov. 88.

Peña, Lito. 29 Oct. 80, 3 Dec. 83.
  Suite Antillana. 23 Nov. 68.

Pérez, Ana del Pilar. 29 Apr. 87, 22 Aug. 90.

Pérez, Jorge. 24 Nov. 70.

Pérez, Samuel (pianist). 4 Feb. 81 (c), 13 Nov. 82, 30 Oct. 87, 30 Oct. 90.

Pérez, Samuel (singer). 21 Apr. 85.

Pérez Ayala, José. 3 Oct. 87.

Pérez Frangie, Teresa. 20 July 74, 6 Mar. 76, 7 June 78, 29 Apr. 87.

Pérez Garay, Idalia. 31 Jan. 81, 23 Dec. 88.

Performing Arts Center (Centro de Bellas Artes). 6 June 79, 12 June 80, 18 Apr. 81.

Performing Arts Corporation (Corporación de las Artes de Representación). 12 June 80, 19 Feb. 81.

Pergolesi, Giovanni Battista
La Serva Padrona. 7 Dec. 77.

Perkins, Kenneth. 10 Feb. 68.

Perlman, Itzhak. 9 June 72, 11 June 75.

Perrín, Guillermo. 29 Apr. 87.

Perron, Serge. 25 Nov. 81 (b).

Perugia, Noemi. 11 Mar. 82.

Petkov, Dimiter. 1 Feb. 84.

Photography during events. 25 Apr. 60, 13 Sept. 73, 16 Dec. 78, 14 Dec. 80, 1 Sept. 84, 11 Feb. 86, 23 Oct. 87, 22 Nov. 91.

Piston, Walter
Quintet. 6 Mar. 73.

Plectrum Musica Quartet. 4 Nov. 70.

Polesinelli, Maryann. 2 July 83.

Polish Chamber Orchestra. 10 Feb. 86.

Ponce Historical Society. 30 Oct. 87.

Poulenc, Francis
Sonata for Trumpet, Horn and Trombone. 18 June 88.

Pressler, Menahem. 11 Mar. 87 (a).

Pro Arte Lírico. 22 Aug. 90.

Pro Arte Musical Society. 14 Oct. 78, 26 Oct. 79, 17 Feb. 83, 28 Sept. 83, 6 Jan. 86, 20 Jan. 87, 11 Mar. 87 (a).

Program notes. 19 June 72 (b), 12 June 73, 29 June 74, 14 Dec. 80, 28 Oct. 81, 14 Apr. 82, 19 June 82, 9 Sept. 82, 2 Dec. 82, 23 June 83, 3 Dec. 83, 16 Sept. 86, 17 June 87, 11 Nov. 87, 17 June 89, 27 June 89, 17 June 90, 30 Oct. 90, 7 Nov. 90, 22 May 91, 15 Feb. 92.

Prokofiev, Sergei
    Alexander Nevsky. 14 Nov. 89.
    Concerto No. 3 for Piano and Orchestra. 23 Mar. 66.
    Concerto No. 2 for Violin and Orchestra. 9 June 72.
    Quintet, Op. 39. 7 May 76.
    Sonata for Cello and Piano, Op. 119. 16 Feb. 78 (b).

Pryor, Arthur
    Fantastic Polka. 17 June 90.

Puccini, Giacomo
    La Bohème. 16 Feb. 78 (a) (aria), 6 Sept. 91 (aria).
    Gianni Schicchi. 6 Sept. 91.
    Madama Butterfly. 14 Dec. 73.
    La Rondine. 4 May 85 (aria).
    Tosca. 27 Sept. 72, 14 Sept. 91.
    Turandot. 14 Oct. 78 (aria), 1 Sept. 84.
    Le Villi. 29 Apr. 89 (excerpt).

Puerto Rican Foundation for Zarzuela and Operetta. 23 May 85, 6 Jan. 86, 29 Apr. 87, 18 May 88, 29 Mar. 90.

Puerto Rican music, defined. 21 Sept. 85.

Puerto Rico and contemporary music. 7 Aug. 66.

Puerto Rico Casals Festival. June 57, 13 June 60, 16 June 60, 20 June 60, 3 June 63, 17 June 63, 10 June 66, 8 June 67, 26 May 68, 25 May 69, 7 June 70, 30 May 71, 2 June 72, 7 June 72, 9 June 72, 19 June 72 (a), 19 June 72 (b), 20 June 72, 31 May 73, 9 June 73, 12 June 73, 9 June 74, 14 June 74, 20 June 74, 24 June 74, 29 June 74, 5 June 75, 11 June 75, 16 June 76, 30 June 76, 12 July 76, 13 Nov. 77, 24 June 78, 24 May 79, 30 May 79, 6 June 79, 12 June 80, 22 June 80, 9 June 81, 11 June 81, 18 June 81, 31 May 82, 19 June 82, 23 June 83, 5 June 84, 26 June 85, 21 Sept. 85, 6 Jan. 86, 17 June 87, 7 June 88, 18 June 88, 22 June 88, 13 June 89, 17 June 89, 18 June 89, 12 June 90, 19 June 90, 21 June 90 (restored videotapes), 22 June 90, 25 June 91.

Puerto Rico Chamber Orchestra. 6 Jan. 86.

Puerto Rico Conservatory of Music. 6 June 79, 12 June 80.
    Chorus. 7 June 72, 19 June 72 (a), 24 Oct. 73, 24 June 74, 9 June 81, 29 May 85, 6 Jan. 86, 7 June 88.

Opera Workshop. 21 Apr. 85, 6 Jan. 86.

Puerto Rico International Guitar Festival. 14 Dec. 80, 10 Nov. 87.

Puerto Rico Musical Society. 4 June 74.

Puerto Rico Philharmonic Orchestra. 16 Oct. 85.

Puerto Rico Sings to World Peace. 18 May 73.

Puerto Rico String Quartet (1). 13 Nov. 82.

Puerto Rico String Quartet (2). 2 Feb. 90.

Puerto Rico Symphonic Chorus. 6 Jan. 86.

Puerto Rico Symphony Orchestra. 21 Dec. 59, 23 Mar. 66, 2 Apr. 66, 17 Apr. 70, 28 Apr. 70, 25 Mar. 73, 24 Oct. 73, 2 Feb. 74, 7 Apr. 76, 18 Dec. 77, 20 Jan. 78, 16 Feb. 78 (a), 14 Oct. 78, 29 Mar. 79, 30 May 79, 6 June 79, 12 June 80, 14 Dec. 80, 22 Jan. 81 (a), 4 Feb. 81 (a), 12 Apr. 81, 9 June 81, 18 June 81, 20 June 81, 30 Sept. 81, 28 Oct. 81, 25 Nov. 81 (a), 14 Apr. 82, 31 May 82, 30 Aug. 82, 9 Sept. 82, 10 Nov. 82, 18 Jan. 83, 19 Feb. 83, 17 Sept. 83, 18 Sept. 83, 4 Oct. 83, 3 Dec. 83, 14 Dec. 83, 3 Jan. 84, 1 Feb. 84, 5 June 84, 2 Oct. 84, 4 May 85, 29 May 84, 6 Jan. 86, 11 Feb. 86, 16 Sept. 86, 15 Nov. 86, 18 Feb. 87, 11 Mar. 87, 25 Mar. 87, 25 Apr. 87, 29 May 87, 17 June 87, 10 Nov. 87, 19 Jan. 88, 13 Apr. 88, 7 June 88, 14 Sept. 88, 5 Oct. 88, 9 Oct. 88, 25 Jan. 89, 29 Apr. 89, 17 May 89, 14 Nov. 89, 6 Mar. 90, 23 May 90, 23 May 90, 2 June 90, 19 June 90, 11 Oct. 90, 28 Nov. 90, 25 Sept. 91, 22 Nov. 91, 2 May 92, 13 May 92.

Puerto Rico Youth Choir. 24 Apr. 92.

Puig, Efrén. 18 May 88.

Purcell, Henry
Dido and Aeneas. 30 Nov. 69.
The Fairy Queen. 4 Nov. 70.

Quantz, Johann Joachim
Trio Sonata in C Minor. 7 Nov. 90.

Quilinchini, Evelina (Evelyn). 21 Apr. 85, 23 May 85, 6 Jan. 86, 25 Mar. 87.

Quintet of the Americas (Quinteto de las Américas). 10 Oct. 85.

Quintet of the Commonwealth of Puerto Rico. 6 Jan. 86.

Quintón, José I.
"Una Página de mi Vida." 4 Feb. 81 (c).
String Quartet. 12 July 60, 30 Jan. 69, 17 Oct. 69, 5 Feb. 92.
Quiñones Ledesma, Jesús. 21 Mar. 76.
Quiñones Rivera, Mareia. 15 Feb. 92.
Quivar, Florence. 7 June 88.
Rachmaninoff, Sergei
Cello Sonata, Op. 19. 11 Oct. 68, 28 Sept. 83.
Rahn, Eduardo. 10 Nov. 82.
Rainis, Sergije. 30 Nov. 69, 2 June 72, 7 June 72, 9 June 81.
Rakusin, Fredda. 1 Feb. 84.
Rameau, Jean-Philippe
Concerto No. 6, "La Poule." 15 Feb. 67.
Ramírez, José Raúl. 3 Dec. 83.
Ramírez, Luis Antonio. 4 June 74.
Nine Antillean Songs. 11 June 81.
Sonata Elegíaca. 23 Nov. 68, 16 Feb. 78 (b).
Suite. 2 Feb. 74.
Ramírez, Noel. 7 June 78, 1 Sept. 84, 25 Apr. 87, 17 Sept. 88, 14 Sept. 91.
Ramírez, Roberto. 9 Sept. 82, 18 Feb. 86, 27 June 89.
Ramírez, Rubén. 27 June 89.
Ramos, Bertha. 20 July 74.
Ramos, Hilda. 29 Mar. 90.
Ramos, José Antonio. 24 Apr. 92.
Ramos, Miguel. 18 Jan. 83.
Rampal, Jean-Pierre. 16 June 76, 19 June 76.
Randazzo, Arlene. 24 July 79.
Rapoport, Alan. 14 Mar. 91.
Rattenbach, Augusto
Serenade (flute, clarinet, trumpet, cello). 18 Feb. 86.
Raúl, Luis. 29 Apr. 87.

Ravel, Maurice
> *Don Quichotte à Dulcinée.* 29 Mar. 79.
> *Gaspard de Nuit.* 11 Nov. 86.
> *Piano Concerto for the Left Hand Alone and Orchestra.* 30 Sept. 81.
> *Rapsodie Espagnole.* 18 Dec. 77.
> *Shéhérazade.* 18 June 89.
> *String Quartet.* 5 Feb. 67.
> *Tzigane.* 28 Feb. 88.

Rawie, James. 6 Jan. 86.

Rechani, Jorge. 20 Apr. 89.

Reger, Max. *Sonata for Clarinet and Piano.* 17 Sept. 80.

Rescigno, Joseph. 25 Apr. 87.

Respighi, Ottorino
> *Il Tramonte.* 5 Apr. 69.

Revueltas, Silvestre
> *Redes.* 2 Feb. 74.
> *Sensemayá.* 15 Nov. 86.

Ricciarelli, Katia. 14 Oct. 78, 11 Feb. 87.

Rigacci, Bruno. 1 Sept. 84.

Rimsky-Korsakov, Nicolai
> *Capriccio Espagnol.* 21 Dec. 59, 23 Mar. 66, 9 Oct. 88.

Rivera, Danny. 29 Oct. 80.

Rivera, Graciela. 13 June 60.

Rivera, Miguel. 20 July 74.

Rivera, Mónica. 9 May 86.

Rivera, Nelson. 1 Oct. 81 (b), 11 Mar. 82.

Rivera, Roberto. 18 Feb. 86.

Rivera, William. 7 June 88.

Rivera Capdeville, Gualberto. 16 Oct. 85.

Rivera Guzmán, Félix. 23 May 90.

Rivera Toledo, Pedro
> *Fela.* 25 Aug. 84.

  La Verdadera Historia de Pedro Navaja. 31 Jan. 81.
  Variations on "The Flight of the Bumblebee." 20 Aug. 91.
Robledo, Aura Norma. 20 July 74, 21 Mar. 76, 17 Sept. 80, 19 June 82.
Robles, María Esther. 26 July 60, 21 Apr. 85.
Rodgers, Elizabeth. 16 Feb. 87.
Rodrigo, Joaquín
  Concierto de Aranjuez. 22 June 80, 25 Mar. 87, 9 Oct. 88.
  Fantasía para un Gentilhombre. 9 Oct. 88.
  Invocación y Danza (Homenaje a Manuel de Falla). 13 June 89.
  Para un Códice Salmantina. 16 Sept. 86.
  Pastoral Concerto for Flute and Orchestra. 17 May 89.
  Suite for Castanets and Orchestra (excerpts). 28 Nov. 90.
Rodríguez, Augusto. 29 July 69, 17 Oct. 69, 16 May 70, 24 Dec. 70, 21 Mar. 87.
  "Los Carreteros." 16 May 70.
Rodríguez, Luisita. 5 Apr. 69, 30 Nov. 69, 5 Dec. 78.
Rodríguez, Roberto. 23 Dec. 88.
Rodríguez Alvira, José. 30 Oct. 90, 22 Mar. 91.
  Árboles. 8 Oct. 85.
  Tempus Fugit. 30 Oct. 90.
Rogers, Nigel. 17 June 87, 19 June 90.
Rojas, Pedro. 29 Oct. 80.
Román, Elsa. 29 Mar. 90.
Romano, Patrick. 17 June 87, 19 June 90.
Romero, Alfredo
  Sonata (excerpt). 4 June 74.
Romero, Ángel. 14 Dec. 80.
Rondalla Puerto Rico. 16 May 60.
Rosado, Ana María. 5 Oct. 80, 14 Dec. 80, 1 Oct. 81 (b), 15 Sept. 85, 2 July 86.
Rosales, Rachel. 15 Feb. 92.
Rosario, Harry. 8 Oct. 85, 15 Oct. 86, 9 Oct. 88, 19 June 90.

Rosen, Charles. 27 Oct. 82.

Rosenfeld, Jayn. 13 Feb. 86.

Ross, Walter
    Prelude, Fugue and Big Apple. 17 Sept. 80.

Rossi, Salomone
    Works, arr. 5 June 84.

Rossini, Gioachino
    The Barber of Seville. 30 Aug. 82, 17 June 90 (overture).
    La Cenerentola. 21 Feb. 91 (aria).
    L'Italiana in Algeri. 25 June 91 (overture).
    La regata veneziana. 21 Feb. 91.
    Semiramide. 3 Jan. 84 (overture).

Rostropovich, Mstislav. 30 June 76, 17 June 88, 22 June 88, 18 June 89, 22 June 90.

Rubenstein, Bernard. 21 Sept. 85.

Rubiano, Jorge. 16 May 60.

Rubio, Elio. 9 Oct. 80.

Ruiz, José Antonio. 2 July 83.

Sachs, Joel. 13 Feb. 86, 23 Dec. 88.

Saharrea, Paulino. 19 June 72.

Saint-Saëns, Camille
    Havanaise. 27 Oct. 82.
    Piano Concerto in C Minor. 7 Apr. 76.
    Violin Concerto No. 3, Op. 61. 14 June 74.

Sala Casals. 14 Mar. 91.

Saldaña, Ramón. 31 Jan. 81.

San Basilio, Paloma. 17 June 83.

San Juan Chamber Music Festival. 15 Feb. 67, 21 Feb. 67.

San Juan Children's Choir. 19 June 76, 26 Dec. 81, 23 June 83, 17 June 87, 19 June 90, 28 Dec. 91.

San Juan Consort. 14 Mar. 91.

San Juan Municipal Ballet. 17 Sept. 83, 25 Apr. 87.

San Juan Philharmonic Chorus (Coral Filarmónica de San Juan). 14 Nov. 89, 19 June 90, 13 May 92.

San Juan Pops. 20 Aug. 91.

Sánchez, Isabel. 20 Apr. 89.

Sánchez, Joaquín. 21 Apr. 85.

Sánchez, Tony. 15 Oct. 86.

Sanromá, Jesús María. 25 Apr. 60, 26 July 60, 11 Oct. 68, 29 July 69, 16 Apr. 70, 17 Apr. 70, 18 May 73, 30 Apr. 81, 10 Nov. 82, 2 Dec. 82, 18 Sept. 83, 3 Dec. 83, 13 Oct. 84.

Sanromá Scholarships (APOS). 10 Nov. 82, 18 Feb. 86.

Santa Cruz Wilson, Domingo
Five Tragic Poems. 11 June 81.

Santana, Carmelo. 30 Aug. 82.

Santos, Carle. 8 Dec. 82.

Sarasate, Pablo
"Carmen" Fantasy. 27 Oct. 82.

Sarmientos, Jorge. 29 Mar. 79, 2 Oct. 84.
Ofrenda de Gratitud (Terremoto de 1976). 29 Mar. 79.
RESPONSO (Homenaje II). 2 Oct. 84.

Satoh, Somei
The Heavenly Spheres Are Illuminated by Lights. 15 Feb. 92.

Scarlatti, Alessandro
Concerto Grosso in F. 21 Feb. 67.

Scharrón, Eladio. 8 Oct. 85.

Schedrin, Rodion
Stykhira. 17 June 88.

Scheja, Steffan. 28 Sept. 83.

Schekman, Peter. 24 June 78.

Scherbaum, Adolf. 15 Feb. 67.

Schickele, Peter. 25 Jan. 89.
Eine Kleine Nichtsmusik. 25 Jan. 89.

Schillings, Gunter
Sonata for Violin and Piano. 5 Oct. 80.

Schnebel, Dieter
> *Maulwerke* ("Phonoarticulations"). 4 Feb. 81 (b).

Schneider, Alexander. June 57, 21 Dec. 59, 13 June 60, 16 June 60, 20 June 60, 10 June 66, 8 June 67, 2 June 72, 19 June 72 (a), 31 May 73, 9 June 73, 9 June 74, 24 June 74, 17 June 76, 9 June 81.

Schoenberg, Arnold
> *Fantasy for Violin and Piano.* 1 Oct. 81.
> *Five Piano Pieces, Op. 23.* 23 Feb. 70.
> Four-hand piano pieces. 1 Oct. 81 (a).
> *Kammersymphonie, Op. 9.* 13 Apr. 85.
> *Pierrot Lunaire.* 1 Oct. 81 (a).
> *Second String Quartet.* 1 Oct. 81 (a).
> *Six Little Piano Pieces, Op. 19.* 23 Feb. 70.

Schola Antiqua. 22 May 91.

Schub, André Michel. 31 May 82.

Schubert, Franz
> "Die Forelle." 29 Jan. 86.
> *Quintet in A Major, "The Trout."* 24 June 78, 29 Jan. 86, 18 June 88.
> *Quintet for Two Violins, Viola and Two Cellos.* 9 June 74.
> *Die Schöne Müllerin.* 23 Dec. 88.
> *Die Winterreise.* 30 Ap 81, 29 Apr. 86.
> Songs. 22 Jan. 81 (b).
> *Symphony No. 4, "Tragic."* 23 Mar. 66, 20 June 74.
> *Symphony No. 8, "Unfinished."* 16 May 60, 24 June 74, 27 Oct. 82.
> *Symphony No. 9 in C Major, "Great."* 16 June 60.
> *Wanderer Fantasy.* 31 May 82.

Schumann, Robert
> *Concerto for Cello and Orchestra.* 29 May 87.
> *Stücke im Volkston, Op. 102.* 16 Feb. 78 (b).
> *Symphony No. 4.* 2 June 72.

Schwartz, David. 24 June 78.

Schwartz, Francis. 17 Sept. 80, 1 Oct. 81 (b), 11 Mar. 82, 22 Apr. 84, 3 Mar. 86, 5 Apr. 89.

    Bato. 15 Sept. 85.
    Calígula. 1 Oct. 81 (b).
    Caligula: Twenty Years of Music Theater by Francis Schwartz. 5 Apr. 89.
    "Canción del Nuevo Mundo." 15 Feb. 92.
    "Canción Hemisférica." 15 Feb. 92.
    Cantata Juvenil del Nuevo Mundo. 24 Apr. 92.
    Fantasías Amazónicas. 5 Oct. 80, 1 Oct. 81 (b).
    Gestos. 19 Feb. 83.
    Grimaces. 22 Apr. 84.
    Liberty Fantasy. 30 Nov. 88.
    Mis Cejas No Son Poblados. 1 Oct. 81 (b).
    L'oncle de Baudelaire. 1 Oct. 81 (b).
    Paz en la Tierra. 21 Mar. 87, 30 Oct. 90.
    The Tropical Trek of Tristan Trimble. 6 May 73.
    We've Got (Poly)rhythm. 2 July 86.
Schwarz, Gerard. 23 June 83.
Scriabin, Alexander
    Prometheus: Poem of Fire. 29 May 87.
Segovia, Andrés. 20 June 60.
Seltzer, Cheryl. 13 Feb. 86.
Sereni, Mario. 17 Sept. 83.
Serkin, Rudolf. 16 June 76.
Serrano, Carlos. 19 June 72 (a), 27 Sept. 72, 20 July 74, 18 Dec. 77, 7 June 78.
Serrano, Isabel. 17 June 87.
Shatkin, Judith
    1492 for Piano and Percussion. 15 Feb. 92.
Sheppard, Meg. 25 Nov. 81 (b).
Sherba, John. 4 Oct. 83.
Shiesley, Robert. 20 July 74.
Shostakovich, Dmitri
    Cello Sonata. 11 Oct. 68.

Piano Concerto No. 1. 28 Sept. 83.
   Piano Preludes. 25 Apr. 60.
   Quintet, Op. 57. 30 Jan. 69.
   String Quartet No. 8. 2 Feb. 91.
   Symphony No. 5. 29 Mar. 79, 18 Sept. 83.
   Symphony No. 7. 19 Jan. 88.
Shulman, Harry. 10 June 66.
Sibelius, Jean
   Symphony No. 1. 18 Dec. 77.
Sicardó, Mercedes. 22 Aug. 90.
Siegert, Hans Christian. 5 Oct. 80, 5 Oct. 82.
Sierra, Roberto
   Descarga. 14 Sept. 88.
   Fanfare for Minillas. 12 Apr. 81.
   Glosas para Piano y Orquesta. 13 May 92.
   Quintet for Clarinet and Strings. 15 Mar. 78.
   Salsa para Vientos. 10 Oct. 85.
Silipigni, Alfredo. 14 Sept. 91.
Silva, Conrado
   Equus. 4 Feb. 81 (b).
Silva, Federico. 7 May 76, 4 Feb. 81 (a), 2 Oct. 84, 15 Oct. 86.
Silva-Marín, Guillermo. 24 July 79, 2 July 83.
Simó, Manuel
   String quartet movement. 17 Sept. 80.
Skowronek, Felix. 28 Mar. 66.
Smith, Jennifer. 19 June 90.
Solistas de Puerto Rico. 15 Oct. 86, 3 Oct. 87.
Somohano, Arturo. 16 Oct. 85.
Sor, Fernando
   Songs. 18 Nov. 81.
   Variations on a Theme by Mozart. 5 Oct. 80.
Sorroche, Juan. 13 Sept. 73, 14 Dec. 80, 18 Nov. 81, 9 Sept. 82.
Soto, Danilo. 20 Apr. 89.

Soto, Juan (Johnny). 9 Apr. 70, 30 Apr. 81, 25 Apr. 87.
Soyer, David. 7 June 70.
Spanish National Chorus. 17 June 87.
St. Cyr, Marcel. 10 Feb. 68.
St. John's School Children's Chorus. 14 Sept. 91.
St. Marcoux, Micheline Coulombe. 25 Nov. 81.
Stade, Frederica von. 18 June 89.
Stanienda, Jan. 10 Feb. 86.
Stapp, Olivia. 1 Sept. 84.
Stark, Bruce
    Farewell Song. 15 Feb. 92.
Starker, Janos. 5 June 84, 22 Nov. 89 (a).
Steinberg, Michael. 17 Feb. 83.
Steinhardt, Arnold. 7 June 70.
Stern, Isaac. 8 June 67.
Stern, Maurice. 1 Sept. 84.
Stevens, Milton. 18 June 88.
Stevenson, Robert. 31 Oct. 90.
Storch, Laila. 5 Feb. 67, 21 Feb. 67.
Strauss, Johann II
    Die Fledermaus. 2 July 83.
    Emperor Waltz. 20 Jan. 87.
Strauss, Richard
    Burlesque. 28 Apr. 70, 3 Jan. 84.
    Death and Transfiguration. 27 Oct. 82.
    Don Juan, Op. 20. 20 June 74.
    Der Rosenkavalier. 2 May 92 (excerpts).
    Songs. 4 Apr. 70.
Stravinsky, Igor
    Duo Concertant. 28 Feb. 88.
    Dumbarton Oaks Concerto. 5 Dec. 78.
    Firebird Suite. 3 Jan. 84.

The Soldier's Tale. 2 Oct. 85, 15 Oct. 86, 20 Jan. 87.

Strickler, Fred. 6 Mar. 90.

Sueras, Rafael. 8 Oct. 85.

Takemitsu, Toru
Undisturbed Rest. 11 Nov. 86.

Talavera, Cecilia. 30 Nov. 69, 22 Jan. 81 (b), 14 Mar. 84.

Tannenbaum, Elias
Remembrance II. 11 Nov. 87.

Tauriello, Antonio
Symphonic Overture. 2 Apr. 66.

Tavárez, Manuel Gregorio
Danzas. 16 May 60.
Redención. 22 Mar. 91.

Tavárez Classical Trio. 22 Mar. 91.

Taylor, William (Billy). 15 Nov. 86.
Impromptu. 15 Nov. 86.
Jazz Suite for Piano and Orchestra. 15 Nov. 86.

Tchaikovsky, Piotr Ilyich
Concerto for Violin and Orchestra. 11 June 75, 29 Mar. 79.
Francesca da Rimini Overture. 30 June 76, 13 Apr. 88, 22 June 90.
Hamlet Overture-Fantasy. 22 June 90.
Romeo and Juliet Overture-Fantasy. 11 Feb. 86.
Symphony No. 2. 16 Feb. 78 (a).
Symphony No. 5. 30 June 76, 17 June 88.
Symphony No. 6, "Pathétique." 7 Apr. 76, 22 June 80, 22 Nov. 89, 22 June 90.
Trio in A Minor, Op. 50. 18 June 88.
Variations on a Rococo Theme for Cello and Orchestra. 25 June 91.

Te Kanawa, Kiri. 4 May 85.

Teatro de la Opera. 30 Aug. 82, 1 Sept. 84, 25 Apr. 87, 17 Sept. 88, 12 Mar. 91.

Teatro del Sesenta. 31 Jan. 81.

Telemann, Georg Philipp
    Don Quixote Suite. 10 Feb. 86.
    Suite for Flute and Strings. 19 June 76.
    Trumpet Concerto. 15 Feb. 67.
Televised concerts. 20 June 74, 27 June 75, 23 June 83, 18 June 89.
Téllez, Carmen Helena. 17 June 87.
Temme, Michael. 30 Aug. 82.
Temple University Chorus. 7 June 88.
Tena, Lucero. 28 Nov. 90.
Terán, Rogelio. 21 Sept. 67.
Tessier, Georges. 2 Apr. 66.
Tevah, Victor. 23 Mar. 66, 2 Apr. 66, 17 Apr. 70, 24 Oct. 73, 14 June 74, 28 Apr. 70, 4 Oct. 83.
Texidor, Pedro Juan. 23 May 85.
Theayer, Edwin. 18 June 88.
Thomas, Ambroise
    Hamlet. 12 Mar. 91 (aria).
Thompson, Annie Figueroa de. 5 July 92. Also see Figueroa, Annie.
Thompson, Donald. 4 June 74, 20 July 74, 5 July 92.
Thompson, James. 9 Apr. 70.
Tocata. 6 Jan. 86, 29 Jan. 86, 3 Feb. 87.
Torelli, Giuseppe
    Trumpet Concerto. 15 Feb. 67.
Toro, Orlando. 3 Oct. 87.
Toro, Puli. 14 Dec. 73, 17 Sept. 88.
Torre, Javier de la
    Pequeña Suite Popular. 5 Feb. 92.
Torréns, Rafael. 9 Oct. 80, 25 Aug. 84, 20 Apr. 89, 29 Mar. 90, 22 Aug. 90.
Torres, Aldo. 17 Sept. 80.
Torres, José. 14 Mar. 84.
Torres, José Ramón. 18 Jan. 83, 14 Sept. 91.
Torres, Luis. 14 Mar. 84.

Torres, Raymond
   Canción de las Antillas. 13 May 92.

Torres, René. 30 Aug. 82, 25 Apr. 87.

Trace, Cheryl. 15 Oct. 86, 19 June 90, 2 Feb. 91.

Traffic control in theaters. 6 Feb. 76, 18 Dec. 77, 16 Dec. 78, 5 Oct. 80, 14 Dec. 83, 1 Sept. 84, 16 Sept. 86, 25 Mar. 87, 30 Oct. 87, 6 Sept. 91, 5 Feb. 92, 15 Feb. 92.

Trampler, Walter. 13 June 60, 9 June 74.

Travieso, Héctor. 22 Aug. 90.

Tree, Michael. 7 June 70.

Trigg, William. 15 Feb. 92.

Trío de Puerto Rico. 17 May 67.

Tschudin, Mike. 21 Dec. 59.

Tudor, David. 11 Mar. 82.

Turina, Joaquín
   Danzas Fantásticas. 28 Nov. 90.
   Sinfonía Sevillana. 23 May 90.

University of Puerto Rico
   Chorus. 29 Oct. 80, 29 May 85, 6 Jan. 86, 17 May 86, 16 Sept. 86, 21 Mar. 87, 29 May 87.
   Concert Choir. 30 Oct. 90.
   Cultural Activities Series. 13 Ap 85, 6 Jan. 86, 11 Feb. 86, 13 Feb. 86, 3 Mar. 86, 29 Apr. 86, 9 May 86, 16 Sept. 86, 15 Nov. 86, 16 Feb. 87, 19 Jan. 88, 5 Mar. 88, 17 May 89.
   Department of Music. 4 Feb. 81, 5 Mar. 88.

Urdaz, Mayra. 23 Dec. 88.

Uribe, Blanca. 2 Oct. 84.

Valente, Benita. 2 May 92.

Valentín, Antonio. 2 July 83.

Vallecillo, Irma Luz. 23 Mar. 66, 24 June 78, 11 June 81, 23 June 83.

Varas, Zaida (Zayda). 23 May 85, 29 Apr. 87, 18 June 88, 20 Apr. 89.

Varèse, Edgard
   Octandre. 2 Oct. 85.

Vargas Wallis, Darwin
  Tiempo de Adviento. 4 Oct. 83.
Varon, Lorna Cooke. 23 June 83.
Vásquez, Edmundo
  Créole et Lontaine. 2 July 86.
Vassallo, Vanessa. 3 Oct. 87, 7 Nov. 90.
Vázquez, Alejandro (Alex). 30 Nov. 69, 9 Apr. 70, 30 Apr. 81, 1 Sept. 84, 23 Dec. 88.
Vázquez, Carlos. 5 Oct. 82.
  Two Pieces for Clarinet. 3 Oct. 87.
Vega, Aurelio de la
  Elegía. 2 Feb. 74.
Vega Drouet, Héctor. 29 Apr. 87, 18 May 88, 20 Apr. 89, 29 Mar. 90.
Velázquez, Manuel. 14 Dec. 80.
Venegas, Rocky. 29 Mar. 90.
Veray, Amaury
  Allegro. 23 Nov. 68.
  A Portrait of Juliet. 10 Oct. 86.
  Toccata for Piano. 3 Oct. 87.
  Songs. 5 Dec. 78.
Verdejo, Awilda. 7 June 88.
Verdi, Giuseppe
  Aida. 17 Sept. 83, 11 Mar. 87 (b) (excerpt), 12 June 90 (overture).
  Attila. 18 May 73 (aria).
  Don Carlo. 29 Apr. 89 (excerpt), 12 June 90 (excerpt).
  La Forza del Destino. 14 Oct. 78 ("Pace, Pace, mio Dio").
  Hymns to the Virgin Mary (excerpt). 12 Feb. 76.
  Opera arias. 18 Nov. 81.
  Otello. 21 Mar. 76, 11 Feb. 87 (film), 13 Apr. 88 (aria).
  Requiem. 7 June 72, 3 Jan. 84, 7 June 88.
  Rigoletto. 26 Oct. 79 (excerpts), 12 June 90 (excerpt).
  Simon Boccanegra. 10 Feb. 70 (arias).
Vidaechea, Joaquín. 17 Sept. 80.

Vidal, María Rosa. 4 June 74.

Vidal Caso, Robert. 14 Dec. 80.

Videocameras and concerts. 11 Feb. 86.

Vienna Choirboys. 12 Feb. 76.

Viet-Rock. 24 Nov. 70.

Vieuxtemps, Henri
    Concerto No. 5 for Violin and Orchestra. 19 June 82.

Villafañe, Diana. 17 Sept. 80.

Villa-Lobos, Heitor
    Chôros No. 2. 11 June 81, 10 Oct. 85.
    Concerto for Guitar and Orchestra. 5 Oct. 88.
    Danza. 25 Apr. 60.
    Estudio No. 1. 2 July 86.
    Fantasia Concertante. 4 May 84.
    Mômoprecóce. 4 Oct. 83.
    Piano Concerto No. 1. 31 May 73
    Preludio No. 1. 2 July 86.

Villamil, Victoria. 1 Oct. 81 (a), 13 Feb. 86.

Villarojo, Jesús
    Graphic Games. 4 Feb. 81 (b).

Vivaldi, Antonio
    Concerto for Three Violins and Orchestra. 21 Feb. 67.
    Concerto for Two Mandolins and Orchestra. 16 May 60.
    Concerto for Two Trumpets and Orchestra (excerpt). 28 Sept. 83.
    Concerto in D Major for Guitar. 25 Mar. 87.
    Concerto in A Minor. 6 Mar. 73.
    Gloria. 30 Nov. 69.
    The Seasons. 10 Feb. 86.

Vives, Amadeo
    Doña Francisquita. 23 May 85.

Vizcarrondo, Leocadio. 29 Oct. 80.

Vlaun, Kim Daniel.
    Suite Antiyano. 4 May 84.

Wagner, Richard. 17 Feb. 83.
>   "Der Engel." 18 Nov. 81.
>   *Die Meistersinger* (overture). 5 June 84.
>   *Parsifal*. 5 June 84 (excerpts, arr.).
>   *Rienzi* (overture). 28 Apr. 70.
>   *Siegfried Idyll*. 24 June 74, 23 June 83.
>   "Stehe still." 18 Nov. 81.
>   "Träume." 18 Nov. 81.
>   *Die Walküre*. 12 June 90 (excerpt).

Walter, David. 24 June 78.

Walters, William. 25 Jan. 89.

Wanhall, Johann
>   *Clarinet Sonata*. 11 May 60.

Warfield, William. 17 June 63.

Warsaw Symphonic Chamber Orchestra. 25 June 91.

Waverly Consort. 23 June 83.

Webber, Andrew Lloyd
>   *Evita*. 27 June 83.

Weber, C.M. von.
>   *Concerto in E Flat for Clarinet and Orchestra*. 11 Oct. 90.
>   *Der Freischütz* 13 June 60 (overture), 18 June 66 (overture).
>   *Duo Concertante*. 11 May 60.

Webern, Anton
>   *Five Orchestral Pieces, Op. 10*. 11 June 75.
>   *Three Little Pieces for Cello and Piano*. 15 Mar. 78.

Weigelt, Hannelott. 17 June 89.

Welting, Ruth. 18 Jan. 83.

Wilson, Neil. 7 June 88.

WIPR, programming policy. 16 Mar. 73.

Wu, Mia. 13 Feb. 86.

Wyttenbach, Jarg
>   *Three Pieces for Piano*. 11 Nov. 86.

Xenakis, Iannis
Mikka. 5 Oct. 80.

XXX, M.D. 5 Feb. 80.

Yepes, Narciso. 25 Mar. 87, 9 Oct. 88, 13 June 89.

Young, Susan. See Pabón, Susan.

Yumaha, Akira
Divertimento for Alto Saxophone and Marimba. 15 Oct. 86.

Zabaleta, Nicanor. 5 Feb. 83.

Zanetti, Miguel. 2 Apr. 79, 23 Oct. 87.

Zarabanda. 17 June 87.

Zarzuela. 9 Oct. 80, 23 May 85, 6 Jan. 86, 29 Apr. 87, 18 May 88, 20 Apr. 89, 22 Aug. 90.

Zayas, Edgardo. 24 Apr. 92.

Zayas, Glenn. 29 Mar. 90.

Zeffirelli, Franco. 11 Feb. 87.

Zervigón, Pedro. 16 Sept. 86.

Zubillaga, Luis
Canciones y Recuerdos. 5 Dec. 78.

Zukerman, Pinchas. 9 June 73.

Zukovsky, Michelle. 9 June 74.